READING RESEARCH REVISITED

LANCE M. GENTILE
North Texas State University

MICHAEL L. KAMIL
University of Illinois at Chicago

JAY S. BLANCHARD
Texas Tech University

CHARLES E. MERRILL PUBLISHING COMPANY
A Bell & Howell Company
Columbus Toronto London Sydney

Published by
CHARLES E. MERRILL PUBLISHING COMPANY
A Bell & Howell Company
Columbus, Ohio 43216

This book was set in Sabon and Avant Garde.
Text Design: Joan Jaschke
Cover Photograph: Jean Greenwald
Cover Design Coordination: Tony Faiola
Cover Credit: The **Journal of Reading Behavior**, a publication of the National Reading Conference, 1070 Sibley Tower, Rochester NY 14604 (published quarterly); and the International Reading Association.

Library of Congress Catalog Card Number: 82–62994
International Standard Book Number: 0–675–20028–8
Printed in the United States of America
2 3 4 5 6 7 8 9 10 — 87 86 85 84

We wish to dedicate this book to our mothers and fathers:

Alfonso F. Gentile
Mary A. Gentile
Harry Kamil
Annette L. Kamil
John T. Blanchard
Jeanne Blanchard

Lance M. Gentile is professor of Education in reading and Director of the Pupil Appraisal Center at North Texas State University. He earned his Ph.D. in Reading at Arizona State University. He is a former elementary, middle, high school, and adult teacher. He authored *Using Sports and Physical Education to Strengthen Reading Skills* (1980), *Using Sports for Reading and Writing Activities: Elementary and Middle Grades* (1983), and *Using Sports for Reading and Writing Activities: Middle Grades and High School* (1983), as well as numerous research and practitioner-based articles in professional journals, book chapters, and reviews. Dr. Gentile is founding editor (1978) of *Reading Psychology,* an International Quarterly Journal. He is active in various professional organizations including the International Reading Association, in which he is currently on the Research Award Committee.

Michael L. Kamil is associate professor of Education at the University of Illinois at Chicago. He received his Ph.D. from the University of Wisconsin. He has been director of reading clinics at Arizona State and Purdue Universities. Dr. Kamil is past editor of the *National Reading Conference Yearbook* and served on the Editorial Advisory Board for *Reading Research Quarterly.* He is currently an associate editor of *Reading Psychology* and the *Handbook of Reading Research.* Dr. Kamil has published many research articles, book chapters, and reviews. His research interests are in the application of technology to education, processes underlying instructional techniques like the cloze procedure, and models and theories of reading.

Jay S. Blanchard is assistant professor of Reading in the College of Education at Texas Tech University. He received his B.A. and M.S.T. in Elementary Education from Drake University and Ph.D. in Reading Education from the University of Georgia. He coauthored *Computer Applications in Reading* (1979) and has authored numerous articles in professional reading journals. He is active in various professional organizations, including the International Reading Association, American Reading Forum, and the College Reading Association.

PROLOGUE

NICHOLAS J. SILVAROLI
Arizona State University

Reading Research Revisited is committed to the premise that reading educators should take an in-depth view of all research in reading. This prologue will emphasize how this book is unique and how it significantly contributes to the field of Reading Education.

Reading Research Revisited is unique because it relieves some of the reader's traditional responsibility. Until now, authors have provided reading educators with collections of readings—the work of one or more scholars—on various aspects of specific topics. Another common approach has been to provide pro and con reactions to specific topics. In both approaches the reader was required to independently add his or her personal insights and observations to the author's intentions. This work provides as many as three different authors' reactions to a single classical study. These reactions are called "Critique," "For Further Learning," and "Commentary." As a result, the reader is supplied with additional insights the classical study may have overlooked or was forced to ignore at the time of its original presentation.

The professionals who wrote the Critiques, For Further Learnings, and Commentaries for each classical study were people directly involved in the study or whose expertise was directly related to the study.

Reading Research Revisited is significant in offering a model for future authors interested in a more comprehensive approach to reporting research findings, and because it attempts to teach as well as report research findings.

It is hoped that this unique and significant work will encourage future authors to adopt a similar mode of presentation.

INTRODUCTION

LANCE M. GENTILE
MICHAEL L. KAMIL
JAY S. BLANCHARD

Research involves the continual testing and retesting of data, theory, and results, but the longevity or strength of belief in a set of findings is never beyond criticism. Reading research is no different. What can be accepted as true today may be proven false or inaccurate in the future.

Between 1978 and 1982, more than 2000 empirical reading research studies were conducted in this country alone. Although this figure represents a substantial fraction of all the studies ever done in reading, real progress in the quest for knowledge can only occur if these studies are integrated into what is already known about reading and reading-related processes.

Considering the current wave of interest in this field, it is important to stress that if researchers are going to advance existing knowledge they must avoid performing repetitious, meaningless, or spurious studies. To do so requires a keen perspective of what has already been accomplished, what must be repeated or improved, and what remains to be done. Only in this way can research lead us to a greater theoretical and practical understanding of those features of the reading process that make a real difference in teaching and learning.

This has been our primary motivation for producing *Reading Research Revisited.* The book is a result of our conviction that to move forward in reading and shun the aforementioned pitfalls, we need to examine and understand the significant elements of historical research. To do this we have solicited the criticism of some of today's recognized researchers on a representative body of pivotal or influential studies. The process of critiquing these studies in this manner does not necessarily entail fault-finding, but rather is vital to integrating the findings into theory and practice. It has been used as a means to explore or expose different perspectives of the same problems and issues. Each perspective, including the original, may have its use, and each may be correct and contribute measurably to our understanding.

At times, however, the authors do contest or repudiate portions of the original studies. Where this happens they have been careful to document opposing evidence and to propose alternatives which may have corrected these discrepancies. Some of the studies have withstood the tests of time and scrutiny. On the other hand, although some of the studies strongly influenced educational practices in their day, researchers have since developed more reliable research methods and tools which, when applied to the same problems, yield contradictory results. Consequently, the authors often argue the strengths and weaknesses of some studies, pinpoint flaws and question the validity of others, or go beyond the original research itself.

The book is divided into thirteen topical sections; a wide range of studies is critiqued. These begin with James M. Cattell's 19th-century work on eye movements and advance to contemporary observational studies of comprehension instruction by Dolores Durkin.

Reading Research Revisited selections cross the following four strands:

1. Original research articles reprinted by special permission of the first published. (In some instances summaries of the original studies appear in lieu of the studies themselves; these have been written exclusively for this book.)
2. A critique of these studies written by one of today's leading reading researchers.
3. Suggested readings for further learning.
4. A commentary on the critique written by another well-known reading researcher.

We would like to thank all the authors who contributed their time and expertise to the development of this work. Thanks also to the early reading researchers for paving the way for those of us who follow; and special thanks to Carol Schrader for typing the manuscript and demonstrating great patience in completing a difficult task.

CONTENTS

READING RESEARCH REVISITED

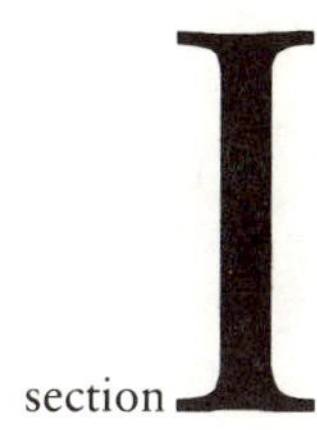

section I

THEORETICAL MODELS OF READING

SUMMARIES by J. Cortina and R. Robinson, of *Substrata-Factor Theory of Reading,* and *Conceptual Ability in the Substrata Theory of Reading*

CRITIQUE by Harry Singer

FOR FURTHER LEARNING

COMMENTARY by John Downing

SUMMARY by Lynda Melton, of *Toward a Theory of Automatic Information Processing in Reading*

CRITIQUE by S. Jay Samuels and David LaBerge

FOR FURTHER LEARNING

COMMENTARY by Wayne Otto

This section introduces the reader to Jack Holmes's *Substrata-Factor Theory of Reading* and S. Jay Samuels and David LaBerge's *Theory of Automatic Information Processing in Reading.* Singer critiques Holmes's work and develops a point-for-point comparison with each concept of Rumelhart's interaction theory of reading. Essentially, Singer claims Holmes's theory is identical to Rumelhart's, whose ideas were developed long after Holmes's. However, Rumelhart has never acknowledged any connection. Downing makes the point that Jack Holmes's theory is as applicable today as it was 30 years ago and shows its potential for stimulating further theoretical considerations in the field of reading.

In an interesting review of their earlier work, Samuels and LaBerge consider their original theory's strengths and weaknesses after the passage of a decade. They point to some of the features of *Automatic Information Processing* that need to be revised and those that have withstood the test of time. Otto considers Samuels and LaBerge's ideas noteworthy and offers several suggestions for further development of this model of the reading process.

A SUMMARY OF JACK A. HOLMES'S AND HARRY SINGER'S STUDIES: FACTORS UNDERLYING MAJOR READING DISABILITIES AT THE COLLEGE LEVEL AND CONCEPTUAL ABILITY IN THE SUBSTRATA THEORY OF READING

JOSEPH CORTINA

Cedar Valley College

ROY A. ROBINSON

Keene Independent School District

Jack A. Holmes presented a theoretical design in 1948 to explain the various mental processes involved in reading. His Substrata-Factor Theory attempted to show the degree of contribution each reading subskill made to success in reading. In addition, Holmes sought to determine the manner in which the skills interrelated as one's reading ability progressed toward maturity. To support his ideas, Holmes developed a statistical method of analysis to substantiate the Substrata-Factor Theory. His original research is considered the "embryo" of investigations attempting to relate significant reading-related factors to specific developmental stages.

Beginning in 1962, Harry Singer collaborated with Holmes, and extended their analysis of the substrata factors related to reading. Both researchers were interested in determining to what extent various reading skills contributed to reading comprehension; both wanted to map the sequential development of a hierarchical organization of reading skills.

From his review of prior research, Holmes concluded that several factors corresponded with incidences of reading disability. According to Holmes, these comparisons had been recognized previously, but no one had determined how they might be organized in relation to speed and power of reading. In response to this void in the research, Holmes (1948) launched the first large-scale study designed to analyze how these factors corresponded to differences observed among students reading at different levels.

Holmes first assumed that initial subskills in reading are organized into sets of subskills or working systems. (A working system is defined as a hierarchy of a set of predictors. Holmes and Singer, 1964.) He also believed that not all students organize these subskills into identical working systems. Nevertheless, they may experience equal success with similar intellectual problems. Holmes theorized that as students' reading skills mature, initial working systems are incorporated into higher-order networks (Geyer, 1972), and that once they are effectively organized, they are employed spontaneously by the student. However, this "automatic" response system is subject to the level of difficulty and purpose of the reader for completing a specific task (Singer, 1962).

To demonstrate his Substrata-Factor Theory statistically, Holmes (1948) constructed a correlational matrix of all the variables (skills previously suggested to be primary factors contributing to comprehension) and showed how these correlated with two criterion variables: speed of comprehension and power of comprehension. Next, he developed a statistical technique known as the substrata-factor analysis (Holmes, 1965), which was an extension of the *Wherry-Doolittle Test Selection Technique*. This technique provided partial regression coefficients for the independent variables shown to be the best predictors of the two criterion variables: speed of comprehension and power of comprehension.

The term "partial regression" means that once the variables demonstrating a significant correlation with (or proving to be the best predictors of) the criterion variables are determined, they are removed from the set of predictors and become "sub-criterions" (see Summary/Figure 1). The process is then repeated to determine which of the remaining variables show a significant correlation to the subcriterions. It continues until no variables are left in the matrix. In essence, the process is a multiple regression analysis repeated continuously without replacement (Cohen, 1968).

Though the Substrata-Factor analysis identified the best predictor, the next best predictor, etc., application of an F-test determined whether the contribution each skill made to the criterion was statistically significant. When the F-test indicated that the contribution of each variable's predictability of a specific cri-

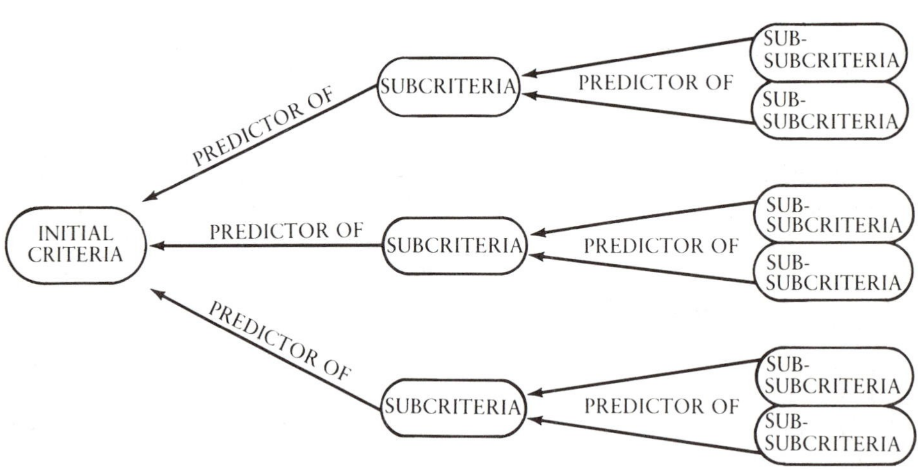

SUMMARY/FIGURE 1.
Illustration of Partial Regression Showing the Selective Process for Identifying Predictive Subcriteria According to Holmes's and Singer's Substrata-Factor Theory.

terion was not significant, the selection of predictors for that particular criterion or subcriterion was terminated.

Thanks to Karl Pearson who, according to Ferguson (1967) redefined correlation as a mutual relationship (Pearson Product Moment Correlation Coefficient), the limitations imposed by the "identical or overlapping elements" concept was no longer a major obstacle in developing substrata analysis procedures (Ezekiel, 1941).

With these correlational questions resolved, Holmes was able to carry out his Substrata-Factor analyses. The initial model first appeared in his doctoral dissertation which investigated the differences in substrata abilities among college students (1948).

Holmes adapted the substrata analysis for use in a government-commissioned project investigating differences in reading ability among various groups at the high-school level (Holmes and Singer, 1966). Harry Singer, then a graduate student, assisted Holmes in this research project. Their research at the high-school level was followed by additional studies by Singer which led to the Substrata-Factor model for grade four (Singer, 1962), and later to an expansion of the model to include grades three through six (Singer, 1964) as well.

In an effort to broaden the scope of Jack Holmes' Substrata-Factor Theory, Singer sought to discover patterns of predictors of reading power at various grade levels which would account for differences in abilities and processes between the beginning and mature readers (Williams, 1971). The models from Singer's efforts provided statistically significant predictors of reading abilities at various levels of achievement. This means that a certain skill may be of primary importance at one level of comprehension, but may be merged with, or have its primary position of importance replaced by, a skill that corresponds more directly to the increased demands accompanying reading comprehension at higher or more mature levels.

In 1964, Singer completed a study that extended the pattern of Substrata Factors accompanying reading development to grades three through six (Singer, 1964). The model that evolved from this investigation illustrates a particular hierarchy of skills or factors that account for the variance in power of reading observed at each consecutive grade level. To construct this model, Singer tested 250 pupils in grades 3 through 6 with a battery of scales that measured mental abilities, listening comprehension, linguistic meaning, word recognition, and visual and auditory perception. Data from the testing were subjected to Holmes and Singer's Substrata-Factor Analysis. By using this technique, Singer, like Holmes, attempted to determine:

(1) *Which* subabilities, or subskills, are used at each grade level?

(2) *How much* are they used at each grade level?

This model illustrated, for example, that from an analysis of the data, 66 percent of the variance accounted for various levels of power of reading at grade three. The proportion of contribution each subability made to the variance in power of reading was represented by the following percentages: word recognition in context, 26 percent; auditory-visual verbal conceptualization, 10 percent; visual-verbal meaning, 16 percent; auding, 7 percent; and syllabication consistency, 7 percent. At the sixth grade level, only three factors accounted for 73 percent of the variance in power of reading (Singer, 1964). The entire model presents the year-to-year changes in the percent contribu-

summary

tions of the various substrata factors that accompany reading development from grades three through six. The model indicates that: the skill of visual-verbal meaning, or visual-verbal association, generally is more significant by grade six; auding is only slightly significant at grades three, four, and five and is even less significant at grade six; meaning of affixes is significant at grades five and six; and word recognition in context is highly significant at grades three and five.

Singer (1964) presented data to show that certain subabilities contribute less and less toward the variance in power of reading. His explanation for these intermittent adjustments of specific subabilities indicates that certain primary factors have been reorganized to lower level positions and make only indirect contributions to the variance in power of reading. Singer refers to this process of reorganization as "subordinate integration" (similar to Holmes's "mobilization") and shows that factors tend to reorganize as one's reading skills mature.

For example, if a reading task required fourth-grade students to recall literal details (a more mature skill) from a particular phrase, the model demonstrates that students would be more likely to comprehend if they were able to discriminate differences among strings of words. Concomitantly, the students would be able to distinguish one word from another if they were able to recognize differences in each word's spelling pattern, and, more importantly, if they were able to associate a printed word with the words they use in spoken language.

In 1964, Singer organized broader representations or models of the Substrata-Factor Theory. In these broadened versions, Singer compared and contrasted the percent certain specific reading-related factors contribute to reading at the sixth-grade level, high-school level, and college level (Singer, 1964). Both Holmes and Singer hypothesized that throughout the grades, subordinate integration within subabilities continues, and that the mature reader becomes more and more flexible and efficient in organizing and reorganizing his subabilities. Singer's extension of the Substrata-Factor Theory proposed that a "mature organization" characteristic occurs for vocabulary at grade six, auding assumes a subordinate position at the high school and college levels, and visual modality supercedes auditory modality when processing input stimuli (Singer, 1964).

Each of these extended theoretical models developed by Singer demonstrates the patterns that accompany reading power and highlights the relationship between the development of intelligence and power of reading. Athey (1977) suggested that Singer's Substrata-Factor Analysis models show that although the correlation between IQ and reading diminishes from grade one to grade four, the correlation between IQ and reading *increases* after grade four (p. 88).

Through their Substrata-Factor Theories, Holmes and Singer were able to suggest practical instructional procedures. Also, Holmes's and Singer's illustrations of patterns of reading development provide statistically constructed models for identifying subskills that may significantly affect the development of reading power. Moreover, they reinforce ecclectic instructional approaches and encourage working individually with students whose abilities and purposes for reading at various grade levels differ.

---

summary

REFERENCES

Athey, I. Syntax, semantics, and reading. In J. T. Guthrie (Ed.), *Cognition, curriculum, and comprehension*. Newark, DE: International Reading Association, 1977.

Cohen, J. Multiple regression as a general data-analytic system. *Psychological Bulletin,* 1968, *70,* 426–443.

Ferguson, G. A. *Statistical analysis in psychology and education* (4th ed.). New York: McGraw-Hill Book Co., 1967, 102.

Ezekiel, M. *Methods of correlation analysis.* New York: John Wiley and Sons, 1941.

Geyer, J. J. Comprehension and partial models related to the reading process. *Reading Research Quarterly,* 1972, 7(4), 446.

Holmes, J. A. *Factors underlying major reading disabilities at the college level.* Unpublished doctoral dissertation, University of California, Berkeley, 1948.

Holmes, J. A. Basic assumptions underlying the substrata-factor theory. *Reading Research Quarterly,* 1965, *1*(1), 5–27.

Holmes, J. A., & Singer, H. *Speed and power of reading in high school.* Washington: U.S. Dept. of HEW, Office of Education. (Catalog number SF5 230:30016.)

Singer, H. *Conceptual ability in the substrata theory of reading.* Unpublished doctoral dissertation, University of California, Berkeley, 1960.

Singer, H. Substrata-factor theory of reading: Theoretical design for teaching reading. In J. A. Figurel (Ed.), *Challenge and experiment in reading,* 1962, 7, 226–232.

Singer, H. Substrata-factor patterns accompanying development in power of reading, elementary through college level. In E. Thurston & L. Hafner (Eds.), *Philosophical and sociological bases of reading.* Fourteenth yearbook of the National Reading Conference, 1964, 41–56.

Williams, J. P. Learning to read: A review of theories and models. In F. B. Davis (Ed.), *The literature of research in reading with emphasis on models.* New Brunswick, N. J.: Graduate School of Education, Rutgers University, 1971.

A Critique of Jack Holmes's Study: The Substrata-Factor Theory of Reading and Its History and Conceptual Relationship to Interaction Theory

HARRY SINGER

University of California, Riverside

Research in reading was atheoretical for its first 75 years. As Holmes (1953) pointed out some 28 years ago, "if one wishes to review *theories of reading* . . . he will, to his amazement, search in vain for likely leads. A close scrutiny of the index of such an early classic as Huey's (1908) *The Psychology and Pedagogy of Reading*, or the indices of . . . basic textbooks . . . or even in the index of such a modern treatment of the subject as that given by Anderson and Dearborn (1952) in *The Psychology of Teaching Reading* will not reveal any reference to either 'Theory . . . of reading' or 'Reading in theory' " (chap. 15). However, Holmes also recognized that in the preceding years, research laid the foundations for the formulation of theory.

The beginning of research in reading started with Javal's (1879) discovery that eye-movement behavior in reading consisted of jerky movements which he called by the French term *saccades*. Subsequently, some 12,000 studies, 4,000 alone on the psychology and physiology of reading, were done by various researchers whose works were summarized by Gray (1972), but only some of the studies were landmark investigations (Singer, 1980, 1981). A few of the studies that were highly relevant to the substrata-factor theory will be cited in this critique.

Buswell (1922) came close to formulating a theory of reading when he plotted three curves—number of fixations, average duration of fixations, and number of regressions per 100 words—for average groups of readers from grades 1–12. He interpreted these developmental curves as the common routes toward the ultimate goal of maturity in reading around which individuals deviated; the direction of the route over which the pupils travel depends largely on the method of instruction. Judd and Buswell (1922) added a theory of reading with their discovery that eye-movement behavior varied with changes in the content and difficulty of the material, and with the reader's purposes in reading. Gates (1947) constructed a wide battery of tests for the elementary-school level. The correlations between these tests and comprehension ranged from less than 0.15 for motor abilities to more than 0.80 for phrase recognition. Although Monroe (1932, p. 110) did not use multiple-regression statistics in her study of *Children Who Cannot Read*, she nevertheless reached the conclusion that a "reading defect may result in those cases in which the number and strength of the impeding factors is greater than the number or strength of the facilitating factors." Phelan (1940) was among the first to use factor analysis to find a set of factors (rote memory for words, cognition, and visual perception for words) that correlated with reading comprehension. Lazar (1942), relying only upon her insight as a practitioner in the New York City school system, came close to anticipating the substrata-factor theory when she wrote:

> the origin of reading failure . . . is to be sought in a constellation of causes. . . . The factors in a constellation differ in magnitude. . . . The most constructive approach that can be taken in the study of reading failure is to investigate these causes in their interdependence in order to find, if possible, which carry the most weight. . . . No clear and definite "method" exists for specifically isolating the most significant element from the combination of many.

Several years after Lazar's insightful publication, Holmes (1948, 1954) invented a statistical model, substrata analysis, to accomplish what Lazar noted would be necessary to discover the constellation of factors and their magnitude. Holmes first used substrata analysis in his doctoral dissertation (1948). Later, he published his substrata-factor theory of reading (1953) and used it to interpret the results reported in his doctoral dissertation. Over a decade passed before Holmes (1965) published the basic assumptions underlying the substrata-factor theory, which include his theory on the organization and dynamics of the mind. In the meantime, Holmes and Singer (1961, 1966) tested a basic hypothesis of the substrata-factor theory at the high-school level, and Singer (1960, 1962, 1965c) expanded the theory to include the conceptual domain, tested the central hypothesis of substrata-factor theory at the elementary level, and adduced evidence for its developmental validity. Then, Athey and Holmes (1969) investigated personality factors in reading and Kling (1966) showed the compatability of substrata-factor theory with general open-system theory. More recently, Katz and Singer (1981) tested an hypothesis from the substrata-factor theory at the first-grade level.

Thus, the substrata-factor theory has been applied at each level of education from college to first grade. The statistical models constructed at these levels represent developmental changes in the general routes to maturity in reading. Psychological, neurological, and developmental explanations have been formulated to explain the statistically constructed substrata model. There are four integrated models: statistical, psychological, neurological, and developmental. A brief review of each model appears in this critique, accompanied by excerpts from the original publications. However, to really "revisit research," the publications should be read in their entirety.

STATISTICAL MODEL

Holmes began his work with a thorough review of the research literature. He appreciated the groundwork prepared by previous investigators "whose background work made possible the thinking through of the present study" (Holmes, 1954, p. 17). But, consistent with his background as chairperson of a high-school chemistry and physics department, and his work as a synthetic chemist on the Manhattan Project, Holmes (1954, p. 17) wrote that the "*justification of the present study rests in its experimental attack on the problem of integrating the fragmentary bits of knowl-*

critique

edge which have been screened from the foregoing review of the literature" [italics in the original]. Thus, he applied his interest in synthesis to research in reading.

From his review of the research literature, Holmes selected 37 independent variables, each of which had a significant zero-order correlation with the dependent variables of speed and/or power of reading. The independent variables fit into five categories: mental ability, linguistic abilities (vocabulary, general information, spelling, phonetic association, word discrimination, affixes, word sense, etc.), small motor ability, oculomotor functional control (eye-movement behavior), and personality factors (assessed by the *Bell Adjustment Inventory, Johnson Temperament Analysis,* and *California Test of Personality*). Rate of reading was measured by the *Van Wagenen Rate of Comprehension* and the *Minnesota Speed of Reading*. Power of reading was determined by the total score on the *Van-Wagenen Dvorak Diagnostic Examination of Silent Reading Abilities*, which consists of the subtests of central thought, clearly stated details, interpretation, integration of dispersed ideas, and ability to draw inferences.

These tests were administered to a sample of college students, whose scores formed a correlational matrix. The Wherry-Doolittle (1947) multiple correlation technique determined the minimal number of variables that predict or account for the maximum variance in speed or power of reading. Typically, the Wherry-Doolittle technique selects only three or four variables from the entire correlational matrix as first-level predictors of speed or power of reading. But, in a simple yet brilliant contribution to statistical technique, Holmes extended the Wherry-Doolittle technique to a second level of analysis to determine which of the remaining variables in the matrix predicted each of the first-level predictors. He then went on to a third level of analysis. Holmes named this extension *substrata analysis*. (For a more detailed explanation of the method, see Singer, 1969.) The results of this analysis are shown in Critique/Figure 1 (Holmes, 1954, p. 80).

On the right-hand side of the figure, at the first substrata level, four factors predict power of reading: perception of verbal relations, intelligence, vocabulary in context, and fixations. At the second substrata level, general information, vocabulary in isolation, and prefixes predict vocabulary in context. At the third level, general information, phonetics, word discrimination, and suffixes predict vocabulary in isolation. The left-hand side of the chart is read in the same way for the substrata analysis of speed of reading.

The flow chart represents a cross-section of the subabilities that an average member of the group can *mobilize* for attaining speed and power of reading. Note that at the bottom of the flow chart Holmes thought the still unaccounted variance for power of reading might be "sustained effort and desire to know" and, for speed of reading, "motivational habit and desire for speed."

Holmes (1953, Chap. 32, p. 9) pointed out that the flow chart "samples the dynamic continuum of reading and represents for an age group the best selection of factors and the best organization of these factors as they are integrated into the average working system of the group. From the hundreds of factors available, it gives the teacher some realistic basis for selecting and stressing the various abilities. Of course . . . the teacher . . . must take care of the individual difference which theory predicts and experience confirms. All children do not need to learn the same

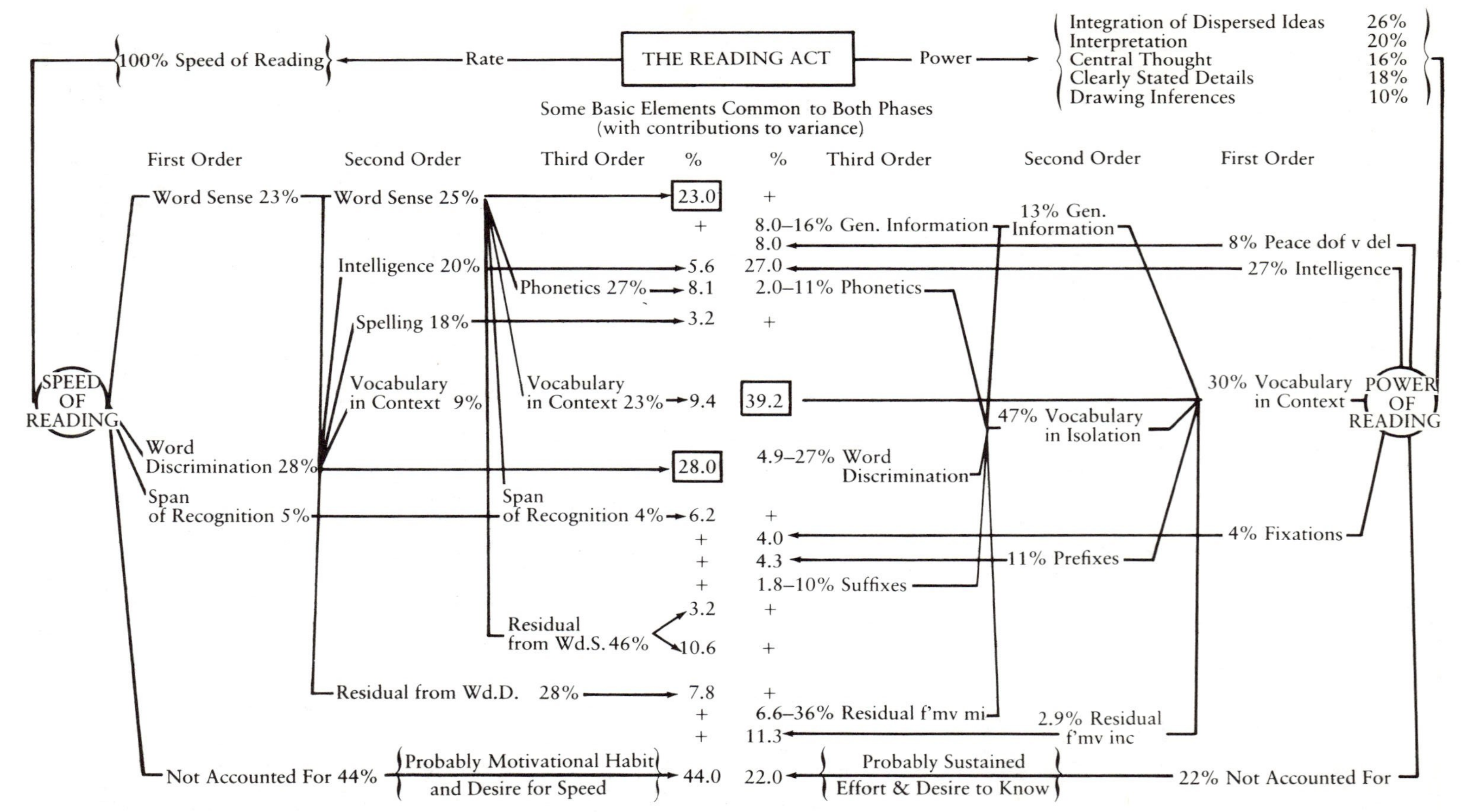

CRITIQUE/FIGURE 1.
Flow Chart for the Tasks Involved in the Reading Act with Breakdown for Underlying Factors (Holmes, 1948).

things to the same degree to perform a more complicated task to the same degree of perfection." Or, in current terminology, they do not have to *master* each separately defined skill.

Holmes (1954, p. 7) interpreted the flow chart as supporting the hypothesis that: "the general reading ability of college students is a composite of 'speed' and 'power' of reading, and that underlying each component is a multiplicity of related and measurable factors. Disabilities in reading should, therefore, bear an inverse relationship to the quantitative levels of each such component and hence manifest detectable deficiencies in such underlying factors." This hypothesis refers to the *structure* of the statistical model. The *dynamics* of the psychological model, that is, how the model works in the process of reading, was explained in *The Substrata-Factor Theory of Reading* (Holmes, 1953).

PSYCHOLOGICAL MODEL

The theory states that, in trying to attain power or comprehension in reading, an individual mobilizes his or her substrata factors into a momentary working system to solve a problem, such as identifying a printed word, selecting an appropriate meaning for a word, or making an inference or an interpretation. If one working system does not solve the problem, then another set of substrata factors, perhaps at a second or third level, is mobilized to solve the problem. For example, if the reader cannot recognize a word as a whole word, then the reader must organize a set of subabilities at the next level, such as phonene-grapheme correspondence and blending ability, to sound out and then synthesize the word. (Schema theory would assert that the reader activates a word-recognition problem-solving schema.) Moreover, as the reader's purposes, the difficulty of the material, or the type of content changes, even within the same passage, the reader organizes and reorganizes substrata factors into momentary working systems in response. Thus, we can envision that as a reader's eyes jump across the line of print from one fixation to the next, at each fixation the reader is mobilizing different substrata factors into momentary working systems at one or more substrata levels to solve a task in reading. In Holmes's words (1953, Chap. 32, p. 1):

> *The Substrata-Factor Theory of Reading* is predicated on the fundamental hypothesis that the reading ability of an individual, in a particular field, is a dynamic and complex skill, compounding and recompounding for each new task an appropriate integration of a multiplicity of related and underlying factors. Upon this basic assumption the rationale of the generalized theory must stand or fall.
>
> [He added that] different amounts of each [factor], at different times, are momentarily unified or integrated into a *working-system* of subabilities which are directed toward the solution of a problem. The problem organizes the abilities as the abilities determine what may be organized. That is, the particular kind of problem requires a certain organization of abilities, as the individual's possession of certain abilities limits what he may organize. . . . efficient reading . . . depends upon the synthesis of many subabilities. The synthesizing and integrating process is the crux of the reading process, i.e. the quick comprehension of the printed page. Whenever the smooth and

> rapid flow of thought-intake is interrupted in the reading process by incomprehension or confusion . . . then the reader must slow down and reread in this effort to resolve the problem by analysis . . . in power of reading the analytical process is more to the fore than is synthesis. Nevertheless, both speed and power of reading are dependent upon the integration of a set of subskills which cluster on at least three levels of complexity.

Next, Holmes and Singer (1966, pp. 155–159) summarized the substrata-factor theory in the following way:

> The Substrata-Factor Theory holds that general reading is a composite of Speed and Power of Reading and that underlying each component is a multiplicity of related and measurable factors. Further, the Theory states that, in essence, excellence in reading is normally an audiovisual verbal-processing skill of symbolic reasoning, sustained by the interfacilitation of an intricate hierarchy of substrata factors which are mobilized as a psychological working-system and pressed into service in accordance with the purposes of the reader.
>
> The key concepts in the Theory . . . are (a) *substrata factors*, or closely related sets of information stored in neurological subsystems of cell-assemblies; (b) *audio-, visual-,* and *kinesthetic-modalities*; (c) *mobilizers* arising from the focusing of deep-seated value systems; (d) *interfacilitation* of substrata factors; (e) intracerebral communication, or *working-systems*; (f) nature, sequence, and scope of information input; (g) *associative conceptualization* stimulated by the cortical activity of *perception*; (h) *gradient shift* and its attendant alteration of the hierarchy of the working system; (i) *mutual-and-reciprocal causation*; and (j) *initial kick differential* with accrued amplication from monitored feedback which results in variation in output.

Then they tested these theoretically derived hypotheses at the high-school level:

1. Different known-groups [total, boy vs. girl, bright vs. dull, fast vs. slow, and powerful vs. nonpowerful] will mobilize different substrata-factor hierarchies for the purpose of reading with speed and/or power. The result of the substrata analysis will be assumed to be the pattern of abilities underlying speed and/or power of reading in the "theoretically most representative individual of each such known-groups." Differences in patterns between representative individuals will indicate "there is more than one way to solve an intellectual problem."
2. The minor hypothesis is that since a student can bring to "focus in the reading process only those skills and abilities in his particular repertoire, he must learn to read by learning to *integrate* that characteristic hierarchy or working system of substrata factors which will maximize his strengths and minimize the use of his weak ones."

To test these hypotheses, 400 high-school students took a battery of 56 variables, including mental, linguistic, visual perceptual, listening, and auditory-perceptual abilities. They were also assessed on academic attitudes, interests, emotional-social problems, and musicality.

The study confirmed again the major hypothesis of the substrata-factor theory. Known-groups may indeed mobilize different sets of subabilities to attain identical success in their speed and/or power of reading. Thus, there is more than one way to solve an intellectual problem or more than one route to success in reading achievement.

critique

However, the minor hypothesis was not substantiated. Both the substrata analysis and the factor analysis indicated the hypothesis had to be revised in the following way: to read "at all with speed and/or power of reading at the high-school level, a student must be able to mobilize minimum amounts of certain basic audiovisual verbal processing abilities, particularly word recognition abilities, even though these may be among his weakest. However, as his proficiency increases, to surpass mounting competition, he must mobilize into his working-system increasing amounts of his appropriate strengths, even though such assets may be only remotely associated with reading success for people in general, and even though these strengths may be relative weaknesses for his known group."

Holmes's work created immense interest. In 1960, he presented a paper at the International Reading Association's Annual Conference, entitled "The Substrata-Factor Theory of Reading: Some Experimental Evidence" (Holmes, 1960). Constance McCullough wrote in *Reading for All*, "At IRA's annual convention in May 1960, Jack Holmes spoke on his Substrate [sic] Factor Theory of Reading and stole the headlines in every report on that gathering" (Jerrolds, 1977, p. 64).

On its front page, the *New York Times* published the Substrata-Factor Theory's major hypothesis and a terse comment that it represented a definition of reading that had been presented at the conference.

Subsequently, Theodore Clymer and Edward Summers (editor and associate editor, respectively) invited Holmes and Singer to help them launch *The Reading Research Quarterly* by submitting articles on their research. Holmes' paper, "Basic Assumptions Underlying the Substrata-Factor Theory of Reading," (1965) was published as the first article and Singer, drawing upon data from his cross-sectional research, presented "A Developmental Model for Speed of Reading in Grades Three Through Six" (1965a) as the second article in the new journal. The developmental model for power of reading was published elsewhere (Singer, 1964). Its basic assumptions constituted Holmes's neurological model.

NEUROLOGICAL MODEL

Holmes (1965) introduced his neurological model, which was implicit in his statistical and psychological model, by criticizing the statistical and implicit neurological models in the factor analytic models of Spearman, Thurstone, and Thomson. Holmes published a succinct summary of his 1965 paper in the appendix to Holmes and Singer's monograph (1966, pp. 178–179). Holmes's first assumption is that the "cognitive complex of the brain is thought of as constituting a cosmos of subability systems which became dynamically associated in a multitude of working systems in accordance with the requirements of the task and the purposes of the individual." The second assumption, a statistical one, is that "a meaningful correlation in the present context merely reflects a mean mutual interaction of two sets of test scores which in turn represent the dynamic interplay of (a) two macrosystems, (b) a system with one of its subsystems, or (c) two subsystems . . . correlations simply reflect the interdependence of two cortical systems. . . . The correlation . . . arises from the interaction of two *organized* bodies of information."

critique

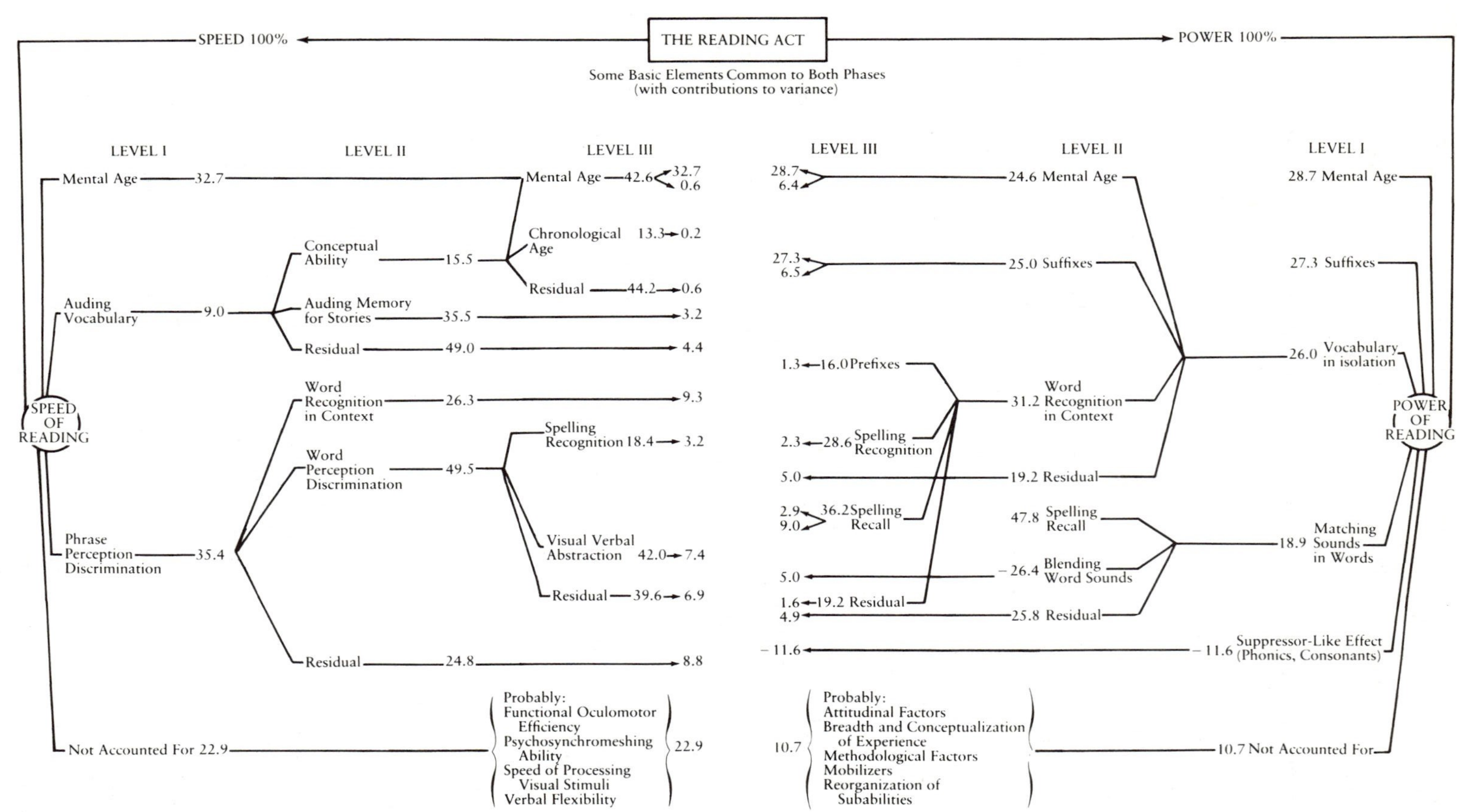

Note: All values expressed in percent.

CRITIQUE/FIGURE 2.
Flow Chart to Show the Results of the Substrata Analysis of Speed and Power of Reading at the Fourth Grade Level (H. Singer, 1960.)

Thus, Holmes perceived the brain as consisting of microsystems of cell assemblies that may be conjoined or organized into hierarchically structured working-systems, then reorganized into other working-systems according to moment-to-moment changes in the tasks and purposes of the reader. Singer then tested the developmental validity of the main hypothesis of the Substrata-Factor Theory.

DEVELOPMENTAL MODEL

Drawing upon the substrata-factor theory and its models, Singer (1960) found that the major hypothesis of the Substrata-Factor Theory was tenable at the fourth-grade level. The flow chart of this investigation appears in Critique/Figure 2.

The flow chart shows that four systems underlie power of reading; in current terminology these systems are graphophonemic (matching word sounds), semantic (vocabulary), morphemic (suffix), and reasoning (mental age). For speed of reading, there are three systems: speed and span of perception (phrase perception discrimination), semantics (vocabulary), and reasoning (mental age).

Singer (1966, 1976) also demonstrated that (1) conceptualization, for example, use of a concept such as "flower" to select four exemplars, "rose" "daisy," "tulip," and "pansy," from a list of ten items, and (2) perceptual abstraction and generalization ability, for example, auditory abstraction from words such as *ch*eese, *ch*urch, and *ch*ew, were among the factors underlying speed and power of reading.

Subsequently, Singer (1962, pp. 228–231) explained how the substrata model for the fourth grade could serve as a theoretical design for teaching reading—for curriculum design, grouping students for instruction, and for evaluation. Singer (1965b) also explained how the model could be used for diagnosis by applying it to a precocious reader, a five-year-old girl who could read at the fourth-grade level on the *Gates Reading Survey.* She had relative strengths in word recognition and a relative weakness in conceptual ability when compared with fourth-grade good and poor readers. Her profile pattern is shown in Critique/Figures 3 and 4.

Singer (1965c) then tested a developmental hypothesis in grades 3, 4, 5 and 6. To show developmental changes from grades 3 to 6, he used the first-level predictors from each of these grades to construct developmental models for speed and power of reading. These models are shown in Critique/Figures 5 and 6.

Singer (1965c, p. 17) interpreted these data as supporting the major *developmental* hypothesis of the substrata-factor theory: "a sequential development of a hierarchical organization of substrata factors does, in fact, accompany improvement in speed and power of reading. Moreover, a reorganization of substrata factors tends to occur in which first level factors at lower grade levels become subsumed within substrata factors at higher grade levels. . . . However, some first level factors, such as Visual Verbal Meaning [vocabulary] for Speed and Power of Reading, and Speed of Word Perception for Speed of Reading are first level factors throughout the intermediate grades."

How does this development occur? After 12 years, further research on the substrata-factor theory was conducted. Singer investigated reading and learning

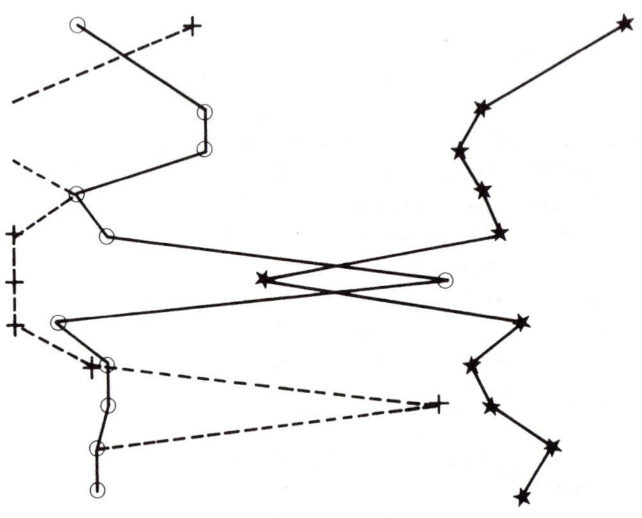

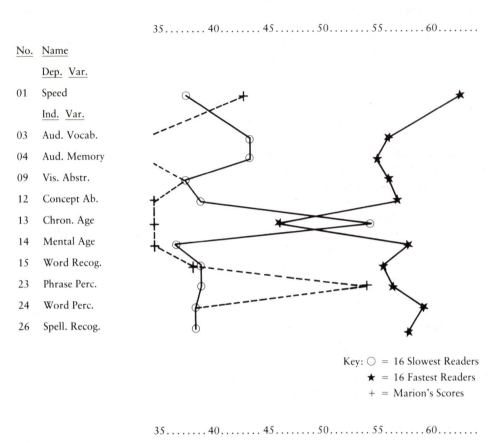

CRITIQUE/FIGURE 3.
Psychograph of Selected Substrata Elements for Speed of Reading for a Precocious Reader.

from text at the high-school level (Singer, 1973; Singer & Donlan, 1980). Then Katz and Singer (1976) retested the first-grade study data (Bond & Dykstra, 1967) to test a substrata-factor theory hypothesis, but the data were not adequate. Katz (1980) subsequently did a doctoral dissertation which had adequate data to test a substrata-factor hypothesis on the relationship between methods of instruction and development of subsystems underlying achievement at the first-grade level.

Interactions between methods of instruction and development of subsystems underlying achievement. Essentially, Katz tested the substrata-factor hypothesis by conducting a study in two phases. 1) Four teachers, not employed by the school system, provided supplemental instruction to first graders who had been randomly assigned within two schools to supplementary instruction in each of four subsystems: graphophonemics, morphophonemics, semantics, and syntax. After ten weeks of

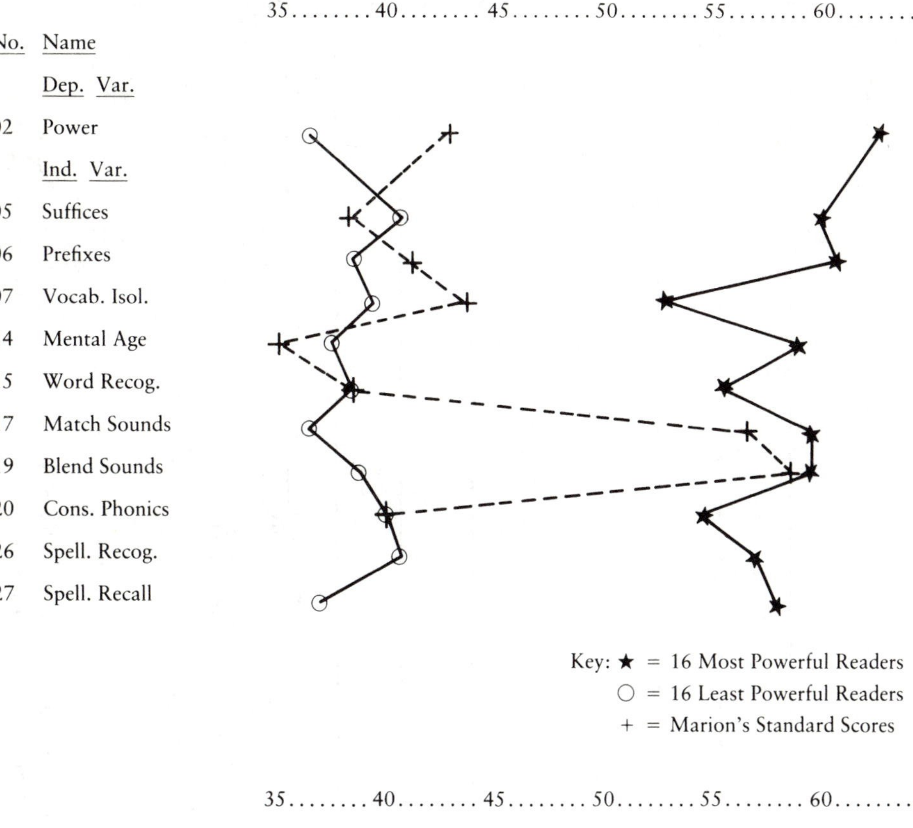

CRITIQUE/FIGURE 4.
Psychograph of Selected Substrata Elements for Power of Reading for a Precocious Reader.

supplementary instruction, an analysis of variance design revealed significant systematic differences among the criterion-referenced tests given to all the groups. Each group was significantly superior to the others on the supplementary method it had been taught.

2) For each group, she computed a multiple-regression equation for determining the predictors of comprehension. Her data, derived from her criterion-referenced tests and the *Metropolitan Reading Instructional Tests*, revealed that each group's multiple-regression equation for predicting reading comprehension contained the same predictors, but each group's lowest predictor was in the very subsystem in which the group had received supplementary instruction.

Katz interpreted the data as supporting the substrata-factor hypothesis: methods of instruction interact with students' capabilities to differentially develop subsystems underlying reading achievement. The subsystems of graphophonemics, syntax,

Grade 3		Grade 4		Grade 5		Grade 6	
Visual verbal meaning	14%			Visual verbal meaning	20%	Visual verbal meaning	18%
		Auditory picture meaning	8%			Auditory picture meaning	15%
		Meaning of affixes	19%	Meaning of affixes	11%		
Recognition of affixes and roots	9%						
Speed of word perception	23%	Speed of word perception	16%	Speed of word perception	14%	Speed of word perception	19%
		Spelling recognition	15%	Spelling recognition	16%	Spelling recognition	17%
		Spatial relations	−1%				
Dot-figure ground configuration	3%						
Word reversals	2%						
				Visual verbal abstraction	6%		
				Auditory verbal abstraction	−6%		
Variance explained:	47%		57%		61%		69%
Variance *not* accounted for:	53%		43%		39%		31%
Total:	100%		100%		100%		100%

Speed of Reading

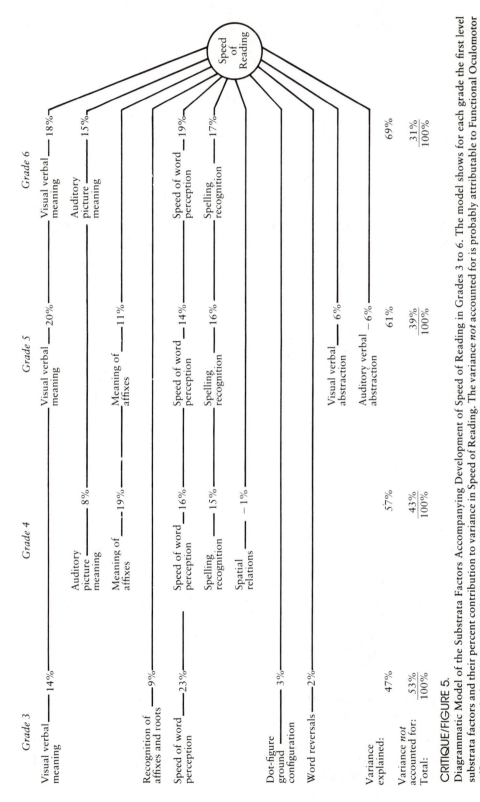

CRITIQUE/FIGURE 5.

Diagrammatic Model of the Substrata Factors Accompanying Development of Speed of Reading in Grades 3 to 6. The model shows for each grade the first level substrata factors and their percent contribution to variance in Speed of Reading. The variance *not* accounted for is probably attributable to Functional Oculomotor Efficiency, Speed of Processing Visual Stimuli, Mobilizers, Biological Support System, and Verbal Flexibility.

Grade 3		Grade 4		Grade 5		Grade 6	
Visual verbal meaning	16%	Visual verbal meaning	19%	Visual verbal meaning	18%	Visual verbal meaning	36%
Auding	7%	Auding	6%	Auding	8%		
		Meaning of affixes	11%	Meaning of affixes	20%	Meaning of affixes	17%
		Visual verbal conceptualization	9%				
Auditory-visual verbal conceptualization	10%						
Word recognition in context	26%	Word recognition in context	12%	Word recognition in context	14%		
		Matching sounds in words	14%			Matching sounds in words	20%
				Blending word elements	9%		
Syllabication consistency	7%						
Variance explained:	66%		71%		69%		73%
Variance *not* accounted for:	34%		29%		31%		27%
Total:	100%		100%		100%		100%

Power of Reading

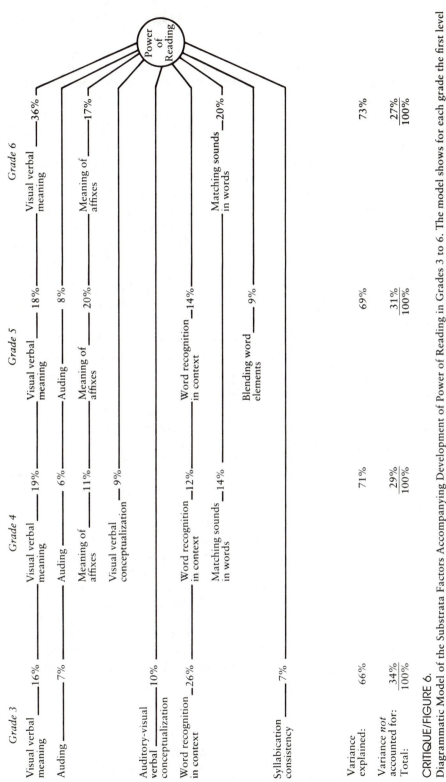

CRITIQUE/FIGURE 6.

Diagrammatic Model of the Substrata Factors Accompanying Development of Power of Reading in Grades 3 to 6. The model shows for each grade the first level substrata factors and their percent contribution to variance in Power of Reading. The variance *not* accounted for is probably attributable to Attiitudinal Factors, Verbal Flexibility, and Mobilizers.

and semantics developed at the first-grade level are initially functionally related to differences in methods of instruction. This finding, in agreement with Buswell's (1922) early study and Barr's (1974–75) more recent investigation, has important implications for diagnosis and improvement of reading. Katz (1980) also found, through principal components factor analysis, that at the end of first grade, the *Metropolitan Reading Achievement Test* correlated only 0.27 with a word recognition factor, but 0.73 with a reasoning-in-reading factor heavily saturated with semantics and syntax, perhaps because Katz's students had received considerable instruction in their classrooms in graphophonemics. Further research is necessary to fill in the gap in substrata models between grades 1 and 3 and to determine, through a longitudinal study, whether the methodologically induced differences in subsystems underlying achievement lead towards convergence in the third or fourth grades. Singer (1970) predicted that variations in "stimulus models" for teaching reading might produce initial differences in the routes to reading comprehension, but that convergence is likely to occur in subsequent grades. Later, Guthrie (1973) inferred from his cross-sectional data that such convergence did occur. However, he did not perform a longitudinal study of groups that had started off with systematic instructional differences.

Thus, the substrata-factor theory continues to provide data which have implications for further research and instruction. However, the statistical model does have a limitation which should be defined.

Limitations in the Statistical Model. Substrata analysis is applied to norm-referenced tests. Both the method of analysis and the tests stress individual differences, not similarities. Indeed, as students learn and become alike in a close-ended variable, such as symbol-sound correspondences, which students can master (Bloom, 1971) given adequate instruction and time to learn (Carroll, 1963), the close ended variable drops out as a predictor of reading achievement. But it still operates in the process of reading, even though it no longer appears in the statistical model at a subsequent grade level. Hence, it is necessary to consider the sequence of statistical models from grade 1 and up when attempting to determine *all* the substrata factors underlying reading achievement. For example, we do not find syntax as a first-level predictor after grade 1, nor graphophonemics after grade 6. Syntax tends to become asymptotic to maturity about grade 1 or 2 and graphophonemics stops differentiating readers at some developmental point between grade 6 and high-school level. But semantics, an open-ended variable is a first-level predictor throughout the grades. Therefore, all factors that occur at one grade level as substrata factors can still be mobilized into working systems at higher grade levels. Indeed, factor analytic studies at all grade levels show that reading comprehension loads to some degree on all the variables in the major systems of syntax, semantics, and reasoning-in-reading.

CONCLUSION

The substrata-factor theory has a productive career. Holmes and Singer (1964) perceived the formulation of other "theoretical models and a trend to more basic

critique

research in reading." They predicted this trend would lead to a spirit of creative activity. The results were even greater than they anticipated; some were included in a *festschrift* for Holmes (Singer & Ruddell, 1970, 1976). The postulates, hypotheses, and concepts of substrata-factor theory also have a close resemblance to other theoretical formulations and models, such as Rumelhart's (1976) interaction model and schemata theory (1981).

Note the similarities between substrata theory concepts with Rumelhart's interaction model and theory. Rumelhart's concepts are stated in parentheses in the next sentences. Holmes defined a substrata factor as "a system of subsystems," each with its "special information and rich associations (knowledge structures) which has a *functional integrity* of its own and at the same time may contribute to larger and more complex working systems which have functional integrities of their own (embedded hierarchies of schemata). The "systems may be mobilized (activated) into a hierarchy of a more comprehensive working system" . . . in accordance with the requirements of the task and the purposes of the individual" (interaction between text-based and reader-based resources) (Holmes & Singer, 1966, p. 177). However, instead of simply postulating the systems within the reader that simultaneously and mutually interact with each other and with the text, Holmes created a statistical model to empirically determine what these factors are and their relative contributions to each other and to speed and power of reading. Therefore, we conclude that although the substrata-factor theory has appeared inactive for the past decade, it is very much alive and well.

FOR FURTHER LEARNING

Those readers who are interested in continuing to explore the topic of theoretical models of reading would find the following references helpful:

Singer, H. Substrata-factor theory of reading: Theoretical design for teaching reading. In J. A. Figurel (Ed.), *Challenge and experiment in reading*. New York: Scholastic Magazines, 1962.

Singer, H. Substrata-factor evaluation of a precocious reader. *The Reading Teacher*, 1965b, *18*(4), 228–296.

Singer, H. *Substrata-factor reorganization accompanying development in speed and power of reading at the elementary school level.* (Cooperative Research Project No. 2011), U.S. Department of Health, Education, and Welfare (Office of Education), 1965c.

Singer, H. Conceptualization in learning to read. In G. Schick & M. May (Eds.), *New frontiers in college-adult reading*. Fifteenth Yearbook of the National Reading Conference. Marquette, Wisconsin: The National Reading Conference, 1966.

Singer, H. Roundtable review: Reply to John Carroll's critique of the substrata-factor theory of reading. *Research in the Teaching of English*, 1969, *3*(5), 87–102.

Singer, H. Conceptualization in learning to read. Reprinted in H. Singer & R. B. Ruddell (Eds.), *Theoretical models and processes of reading*. Newark, Del.: International Reading Association, 1976.

REFERENCES

Anderson, I. H., & Dearborn, W. F. *The psychology of teaching reading.* New York: Ronald, 1952.

Athey, I., & Holmes, J. A. *Reading success and personality characteristics in junior high school students.* (University of California Publications in Education, Vol. 18.) Berkeley: Unversity of California Press, 1969.

Barr, R. The effect of instruction on pupil reading strategies. *Reading Research Quarterly,* 1974–75, *10,* No. 4.

Bloom, B. S. Mastery learning and its implications for curriculum development. In E. Eisner (Ed.), *Confronting curriculum reform.* Boston: Little, Brown, 1971.

Bond, G. L., & Dykstra, R. The cooperative research program in first-grade reading instruction. *Reading Research Quarterly,* 1967, *2,* 5–142.

Buswell, G. T. Fundamental reading habits: A study of their development. *Supplementary Educational Monographs,* No. 21, University of Chicago Press, 1922.

Carroll, J. B. A model of school learning. *Teachers College Record,* 1963, *64,* 723–733.

Gates, A. I. *The improvement of reading.* New York: Macmillan, 1947.

Gray, W. S. In Bonnie M. Davis (Ed.), *A guide to information sources for reading.* Newart, Del.: International Reading Association, 1972.

Guthrie, J. Models of reading and reading disability. *Journal of Educational Psychology,* 1973, *65,* 9–18.

Holmes, J. A. *The substrata-factor theory of reading.* Berkeley: California Book Co., Multilithed, 1953. (Out of print.)

Holmes, J. A. Factors underlying major reading disabilities at the college level. (Doctoral dissertation, University of California, Berkeley, 1948.) Published in *Genetic Psychology Monographs,* 1954, *49,* 1–95.

Holmes, J. A. The substrata-factor theory of reading: Some experimental evidence. In J. A. Figurel (Ed.), *New Frontiers in Reading* (Proceedings of the Fifth Annual Conference of the International Reading Association). New York: Scholastic Magazine, 1960.

Holmes, J. A. Basic assumptions underlying the substrata-factor theory of reading. *Reading Research Quarterly,* 1965, *1*(1), 5–28.

Holmes, J. A., & Singer, H. *The substrata-factor theory: Substrata-factor differences underlying reading ability in known groups.* U.S. Office of Education, Final Report No. 538, SAE 8176, 1961.

Holmes, J. A., & Singer, H. Theoretical models and trends toward more basic research in reading. *Review of Educational Research,* 1964, *34*(2), 127–155.

Holmes, J. A., & Singer, H. *Speed and power of reading in high school.* U.S. Department of Health, Education, and Welfare, Office of Education, Cooperative Research Monograph No. 14. Washington, D.C.: U.S. Government Printing Office, Superintendent of Documents Catalog No. FS 5.230:30016, 1966.

Huey, E. B. *The psychology and pedagogy of reading.* New York: Macmillan, 1908.

Javal, E. Essai sur la physiologie de lecture. *Annales d' Oculistique,* 1879, *82,* 242–253.

Jerrolds, B. W. *Reading reflections.* Newark, Del.: International Reading Association, 1977.

Judd, C. H., & Buswell, G. T. Silent reading: A study of the various types. *Supplementary Educational Monographs,* No. 23. Chicago: University of Chicago Press, 1922.

Katz, I. C. *The effects of instructional methods on reading acquisition systems.* Unpublished doctoral dissertation, University of California, Riverside, 1980.

Katz, I. C., & Singer, H. Effects of instructional methods on reading acquisition systems: A reanalysis of the first grade studies data. Paper presented at the International Reading Association's Conference, Anaheim, May 1976. In Educational Retrieval of Information Center, 1976.

Katz, I. C., & Singer, H. The substrata factor theory of reading: Differential development of subsystems underlying reading comprehension in the first year of instruction. Paper submitted to the National Reading Conference. Dallas: 1981.

Kling, M. General open systems theory and the substrata-factor theory of reading. In A. J. Kingston (Ed.), *Institute V: Use of theoretical models in research.* (Highlights of the Preconvention Institute.) Newark, Del.: International Reading Association, 1966.

Lazar, M. A diagnostic approach to the reading program, Part I. *Educational Research Bulletin,* No. 3. Bureau of Reference, Research and

Statistics. New York: New York Board of Education, 1942.

Monroe, M. *Children who cannot read.* Chicago: University of Chicago Press, 1932.

Phelan, Sister M. B. Visual perception in relation to variance in reading and spelling. *Educational Research Monograph*, Catholic University of America, 1940, *12*(No. 3), 1–48.

Rumelhart, D. E. *Toward an interactive model of reading.* Technical Report No. 56. San Diego: Center for Human Information Processing, University of California, 1976.

Rumelhart, D. E. Schemata: The building blocks of cognition. In J. T. Guthrie (Ed.), *Comprehension and teaching.* Newark, Del.: International Reading Association, 1981.

Singer, H. *Conceptual ability in the substrata-factory theory of reading.* Unpublished doctoral dissertation, University of California, Berkeley, 1960.

Singer, H. Substrata-factor theory of reading: Theoretical design for teaching reading. In J. A. Figurel (Ed.), *Challenge and experiment in reading.* New York: Scholastic Magazines, 1962.

Singer, H. Substrata-factor patterns accompanying development in power of reading, elementary through college levels. In E. Thurston & L. Hafner (Eds.), *The philosophical and sociological bases of education.* Fourteenth Yearbook of the National Reading Conference. Marquette, Wis.: The National Reading Conference, 1964.

Singer, H. A developmental model for speed of reading in grades three through six. *Reading Research Quarterly*, 1965a, *1*(1), 29–49.

Singer, H. Substrata-factor evaluation of a precocious reader. *The Reading Teacher*, 1965b, *18*(4), 288–296.

Singer, H. *Substrata-factor reorganization accompanying development in speed and power of reading at the elementary school level.* (Cooperative Research Project No. 2011), U. S. Department of Health, Education, and Welfare (Office of Education), 1965c.

Singer, H. Conceptualization in learning to read. In G. Schick & M. May (Eds.), *New Frontiers in College-Adult Reading.* Fifteenth Yearbook of the National Reading Conference. Marquette, Wis.: The National Reading Conference, 1966.

Singer, H. Roundtable review: Reply to John Carroll's critique of the substrata-factor theory of reading. *Research in the Teaching of English*, 1969, *3*(5), 87–102.

Singer, H. Stimulus models for teaching reading. In M. Clark & S. Maxwell (Eds.), *Reading: Influence on Progress. Proceedings of the Fifth Annual Study Congress of the United Kingdom Reading Association*, 1970, 112–119.

Singer, H. Conceptualization in learning to read. Reprinted in H. Singer & R. B. Ruddell (Eds.), *Theoretical Models and Processes of Reading.* Newark, Del.: International Reading Association, 1976.

Singer, H. *Preparing content reading specialists for the junior high school level: Strategies for meeting the wide range of individual differences in reading ability.* Final Report to the U.S. Office of Education, EPDA Project, Fall, 1973. ERIC ED 088003, CS000 924.

Singer, H. A century of landmarks in reading and learning from text at the high school level: Theories, research, and instructional strategies. Invitational paper presented to the California Professors of Reading, at the California Reading Association's annual meeting, Sacramento, Nov. 6, 1980.

Singer, H. Hypotheses on reading comprehension in search of classroom validation. Presidential Address, National Reading Conference. In M. Kamil (Ed.), *30th Yearbook of the National Reading Conference.* Chicago: The National Reading Conference, 1981.

Singer, H., & Donlan, D. *Reading and learning from text.* Boston: Little, Brown, 1980.

Singer, H. & Ruddell, R. B. *Theoretical models and processes of reading.* (1st ed., 1970; 2nd ed., 1976). Newark, Del.: International Reading Association, 1970, 1976.

The Wherry-Doolittle Test Selection Technique. In H. E. Garrett, *Statistics in psychology and education.* New York: Longmans Green, 1947.

A Commentary on Jack Holmes's Substrata-Factor Theory of Reading: Novelty, Novelty, Novelty

JOHN DOWNING

University of Victoria, Canada

This commentary is a summons to reading professionals to maintain rigorous standards of logic in theory and theory-based research. In particular, they should not reject or neglect theory because it is old. Holmes's Substrata-Factor Theory of Reading is a case in point: This commentary reviews the statistical, neurological, and psychological models in Holmes's theory and shows their potential for stimulating further theoretical thought in the field of reading.

Thomas Hood wrote in the *Announcement of Comic Annual for 1836:* "There are three things which the public will always clamour for, sooner or later: namely, novelty, novelty, novelty." This remains true nearly 150 years later. Unfortunately, this popular whim is rampant in education and even in educational psychology. Psychologists, in their scientific training, learn that the soundness of a theory depends on its logical congruity. Neither the date when the theory was propounded nor the year in which the research on it was reported are relevant in judging the worth of a theory. Yet, in reading research, recent findings commonly are more highly regarded than those from earlier studies. This is counterproductive in our field. It stunts the growth of knowledge of the psychology of reading that could sprout from the theoretical genius of outstandingly creative people in this field. "The evil that men do lives after them, the good is oft interred with their bones." So it frequently is with good theories. A remarkable example of this is Professor Jack Holmes's Substrata Factor Theory of Reading. His death came at the height of his development of his theory. His theory was *and still is* a theoretical goldmine. It is far from being exhausted by what has been extracted thus far. Indeed, there are rich veins that, as yet, have barely been explored in our thinking. But since Holmes' death sixteen years ago, little new word on the Substrata-Factor Theory has been initiated.

Portions of this paper were first published in *Reading Psychology*, Spring 1981, 2(2), and are reprinted by permission of the publisher.

HOLMES'S SUBSTRATA-FACTOR THEORY

Holmes wrote this succinct statement of his own theory in a paper for the fifth annual convention of IRA at New York in 1960:

> In essence, the Substrata-Factor Theory holds that, normally, reading is an audio-visual verbal-processing skill of symbolic reasoning, sustained by the intrafacilitations of an intricate hierarchy of substrata factors that have been mobilized as a psychological working system and pressed into service in accordance with the purposes of the reader (Holmes, 1970, 178–188).

Holmes developed three complementary models from this theory. They were, respectively, statistical, neurological, and psychological.

The Statistical Model

The statistical model captured the greatest interest among Holmes' colleagues in the educational psychology and reading professions during his own lifetime. This coincided with the popularity of factor-analytic research methods in educational psychology in that period. Holmes himself was fascinated by the technology of scientific research, its design, its apparatus, its treatment of results, and so on. Thus Holmes and his students became deeply involved in research on the statistical model. Some (but not all) of Holmes' students appear to have become so enamoured of the then-fashionable factor-analytic aspect that they lost sight of the essential logic at the base of the Substrata-Factor Theory.

Holmes used a type of factor-analytic technique to try to identify the "subability" elements that can be mobilized into different "working systems." In his 1960 paper, cited above, he had isolated thirteen crucial variables. Other analyses were made subsequently. These statistical results were subjected to methodological criticism by other researchers (notably Carroll, 1968). As a result, most of the literature on the Substrata-Factor Theory is related to Holmes's statistical model. Neglect of Holmes's theory in the past decade can be due to both the original emphasis on the statistical model and the decline of interest in factor analysis. Although the neurological and psychological models had considerable potential for future development, they were never given the attention that they deserved. Now they languish, perhaps in part because Holmes was so far ahead of his time.

The Neurological Model

Holmes's neurological model could provide the basis for a resolution of the controversy between medically-oriented views of "congenital dyslexia" and psychologically-oriented views of reading disability.

commentary

Burt's (1966) article, "Counterblast to Dyslexia," is rather typical of the strongly negative attitudes of educational psychologists to the neurologically based concept of congenital dyslexia. Burt wrote: "Indeed, the whole attempt to interpret these highly intricate activities in terms of 'brain functions' is in the present state of knowledge gravely misleading. I find it extremely hard to believe that some process of natural selection, operating during the last few centuries, has produced in the general population a specific "brain centre' (or 'cortical area') for reading" (p. 3). Burt went on to cite the evidence against localization of function in the cortex, and concluded that "the term 'congenital' is quite unwarranted, and that, with rare exceptions, the cases commonly grouped under the name 'dyslexia' present educational problems rather than medical or neurological" (p. 4).

Holmes's Substrata-Factor Theory, however, makes it quite unnecessary to posit any special cortical area for reading. His concept of "mobilizers" explains how reading may be influenced by neurological dysfunctions even though the reading of text is far too new historically in the repertoire of human behavior for it to have evolved any specfic neural system or organ of its own. Holmes states that "mobilizers" are "conative tendencies . . . that function to select from one's repertoire of subabilities those which will maximize one's chances of solving a specific problem . . ." (Holmes, 1970, p. 188). Thus, if reading skill involves no subabilities that are not modules of other skills that existed long before the invention of writing, then Burt's objection to the hereditability of a neurologically based dyslexia is removed.

In our book, *Psychology of Reading,* my colleague Che Kan Leong and I have discussed the face validity of Holmes's theory in this respect. We noted that, as well as reading books and other textual material, people read road signs that contain no text. They also read maps, charts, and graphs. Palmists read the lines in people's hands. The old farmer reads the sky to forecast the weather. The deaf read lips. Hunters read the spoor of game. All these forms of reading have the common characteristic of interpretation of visible signs. Some reading (for example, Braille) is not through the visual mode, but we concluded that "*reading is always the interpretation of signs.*" However, we found one difference between reading text and some of these other kinds of reading activities. The signs read by palmists, hunters, and farmers have not been deliberately created with any communication intent. In contrast, signs such as those used in maps and printed or written text are arbitrary *symbols* deliberately created for the purpose of communication. Therefore, we decided that the basic definition of reading for our book on the psychology of the reading behavior of concern to educators should be, "*reading is the interpretation of symbols*" (Downing and Leong, 1982). Hence, none of the subabilities of reading text is unique to that skill. Even the one special feature of text, maps, and charts—that they are deliberately created for the purpose of communication—is not unique. Communication purposes existed in speech prior to the invention of written language. Also, concepts of intentions in general must have existed. Therefore, Holmes's premise that reading behavior consists in the mobilization of more general subabilities seems feasible. These subabilities are subject to the general laws of genetics, and hence individuals may suffer neurological deficiencies in them that can cause reading problems of the type referred to in theories of congenital dyslexia.

The Psychological Model

It is Holmes's psychological model that provides the most interesting integrative insights for the study of the processes of reading and learning to read. Three attributes of the Substrata-Factor Theory should be signposts for future development in theory and research in the psychology of reading: 1) reading as *a skill*; 2) the *modular* nature of subabilities; 3) *conceptual reasoning* in reading acquisition.

1) Reading as *a Skill.* In the quotation at the beginning of this article, Holmes described reading as *a skill*, and he specifically viewed reading as belonging to an "audio-visual verbal-processing skill." To many reading researchers this may be obvious, and they may feel that others such as Clay (1972, p. 8) and Lansdown (1974, p. 4) have also categorized reading as "a skill." But, nevertheless, it is important for reading researchers to assert strongly that reading *is a skill.* There are two reasons why this should be made explicit.

First, the loose usage of the plural form "reading skills" by teaching methods specialists gives students and teachers a false picture of the learning-to-read process. These specialists use the term "skills" to refer to either mental or motor activities that they claim must be taught as part of the reading curriculum. This gives the false impression that these activities are isolated and independent behaviors that can be linked together to create reading ability. Worse, this view distorts everything that psychological research has discovered about the characteristics of a skill—that it is *a whole, integrated, goal-directed complex* of a wide range of behaviors. This is also a serious practical problem because a great deal of damage is being done in classrooms by fragmenting the skill of reading into these alleged elements, many of which have no reality in normal reading behavior.

The second reason why Holmes's view of reading as *a skill* should be made more explicit has much wider significance for theory and research as well as practice. Research on skill learning is one of the oldest interests of scientific psychology. Well-designed experiments on the acquisition of skill were begun toward the end of the nineteenth century, and continuous progress in this aspect of research has been made since then to the present day. A valuable source of general psychological knowledge is thus available that can be applied to the acquisition of the specific skill of reading. This viewpoint was implicit in and runs throughout Holmes's Substrata-Factor Theory. Let us consider two examples of how viewing reading as *a skill* puts general psychological theory and research on skill development to work for understanding the specific process of learning to read.

As a first example, consider Holmes's description of "substrata factors" and the "working system." He wrote that the "substrata factors" are "neurological subsystems" that are "tied together in a working system, and, as their interfacilitation in the working system increases, the efficiency of the child's reading also increases. Here is an explanation, then, of what may take place when the child learns to read better, by reading" (Holmes, 1970, p. 188). Here Holmes is applying and explaining the general principle from educational psychology that appropriate practice is important for skill development. Similarly, Samuels (1976) states: "Students will learn to read only by reading" (p. 325). Bamberger (1976) found that "many children do not read books because they cannot read well enough. They cannot read well because they do not read books" (p. 61). To the problem of Bamberger's paradox, we can bring to bear a vast array of psychological research findings on the effects of practice in the acquisition of skill.

For our second example of how viewing reading as a skill was productive in Holmes' theory, let us consider his concept of "gradient shift." He postulated that "the pattern of substrata factors in a child's reading hierarchy will undergo a *gradient shift,* or orderly change, as he advances through the grades. As a child increases his proficiency over a succession of newly learned subskills, the substrata factor patterns which underlie his developing ability to read will also change" (Holmes, 1970, p. 190). Here, Holmes is applying to reading the well established general principle from educational psychology that the characteristics of behavior in a skill change as the learner moves from being a beginner to becoming a proficient performer.

This fact is overlooked by many reading specialists. Also, certain theorists have taken a rather large leap from observations of fluent reading behavior to prescriptions for teaching beginners. For example, Goodman (1976) writes that the essence of reading is a "constructive search for meaning" (p. 58) in which the readers' "language competence enables them to create a grammatical and semantic prediction in which they need only sample from the print to reach meaning" (p. 59). But does that observation justify Goodman's claim that "instructional reading programs that begin with bits and pieces abstracted from language, like words or letters . . . make learning to read harder because it isn't language anymore?" (p. 59).

The Soviet educational psychologist Elkonin (1973) states the principle that is much more in accord with the weight of evidence from research on skill acquisition in general. He points out that "it is only the summarized, abbreviated and highly automated nature of the perfected form of this skill that gives the impression of a simple association between spoken and written language. Prior to this level of performance, the skill must go through a long period of development and its initial form is not in the least like its final one. One of the most flagrant errors in methods of reading instruction, in our view, is the belief that the initial and final forms of a skill are identical. Their processes are always very different" (p. 17).

2) The *Modular* Nature of Subabilities. A second signpost from Holmes's Substrata-Factor Theory was in his thinking about the "hierarchy of subskills." At the time Holmes was writing, the popular view of this hierarchy was derived mainly from the work of one of his colleagues at Berkeley—Gagné. Its typical expression can be seen in the claim that "we must learn all the subordinate (S–R) chains before we can perform a particular skill" (De Cecco & Crawford, 1974, p. 249). Teaching methods specialists who espouse rigid scope and sequence programs may feel comforted by such assertions, but Gagné's conception of S–R chains was and is open to question. Holmes's scepticism was justified by such views as those expressed by Borger and Seaborne (1966): "It seems likely that the structure of organisms is hierarchical in character, with control shifting between levels according to the demands of the situation" (p. 149). Elliott and Connolly (1974) have shown how the structure of a skill may be hierarchical without implying a rigid sequence for the learning of its subskills. They argue that subskills may be "hierarchically organized in the pursuit of activities that are voluntary with respect to their guiding plan. Practiced sequences of acts would be definable as subroutines, comprised in turn of lower order behavioural elements available to more than one higher order sequence" (p. 139).

Holmes had already applied this viewpoint to reading when he wrote: "A working system may be described as a dynamic set of subabilities which have been mobilized for the purpose of solving a particular problem. Neurologically, a working system is conceived of as a nerve-net pattern in the brain that functionally links together the various substrata factors that have been mobilized into a workable communications system," and that "an individual will solve the same problem at different times in his life by using different working systems. Moreover, different individuals may perform the same task to an equal degree of success by drawing upon different sets of sub-abilities. In other words, we hypothesize that there is more than one way to solve an intellectual problem" (Holmes, 1970, p. 189). Although Holmes and Singer (1961) discovered a common set of basic subskills in reading, they believed that their studies substantiated completely the hypothesis that "different individuals may perform the same task (reading) with equal success by mobilizing different sets of sub-abilities" (Holmes & Singer, 1964, p. 132). Lansdown puts it in more graphic language: "reading is a skill . . . organized in a hierarchy of subskills" but "unfortunately, this hierarchy of skills does not unfold, layer after layer, like an onion. It is more like a plate of spaghetti, with a recognizable top and bottom and many overlapping bits in the middle" (p. 5).

3) ***Conceptual Reasoning* in Reading Acquisition.** Possibly, Holmes's most valuable contribution in his Substrata-Factor Theory was in his insight into the psychological link between conative and cognitive aspects of human development. Let us consider his statements on these respective aspects:

1. "*Mobilizers* are psychologically defined in terms of deepseated value systems, the fundamental ideas that the individual holds of himself, and his developing relationship to his environment. As conative tendencies, with or without conscious awareness, mobilizers function to select from one's repertoire of sub-abilities those which will maximize one's chances of solving a problem in particular, and forwarding the realization of self-fulfillment in general" (Holmes, 1970, p. 188).

2. "Other things being equal, then, individual differences in the ability to reason about what is being read . . . depend not only upon the essential nature of the stored information, but more importantly, upon the *associative logic of the conceptualizing activity of perception* stimulated within the brain, by the meaningfulness of the sequential input at the time of *presentation* and *reception*." Therefore, "the careful selection of meaningful material, the logic of our explanations, the continuity of our theme in the classroom lesson, the unit, and the total curriculum are important not only because they foster clarity and understanding at the time of presentation, but because the logic and fact of the sequential input is the essential element in teaching that leads the child *himself* to develop these habits of cortical association which determine not only the nature

and efficiency of recall, but also the degrees of freedom or versatility a child may have for reorganizing his working systems later on when, in fact, reorganization is necessary and desirable, if the process of symbolic reasoning is to be both logical and creative—that is, if it is to maximize creativity in the transfer of training process" (Holmes, 1970, p. 191).

These two premises in the Substrata-Factor Theory provide an explanation of a phenomenon in reading that has long been recognized but not well understood. Let us recollect the well-established fact that the purpose of the reading act is an integral part of the psychological process of reading. Purpose in reading is like the gear shift system in an automobile. The total process cannot be separated from the essential shift system that changes dynamically according to the driver's (or reader's) purpose and the level of difficulty of the road (or book).

Consider Thorndike's (1917) description of reading comprehension: "The mind is assailed as it were by every word in the paragraph. It must select, repress, soften, emphasize, correlate, and organize, all under the influence of the right mental set or purpose or demand" (p. 329). Other classic studies, such as those of Gray (1917) and Judd and Buswell (1922), found that eye movements in reading change according to the purpose, indicating that a change of brain processing is occurring with the shift of purpose. Recent studies continue to underscore this fact (for example, Rickards & August, 1975). Russell (1970) in his final book concluded: "The dominant factor in comprehension . . . is the purpose of the reader, stated or unstated" (p. 170). Holmes's theory provides the explanation for this very important fact.

Holmes's theory also explains how this purposeful reading develops through experience and practice with reading activities—as stated in his two premises quoted above. Holmes spelled out this learning process in his paper presented at the fifteenth annual meeting of the National Reading Conference at Dallas, Texas, in 1965. "When the *child begins* to talk, these somatesthetic areas and the uncommitted area (Penfield, 1964) of the cortex begin to form the necessary neurological connections and psychological associations to shape up his command of the language. But as the educative process really begins to take hold, the child is required to associate meaning to abstract *visual* symbols representing abstract *auditory* symbols which, in turn, represent *pictures* of objects which the child must *handle* to know. And so one of the developmental tasks the school must present to the tactile-kinesthetically minded child is a problem-enriched environment demanding auditory-*verbal,* visual-*verbal,* and manipulatory-*verbal* responses to multifaceted stimuli objects. If the concepts he is forming are to have much meaning, then actual object 'touch stones' must be present. Although first-hand experience is basic, experience talked about by the child himself makes for a better learning situation" (Holmes, 1966, p. 110).

The importance of other aspects of logical reasoning in learning a skill also has been given greater recognition in the literature of psychological theory and research in recent years. For example, Cronbach (1977), in his review of studies of skill acquisition, states that the learner "must find out what to do" (p. 396), and the beginner "is getting in mind just what is to be done" (p. 398). Even earlier, Fitts (1962) had concluded that the initial phase of skill learning is a "cognitive" one. Vernon (1971) has arrived at the same conclusion in regard to the specific skill of reading. She states that learning the alphabetic principle "necessitates a fairly advanced stage of conceptual reasoning" and "intelligent comprehension" of the task (p. 82). In her earlier review of the causes of reading disability, Vernon (1957) had concluded that "the fundamental trouble appears to be a failure in development of this reasoning process" (p. 48), and she named this failure "cognitive confusion" (p. 71). The present author has reviewed elsewhere (Downing, 1979) the numerous investigations that have indicated that in all the various languages studied thus far, children normally enter the task of acquiring the skill of reading in a state of cognitive confusion about its purposes and about the features of speech that are represented by the orthography.

In Conclusion

Holmes's professional life was strongly motivated by his interest in the creative development of theories and their testing through scientific research. Singer and Ruddell (1970) have provided a tribute to Holmes in their volume of *Theoretical Models and Processes of Reading* that is formally dedicated to his memory. In that book, Singer and Kling (1970, p. vii) ask us to remember Holmes "as a spurt of creative productivity" in integrating theory construction and experimental research. Holmes's work is not done yet. His thoughts are still with us. They still have great potential for stimulating further creative theory development. But we must insist on rigorous standards of logic in theory and theory-based research, and we should resist the public demand for novelty with its concomitant rejection of theory and research just because it's old or out of fashion.

REFERENCES

Bamberger, R. Literature and development in reading. In J. E. Merritt (Ed.), *New horizons in reading*. Newark: International Reading Association, 1976.

Borger, R., & Seaborne, A.E.M. *The psychology of learning*. Harmondsworth: Penguin, 1966.

Burt, C. Counterblast to dyslexia. *Association of Educational Psychologists Newsletter,* March 1966, No. 5, 2–6.

Carroll, J. B. (Review of *Speed and power of reading in high school* by Holmes and Singer). *Research in the Teaching of English,* 1968, 2, 172–184.

Clay, M. M. *Reading the patterning of complex behaviour*. Auckland: Heinemann, 1972.

Cronbach, L. J. *Educational psychology*. New York: Harcourt, Brace & Jovanovich, 1977.

De Ceddo, J. P., & Crawford, W. R. *The psychology of learning and instruction.* Englewood Cliffs: Prentice Hall, 1974.

Downing, J. *Reading and reasoning*. Edinburgh: Chambers, and New York: Springer, 1979.

Downing, J., & Leong, C. K. *Psychology of learning to read.* New York: Macmillan, 1982.

Elkonin, D. B. Further remarks on the psychological bases of the initial teaching of reading (in Russian). *Sovetskaia Pedogogika,* 1973, 14–23.

Elliott, J., & Connolly, K. Hierarchical structure in skill development. In K. Connolly & J. S. Bruner (Eds.), *The growth of competence*. London: Academic Press, 1974.

Fitts, P. Factors in complex skill training. In R. Glaser (Ed.), *Training research and educa-*

references

tion. Pittsburgh: University of Pittsburgh Press, 1962.

Goodman, K. S. What we know about reading. In P. D. Allen & D. J. Watson (Eds.), *Findings of research in miscue analysis: Classroom applications*. Urbana: National Council of Teachers of English, 1976.

Gray, C. T. *Types of reading ability as exhibited through tests and laboratory experiments*. (Supplementary Educational Monographs, No. 5.) Chicago: University of Chicago Press, 1917.

Holmes, J. A. Toward the generalizations of the substrata-factor theory to include a deterministic-nondeterministic learning theory. In G. B. Schick & M. M. May (Eds.), *New frontiers in college-adult reading*. Milwaukee: National Reading Conference, 1966.

Holmes, J. A. The substrata-factor theory of reading: Some experimental evidence. In H. Singer & R. B. Ruddell (Eds.), *Theoretical models and process of reading*. Newark: International Reading Association, 1970.

Holmes, J. A., & Singer, H. *The substrata-factor theory: Substrata factor differences underlying reading ability in known groups at the high school level*. (Final report covering contracts no. 538, SAE-8176 and no. 538A, SAI-8660, U. S. Department of Health, Education and Welfare, Office of Education.) Berkeley: School of Education, University of California, 1961.

Holmes, J. A., & Singer, H. Theoretical models and trends toward more basic research in reading. *Reivew of Educational Research*, 1964, *34*, 127–255.

Judd, C. H., & Bushwell, G. *Silent reading: A study of the various types*. (Supplementary Education Monographs, No. 23.) Chicago: University of Chicago, 1922.

Lansdown, R. *Reading: Teaching and learning*. London: Pitman, 1974.

Penfield, W. The uncommitted cortex. *The Atlantic*, 1964, *7*, 77–81.

Rickards, J. P., & August, G. J. Generative underlying strategies in prose recall. *Journal of Educational Psychology*, 1975, *67*, 860–865.

Russell, D. H. *The dynamics of reading*. Waltham: Ginn-Blaisdell, 1970.

Samuels, S. J. Automatic decoding and reading comprehension. *Language Arts*, 1976, *53*, 323–325.

Singer, H., & Kling, M. Dedication: Jack Alroy Holmes, 1911–1967. In H. Singer & R. B. Ruddell (Eds.), *Theoretical models and processes of reading*. Newark: International Reading Association, 1970.

Singer, H., & Ruddell, R. B. (Eds.) *Theoretical models and processes of reading*. Newark: International Reading Association, 1970.

Thorndike, E. L. Reading as reasoning: A study of mistakes in paragraph reading. *Journal of Educational Psychology*, 1917, *8*, 323–332.

Vernon, M. D. *Backwardness in reading*. London: Cambridge University Press, 1957.

Vernon, M. D. *Reading and its difficulties*. London: Cambridge University Press, 1971.

SUMMARY OF D. LABERGE AND S. J. SAMUELS'S STUDY: TOWARD A THEORY OF AUTOMATIC INFORMATION PROCESSING IN READING

LYNDA MELTON

Irving Independent School District

The LaBerge and Samuels model of automaticity in reading is based on the premise that the interpretation of graphic stimuli into meaning involves sequential stages of information processing. LaBerge and Samuels's purpose was to describe and evaluate the processing of information at each of the following stages: visual memory, phonological memory, and episodic memory. They stressed that meaning from written symbols cannot be readily obtained if the reader's attention is focused at these other levels.

In their visual memory model, LaBerge and Samuels stated that we may process several perceptual codes at one time, but we can focus our attention on just one of those codes. This perceptual code is acted upon by the feature detectors, then processed into letter codes, spelling codes, word codes, and eventually into word-group codes.

To interpret these visual codes into meaning, LaBerge and Samuels relied on Gibson's (1969) and Rumelhart's (1970) research on processing individual features such as line, angle, intersections, and directional features of left, right, up, and down. The attention center is crucial in the beginning stages of perceptual learning, but it is not required in the later stages. To focus attention on the meaning or semantic stage, these visual codes must be processed automatically.

LaBerge (1973) wanted to know whether a person could recognize a letter or letter pattern automatically. He decided the best way to determine this was to show the person the letter or letter patterns when they were expecting a different letter. The amount of time or latency between the stimulus and the response would indicate automaticity or whether attention was required for recognition. In this particular study, the unfamiliar letters were ⇂, ⇃, ↿, ↾, and the familiar ones were *b, d, p, q*. They chose the letters *a, g, n, s* as cues to focus the reader's attention. Sixteen college students were shown the letters. On the first trial, they recognized the familiar letters automatically, but with practice over the four days, there was no difference in the latencies. These data indicate that the perceptual process can become automatic with focused practice.

To measure the role of attention in associative processing, LaBerge and Samuels used latency as the gauge of learning time. (Latency refers to a period of delay in response time to the appearance of the letters.) This experiment directly followed the one measuring automatic perceptual processing, using the same familiar and unfamiliar letters. The unfamiliar letters ⇂, ⇃, ↾, ↿, were practiced until automaticity was achieved in the previous experiment. The familiar letters were given names, bee, dee, pea, and cue. The unfamiliar ones were named one, two, three, and four. LaBerge and Samuels theorized that to control the reader's attention, they needed to present the letter when another letter was expected. Eight subjects were shown successive pairs of common words. When the second word matched the first, they were to push a button. Occasionally an unfamiliar or familiar letter was presented in place of a pair of common words, and the subject was asked to name it by speaking into a microphone. Since the individual could not anticipate when the letters would appear, the latency measure identified the amount of time required to recognize them. After the initial trial, 20 days of practice naming the new letters followed. At the end of the 20 days, the college students did not name the unfamiliar letters as quickly as they did the familiar ones. The results indicate that some measurable time was still required to make these associations.

LaBerge and Samuels (1974) indicated that the fluent reader has practiced processing these perceptual codes or subskills until they are automatic and do not require focused attention for purposes of identification. Because "automaticity" has been achieved, the fluent reader views reading as a holistic process. The authors emphasized the importance of practicing these subskills until students reach this level of automaticity. At this point the reader's attention can be focused on the ultimate goal of reading, that of meaning.

REFERENCES

Gibson, E. J. *Principles of perceptual learning and development.* New York: Appleton-Century-Crofts, 1969.

LaBerge, D. Attention and the measurement of perceptual learning. *Memory and Cognition,* 1973 (b), *1,* 268–275.

LaBerge, D., & Samuels, S. J. Toward a theory of automatic information processing in reading. *Cognitive Psychology,* 1974, *6,* 293–323.

Rumelhart, D. E. A multicomponent theory of the presentation of briefly exposed visual displays. *Journal of Mathematical Psychology,* 1970, *7,* 191–218.

references

A Critique of, A Theory of Automaticity in Reading: Looking Back: A Retrospective Analysis of the LaBerge-Samuels Reading Model

S. JAY SAMUELS AND DAVID LABERGE

University of Minnesota

INTRODUCTION

The LaBerge-Samuels reading model had its origin in a concept which serves to bring together faculty from a number of related disciplines who are members of the Center for Research in Human Learning. Unfortunately, scientists in different disciplines often fail to communicate with each other even though the cross-fertilization of ideas can bring new insights and solutions to problems of scientific importance. The learning center at Minnesota encourages its members to work collaboratively.

LaBerge is an experimental psychologist with interests in memory, learning, and attention. Samuels is an educational psychologist with interests in the reading process. What began as casual meetings in which they discussed reading, culminated in the development of the model and ultimately in a series of investigations as to how words are recognized.

The decade in which LaBerge and Samuels worked together was an exciting period. During this time psychologists were loosening their ties with behaviorism and a movement toward cognitive and information processing approaches. While interest remained high in studies of the word recognition process, new theories of how information is stored and retrieved from semantic memory were developed and tested. This was a period in which new knowledge about the reading process rapidly appeared. As mentioned in the article itself, the LaBerge-Samuels model of reading is a partial model that makes no attempt to include all aspects of what is known about reading. However, model building is a dynamic process and major revisions may come at a later date.

A RETROSPECTIVE ANALYSIS

Seldom have researchers been given the opportunity to do a retrospective analysis of their own work, to determine what aspects, in their opinion, have withstood the test of time and what they would do differently if given the opportunity. In this retrospective analysis, we will present a brief overview of our model, and discuss which aspects of our model on automatic information processing in reading we think have withstood the test of time and which aspects we would like to revise. We will also discuss studies which have been done since the publication of the article that supports the model, and which aspects of the model have lent themselves to practical applications.

COMPREHENSIVE VERSUS PARTIAL MODELS

Nearly a decade ago, we began a year-long series of discussions on the nature of the reading process. These discussions were directed at a number of questions such as the role of attention in decoding and comprehension, differences in how unskilled and skilled readers might deploy attention, and alternative routes information might take on its journey from print to meaning. Other topics included components of an information processing system and the size of the visual processing unit used in word recognition by readers with different degrees of skill who are reading for different purposes. The discussions culminated in an article that took on the form of a model.

Articles that model the reading process were certainly not new at that time, as a considerable number of such models were already available. These models can be categorized as either comprehensive or partial. Comprehensive models attempt to describe the entire reading process, from decoding to comprehension, with rather broad brush strokes. While the numerous factors that affect reading appear in the models, the major shortcoming of comprehensive models is that it may be difficult, if not impossible, to formulate precise hypotheses to test their validity. Thus, what these models gain in comprehensability, they lose in testability.

On the other hand, the partial models only describe some small aspect of the total process but they attempt to do so with enough precision that hypotheses can be derived to test their validity. Thus, what the partial models lose in comprehensability, they gain in testability. Since one of the most important characteristics of a good model is that it can be tested to determine its validity, it is better to err by being less comprehensive and devise models that can be tested. We decided, therefore, to sacrifice comprehensiveness to gain testability.

The LaBerge-Samuels model is, therefore, a partial, rather than a comprehensive, model. For example, in comparing the degree of detail shown in our figures for visual memory in contrast with semantic memory, one can note that there is a detailed internal structure for visual but not for semantic memory. The reason for greater detail in visual memory is that, at the time the model was constructed, more was known about how the visual input was processed than about how meaning was derived from the visual input. In time, as we learn more about semantic memory, we will be able to provide richer detail. Thus, our model has much more to say about particular aspects of reading, but this was done by design rather than by default.

Theory or model building should be conceptualized as a continuous rather than a static process, one aspect of which is the creation of a structure based upon what is known at the time. Other aspects include the testing of that structure and its revision based upon new evidence. With this in mind, our model appears to serve several useful functions. Certain aspects of the model have suggested hypotheses which have led to experimental tests (Schwartz, 1980; Klein, 1976; Samuels, LaBerge, & Bremer, 1978); the model also provided a base which others have used to devise alternative models (Rumelhart, 1977; Stanovich, 1980).

OVERVIEW OF THE MODEL

Before engaging in the retrospective analysis, a brief description of this model is required. As seen in Critique/Figure 1, the model has the form of an information processing paradigm. [Note: The feedback loops in the figure that goes from semantic memory (SM) to phonological memory (PM) and to visual memory (VM) were not part of the original 1974 article but were added later (Samuels, 1977)].

Perhaps the best way to explain an information processing model is to use an analogy. A factory is a place where raw material enters at one point and a product leaves at some other location. As the raw material moves through the factory, a variety of machines, each with a different function, transforms the raw material into its final form. Since some of the machines work faster than others, the material must be stored until the next process can begin. Obviously, in this complex process, a strategic control device is needed to supervise and manage the entire system. Thus, the factory has four basic elements: raw material, machines, storage units, and a strategic control manager. The four elements in a factory can also be found in the LaBerge-Samuels information processing model.

Let us examine how the LaBerge-Samuels model incorporates these elements. We will begin by describing the raw material used in reading. Then we will describe the machines which process the material and how attention is strategic control manager. Finally, we will describe how information is stored and retrieved.

Visual information, the raw material of reading. In Critique/Figure 1, the raw material used by the information processing system is represented by the arrows on the left, which strike the sensory surface of the eye. This raw material consists of letters, words, figures, tables, pictures, and other sources of information which the writer has placed on the printed page.

The machines: visual memory. In addition to the sources of information on the page which serve as the raw material of reading, there are other elements in the model we need to identify. In the model there are four "machines" that process the information on the page. These are represented in Critique/Figure 1 by visual memory (VM), phonological memory (PM), episodic memory (EM), and semantic memory (SM). Each machine has a unique function. Visual memory takes the marks on the page,

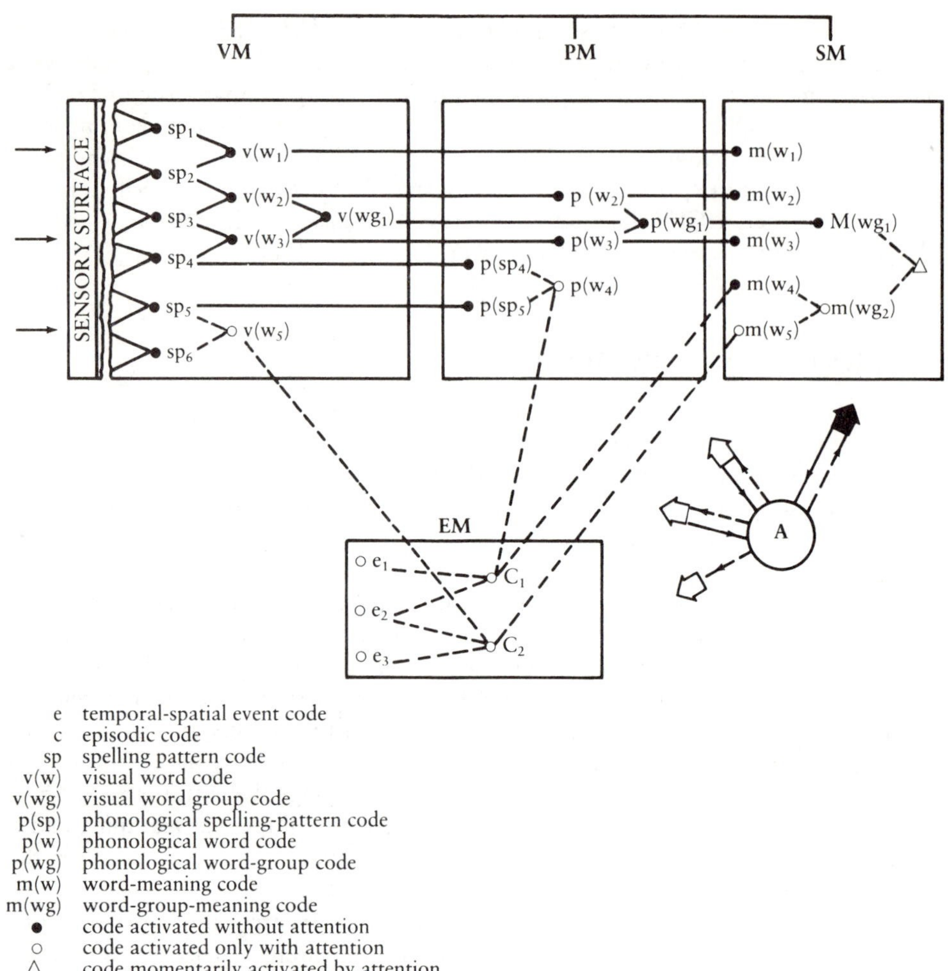

e temporal-spatial event code
c episodic code
sp spelling pattern code
v(w) visual word code
v(wg) visual word group code
p(sp) phonological spelling-pattern code
p(w) phonological word code
p(wg) phonological word-group code
m(w) word-meaning code
m(wg) word-group-meaning code
● code activated without attention
○ code activated only with attention
△ code momentarily activated by attention
➧ momentary focus of attention
—— information flow without attention
— — information flow only with attention

CRITIQUE/FIGURE 1.
Information Processing Model.

such as the letters, spelling patterns, and words, and extracts the visual information they contain.

Critique/Figure 2 shows a more detailed description of visual memory, including the variety of visual units which can be used in word recognition. Unlike some models of word recognition that claim word recognition is a holistic process or others that claim it is a component letter process, the model of visual memory shows that various size units may be used in recognizing a word. As seen in this illustration, for example, symbols f_3 through f_8 indicate that combinations of features can be put

critique

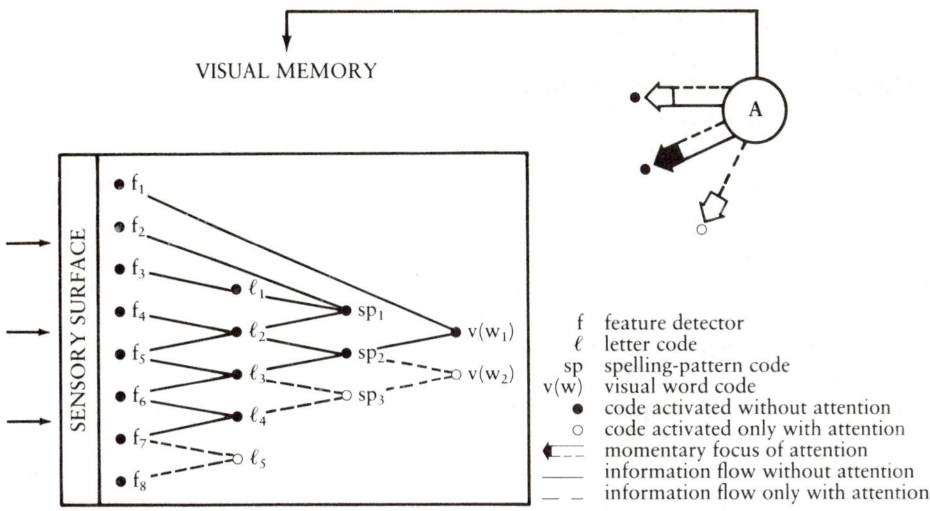

CRITIQUE/FIGURE 2.
The Machines: Visual Memory.

together to form a letter. To illustrate this, imagine a vertical line such as "l" with a circle "o" located at the bottom right of the vertical. This combination of features would give us the letter "b," while a vertical line with a circle located at the bottom left would give us the letter "d." As skilled readers, we see these letters as a single unit, but when first learning the alphabet, the student would identify the smaller features before cementing these features together to form a single letter unit.

Critique/Figure 2 shows that letters combine to form spelling patterns, and these patterns, which consist of frequently seen combinations of letters, are processed as a single visual unit. Symbols l1 through l5 and symbols sp1 through sp3 ("l" for letter and "sp" for spelling pattern) represent this. We encounter these spelling patterns with consonant digraphs such as "ch" as in "cheese" and "sch" as in "school," or with vowel diagraphs such as "oi" as in "boil." These letter combinations must be processed as a single visual unit even though they comprise several individual letters. There are still other spelling patterns, such as prefixes and suffixes, which are processed as single visual units even though they contain several letters.

In the model of visual memory, one also notices that spelling patterns "sp1" and "sp2" can combine to form a word, as represented by v(w1). To see how this works, imagine a spelling pattern such as "scr" in combination with other patterns such as "ee" and "ch" to give us the word "screech."

In this figure, one should also note features f_1 and f_2. The feature designated by f_2 hooks up directly with spelling pattern (sp1) and indicates that under some circumstances the reader may identify a spelling pattern without first identifying the individual letters. In other words, some features for spelling patterns permit direct recognition. Similarly, the feature designated by f_1 hooks up directly with a word, designated by v(w1). The linkage between a word feature and the word indicates there are certain features for words such that the reader can recognize a word without identifying all of its constituent letters.

Haber and Haber (1981) have provided an explanation as to how holistic recognition of words without prior identification of all the constituent letters might occur as the result of context, familiarity with spelling patterns, the shape or outline of a word, and the sparing use of a few letters such as its first or last letters. To illustrate a similar type of holistic recognition, one can often recognize the figure of a friend at a distance from a combination of features such as the person's shape, size, and manner of walking. This recognition may occur at a distance at which smaller features such as eye color and shape of eye, nose, and mouth are unrecognizable. Similarly, in the holistic recognition of a word, we can use a combination of features such as its shape or configuration, its length, and its beginning letter, as well as its context.

Thus, in the LaBerge-Samuels model of visual memory, one can use a number of visual units in word recognition. Exactly which one is used depends on factors such as reader skill, word frequency, and purpose for reading. In a later section, we will discuss how these factors influence the recognition process. For now, however, we will move on to a description of phonological memory.

The machines: phonological memory. Phonological memory translates the printed symbols on the page into their corresponding sound values. This translation of print into sound may occur at several levels such as the letter level, the spelling pattern level, or the whole word level. For example, the combination of letters "s" and "e" would give the phonological representation /se/, the printed symbols "boat" would be translated to the representation /boat/, and the spelling pattern "-ing" at the end of a word like "boating" would be /boating/.

The machines: semantic memory. So far, we have shown how the reader gets from the visual symbols on a page to their corresponding sound representations, but we still have to show how meaning is derived. Comprehending the text is a function performed by semantic memory. Stored within semantic memory are word meanings and procedures for taking strings of these words that conform to the rules of grammar and using them to make sense out of sentences and longer forms of discourse.

The machines: episodic memory. The last machine we will describe is episodic memory. This machine keeps a record of the time, place, and setting during which a particular event or piece of information was acquired. Thus, the knowledge contained in episodic memory is tied to a particular setting. For example, a child who learned to read using a particular typeface might have difficulty reading an unfamiliar type. For word recognition knowledge to be useful, however, one must be able to recognize words in a wide variety of typefaces; that is, for knowledge to be maximally useful, it must be generalizable across numerous conditions and not specific to a particular time, place, or setting.

Thus, a critical difference between episodic and semantic memory is that semantic memory contains general, abstract knowledge which is usable across a variety of situations and settings, whereas episodic memory contains information which

critique

can be used only when a new situation matches rather closely the setting where the information was learned originally. Obviously, to be a good reader one must be able to use one's skills across a broad spectrum of situations, and consequently, it is semantic memory that is most useful in skilled reading.

For purposes of reading, the more important of the four machines are visual, phonological, and semantic memory. These will take the raw material from the printed page, extract the visual information, translate this to the corresponding sound units, and then derive its meaning. However, as apparent from an examination of Critique/Figure 1, the information can take a number of alternative routes on its journey from print to meaning, so that, as important as phonological memory is, it can be bypassed. Also, as we noted in the discussion of visual memory and the different size units used in word recognition, several alternative ways to recognize a word exist. Thus, in the journey from print to meaning, the information may take a number of different paths.

The strategic control manager: attention. One of the most important factors in the model is attention, which is symbolized by the circled "A" in both figures. Attention is a concept psychologists use to explain the cognitive requirements for performing a variety of tasks ranging from reading to driving an automobile. As the term is currently used, it usually refers to the amount of mental energy or effort required to perform tasks. Unfortunately, the amount of attention each of us has available at any given instant is limited. Consequently, if the task we wish to perform requires less attention than we have available, there is no problem since the energy cost is less than our capacity to perform the task. But, if the energy cost for a task exceeds attention capacity, we have to resort to a strategy to overcome our energy limitations.

One useful strategy to use when energy costs exceed capacity is dividing the task into smaller units, being careful that the energy demands of the subunits are less than our capacity limitations. Through this strategy of divide and conquer, the unskilled person can perform complex tasks by doing one subunit at a time. Although the unskilled person can now perform complex tasks, the procedure is slow and difficult. As the unskilled person continues to practice the subunits, the attention demands for the subunits decrease, enabling the student to group the subunits into larger and larger chunks until the entire task can be handled as a single unit.

The basic concepts just described help us understand differences between unskilled and skilled readers. Let us assume that reading is a complex activity, that the attention demands for the unskilled reader to decode the words, extract the meanings of individual words, combine the meanings of all the words to comprehend the sentence as a whole, and to relate the meaning of the sentence to the rest of the text exceeds the student's capacity. Consequently, the student must divide the task into subunits of decoding and comprehension. One strategy the unskilled reader can use is to put attention first on the decoding task and, when it is done, switch attention to comprehension. By switching attention back and forth from decoding to comprehension, the poor reader can read a text with understanding.

Not only must the poor reader subdivide the task into decoding and comprehension, but often must break the words themselves into smaller units. Dividing the words into smaller units for decoding purposes and switching attention back and forth from decoding to comprehension is a slow, difficult process that puts a heavy load on attention and memory systems. The size of the visual unit used for decoding, whether it is a letter, group of letters, or the whole word, depends on the energy demands. Generally, the less skilled the reader, the smaller the unit of visual processing. Also, the less familiar the words that the reader has to decode, the greater the energy costs as the reader processes smaller units. Evidence to support the contention that beginning readers forced to recognize unfamiliar words resort to a strategy of processing at the letter level will be presented in a later section of this article.

With practice, the attention demands for decoding decrease. Then the student will decode larger units and, eventually, decode and comprehend simultaneously. When the decoding task requires so little attention that the student can decode and comprehend simultaneously, we say the decoding is automatic. This automaticity stage is an important characteristic of skilled reading; however, it is important to emphasize that although automatic decoding is a necessary condition, it is not sufficient to guarantee good comprehension. To read with comprehension, numerous comprehension skills are necessary; just having the ability to decode automatically does not ensure that the student can understand the text. Two recent studies in which poor readers still had comprehension difficulties despite receiving training in high-speed word recognition supports the contention that comprehension is a complex process and that automatic decoding is just one of the many skills which must be mastered (Fleisher, Jenking, & Pany, 1979; Dahl & Samuels, 1979).

With regard to the role of attention in reading, we have discussed the delicate balance that must be maintained between task demands and attention capacity. One additional point must be made on how attention maintains strategic control. As stated before, one of the functions of strategic control is to determine when certain processes will begin and when they will terminate. In human information processing, this function is governed by directing attention to the task one wishes to accomplish. For example, when the beginning reader focuses attention on decoding a particular group of words, this task is set in motion. When the reader switches attention to comprehension, the decoding stops. Thus, when attention is focused on a task, it is set in motion and, when attention is withdrawn, the process stops.

It is important to add, however, that under certain conditions a process may be set in motion without the guiding influence of attention. This can occur when a process is so well learned that it is automatic and requires little attention. Then, all that is required to start the process is a stimulus, such as a road sign. For example, when a skilled reader with many years of driving experience sees a sign that says "stop," the necessary actions are instituted without focusing attention on each of the sub-units of behavior. Also, when driving on a highway where there are advertisements, the fluent reader can read them without conscious intention or awareness of effort. For purposes of strategic control, then, attention directs behavior for tasks that are not automatic and require effort and energy. Automatic tasks seem to be completed without the directing influence and control of attention.

Information storage and retrieval. When humans process information, they need some mechanism to store and retrieve it. In the LaBerge-Samuels model, information is stored and retrieved in two ways. Paying attention is one way to store information,

critique

but the storage is temporary. For example, when instructing the beginning reader, the teacher may write CAT on the board and say this word is "cat." To prevent immediate forgetting, the student must pay attention to what the teacher is saying, attend to the writing on the board, and rehearse the association between the visual and phonological representation of the word. During the learning phase, each time the student sees CAT the phonological representation can be retrieved from memory using a considerable amount of attention. Thus, during the learning phase, attention is used to store and retrieve information. During this acquisition phase, reaction time tends to be slow, considerable attention is required for the execution of the response, and often the student has difficulty retrieving the desired response when the stimulus appears.

With enough practice, however, the student can recognize the word and retrieve its meaning from memory using little attention and with faster and more accurate reaction time. The first situation, in which the student only recognizes the word using considerable amounts of attention corresponds to what we ordinarily think of as short-term memory. The second situation, in which the student recognizes the word and retrieves it from memory with little attention corresponds to what we think of as long-term memory.

Once again we note the importance of attention. When we want to store and retrieve new information, the task requires focusing considerable amounts of attention. On the other hand, well learned information can be retrieved from memory using little attention.

SUMMARY

Visual information from the page strikes the sensory surface of the eye, and this information must be decoded. However, because of differences in attentional demands for decoding between unskilled and skilled readers, somewhat different processes are used. Unskilled readers tend to use smaller units, whereas skilled readers use larger units. However, when the skilled reader encounters an unfamiliar word, smaller units are used. Thus, the good reader uses either larger or smaller size visual units, depending on familiarity with the text and purpose for reading. When the skilled reader's purpose for reading is for meaning, holistic processing is used, but when the purpose is to detect spelling errors, component-letter processing is used.

Once the visual information is decoded, it moves on to phonological memory where the units are processed into their corresponding sound representations. When the visual units are smaller than a word, their component sounds blend together in phonological memory to form a word and, when the visual unit is an entire word, its phonological representation is found. However, when the skilled reader recognizes highly familiar words, the phonological recoding stage may be bypassed and the processing route may go directly from visual memory to semantic memory, that is, from print to meaning.

Once phonological processing is completed, the phonological information is sent to semantic memory where it is processed for meaning.

critique

In this journey from print to meaning, attention occupies a critical role. Because the decoding demands exceed the attentional capacity of beginning readers, attention is focused first on decoding and then on comprehension. On the other hand, because the attentional demands for decoding fall well within the skilled reader's capacity, both decoding and comprehension can be done at the same time. In concluding this sketch of information processing in reading, however, it is important to point out that the comprehension process uses considerable amounts of attention for both unskilled and skilled readers. Although one can become automatic at decoding, one does not become automatic at comprehension.

ASPECTS OF THE MODEL THAT HAVE WITHSTOOD THE TESTS OF TIME

To discuss aspects of the model that we think have stood up well, it is imperative to outline some of the goals that we had hoped to accomplish. First, we wanted to explain how attention was used in the reading process. Second, we wanted to suggest a structure for visual memory to show how various sized units might be used in word recognition. Third, we wanted to indicate a variety of routes that information might take on its journey from the printed page to meaning.

Deployment of attention by unskilled and skilled readers. One of our goals when we created our model was to explain developmental trends in reading skill by means of attentional constructs. Even casual observation of skills such as tying one's shoelace or typewriting reveals substantial differences in how these skills are performed as one practices and advances from unskilled to skilled levels of performance. To describe these changes, let us examine how these skills are performed as one becomes more expert. At the first stage, which we call the non-accurate, non-automatic stage, despite considerable amounts of attention and effort, the beginner usually makes many errors. At stage two, which we call the accurate, non-automatic stage, when accurate and appropriate motions are made, visual guidance, attention, and effort are still required. As practice continues in stage three, which we call the accurate, automatic stage, accuracy continues to remain high, visual guidance is no longer needed, motions are executed quickly, and less attention and effort are required.

At the accurate, automatic stage, in the case of tying one's shoelace, the student finds that the lace can be tied and another behavior can take place simultaneously, such as watching television. In the case of typing, the student can simultaneously type from good copy while listening to questions and responding orally to them. Prior to the accurate, automatic stage, the student could not engage simultaneously in two behaviors. When the student can engage simultaneously in behaviors A and B, the automatic stage for A has been reached. At A's automatic stage, the skill being performed requires so little attention that the remaining attention can be used to execute another task at the same time. Of course, the energy costs for A and B can not exceed the student's attention capacity.

The kinds of developmental changes observed in shoelace tying and typing that are outgrowths of practice can also be observed in the word-recognition process.

During stage one, the non-accurate, non-automatic stage, the student makes many word recognition errors despite considerable attention and effort. In stage two, the accurate, non-automatic stage, the student is accurate in word recognition but large amounts of attention are required. During stage three, the accurate, automatic stage, the student is accurate and little attention is required for word recognition.

When the automatic word recognition stage is reached, the student can simultaneously recognize the words and use the available attention for comprehension. The manner in which attention is deployed is one of the important factors in understanding processing differences between the unskilled and the skilled reader. The unskilled reader must first use considerable amounts of attention for word recognition and then switch attention to the comprehension task. This switching of attention back and forth from word recognition to comprehension places considerable strain on the memory system. The skilled reader, on the other hand, can simultaneously recognize words and comprehend, which lifts the burden on the memory systems.

Thus, one of the crucial differences between the unskilled and the skilled reader is the deployment of attention. A recent study by Schwartz (1980) illustrates how skilled and unskilled readers allocate attention differently. In this study, three age groups—second graders, fifth graders, and college students—had to read and recall texts under four different conditions. The four different conditions varied from normal reading, with emphasis on recalling the ideas contained in the text, to reading under conditions that forced the student to focus attention away from meaning and on to mechanical features. To get the readers to attend to mechanical features, every so often the text contained a word printed backwards or they had to perform a letter-matching task. Schwartz was testing the hypothesis that college students focus attention on meaning and not on the mechanical aspects of decoding, while the younger students were still attending to the mechanical aspects of decoding. He found that the college students who, according to automaticity theory, focus attention on meaning, had good recall for the conditions that permitted them to attend to the meaning of the text. The younger students, however, were focusing attention on making mechanical, word-level decisions. Thus, the data supported the model, which states that skilled readers can attend to meaning while automatically decoding, while the beginning reader must devote large amounts of attention to the mechanical aspects of decoding.

Visual memory. The model of visual memory in Critique/Figure 2 indicates that a word may be decomposed into one of several units. These units consist of features, letters, spelling patterns, and words.

The lines connecting the different units in visual memory serve much the same purpose as a road map. Just as a map indicates the routes one may take in moving from one location to another, the model of visual memory indicates the different routes one may take from visual input to word recognition.

In general, in attempting to recognize a word, the reader attempts to use the largest unit that can be processed automatically. What size unit one uses depends in part on reading skill. If the student is automatic in word recognition, then the word can be the unit of recognition, but if the student is not at this level, then some smaller unit which is automatic to the student serves as the unit of recognition.

What we are saying is that in the perceptual learning tasks we encounter in learning to read, there are several levels, ranging from the letter to the entire word, and each level can be automatic. For example, in learning the letters of the alphabet, the child learns the combinations of features that each letter contains. With time and practice, the individual features of each letter fuse together and the student responds to the letter as a single unit. With additional practice the student becomes automatic at letter recognition. In this step-by-step progression, we have shown how a student goes through stages for letter identification.

However, there is more to reading than letter recognition. The student must learn to recognize consonant and vowel digraphs and respond to them as individual perceptual units, then to recognize spelling patterns and words and respond to them as individual perceptual units. Each of these—digraphs, spelling patterns, and word recognition—represents a separate learning task and, with each task, the student goes through the three stages of perceptual development. Thus, the student may be at the automatic stage in letter recognition and at the accurate, non-automatic stage in digraph recognition. Even the skilled reader at the automatic stage for most common words will, on occasion, encounter unusual words which will necessitate the expenditure of considerable amounts of attention.

Still other factors besides reading skill affect the size of the visual processing unit used in word recognition, for example, the legibility of the print and the familiarity of the words. If the text is hard to read because it is degraded in some manner, or if the words are unfamiliar, the skilled reader may not be able to process them at the whole word level. In the case of degraded text, the reader must drop down to a lower level such as letter features and piece the information together to arrive at the word. When the word is unfamiliar (as when we encounter a foreign word), the reader may have to go to the letter or to the spelling-pattern level and blend the patterns and sounds together to recognize the word.

Another factor that can influence the size of the processing unit is the condition under which the word is to be recognized, whether in context or in isolation. With powerful contextual constraints, even a poor reader may recognize the word as a single unit, but when the word is to be recognized either in isolation or in a weak context, the poor reader will use a letter-by-letter process.

An interesting aspect of the model of visual memory (Critique/Figure 2) is the arrow that goes directly from a feature (f-1) to the word (w_1). Just as a letter has a bundle of features that describe it, so too a word. The arrow that goes directly from the features to the word suggests that global features of a word, such as configuration and length, can be used in recognition. For a considerable time, global features such as word contour (penny versus built) and length (penny versus pay) were thought to be poor cues for word recognition. There is growing evidence, however, that global features, in conjunction with context, may provide useful word-recognition cues, especially for skilled readers (LaBerge & Lawry, 1981; Haber & Haber, 1981).

In closing, one final factor influences the size of the visual unit used, and this is the purpose one has for reading. If a skilled reader is reading for meaning and the words are familiar, the visual unit is the whole word; if the reader is proofreading for spelling errors, units smaller than the word are used. Also, it is important to point out that even though the model of visual memory is laid out as a hierarchy, no mandatory sequence of information flows from smaller to larger units. Whereas the beginning reader tends to have information flow in this sequence, the skilled reader has optional routes.

Routes from print to meaning. The information processing model shows several routes that information may take as it makes its way from input to meaning. For example, the most direct route would be from the word unit in visual memory to the meaning of the word in semantic memory.

A somewhat different route would have the input originate at the word level in visual memory, then go on to the representation of the word in phonological memory, and finally to its meaning in semantic memory. This route from visual to phonological to semantic might be used when one sees a word and says it before attaining meaning.

Still a third route from print to meaning might include episodic memory, as shown in Critique/Figure 1. Just as the model of visual memory shows a variety of routes one might use to get from the visual input to the formation of a visual word unit, so too does the entire information processing system show a variety of routes available once the visual word unit is formed until its meaning is attained in semantic memory. The particular route one uses from visual input to meaning depends on four factors: reader skill, purpose for reading, a materials factor such as word familiarity or legibility, and a contextual factor such as identifying words in isolation or in context.

AN ASPECT OF THE MODEL WE WOULD HAVE CHANGED

In 1974, when the LaBerge-Samuels model was first published, semantic memory had no feedback loop to the other components. Thus, the model suggested that the flow of information would be in a linear fashion from visual memory to phonological memory to semantic memory.

Little attempt was made to show how information in semantic memory might influence processing in other components such as visual memory. To illustrate how this might happen, let us assume that the student has read the following words: "In the year 1492 Christopher Columbus sailed to the New World in the Pinta, the Nina and the ------ ------." The student's task is to recognize the two words designated by the dotted lines. What we have is a situation in which the knowledge structures for Columbus and the ships he used are already in semantic memory. As the student reads this sentence, certain words such as "Columbus," "Pinta," and "Nina," and numbers such as "1492" act as powerful contextual cues which will aid the student in recognizing the two target words. Actually, the word-recognition task is quite simple because the information contained in semantic memory aids the word-recognition task that occurs in visual memory. Thus, we see how information in semantic memory, the last component of the system, can aid the processing that occurs in visual memory, which is located earlier in the system. To indicate how this occurs in the model, one simply needs to put in feedback loops so that all the components are interconnected. These feedback loops were added in a 1977 article (Samuels, 1977).

Since publication of our model, Rumelhart (1977) and Samuels (1977) have shown how components in a system can interact and share information with another component, and how a well-developed subskill can aid and compensate for the processing of a poorly developed subskill (Stanovich, 1980).

TESTS OF THE MODEL

We have done several experiments to test the validity of the model of visual memory. In one study (Terry, Samuels, & LaBerge, 1976), skilled readers were given a semantic categorization task in which they pressed a button if the word they saw on the screen was an animal word. The computer measured how long it took the student to decide if the word was a member of the category "animal." Our animal words varied in length from three to six letters. If our skilled readers were using the entire word as the unit of recognition, then latency of response should be unrelated to word length, but if the readers were doing letter-by-letter component processing, then latency should be sensitive to length. In other words, if the skilled readers were using the word as the unit of recognition, then three-letter words and six-letter words should have the same response latency. On the other hand, if the readers were using component-letter processing, then response latency should be faster for the shorter words and slower for the longer words.

We found that when the words were presented in regular print, they were processed as holistic units; that is, both short and long words had the same latency of response, indicating that the word, not the individual letters, was the unit. But when the words were presented in mirror image, they were processed letter-by-letter. For the mirror-image words, the shortest words had the fastest response latency. This finding suggested that skilled readers had a variety of options available for recognition, depending upon the familiarity of the word.

A second study examined developmental trends in the unit of word recognition (Samuels, LaBerge, & Bremer, 1978). This study used the same semantic categorization task as the first study in which the student pressed a button if an animal word appeared, except all the words were in regular print. Our subjects were selected from grades 2, 4, 6, and college. We found that second graders did component-letter processing, sixth graders and college students did holistic processing, and the fourth graders were at a transition point between component and holistic processing. This study provided evidence that as reading skill developed, the unit of visual processing increased in size from the letter up to the entire word.

Other studies examined the effect of word familiarity on the size of the unit of word recognition. Second graders were shown words selected from the basal reading series they were using in school, which varied in familiarity. Some of the words were relatively unfamiliar because they had just been introduced that school year, whereas the other set of words was familiar because they had been introduced a year before.

critique

These second graders, in general, used component-letter processing, but with the highly familiar words, there was a tendency for more holistic processing (McCormick & Samuels, 1979).

Another study used highly skilled readers forced to read words presented in mirror image (Samuels, Miller, & Eisenberg, 1979). At first, the subjects performed component-letter processing, but with repeated exposure to the mirror-image words, the subjects rather quickly increased the size of the visual processing unit. This effect was specific to the practiced words because when new words were shown in mirror image, the subjects again used component processing.

The studies described in this section all used a task in which the words were presented in isolation. A logical question arises as to what happens to the unit of recognition when context is present. The next study described here looked at the size of the visual processing unit when context was present or absent. It also varied reading skill. In this investigation of the size of the unit of word recognition, subjects in grades 2 and 4 were classified as either good or poor readers. The subjects had to pronounce words that varied in length and were presented either in isolation or in context. Voice-onset latency was the dependent variable.

We found that poor readers from the second grade did component-letter processing whether the word was in isolation or in context, while the good readers from grades 2 and 4 did holistic processing in either case. The finding that the worst readers in the study—poor second graders—did component-letter processing whether the word was in isolation or in context or that the good readers did holistic processing is not all that surprising. The most interesting finding in this study was that the poor readers in the fourth grade did two completely different kinds of processsing, depending on the manner in which the words were presented. For words presented in isolation, they did component-letter processing, but for words presented in context, they did holistic processing (Patberg, Dewitz, & Samuels, 1981). The implication is that the context effect, located in semantic memory, influenced the word recognition process in visual memory. Thus, the experimental evidence supported the hypothesized feedback loops in the model. These studies indicate that the size of the unit used for word recognition depends on reader skill, word familiarity, and context.

PRACTICAL APPLICATIONS OF THE MODEL

Automaticity theory has been useful in the diagnosis of certain kinds of reading problems and has provided the theoretical underpinnings for a reading method to develop reading fluency. With regard to diagnosis, some teachers have observed that some beginning readers may recognize words accurately but have difficulty comprehending what they have read. Teachers call this problem "barking at print." Automaticity theory suggests that one cause for the problem may be that decoding uses too much attention and interferes with comprehension. To overcome this problem, the student must continue to read easy material until decoding becomes automatic.

Another common problem occurs with skilled readers. College students, for example, often complain that even though they read the text with care, they cannot remember what was read. Because they are skilled readers, the actual decoding of words takes place without much attention, thus freeing attention to be directed elsewhere. Instead of focusing attention on deriving meaning from the text and understanding and recalling the author's viewpoints, the student's attention wanders elsewhere, to matters entirely unrelated to the text. The solution to this problem is to force the student to process the text for meaning, for example, having the student summarize each page before going to the next page.

With regard to helping students develop reading fluency, the method of repeated reading has been an outgrowth of automaticity theory, and a number of reports now in the literature describe the method, its theory base, and its effectiveness (Samuels, 1976; Chomsky, 1976; Carver & Hoffman, 1980; Schreiber, 1980). In essence, the student rereads a short, easy passage a number of times, either silently or aloud, until the student becomes accurate in recognizing the words in the passage and the speed of reading meets some preset standard. When the passage is read aloud, one notices rather rapid improvement in accuracy, speed, and expression.

Finally, automaticity theory has a rather direct implication for reading instruction. Although accuracy in word recognition is important, there is a stage beyond accuracy—automaticity—which should be our instructional goal, and it is only through practice that our students will achieve this level of performance. In closing, we hope that this retrospective analysis has been a useful vehicle for evaluating the strengths and weaknesses of the LaBerge-Samuels model of reading.

FOR FURTHER LEARNING

Those readers who are interested in continuing to explore the topic of theoretical models of reading would find the following references helpful:

Chomsky, C. After decoding, what? *Language Arts*, 1976, *53*, 288–296.

LaBerge, D., & Lawry, J. Explorations of changing perceptual modes due to attention factors induced by task demands. In D. Sheer (Ed.), *Attention: Theory, brain mechanisms, and clinical application*. Hillsdale, N.J.: Erlbaum, 1981.

Rumelhart, D. Toward an interactive model of reading. In S. Dornic (Ed.), *Attention and performance*. Hillsdale, N.J.: Erlbaum, 1977.

Samuels, S. J. Introduction to theoretical models of reading. In W. Otto (Ed.), *Reading problems*. Boston: Addison Wesley, 1977.

Samuels, S. J. The method of repeated reading. *The Reading Teacher*, 1979, *32*, 403–408.

Schreiber, P. On the acquisition of reading fluency. *Journal of Reading Behavior*, 1980, *12*, 177–186.

Stanovich, K. Toward an interactive-compensatory model of individual differences in the development of reading fluency. *Reading Research Quarterly*, 1980, *16*(1), 32–71.

REFERENCES

Carver, R., & Hoffman, J. The effect of practice through repeated reading on gain in reading ability using a computer-based instructional system. *Reading Research Quarterly,* 1981, *16,* 374–390.

Chomsky, C. After decoding, what? *Language Arts,* 1976, *53,* 288–296.

Haber, R., & Haber, L. The shape of a word can specify its meaning. *Reading Research Quarterly,* 1981. *16,* 334–345.

Klein, G. A. Effect of attentional demands on context utilization. *Journal of Educational Psychology,* 1976, *68,* 25–31.

LaBerge, D., & Lawry, J. Explorations of changing peceptual modes due to attention factors induced by task demands. In D. Sheer (Ed.), *Attention: Theory, brain mechanisms, and clinical application.* Hillsdale, N.J.: Erlbaum, 1981.

McCormick, C., & Samuels, S. J. Word recognition by second graders: The unit of perception and interrelationships among accuracy, latency, and comprehension. *Journal of Reading Behavior,* 1979, *11,* 107–118.

Patberg, J., Dewitz, P., & Saumels, S. J. The effect of context on the size of the peceptual unit used in word recognition. *Journal of Reading Behavior,* 1981, *13,* 33–48.

Rumelhart, D. Toward an interactive model of reading. In S. Dornic (Ed.), *Attention and performance.* Hillsdale, N.J.: Erlbaum, 1977.

Samuels, S. J. Introduction to theoretical models of reading. In W. Otto (Ed.), *Reading problems.* Boston: Addison Wesley, 1977.

Samuels, S. J. The method of repeated reading. *The Reading Teacher,* 1979, *32,* 403–408.

Samuels, S. J., LaBerge, D., & Bremer, C. Units of word recognition: Evidence for developmental changes. *Journal of Verbal Learning and Verbal Behavior,* 1978, *17,* 715–720.

Samuels, S. J., Miller, N., & Eisenberg, P. Practice effects on the unit of word recognition. *Journal of Educational Psychology,* 1979, *4,* 514–520.

Schreiber, P. On the acquisition of reading fluency. *Journal of Reading Behavior,* 1980, *12,* 177–186.

Schwatz, R. Levels of processing: The strategic demands of reading comprehension. *Reading Research Quarterly,* 1980, *15,* 433–450.

Stanovich, K. Toward an interactive-compensatory model of individual differences in the development of reading fluency. *Reading Research Quarterly,* 1980, *16*(1), 32–71.

Terry, P., Samuels, S. J., & LaBerge, D. The effects of letter degradation and letter spacing on word recognition. *Journal of Verbal Learning and Verbal Behavior,* 1976, *15,* 577–585.

A Commentary on Laberge and Samuels's Retrospective Analysis of the Theory of Automaticity in Reading

WAYNE OTTO

University of Wisconsin-Madison

Samuels himself has expressed high expectations for theoretical models: "Theoretical models . . . (are) capable of summarizing the past, elucidating the present, and predicting the future" (Samuels, 1977, p. 11). In other words, well-constructed models (1) summarize, in a simplified form, many findings and facts in a few principles or generalizations, (2) help us to understand current and ongoing happenings, events, and processes, and (3) enable us to generate predictions and hypotheses about future events. With specific regard for the reading process, Samuels says "A model of the reading process should be able to mirror or represent to some degree what goes on when we read" (1977, p. 15).

The LaBerge-Samuels Reading Model comes close to fulfilling Samuels's high expectations. Certainly the model, which Samuels and LaBerge acknowledge as partial, does an adequate job of "representing to some degree what goes on when we read." Within its acknowledged limits, the model does indeed summarize and elucidate. After a decade or so, it appears robust and capable of additional growth.

If there is a flaw in the model, it may be mainly a figment of this author's own expectations. As I see it, the LaBerge-Samuels Reading Model has a serendipitous aspect. It goes beyond elucidation to application in that it offers direction for helping students improve their reading performance. Yet the model falls short in at least two areas of application where it could, perhaps with only a bit of tinkering, address important instructional concerns. Such may not be the responsibility of model makers. I will, however, return to the point in a spirit of constructive and optimistic criticism. But first consider some of the salient positive features of the model.

POSITIVE FEATURES

The LaBerge-Samuels "automaticity model" has, I think, enjoyed almost a decade of growth, application, and generally positive regard by both researchers and practitioners because it combines good scholarship and good common sense. It conveys sound principles from relevant research and theory with an emphatic sense of how real people learn to read.

First, there is concurrent concern for *decoding* and for *comprehending*. This in itself is a worthwhile common-sense acknowledgement. Too often the decoding aspect of the reading process seems to be dismissed—particularly by "psycholinguists"—as too mundane to be worth much bother. In fact, Samuels and LaBerge do not seem reluctant to suggest that, at least some of the time, reading is a "two-stage" process, where the reader first converts print to sound and then attaches meaning to the spoken or silently decoded words. Bateman, (see page 111) makes the same point and underscores it nicely:

> True, we read for the purpose of extracting meaning from print. However, to say so overlooks the vital fact that early reading (and some if not all, of later reading) is a two-stage process. In reading an alphabetic language we first convert the print to sound (words) and *then* we attach/derive meaning from the spoken *word* or its silently decoded equivalent. Phonics has nothing to do with helping us attach or derive meaning from a spoken word such as "blip." It has everything to do with helping us know that the letters b–l–i–p say "blip" and do not say "pig" or "girl" or "bid" or "lip" or anything but "blip."

True, Bateman is talking phonics when she makes her point, and Samuels and LaBerge never say "phonics" when they discuss print-to-sound decoding. But the dual-process point is equally clear. More about this later.

Second, according to LaBerge and Samuels, a reader may employ alternate routes in the "journey from print to meaning." The authors address this point in their discussion of the deployment of attention by unskilled and skilled readers. LaBerge and Samuels have made their concern explicit by their provision of feedback loops in the model.

Third, automatic decoding is presented as but one step along the way to understanding what one reads. Samuels says "although automatic decoding is a necessary condition, it is not sufficient to guarantee good comprehension." While the partial model offered by LaBerge and Samuels does not adequately specify exactly how to guarantee good comprehension, it is good to acknowledge the limitation. With acknowledged limitations a dynamic model offers, at the very least, a promise of growth.

Fourth and finally, the development of information-storage and retrieval mechanisms related to reading is conceived as a three-stage process. The three stages are:

> **Acquisition**, where attention is directed to the storage and retrieval of symbol-sound relationships. The neophyte reader has difficulty retrieving desired responses.
> **Accuracy**, where attention is directed to the execution of appropriate responses. The developing reader "recognizes" any words but continues to devote much attention to the decoding process.
> **Automaticity**, where word recognition is accurate and little attention is required for the word recognition task. The reader uses the available attention for comprehension.

The model acknowledges changes in readers' ability to attend to different aspects of the complex task of reading for meaning as they acquire the component skills of successful reading. In describing three stages, the model elucidates not only the developmental sequence but also the need for changes in the focus of instruction.

Of course this list of positive features reflects this writer's bias in stressing the model's common-sense appeal and in looking for its practical application. The model gets high marks for its awareness of how real people read and its sensitivity to practical applications. In line with my bias, then, I would like to suggest two areas in which further development of the model would seem particularly promising.

Further Development

My concerns center on the "divide-and-conquer" strategy that Samuels and LaBerge describe, first at the acquisition stage, then in the transition from accuracy to automaticity in their three-stage model.

Divide and Conquer: Acquisition Stage

At the acquisition stage, decoding tasks exceed the neophyte reader's attention capacity. Samuels and LaBerge suggest that the reader "divide the task into smaller units, being careful that the energy demands of the sub-units are less than . . . (the reader's) capacity, limitations." My concern is that although the suggestion is perfectly sensible—even potentially useful in a rather general way—it is far too demanding to be directly useful to any but the most gifted "natural learners" of the reading process. Told to "divide and conquer," neophyte readers would wonder what to divide into what and how to do it. But even given that it is *words* that should be divided into their component letters and sounds, the task is likely to be a formidable one both for the reader and for the teacher who wants to help.

Apparently Samuels and LaBerge feel it is sufficient to point the way; they do not offer any explicit directions. While the map with better directions remains to be drawn, I can offer two observations and a suggestion.

First, reading educators have been a lot more successful in taking the reading process apart than in putting it back together. (I claim no personal exemption. As evidence I offer a disassembled MGB, a partially assembled Bang and Olafson turntable, and the *Wisconsin Design of Reading Skill Development.*) Any further suggestions for dealing with the complex task of word analysis must give as much attention to putting words together as to taking them apart.

Second, many of the points addressed in the discussion of *intensive* versus *gradual* phonics instruction in Section II are relevant when one contemplates strategies to divide and conquer words at the acquisition stage. While I do not want to lock myself in with the phonics fanatics, I think the three points that follow are particularly pertinent. First, Dykstra's conclusion (quoted from Walcutt, Lamport, & McCracken, 1974) that early systematic (intensive) instruction in phonics provides the child with the skills necessary to become an independent reader at an earlier age than is likely if instruction is delayed (gradual) and less systematic" (p. 397). Second, John's (see page 103) observation that "The recurring debate on the benefits or limitations of phonics instruction seems unproductive because it focuses on such a narrow aspect of reading behavior." And third, Bateman's (see page 108) tentative generalizations that "the further away from mastery the learner is, the more likely that learner may be to benefit from a deductive, rule-centered approach and conversely, the closer the learner is to mastery, the more likely he or she may be to benefit most from an inductive or example-centered approach." All this suggests to me that instruction at the acquisition stage might take the form of early, emphatic, and explicit phonics instruction. Dykstra's conclusion suggests explicit phonics as a systematic way to direct the neophyte reader's attention to the storage and retrieval of basic decoding skills; Bateman's generalizations—which are tentative but gaining support—underscore the desirability of such a deductive, rule-centered approach at the acquisition stage; and Johns can be reassured by the deliberately narrow focus of the acquisition stage in the model.

The acquisition stage is particularly important in the LaBerge-Samuels model because it is the stage on which all of the subsequent action takes place. The entire model would be bolstered by a strengthening of the acquisition stage. The model-makers ought to consider (*a*) dealing with (or at least acknowledging) the need for synthesis as well as analysis in basic decoding, and (*b*) suggesting (or at least examining) intensive phonics instruction as an explicit approach to basic decoding. The intensive phonics approach, as described by Gurren and Hughes (this volume, pages 83–96), seems to be remarkably well-suited for the acquisition stage described by Samuels and LaBerge. Samuels and LaBerge assert that well-learned information can be retrieved from memory using little attention; so they call for well-learned decoding skills at the acquisition level so attention can be directed elsewhere, to the more important matter of comprehending. The accumulated evidence suggests that intensive phonics instruction is the best way to ensure that basic decoding skills are well-learned.

Divide and Conquer: Transition

At the point of transition from the accuracy to the automaticity stage, Samuels and LaBerge again suggest a divide and conquer strategy: "the student must divide the task into sub-units, these being decoding and comprehension. By switching attention back and forth from decoding to comprehension, it is possible for the poor reader to read a text with understanding" (see page 45). Again, the suggestion seems sensible and even useful in a general way; but it is too simplistic to go very far in explaining how comprehending takes place or why the method of repeated reading "works."

In fairness, Samuels and LaBerge do acknowledge that "To read with comprehension numerous comprehension skills are necessary; just having the ability to decode automatically does not ensure that the student can understand the text." The model-makers clearly are aware that "dividing" is one thing and "conquering" is still another. But they offer only support for the acknowledged limitation and no further elucidation of what must be involved in "understanding the text." Presumably the model-makers are exercising their prerogative in offering a "partial" model.

To their credit, Samuels and LaBerge do describe a procedure for helping readers develop reading fluency, which moves readers beyond mere "barking at print" to giving attention to comprehending the text. The method of repeated readings is an outgrowth of the automaticity construct of the LaBerge-Samuels model whose effectiveness has been demonstrated. Schreiber (1980) has, however, questioned Samuels's explanation of *why* repeated readings "work." Samuels offers an analogy where the reader, like the athlete or the musician, is "given a small unit of activity and this unit is practiced over and over until it is mastered" (1979, p. 407). What the method of repeated readings does, then, "is to give the student the opportunity to master the material before moving on." Schreiber (1980, pp. 179–180) says that:

> if we examine this analogy carefully, we can see that in part at least it begs precisely the questions it is intended to answer. Why should mere repetition of the same passages produce the kinds of impressive gains in reading speed and accuracy that are found *across new reading samples*? It will not do to say simply that there has been a generalization of habits from one set of stimuli to another, since the question remains why and how such a generalization can take place.

The LaBerge-Samuels model does not identify the particular skills acquired through repeated readings, nor does it elucidate the process.

Again, it may not be the responsibility of a partial model to identify and explain everything that it implies. But Schreiber does offer an explanation for the success of the method of repeated readings that the model-makers ought to consider. The gist of Schreiber's explanation is that readers attain reading fluency when they learn to compensate for the absence of prosodic cues in printed material. The method of repeated readings succeeds, then, because it permits readers to (*a*) see that they must rely on cues other than prosodic ones to discover appropriate syntactic phrasing, and (*b*) make better use of "other kinds of signals that are preserved such as function words, inflectional endings and other morphological signals, and the form-class membership of lexical items, as well as the various perceptual strategies that may be based on the use of these formal signalling devices" (1980, pp. 182–183). Schreiber's explanation fits well with the model's three stages of development and suggests a worthwhile corollary to the model.

Since Samuels had the first word in this commentary, he should also have the last. Samuels (1977 and elsewhere) says "there is nothing so practical as a good theory." I agree.

REFERENCES

Samuels, S. J. Introduction to theoretical models of reading. In W. Otto, C. W. Peters, & N. Peters (Eds.), *Reading problems: A multidisciplinary perspective*. Boston: Addison Wesley, 1977, 7–41.

Samuels, S. J. The method of repeated readings. *The Reading Teacher*, 1979, *32*, 403–408.

Schreiber, P. A. On the acquisition of reading fluency. *Journal of Reading Behavior*, 1980, *12* 179–180.

Walcutt, C. C., Lamport, J., & McCracken, G. *Teaching reading: A phonic/linguistic approach to developmental reading*. New York: Macmillan, 1974.

references

section 

WORD RECOGNITION STUDIES

SUMMARIES by James F. Baumann, of *The Time Taken up by Cerebral Operations,* and *Studies on Speed of Letter and Word Recognition*

CRITIQUE by Michael L. Kamil

FOR FURTHER LEARNING

COMMENTARY by James F. Baumann

RESEARCH by Louise Gurren and Ann Hughes, *Intensive Phonics vs. Gradual Phonics in Beginning Reading: A Review*

CRITIQUE by Jerry L. Johns

FOR FURTHER LEARNING

COMMENTARY by Barbara Bateman

RESEARCH by Theodore Clymer, *The Utility of Phonic Generalizations in the Primary Grades*

CRITIQUE by Thomas Barrett

FOR FURTHER LEARNING

COMMENTARY by Nicholas J. Silvaroli

This section introduces the reader to classic word recognition studies by J. M. Cattell and E. B. Huey. Kamil's critique of these studies points to some unwarranted leaps from data to practice. He claims the results of this research were used to support what has become known as the "look-say" method of teaching reading. Kamil cautions the reader that teaching methods should be validated in actual classrooms and not simply derived from isolated sets of "marginally relevant data." Baumann concurs with Kamil and describes a replication of one of Cattell's studies on letter and word perception. He notes that the results exemplify how again educators have failed to critically analyze classic reading research and have gone too far in their interpretations and generalizations.

In his critique of Gurren and Hughes's study, Johns argues that phonics is a persistent problem which has permeated much of reading instruction since the 1930s. He focuses on 3 areas: 1) the historical background of phonics, 2) a summary and critique of 18 studies reviewed by Gurren and Hughes, 3) a perspective of phonics today. Bateman offers a point-by-point argument defending Gurren and Hughes's position and supports the notion that intensive early phonics in early reading instruction is the most effective approach for the majority of children.

Finally, Barrett critiques Clymer's study, *The Utility of Phonic Generalizations in the Primary Grades*. He notes that Clymer intended to conduct studies to answer 3 related questions: 1) What generalizations are being taught in basic reading programs for the primary grades?, 2) To what extent are these generalizations useful in meeting a reasonable degree of application to words in primary grade material?, and 3) Which of the generalizations that stand the test of (2) can primary children learn and successfully apply to unknown words? However, Barrett notes that Clymer only researched the first 2 questions. Silvaroli offers the view that Clymer's study may be responsible for a drastic reduction in the number of phonic generalizations that appear in today's basal readers.

SUMMARY OF EARLY WORD RECOGNITION STUDIES CONDUCTED BY J. M. CATTELL AND E. B. HUEY

JAMES F. BAUMANN

Purdue University

Around the turn of the century, during the period Woodworth (1944) characterizes as the emergence of second-generation American psychologists, several of these budding scholars began to investigate visual perception reaction times. Such pursuits inevitably led to much experimentation of reaction times during reading. Although a number of researchers pursued this new line of inquiry, the most significant contributions were made by James McKeen Cattell and Edmund Burke Huey, and this collective work is commonly referred to as the "early word recognition studies."

In a series of experiments, Cattell and Huey laid the groundwork for later research on visual processes in reading. Although their experimental apparatus was rudimentary and their procedures less than rigorous (by contemporary standards), the impact of these classic studies was unquestionably significant, as evidenced by the numerous citations of Cattell's work and Huey's *The Psychology and Pedagogy of Reading* (1908, reprinted 1968) in subsequent reading and psychological literature.

References and footnotes for this section can be found at the conclusion of Baumann's commentary.

What follows is a discussion of studies by Cattell and Huey that are relevant to the following critique and commentary by Kamil and Baumann, respectively. This review primarily details experiments by Cattell (as opposed to Huey's work) because Cattell's research has frequently been misunderstood or misinterpreted. Readers interested in a comprehensive discussion of work by either Huey or Cattell are referred to Huey's book (1908, reprinted 1968) and a fine compendium of Cattell's research by Poffenberger (1947).

JAMES McKEEN CATTELL

While studying in Leipzig in the 1880s under Wilhelm Wundt, James McKeen Cattell conducted several experiments in the area of visual perception reaction times.[1] In one of these experiments (1885), he investigated the exposure time necessary to perceive colors, pictures, letters, and words. Cattell constructed a tachistoscopic device, which he labeled a gravity chronometer,[2] that permitted subjects brief, accurately timed exposures to various sets of stimuli. In reporting the letter and word perception tasks,

Cattell (1885a) found: (a) isolated words and randomly arranged letters were identified (read) in about the same amount of time (p. 34); (b) not all letters were equally legible (p. 37); (c) three times as many letters could be identified when they made words than when there was no connection (p. 39); and (d) twice as many words could be grasped when they were in context as opposed to a random ordering (p. 40).

Various Interpretations of Cattell's Results

Cattell's findings, although not necessarily intended to describe the reading process, have been frequently cited as "proof" of a basic premise of current psycholinguistic theory: Reading requires both visual and nonvisual information. In other words, a reader's prior knowledge of an experience with language—supplied in the form of orthographic, syntactic, and semantic redundancy—contributes at least as much to the reading process as does the visual input (print). Reading, therefore, is not simply the recognition of individual letters and subsequent decoding of composite words; rather, reading is an integrative process involving a multitude of learned language skills.

Cattell's 1885a experiment, as well as other studies he conducted while at Leipzig (1885b, 1886a, 1886b), has been cited frequently in subsequent reading literature. Unfortunately, various references to Cattell's work have often been inconsistent or even contradictory with one another.

Huey (1908, reprinted 1968), for example, described the "Cattell Fall Apparatus" (i.e., the device used in the 1885a experiment) as determining "how much of the line can be read at a single peep" (1968, p. 54). He noted that Cattell found a particular reader who read up to seven words in a single exposure when the words composed a sentence. Huey qualified this remark, however, by reminding us that Cattell's results illustrated only maximal amounts that could be perceived at a "peep" (1968, p. 52).

Woodworth (1944), supported by Carroll (1972), reported that Cattell demonstrated that the time required to read a short familiar word was equal to or less than the time needed to read a single letter. This evidence has frequently been used to argue for a "whole-word" or "look-say" approach to reading instruction. To paraphrase the argument, since the amount of time needed to read an entire word does not exceed the amount of time for individual letter perception, reading cannot be a letter-by-letter process. Therefore, words are read as units ("wholes"), hence the legitimacy of a whole-word or look-say reading instructional methodology. Cattell himself (1885a), after presenting his data on recognition speed for letters and words, commented that:

> Children are now generally taught to read words as words, and we are not required to spell out the letters [i.e., a look-say reading methodology was in vogue at this time]; but it is well to prove that we read a word as a whole. (pp. 34–35)

(Apparently, Cattell believed any controversy between phonic/alphabetic reading instruction and whole-word/look-say instruction had been resolved at this time (1885), perhaps as a result of his research. If only he could have envisioned the decades of debate that were to follow.)

Many other researchers have cited Cattell's work. Brewer (1972), for example, states that:

summary

> Cattell rejected the letter-by-letter (serial) theory of word perception in favor of the whole-word (parallel) approach on the basis of the following kinds of evidence: (a) Words in prose passages can be read almost as fast as lists of letters. (b) The immediate visual apprehension span for letters in prose is much greater than for random letters. (c) Latencies to initiate pronunciation of words are shorter than those for letters. (d) Visual recognition thresholds for words are lower than the thresholds for letters. (p. 359)

Smith and Holmes (1971) refer to Cattell's 1885b study to reinforce the idea that, from a single tachistoscopic exposure, a skilled reader can identify "(a) four or five unconnected letters; (b) two unconnected words; or (c) four or five words in a meaningful sequence (a phrase or short sentence)" (p. 56).

Frank Smith (1971, 1975, 1978), however, has been most responsible for popularizing Cattell's work. In *Understanding Reading* (1978, pp. 30–31; 153), Smith explicitly describes Cattell's (1885b) "classic study" as a tachistoscopic experiment that showed:

> If random letters of the alphabet were presented . . . then only four or five letters might be reported. But if words were presented, two or three might be reported comprising a total of perhaps 12 letters. And if the words happened to be organized into a short sentence, then four or five words, a total of perhaps 25 letters, might be perceived from one exposure. (p. 30)

A Confusion of Studies

Upon close examination of Cattell's experiments, some confusion exists as to exactly what he found regarding the identification of letters and words. After reviewing the frequently cited 1885b experiment (e.g., Smith, 1971, 1975, 1978; Smith & Holmes, 1971), it was noted that Cattell used a kymograph[3]—not a tachistoscope— to determine the speed with which his subjects could name letters and words. Cattell reported that words in context were read about twice as fast as either unrelated words or random letters (1885b, p. 23). (Biemiller, 1978, reported similar findings after testing adults and children.) However, since a kymograph does not necessarily limit a subject to one eye fixation, and only measures reading rate, inferences drawn about the number of letters and words that can be perceived in one eye fixation are rather speculative.[4]

It is actually Cattell's 1885a study (in which he used the tachistoscopic device) that more directly addresses the relationship between visual and nonvisual information with regard to reading. Thus, some contemporary interpretation of Cattell's research (e.g., Smith, 1971, 1975, 1978; Smith & Holmes, 1971) are in conflict with Cattell's original findings; although in all fairness, while both Smith and Holmes refer to the 1885b study and not the 1885a study, their analyses of Cattell's results are reasonable.

Some Methodological Limitations

In addition to the confusion concerning Cattell's findings on letter and word perception, some severe limitations can be found in his experimental methodology. Upon closer inspection of the 1885a study, for example, it was noted that Cattell did not provide any numerical data to support his statements about the effect context has on identification of words. In addition, he reported considerable intersubject variations in performance:

> The determinations made on eight individuals show a considerable personal difference, but an average consciousness can at one time grasp four numbers, three to four letters, or a sentence composed of four words (p. 39).

Given Cattell's own admission of subjects' individual difference, coupled with lack of numerical data, small sample size, lack of specific information regarding construction of stimuli, and confusion over the identity of the subjects [Cattell, Dr. Berger, a professor at Leipzig, fellow students, "an educated young lady, the wife of a mechanic, and two rather obtuse porters" (1885a, p. 40)], any general statements about Cattell's "findings" regarding the effect of context on limited-time word perception are at best tenuous, and at worst, scientifically unfounded.

In summary, Cattell conducted a number of pioneering psychological experiments in the area of visual perception reaction times during reading. The generalizability of his findings, however, must be tempered because of imprecise apparatus and limiting experimental methods. Nevertheless, his classic experiments were some of the first to probe visual processes in reading, and much of his research has withstood subsequent replication.

EDMUND BURKE HUEY

Although Huey and Cattell never formally collaborated, they were contemporaries and very much aware of each other's work. Huey was especially cognizant of Cattell's research, and he made numerous references to Cattell's experiments in the "Psychology of Reading" section of *The Psychology and Pedagogy of Reading* (1908, reprinted 1968). In addition, Huey conducted several experiments that replicated some of Cattell's prior findings on speed of letter and word recognition.

In one of these experiments, Huey (1908, reprinted 1968, pp. 100–101) required adults to orally read list of individual letters, 4-letter words, 8-letter words, 12-letter words, and 16-letter words (see examples of individual letters and 4-, 8-, and 12-letter words below reproduced from Huey, 1968, p. 100).

y pool analysis anthropology
w rugs habitual independence
u mark occupied histological
s send inherent astronomical

Using lists of 50 such items, Huey reported the following average total reading times per list in seconds: individual letters = 15.7 sec.; 4-letter words = 17.3 sec.; 8-letter words = 19.6 sec.; 12-letter words = 28.5 sec.; 16-letter words = 54.1 sec. Although increased numbers of letters did result in added reading times, Huey argued that these times did not indicate letter-by-letter reading.

> It will be evident that the multiplication of letters makes proportionately little difference in the ease or speed of recognition. . . . Since part of the slightly lessened speed of reading eight-letter words as compared with those of four letters must probably be due to the utterance of the additional syllable or syllables in the former case, it seems certain that the recognition of familiar and comparatively short words is little affected by doubling the number of letters; and this seems confirmatory of the view that such words are recognized in one unitary act, as wholes. (1968, p. 101)

In other words, if 50 individual letters are recognized on the average in 15.7 seconds, one would expect a reader to take four times as long to read 50,

summary

4-letter words, or a time of 62.8 seconds. Using this same procedure, expected reading times for 8-, 12-, and 16-letter words would be 78.4, 114.0, and 216.4 seconds respectively—times significantly longer than the actual reading times obtained empirically. Thus, on the basis of these data, Huey argued that reading indeed is not a letter-by-letter process, and that words therefore must be read as units or wholes.

CONCLUSIONS

Viewed collectively, research by Cattell and Huey lead toward three conclusions:

1. Isolated letters and individual words can be read with approximately the same speed (Cattell, 1885a; Huey, 1908, reprinted 1968).
2. Many more letters are identifiable when they comprise words as opposed to random orderings of letters (Cattell, 1885a).
3. More words can be grasped when arranged in a meaningful sequence compared to random orderings of words (Cattell, 1885a).

These findings have repeatedly been used to support the contention that reading is not a letter-by-letter process, and that surrounding word context is a powerful aid in word recognition. Interestingly, given the methodological limitations of these classic studies, it has only been recently that these long-held tenets have been challenged.

A Critique of Cattell and Huey's Early Word Recognition Studies

MICHAEL L. KAMIL

University of Illinois, Chicago

INTRODUCTION

Perhaps the most elusive goal in educational research has been the attempt to determine optimal pedogogical practice from empirical experimentation. There is a recurrent tension between researchers and practitioners: practitioners have demanded relevance; researchers have wanted to be unconstrained. The result has been a short circuit of the normally self-correcting methodology of the researcher. Either educational practice has been impervious to empirical refutation or it is inferred too hastily. One such example can be seen in the effects of basic word recognition studies on the adoption of methods for teaching beginning reading.

Cattell (1886) was interested in determining the amount of time required to perform certain cerebral operations. He chose to study the "perception time" necessary to deal with letters and words by the subtractive method of reaction time (a rather complete discussion of this methodology can be found in Woodworth, 1938). Basically the argument is that simple reaction time (RT) is quickest. If a decision is required, the difference between the simple and "complex" RTs represents the time necessary for the decision.

In his studies, Cattell compared RTs for letters, short words, and long words. Two of Cattell's conclusions have had far-reaching consequences. First, Cattell concluded that

> ". . . the perception time is only slightly longer for a word than for a single letter; we do not therefore perceive separately the letters of which a word is composed, but the word as a whole. The application to teaching children to read is evident . . ." (p. 387)

His second conclusion was related to the first:

> "We find further that . . . named a word in less time than a letter. This is not surprising; we are constantly reading and using words, much more than letters, so the association between the concept and the name has become closer and takes place in less time." (pp. 531–532)

Portions of this paper were first published in *Reading Psychology*, 1980, *1*(2), 133–136, and are reprinted by permission of the publisher.

While Cattell was not primarily interested in pedagogical implications, his work was used to support what has become known as the "look-say" method of teaching reading.

The impact of these findings can be measured by the following comments from Anderson and Dearborn (1952):

> "The psychological rationale of the word method has been demonstrated numerous times by laboratory studies of the psychology of reading."
>
> "Cattell's results were confirmed by Erdmann and Dodge (1898)."
>
> "These findings of Cattell and of Erdmann and Dodge delivered a damaging blow to the alphabet method and gave support to the movement already under way to revolutionize methods of teaching reading. The older notion had been that words are read by compounding letters. That this is not the case was clearly demonstrated by the finding that words can be read when there is not time to group all the letters. . . . Cattell believed that the cue for recognition was the 'total word picture,' while Erdmann and Dodge used the expression 'general word shape.'" (pp. 212–213)

Huey (1908) reported confirming evidence for Cattell's results (p. 101). The impact of the "look-say" method is still felt today (see, for example, Flesch, 1981). To assess the validity of the evidence for the "look-say" method, we need to examine the details of the original studies.

CATTELL'S PROCEDURES

In his studies Cattell used a simple verbal sound key response. The subject was to respond by naming the stimulus when it was presented. There were 26 items in each set and 3 different types of stimuli: letters, short words (4–5 letters) and long words (9–12 letters). There were 2 subjects, Cattell himself and a colleague. In one study Cattell used both German and English words. [Some of this discussion is based on a paper by Theios and Muise (1975).]

HUEY'S PROCEDURES

Huey used a total of 4 adult subjects, each reading lists of 50 letters or words. Timing was manual, using a stopwatch. No control for frequency was used.

CATTELL'S RESULTS

For the first study, using manual responding, the data can be summarized as follows:

> The mean recognition latencies (across the 26 stimuli) for single letters was 318 msec, for short words 346 msec, and for long words 354 msec.

The results from the second study are summarized in Critique/Table 1. (These data are computed from Cattell's original tables.)

CRITIQUE/TABLE 1

	Single Letters	Short Words	Long Words
First Language	410	388	432
Second Language	478	414	464
Difference	68	26	32
Mean	444	401	448

HUEY'S RESULTS

Huey's results are summarized in Critique/Table 2. (These data are computed from Huey's original tables.)

CRITIQUE/TABLE 2

Stimulus	Total Reading Time in sec.
50 letters	15.7
50 4-letter words	17.3
50 8-letter words	19.6
50 12-letter words	28.5
50 16-letter words	54.1

CRITIQUE

Some simple transformations of the data reveal some interesting findings overlooked by the original investigators. In Cattell's first study, the mean latency difference between letters and long words is 36 msec or about 4 msec per letter.

In the second study, naming single letters always took more time than short words. However, in the first language, the difference between short and long words was 43 msec or about 7 msec per letter. For the second language, the difference was 50 msec or about 8 msec per letter.

The Huey data can be converted into similar comparisons as in Critique/Table 3.

CRITIQUE/TABLE 3

Stimuli	Msec/letter
50 letters	314
50 4-letter words	87
50 8-letter words	49
50 12-letter words	48
50 16-letter words	68

Given these conversions, in all instances, long words take more time to recognize (and/or pronounce) than short words. Cattell's data are to be trusted more than Huey's, simply for the inaccuracy in Huey's use of a stopwatch. Cattell's data show approximately the same 4–8 msec/letter figure across several conditions. This agrees with more precise data reported by Steward, James, and Gough (1968) of about 9 msec per letter.

In summary, the Cattell data might be used to argue that word recognition is a letter-by-letter process. (Technical reasons for not admitting such types of evidence can be found in Townsend, 1974). What is important is that the data do not clearly support the notion that the word is the unit of perception.

The "aberrant" single letter data are not readily explainable. Baron and Thurston (1973) have suggested that the effects are connected with regularity of spelling patterns. Research is still being conducted, but it is not conclusive.

Other considerations militate against accepting the Cattell-Huey evidence as support for pedagogical practice. Among these are 1) the use of adult subjects to infer practices for beginning readers; 2) the confounding of frequency with length; 3) the use of a very small number of subjects; and 4) the use of isolated words and tachistoscopic presentations.

CONCLUSIONS

This is an example of an unwarranted jump from data to practice. The development of teaching practices should be based in theory and data. However, teaching methods must be validated in classroom contexts and not simply derived from isolated sets of marginally relevant laboratory data. Cattell and Huey's work seems to continue to be, in principal, supported by contemporary experimentation in word recognition. The interpretation of this data is, even today, not totally umambiguous. Its relevance to pedagogy is even more tenuous.

Ultimately, pedagogy will have to reflect, somehow, the findings of Cattell, Huey, et al. The question of how they will be reflected is still unanswered; the key lies in further research, expanded to validate educational practice.

FOR FURTHER LEARNING

Those readers who are interested in continuing to explore the topic of word recognition studies would find the following references helpful:

Brewer, W. F. Is reading a letter-by-letter process? In J. F. Kavanaugh & I. G. Mattingly (Eds.), *Language by ear and by eye*. Cambridge, Mass.: M. I.T. Press, 1972.

Huey, E. B. *The psychology and pedagogy of reading*. New York: Macmillan, 1908. (Reprinted, M.I.T. Press, 1968).

James McKeen Cattell, man of science: 1860–1944 (Vol. 1). Lancaster, Pa.: Science Press, 1947.

Smith, F. *Understanding reading: A psycholinguistic analysis of reading and learning to read* (2nd ed.). New York: Holt, Rinehart, & Winston, 1978.

Smith, F., & Holmes, D. L. The independence of letter, word, and meaning identification in reading. *Reading Research Quarterly,* 1971, 6, 394–415.

REFERENCES

Anderson, I. H., & Dearborn, W. F. *The psychology of reading.* New York: Ronald Press, 1952.

Baron, J., & Thurston, I. An analysis of the word-superiority effect. *Cognitive Psychology,* 1973, *4,* 207–228.

Cattell, J. M. The time taken up by cerebral operations. *Mind,* 1886, *11,* pp. 220–242; 376–392, 524–538.

Flesch, R. *Why Johnny can't read.* New York: Harper & Row, 1981.

Huey, E. B. *The psychology and pedogogy of reading.* New York: Macmillan, 1908. (Reprinted, M.I.T. Press, 1968).

Pearson, P. D., & Kamil, M. L. Word recognition latencies as a function of form class, stem length and affix length. *Visable Language,* 1974, *8,* 241–246.

Stewart, M. S., James, L. T., & Gough, P. B. *Word recognition latency as a function of word length.* Paper presented at Midwestern Psychological Association, Chicago, May 1969.

Theios, J., & Muise, J. The word identification process in reading. In J. Castellan, D. Pisoni, & G. Potts (Eds.), *Cognitive theory,* Vol. II. Hillsdale, N.J.: Lawrence Erlbaum, 1975, pp. 289–327.

Townsend, J. T. Issue and models concerning the processing of a finite number of inputs. In B. Kantowitz (Ed.), *Human information processing: Tutorials in cognition.* Hillsdale, N. J.: Lawrence Erlbaum, 1974, pp. 133–185.

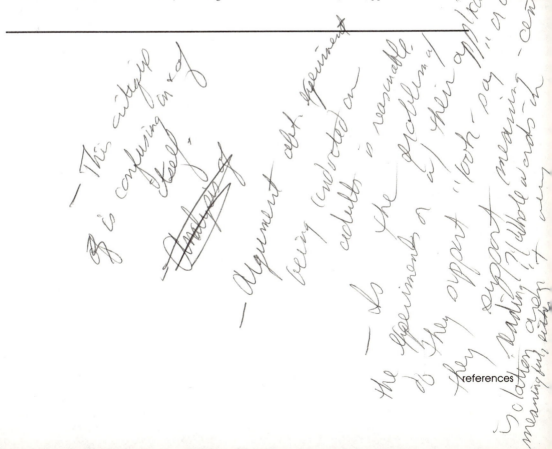

A Commentary on Kamil's Critique of Early Word Recognition Studies: From Cattell and Huey to the Psycholinguists by Leaps and Bounds

JAMES F. BAUMANN

Purdue University

Kamil's critique of the classic word recognition studies by J. M. Cattell (1886a) and E. B. Huey (1908, reprinted 1968) is rather interesting. Based upon a reanalysis of the data from these studies, Kamil concluded that the common interpretation of the results of these investigations—namely, that skilled word recognition is a holistic rather than a letter-by-letter process—could be challenged with these same data. Kamil argued that Cattell and Huey overlooked the fact that, in both of their studies, it took longer to recognize long words than short words; hence, he suggested that the "data might be used to argue that word *recognition is a letter-by-letter process* (see page 74). Since these early studies are commonly cited as support for a whole word or "look-say" method of teaching reading, Kamil stated that "this is an example of an unwarranted jump from data to practice" (see page 74) and cautioned educational practitioners from inferring pedagogical applications too hastily.

I also share Kamil's concern, for it is not uncommon for educators (or researchers themselves) to infer too much from extant research, or to simply misinterpret it. Interestingly, another example of an unjustified data-to-theory/practice leap has occurred with respect to Cattell's work on letter and word perception (see Baumann summary). Again, reading educators have failed to critically analyze classic research and have gone too far in their interpretations and generalizations of the results.

A REPLICATION STUDY

Because of the lack of scientific rigor in Cattell's methodology and the confusion in interpreting the results of his experiments, Karen Wilson-Schneider and I conducted a replication (Baumann and Wilson-Schneider, 1979) of Cattell's 1885a study. Since Cattell's report of the experiment offers rather sketchy information about instrumentation and procedure, we decided to model the replication after Smith's (1978, pp. 30–31; 153) description of Cattell's study. Smith describes an experiment in which fluent readers are tachistoscopically presented three sets of stimuli (strings of random letters, sets of unrelated words, and words in context) and are directed to orally report as many letters or words as possible.

Method

Twenty-four university students participated in the study. Subjects were tested individually and required to respond orally to tachistoscopic flashes of letters and words. Each of the three sets of stimuli (random letters, unrelated words, and words in context) consisted of ten strings of 25 letters that reflected English letter frequency counts. The only differences among the three sets of stimuli were the addition of orthographic regularity in the case of the unrelated words, and the inclusion of orthographic and semantic regularity for the words in context.

The sets of stimuli were presented to the subjects in a counterbalanced manner, and a practice session preceded the actual testing. Thus, each subject was required to respond to ten flashes of 25 random letters, ten flashes of sets of unrelated words, and then flashes of words in context (sentences). Responses were scored as number of letters correctly identified. For the random letter condition, this involved a simple tabulation of correct responses; for the unrelated words and words in context conditions, the words correctly identified were converted to letters to permit statistical comparisons. (Refer to the Baumann and Wilson-Schneider report, 1979, for a complete description of the experimental methodology.)

Results

Commentary/Table 1 presents the mean scores and standard deviations of letters correctly identified for each treatment. Recall that the maximum possible score per condition is 250 (25 letters per string times ten strings). An analysis of variance revealed a statistical significance due to conditions, $F(2,46) = 212.44, p < .001$. *Post hoc* comparisons using Tukey's procedure revealed significance for all three simple comparisons: Random letters versus unrelated words, $F(2,46) = 20.10, p < .001$; random letters versus words in context, $F(2,46) = 28.35, p < .001$; and unrelated words versus words in context, $F(2,46) = 8.23, p < .001$.

COMMENTARY/TABLE 1
Means (and Standard Deviations) of Numbers of Letters Correctly Identified

Condition[a]	Number Correct
Random letters	37.2 (7.5)
Unrelated words	92.5 (17.8)
Words in context	115.2 (28.7)

Note: Maximum score per condition = 250.
[a]n = 24 for each condition.

Discussion

The data clearly indicate that adult fluent readers apprehend many more letters when the letters are organized into unrelated words than when they are presented in random order, and that apprehension span is even greater when the words are contextually meaningful. These findings are consistent with Cattell's (1885a) data on the perception of random letters and unrelated words and Smith's (1971, 1975, 1978) interpretation of them. We found that an average of 3.7 letters were apprehended per flash when presented in random order, and an average of 9.3 letters (2.0 words) were recalled when the stimuli were fashioned into a series of unrelated words. (These averages were computed by dividing the means of correct responses by 10; see Commentary/Table 1. The letter count can be converted to words by dividing by 4.7, the mean number of letters per word.) These results correspond proportionally to the two to three letters and two words that Cattell reported, and the four or five letters and ten to twelve letters that Smith proposed could be read in one eye fixation under these conditions. Apprehension span for words in context, however, averaged only 11.5 letters (2.5 words) as compared to the four words Cattell reported and the four or five words Smith insists can be read.

In summary, our replication study did support the psycholinguistic principle that orthographic and semantic regularities permit increasingly greater apprehension spans in reading, but the results did not indicate that context contributes as much to this increased apprehension span as had been previously reported. In other words, our results were not in complete agreement with Cattell's findings. They conflict to some extent with popular thought concerning the impact context has on apprehension span.

Conclusions

After critiquing Cattell's and Huey's studies, Kamil concluded that an unwarranted jump from data to practice had occurred concerning the efficacy of the whole word approach to reading instruction. The replication study described above also demonstrated an unjustified leap—a leap from data to theory. That is, the psycholinguistic interpretations of the power of context were not nearly as powerful as believed.

What is the significance of these findings? I believe three "lessons" can be learned from these examples. First, researchers should review classic studies more critically and be more cautious in drawing implications from them. Although the contributions made by historical scientific figures like Cattell are unquestionably great, one must consider the differing levels of scientific rigor between classic and current behavioral research. Due to a lack of accurate physical apparatus and knowledge of modern research design and statistical procedures, the precision of classic research does not compare to that of current experimentation. Consequently, interpreting classic studies as though they are contemporary can be dangerous.

Second, researchers should replicate research more frequently. This applies to classic as well as more recent investigations. No single one-shot experiment should serve to prove or disprove any theory, yet frequently this is the case. Unfortunately, we seldomly replicate our own research or that of others. Pearson (1978) discusses this very issue and states that "somehow data get lost, but the conclusions live on, regenerating themselves. . . . Replication ought to be encouraged; however our present system of refereed publication systematically discourages it (e.g., 'this article adds nothing new to the literature')" (pp. 355–356). We can only hope that journal editors realize the value of replication studies—both those that support and those that challenge prior research.

And third, when implications for educational practice are intended, studies must be constructed such that they possess high levels of external or ecological validity; that is, applied educational research should be conducted such that the subjects, instrumentation, procedures, and experimental tasks are similar to those situations (or environments) to which one wishes to generalize. For example, as Kamil appropriately noted, to make generalizations to beginning reading instructional strategies from the results of Cattell's and Huey's studies is indeed foolhardy because adults, not children, were subjects in the study, and the use of isolated words and a tachistoscopic presentation hardly simulates the task facing a beginning reader.

In summary, classic research has a great potential value, but one must consider the time and circumstances under which the research was conducted. The responsibility lies with the reader of research to ascertain what implications can be justifiably drawn from particular studies. Educational theorists and practitioners must not be overzealous in their desire to prove a theory or justify an educational practice so that they end up fitting research to theory or practice, rather than the reverse.

NOTES

1. The references in this paper to Cattell's studies will direct you to the original publications. However, since several of the original studies were published in German and many of the articles may be difficult to retrieve due to their age, I have listed page numbers that correspond to the 1947 compendium of Cattell's work: *James McKeen Cattell, Man of Science: 1860–1944* (Vol. 1), A. T. Poffenberger (Ed.). Science Press, Lancaster, Pa., 1947. This volume contains all the cited articles, either as they originally appeared (if published in English) or translated from German.
2. The gravity chronometer, which Huey called the "Cattell Fall Apparatus," is a guillotine-like mechanism. A vertically sliding plate with a horizontal opening is released and dropped from varying heights, allowing subjects a brief view of the stimuli (letters and words typed on cards) behind the opening. Exposure time was calculated by considering the height of the opening and the height (and hence speed) from which the plate was dropped. Cattell claimed (1885a, p. 29) that the device was accurate to within .0001 of a second. In later experiments (1886a), Cattell refined the apparatus by including an electromagnet that held the plate up, permitting smoother release when the current was cut off.
3. Cattell's kymograph is a serial exposure apparatus that consists of a vertical rotating cylinder, the speed of which can be variably controlled. A sheet of metal with a horizontal, adjustable opening built in is used to mask the moving drum. This slit allows subjects only a limited view of the stimuli (letters and words). The adjustable opening permits exposure of from one to six letters. Cattell calculated "exposure times" by dividing the number of letters exposed by the speed of the rotation.

4. Cattell collected the data reported in the 1885b experiment while he was a graduate fellow at Johns Hopkins (1882–1883). Interestingly, his subjects for this experiment were fellow graduate students and faculty that included Joseph Jastrow, John Dewey, G. Stanley Hall, and Cattell himself.

REFERENCES

Baumann, J. F., & Wilson-Schneider, K. *Apprehension span of adult fluent readers: A clarification of J. M. Cattell's classic research in letter and word perception.* (Technical Report No. 520). Madison, Wis.: Wisconsin Research and Development Center for Individualized Schooling, September 1979. (ERIC Document Reproduction Service No. ED 178 877.)

Biemiller, A. Relationships between oral reading rates for letters, words, and simple text in the development of reading achievement. *Reading Research Quarterly,* 1978, *13,* 223–253.

Brewer, W. F. Is reading a letter-by-letter process? In J. F. Kavanagh & I. G. Mattingly (Eds.), *Language by ear and by eye.* Cambridge, Mass.: M.I.T. Press, 1972.

Carroll, J. B. The case for ideographic writing. In J. F. Kavanagh & I. G. Mattingly (Eds.), *Language by ear and by eye.* Cambridge, Mass.: M.I.T. Press, 1972.

Cattell, J. M. Uber die Trageit der netzhaut und des Sechentrums. *Philosophische Studien,* 1885, *3,* 94–127. Translated and reprinted as, The inertia of the eye and brain. *Brain,* 1885, *8,* 295–312. Also in A. T. Poffenberger (Ed.), *James McKeen Cattell, man of science: 1860–1944* (Vol. 1). Lancaster, Pa.: Science Press, 1947(a).

Cattell, J. M. Uber die Zeit der Erkennung and Benennung von Schriftzeichen, Bildern und Farben. *Philosophische Studien,* 1885, *2,* 635–650. Also in A. T. Poffenberger (Ed.), On the time required for recognizing and naming letters and words, pictures and colors. *James McKeen Cattell, man of science: 1860–1944* (Vol. 1). Lancaster, Pa.: Science Press, 1947.

Cattell, J. M. Psychometrische Untersuchungen. *Philosophische Studien,* 1886, *3,* 305–335; 452–492. Translated and reprinted as, The time taken up by cerebral operations. *Mind,* 1886, *11,* 220–242; 377–392; 524–538. Also in A. T. Poffenberger (Ed.), *James McKeen Cattell, man of science: 1860–1944* (Vol. 1). Lancaster, Pa.: Science Press, 1947. (a)

Cattell, J. M. The time it takes to see and name objects. *Mind,* 1886, *11,* 63–65. Also in A. T. Poffenberger (Ed.), *James McKeen Cattell, man of science: 1860–1944* (Vol. 1). Lancaster, Pa.: Science Press, 1947 (b).

Huey, E. B. *The psychology and pedagogy of reading.* New York: Macmillan, 1908. Republished by M.I.T. Press, Cambridge, Mass., 1968.

Pearson, P. D. On bridging gaps and spanning chasms. *Curriculum Inquiry,* 1978, *8*(4), 353–363.

Poffenberger, A. T. (Ed.). *James McKeen Cattell, man of science: 1860–1944* (Vol. 1). Lancaster, Pa.: Science Press, 1947.

Smith, F. *Understanding reading: A psycholinguistic analysis of reading and learning to read.* New York: Holt, Rinehart, & Winston, 1971.

Smith, F. *Comprehension and learning: A conceptual framework for teachers.* New York: Holt, Rinehart, & Winston, 1975.

Smith, F. *Understanding reading: A psycholinguistic analysis of reading and learning to read* (2nd ed.). New York: Holt, Rinehart, & Winston, 1978.

Smith, F., & Holmes, D. L. The independence of letter, word and meaning identification in reading. *Reading Research Quarterly,* 1971, *6,* 394–415.

Woodworth, R. S. James McKeen Cattell, 1860–1944. *Psychological Review,* 1944, *51,* 201–209. Reprinted in A. T. Poffenberger (Ed.), *James McKeen Cattell, man of science: 1860–1944* (Vol. 1). Lancaster, Pa.: Science Press, 1947.

INTENSIVE PHONICS VS. GRADUAL PHONICS IN BEGINNING READING: A REVIEW

LOUISE GURREN

New York University

ANN HUGHES

Reading Reform Foundation

ABSTRACT

Drawing from unpublished as well as published research, this review presents 22 comparisons between intensive-phonics groups and gradual-phonics groups. It differs from standard reviews in two respects. First, it restricts itself to comparisons meeting certain rigorous statistical criteria and gives specific reasons for excluding various less-rigorous studies. Second, instead of quoting the conclusions of the various investigators, it tabulates their findings in terms of significant differences.

On the basis of this tabulation, 19 comparisons favored intensive phonics, three favored neither method, and none favored gradual phonics. The reviewers conclude that early and intensive phonics instruction tends to produce superior reading achievement. They recommend that vowel sounds as well as consonant sounds be taught intensively from the start of reading instruction.

Large numbers of American schools have recently altered their reading programs by adding intensive phonetic training from the start of the program. At the same time, a number of scholars have carried out carefully controlled research to determine the practical value of such an addition. There seems great need that the results of such research should now be comprehensively reviewed so that they may serve as a guide to educators concerned with teaching reading as effectively as possible.

The present review is both selective and comprehensive. It is selective in that it excludes opinion surveys, word-count studies, purely theoretical discussions, correlational studies, and loosely-controlled experiments. It is comprehensive in that it includes all the rigorous evaluations the authors could locate which compare actual performance of a group which has had intensive phonics from the start with that of a group which has not.

From *The Journal of Education Research*, April 1965, *58* (8), pp. 339–346.

THE QUESTION

The rigorous comparisons in this review furnish direct evidence on the following question:

Does the intensive teaching of all the main sound-symbol relationships, both vowel and consonant, from the start of formal reading instruction have a beneficial effect on reading comprehension, vocabulary and spelling?

For convenience, such intensive teaching will be referred to in this review as a "phonetic" approach. It forms one element of many very different reading programs without being the only element of any of them. For instance, it is basic to programs involving such materials as the following: the Economy Company basic reading series, the various linguistic materials in the Bloomfield tradition, the Hay–Wingo materials, various Boston University auditory discrimination and homophone materials, and others.[1]

On the other hand, an intensive "phonetic" approach is definitely *not* an element of traditional basal programs such as the American Book Company program, the Ginn program, the Row Peterson program or the Scott, Foresman program. Such programs are often referred to as involving an eclectic or combination method, but it should be noted that the phonics in such combinations consists of gradual phonics rather than intensive phonics.

Thus a clear contrast exists between reading programs which do include an intensive "phonetic" approach and ones which do not. Rigorous comparisons of results from such contrasting programs should furnish a basis for deciding the relative value of the two approaches.

[1]Four of the most recently-published reading series also include, among other elements, an intensive "phonetic" approach: the new Lippincott series (1963), the Mazurkiewicz–Tanyzer i/t/a series (1963), the Open Court series (1963) and the Reardon–Baer parochial series (1960).

THE MAIN DIFFERENCES

Most "conventional" methods do include training in phonics, and some are even referred to as being very strong in phonics, but they still differ from "phonetic" methods in three ways:

Timing. The "phonetic" methods teach all the main vowel and consonant sounds from the start of reading instruction in first grade, while the "conventional" methods delay the teaching of most vowel sounds and some consonant sounds until second grade.

Emphasis. The "phonetic" methods involve constant phonetic review, while "conventional" methods involve much less.

Method of Attacking an Unfamiliar Word. "Phonetic" methods train the beginning reader to pronounce all the sounds of an unfamiliar word in the normal order and to use context for confirming the result, while "conventional" methods train him to analyze the sounds of parts of the word (usually the first and last consonants) and then guess the rest from context.

Some "phonetic" methods provide specific training in blending sounds into whole words, e.g., the Economy method and the Hay–Wingo method, while others leave this to the ingenuity of the individual child or teacher.

PROCEDURE

The first step in preparing this review was to examine all the studies on phonics which could be located and to list all those which compared an intensive "phonetic" instructional group with a conventional-method instructional group.

A group was considered "phonetic" if it received intensive teaching of all the main sound-symbol relationships, both vowel and consonant, from the start of formal reading instruction; it was considered "conventional" if it did not. The various "phonetic" methods identified all include such intensive teaching, but are not implied to be alike in other respects. The various "conventional" methods all fail to include it, but are also not implied to be alike in other respects.

The second step was to examine the research design of these studies and to exclude from the tabulation all which were not rigorous in their design. In this review, a comparison is considered rigorous only if it has the four following characteristics:

1. *Appropriate Type of Comparison.* Compares the actual performance of a "conventional" group with that of a "phonetic" group of comparable IQ, a group which has had intensive sound-symbol teaching from the start of first grade.
2. *Proper Sample.* Uses whole groups with equivalent IQ, or uses random selection resulting in equivalent IQ, or matches as many pairs as possible by IQ.
3. *Adequate Testing.* Uses tests of appropriate difficulty, administers the same tests to both groups at the same stage, and gives reading scores and IQ's of both groups.
4. *Standard Tests of Statistical Significance.* Evaluates the differences between the means in terms of t-values or F-values.

Only 18 of the investigations contained comparisons which could qualify as rigorous by this definition.[2] There were, however, 22 rigorous comparisons in the 18 investigations, since two compared more than one pair of groups. One investigator compared the same pair of groups at two different grade levels. The studies were published in several articles in educational journals, two reports to school boards, and ten doctoral dissertations, five of which have received little or no attention from earlier reviewers.

The third step was to tabulate the statistically significant differences in reading comprehension, vocabulary and spelling for each of the 22 rigorous comparisons. This step was accomplished by examining the tables in each study and was therefore completely objective, having no dependence on the opinions or conclusions of the various investigators. The word *significant* is used throughout this review in its technical sense, to indicate statistical significance at or beyond the 5 per cent level. Subtests showing differences which were significant at or beyond the 1 per cent level were also noted.

The fourth step was to classify each rigorous comparison as a whole as favorable to intensive phonics or not. A comparison was considered favorable to a certain group if that group was *significantly* superior in at least half the subtests of comprehension, vocabulary and spelling given. This classification was therefore also completely objective, having no dependence on the opinions or conclusions of the various investigators

[2] A full bibliography of the non-rigorous studies which were excluded from this review may be obtained from the junior author, Ann Hughes, Director of Statistical Research, Reading Reform Foundation, 36 West 44th St., New York 36, N.Y.

or on the opinions of the present reviewers.

FINDINGS

An analysis of the 22 rigorous comparisons is shown in Research/Table 1. Each comparison in the table represents a different sample, except for Bear's '64 follow-up study, and each has been listed beneath the group it favors.

It should be noted that the authors of this review were unable to find *any* rigorous comparisons which favored a "conventional" group. In other words, there were no rigorous comparisons in which a "conventional" group was significantly superior in half the subtests of comprehension, vocabulary and spelling.

RESEARCH/TABLE 1.
Results of 22 rigorous comparisons in 18 studies comparing "conventional" and "phonetic" reading programs

Favorable to Neither Group[a]	Favorable to the "Conventional" Group[a]	Favorable to the "Phonetic" Group[a]
E-3[b] Morgan & Light '63 E-4 Sparks '56 L-4 McDowell '53	None	E-1 Sparks '56 E-2 Sparks '56 E-2 Kelly '58 E-3 Henderson '55 E-3 Duncan '64 E-4 Wollam '61 L-1 Wohleber '53 L-2 Wohleber '53 L-3 Wohleber '53 L-4 Dolan '63 H-1 Bear '59 H-6 Bear '64 Q-2 Wood '55 O-1 Russell '43 O-1 Murphy '43 O-1 Crossley '48 O-1 Durrell et al '58 O-1 Santeusanio '62 O-3 Agnew '39
Total: 3	0	19

[a]For basis of classifications, see section on procedure and Table 2. See annotated bibliography for special details.

[a]Key to symbols:
E, L, H, Q, O = Materials used by "phonetic" group, as follows:
E = Economy Company's Phonetic Keys to Reading
L = Linguistic, various modifications of Bloomfield's plan
H = Hay, J. and Wingo, C., *Reading with Phonics*, Lippincott Co.
Q = Queensland Readers, Australia
O = Other "phonetic" materials
1, 2, 3, 4, 6 = Grade level at which tested

In evaluating results from achievement tests such as those used in the studies cited in Research/Tables 1 and 2, it is necessary to remember the human variables. Even the most foolproof system can occasionally be poorly installed. Conversely, poor materials can occasionally be surprisingly effective in the hands of an inspired teacher. One cannot expect a superior method to produce superior results under any and all conditions. However, one *can* expect it to produce superior results most of the time.

Thus, if the "conventional" method were actually superior, most of the rigorous comparisons could be expected to fall in the "conventional" column, with a few in the other columns. If both methods were equally good, most of the comparisons could be expected to fall in the "neither" column, with a few in the others.

What actually happens, is that most of the comparisons in Research/Table 1, 19 out of 22, fall in the "phonetic" column, while three fall in the "neither" column and not one falls in the "conventional" column. This distribution of results strongly indicates an actual superiority of the "phonetic" approach over the "conventional" approach. The three comparisons in the "neither" column cannot legitimately be considered to negate the 19 in the "phonetic" column, since a certain amount of spill must be expected in any situation where there are human variables.

Research/Table 2, which demonstrates why each of the 22 comparisons was so classified in Research/Table 1, also provides material for evaluating the widespread belief that a "phonetic" approach aids in word attack but damages comprehension.

If it were true that a "phonetic" approach damaged comprehension, most of the comprehension subtests would be expected to appear in the "conventional" column in Research/Table 2, with a few in the others. If neither approach actually tended to produce superior comprehension, most should appear under "no-significant-difference," with a few in the other columns.

Actually, more than half the c symbols fall in the "phonetic" column. Sixteen comparisons favor the "phonetic" group as to comprehension, while not one favors the "conventional" group.

DISCUSSION

The belief that early emphasis upon phonics may damage growth in comprehension is only one of a number of frequently-voiced criticisms of "phonetic" methods. Further analysis of other information in the rigorous studies supplies an objective basis for evaluating several other criticisms.

1. *Does the "Phonetic" Method Slow Down Fast-Learners?* The criticism that a "phonetic" approach slows down fast-learners is not supported by the data. Of the six comparisons in Research/Table 1 in which mean IQ's were above 110, (see annotated bibliography for IQ's,) five favored the "phonetic" group, while one favored neither.

In addition, five investigators, Dolan, Wollam, Bear, Sparks and Duncan,[3] took the further step of stratifying their

[3]Bear divided his fast-learners into two levels. His moderately-fast level (IQ 101 to 120) showed significant differences on every subtest, both in first grade and in sixth, all favoring the "phonetic" children; his top level (above IQ 120) showed none. Sparks included both these ranges in a single category and found the same number and kind of significant differences as he had found in his total groups.

RESEARCH/TABLE 2.
Analysis of subtests in 22 rigorous comparisons in 18 studies comparing "conventional" and "phonetic" reading programs[a]

Method	Comparison	Subtests Showing No Signif. Difference	Subtests Showing Sig. Diffs. Favoring "Conventional" Group	Subtests Showing Sig. Diffs. Favoring "Phonetic" Group	Total Subtests Given[a]
Economy:	E-1[b] Sparks '56			*c, v*[c]	2
	E-2 Sparks '56	v		*c*	2
	E-2 Kelly '58			*c*	1
	E-3 Henderson '55			ccc, *vvv, s*	7
	E-3 Morgan & Light '63	ccc	*c*, v		5
	E-3 Duncan '64			c	1
	E-4 Sparks '56	c, v, s			3
	E-4 Wollam '61	c, v		v, *s*	4
Linguistic:	L-1 Wohleber '53	c		*c, v*	3
	L-2 Wohleber '53			*c, v*	2
	L-3 Wohleber '53			*c, v*	2
	L-4 McDowell '53	cccc, v	*c*, v	*s*	8
	L-4 Dolan '63	cc, v		*cc, vvvv*v	10
Hay–Wingo:	H-1 Bear '59	vv		*cc, vv*v	7
	H-6 Bear '64	c		v, *ss*	4
Queensland:	Q-2 Wood '55	c		c	2
Other:	O-1 Russell '43			*c, vvvv, ss*	7
	O-1 Murphy '43			*v*	1
	O-1 Crossley '48	v		cc, v	4
	O-1 Durrell et al. '58	c, v		*c*, v	4
	O-1 Santeusanio '62			c, *vv*v	4
	O-3 Agnew '39	cc		*cc, v*	5
Total no. subtests:		27	4	57	88

[a]Including subtests of comprehension, vocabulary and spelling, but not other tests such as phonics, letter names, work-study skills, speed, accuracy, oral reading, and word pronunciation. Word discrimination and visual discrimination subtests have been counted as vocabulary. Subtests showing differences significant at the .01 level are italicized.

[b]For key to symbols E-1, L-4, etc., see key to Research/Table 1.

[c]c = comprehension subtest; v = vocabulary subtest; s = spelling subtest.

groups by IQ. In these sub-group comparisons in which the fast-learners in the "phonetic" groups were compared with the fast-learners in the "conventional" groups, all the significant differences in comprehension, vocabulary and spelling favored the "phonetic" approach. Four of the five investigators found such differences in comprehension, and three found them in vocabulary.

2. *Is a "Phonetic" Approach Too Hard for Slow-Learners?* In every instance where the slow-learners in the "phonetic" groups were compared with the slow-learners in the "conventional" groups, all the significant differences again favored the "phonetic" approach. Four of the five investigators found such differences in comprehension, and three found them in vocabulary.

3. *Do "Phonetic" Groups Read More Slowly?* While speed is not included in our basic question, it deserves mention because it is a key goal of the "conventional" method. It is true that the "conventional" method tends to develop facile reading in pre-primers, but experimental evidence suggests that such early speed in easy materials may have little relationship to eventual speed. Seven of the rigorous comparisons in Research/Table 1 included measures of speed. In two, the "conventional" group read significantly faster, Agnew '39 and McDowell '53; in two, the "phonetic" group read significantly faster, Wollam '61 and Dolan '63; in the other three, there was no significant difference in speed: Wood '55, E–5 Sparks '56 and Bear '64.

4. *Can the Success of the "Phonetic" Groups Be Explained by the Hawthorne Effect?* Much has been said about the factor of teacher enthusiasm for a new method, the so-called Hawthorne or honeymoon effect, which is said to help any experimental group. Little has been said about two compensating factors: first, possible teacher distaste for change and extra work, and second, the initial awkwardness of teachers using an unfamiliar method.

If the Hawthorne effect were actually dominant, then teachers who were new to the "phonetic" method could be expected to get better results than teachers using it for the second or third time (or habitually); i.e., we would expect "phonetic" pilot groups to be superior almost every time, while we would expect "phonetic" non-pilot groups to achieve superiority much less often.

This was not the case. Of the 13 "phonetic" groups in Research/Table 1 which were pilot groups, ten were superior.[4] Of the eight "phonetic" groups which were *not* pilot groups, *all* were superior.[5] It seems logical to conclude that the "phonetic" method does not owe its success to novelty.

5. *Does the Early Advantage Disappear Later?* The best evidence on whether an early advantage from a "phonetic" start evens out later would come from longitudinal (or follow-up) studies. Only two investigators from Research/Table 1 measured the same groups of children both early and late and published both first-grade and sixth-grade scores: Bear and Henderson.[6] In both cases, the "phonetic" group had an early advantage and maintained it.

[4]Bear's pilot group was superior in two comparisons in Research/Table 1, but counts as only one group.

[5]The eight comparisons in Research/Table 1 in which the "phonetic" group was not a pilot group are the following: E–1 Sparks '56, E–2 Sparks '56, L–1 Wohleber '53, L–2 Wohleber '53, L–4 Dolan '63, Q–2 Wood '55, O–1 Russell '43, and O–3 Agnew '39. In each of these cases, the "phonetic" group had teachers with at least one year's previous experience with the "phonetic" approach.

[6]Margaret Henderson Greenman's "phonetic" pilot group was superior in each grade from first through sixth, though only the third-grade comparison included tests of significance. Her follow-up is described in her February, 1959, report to the American Educational Research Association Conference (obtainable from School District No. 4, Champaign, Illinois) and in an article by Theodore L. Harris in the September, 1962, *Journal of Educational Research.*

The wide-spread belief that an early advantage dissipates rests largely on the Sparks '56 study, summarized by Sparks and Fay in 1957, which has been widely misunderstood. The comparisons in Sparks '56 were not longitudinal, but multilevel, all four grades being tested the same year. (See Research/Table 1.) The only longitudinal study of any of these children was done by Fay, who followed the pilot group's progress in fifth and sixth grade, but did not follow the younger, more successful non-pilot groups.[7] It should be noted that the total longitudinal span here was fourth grade through sixth, not first through sixth. We know only that this particular pilot group showed no significant difference from its control group in either fourth, fifth or sixth grades. It would be unsound to assume that a significant difference had existed in first grade and had dissipated.

The authors of this review know of no instance where an early "phonetic" advantage (rigorously measured) has later disappeared.

6. *Are "Phonetic" Groups Usually Superior in Grade 3 and Above?* Although only Bear and Henderson made wide-span longitudinal studies, several others chose to make single comparisons at the third-grade level or higher. Altogether, there are ten rigorous upper-grade comparisons in Research/Table 1: seven favor the "phonetic" group, and three favor neither. Not one favors the "conventional" group.

Thus the rigorous comparisons indicate that "phonetic" groups tend to be superior in later grades as well as in first and second grade.

[7]Leo Fay's fifth- and sixth-grade follow-up of Sparks' pilot group was reported in the 1961 *International Reading Association Conference Proceedings,* without scores or critical ratios.

SOME NON-RIGOROUS STUDIES

Previous reviews on phonics have concentrated largely on a group of studies from the 1920's and 1930's which have been cited as supporting the "conventional" method. Several of these as well as some of their modern successors are irrelevant in that they did not actually compare a "phonetic" group with a "conventional" group, but made some other type of comparison and then hypothesized freely. Others used highly selected samples or failed to give IQ's. Fourteen such studies will be mentioned below, simply to point out why they cannot be considered rigorous as previously defined.

A. The studies listed below were omitted from Research/Tables 1 and 2 because they did not employ appropriate types of comparison. The first four, for instance, failed to include any group which had been intensively "phonetic" from the start.

1. *Dolch and Bloomster,* 1937, ESJ.[8] All the children had gradual phonics. The only actual comparison was between bright children and dull children.

2. *Tate,* June, 1937, ESJ. All the children had gradual phonics except during the eight-week experiment in the spring.

3. *Tate, Herbert and Zeman,* March, 1940, ESJ. The study compared gradual phonics with no phonics.

4. *Mills,* January, 1956, ESJ. Various children were given a single lesson

[8]The dates listed are dates of publication. The initials NM refer to Gates' book, *New Methods in Primary Reading.* The other initials refer to the following periodicals: ESJ—*Elementary School Journal,* RT—*Reading Teacher,* JEP—*Journal of Educational Psychology,* PJE—*Peabody Journal of Education.*

in phonics by the experimenter. No attention was paid to methods used by regular teachers.

5. *Gates'* Carden study, March, 1961, RT. The study failed to include a "conventional" group for comparison.

6. *Tensuan and Davis,* October, 1964, RT. The study did not deal with English-speaking children.

B. The next three were omitted because they discarded most of one group or the other (or both) while matching. This procedure can result in a final sample which is not representative because it is loaded with over-achievers or under-achievers.

1. *Gates'* study of 25 matched pairs, 1928, NM. The comparison was not based on a proper sample, because the experimenter used only a selected fourth of his 111 "conventional" children.

2. *Gates and Russell,* October, 1938, ESJ. The comparison was not based on a proper sample, because the experimenters used only a selected third of their "phonetic" group. They compared 146 children from four "conventional" classes with 51 children selected from four "phonetic" classes.

3. *McCollum's* report to the Berkeley School Board on 20 matched pairs, June, 1962. The comparison was not based on a proper sample, because the experimenter used only a selected third of each group.

C. The four studies below were omitted because they failed either to administer IQ tests or to report IQ's. This failure is a serious one, since IQ differences have been shown to produce differences in reading ability which have no connection with method.

1. *Sexton and Herron's* Newark study, May, 1928, ESJ.

2. *Gates'* split-class experiment, 1928, NM.

3. *Mosher and Newhall,* October, 1930, JEP.

4. *Garrison and Heard,* July, 1931, PJE.

D. The study below was omitted because inappropriate statistical techniques were used.

1. *Cleland and Miller,* February, 1965, ESJ. The test which was treated as a pretest was given during the second half of February, five months after the experiment had begun. The present reviewers applied ordinary t-tests to the raw data given in the original study, (Harry B. Miller's doctor's dissertation, University of Pittsburgh, 1962,) and discovered that the "phonetic" group was actually significantly superior to the "conventional" group both in February and in May.

In addition, six of the studies already listed failed to include tests of significance: Dolch and Bloomster; Tate; Tate, Herbert and Zeman; Gates '61; Sexton and Herron; and Gates and Russell. In another of these studies, Garrison and Heard, the tests of significance were improperly applied to scores from tests that were so easy that both groups averaged almost perfect scores. This was true of 11 of the 20 tests of comprehension, vocabulary and spelling.

Many of the non-rigorous studies just listed have other major faults, both of design and of interpretation, too numerous to explore in this review. Their irrelevance or statistical inadequacy has received little attention from advocates of the "conventional" method. No attempt has been made in this review to take into account the many non-rigorous studies which are frankly favorable to the "phonetic" approach.

CONCLUSIONS

1. It can be seen from Research/Table 1 that rigorous controlled research clearly favors intensive teaching of all the main sound-symbol relationships, both vowel and consonant, from the start of formal reading instruction.

2. It can be seen from Research/Table 2 that such teaching benefits comprehension as well as vocabulary and spelling.

3. It can be seen from the ten upper-grade comparisons in Research/Table 1 that "phonetic" groups are usually superior in grades 3 and above.

RECOMMENDATIONS

Since the results of this comprehensive and objective review of rigorously controlled research indicate that a gradual phonics approach is significantly less effective than an intensive phonics approach in beginning reading instruction, the authors recommend that an intensive "phonetic" approach be generally accepted as one of the most essential components of a good reading program. It is specifically suggested:

1) that all the main sound-symbol relationships, both vowel and consonant, be taught intensively from the start of reading instruction.

2) that schools provide their teachers with suitable materials and in-service training for using an intensive phonetic approach, and

3) that colleges and universities offer training in the necessary techniques, both in summer workshops and in regular courses.

ANNOTATED BIBLIOGRAPHY

(The note after each reference gives group sizes, IQ levels, and the proportion and direction of significant differences on the subtests relevant to comprehension, vocabulary and spelling. Symbols are explained in the key to Research/Table 1.)

1. **Agnew, Donald C.** *The Effect of Varied Amounts of Phonetic Training in Primary Reading,* Duke University Research Studies in Education No. 5. Durham, N.C.: Duke University Press, 1939. (Also condensed in Hunnicutt, C. W. and Iverson, W. J., *Research in the Three R's.* New York: Harper, 1958.)

   (O–3) The majority of the relevant subtests, three out of five, showed significant differences favoring the 89 third-graders from Durham, where phonics was emphasized. There were no such significant differences favoring the 89 "conventional" third-graders from Raleigh. Mean IQ's were 111 and 112, respectively. Tests used: Gates Basic Silent Reading, Pressey Vocabulary, Otis IQ.

2. **Bear, David E.** "Phonics for First Grade: A Comparison of Two Methods," *Elementary School Journal* LIX (April 1959), pp. 394–402. (Summary of the author's "A Comparison of a Synthetic with an Analytic Method of Teaching Phonics in First Grade." Unpublished doctor's dissertation, Washington University, St. Louis, 1958.)

   (H–1) The majority of the relevant subtests, five out of seven, showed significant differences favoring the 136 first-graders who had used Hay–Wingo materials. There were no significant differences favoring the 139 "conventional" first-graders. Mean IQ's were 112 and 113, respectively. Tests used:

Gates Primary; Metropolitan Achievement Primary I; Durrell Visual Discrimination; California Test of Mental Maturity, Primary.

3. **Bear, David E.** "Two Methods of Teaching Phonics: A Longitudinal Study," *Elementary School Journal* LXIV (February 1964), pp. 273–9.

 (H–6) In this follow-up of Bear's '59 study, the majority of the relevant subtests, three out of four, showed significant differences favoring the 96 sixth-graders who had used Hay–Wingo in first grade. There were no significant differences favoring the 90 "conventional" sixth-graders. No significant difference was found between the mean IQ's of these diminished groups. Tests used: Gates Reading Survey, local spelling tests.

4. **Crossley, Beatrice A.** "An Evaluation of the Effect of Lantern Slides on Auditory and Visual Discrimination of Word Elements." Unpublished doctor's dissertation, Boston University, 1948.

 (O–1) The majority of the relevant subtests, three out of four, showed significant differences favoring the 204 first-graders who had systematic auditory training. There were no significant differences favoring the 212 "conventional" first-graders. Mean IQ's were 106 and 105, respectively. Tests used: Gates Primary, Boston University test of visual discrimination, Kuhlmann–Anderson IQ for Grade One.

5. **Dolan,** Sister **Mary Edward.** "A Modified Linguistic Versus a Composite Basal Reading Program," *Reading Teacher* XVII (April 1964), pp. 511–5. (Summary of the author's "A Comparative Study of Reading Achievement at the Fourth Grade Level under Two Methods of Instruction: Modified Linguistic and Traditional Basal." Unpublished doctor's dissertation, University of Minnesota, 1963.)

 (L–4) The majority of the relevant subtest, seven out of ten, showed significant differences favoring the 403 Detroit fourth-graders who had followed a modification of Bloomfield's plan. There were no significant differences favoring the 407 Dubuque "conventional" fourth-graders. Mean IQ's for the boys were 104 and 106, respectively. Mean IQ's for the girls were 111 for both groups. Tests used: Gates Reading Survey; Bond, Clymer, Hoyt Diagnostic Test; Bond, Clymer, Hoyt Developmental Tests; Lorge–Thorndike Non-Verbal IQ.

6. **Duncan, Roger L.** "A Comparative Study: Two Methods of Teaching Reading", *Tulsa School Review* XXI (September 1964), pp. 4–5. (Also condensed in *School Management* VIII (December 1964), pp. 46–7.)

 (E–3) Duncan applied the median test to second- and third-grade scores of the 882 children in the Phonetic Keys pilot group and the 878 "conventional" children. He found highly significant differences favoring the "phonetic" group on every subtest of comprehension, vocabulary, spelling and language at both levels. He applied t-tests only to third-grade comprehension and language and found significant differences on both, again favoring the "phonetic" group. Mean IQ for both groups was 103. Tests used: Metropolitan Achievement Primary II, Metropolitan Achievement Elementary, Kuhlmann–Anderson Intelligence.

7. **Durrell, Donald D. and others.** "Success in First Grade Reading," *Journal of Education* CXL (February 1958), pp. 1–48. (Summary of doctor's dissertations at Boston University by Alice Ni-

cholson, Arthur V. Olson, Sylvia R. Gavel and Eleanor B. Linehan.)

(O–1) Half the relevant subtests, two out of four, showed significant differences favoring the 314 first-graders who had systematic training in letter names and phonics. There were no significant differences favoring the 300 "conventional" first-graders. Mean mental ages were 81 and 82 months, respectively. Tests used: Detroit Word Recognition, Boston University tests, Otis Alpha, California Test of Mental Maturity.

8. **Henderson, Margaret G.** *Progress Report of Reading Study 1952–55.* Champaign, Illinois: Board of Education, 1955. (Also condensed in *Chicago Schools Journal,* January–February 1956, pp. 141–7.)

(E–3) All seven relevant subtests showed significant differences favoring the 87 third-graders who had used Phonetic Keys to Reading over the 195 "conventional" third-graders. Mean IQ's were 109 and 106, respectively. Tests used: Metropolitan Achievement Elementary, Stanford Elementary, Iowa Basic Skills, California Test of Mental Maturity.

9. **Kelly, Barbara C.** "The Economy Method Versus the Scott Foresman Method in Teaching Second-Grade Reading in the Murphysboro Public Schools," *Journal of Educational Research* LI (February 1958), pp. 465–8.

(E–2) The one relevant test showed a significant difference favoring the 100 second-graders who had used Phonetic Keys to Reading over the 100 "conventional" second-graders. The mean mental ages were 100 months and 101 months, respectively. Tests used: California Achievement, California Test of Mental Maturity.

10. **McDowell, Rev. John B.** "A Report on the Phonetic Method of Teaching Children to Read," *Catholic Education Review* LI (October 1953), pp. 506–19.

(L–4) The majority of the relevant subtests, five out of eight, showed no significant difference between the 142 fourth-graders who had used a modification of Bloomfield linguistics and the 142 "conventional" fourth-graders. (Of the other three relevant subtests, one showed a significant difference favoring the "phonetic" group, and two showed significant differences favoring the "conventional" group.) Mean IQ's were 116 and 115, respectively. Tests used: Iowa Silent Reading, Metropolitan Achievement, California Test of Mental Maturity.

11. **Morgan, Elmer F. and Light, Morton.** "A Statistical Evaluation of Two Programs of Reading Instruction," *Journal of Educational Research* LVII (October 1963), pp. 99–101.

(E–3) The majority of the relevant subtests, three out of five, showed no significant difference between the third-graders who had used Phonetic Keys to Reading and the "conventional" third-graders. (The other two subtests showed significant differences favoring the "conventional" group.) Group sizes were not given, but combined groups totaled about 150. Mean IQ of both groups was 102. Tests used: Gates Basic Reading, California S-Form IQ. The second and third comparisons in the study did not include IQ's and therefore do not qualify as rigorous.

12. **Murphy, Helen A.** "An Evaluation of the Effect of Specific Training in Auditory and Visual Discrimination on Beginning Reading." Unpublished doctor's dissertation, Boston University, 1943.

(O–1) The one relevant subtest showed a significant difference favoring the 144 first-graders who had systematic auditory training over the 73 "conventional" first-graders. Mean mental age was 71 months for both groups. Tests used: Detroit Word Recognition, Detroit First Grade IQ, Pintner–Cunningham IQ.

13. **Russell, David H.** "A Diagnostic Study of Spelling Readiness," *Journal of Educational Research* XXXVII (December 1943), pp. 276–83.

(O–1) All seven relevant subtests showed significant differences favoring the 61 first-graders who had "much phonics" over the 55 "conventional" first-graders. Mean IQ's were 104 and 105, respectively. Tests used: Gates Primary, Gates Reading Diagnosis Tests, New Stanford Dictation Spelling, informal spelling test, Detroit First Grade IQ, Pintner–Cunningham IQ.

14. **Santeusanio, Nancy C.** "Evaluation of a Planned Program for Teaching Homophones in Beginning Reading." Unpublished doctor's dissertation, Boston University, 1962. (Summary in *Dissertation Abstracts* XXIII (February 1963), pp. 2820–1.)

(O-1) All four relevant subtests showed significant differences favoring the 202 first-graders who had training in homophones over the 202 "conventional" first-graders. Mean IQ for both groups was 106. Tests used: Metropolitan Achievement Primary I; Boston University Visual Discrimination Test; Lorge–Thorndike IQ, Level 1.

15. **Sparks, Paul E.** "An Evaluation of Two Methods of Teaching Reading." Unpublished doctor's dissertation, Indiana University, August, 1956. (Summary in an article with the same title by Sparks, Paul E. and Fay, Leo C. in the *Elementary School Journal* LVII (April 1957), pp. 386–90.)

(E–1) Both the relevant subtests showed significant differences favoring the 124 first-graders who had Phonetic Keys to Reading over the 122 "conventional" first-graders. Mean IQ's were 110 and 105, respectively. Tests used: California Reading Test, Primary, Form CC; Otis Alpha IQ, Short Form.

(E–2) One of the two relevant subtests showed a significant difference favoring the 122 second-graders who had Phonetic Keys to Reading. There were no significant differences favoring the 104 "conventional" second-graders. Mean IQ's were 105 and 108, respectively. Tests used: California Reading Test, Primary, Form CC; Otis Alpha IQ, Short Form.

(E–4) None of the three relevant subtests showed a significant difference favoring either the 84 fourth-graders who had formed the phonetic Keys pilot group or the 89 "conventional" fourth-graders. Mean IQ for both groups was 106. Tests used: Gates Reading Survey; Stanford Achievement Intermediate Spelling; Otis Alpha IQ, Short Form.

N.B. Sparks' third-grade comparison made use of tests that were too easy to measure the ability of the better half of either group: California Reading Test, Primary, Form CC. Therefore the third-grade comparison does not qualify as rigorous.

16. **Wohleber, Sister Mary Louis, R.S.M.** "A Study of the Effects of a Systematic Program of Phonetic Training on Primary Reading." Unpublished doctor's dissertation, University of Pittsburgh, 1953.

(L–1) The majority of the relevant subtests, two out of three, showed significant differences favoring the 65 first-graders who had used a modified linguistic program. There were no significant differences favoring the 65 "conventional" first-graders. Mean IQ's were 114 and 115, respectively. Tests used: Gates Primary, Detroit Advanced First Grade IQ.

(L–2) Both the relevant subtests showed significant differences favoring the 80 second-graders who had used a modified linguistic program over the 80 "conventional" second-graders. Mean IQ's were 105 and 106, respectively. Tests used: Gates Advanced Primary, Otis Alpha IQ.

(L–3) Both the relevant subtests showed significant differences favoring the 79 third-graders who had formed the linguistic pilot group over the 79 "conventional" third-graders. Mean IQ's were 105 and 106, respectively. Tests used: Gates Advanced Primary, Otis Alpha IQ.

17. **Wollam, Walter A.** "A Comparison of Two Methods of Teaching Reading." Unpublished doctor's dissertation, Western Reserve University, 1961. Abstract available from author: Superintendent of Schools, Alliance, Ohio.

(E–4) Half the relevant subtests, two out of four, showed significant differences favoring the 301 fourth-graders who had used Phonetic Keys to Reading in grades one through three. There were no significant differences favoring the 306 "conventional" fourth-graders. Mean IQ's were 107 and 109, respectively. Tests used: Diagnostic Reading Tests, Survey Section, Lower Level; sixty-word sample from spelling manual; California Test of Mental Maturity.

18. **Wood, W.** *An Investigation of Methods of Teaching Reading in Infants' Schools*, Bulletin No. 9. Brisbane, Australia: Research and Guidance Branch of the Queensland Department of Public Instruction, March, 1955.

(Q–2) One of the two relevant subtests showed a significant difference favoring the 168 second-graders who had used the usual Queensland Readers, a program which included an intensive "phonetic" approach. There were no significant differences favoring the 193 second-graders whose teachers were experimenting with gradual phonics. Mean IQ's were 110 and 107, respectively. Tests used: A.C.E.R. Reading Comprehension; Ohio Department of Public Instruction Reading for Meaning Test; Terman–Merrill Binet IQ, Form L; Melbourne General Ability Test.

N.B. A later Queensland study, in 1958, did not include IQ's and therefore does not qualify as rigorous.

A Critique of Louise Gurren and Ann Hughes's Study: Intensive Phonics vs. Gradual Phonics in Beginning Reading: A Review

JERRY L. JOHNS

Northern Illinois University

PART I: SETTING THE STAGE

Historical Background on Phonics Instruction

The history of reading instruction provided by Smith (1965) makes it clear that the impact of phonics on the teaching of reading changed over the years. In some periods, phonics was strongly emphasized, while in others it was considered an outmoded procedure. Near the close of the nineteenth century, Pollard's synthetic method, with its stress on the sounds of the vowels and consonants, was popular (Robinson, 1977). Her method was the first of the elaborately organized systems of phonics (Cordts, 1965).

At the beginning of the twentieth century, phonics was in wide use. By the 1920s, silent reading was emphasized. With the introduction of experience charts, students dictated stories that formed the basis for reading. Phonics, however, was still introduced "during the first three or four weeks of reading instruction, and considerable attention was given to it throughout the primary grades" (Smith, 1965, p. 183). The usual method of teaching phonics was to "introduce the sounds of letters and combinations by oral exaggeration of similar sounds in rhymes and jingles; and later have the children sound separate letters, diphthongs, and families, consisting of vowels attached to their succeeding consonant" (Smith, 1965, pp. 182–83). By the late 1920s, interest in phonics changed from "a debate on whether or not phonics should be taught to a controversy over how and when to teach it" (Walcutt, Lamport, & McCracken, 1974, p. 378).

In the 1930s, intensive phonics was displaced by whole-word instruction. Reading programs delayed phonics until children were able to note similarities and differences in words. According to Smith, phonics was taught much more moderately than in former periods and was subordinated to other phases of reading instruction.

By the 1940s, phonics was used with context clues and structural analysis to form a group of word recognition skills. Although phonics was included in all basal reading programs, it was not uncommon to delay phonic analysis until students had acquired a stock of sight words. Phonics, then, became part of a triad (with context clues and structural analysis) that aided in the pronunciation of words that were not recognized at sight.

The 1950s and 1960s witnessed a combination of phonics and whole-word methods. Critics of the whole-word or look-and-say method became vocal. Flesch's name was well-known to both educators and parents. His book, *Why Johnny Can't Read,* "took the nation by storm. It stayed on the best-seller lists for over thirty weeks and was serialized in countless newspapers" (Chall, 1967, p. 3). Flesch characterized reading instruction in schools as a look-and-say or sight method and identified phonics-first as *the* method to teach reading.

Many publishers responded with renewed vigor by producing basal programs and supplementary materials that focused heavily on intensive phonics. Chall's classic study *Learning to Read: The Great Debate* (1967) was, to a large degree, stimulated by the bitter debate between advocates of whole-word and intensive-phonics methods.

The 1970s and early 1980s can be characterized by inflation, recession, and a lowered national birth rate. Schools closed. A renewed period of conservatism entered the educational system and the back-to-basics movement received considerable publicity. Flesch's article in the November 1, 1979 issue of *Family Circle* called for a renewed effort to use phonics-first programs in our nation's schools (Johns, 1980). That same thrust was repeated in Flesch's most recent volume (1981).

This brief historical overview of phonics instruction since the 1900s should make it clear that phonics has been a persistent and controversial topic in the field of reading. The role of phonics in reading instruction is certainly a recurring theme—it seems to cycle into favor and disfavor.

In 1965 when Gurren and Hughes published their review, phonics was certainly a topic of concern. Two years later, Chall's book appeared and was widely reviewed in educational journals (Johns, 1969). Chall's work and the now famous first-grade studies were at least partially concerned with the basic question posed by Gurren and Hughes in their review of phonic studies: "Does the intensive teaching of all the main sound-symbol relationships, both vowel and consonant, from the start of formal reading instruction have a beneficial effect on reading comprehension, vocabulary, and spelling?"

A Brief Summary of the Gurren-Hughes Review

In 1965, Gurren and Hughes reviewed 18 published and unpublished studies that compared intensive-phonics groups and gradual-phonics or so-called "look-say" groups. According to Gurren and Hughes, each study included in the review met four criteria: (1) a true comparison of intensive phonics versus gradual phonics; (2) a sampling procedure that ensured that both groups were equivalent in intelligence; (3) adequate and similar testing of both groups; and (4) the use of statistical tests to determine the significance of the differences between the means in the two groups.

Gurren and Hughes concluded that none of the 22 comparisons (some studies had more than 1 comparison) favored the gradual-phonics groups, 3 favored neither group, and 19 favored the intensive-phonics groups. Of the 88 subtests dealing with comprehension, vocabulary, and spelling that were used in the 22 comparisons, 4 favored the gradual-phonics groups, 27 favored neither group, and 57 favored the intensive-phonics groups.

From their analysis of the data, Gurren and Hughes concluded that intensive phonics was superior to gradual phonics; moreover, intensive phonics benefited comprehension and vocabulary from the start of formal reading and in grades three and above. They then recommended that all the main sound-symbol relationships (vowel and consonant) be taught intensively from the beginning of reading instruction. To help implement intensive phonics, they urged schools and institutions of higher learning to offer appropriate training, techniques, and materials in an intensive-phonic approach.

PART II: THE CRITIQUE

A number of issues and questions raised by the Gurren-Hughes review will be considered. For convenience, headings are provided.

The Title

Look at the title. The authors are contrasting intensive phonics and gradual phonics in *beginning* reading instruction. Consult their annotated bibliography and observe that the first study cited deals with third-grade students. Are these students beginning readers? Doesn't *beginning* reading instruction occur in the first grade? Are Gurren and Hughes guilty of false advertising? Should they have offered a title that more accurately reflected the content of their review? Look over the remaining annotations in the bibliography. The studies dealt with students in grades one, two, three, four, and six. Less than half of the studies are at the level where Gurren and Hughes, according to their chosen title, were supposed to concentrate their review. Perhaps a caution flag should be raised.

The Authors

Many researchers have organized the world of reading to fit their beliefs. They may find research that confirms their views, and sometimes they interpret research in such a way that it supports them. They may also unfairly criticize research that supports a different point of view. Would you be surprised to see Kenneth Goodman or Frank Smith conduct a research review along the lines of Gurren and Hughes? Goodman and Smith do not seem to have much use for phonics instruction. Perhaps they have a bias; however, they also have reasons and research to support *their* views.

Notice that Ann Hughes is affiliated with the Reading Reform Foundation. Did you know that the sole aim of that foundation is to restore intensive phonics to the teaching of reading throughout the nation? She may have a vested interest in the outcome of the review she undertook. Was her bias operating when evaluating studies for inclusion or exclusion in the review? Raise another caution flag, but also remember that all researchers operate from a particular set of beliefs or assumptions. The main concern should be whether those beliefs influence the study to the point of distortion or whether the influence is kept to a minimum.

The Time Span

There is a wide span (1939 to 1964) covered by the studies included in the Gurren-Hughes review. The historical background on phonics instruction provided earlier in this critique should help you see that there is no period of phonics instruction that can be labeled as purely "intensive" or purely "gradual" with any degree of certainty. Emans (1968) contends that phonics has had various forms throughout the years. In short, had the approach to teaching phonics changed during the time span covered by the Gurren-Hughes review? It is difficult to believe that the instructional methods for teaching intensive and gradual phonics remained unchanged or reflected common practices during the 25-year time span covered in their review.

Distinctions between Intensive and Gradual Phonics

Gurren and Hughes distinguish between intensive and gradual phonics in three ways: timing, emphasis, and method of attacking an unfamiliar word. But the distinction between these two approaches to phonics is not as clear-cut as Gurren and Hughes make it; furthermore, some would argue that the Gurren and Hughes distinction is a false one. A look at the studies Gurren and Hughes cite leads one to ponder whether evidence is provided that timing, emphasis, and methods of word attack in these studies are similar or comparable. Consider the study by Dolan, who compared a modified Bloomfield program and a composite basal reading program. Although Bloomfield's material does not seem compatible in phonic emphasis with the studies reported by Murphy and Russell, Gurren and Hughes regard all these studies as comparable.

Classifying studies as having intensive or gradual phonics also presents a problem. Gurren and Hughes classified the Bloomfield program as intensive phonics. Chall recognized the difficulty of classifying such programs; furthermore, she decided to classify the Bloomfield program as an analytic or gradual phonics program "because, after awhile, the words are read as wholes and letter-sound correspondences are not specifically taught, but are to be induced by the child" (Chall, 1967, p. 346).

Perhaps the basic consideration is whether Gurren and Hughes lumped together some studies that are not as compatible as they should be for the type of comparison they undertook.

critique

The Selection/Exclusion of Studies

What criteria should Gurren and Hughes have used to select studies for the review? They used four characteristics as criteria for selecting rigorous studies. In a critique of the Gurren-Hughes review, Weintraub (1966) criticized a number of the studies they included; however, he used different criteria. Were the criteria used by Gurren and Hughes too restrictive or too loose? The basic question concerns the criteria that are used to judge studies. You probably agree that the criteria should be rigorous, but what makes a study rigorous?

Consider two other studies—one by Agnew and one by Wollam. It is possible that some teachers in the Agnew study spent twenty minutes more each day in reading instruction than did other teachers. This would amount to more than two hours of additional instruction per week. Could this time difference help account for the observed differences in the study?

In the Wollam study, teachers using the new phonics program spent more time in preparation for reading instruction than did those who used the conventional program. Were the teachers in the new program better prepared for teaching the new program? Were they enthusiastic? Was the Hawthorne effect operating? Could these factors help explain the results of the study?

Many studies have limitations that restrict their results. Although one can disagree with the criteria used by Gurren and Hughes, they did offer, and apparently followed, the criteria they set forth, except for including groups above the first-grade level.

Statistical Significance

Gurren and Hughes tabulated the findings from the 18 studies included in their review on the basis of *statistically* significant differences. Statistical tests reveal to what degree the observed findings might be due to chance. When Gurren and Hughes reported levels of significance at the .05 and the .01 levels, they used only differences that have a chance occurrence of five or less, or one or less, in a hundred. Although these levels of significance are commonly used in educational research, such differences may not be inherently meaningful or important. In short, statistically significant differences may or may not have practical importance.

Some of the studies included by Gurren and Hughes appear to have *both* statistical and practical significance (for example, the study by Kelly). But the study by Bear (1959), although containing statistically significant differences, may lack practical significance. Why? The grade-equivalent scores for the experimental group averaged only about two months higher than the grade-equivalent scores for the control group.

Means Mask

What works for one student may not work equally well for another. When we use mean achievement levels to compare groups, individual differences in achievement often become masked or submerged in the group average.

critique

For example, Johns (1977) found a considerable range of individual differences in an investigation of children's concepts of spoken words and urged a cautious interpretation. Does it seem likely that some students in the intensive-phonics group performed more poorly than some students in the gradual-phonics group? Is the reverse also likely to be true? Although Gurren and Hughes only reported the results from the studies, they did recommend that intensive phonics be taught from the start of reading instruction. From this recommendation one might conclude that *all* children would profit from such an emphasis. Look at Research/Table 2 in their review and note that 31 of the subtests did not give an advantage to the intensive-phonics groups. That same table does support an overall advantage to such groups, but it is not an all-inclusive advantage. Should Gurren and Hughes have exercised more caution in their recommendation?

Synthesis of Critique

The Gurren and Hughes review concerns two types of phonics programs (intensive and gradual) that have frequently been debated. After examining many studies, Gurren and Hughes included in the review only those that met their criteria for rigor. They found that the bulk of the comparisons favored the intensive-phonics groups in comprehension, vocabulary, and spelling.

This critique, while not an exhaustive treatment of the Gurren-Hughes review, contains a number of questions and issues to consider when examining their work. The main areas of concern include the following: (1) whether studies above first grade are appropriate to include in a review concerned with beginning reading instruction; (2) possible author bias (deliberate or non-deliberate); (3) whether the time span covered by the studies (25 years) makes similar intensive- and gradual-phonics instruction questionable; (4) the difficulty of establishing clear distinctions between the phonics emphases; (5) the appropriateness of the criteria used for selecting studies; (6) statistical versus practical significance in interpreting results; and (7) conclusions and recommendations that may be too global.

PART III: THE BIG PICTURE

Research and reviews of research are not easy undertakings. Critics abound. Borg and Gall, after reviewing a number of studies on the quality of educational research, concluded that "a substantial percentage of studies published in education have serious deficiencies" (1979, p. 145). Those studies without serious deficiencies could be challenged by people who see other ways to explore the topic, gather data, conduct data analysis, and manipulate variables.

Gurren and Hughes presented a review of phonic studies about which a number of valid criticisms can be raised. Weintraub (1966) severely criticized seven comparisons included by Gurren and Hughes; nevertheless, if we eliminate these comparisons, those remaining still favor the intensive-phonics groups. Other studies have produced similar findings.

critique

The 27 first-grade studies include some data that may answer the basic question posed by Gurren and Hughes. In a speech to the 16th Annual Conference of the Reading Reform Foundation, Dykstra (1977) noted that a primary purpose of the 27 first-grade studies was to evaluate the effectiveness of many approaches to teaching children to read. Dykstra said that "children who learn to read in instructional programs emphasizing early and intensive teaching of phonics demonstrated superior ability, in word recognition skills particularly, at the end of both grades one and two" (1977, p. 12).

Karlin (1980) reviewed the first-grade studies, Chall's large-scale study of beginning reading, and a group of studies concerning intensive-phonics and gradual-phonics programs. He noted that although reading scores for the programs stressing intensive phonics did not have consistent, marked superiority, the findings leaned in the direction of those programs.

Dykstra also drew a similar conclusion when he summarized the results of sixty years of research dealing with beginning reading instruction for Walcutt, Lamport, & McCracken (1974). He said that "early systematic (intensive) instruction in phonics provides the child with the skills necessary to become an independent reader at an earlier age than is likely if phonics instruction is delayed (gradual) and less systematic." Dykstra's conclusion was also supported by Weaver and Shonkoff who, after acknowledging the difficulties encountered in conducting and interpreting reading program comparisons, concluded that "results tend to favor early and systematic code instruction" (1978, p. 65).

Phonics is one of several important cue systems that play a role in helping students to reconstruct meaning from print. Critics and advocates of phonics seem to polarize themselves, thereby making dialogue strained or impossible. The recurring debate on the benefits or limitations of phonics instruction seems unproductive because it focuses on such a narrow aspect of reading behavior.

The process of learning to read is influenced by factors over and above the materials or methods used. The first-grade studies produced evidence that the effectiveness of the same instructional program (for example, intensive phonics) in different school systems led to varied reading achievement, even when students appeared to share similar readiness, socio-economic status, and intelligence. To yield more generalized findings, research in reading must systematically consider schools, classrooms, and materials. Research must identify characteristics of good schools, good classrooms, and effective instruction. Until more effort is aimed in that direction, there will be studies like the Gurren and Hughes review—an instructional study conducted in a type of vaccum. Such studies will, at best, offer very limited insight into the teaching of reading. But perhaps limited insights are the best that can be achieved as the mysteries and problems of reading are investigated. Or, as Huey (1968, p. 5) said, "problem enough, this, for a life's work, to learn how we read!"

FOR FURTHER LEARNING

Those readers who are interested in continuing to explore the topic of phonics would find the following references helpful.

for further learning

Artley, A. S. Progress report on the Champaign reading study 1952–55: A review and discussion. *Elementary English,* Feb. 1957, *34,* 102–105.

Bond, G. L., & Dykstra, R. The cooperative research program in first-grade reading instruction. *Reading Research Quarterly,* Summer 1967, *2,* 5–142.

Chall, J. S. *Learning to read: The great debate.* New York: McGraw-Hill, 1967.

Flesch, R. *Why Johnny still can't read.* New York: Harper & Row, 1981.

Robinson, H. M. News and comments: Methods of teaching beginning readers. *The Elementary School Journal,* May 1959, *59,* 419–435.

Weintraub, S. A critique of a review of phonics studies. *The Elementary School Journal,* Oct. 1966, *67,* 34–40.

REFERENCES

Bear, D. E. Phonics for first grade: A comparison of two methods. *The Elementary School Journal,* April 1959, *59,* 394–402.

Borg, W. R., & Gall, M. D. *Educational Research* (3rd ed.). New York: Longman, 1979.

Chall, J. S. *Learning to read: The great debate.* New York: McGraw-Hill, 1967.

Cordts, A. D. *Phonics for the reading teacher.* New York: Holt, 1965.

Dykstra, R. What the 27 studies said. *The Reading Informer,* Conference report, Nov. 1977, *5,* pp. 11–12; 24.

Emans, R. History of phonics, *Elementary English,* May 1968, *45,* 602–608.

Flesch, R. *Why Johnny still can't read.* New York: Harper and Row, 1981.

Huey, E. G. *The psychology and pedagogy of reading.* New York: M.I.T. Press, 1968. (Originally published by Macmillan, 1908.)

Johns, J. L. Reviews of *Learning to read: The great debate. Elementary English,* May 1969, *46,* 635–638.

Johns, J. L. Children's conceptions of a spoken word: A developmental study. *Reading World,* May 1977, *16,* 248–257.

Johns, J. L. It's only a Flesch wound. *Illinois Reading Council Journal,* March 1980, *8,* pp. 3–4; 10.

Karlin, R. *Teaching elementary reading* (3rd ed.). New York: Harcourt, 1980.

Research critiques. In P. Groff (Ed.), *Elementary English,* April 1968, *45,* pp. 507–512; 517.

Robinson, H. A. (Ed.). *Reading & writing instruction in the United States: Historical trends.* Newark, Del.: International Reading Association, 1977.

Smith, N. B. *American reading instruction.* Newark, Del.: International Reading Association, 1965.

Walcutt, C. C., Lamport, J., & McCracken, G. *Teaching reading: A phonic/linguistic approach to developmental reading.* New York: Macmillan, 1974.

Weaver, P., & Shonkoff, F. *Research without reach: A research-guided response to concerns of reading educators.* Newark, Del.: International Reading Association, 1978.

Weintraub, S. A critique of a review of phonics studies. *The Elementary School Journal,* Oct. 1966, *67,* 34–40.

A Commentary on Johns's Critique of Gurren and Hughes's Study: Measuring the Effects of Intensive Phonics vs. Gradual Phonics in Beginning Reading

BARBARA BATEMAN

University of Oregon

Johns's critique of Gurren and Hughes's article raises interesting and provocative issues that invite further comment. This author will use the same headings as they appear in the critique itself.

THE TITLE

If, as the critique suggests, a caution flag should be raised by the authors' term "beginning reading instruction," it must be a very tiny flag. Certainly some of the studies reviewed by Gurren and Hughes use students in grades beyond the first. The point is that those students were taught by intensive or by gradual phonics when their beginning reading instruction occurred. Gurren and Hughes clearly state they were comparing groups that had intensive phonics "from the start" with groups that did not. Had the authors limited their review to studies of first graders, one can readily predict that their effort would have been dismissed on the grounds that any differences might have quickly disappeared after first grade.

Whether intensive scrutiny of the title of any article is worthwhile is itself debatable and one hesitates to dignify unduly a questionable undertaking by belaboring the point. However, had the authors not qualified "reading" by using the word "beginning," the reader might have thought they were reviewing the role of phonics in teaching remedial reading or in teaching study skills to college freshmen. Furthermore, who is to say that "beginning" conveys *only* first grade—many might argue that even old-timers like third graders are "beginning" their lifelong reading experience.

THE AUTHORS

An important point made in Johns's critique is that all researchers operate from a particular point of view. A related question is whether that point of view is itself research-based. For example, it is theoretically possible that Hughes became affiliated with the Reading Reform Foundation *after* her research revealed that intensive early phonics produced better readers. To put it another way, sometimes research produces a point of view and sometimes a point of view produces research. Rather than dismiss or downplay a study because of the authors' known affiliation or position, the sophisticated consumer of research should examine the study itself.

THE TIME SPAN

One of the essential skills in interpreting and evaluating research is careful usage of the authors' definitions of terms. In this case, Gurren and Hughes define the phonetic approach as the "intensive teaching of all the main sound-symbol relationships, both vowel and consonant, from the start of formal reading instruction" (p. 165). They acknowledge that this is but one element in some reading programs that differ otherwise. They further recognize that many traditional programs that do *not* teach sound-symbol relationships intensively from the beginning also differ widely among themselves.

Thus, the proper "time span" question is whether it was possible, during the 25-year period reviewed, to divide reading programs into those that taught the sound values of vowels and consonants from the beginning and those that did not. The issue is neither *how* sound values of vowels and consonants were taught by a given program nor what was done in programs that did not teach these values. It is simply yes or no—did a program do it? Few reasonable people dispute that such a distinction was possible in 1939, 1964, and today. Furthermore, a reader who doubts the validity of Gurren and Hughes's distinction may examine the programs used in each of the studies reviewed and, if desired, reanalyze the data. Gurren and Hughes's responsibility was to describe what they did so someone else could do the same thing. Researchers are not required to function in a way that pleases everyone, only to describe their procedures accurately and fully enough to permit replication.

DISTINCTIONS BETWEEN INTENSIVE AND GRADUAL PHONICS

In suggesting that it is difficult or impossible to make distinctions between programs that use intensive (emphasis) teaching of sound-symbol relationships (method) at the beginning (timing) from those that do not, Johns uses the only remotely possible "gray area" program—Bloomfield. Indeed Chall (1967) correctly classified Bloomfield's program as an analytic or gradual phonics program. Gurren and Hughes just as correctly classified the *modification* of Bloomfield's program used by Dolan as an intensive-phonics program (p. 167). Bloomfield's program does *not* directly teach sound-symbol correspondences; the many modifications of it *do*. That is the basis for modifying it. (For discussion of this issue see Bateman and Wetherell, 1964, pp. 98–104.)

THE SELECTION/EXCLUSION OF STUDIES

Johns's critique accurately concludes that Gurren and Hughes did what they should have done—they specified clearly the criteria they used and they followed their own guidelines. I cannot agree with Johns that they erred in including studies above first grade, since their relevant criterion states they included studies of groups that had had intensive phonics "from the start of first grade." All groups met that criterion although some were past first grade at the time data were collected. It is as if one studied (and titled the research report) "The effects of fluoride administered to preschoolers" and then reported on the number of cavities found in children 5 years of age through 12 years, where the experimental group had had fluoride treatments *during the preschool year* and the control group had not. To study only five-year-olds who have had a year of fluoride treatment is to learn less than to study older children who also had the treatment.

STATISTICAL SIGNIFICANCE

Statistical significance (the probability that the obtained differences or relationship would have occurred just by chance if in fact there was no "real" difference or relationship) and practical significance do not necessarily go hand in hand. Johns's critique presents an excellent example of a statistical significance with no practical value. It can also be noted that one can have practical significance without statistical significance—a point widely overlooked until recently. For example, suppose two new reading programs (A and B) are introduced, each claiming to be the finest program ever. Program A costs only half as much as B. Each of ten independent researchers undertakes a comparison of program efficacy. Each study finds that A is superior to B, but *not* at the level of statistical significance. That is, each finds the mean reading achievement to be higher in A than B, but the likelihood of the observed difference occurring by chance ranges from .09 to .06, and in no study reaches the "magic" level of .05. Each study reports "no significant difference" between the programs and yet common sense tells us that if there is really no difference we would expect about half the studies, by chance, to favor B. Given that all ten favor A and that A is less expensive, we would be foolish to buy B. So we have great practical significance without traditional statistical significance.

Dr. Johns's critique minimizes the value of Bear's findings that first graders taught by intensive phonics averaged "only about two months higher" in reading than the controls. This evaluation is somewhere between unusual and astonishing. The intensive phonics group was about 25% ahead of the conventional group! If superior teaching methodology produced that kind of advantage throughout 12 years of schooling, our high-school graduates would be achieving at the level of students entering their senior year of college. For a short-term view, ask any experienced second-grade teacher how much more can be accomplished with a group entering at an average 2.2 grade level versus one entering at a 1.9 grade level.

MEANS MASK

The few paragraphs under this heading in the critique raise an issue perhaps as large as all the others combined; that is, whether it is conceivable that there is *a* best method of teaching any skill, in this case initial reading of the English language, to all students. The traditional catechism says that there is no one best method. A full exploration of the theory and evidence on this point (known in scholarly language as "aptitude-treatment interaction" and variations on that theme) would require literally a large volume of small print. Before I attempt to summarize the state of the issue succinctly, the reader should be aware that early in my professional career, I believed as I had been taught and as my intuition suggested—there is no one best method for teaching anything to everyone. After all, we are individuals uniquely different from all other individuals, aren't we? However, my own research and my interpretation of others' studies have convinced me that for some tasks, including early reading, there may indeed be *a* best method for at least 99% of us. This is a growing, but still a minority, view. With this background, the reader is invited to examine the following brief summary critically.

The overwhelming majority of studies of the proposition that some methods are best for some learners and others are best for other learners fails to support that proposition. Many believe that methodological difficulties have caused this failure, and that, when those are surmounted, we *will* find more aptitude-treatment interactions, i.e., that one method will be found better for some learners and another method better for others. This may be true; no one can prove it is not. But as study after study attempts to refine and correct the procedures of earlier studies and still finds little support for the individual differences approach, one must have some doubts.

One very tentative generalization gleaned from those few academic achievement studies that do find differential effectiveness of method as a function of characteristics of learners is this: the further away from mastery the learner is, the more likely that learner may be to benefit from a deductive, rule-centered approach. Conversely, the closer the learner is to mastery, the more likely he or she may be to benefit most from an inductive- or example-centered approach. Even if this generalization about a possible exception to the general rule of "one best method for all" is true, it still follows that all beginning readers are a long way from mastery of reading and therefore need a direct, intensive, rule-centered (i.e., phonic) approach to reading.

Thus, we question the wisdom of recommending any approach for beginning reading instruction other than the one that is found best "on the average," that is, intensive, early phonics.

Flesch (1981) has clearly and candidly examined the research on the "no one method is best" issue in regard to phonics in early reading. Every interested reader should read his treatment of the matter.

Having said all this, let us say it yet one more way. If two very different reading methods (programs) were used in two comparable first-grade classrooms, we would find that the results would (a) be more or less normally distributed, i.e., some children would perform very well in each, some very poorly in each, and most would do reasonably well; and (b) one method would probably produce better results, on the average, than the other. Graphically, our results might look roughly like this:

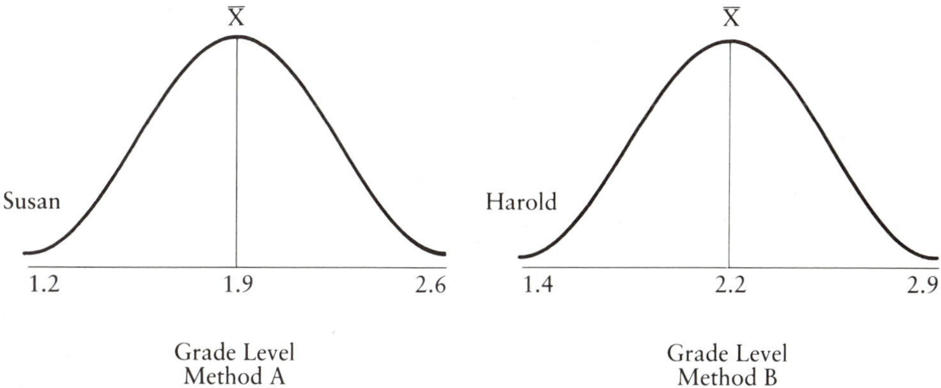

COMMENTARY/FIGURE 1.
Two Low Performers in Two Reading Programs.

Our question is whether first-grade Susan, who fared poorly under Method A (1.2 grade level), might have done better under Method B, and whether Harold, who did poorly under Method B (1.4), might have done better with A. We tend to answer yes to both. If A does not work well with Susan, try B. If B does not work well with Harold, try A. However, considerable research in early reading and in aptitude treatment interaction suggests that if Method B is better on the average, then both Harold and Susan would be better off with B than A.

SYNTHESIS OF CRITIQUE

As Johns's critique highlights, Gurren and Hughes contrasted what they call gradual versus intensive phonics. Today's jargon would say they contrasted phonics programs with whole-word and/or eclectic programs. One must realize that most reading "experts" (with the notable exception of a few psycholinguists) recognize that, because English is an alphabetic language, sound-symbol correspondences are essential to efficient decoding of that language. The crucial difference between phonics and other programs is, as Gurren and Hughes said 15 years ago, a matter of timing, emphasis, and method. Flesch (1981) has analyzed with great clarity the claim of the present "traditional" programs that they *do* teach phonics; he concludes they teach phonics far too little and too late.

Johns's critique of the Gurren and Hughes article raises legitimate and proper questions, but all of them must be resolved in favor of Gurren and Hughes. The skeptics are invited to (a) establish their own definitions of intensive phonics programs; (b) examine the studies conducted from 1964 to the present (or any other time period) that contrast intensive phonics to all other forms of initial reading instruction in a controlled manner; and (c) report the results. Every indication is that Gurren and Hughes's conclusions and recommendations will be repeated.

THE BIG PICTURE

A few comments must be made in response to Part III—The Big Picture. While citing only reviewers whose overall conclusions are the same as Gurren and Hughes's (i.e., intensive, early phonics produces better readers), Johns still insists that he is not a strong proponent of phonics. This disclaimer is puzzling to the reader who is first exploring these issues. If those who have conducted or reviewed serious research agree that more phonics instruction is better than less, how can anyone disclaim strong advocacy? This difficult question has never been fully answered. Flesch (1981) has disrobed several alibis for the failure to use and/or advocate intensive phonics instruction. Many would simply brush aside the overwhelming body of pro-phonics data, saying that research does not matter because one can find studies to support anything. If this is true, why hasn't a body of research that supports no phonics, slight phonics, or gradual phonics been offered? Simply because no such body of evidence exists. Yet another claim is that it is the teacher, not the method, that makes the difference. As cited in Johns's critique (page eleven), Dykstra has refuted this position quite decisively. But it persists. It is often expressed as "There is more difference in effectiveness within reading programs (i.e., teacher differences in using any one program) than between programs." This is a very dangerous statement because, while it is true, the conclusions usually drawn from it are devastatingly false. One false conclusion is that "therefore, it's the teacher, not the method, that makes the difference and teachers should use those programs or methods with which they are most comfortable."

To show the truth of the claim and the falsity of the conclusion, we need only hypothesize that programs A and B are each used in 1,000 first-grade classes, then plot the *average* reading achievement scores for each of the 1,000 A classes and the 1,000 B classes. We will find something like this:

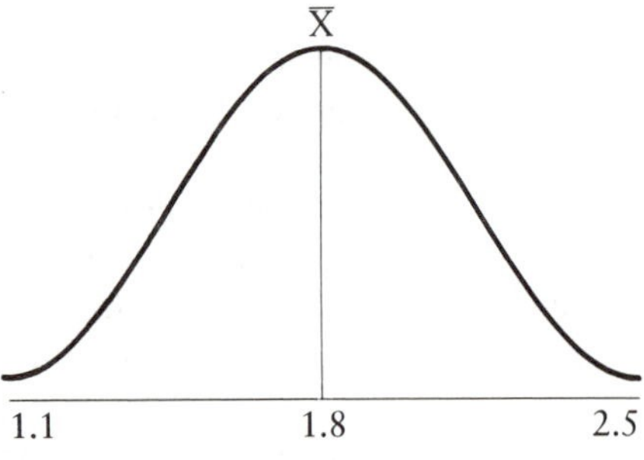

Average Grade Level in Class
Program A

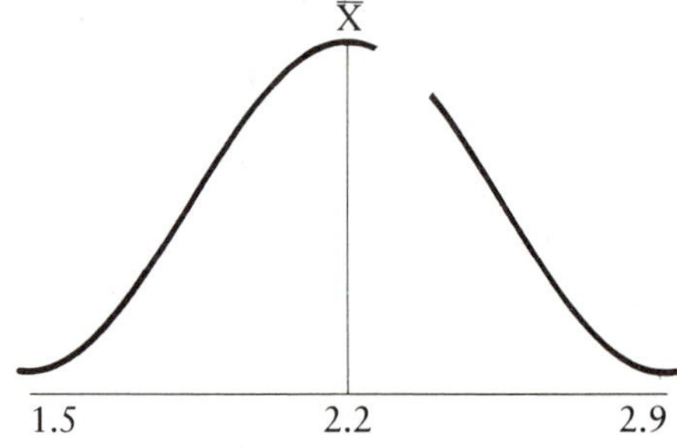

Average Grade Level in Class
Program B

COMMENTARY/FIGURE 2.
Hypothetical Comparison of Two Reading Programs.

In both cases, the classes using a program (A or B) show a 1.4 grade-level difference between the highest and lowest achieving classes. Thus the within-program range and variance, caused by teachers and other factors, are large. In fact, the range is 3.5 times larger than the 0.4 years' mean difference between programs. And yet, can one possibly say there is no real difference between programs and, therefore, that teachers should be allowed to use A because they "like it"? Of course not. Yet that is what is said and done in thousands of school districts every year.

After disavowing strong advocacy of phonics, Johns indicates that phonics is but one cue system which helps complete the ultimate act of reading, i.e., extracting meaning from print. True, we read for the purpose of extracting meaning from print. However, to say so overlooks the vital fact that early reading (and some, if not all, of later reading) is a two-stage process. In reading an alphabetic language we first convert the print to sounds (words) and *then* we attach/derive meaning from the spoken *word* or its silently decoded equivalent. Phonics has nothing to do with helping us attach or derive meaning from a spoken word such as "blip." It has everything to do with helping us know that the letters b–l–i–p say "blip" and do not say "pig" or "girl"or "bid" or "lip" or anything but "blip."

Some children learn to read without early, intensive, systematic instruction in phonics. Many of them can be recognized in later years by their unique spelling habits. Of the many children in this country today who do not learn to read well easily, the evidence is abundantly clear that their chances would have been far better had they had more early phonics instruction. Gurren and Hughes's review is a good example of that evidence.

REFERENCES

Bateman, B., & Wetherell, J. A critique of Bloomfield's linguistic approach to the teaching of reading. *The Reading Teacher*, Nov. 1964, 98–104.

Chall, J. *Learning to read: The great debate*. New York: McGraw-Hill, 1967.

Flesch, R. *Why Johnny still can't read*. New York: Harper and Row, 1981.

THE UTILITY OF PHONIC GENERALIZATIONS IN THE PRIMARY GRADES

THEODORE CLYMER

The origins of this study go back to Kenneth, an extraordinary elementary pupil. Prior to my encounter with Kenneth I had completed a reading methods course in a small teachers college which provided a background in the principles of teaching reading as well as a good introduction to techniques. Among these techniques were procedures to develop phonic generalizations and also *the* list (not *a* list) of the most valuable generalizations to develop. (To those of you who might like copies of the list, I am sad to report that somehow through the years it has been lost.)

Difficulties with Kenneth began as the class reviewed phonic generalizations at the start of the school year. Our procedures were like those used in many classrooms: Groups of words were presented, and the class analyzed their likenesses and differences with a view toward deriving a generalization about relationships between certain letters and sounds or the position and pronunciation of vowels.

Throughout these exercises, following the dictum of my reading methods teacher, we were careful not to call the generalizations "rules," for all our statements had a number of exceptions. As the class finally formulated a generalization regarding the relationships of letters, letter position, and sounds, such defensive phrasing as "most of the time," "usually," and "often" appeared as protective measures. We also spent time listing some of the exceptions to our generalizations.

At this point Kenneth entered the discussion. While the class was busily engaged in developing the generalization, Kenneth had skimmed his dictionary, locating long lists of exceptions to the generalization. In fact, he often located more exceptions than I could list applications. When I protested—somewhat weakly—that the dictionary contained many unusual words, Kenneth continued his role as an educational scientist. He turned to the basic reader word list in the back of his text and produced nearly similar results. Today, of course, Kenneth's behavior would be rated as "gifted," "talented," or "creative"—although I remember discussing him in other terms as I sat in the teacher's lounge.

From *The Reading Teacher*, Vol. 16, January 1963, pp. 252–58. Reprinted with permission of the author and the International Reading Association.

This paper is an extension of a report given at a joint meeting of the International Reading Association and the National Conference of Research in English, May 1961. Thomas Barrett, Harriette Anderson, Joan Hanson, and David Palmer provided invaluable assistance in various phases of the study.

As Kenneth had provided a memorable and even a "rich" learning experience for me, he furnished the impetus for a series of studies which will attempt to answer three questions: (1) What phonic generalizations are being taught in basic reading programs for the primary grades? (2) To what extent are these generalizations useful in having a "reasonable" degree of application to words commonly met in primary grade material? (3) Which of the generalizations that stand the test of question 2 can be learned and successfully applied to unknown words by primary children?

WHAT GENERALIZATIONS ARE TAUGHT?

Four widely used sets of readers were selected to determine the phonic generalizations being taught in the primary grades. After a preliminary study of the manuals, workbooks, and readers, the manuals were selected as the source of the generalizations. The manuals presented the generalizations in three ways: (1) statements to be taught to the pupils, (2) statements to be derived by the pupils after inductive teaching, and (3) statements with no clear indication as to what was to be done. Generalizations presented by all three means were included in the analysis.

Five general types of generalizations emerged from the study of the teachers manuals. These types dealt with (1) vowels, (2) consonants, (3) endings, (4) syllabication, and (5) miscellaneous relationships. Arbitrary decisions were made in assigning some generalizations to one or another of the five types since certain statements might easily be classified under two or more headings.

If we eliminate from our consideration the miscellaneous type of generalization, a total of 121 different statements were located. There were 50 vowel generalizations, 15 consonant generalizations, and 28 generalizations in each of the ending and syllabication groups. In evaluating these figures it should be kept in mind that any statement was considered a separate generalization when its phrasing excluded or included different sets of words than another statement. For example, the generalization, "When there are two vowels side by side, the long sound of the first is heard and the second one is usually silent" and "When *ea* come together in a word, the first letter is long and the second is silent" were counted as two separate generalizations, although the second statement is a special application of the first.

While not directly related to our discussion here, note should be made of the wide variation of grade level of introduction, emphasis, and phrasing of the generalizations. Of the 50 different vowel generalizations, only 11 were common to all four series. None of these 11 was presented initially at the same half-year grade level in all four series. Some series gave a much greater emphasis to the generalizations than did other series. One publisher introduced only 33 of the 121 generalizations, while another presented 68. These comments are not meant to detract from the usefulness of basic materials, but simply to point out some of their differences. These differences do call for careful adjustments in the classroom when pupils are moved from one set of materials to another. The teacher who changes from series X to series Y may need to make some important revisions in his word recognition program. These findings may indicate also the need for further experimentation on emphasis and the developmental aspects of our word recognition program.

WHICH GENERALIZATIONS ARE USEFUL?

Forty-five of the generalizations given in the manuals were selected for further study. The selection of these was somewhat arbitrary. The main criterion was to ask, "Is the generalization stated specifically enough so that it can be said to aid or hinder in the pronunciation of a particular word?" An example or two will make our criterion clear. The generalization, "Long *o* makes a sound like its name," is undoubtedly a valuable generalization, but it was not specific enough to meet our criterion. On the other hand, the statement, "When a vowel is in the middle of a one syllable word, the vowel is short," was included because we could judge by reference to a word list how often one syllable words with a vowel in the middle do in fact have a short vowel sound.

Our next problem was to develop a word list on which we could test the generalizations. A reasonable approach seemed to be that of making up a composite list of all the words introduced in the four basic series from which the generalizations were drawn, plus the words from the Gates Reading Vocabulary for the Primary Grades. Once this list of some twenty-six hundred words was prepared, the following steps were taken:

1. The phonetic respelling and the syllabic division of all words were recorded. Webster's *New Collegiate Dictionary* was used as the authority for this information.

2. Each phonic generalization was checked against the words in the composite list to determine (*a*) the words which were pronounced as the generalization claimed and (*b*) the words which were exceptions to the generalization.

3. A "per cent of utility" was computed for each generalization by dividing the number of words pronounced as the generalization claimed by the total number of words to which the generalization could be expected to apply. For example, if the generalization claimed that "When the letters *oa* are together in a word, *o* always gives its long sound and the *a* is silent." All words containing *oa* were located in the list. The number of these words was the total number of words to which the generalization should apply. Then the phonetic spellings of these words were examined to see how many words containing *oa* actually did have the long *o* followed by the silent *a*. In this case thirty words were located which contained *oa*. Twenty-nine of these were pronounced as the generalization claimed; one was not. The per cent of utility became 29/30 or 97. This procedure was followed for generalizations.

When the per cent of utility was computed for each generalization, we set two criteria as to what constituted a "reasonable" degree of application. We have no scientific evidence to demonstrate that these criteria are valid; it can only be said that they seem reasonable to us.

The first criterion was that the composite word list must contain a minimum of twenty words to which the generalization might apply. Generalizations with lower frequencies of application do not seem to merit instructional time.

The second criterion was a per cent of utility of at least 75. To state the matter another way, if the pupil applied the generalization to twenty words, it should

The Utility of Forty-Five Phonic Generalizations

*Generalization	No. of Words Conforming	No. of Exceptions	Per Cent of Utility
1. When there are two vowels side by side, the long sound of the first one is heard and the second is usually silent.	309 (bead)†	377 (chief)†	45
2. When a vowel is in the middle of a one-syllable word, the vowel is short.	408	249	62
middle letter	191 (dress)	84 (scold)	69
one of the middle two letters in a word of four letters	191 (rest)	135 (told)	59
one vowel *within* a word of more than four letters	26 (splash)	39 (fight)	46
3. If the only vowel letter is at the end of a word, the letter usually stands for a long sound.	23 (he)	8 (to)	74
4. When there are two vowels, one of which is final *e*, the first vowel is long and the *e* is silent.	180 (bone)	108 (done)	63
*5. The *r* gives the preceding vowel a sound that is neither long nor short.	484 (horn)	134 (wire)	78
6. The first vowel is usually long and the second silent in the digraphs *ai*, *ea*, *oa*, and *ui*.	179	92	66
ai	43 (nail)	24 (said)	64
ea	101 (bead)	51 (head)	66
oa	34 (boat)	1 (cupboard)	97
ui	1 (suit)	16 (build)	6
7. In the phonogram *ie*, the *i* is silent and the *e* has a long sound.	8 (field)	39 (friend)	17
*8. Words having double *e* usually have the long *e* sound.	85 (seem)	2 (been)	98
9. When words end with silent *e*, the preceding *a* or *i* is long.	164 (cake)	108 (have)	60
*10. In *ay* the *y* is silent and gives *a* its long sound.	36 (play)	10 (always)	78
11. When the letter *i* is followed by the letters *gh*, the *i* usually stands for its long sound and the *gh* is silent.	22 (high)	9 (neighbor)	71
12. When *a* follows *w* in a word, it usually has the sound *a* as in *was*.	15 (watch)	32 (swam)	32
13. When *e* is followed by *w*, the vowel sound is the same as represented by *oo*.	9 (blew)	17 (sew)	35
14. The two letters *ow* make the long *o* *sound*.	50 (own)	35 (down)	59

research

The Utility of Forty-Five Phonic Generalizations (continued)

*Generalization	No. of Words Conforming	No. of Exceptions	Per Cent of Utility
15. *W* is sometimes a vowel and follows the vowel digraph rule.	50 (crow)	75 (threw)	40
*16. When *y* is the final letter in a word, it usually has a vowel sound.	169 (dry)	32 (tray)	84
17. When *y* is used as a vowel in words, it sometimes has the sound of long *i*.	29 (fly)	170 (funny)	15
18. The letter *a* has the same sound (ô) when followed by *l*, *w*, and *u*.	61 (all)	65 (canal)	48
19. When *a* is followed by *r* and final *e*, we expect to hear the sound heard in *care*.	9 (dare)	1 (are)	90
*20. When *c* and *h* are next to each other, they make only one sound.	103 (peach)	0	100
*21. *Ch* is usually pronounced as it is in *kitchen*, *catch*, and *chair*, not like *sh*.	99 (catch)	5 (machine)	95
*22. When *c* is followed by *e* or *i*, the sound of *s* is likely to be heard.	66 (cent)	3 (ocean)	96
*23. When the letter *c* is followed by *o* or *a* the sound of *k* is likely to be heard.	143 (camp)	0	100
24. The letter *g* often has a sound similar to that of *j* in *jump* when it precedes the letter *i* or *e*.	49 (engine)	28 (give)	64
*25. When *ght* is seen in a word, *gh* is silent.	30 (fight)	0	100
26. When a word begins *kn*, the *k* is silent.	10 (knife)	0	100
27. When a word begins with *wr*, the *w* is silent.	8 (write)	0	100
*28. When two of the same consonants are side by side only one is heard.	334 (carry)	3 (suggest)	99
*29. When a word ends in *ck*, it has the same last sound as in *look*.	46 (brick)	0	100
*30. In most two-syllable words, the first syllable is accented.	828 (famous)	143 (polite)	85
*31. If *a*, *in*, *re*, *ex*, *de*, or *be* is the first syllable in a word, it is usually unaccented.	86 (belong)	13 (insect)	87
*32. In most two-syllable words that end in a consonant followed by *y*, the first syllable is accented and the last is unaccented.	101 (baby)	4 (supply)	96
33. One vowel letter in an accented syllable has its short sound.	517 (city)	356 (lady)	61

The Utility of Forty-Five Phonic Generalizations (continued)

*Generalization	No. of Words Conforming	No. of Exceptions	Per Cent of Utility
34. When *y* or *ey* is seen in the last syllable that is not accented, the long sound of *e* is heard.	0	157 (baby)	0
35. When *ture* is the final syllable in a word, it is unaccented.	4 (picture)	0	100
36. When *tion* is the final syllable in a word, it is unaccented.	5 (station)	0	100
37. In many two- and three-syllable words, the final *e* lengthens the vowel in the last syllable.	52 (invite)	62 (gasoline)	46
38. If the first vowel sound in a word is followed by two consonants, the first syllable usually ends with the first of the two consonants.	404 (bullet)	159 (singer)	72
39. If the first vowel sound in a word is followed by a single consonant, that consonant usually begins the second syllable.	190 (over)	237 (oven)	44
*40. If the last syllable of a word ends in *le*, the consonant preceding the *le* usually begins the last syllable.	62 (tumble)	2 (buckle)	97
*41. When the first vowel element in a word is followed by *th*, *ch*, or *sh*, these symbols are not broken when the word is divided into syllables and may go with either the first or second syllable.	30 (dishes)	0	100
42. In a word of more than one syllable, the letter *v* usually goes with the preceding vowel to form a syllable.	53 (cover)	20 (clover)	73
43. When a word has only one vowel letter, the vowel sound is likely to be short.	433 (hid)	322 (kind)	57
*44. When there is one *e* in a word that ends in a consonant, the *e* usually has a short sound.	85 (leg)	27 (blew)	76
*45. When the last syllable is the sound *r*, it is unaccented.	188 (butter)	9 (appear)	95

†Words in parentheses are examples—either of words which conform or of exceptions, depending on the column.

*Generalizations marked with an asterisk were found "useful" according to the criteria.

aid him in getting the correct pronunciation in fifteen of the twenty words.

The table gives the results of our analysis of the forty-five phonic generalizations. An inspection of the data leaves me somewhat confused as to the value of generalizations. Some time-honored customs in the teaching of reading may be in need of revision.

Certain generalizations apply to large numbers of words and are rather constant in providing the correct pronunciation of words. (See, for example, generalizations 19, 35, and 36.)

A group of generalizations seem to be useful only after the pupil can pronounce the word. Generalizations which specify vowel pronunciation in stressed syllables require that the pupil know the pronunciation of the word before he can apply the generalization. (See, for example, generalization 33.) This criticism assumes, of course, that the purpose of a generalization is to help the child unlock the pronunciation of *unknown* words.

The usefulness of certain generalizations depends upon regional pronunciations. While following Webster's markings, generalization 34 is rejected. Midwestern pronunciation makes this generalization rather useful, althrough we reject it because we used Webster as the authority. Such problems are natural, and we should not hold it against Mr. Webster that he came from New England.

If we adhere to the criteria set up at the beginning of the study, of the forty-five generalizations only eighteen, numbers 5, 8, 10, 16, 20, 21, 22, 23, 25, 28, 29, 30, 31, 32, 40, 41, 44, and 45 are useful. Some of the generalizations which failed to meet our criteria might be useful if stated in different terms or if restricted to certain types of words. We are studying these problems at the present time. We are also examining other generalizations which we did not test in this study.

CONCLUSION

In evaluating this initial venture in testing the utility of phonic generalizations, it seems quite clear that many generalizations which are commonly taught are of limited value. Certainly the study indicates that we should give careful attention to pointing out the many exceptions to most of the generalizations that we teach. Current "extrinsic" phonics programs which present large numbers of generalizations are open to question on the basis of this study.

This study does not, of course, answer the question of which generalizations primary children can apply in working out the pronunciation of unknown words. The answer to the question of the primary child's ability to apply these and other generalizations will come only through classrroom experimentation. Also, this study does not establish the per cent of utility required for a generalization to be useful. The percentage suggested here (75) may be too high. Classroom research might reveal that generalizations with lower percentages of utility should be taught because they encourage children to examine words for sound and letter relationships.

The most disturbing fact to come from the study may be the rather dismal failure of generalization 1 to provide the correct pronunciation even 50 percent of the time. As one teacher remarked when this study was presented to a reading methods class, "Mr. Clymer, for years I've been teaching 'When two vowels go walking, the first one does the talking.' You're ruining the romance in the teaching of reading!"

A Critique of Theodore Clymer's Study: The Utility of Phonic Generalizations in the Primary Grades

THOMAS C. BARRETT

University of Wisconsin–Madison

PROLOGUE

After accepting the assignment to critique the Clymer study, I began to think about the task at hand. The first thing that crossed my mind was that I might not be the best choice since I was the person who located and categorized the generalizations used by Clymer. But several thoughts struck me as I reread Clymer's article. First, a number of questions can be raised about the study. Second, the author's report was relatively brief because of restricted space in the journal. Third, since I had firsthand acquaintance with the study and the author, I could add some insights about the study not contained in the article.

ORIGINS OF THE STUDY

Clymer intended to conduct a series of studies to answer three related questions: (1) What generalizations are being taught in basic reading programs for the primary grades? (2) To what extent are these generalizations useful in meeting a reasonable degree of application to words in primary grade material? (3) Which of the generalizations that stand the test of (2) can primary children learn and successfully apply to unknown words. As Clymer stated in his conclusion, only the first two questions were answered by the study. To my knowledge Clymer did not conduct a study dealing with the third question. This is unfortunate because such an investigation might have provided invaluable information about the utility of phonic generalizations for actual use in the classroom.

Clymer suggested that the impetus for his intended studies came from one of his elementary school pupils named Kenneth. Although Kenneth undoubtedly did influence Clymer, I am certain Clymer was aware of two earlier studies that also had implications for his work.

The first of these studies was conducted by Sartorious (1931) in the area of spelling. Three of her findings are worth noting here:

1. A total of 110 different rules were located in 20 spellers.
2. Two of the spellers contained no rules, seven had 1 to 19 rules, three had 20 to 29 rules, four had 30 to 39 rules, and four had 40 to 43 rules.

3. Thirty-eight rules were common to five or more of the spellers. When these rules were refined further, 11 were eliminated because they were categorized as definitions. The 27 remaining rules were analyzed for their applicability to words in a list developed by the author.

Oaks (1952) reported the second of these precursory investigations. She found that the following generalizations appeared to operate in the pronunciation of vowels contained in the primer, first-grade, second-grade, and third-grade reading vocabularies used in the study:

1. When a stressed syllable ends in *e*, the first vowel in the syllable has its own long sound and the final *e* is silent.
2. When a stressed syllable containing only one vowel ends with that vowel, the vowel has its own long sound.
3. When there is only one vowel in a stressed syllable and that vowel is followed by a consonant, the vowel has its short sound.
4. When a word of more than one syllable ends with the letter *y*, the final *y* has a sound of short *i;* when a word of more than one syllable ends with the letters *ey*, the *e* is silent and the *y* again has the sound of short *i*.
5. When a syllable contains only the one vowel, *a*, followed by the letters *l* or *w* the sound of the *a* rhymes with the word saw.
6. When there are two adjacent vowels in a syllable, the first vowel has its long sound and the second vowel is silent.
7. When a word of more than one syllable ends in the letters *le*, the *l* becomes syllabic, i.e., it functions as a vowel and is pronounced, but the *e* is silent.
8. When a word of more than one syllable ends in the letters *en*, the *n* becomes syllabic and is pronounced, but the *e* is silent.

Oaks then studied the applicability of the generalizations to the vowel situations in the vocabularies she used. She concluded that generalization 3 should be introduced at the primer level, generalizations 1, 2, 4, and 5 at the second-grade level, and generalization 7 at the third-grade level. Generalizations 6 and 8 were eliminated because of a high number of exceptions to 6 and a low number of applications for 8. It is interesting to note that Clymer came to the same conclusion as Oaks about the infamous generalization "when two vowels go walking" approximately ten years later.

WHAT GENERALIZATIONS ARE TAUGHT?

Clymer indicated that the four series of readers analyzed were in wide use. He did not mention that the series were also selected because they placed varying degrees of emphasis on word identification and were the products of highly regarded experts in the reading field.

critique

Since one of the criteria used to select the series depended upon the varying degrees of emphasis they placed on word identification, it is not surprising that there was considerable variability in the number of generalizations found in each. (One introduced 33 generalizations and another 68.) Would this finding have appeared had the four series been randomly selected from the total population available at that time? Possibly, but we cannot be certain. Nor can we be certain that the number and types of generalizations studied would have been the same had a random sample of series been employed. Even without random sample, the number and types of generalizations located might have been altered had one or two intensive phonic programs been added to the study.

As a point of information, the miscellaneous generalizations Clymer eliminated dealt with digraphs, spelling of words, definitions, blends, and the apostrophe. They included (1) when *c* and *h* are next to each other they make one sound; (2) names of persons begin with capital letters; (3) a root word is a word from which other words are made; (4) *Th* and *r* blend together into two sounds before the vowel in each word is presented; (5) when an *'s* is added to a proper noun it makes the noun possessive. Clymer correctly eliminated 21 miscellaneous generalizations from the study.

One final point will be offered before leaving this part of the study. It has to do with variation of the point of introduction of generalizations across the four series. The author indicated that 11 vowel generalizations were common to all four series but that none was presented initially at the same half-year level. His initial data indicated that nine generalizations that dealt with the long and short sounds represented by the vowel letters were common to all the series, but that the series did not present the generalizations at the same level or in the same order. Thus, one series presented short vowel generalizations at level 1 and long vowel generalizations at the 2–2 level. A second series presented long vowel generalizations at level 1 and short vowel generalizations at the 2–1 level. The third series was similar to the second only at the next higher levels, 2–1 and 2–2. In contrast to the above mentioned methods of presentation, the fourth series did not separate the long and short generalizations but presented them simultaneously. These observations underscore Clymer's point about the lack of consistency in the scope and sequence of phonic skills across programs at the time the study took place. It would be of some interest to find out what changes have occurred in the scope and sequence of phonic skills in present-day basal series and what, if any, empirical evidence supports present-day practices.

WHICH GENERALIZATIONS ARE USEFUL?

Clymer determined which of the 121 generalizations were useful in the following manner. First, he reduced the number of generalizations for further study to 45 by asking the question, Is the generalization stated specifically enough so that it can be said to aid or hinder in the pronunciation of a particular word? Next, he developed a list of 2600 words by combining the words from the four series with those from the Gates Reading Vocabulary for the Primary Grades. Third, using Webster's New

Collegiate Dictionary as the standard, he applied each of the 45 generalizations to the appropriate words in the list to determine which ones were pronounced in accordance with the generalization and which ones were exceptions. Fourth, Clymer determined a percentage of utility for each generalization by dividing the number of words pronounced in accordance with the generalization by the total number of words to which the generalization should have applied. Finally, he determined which generalizations had a reasonable degree of application by locating those that applied to a minimum of 20 words in the list and had at least a 75% level of utility. As the end result, 18 of the 45 generalizations (5, 8, 10, 16, 20, 21, 22, 23, 25, 28, 29, 30, 31, 32, 40, 41, 44, and 45) were designated as useful.

Although the procedures were straightforward and detailed enough to permit replication of the study, some of the decisions, according to the author, were made arbitrarily with little empirical evidence to support them. For this and other reasons, parts of the investigation are open to question and will be addressed at this point.

critique

Some of the generalizations in the final sample of 45 did not appear to meet the criterion for retention; namely, is the generalization stated specifically enough so that it can be said to aid or hinder in the pronunciation of a particular word? For example, consider generalization 15—*w* is sometimes a vowel and follows the vowel digraph rule. It is difficult to see how this generalization is specific enough to aid or hinder the pronunciation of a particular word if the digraph rule, whatever it is, is not stated. Clymer was aware of this problem when he pointed out that a group of generalizations in the final sample seemed useful only if the reader could pronounce the word (e.g., those generalizations that specified vowel pronunciation in stressed syllables). Such problematic generalizations might have been eliminated from the study if a group of independent judges had been involved in the selection of the final sample of generalizations.

The two criteria that determined whether a generalization had a reasonable degree of application also appear open to further examination. The first criterion was that the word list must contain a minimum of 20 words to which a given generalization might apply. When one considers that 20 words constitute less than 1% of 2600 words studied, it seems that the criterion might have been a bit low. If the criterion had been set at 50 words, which would constitute approximately 2% of the words studied, generalizations 10, 25, 29, and 41 would not have been included among the 18 useful generalizations. In contrast, it could be argued that the second criterion to determine the usefulness of a generalization was set too high. Why did Clymer select a 75% utility level rather than 60%? If he had selected 60% generalizations 2, 4, 6, 9, 24, and 33 would have been on the list of 18 useful generalizations.

We could go on with this exercise but that would not resolve the issue. The problem with the two criteria may be that they only dealt with the number of different words to which a generalization applied rather than with the number of different words and the number of times each of the different words was repeated in the four series. If Clymer had counted the number of repetitions for each word in the four series and applied criteria to the two variables to determine the usefulness of each generalization, one could have more confidence in his findings. However, counting the number of repetitions for each word would have been a superhuman task at the time the study was conducted.

Maybe the usefulness of Clymer's 45 generalizations should be cross-validated to a word list similar to the *Computational Analysis of Present-Day American English* (Kucera and Francis, 1967). Their list contains a rank ordering of 50,406 words from a corpus of 1,014,232 words drawn from 500 samples of approximately 2,000 words each selected from 15 different genre (e.g., press reportage, skills and hobbies, science fiction, bibliographies, etc.), to ensure representativeness. The rank ordering of a word in the list is related to the number of times it was repeated in the 1,014,232 running words. Thus, the Kucera and Francis word list would permit one to use the two variables of number of words and number of repetitions to cross-validate Clymer's results.

One of the criticisms directed at Clymer's findings when the study was first published was that they might not be valid above the third-grade level. Fortunately, Bailey (1967), who applied Clymer's generalizations to 5,773 words that appeared in two or more of eight series for the six grades, and Emans (1967), who used a random sample of 10% of words (1,944) beyond the primary level in *The Teacher's Word Book of 30,000 Words* by Thorndike and Lorge, helped to answer this criticism.

As shown in Critique/Table 1, Bailey's results were consistent with Clymer's for the 18 useful generalizations, while Emans (1967) supported Clymer's results in 15 instances. If Clymer's criteria for determining which generalizations had a rea-

CRITIQUE/TABLE 1
A Comparison of Clymer's Results With Those of Bailey and Emans for the Eighteen Useful Generalizations

Number of Generalization	No. of Words Conforming			No. of Exceptions			Percent of Utility		
	C*	B	E	C	B	E	C	B	E
5	181	1,378	459	134	226	99	78	86	82
8	85	148	24	2	23	0	98	87	100
10	36	44	6	10	6	0	78	88	100
16	169	462	265	32	56	5	84	89	98
20	103	225	53	0	0	0	100	100	100
21	99	196	35	5	29	17	95	87	67
22	66	260	79	3	24	9	96	92	90
23	143	428	151	0	0	0	100	100	100
25	30	40	3	0	0	0	100	100	100
28	334	809	274	3	17	26	99	98	91
29	46	80	9	0	0	0	100	100	100
30	828	1,906	396	143	439	134	85	81	75
31	86	336	179	13	62	36	87	84	83
32	101	190	57	4	5	0	96	97	100
40	62	196	53	2	15	15	97	93	78
41	30	74	44	0	0	0	100	100	100
44	85	137	15	27	12	3	76	92	83
45	188	601	165	9	160	7	95	79	96

*C = Clymer, B = Bailey, E = Emans

sonable degree of application were interpreted strictly, Bailey would have added numbers 3, 19, 24, 25, and 38 to the most useful list, while Emans would have added numbers 24, 28, and 36. The discrepancies in the number of words found for generalizations 10, 25, and 29 by the three authors, and for some of the other generalizations not shown in the table, again raise questions about the types and sources of vocabularies that may be employed for such studies. Nevertheless, it is safe to say that Bailey and Emans extended and gave support to Clymer's findings.

CONCLUSION

Clymer's study accomplished two of the three things he believed significant regarding phonic generalizations. Questions can be raised about certain procedural decisions that were made, but it was a straightforward effort that stimulated other research efforts (as indicated in the list of additional readings that follows). It does, however, remain to be seen which useful generalizations can be learned and successfully applied to unknown words by primary children.

FOR FURTHER LEARNING

Those readers who are interested in continuing to explore the topic of the utility of phonic generalizations would find the following references helpful:

Bailey, M. H. The utility of phonic generalizations in grades one through six. *Reading Teacher*, Feb. 1967, *20*, 413–418.

Burmeister, L. E. Usefulness of phonic generalizations. *Reading Teacher*, Jan. 1968, *21*, pp. 349–356; 360.

Burmeister, L. E. Vowel pairs. *Reading Teacher*, Feb. 1968, *21*, 445–452.

Burmeister, L. E. Final vowel-consonant-e. *Reading Teacher*, Feb. 1971, *24*, 439–442.

Burrows, A. T., & Lourie, Z. When 'two vowels go walking.' *Reading Teacher*, Nov. 1963, *17*, 79–82.

Emans, R. The usefulness of phonic generalizations above the primary grades. *Reading Teacher*, Feb. 1967, *20*, 419–425.

REFERENCES

Bailey, M. H. The utility of phonic generalizations in grades one through six. *The Reading Teacher*, Feb. 1967, *20*, 413–418.

Emans, R. The usefulness of phonic generalizations above the primary grades. *The Reading Teacher*, Feb. 1967, *20*, 419–425.

Kucera, H., & Francis, W. N. *Computational analysis of present-day American English*. Providence: Brown University Press, 1967.

Oaks, R. E. A study of the vowel situations in a primary vocabulary. *Education*, May 1952, *72*, 604–617.

Sartorious, I. C. *Generalizations in spelling*. Teachers College, Columbia University Contributions to Education, *472*, 1931.

references

A Commentary on Barrett's Critique of Clymer's Study Regarding the Utility of Phonic Generalizations in the Primary Grades

NICHOLAS J. SILVAROLI

Arizona State University

Barrett's critique of Clymer's study was interesting because it provided valuable insights about the procedures used in the study.

Clymer had three research questions in his 1963 original study. The study dealt with two of the research questions but never did address the third question which was, "Which of the generalizations that stand the test of Question 2 can be learned and successfully applied to unknown words by primary children?" The fact that the original study neglected to deal with this question escaped me until Barrett pointed it out.

Barrett's observation regarding the actual selection of four popular reading series rather than a random selection from all existing series points out a significant procedural problem with the Clymer study. However, Barrett's extensive discussion of the criterion for selection of generalizations seems a bit overworked. His emphasis on the straightforwardness of Clymer's study are well-taken, though later studies of Bailey (1967), Emans (1967), and Burmeister (1968) essentially supported Clymer's conclusion: basal reading series lacked consistency when presenting phonic generalizations.

My critique could be lengthened considerably if I were to discuss each aspect of each generalization or argue whether the word "generalization" is more or less appropriate than the word "rule." However, I believe that Clymer's work should be regarded as classic because it provides reading educators with three essential concepts. I believe that prior to the Clymer study, with its procedural limitations, we acted as if phonic generalizations were scientifically determined. We also suffered from what I call an additive fixation and were unwilling to deal with the notion of priorities. Allow me to be more specific about these concepts.

Before Clymer's study, reading educators such as classroom teachers, reading specialists, and university faculty often used such qualifying terms as "usually" and "not always" when introducing a phonic generalization. In addition, we tended to select only those words that fit the generalization, giving the impression that the generalization was consistent and had wide application. We also expected students to learn the generalization without exception, thus implying that it was scientifically determined. Since the Clymer study, I believe we are less inclined to treat generalizations as being scientifically determined. We now recognize the importance of the utility of phonic generalizations and are less inclined to present generalizations that apply to a small number of words. We are also aware that phonic generalizations are merely teacher inventions used to describe sounds within words. In other words, phonic generalizations are not the products of long years of scientific research and study.

Reading educators have also suffered from an additive fixation. If we found a generalization used by the ancient Druids we would have been compelled to add it to the reading curriculum. Not only would we have felt academically pure, we would have defended our actions on the basis of academic depth and rigor. The Clymer study, in my view, made reading educators a little less additive; we began to recognize the value of eliminating obscure, low-utility items. An excellent example of this comes from the Clymer study itself. He found 121 generalizations in the four basic readers but could only understand 45 because so many of them overlapped or described the same sound in different ways. This is additive fixation. A teacher states a generalization in a unique way, another states the identical generalization in another way. Given our fixation, we tended to include all of these unique statements until we could only understand 45 of a possible 121 generalizations. A review of basal readers with 1980 or later copyrights reveals a drastic reduction in the number of phonic generalizations. In my view, this was a direct result of the Clymer study.

Finally, reading educators now seem more willing to establish priorities in all aspects of the reading curriculum. We have significantly reduced the number of phonic generalizations in current reading series and seem to be applying the importance of establishing priorities and balance with the area of comprehension instruction.

In summary, if the Clymer study really helped us become skeptical, and overcome an additive fixation, and taught us the importance of prioritization and balance, then, indeed, it has served us well.

REFERENCES

Bailey, M. H. The utility of phonic generalizations in grades one through six. *The Reading Teacher,* Feb. 1967, *20,* 413–418.

Burmeister, L. E. Usefulness of phonic generalizations. *The Reading Teacher,* Jan. 1968, *21,* 349–356.

Emans, R. E. The usefulness of phonic generalizations above the primary grades. *The Reading Teacher,* Feb. 1967, *20,* 419–425.

references

BEGINNING READING

SUMMARIES by Linnea C. Ehri, of *The Effect of Letter-Name Knowledge on Learning to Read, Comparisons of Letter-Name and Letter-Sound Training as Transfer Variables, The Effect of Training in Letter Names on Success in Beginning Reading for Children of Differing Abilities, The Effects of Kindergarten Instruction in Alphabet and Numbers on First Grade Reading,* and *The Effects of Letter Knowledge on Achievement in Reading in the First Grade*

CRITIQUE by Linnea C. Ehri

FOR FURTHER LEARNING

COMMENTARY by Elizabeth Sulzby

RESEARCH by Mabel V. Morphett and Carleton Washburne, *When Should Children Begin to Read?*

CRITIQUE by Lance M. Gentile

FOR FURTHER LEARNING

COMMENTARY by Lloyd O. Ollila

This section introduces the reader to studies of letter-name knowledge by S. Jay Samuels; J. R. Jenkins, R. B. Bausell, and L. M. Jenkins; Ronald J. Johnson; N. E. Silberberg and I. A. Iversen; and Dorothy C. Ohnmacht. Ehri summarizes and critiques this work. Her critique focuses on the question of whether knowing the names of alphabet letters makes it any easier for children to learn to read. She cites the following several reasons for believing that letter-name knowledge contributes: evidence that decoding skills are central to learning to read, evidence that beginners use sounds they detect in letter names to invent spellings for words, evidence that learning arbitrary letter-sound pairs is a difficult task for prereaders but becomes much easier if letter names are already known. Ehri claims that a re-analysis of these studies reveals they are flawed in numerous respects, and as a result their conclusions may not be valid. Sulzby commends Ehri's use of linguistic theory and research to critique these five studies but questions her attempt to infer positive evidence for such an effect from these studies. Sulzby feels these studies are conceptually, rather than procedurally, flawed. She offers a review of research to defend her position which, in her view, represents a more developmental view of reading and writing acquisition. Moreover, Sulzby suggests further research based upon clearer definitions of beginning reading and writing.

Additionally, the original research study, *When Should Children Learn to Read?*, by Morphett and Washburne is reprinted. Gentile's critique questions the validity of 6.5 years as being the proper age for all children to learn to read and rejects the authors' reliance on one single variable, i.e., mental age, to answer the problem of when a child should begin learning to read. Ollila's comments make further reference to and expand upon the issues and problems Gentile raised with Morphett and Washburne's study. Finally, Ollila provides a unique focus in three other areas: 1) the statistical procedures of the study; 2) changes that have occurred meanwhile in children's backgrounds; 3) relevant research on beginning reading.

SUMMARY OF S. J. SAMUELS'S STUDY: THE EFFECT OF LETTER-NAME KNOWLEDGE ON LEARNING TO READ

LINNEA C. EHRI

University of California at Davis

Teaching children to name alphabet letters is commonly included in reading readiness programs. Durrell and Murphy (1964) have claimed that because most letter names contain their sounds, children who know names will relate letters to phonemes and learn to read words more easily. The belief that letter names facilitate learning to read has a long history. The alphabetic method of teaching reading was nearly universal in America until about 1870. Current belief in the benefits of letter names rests upon numerous studies revealing a high positive correlation between letter-name knowledge upon entry into first grade and end-of-the-year reading achievement. The addition of factors such as mental age, auditory and visual discrimination, and socio-economic status (SES) accounts for little additional variance (Silvaroli, 1965). However, experimental classroom studies have failed to demonstrate a causative relationship (Johnson, 1969; Ohnmacht, 1969), indicating that it may be a mistake to impute causation to correlational findings.

Two experiments employing a training-transfer design were conducted to determine under laboratory conditions whether specific components of letter-name training might facilitate reading acquisition. The graphemes were four artificial letters. The names were those of the Standard English letters S, M, E, A. The words taught during the transfer task were "see," "say," "me," "may." In Experiment 1, 100 mid-year first-graders were assigned randomly to one of four treatment groups: (1) a letter-name learning group; (2) a letter-discrimination group who learned which of four geometric forms (square, circle, cross, triangle) was the mate of each grapheme; (3) a control group who learned to name four dogs; (4) a control group who performed the transfer task before the training task to assess learning speed without prior training. Training and transfer continued to a criterion of one perfect trial with 40 trials maximum. Incorrect responses were corrected. Subjects failing to reach criterion during the training phase were replaced.

The dependent variable, number of trials to criterion, was subjected to an analysis of variance in each task. Mean performances of the groups did not differ significantly on the training task nor on the transfer task where $X = 17.24$ trials (letter name) vs. 19.80 (letter discrimination) vs. 17.36 (dog name) vs. 16.56 (no training).

The experiment was repeated a year later with a different experimenter and different schools. Mid-year first-graders were assigned to one of three treatment groups, 25 subjects per group: (1) letter-name group, (2) letter-discrimination group, (3) no-training control group. (The dog-name control group in Experiment 1 was not included here.) Again, the groups did not differ significantly in their mean performance on the transfer task: X = 16.84 trials to criterion (letter names) vs. 19.88 (letter discrimination) vs. 22.24 (control). The power of these statistical tests was examined in two ways, and the conclusion was that a Type II error was highly unlikely.

Findings of both studies indicate that "letter-name knowledge does not facilitate learning to read words made up of the same letters." The fact that subjects were first graders and well into the process of reading acquisition rules out the possibility that failure in this study resulted because the subjects did not know that graphemes map phonemes in words. The failure of this experimental study, as well as others, indicates that correlational findings between letter-name knowledge and reading achievement may be a product of uncontrolled organismic or environmental conditions such as paired associate learning ability, intelligence, or home background variables.

Although letter-name training does not appear to contribute, studies by Jeffrey and Samuels (1967), Linehan (Durrell, 1958), and Ohnmacht (1969) indicate that letter-sound training is beneficial. However, Jeffrey and Samuels (1967) performed a task analysis in their study and concluded that for letter-sound training to facilitate word decoding, it must be combined with training in two other subskills, left-to-right scanning and phonic blend training. The importance of performing such a task analysis to identify specific terminal behaviors and prerequisite subskills in the field of reading is stressed.

REFERENCES

Durrell, D. Success in first grade reading. *Boston University Journal of Education,* 1958, *3,* 2–47.

Durrell, D., & Murphy, H. Speech to print phonics. *Teachers manual.* New York: Harcourt, Brace and World, 1964.

Jeffrey, W. E., & Samuels, S. J. The effect of method of reading training on initial learning and transfer. *Journal of Verbal Learning and Verbal Behavior,* 1967, *6,* 354–358.

Johnson, R. J. The effect of training in letter names on success in beginning reading for children of differing abilities (Doctoral dissertation, University of Minnesota, 1969).

Ohnmacht, D. D. The effects of letter-knowledge on achievement in reading in the first grade. Paper presented at American Educational Research Association in Los Angeles, 1969.

Silvaroli, N. J. Factors in predicting children's success in first grade reading. *Reading and Inquiry, Proceedings of International Reading Association,* 1965, *10,* 296–298.

SUMMARY OF JENKINS, BAUSELL, AND JENKINS'S STUDY: COMPARISONS OF LETTER-NAME AND LETTER-SOUND TRAINING AS TRANSFER VARIABLES

LINNEA C. EHRI

University of California at Davis

Although letter-name knowledge is the best single predictor of beginning reading achievement (Dykstra, 1970), experimental studies have failed to demonstrate facilitation (Johnson, 1970; Samuels, 1970). Jeffrey and Samuels (1967) found that letter-sound training boosted word recognition, but Samuels (1970) indicated later that only two of the four letter-sounds examined accounted for the effect.

Four experiments explored the effects of letter-name and letter-sound training on word recognition using a two-stage learning-transfer design. In Experiment 1, 96 first-graders (eighth month of school) were assigned to one of the three treatment groups. During the first stage, subjects learned to associate either letter names (Group N) or letter sounds (Group P for phonemic) with four letter-like symbols. The names for these symbols were names of the English letters, I, A, N, T. The sounds were the lax (short) vowels /I/ and /æ/, plus /n/ and /t/. Control subjects performed an unrelated paired-associate task. All groups were taken to criterion (two consecutively correct trials). Twelve of the subjects, eight in Group P and four in Group C, were replaced because they failed to reach criterion in 30 trials. Between the learning and transfer stages, subjects were taught to pronounce and blend the sounds in the transfer words (e.g., say /æ/, say /t/, say what word /æ/—/t/ makes). During the transfer stage, all subjects were taught to read four words (i.e., in, it, an, at), each spelled with two of the four letter-like forms. Since letters were recombined across spellings, subjects could not discriminate a word on the basis of a single letter.

Analyses of variance were used to compare performances of the three groups during the learning and transfer stages. The dependent measure was the number of trials to criterion. During learning, Group N learned its associations significantly faster than the other two groups, who did not differ (X = 5.63 trials for N, 11.59 for P, 12.03 for C). On the transfer task, Groups N and P learned to read the words at comparable rates, and both were significantly faster than Group C (X = 12.00 trials for N, 9.19 trials for P, 19.63 trials for C). Such positive findings contrast with Samuels's (1970) failure to observe transfer among letter-name learners. A comparison of IQ scores across groups ruled out one explanation for the results, that the letter-name condition included faster learners.

A second experiment ruled out the possibility that the letter-name subjects' knowledge of conventional target-word spellings helped them succeed on the transfer task. The sample was limited to first-graders who were unable to read all four transfer words on a pretest. However, because subjects in Group P had so much difficulty learning the letter-sound relations (i.e., 12 out of 20 subjects failed to reach criterion), comparable experimental groups could not be formed to study transfer performances.

To make it possible for all subjects to complete the learning stage, the procedures used in Experiment 1 were modified in a third experiment. First-graders who could name the four Standard English letters but could not read any of the four transfer words were selected during the second month of school. A more effective method of teaching letter-sound relations to Group P was employed. Between learning and transfer stages, Group P received blending practice as before, while Groups L and C were given spelling practice (i.e., say "at," say "A, T spells AT"). During the subjects' first exposure to words in the transfer task, either the names of the letters (for Groups N and C) or the sounds of the letters (for Group P) were repeated three times, followed by a statement that the letters or sounds spell the word (i.e., "A, T spells AT"). Otherwise, procedures were the same as in Experiment 1.

Analysis of variance of the number of correct responses across 20 trials in the transfer task revealed that Group P outperformed Groups N and C, who did not differ ($X = 44.08$ for P, 26.33 for N, 25.75 for C). In contrast to Experiment 1, letter-sound knowledge, not letter-name knowledge, facilitated word learning. Since Experiment 3 differed from Experiment 1 in several respects, which difference was responsible for these results is not clear.

A fourth experiment replicated and extended findings to a more natural school task involving real, rather than artificial, orthography. First-graders (second month of school) who could not read any of the transfer words learned to identify the names or sounds of the four Standard English letters. (Nearly all subjects in Group N already knew the letter names so they simply reviewed them during this stage.) The procedure to train Group P on the letter-sound relations was the same as that used in Experiment 3. No subjects failed to learn them. No blending or spelling training was provided between training and transfer stages except that, prior to the first transfer trial, the experimenter named the letters or sounds in the words and then pronounced the blends as in Experiment 3. Results duplicated those in Experiment 3. Group P identified significantly more words correctly during the first 20 trials than Group N ($\overline{X} = 43.58$ correct for P, 27.25 for N).

These experiments lead to several conclusions. Learning grapheme-sound relations is much more difficult than learning grapheme-name relations. However, knowledge of letter-sound relations facilitates acquisition of a reading vocabulary more than letter-name knowledge does. It suggests that "letter name instruction and similar readiness activities may be of limited value in reading programs" (Jenkins et al., 1972, p. 85).

---

summary

REFERENCES

Dykstra, R. Relationships between readiness characteristics and primary grade reading achievement in four types of reading programs. Paper presented at American Educational Research Association at Minneapolis, 1970.

Jeffrey, W. E., & Samuels, S. J. The effect of method of reading training on initial learning and transfer. *Journal of Verbal Learning and Verbal Behavior,* 1967, 6, 354–358.

Johnson, R. J. The effect of training in letter names on success in beginning reading for children of different abilities. Paper presented at Annual Meeting of American Educational Research Association, Minneapolis, 1970.

Samuels, S. J. Letter-name vs. letter-sound knowledge as factors influencing learning to read. Paper presented at Annual Meeting of American Educational Research Association, Minneapolis, 1970.

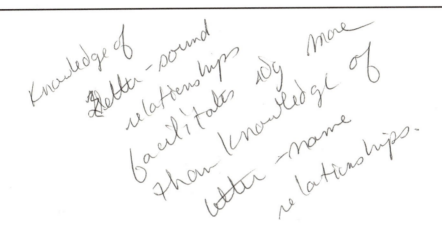

Knowledge of letter-sound relationships facilitates rdg more than knowledge of letter-name relationships.

references

SUMMARY OF F. J. JOHNSON'S STUDY: THE EFFECT OF TRAINING IN LETTER NAMES ON SUCCESS IN BEGINNING READING FOR CHILDREN OF DIFFERING ABILITIES

LINNEA C. EHRI

University of California at Davis

A review of letter-name studies provides several conclusions. Correlation coefficients between letter-name knowledge and reading achievement tend to cluster around 0.50 across studies. Tasks requiring children to name letters shown or to identify letters named are better predictors of reading achievement than simple letter-matching tasks. Although some classroom experiments have found significant differences favoring groups pretrained in letter names (Linehan, 1958), controlled laboratory experiments have found no significant advantage for groups pretrained in letter names (Samuels, 1969). In contrast, training in letter sounds seems to enhance reading achievement, which may be responsible for the significant differences attributed to letter-name training in some investigations where the two variables were confounded.

Interpretations of the correlation between early letter-name knowledge and later success in learning to read have varied. Barrett (1966) cautioned that letter-name knowledge might not be a causal factor but might simply reflect "a rich experience with a variety of written materials." Hence, teaching children letter names may not ensure success in learning to read. In contrast, Chall (1967), in her review of the literature, concluded that letter-name knowledge was an important factor helping children learn to read in the beginning stages, regardless of whether the teaching method emphasized code or meaning.

Johnson's investigation examined the effects of letter-name instruction upon first-grade reading achievement. In the experimental condition, one or another of two standard programs to teach letter names was administered to six classrooms of first graders. The control treatment consisted of listening activities administered to 12 classrooms of first graders. Treatments were assigned randomly to the classrooms. The sample included 424 middle- to upper-middle-class Caucasians, half girls, half boys. Pretests were administered during the first three weeks of the first semester of first grade: the Murphy-Durrell Reading Readiness Analysis and the Lorge-Thorndike Intelligence Test. Also, an informal test of uppercase and lowercase letter-name knowledge which had been given at the end of kindergarten was re-administered. During the next three weeks of the semester, experimental groups received letter-name instruction while control groups performed listening activities for 15 minutes each day. The letter-name test was re-administered. Then both groups began formal reading instruction in a basal program. At the end of the fall semester, students' reading achievement was measured with the Gates-MacGinitie Reading Tests of Vocabulary and comprehension.

Analysis of variance of pretest and post-test scores were conducted. Children were blocked by ability levels according to intelligence, pretraining knowledge of letter names, and reading readiness in separate analyses. Analysis of pretest scores revealed no significant differences among the groups on any measure. Analysis of post-test performances on both uppercase and lowercase letter names revealed significant differences favoring the experimental groups. Interactions with ability revealed that the children who knew the fewest letters at the outset of training made the greatest gains. The analysis of reading vocabulary and comprehension post-tests detected no significant main effects or interactions, indicating that experimental subjects had not acquired superior reading skills by the end of the first semester. From these results, Johnson (1969) concluded that "if the improvement of reading achievement is the criteria, there appears to be little value in teaching children the names of the letters."

Correlations among the various tests were examined. The best predictor of reading vocabulary and comprehension scores at the end of the first semester was the total score on the reading readiness test (sum of scores on the phonemes test, the letters test, and the learning-rate test; r = .72 and .62). The measure of lowercase letter-name knowledge taken in kindergarten followed closely as the second best predictor (r = .66 and .59). The correlations between intelligence, vocabulary, and comprehension were much lower (r = .33 and .31). Few differences were found between performances and males and females.

REFERENCES

Barrett, T. C. Performance on selected prereading tasks and first-grade reading achievement. *Vistas in Reading,* 1966, *11,* 461–464.

Chall, J. S. *Learning to read: The great debate.* New York: McGraw-Hill, 1967.

Linehan, E. B. Early instruction in letter names and sounds as related to success in beginning reading. *Journal of Education,* 1958, *140,* 44–88.

Samuels, S. J. Personal correspondence. Minneapolis: University of Minnesota, 1969.

SUMMARY OF SILBERBERG, SILBERBERG, AND IVERSEN'S STUDY: THE EFFECTS OF KINDERGARTEN INSTRUCTION IN ALPHABET AND NUMBERS ON FIRST GRADE READING

LINNEA C. EHRI

University of California at Davis

The question of what to include and how to structure preschool reading readiness programs has remained a topic of debate. Recent research indicates that reading readiness skills can be effectively trained, that a formalized readiness program is superior to an incidental approach (Angus, 1962), and that effects may persist through the primary grades (McKee, Brezeinski, & Harrison, 1966). However, the effects of readiness training on later reading skills have been negligible in most studies except on children from bilingual homes (Silberberg, 1966). In a re-analysis of the data from Silberberg's study (1966) using stepwise linear regression procedures applied to Gates Reading Readiness Test Scores, Silberberg, Iversen, and Silberberg concluded that "the Letter and Number Subtest alone is nearly as efficient as all five subtest scores in predicting end-of-first-grade reading scores, and the additional information, age and IQ, contributes little if anything to increased precision in prediction" (1968, p. 6).

The purpose of the present experimental study was to determine whether formal training in letter and number recognition in kindergarten would result in higher reading levels by the end of the first grade. The subjects were 109 middle-class kindergarteners from four classes in two schools, an experimental class and a control class in each school, each class having a different teacher. The experimental group received special instruction lasting eight weeks during April and May which consisted of 15 minutes of formal lessons daily. Letters and numbers were printed on the chalkboard and traced in the air, their shapes were named and discussed, and various games were played. The control-group classrooms and teachers were not aware that an experiment was taking place, and they adhered to the regular informal kindergarten program.

Before first grade, all subjects were administered the Gates Reading Readiness Test on three separate occasions: (1) as a pretest immediately before the experimental procedure; (2) as a post-test immediately following the completion of the experimental procedure; and (3) as a second post-test at the beginning of first grade. At the end of first grade, all subjects were administered the Metropolitan Achievement Test (MAT) and Wide Range Achievement Test, Word Recognition section (WRAT).

Analysis of performances on the readiness tests revealed that the experimental subjects "made significant gains in learning the names of letters and numbers" as a result of training while control subjects "made only the usual modest gains in learning the same information" (Silberberg et al., 1972). Furthermore, experimental subjects maintained their superiority over the control subjects throughout the summer between kindergarten and first grade. (For details of this analysis, refer to Orensteen, 1968.)

In the analysis of performance on the MAT reading test given at the end of first grade, subjects were grouped according to Gates readiness pretest scores (low, intermediate, high). Sex and treatment group were also factors in the analysis. Reading scores obtained prior to the experimental treatment were positively and significantly related to reading achievement. Sex was a significant factor, with girls outperforming boys. However, effects involving the experimental treatment were not significant. The same analysis was performed on the WRAT scores. Only the readiness level effect was significant. No main effects or interactions involving sex or experimental treatment were significant.

These results indicate that although accelerated training in reading readiness improves children's scores on readiness tests following training, it does not affect their subsequent ability to read. Although readiness training has benefits, they are transitory. It would seem that "at least for children of middle class homes, formalized training in letters and numbers recognition is a questionable educational practice when end-of-the-first-grade reading is taken to be the appropriate criterion of utility" (Silberberg et al., 1972, p. 11). Interpretation of the results raise doubts about the value of other readiness training and of kindergarten itself.

Stepwise regression procedures examined the relationship between various readiness tests given in kindergarten and reading achievement at the end of first grade. The Letters and Numbers Subtest of the Gates test survived as the best single predictor, just as before (Silberberg et al., 1968). This test may be used alone in place of the total Gates test without too much loss of information.

REFERENCES

Angus, M. *An investigation of the effects of a systematic reading readiness program at the Kindergarten A level.* Unpublished dissertation, Wayne State University, 1962.

McKee, P., Brezeinski, J. E., & Harrison, M. L. The effectiveness of teaching reading in kindergarten, Cooperative Research Project No. 5-0371. Denver: Denver Public Schools, 1966.

Orensteen, R. *The effect of teaching alphabet and numerals in kindergarten on measured reading readiness.* Unpublished master's thesis, University of Minnesota, 1968.

Silberberg, M. The effect of formal reading readiness training in kindergarten on development of readiness skills and growth in reading. Unpublished doctoral dissertation, University of Minnesota, 1966.

Silberberg, N., Iversen, I., & Silberberg, M. The predictive efficiency of the Gates Reading Readiness Tests. *Elementary School Journal,* 1968, *68*(4), 213–218.

SUMMARY OF DOROTHY C. OHNMACHT'S STUDY: THE EFFECTS OF LETTER KNOWLEDGE ON ACHIEVEMENT IN READING IN THE FIRST GRADE

LINNEA C. EHRI

University of California at Davis

This study evaluated the effects of three types of instruction on first-grade reading achievement. *Letter-name instruction* included various activities: "distinguishing letter forms from one another, finding specific letters in words, matching letters, associating upper-case and lower-case letters, checking ability to identify letter names and to name letters shown." *Letter-name-and-sound instruction* included some of these activities plus "listening for beginning sounds in words, associating letter sounds and forms, and matching beginning sounds and letters" (Ohnmacht, 1969, p. 3). *Sight-word instruction* involved "activities in visual and auditory perception of whole words, configuration clues, whole words in sentences, relation of oral expression to written expression, and activities in matching like words and noting details in words without reference to letter names or sounds. Some lessons were designed to reinforce knowledge of sight words and associate sight words with meaning in different contexts."

Classrooms of first-graders from three schools ($N = 208$) were assigned to one of three treatment groups. Each treatment group included three classrooms of children from one school, one class considered high in reading readiness, one average, and one low. *Treatment Group A* received instruction in letter names followed by instruction in sight words. *Treatment B* received instruction in letter names and sounds followed by sight words. *Treatment C* received instruction in sight words followed by letter-name-and-sound instruction.

Several pretests measured readiness skills during the first three weeks of first grade: letter-name and letter-sound knowledge; Metropolitan Readiness Test; phoneme and letter tests of Murphy-Durrell Readiness Analysis; Lorge Thorndike intelligence test. Treatment instruction began during the second week. The time allocated for the experimental treatment was held constant across all the classrooms. Children were taught to read concurrently. "All treatment groups used the same basal materials for reading instruction during instructional time not devoted to the experimental variable" (Ohnmacht, 1969, p. 3). During the 18th week of first grade, the Metropolitan Achievement Test was administered to measure the criterion variables: word recognition, word discrimination (letter-sound associations), and reading comprehension.

An analysis of covariance technique was used. Statistically controlled variables were: prior knowledge of letter names and letter sounds, information and oral language comprehension, and intelligence. On the measures of word recognition and word discrimination, Group B significantly outperformed Groups A and C, who did not differ. On the measure of reading comprehension, Groups B and C performed comparably and outperformed Group A. These findings indicate that subjects given letter-name instruction (Group A) were not as far along in learning to read by the 18th week as the two groups given instruction in letter-name-and-sound relations (Groups B and C). Regarding the latter two treatments, subjects given letter-name-and-sound instruction before sight-word instruction achieved superior word discrimination and recognition skill than subjects given sight-word instruction first and letter-name-and-sound instruction second. However, this manipulation had no differential effect on achievement in reading comprehension.

The performances of various subgroups of subjects were compared to determine whether the general pattern of differences reported above was evident among subjects at varous IQ levels and reading readiness levels. When subjects were grouped by IQ, the superior performance of Group B over Group A was apparent on all three criterion measures for high and average IQ subjects, but not for low IQ subjects, where there were no differences. When subjects were grouped by reading readiness scores, the superior performance of Group B over Group A was evident on all three measures for above-average and average readiness subjects. However, among below-average readiness subjects, a reversal occurred. On one measure, the word recognition test, Group A significantly outperformed Group B. The two groups did not differ on the other two criterion measures. From these results, one can conclude that the pattern of lower reading achievement of letter-name subjects as compared to letter-name-and-sound subjects held up across subgroups except in one case. Differences between Group C and the other two groups were not consistent across subgroups and measures.

Several implications for instruction are drawn. Early emphasis on letter-name-and-sound instruction yields an advantage in learning to recognize words over early sight-word instruction. However, it makes little difference to reading comprehension which type of instruction begins first. In contrast, instruction in letter-name knowledge yields no benefits over the other two types, except perhaps among children who are least ready for reading. This suggests that the time may be better spent on other beginning reading activities.

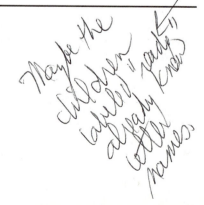

summary

A Critique of Five Studies Related to Letter-Name Knowledge and Learning to Read

LINNEA C. EHRI

University of California at Davis

Numerous studies report high positive correlations between knowledge of alphabet letter names and learning to read (Chall, 1967). In fact, knowledge of letter names is the best single predictor of beginning reading achievement, even better than intelligence. Researchers, though, have been reluctant to conclude that letter-name knowledge facilitates reading acquisition (Gibson & Levin, 1975; Venezky, 1975), primarily because several experimental studies failed to demonstrate an advantage for letter-name-trained subjects over controls in learning to read (Jenkins, Bausell, & Jenkins, 1972; Johnson, 1969; Muehl, 1962; Ohnmacht, 1969; Samuels, 1972; Silberberg, Silberberg & Iversen, 1972). However, these studies were performed a decade ago, and since then our knowledge of reading acquisition has advanced. This paper carves out a role for letter-name knowledge in learning to read based on current theory and research, and then re-examines the old evidence for its adequacy in assessing whether letters contribute in the way specified.

ROLE OF LETTER-NAME KNOWLEDGE

The current view of reading acquisition emerging from several quarters is that the skills that are central and distinguish children who make progress from those who lag behind are skills that involve facility with the letter-sound mapping system (Ehri & Wilce, 1979; Guthrie, 1973; Guthrie & Siefert, 1977; Liberman, Shankweiler, Liberman, Fowler, & Fischer, 1977; Mason, 1976; Perfetti and Hogaboam, 1975; Venezky, 1974). This is because English orthography is alphabetic (Gleitman & Rozin, 1977; Rozin & Gleitman, 1977). For word spelling to appear sensible rather than arbitrary to learners, the learners must be able to distinguish individual letters in printed words and process the letters as symbols for sounds in pronunciations. Letter-name knowledge provides the foundation for acquiring this alphabetic system. In learning the names of letters, children must discriminate and remember their shapes. Learning names also helps children attach relevant sounds to letters since most, if not all, of the names contain sounds commonly symbolized by the letters in

Gratitude is expressed to S. Jay Samuels and his remarkable filing system for instantly locating and delivering copies of the Johnson and Ohnmacht papers, which were reports of unpublished presentations given at meetings of the American Educational Research Association over ten years ago.

word spellings. Even H, Q, W, and Y, considered to be exceptions by Durrell (1980) contain relevant sounds: the name of H contains /č/ as in chair;" Q contains /k/ as in "queen;" /w/ can be found as a final glide in W, and likewise /y/ as a final glide in Y; Y also contains /ay/ as in "fly." Although these relations are less obvious, they are nonetheless available to learners (who know the names) in search of a nonarbitrary basis for associating sounds and letters.

Use of letter names by beginners to spell words has been documented by Read (1971, 1975), Chomsky (1977), and Henderson and Beers (1980), among others. Some interesting inventions that illustrate children's reliance on letter names are: HEK (truck), JAGN (dragon), PRD (pretty), SHU (shoe), TLFON (telephone). Of course, this strategy can lead to mistakes when the wrong sounds for letters are picked out of their names. For example, children have been mislead by /w/ in the name of Y and have spelled "water" as YTR, "while" as YL. Obviously, letter-name knowledge must be adapted and used selectively to build knowledge of the system. Whereas the beginner might entertain many possible letter-sound mappings, the ones that survive are those reinforced by exposure to conventional spelling patterns. Of course, the system consists of more than can be derived from letter-name knowledge. Many letters map sounds not contained in their names, most importantly, the letters for short vowels.[1] Also, the English spelling system includes regularities extending beyond single grapheme-phoneme relations (i.e., morpheme spelling, lexically derived spellings) (Chomsky, 1970; Venezky, 1970). Although knowing letter names does not provide complete knowledge of the system, it does provide important building blocks enabling children to make sense of the system at the outset of reading instruction (Durrell & Murphy, 1978; Mason, 1980).

Probably the main reason that knowledge of letter names puts children ahead in learning to read when they enter first grade is that the task of learning the names or sounds for alphabet letters is quite difficult and very time-consuming. The number of associations to be mastered is considerable: 26 names and 40 or more sounds for 52 visual figures. Many of the lowercase letters are visually similar and hard to discriminate. The associations themselves are totally arbitrary. That is, there is nothing inherent in the symbol which suggests its name or sound. Ehri and Wilce (1979) found that first-graders had trouble with a paired-associate learning task where the stimuli were four distinctive figures and the responses were meaningless sounds (e.g., mav, rel, kip, guz). The majority (67%) could not learn the four sounds even after 15 practice trials. This shows that learning arbitrary associations between meaningless stimuli and responses, which is what letter-name or letter-sound learning requires, takes children a long time. To the extent that children enter first grade knowing letter names, they have already mastered many of these hard-to-learn associations. In a recent study with kindergarten prereaders, we had no trouble teaching letter-sound associations to children who could already name the eight target letters. We had a great deal of trouble, and in fact gave up training, children who could not name the letters. Extracting sounds from letter names is a much easier task than learning letter-sound relations from scratch.

Not all methods of reading instruction teach letter-sound relations explicitly. Yet all beginners are thought to acquire knowledge of the basic relations in the course of learning to read, perhaps because the relations are induced implicitly.[2]

critique

That is, beginners figure out the relations on their own as they become familiar with printed words (Gibson & Levin, 1975). For induction, however, a foundation is required. That is, existing knowledge must provide a basis for detecting the regularities (Rohwer, Ammon, & Cramer, 1974). Such a basis lies in letter-name knowledge. Evidence is provided by Mason's (1980) longitudinal study of early readers. She reports that at an early point in learning to read, after children had mastered the names of the letters but before they knew many printed words, they first exhibited knowledge of consonant letter-sound relations in their attempts to read unfamiliar words. Interestingly, this appeared *before* teachers and parents reported teaching them any letter sounds. Very likely, beginners figured out the relations using letter-name knowledge just as Read (1971, 1975) and others have observed them do in spelling words.

Having an adequate foundation for inducing the letter-sound system may require more than simply knowing letter names. Beginners may need other skills to make use of their letter-name knowledge, such as sensitivity to phoneme-size units in pronunciations and how they are blended (Liberman et al., 1977). Another requirement may be having the letter names at the "tip of the tongue" so that sight of the letters evokes their names automatically without conscious attention and thought. LaBerge and Samuels's (1974) model of automatic information processing indicates that lower-level information must be known automatically to contribute to higher-level processing. In a reading task, printed words, not letter names or sounds, are seen and pronounced. For beginners reading text to process graphic cues along with context cues (Biemiller, 1970), automatic letter-name knowledge may be required. Evidence suggesting the importance of letter-naming fluency is mainly correlational yet the relationships are very high, in fact, somewhat higher than the correlations between letter-name accuracy and reading achievement (i.e., $r = .51$ to $.60$ for accuracy, Bond & Dykstra, 1967; vs. $r = .79$ to $.81$ for speed, Speer & Lamb, 1976).[3]

To initiate use of letter names in the induction process, it may be important to expose beginners to word spellings whose letters have names predicting their sounds (e.g., *be*an, *a*pe, *o*p*en*, *tee*th, dr*ess*, *dee*p) (Durrell, 1980). Since beginners attend mainly to boundary letters in reading and remembering words (Marchbanks & Levin, 1965; Williams, Blumberg, & Williams, 1970) ". . . *it* may be sufficient for letters in initial and final positions to be phonetically plausible *in order* to get induction of the system underway." Also, seeing consonant letters that are invariant in symbolizing only sounds in their names may be more important than seeing vowel letters that symbolize other sounds as well as their names.

ADEQUACY OF LETTER-NAME EXPERIMENTS

The view developed above suggests that, under certain conditions, letter-name knowledge may contribute to learning to read; however, several experiments have been interpreted to show otherwise. We will examine these experiments to determine whether the results dispute the proposed view.

critique

Five studies are considered here. The approach in each was to vary the letter-name experiences of experimental and control groups and then observe whether the groups performed differently on a reading task. The first two experiments were conducted in laboratories with subjects trained and tested individually, the latter three in classrooms with subjects trained and tested in groups.[4]

1. S. J. Samuels, The effect of letter-name knowledge on learning to read. Samuels (1972) taught mid-year first-graders real letter names (S, M, E, A) for four artificial letter-like forms and then examined how long it took the students to learn to read four words spelled with these letters ("see," "say," "me," "may"). He compared their learning to two control groups, one receiving letter discrimination training, the other receiving no letter-name training. The study was performed twice. In both cases, children who received letter-name training did not learn to read the words in fewer trials than any of the control groups.

Samuels asserts that the absence of facilitation is especially telling since his subjects were not novices but well into reading acquisition. However, doubts can be raised about the adequacy of their training and the words they were given to read. Since the letter forms were unfamiliar, since subjects were only taught to an accuracy criterion (i.e., saying the letter names perfectly once), and, since they were exposed to the letters an average of only six times, it is questionable whether children learned the letter-name associations well enough to use this information in the word reading task. Very likely the letters did not evoke their names automatically or even quickly but rather required attention and effort. Furthermore, the words to be read imposed a heavy burden on letter-name knowledge. To benefit, the reader could simply notice the correspondence between one of the letters and the pronunciation of the word (as beginning readers often do with real words), but had to process and discriminate *both* of the letters correctly since the letters were recombined across words, rather than uniquely associated with single words. Not surprisingly, to learners who had just barely overcome the associational confusion in learning individual letter-name pairs, their infirm knowledge of names offered little help.

Another factor limiting the possible value of letter names in this study is that subjects were not taught supplementary skills needed to make use of their letter-name knowledge. In an earlier study, Jeffrey and Samuels (1967) showed that training in letter-sound correspondences facilitated word reading. In their study, subjects were taught subskills such as left-to-right scanning, phonemic segmentation, and blending, which are necessary for subjects to apply their letter-sound training. A similar approach adopted here would have been equally appropriate and might have made a difference.

2. Jenkins, Bausell, and Jenkins, Comparisons of letter-name and letter-sound training as transfer variables. The Jenkins et al. study (1972) taught letter names to one experimental group, taught letter-sound relations to another experimental group, provided an unrelated learning experience to control subjects, and then compared the three groups' success in learning to read words comprised of the letters. They conducted four experiments with first-graders. Only the first used artificial orthography as stimuli for the names or sounds of letters (I, A, N, T). The remaining

critique

experiments used standard capital letters. The transfer words to be read following training were: "in," "it," "at," "an." One stumbling block in E–2 was that letter-sound training proved too difficult. In subsequent experiments, subjects were screened for letter-name knowledge and a better method of teaching letter-sound relations was employed. Results on the word reading transfer task were mixed across experiments as a result of procedural differences. In E–1, subjects were end-of-the-year first-graders, taught with artificial orthography, and all groups were given phonic blending training. Under these conditions, the letter-name group learned to read the words as well as the letter-sound group and both surpassed controls. In E–3 and E–4, the readers were less advanced, the words were presented in standard English print, and phonics assistance in decoding was provided to letter-sound subjects but replaced by spelling practice for letter-name subjects. Under these conditions, the sound group learned to read the transfer words faster than the letter group, which performed no better than controls.

These experiments appear to support the hypothesis that letter-name knowledge contributes to word reading when it is combined with other skills that enable subjects to apply their knowlege. In E–1, when the letter group was taught to blend sounds as well as to name letters, facilitation was observed. However, in subsequent experiments when letter-name subjects were not taught this "enabling" skill, their word reading performances were no better than the control group's performance. This inference is tentative, however, since other features besides blending instruction changed from E–1 to E–3 and E–4.

Although a positive case might be made, some inadequacies in these experiments limit the contribution of letter names. The main problem lies with the particular letters and words used in training. Only two of the letter names, T and N, were potentially useful in reading the target words. The other two letters, I and A, did not map the long vowels in their names but rather symbolized short vowels. Also, the letters whose names were relevant were positioned behind these irrelevant letters, possibly inhibiting detection of the letter-name relations. Furthermore, response competition between letter names and words may have been introduced by the similarity between the letter name for N ("en") and the pronunciations of the words "in" and "an," particularly in later experiments where spellings were recited orally in the transfer task: "I—N spells *in*," "A—N spells *an*." Muehl (1962) observed that letter names created interference because subjects named the letters rather than words. The Jenkins study may have magnified the problem of distinguishing between words and letter names as responses since the words, being function words, evoked little meaning and so probably did not stand out as real words among the sounds (Ehri, 1975, 1976, 1979).

Results are consistent with two points made above, that the task of learning letter-sound associations is very difficult and that knowledge of letter names may facilitate learning letter-sound relations. In E–2, although many trials (30) were given to learn a small number of associations (4), 60% of the subjects were unsuccessful. Interestingly, when letter-name knowledge was used to select subjects in experiments following E–2, the number failing to learn letter-sound relations dropped substantially (from 60% to 33% in E–3 and to 0% in E–4). However, the letter-sound training method was also altered in later experiments, and this may have

critique

reduced failures as well. Also, only two of the letter names were useful in learning letter-sounds, so use of letter name knowledge does not account entirely for the drop in number of failures.

3. R. J. Johnson, The effect of training in letter names. In Johnson's (1969) study, 24 classrooms of entering first-graders received three weeks of training before they began formal reading instruction. The experimental groups received letter-name instruction, the control groups listening instruction. Reading achievement was measured at the end of the first semester. Results of pre- and post-tests measuring letter-name knowledge confirmed that training was effective and that letter-name subjects knew more names at the end of instruction than control subjects did. However, experimental and control groups performed no differently on word recognition and reading comprehension tests given several weeks later.

Since letter training lasted only three weeks and was group-administered in this study, one might wonder whether experimental subjects gained all that much. Comparison of mean scores on letter-naming tests given before and after training revealed that both groups knew most of the letter names before training (i.e., 16–17 uppercase letters and 13–14 lowercase letters), and that mean gains from training differentiated experimental from control groups by only 2 uppercase letters and 2–3 lowercase letters. Thus, a likely reason why differences in reading achievement failed to appear is that the groups were not sufficiently different in their letter-name knowledge. Ideally, such a study should be designed so that experimental subjects know most of the letter names while control subjects know very little. Results would be much more telling.

4. Silberberg, Silberberg, and Iversen, The effects of kindergarten instruction in alphabet and numbers on first grade reading. The study by Silberberg, Silberberg, and Iversen, (1972) involved only four classrooms of children. Training was given at the end of kindergarten. Half of the classes were group-taught letter names (and also numbers) in 15-minute sessions running daily for eight weeks. Practice activities included viewing, naming, and tracing letters, and playing letter games. Control subjects received no special treatment. Reading achievement measured a year later (end of first grade) revealed no differences between the two groups.

Differences may have been absent because, as in the Johnson study (1969), letter training may not have contributed much to differentiating experimental from control subjects' letter-name knowledge. (Since mean scores were not reported, we cannot tell.) Another possible shortcoming of this study is that reading achievement was not measured until a year after training, at a point when even the poorer readers were reading close to a second-grade level. Any benefits of letter-name knowledge may have washed out by then.

5. D. C. Ohnmacht, The effects of letter knowledge on achievement in reading in the first grade. Ohnmacht (1969) employed three treatment groups: one taught letter names followed by instruction in reading sight words; one taught letter names and sounds followed by sight-word instruction; and a control group that received sight-word instruction followed by letter names and sounds. Each group included one

critique

classroom of first-graders at each of three levels of reading readiness. Reading achievement tests were administered four months after instruction began. Comparison of group means revealed that letter-sound subjects outperformed the other two groups on the word recognition test, and both letter-sound and control groups outperformed letter-name subjects in reading comprehension. When scores were examined separately for the three levels of reading readiness, the general pattern was apparent for high and average readers but not for below-average children. Here, surprisingly, the letter-name group did best on the word recognition measure, outperforming the letter-sound group, which in turn outperformed the control group. No differences were detected in reading comprehension.

Ohnmacht's results have been cited by several as providing negative evidence for the letter-name hypothesis. (See Samuels, 1971; also Gibson & Leven, 1975, p. 250, who inaccurately describe the control group as receiving no treatment.) However, the above description does not support this conclusion. First, the control group was not really a control but rather another treatment group receiving letter-name and sound instruction. Second, a difference favoring the letter-name group did surface among subjects at the lowest level of reading readiness. However, this difference cannot be interpreted as support for the letter-name hypothesis since the other groups were supposed to have been taught letter names as well. Johnson (1969) suggests an explanation for the superior performance of the low-level letter-name group. The treatment groups were actually three classes taught by different teachers, so differences in teacher effectiveness may have outweighed effects of the methods. Ohnmacht's study does show that letter-name training, combined with letter-sound training, promotes reading acquisition more than letter-name training alone.

Discussion. The present analysis makes it clear that the negative evidence yielded by these studies does not lay to rest the letter-name hypothesis. Each study has serious flaws that preclude conclusions about the contribution of letter names. More research is needed to settle the matter. This critique identifies factors that should be given greater attention in the design of future experiments. Some of the factors neglected in earlier studies are: how well letter names must be known to be useful (accurately versus automatically); whether specific enabling skills (phoneme segmentation, blending) might be necessary; what characteristics of the words to be read might make a difference (whether they contain letters with names giving clues to sounds, whether all the letters must be discriminated); and what magnitude of difference in letter-name knowledge might make a difference in learning to read.

Researchers did not consider that letter-name knowledge might be functionally inseparable from other factors and that its contribution might require these other factors when they tackled the letter-name hypothesis ten years ago. Rather they were bent on isolating letter-name knowledge and testing it as a single separable cause, especially since its correlations with reading achievement were so impressive. In isolating the variable and operationally defining it in their experiments, researchers took the name literally (i.e., number of letters that could be named). They did not consider aspects such as whether or not names mapped sounds in the words to be read, whether learners could detect the relevant sounds in the names, or whether

critique

differences in letter-name knowledge amounting to two to three letters could be expected to affect reading achievement, as essential. Thus, when experimental evidence turned up negative, rather than revising their narrow view of letter-name knowledge, researchers concluded that letter names did not really contribute, that correlations with reading achievement were probably accounted for by other factors such as "level of cognitive development, emotional stability, attention span, and proper interaction with adults outside of school" (Venezky, 1975). This critique has tried to show that the other options merit empirical investigation before the curtain is lowered on letter names. Studies have shown that letter-name instruction combined with letter-sound instruction does facilitate reading acquisition (Linehan, 1957; Ohnmacht, 1969). Since the two skills are highly correlated, it makes little sense to study them as separate variables. Rather they should be viewed as functionally related skills whose integration may be the factor promoting reading acquisition (Guthrie, 1973).

One implication of the above analysis for instructional practice should be mentioned since it contrasts with earlier views. Whereas letter-name researchers have recommended that letter sounds rather than letter names should be taught in reading readiness programs, the present perspective suggests that it probably makes little difference which is chosen in terms of time to learn the 22 or so associations represented in letter names. This is because the main difficulty of the learning task is not in extracting sounds from names after the names are acquired, but rather in acquiring the names or sounds and their associations with letters in the first place. If both names and sounds are unfamiliar, there is no reason to expect one to take less time to learn than the other. Of course, as with the other possibilities raised above, this too is an empirical question to be answered with data, not logic.

NOTES

1. However, even here, letter-name knowledge may be useful. The major spelling pattern differentiating long and short vowels is that long vowels are symbolized by the letters saying their own names plus a second vowel letter, often final silent *E*, whereas letters for short vowels stand alone. It may be that knowledge of vowel letter names is needed to distinguish long from short vowel sounds (i.e., long vowels are letter names, short vowels are not), which may be helpful in learning the pattern. The importance of knowing this pattern is indicated by Shankweiler and Liberman (1972), who find that errors in reading vowels distinguish skilled from less skilled beginning readers more than errors in reading consonant letters.
2. Many people mistakenly assume that acquisition of letter-sound relations in learning to read is synonymous with phonics instruction. Certainly this is the goal of a phonics program. However, knowledge of letter-sound relations may be acquired by learners in other programs as well. In fact, acquisition of a letter-sound mapping system of some sort is thought to be essential for making progress in learning to read regardless of the method of instruction. Thus, readers should not jump to the mistaken conclusion that this paper is describing only learners in a phonics program.

3. Alternative explanations for the high correlation between letter-naming speed and reading achievement should be acknowledged. The explanation proposed in the text is that letter-naming speed reflects how well subjects have learned the letter names and that this contributes in learning to read. Alternatively, letter-naming speed may be a consequence rather than a cause. Children may become more facile in naming letters as a result of making progress in learning to read. A final possibility is that letter-naming speed reflects more basic differences in encoding speed, distinguishing good and poor readers (Spring & Capps, 1974). Resolution awaits further research.
4. Evaluation of these studies is not comprehensive. Only major inadequacies are identified. In some cases, criticisms mentioned for one study apply to others as well. The study by Muehl (1962) is not discussed since the design was quite different. See Venezky (1975) for a critique of this study.

FOR FURTHER LEARNING

Those readers who are interested in continuing to explore the topic of beginning reading would find the following references helpful:

Beers, J. W., & Henderson, E. H. A study of developing orthographic concepts among first graders. *Research in the Teaching of English,* 1977, *11,* 133–148.

Bond, G. L., & Dykstra, R. The cooperative research program in first-grade reading. *Reading Research Quarterly,* 1967, *2,* 5–142.

Durrell, D. D. Commentary: Letter name values in reading and spelling. *Reading Research Quarterly,* 1980, *16,* 159–163.

Jeffrey, W. E., & Samuels, S. J. Effects of method of reading training on initial learning and transfer. *Journal of Verbal Learning and Verbal Behavior,* 1967, 6, 354–358.

Mason, J. When *do* children begin to read: An exploration of four-year-old children's letter and word reading competencies. *Reading Research Quarterly,* 1980, *15,* 203–227.

Read, C. Pre-school children's knowledge of English phonology. *Harvard Educational Review,* 1971, *41,* 1–34.

Venezky, R. L. The curious role of letter names in reading instruction. *Visible Language,* 1975, 9, 7–23.

REFERENCES

Biemiller, A. J. The development of the use of graphic and contextual information as children learn to read. *Reading Research Quarterly,* 1970, 6, 75–96.

Bond, G. L., & Dykstra, R. The cooperative research program in first-grade reading. *Reading Research Quarterly,* 1967, 2, 5–142.

Chall, J. S. *Learning to read: The great debate.* New York: McGraw-Hill, 1967.

Chomsky, C. Reading, writing and phonology. *Harvard Educational Review,* 1970, *40,* 287–309.

Chomsky, C. Approaching reading through invented spelling. In L. B. Resnick & P. A. Weaver

(Eds.), *Theory and practice of early reading* (Vol. 2). Hillsdale, N.J.: Lawrence Erlbaum Associates, 1977, 43–65.

Durrell, D. D. Commentary: Letter name values in reading and spelling. *Reading Research Quarterly,* 1980, *16,* 159–163.

Durrell, D. D., & Murphy, H. A. A prereading phonics inventory. *The Reading Teacher,* 1978, *31,* 385–390.

Ehri, L. C. Word consciousness in readers and prereaders. *Journal of Educational Psychology,* 1975, 67(2), 204–212.

Ehri, L. C. Word learning in beginning readers and prereaders: Effects of form class and defining contexts. *Journal of Educational Psychology,* 1967, *68,* 832–842.

Ehri, L. C. Linguistic insight: Threshold of reading acquisition. In T. G. Waller & G. E. MacKinnon (Eds.), *Reading research: Advances in theory and practice* (Vol. 1). New York: Academic Press, 1979.

Ehri, L. C., & Wilce, L. S. The mnemonic value of orthography among beginning readers. *Journal of Educational Psychology,* 1979, *71,* 26–40.

Gibson, E. J., and Levin, H. L. *The psychology of reading.* Cambridge, Mass.: The MIT Press, 1975.

Gleitman, L. R., and Rozin, P. The structure and acquisition of reading I: Relations between orthographics and the structure of language. In A. S. Reber and D. L. Scarborough (Eds.), *Toward a psychology of reading.* Hillsdale, N.J.: Lawrence Erlbaum Associates, 1977.

Guthrie, J. T. Models of reading and reading disability. *Journal of Educational Psychology,* 1973, *65,* 9–18.

Guthrie, J. T., & Seifert, M. Letter-sound complexity in learning to identify words. *Journal of Educational Psychology,* 1977, *69,* 686–696.

Henderson, E. H., and Beers, J. W. *Developmental and Cognitive Aspects of Learning to Spell.* Newark, Del.: International Reading Association, 1980.

Jeffrey, W. E., & Samuels, S. J. Effects of method of reading training on initial learning and transfer. *Journal of Verbal Learning and Verbal Behavior,* 1967, 6, 354–358.

Jenkins, J. R., Bausell, R. B., & Jenkins, L. M. Comparison of letter name and letter sound training as transfer variables. *American Educational Research Journal,* 1972, *9,* 75–86.

Johnson, R. J. *The effect of training in letter names on success in beginning reading for children of differing abilities.* (Doctoral dissertation, University of Minnesota, 1969.) (University microfilms)

LaBerge, D., & Samuels, S. J. Toward a theory of automatic information processing in reading. *Cognitive Psychology,* 1974, *6,* 293–323.

Liberman, I. Y., Shankweiler, D., Liberman, A. M., Fowler, C., & Fischer, F. W. Phonetic segmentation and recoding in the beginning reader. In A. S. Reber & D. L. Scarborough (Eds.), *Toward a psychology of reading.* Hillsdale, N. J.: Lawrence Erlbaum Associates, 1977.

Linehan, E. B. Early instruction in letter names and sounds as related to success in beginning reading. (Doctoral dissertation, Boston University, 1957.) (University microfilms)

Marchbanks, G., & Levin, H. Cues by which children recognize words. *Journal of Educational Psychology,* 1965, *56,* 57–61.

Mason, J. M. Overgeneralization in learning to read. *Journal of Reading Behavior,* 1976, *8,* 173–182.

Mason, J. When *do* children begin to read: An exploration of four-year-old children's letter and word reading competencies. *Reading Research Quarterly,* 1980, *15,* 203–227.

Muehl, S. Effects of letter name knowledge on learning to read a word list in kindergarten children. *Journal of Educational Psychology,* 1962, *53,* 181–186.

Ohnmacht, D. C. *The effects of letter knowledge on achievement in reading in the first grade.* Paper presented at American Educational Research Association meeting, Los Angeles, 1969.

Perfetti, C. A., & Hogaboam, T. Relationship between single word decoding and reading comprehension skill. *Journal of Educational Psychology,* 1975, *67,* 461–469.

Read, C. *Children's categorization of speech sounds in English.* National Council of Teachers of English, Research Report No. 17, 1975.

Read, C. Pre-school children's knowledge of English phonology. *Harvard Educational Review,* 1971, *41,* 1–34.

Rohwer, W. D., Ammon, P. R., & Cramer, P. The cognitive approach. *Understanding intel-*

lectual development. Hinsdale, Ill.: Dryden Press, 1974.

Rozin, P., & Gleitman, L. R. The structure and acquisition of reading II: The reading process and the acquisition of the alphabetic principle. In A. S. Reber & D. L. Scarborough (Eds.), *Toward a psychology of reading.* Hillsdale, N. J.: Lawrence Erlbaum Associates, 1977.

Samuels, S. J. Letter-name versus letter-sound knowledge in learning to read. *Reading Teacher,* 1971, *24,* 604–608.

Samuels, S. J. The effect of letter-name knowledge on learning to read. *American Educational Research Journal,* 1972, *9,* 65–74.

Shankweiler, D., & Liberman, I. Y. Misreading: A search for causes. In J. F. Kavanagh & I. G. Mattingly (Eds.), *Language by ear and by eye.* Cambridge, Mass.: The MIT Press, 1972, 293–317.

Silberberg, N. E., Silberberg, M. C., & Iversen, I. A. The effects of kindergarten instruction in alphabet and numbers on first grade reading. *Journal of Learning Disabilities,* 1972, *5,* 254–261.

Speer, O. B., & Lamb, G. S. First grade reading ability and fluency in naming verbal symbols. *The Reading Teacher,* 1976, 572–576.

Spring, C., & Capps, C. Encoding speed, rehearsal, and probed recall of dyslexic boys. *Journal of Educational Psychology,* 1974, *66,* 780–786.

Venezky, R. *The Structure of English Orthography.* The Hague: Mouton, 1970.

Venezky, R. L. Theoretical and experimental bases for teaching reading. In T. A. Sebeok (Ed.), *Current trends in linguistics. Linguistics and Adjacent Arts and Sciences* (Vol. 12). The Hague: Mouton, 1974, 2057–2100.

Venezky, R. L. The curious role of letter names in reading instruction. *Visible Language,* 1975, *9,* 7–23.

Williams, J. P., Blumberg, E. L., & Williams, D. V. Cues used in visual word recognition. *Journal of Educational Psychology,* 1970, *61,* 310–315.

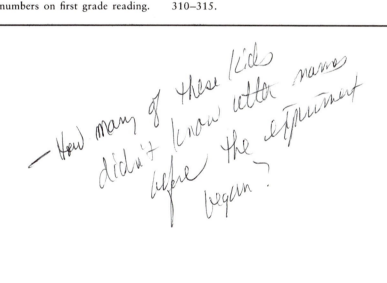

— How many of these kids didn't know letter names before the experiment began?

A Commentary on Ehri's Critique of Five Studies Related to Letter-Name Knowledge and Learning to Read: Broadening the Question

ELIZABETH SULZBY

Northwestern University

Ehri took the position that letter-name knowledge does play a role in learning to read and reviewed research to support her position. She then suggested the need for further research in the role of letter-name knowledge in reading acquisition.

Ehri has broadened the question concerning whether children need to know the names of alphabet letters when they are learning to read from the earlier linguistically naive, correlational, noninteractive paradigms. I will suggest ways in which the question may be broadened further. I will also review other current research that will substantiate Ehri's claim about the importance of letter-name knowledge and will suggest how this research may lead us to refine the question in a number of useful ways. Finally, I will suggest avenues for further research. In all cases, both logic (theory) and empirical evidence (research) are involved. We need to improve both our logic and our evidence; Ehri's chapter is a fine example of the improvement currently possible.

In her critique, Ehri's careful reviews of current research and of the five sets of older studies illustrate the contribution that linguistics can make to the field of reading research. Her analysis of the stimulus items, including words, nonsense syllables, letter names with their associated sounds within words and within the names themselves, positions of letters and sounds within words, is an example of the care researchers should take to ensure that their variables are indeed operationalized in an informative way. In addition, she alludes to developmental issues such as how young children may conceive such relationships.

The sets of older research lead Ehri to make two points: first, that this body of research is flawed and, second, it nevertheless contains some evidence that letter-name knowledge may help children learn to read. The more important of her two points is the flawed nature of the studies. The evidence culled from the review that these studies indicate a role for letter-name knowledge is not very convincing. In my opinion, it is better to discard the findings of these studies on the basis of their flawed designs rather than to try to draw positive evidence. Nevertheless, Ehri's conclusion that buried within these studies is some evidence about the perhaps inseparable nature of the two variables of letter sounds and letter names is an important speculation and the critique does contribute to that argument since many of the studies included both kinds of conditions, either by plan or by flaw.

The older studies were based upon models using letter-name knowledge as a predictor of later success upon a criterion measure, even though the designs were experimental or quasi-experimental. Nurss (1979) reported research connected to revision of a current readiness test. While letter-name knowledge has a long history as a good predictor of subsequent performance on reading achievement tests, Nurss pointed to a shift in the nature of the predictive relationship. More children now come to school already knowing letters and letter names, thus the ability to recognize and match letter names to forms is no longer a predictor if measured in first grade, although it maintains its ability to predict if tested in kindergarten. I will address the issue of when letter-name knowledge is measured in a later section concerning the time of initial learning and time of effective use of letter-name knowledge.

From her reviews of both the older and more recent research, Ehri reasoned that letter-name knowledge seems to be used by some children and should have an effect upon some criterion measure(s). But in her critique, she does not make clear what kinds of criterion measures are appropriate.

In fact, it is not clear in Ehri's critique what her notion of beginning reading is. In the older studies reviewed, the criterion measures included correct pronunciation of isolated words or pseudo-words and performance upon word recognition and comprehension subtests of reading achievement tests. In the reviews of the more current studies, the issues of criterion measures and definitions of beginning reading were not addressed.

Certainly, the issue of what counts as "reading" or "beginning reading" and the issue of how letter-name knowledge might be used in whatever definition of reading is studied are both essential to good theory and research. For example, "reading" at the beginning stage can be defined as reading isolated words or pseudowords; reading from one's own invented spelling; reading from conventional orthography; reading continuous text written or dictated by oneself; reading continuous text written by others; performance on standardized tests of various kinds. Some researchers (Goodman, 1980; Harste, Burke, & Woodward, 1982; Sulzby, 1981a, in press) currently suggest that beginning reading may be measured or relevantly described at points before the oneset of what is usually recognized as reading, or at the point that Sulzby (1981a) calls "independent reading."

It is essential to define and operationalize "reading" to investigate the role of letter-name knowledge in the way Ehri suggests. Her suggestions imply that we need a much finer grained analysis of the notion of "role" in acquisition. She suggests that letter-name knowledge becomes integrated into a broader set of skills and loses its separable identity and thus is not measured by some designs. Perhaps such a suggestion could be tested in interactive designs (Lesgold & Perfetti, 1981).

To investigate Ehri's contention that letter-name knowledge plays a role in reading acquisition, we must also expand the question to a set of related questions. Ehri raised some of these questions in one form or another.

I will suggest some related research and research paradigms to exploit in the future. These questions all assume that letter-name knowledge is important, but more precise research can invalidate this assumption. Each question also points to our need for further empirical evidence.

1. How do children learn letter names?
2. How is letter-name knowledge used by children?
3. What does letter-name knowledge enable the child to learn? (Relevant here is having a meta-language.)
4. When does the child use letter-name knowledge in reading acquisition?
5. Do all children learn and use letter names? Is it possible to bypass letter names, and what are the consequences of bypassing them?

HOW DO CHILDREN LEARN LETTER NAMES?

In spite of the evidence from the invented spelling research that children's early spellings use and reflect letter names, we do not have solid, descriptive research about how children learn letter names prior to school instruction. Ehri found that the task of teaching letter names and letter forms to children who entered first grade knowing no letter names was an arduous, defeating task (Ehri & Wilce, 1979). Yet they found that many children came to school knowing many letter names. This is compatible with the reports of Nurss (1979) and Sulzby (1981a). Such children learn their letters at home and in day-care and nursery schools, we presume, yet we have little observational and longitudinal records of the form of this learning.

Ehri used the term "association" to describe the kind of learning done in learning letter names and their accompanying forms. I would argue that we do not know enough to characterize the form of learning of letter names by young children. A more precise definition of what is meant by association would be helpful. Names and forms are arbitrarily related in the English alphabet, but there is evidence that children attempt to put some system into even these arbitrary relationships. Invented spelling research (Beers & Henderson, 1977; Chomsky, 1979; Read, 1975) presents the systematicity with which children abstract one part of a letter name rather than another for use in spelling (why /b/ rather than /iy/ from B, yet /m/ rather than /ɛ/ from M?). Similarly, children induce relationships in letter forms (Hildreth, 1932, 1936; Sulzby, 1981a) and make similar malformed letters (Simner, 1981). Whether the relationships children abstract in these areas are relevant to the form of their learning of letter names is not known.

Observations of children learning letter names in the home are needed. I have speculated that children first learn from blocks, alphabet books, and the alphabet song. We need to see how this learning takes place before we can use the term association for it, except in a loose sense. Teale[1] reports that in a longitudinal study of Anglo, Black, and Chicano working-class children in San Diego, he and his colleagues found that most of these children learned letter names from the alphabet song in their homes. Blocks and alphabet books, contrary to my speculation based upon middle-class children, were rarely present. They found that children learned the song but had difficulty with part of the string such as the LMNOP sequence. At first, parents laughed about the child's errors, then they would begin to intervene and slow the child down on the problematic part. It was only after the children had mastered the song that parents began to introduce the visual forms of the letters. If children learn letter names with a melodic accompaniment and then later learn to match forms with the names, the learning does not seem to be simple association. Teale also reported that the children often were learning how to write their names at some points simultaneously with the alphabet song so a subset of letters was learned in the context of a meaningful label. He further observed that there were many variations and twists in the patterns of letter-name learning.

We need more careful descriptions of how children do learn letter names and forms in the different settings in which they learn them. If some children learn from blocks and alphabet books, the letter names may be cued by key words which include sound correspondence clues. Thus Ehri's contention that letter names and letter sounds are difficult to separate may have an even earlier origin than her mention of invented spelling. As she stated, we need empirical evidence. We also need to move from observational research's clues to other designs capable of disconfirmation.

HOW IS LETTER-NAME KNOWLEDGE USED BY CHILDREN?

Ehri reviewed evidence from invented spelling research in which there is evidence that letter names are used as a cue to spellings. This research can be expanded to include the voicing that children do while writing continuous text (Graves, 1979; Sulzby, 1981a, 1981b). Voicing often includes children's re-reading to monitor what they have written thus far. In this voicing, children often say sounds and letter names. Records of when and how voicing shows letter-name knowledge is needed to compare to degree of reading competence. Since Ehri has contended that letter-name knowledge gets integrated with other skills, we need longitudinal close observation to detect points of integration or to dispute that such points occur.

I would caution, however, that such protocols will differ according to whether you ask children to write isolated words or to write compositions. Within our data we have samples of the same children doing both tasks in the same session. A child may write text clauses using one letter per word or using pretend cursive, but then may write isolated words in "editing" with many more sounds represented. The voicing during composition may or may not include letter sounds and letter names; absence of voicing cannot be taken as an indication that the child does not use letter names. We can start from protocol clues but we need corroborating research such as that of Read (1975), and particularly that of Mason (1980), done at times keyed to the composition evidence.

WHAT DOES LETTER-NAME KNOWLEDGE ENABLE THE CHILD TO LEARN?

Much has been made of children's metalinguistic confusions. We have not paid enough attention to how children use metalinguistic terms in learning to read and write. Research in early reading and spelling (Clark, 1976; Durkin, 1966; Read, 1975) has indicated that children who learn at home ask their parents questions about reading and writing. We have little evidence of the questions that they ask, yet it would seem that letter names would play a role both in what the parents answer and in the ease with which the children can ask answerable questions. Sulzby (1981b) reports sequences in which five-year-old children pursue questions about how word boundaries work in written texts. These children used letter names with various degrees of proficiency as a means of getting other information about the reading and writing systems. Knowledge of letter names might be more important as part of a means of gaining other knowledge than as a direct source of reading acquisition.

WHEN DOES THE CHILD USE LETTER-NAME KNOWLEDGE IN READING ACQUISITION?

Ehri suggested that we should attend to parts of reading acquisition that occur at the same time as children's learning of letter-name knowledge. Mason (1980) indicated that a spurt in letter-sound knowledge seemed to come soon after children learned letter names.

In her own research, Ehri is very careful to consider the complexity of the notion of prerequisites in reading. The issue of whether or in what way letter-name knowledge may be a prerequisite necessary to reading acquisition, may be an enabling factor, or may be an outcome or by-product, requires longitudinal study with carefully described samples of children of differing backgrounds. Such research should include children before and during formal instruction.

The notion of automaticity may be misleading if introduced without accompanying longitudinal study begun with very young children. Automaticity should be separated from the notion of prerequisites and used with careful definition of what we mean by effect upon reading. If we mean that letter-name knowledge affects achievement test scores at the end of first grade, then automaticity may be a legitimate concept to explore. If we mean that the child uses letter-name knowledge to sound out a few never-before-seen-but-known words, and that this step is used to measure beginning reading, then automaticity may not be a legitimate concept. Learning that you can sound out a few words or that you can read back from your invented spelling may be enough to get the child started in reading. The child may start reading without needing letter names learned to a level of automaticity; automaticity may then become a by-product as reading matures. On the other hand, the child may become stymied in reading for reasons that have nothing to do with letter-name knowledge. Again, we need sharply defined longitudinal evidence.

DO ALL CHILDREN LEARN AND USE LETTER NAMES?

This is an individual differences question and we have increasing indications that individual differences in beginning reading continue to be detected with current research paradigms (Amarel, 1981; Lesgold, Resnick, Roth, & Hammond, 1981). Since we do not know in any detail how letter names are learned and used, we do not know whether letter name knowledge can be bypassed and what the consequences are of bypassing this knowledge. Ehri and Wilce (see page 145) found children who differed widely in letter-name knowledge and gave up teaching letter names to children who knew almost none at the start of their study. Although such children are difficult to work with, they would seem to be fruitful subjects of the effects of bypassing letter-name knowledge at an age that seems optimal for such learning. With better descriptive data on younger children in various learning settings, including the home, we may be able to design better experimental tests of our hypotheses about letter-name knowledge. Ehri points to relevant ways of conducting such research.

NOTE

For more information about this study funded by the National Institute of Education, contact A. B. Anderson, Laboratory of Comparative Human Cognition, University of California, San Diego, or W. H. Teale, Division of Education, College of Social and Behavioral Sciences, University of Texas at San Antonio.

REFERENCES

Amarel, M. Qualities of literacy: The personal dimension. Paper presented at the Vice-presidential Symposium of Division B, American Educational Education Association, Los Angeles: April 1981.

Beers, J. W., & Henderson, E. H. A study of developing orthographic concepts among first graders. *Research in the Teaching of English*, 1977, *11*, 133–148.

Chomsky, C. Approaching reading through invented spelling. In L. B. Resnick & P. A. Weaver (Eds.), *Theory and practice of early reading* (Vol. 2). Hillsdale, N.J.: Lawrence Erlbaum Associates, 1979.

Clark, M. M. *Young fluent readers*. London: Heinemann Educational Books, 1976.

Durkin, D. *Children who read early*. New York: Teachers College Press, 1966.

Ehri, L. C., & Wilce, L. S. The mnemonic value of orthography among beginning readers. *Journal of Educational Psychology,* 1979, *71,* 26–40.

Goodman, Y. The roots of literacy. Paper presented at the Claremont Reading Conference, Forty-fourth Yearbook, 1980.

Graves, D. The growth and development of first grade writers. Paper presented at the Canadian Council of Teachers of English Annual Meeting. Ottawa: May 1979.

Harste, J. C., Burke, C. L., & Woodward, V. A. Children's language and world: Initial encounters with print. In J. Langer & M. Smith-Burke (Eds.), *Bridging the gap: Reader meets author.* Newark, Del.: International Reading Association, 1982.

Hildreth, G. The success of young children in number and letter construction. *Child Development,* 1932, *3,* 1–14.

Hildreth, G. Developmental sequences in name writing. *Child Development,* 1936, *7,* 291–303.

Lesgold, A. M., & Perfetti, C. A. (Eds.), *Interactive processes in reading.* Hillsdale, N.J.: Lawrence Erlbaum Associates, 1981.

Lesgold, A. M., Resnick, L. B., Roth, S. F., & Hammond, K. L. *Patterns of learning to read: A longitudinal study.* Paper presented at the biennial meeting of the Society for Research in Child Development. Boston: April 1981.

Mason, J. When *do* children begin to read: An exploration of four-year-old children's letter and word reading competencies. *Reading Research Quarterly,* 1980, *15,* 203–227.

Nurss, J. R. "Assessment of readiness," T. G. Walker & G. E. MacKinnon (eds.). *Reading research: Advances in theory and practice.* Vol. 1. New York: Academic Press, 1979.

Simner, M. L. *Printing errors in kindergarten and the prediction of academic performance.* Paper presented at the biennial meeting of the Society for Research in Child Development. Boston: April 1981.

Sulzby, E. *Kindergarteners begin to read their own compositions: Beginning readers' developing knowledges about written language project.* Final report to the Research Foundation of the National Council of Teachers of English. Evanston, Ill.: Northwestern University, 1981(a).

Sulzby, E. Kindergarteners deal with word boundaries. Paper presented at the annual meeting of the National Reading Conference. Dallas, Dec. 1981(b).

Sulzby, E. Oral and written language mode adaptations in stories by kindergarten children. *Journal of Reading Behavior,* 1982, *14,* 51–59.

Read, C. *Children's categorizations of speech sounds in English.* Research report #17, National Council of Teachers of English, Urbana, Ill.: 1975.

WHEN SHOULD CHILDREN BEGIN TO READ?

MABEL VOGEL MORPHETT and
CARLETON WASHBURNE (1931)

In tracing back to their origins the reading difficulties of some children and their distaste for the subject, the Department of Educational Counsel in Winnetka found that in several instances the children's mental ages on entering the first grade had been low and that discouragement had resulted from their first attempts to learn to read. This discouragement sometimes resulted in a mental set against reading, which lasted for years and which hampered all their school work. The research department, therefore, with the aid of the primary-grade teachers, set about the task of discovering the period in the mental development of children when, as a rule, there is the best chance of their learning to read readily.

In September 1928, all Winnetka first-grade children, 141 in number, were given the Detroit First-Grade Intelligence Test. The eight first-grade teachers were not told the mental ages of the children and attempted to teach all of them to read. The method, in accordance with the Winnetka technique, was largely individual, so that the slow children did not retard the fast ones. In February 1929, the reading progress of these children was measured for the purpose of determining the amount of progress made by children at each mental level.

In order that the reading progress might be measured, the first large teaching unit was divided into definite steps, which were measurable by the teachers. Twenty-one steps took the children through the beginning reading materials.[1] Each further step represented the reading of a primer or first reader. Reading progress was measured by the number of these steps which the child had completed by February.

In addition to these progress steps the sight-word score of each child was measured. Each child in Winnetka is required to know at least 139 words at sight before passing from first-grade reading to second-grade reading. These words are those most frequently used in primers and first readers. The children were tested individually with flash cards, and the number of words recognized by each child was recorded as his sight-word score. In some cases the children knew some of the second-grade sight words as well as the 139 first-grade words. In such cases the score was the total number of first- and second-grade words recognized.

The first-grade teachers, all of whom had had several years of experience with

Reprinted from *The Elementary School Journal,* 1931, pp. 496–503, by permission of the University of Chicago Press.

[1]Livia Youngquist and Carleton Washburne, Winnetka Primary Reading Materials. Chicago: Rand McNally & Co., 1928.

the reading materials, agreed that children who seemed ready for reading from the beginning of the year had usually completed at least thirteen progress steps and knew at least thirty-seven sight words by February. Therefore, thirteen progress steps and thirty-seven sight words were accepted as the measure of the minimum degree of satisfactory progress.

The Detroit First-Grade Intelligence Test and the Stanford Revision of the Binet-Simon Scale were used to determine the mental ages of the children. The Detroit tests were given to all first-grade children entering in September. The Stanford-Binet test was given later in the year, and the mental ages were calculated as of September 1928. In this way comparison between the mental ages determined by the Detroit and Stanford-Binet tests was made possible.

Research/Table 1 gives the correlations which were found between the sight-word scores and intelligence and between reading progress and intelligence. Since the data proved to be non-linear, the correlation ratios rather than the correlation coefficients are given. When the relation between reading progress and intelligence was calculated, it was necessary to use the rank method of figuring correlations since the intervals of progress were not necessarily of equal difficulty. The correlations show that there is a fairly high degree of relationship between mental age and reading progress. The Detroit test shows more relation to progress than does the Stanford-Binet test. Of the three measures of intelligence—mental age, average of the mental and chronological ages, and intelligence quotient—mental age shows the greatest degree of relationship, although the differences are slight. In the calculations that follow, mental age alone is used as the method of figuring intelligence.

The scores were next divided into groups based on the children's mental ages in September. The percentage of children of each mental age making satisfactory progress (thirteen steps or more) and the percentage making satisfactory sight-word scores (thirty-seven or more) were determined. Research/Tables 2 and 3 show the results.

Research/Table 2 shows that a small percentage of children who began reading with a mental age of less than six years were able to achieve satisfactory

RESEARCH/TABLE 1.
Correlations Between Achievement in Reading of 141 First-Grade Children and Their Intelligence as Measured by Detroit Test and Stanford-Binet Test

Factors Correlated	*Detroit Test*	*Stanford-Binet Test*
Sight-word score and mental age	.65	.58
Sight-word score and average of mental and chronological age as of September 1, 1928	.57	.49
Sight-word score and intelligence quotient	.56	.54
Reading progress and mental age	.59	.51
Reading progress and average of mental and chronological age as of September 1, 1928	.55	.49
Reading progress and intelligence quotient	.50	.53

RESEARCH/TABLE 2.
Number of Children of Each Mental Age and Percentage Making Satisfactory Reading Progress

Mental Age in Years and Months*	Number of Children† Detroit Test	Number of Children† Stanford-Binet Test	Percentage Making Satisfactory Reading Progress‡ Detroit Test	Percentage Making Satisfactory Reading Progress‡ Stanford-Binet Test
4–5 to 4–11	1	1	....	....
5–0 to 5–5	12	1	0	....
5–6 to 5–11	12	12	0	8
6–0 to 6–5	17	22	47	41
6–6 to 6–11	23	38	78	68
7–0 to 7–5	29	31	79	68
7–6 to 7–11	16	15	75	87
8–0 to 8–5	7	11	....	82
8–6 to 9–0	8	2	....	....

*Intervals are half sigmas above and below the mean of the entire group as determined by the Detroit test.

†Because the tests were given on different dates, some children who were given the Detroit test were not given the Stanford-Binet test and vice versa.

‡No percentages were figured for groups of less than ten children.

RESEARCH/TABLE 3.
Number of Children of Each Mental Age and Percentage Making Satisfactory Sight-Word Scores

Mental Age in Years and Months	Number of Children* Detroit Test	Number of Children* Stanford-Binet Test	Detroit Test	Stanford-Binet Test
4–5 to 4–11	1	1	....	....
5–0 to 5–5	12	1	0	....
5–6 to 5–11	12	12	0	8
6–0 to 6–5	17	25	71	52
6–6 to 6–11	23	43	87	77
7–0 to 7–5	31	35	84	89
7–6 to 7–11	23	18	83	94
8–0 to 8–5	10	11	90	91
8–6 to 9–0	12	3	100	....

*The numbers of children whose sight-word progress is compared differ from the numbers whose reading progress is compared in Table II because one group of children not taught by the individual method was omitted from the reading-progress group.

reading progress but that for the group having a mental age between six years and six years and six months there was a sharp rise in the percentage making satisfactory progress. This fact is shown graphically in Research/Figure 1. The curves for the Stanford-Binet and the Detroit tests are essentially alike, although final flattening occurs later on the Stanford-Binet curve.

The curve of the results on the Stanford-Binet test seems to indicate that

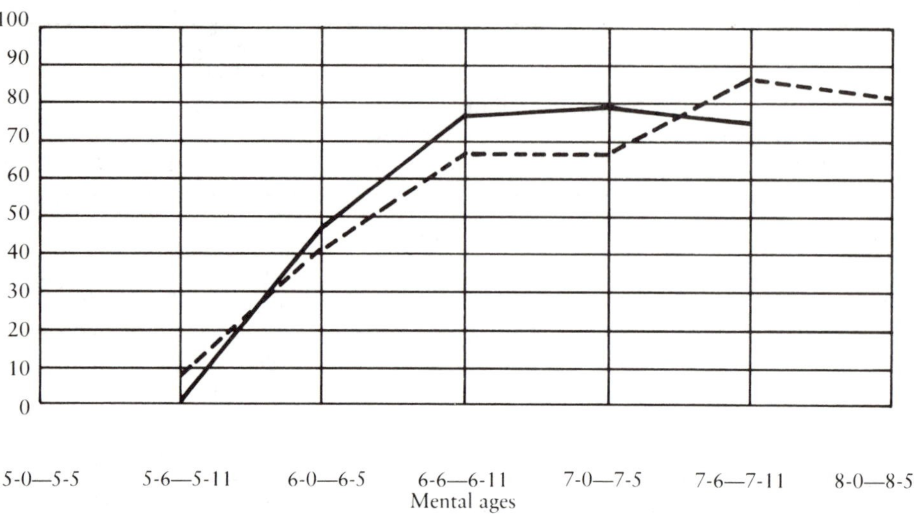

RESEARCH/FIGURE 1.
Percentages of children of various mental ages, as determined by the Detroit First-Grade Intelligence Test (solid line) and by the Stanford Revision of the Binet-Simon Scale (broken line), making satisfactory reading progress in school year 1928–29.

children would gain considerably in speed of learning if they could wait until they had attained a mental age of seven years and six months before beginning to read. However, the curve of the results of the Detroit test shows that the children with mental ages of six years and six months made progress practically as satisfactory as that of the children with higher mental ages. Since the results of the Detroit test show a higher correlation with reading progress than do the results of the Stanford-Binet test and since the Detroit test is more practicable to administer than the Stanford-Binet test, it seems reasonable to use the Detroit test as a basis for determining children's readiness for reading. The mental level of six years and six months is the breaking point in the curve, that is, the point beyond which there is very little gain in postponing the teaching of reading. This break is evident to some extent on the Stanford-Binet curve and markedly true on the curve of Detroit test scores.

Research/Figure 2 points to the same conclusion—that it pays to postpone beginning reading until a child has attained a mental age of six years and six months. If this practice is followed, 78 percent of the children may be expected to make satisfactory general progress, and 87 percent of the children may be expected to make satisfactory progress in learning sight words.

A similar study was carried on during the school year 1929–30 for the purpose of checking the results of the 1928–29 experiment.

All children who were mentally six years of age or more were taught reading from the beginning of the year. The pre-

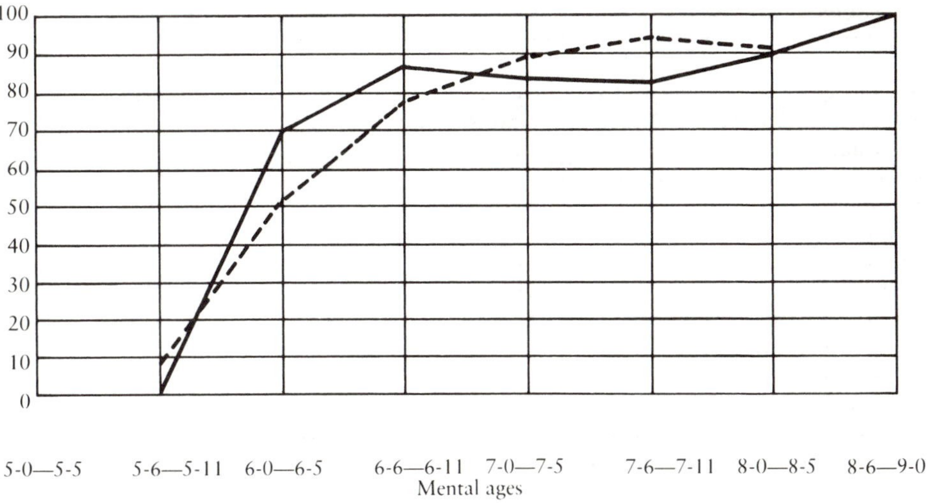

RESEARCH/FIGURE 2.
Percentages of children of various mental ages, as determined by the Detroit First-Grade Intelligence Test (solid line) and by the Stanford Revision of the Binet-Simon Scale (broken line), making satisfactory sight-word scores in school year 1928–29.

vious study made it seem futile to try to teach younger children, but a few with lower mental ages were taught reading for the purpose of the experiment. Mental ages were determined this time by the Detroit First-Grade Intelligence Test and the Pintner-Cunningham Primary Mental Test.

At the end of the year (June, 1930) the children were tested on the sight-word list and the Gray Standardized Oral Reading Check Test. A child was considered to have made satisfactory progress if he knew the entire sight-word list (139 words) and read the Gray test in fifty seconds or less with three errors or less. This standard has been set by Gray for Grade I. Research/Table 4 gives the number of children of each mental age and the percentage of children at each mental level making satisfactory scores in both sight words and oral reading. Research/Figure 3 makes the data of Research/Table 4 graphic. As in Research/Figures 1 and 2, the percentage of children who learned to read satisfactorily is greatest at the mental ages of six years and six months and of seven years. The curve for sight-word scores breaks at the mental age of six years and six months, while the curve on the Gray Standardized Oral Reading Check Test breaks at the mental age of seven.

The second year's experiment, therefore, in which a different set of children, different teachers, a different method of determining mental age, and a different method of determining progress were used and in which a whole year's work instead of a half year's was taken as the measure of progress confirms the experiment of the first year.

RESEARCH/TABLE 4.
Number of Children of Each Mental Age and Percentage Making Satisfactory Sight-Word Scores and Oral-Reading Scores

Mental Age in Years and Months*	Number of Children		Percentage Making Satisfactory Progress	
	Sight-Word Test	*Oral-Reading Test*	*Sight-Word Test*	*Oral-Reading Test*
5–0 to 5–5	1	0	....	....
5–6 to 5–11	10	9	....	....
6–0 to 6–5	25	24	64	58
6–6 to 6–11	23	23	87	83
7–0 to 7–5	23	23	87	91
7–6 to 7–11	12	12	83	92
8–0 to 8–5	5	5	....	....
8–6 to 9–0	1	1	....	....

*Average of scores on Detroit test and Pintner-Cunningham test.

Per cent

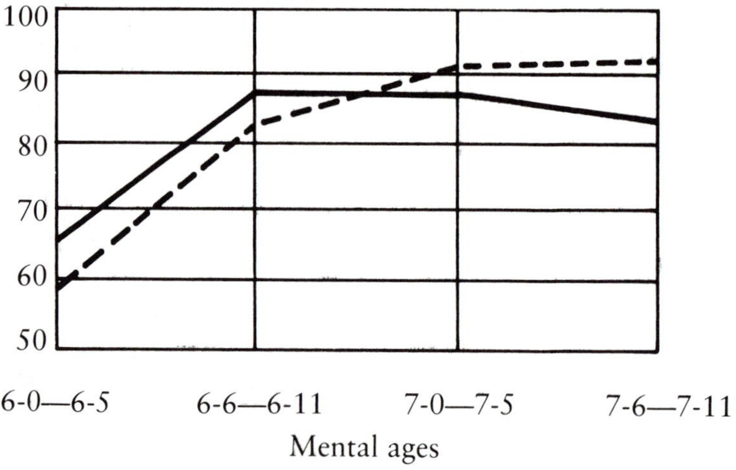

RESEARCH/FIGURE 3.
Percentages of children of various mental ages who in school year 1929–30 made satisfactory sight-word scores (solid line) and satisfactory scores on the Gray Standardized Oral Reading Check Test (broken line).

SUMMARY

1. Correlations between mental age and ability to learn to read, as measured by reading progress and sight-word scores, showed a fairly high degree of relationship. The correlations ranged from .50 to .65.

research

2. The correlations between mental age and reading progress were somewhat higher when mental age was measured by the Detroit First-Grade Intelligence Test than when mental age was measured by the Stanford Revision of the Binet-Simon Scale.

3. Mental age alone showed a larger degree of correlation with reading progress than did the intelligence quotient or the average of mental and chronological ages.

4. When the Detroit test was used as a basis for determining mental-age groups, the children who had a mental age of six years and six months made far better progress than did the less mature children and practically as satisfactory progress as did the children of a higher mental age.

5. When mental age was measured by the Stanford Revision of the Binet-Simon Scale, the children with a mental age of six years and six months again made very much better progress in reading than did those of less maturity, but they made less satisfactory progress than did those whose mental age was six months greater. The gain in ability up to six years and six months of mental age, however, was much greater than the subsequent gain.

6. A repetition of the experiment in 1929–30 with different teachers, different children, and different tests confirmed the earlier experiment in all its basic conclusions.

7. Consequently, it seems safe to state that, by postponing the teaching of reading until children reach a mental level of six and a half years, teachers can greatly decrease the chances of failure and discouragement and can correspondingly increase their efficiency.

A Critique of Mabel V. Morphett and Carleton Washburne's Study: When Should Children Begin To Read?

LANCE M. GENTILE

North Texas State University

The question of when a child should begin to read has been debated for years. In similar ways, many have labored over the issue of when a child should begin to walk or talk. No one has stepped forth to tell parents that their child should walk or talk at precisely 9.5 months; rather, authorities agree that within a range of time somewhere between 9 and 18 months, or even longer, children can be expected to begin walking and talking (Sheppard & Willoughby, 1975). Most people accept the fact that these functions occur at different times for each child and that usually a wide span of individual differences, both in the child and the home environment, are responsible for any accelerated or delayed development.

Unfortunately, however, many parents and educators have shown high anxiety over children's learning to read at exactly the "right" time. That time was stated specifically by Morphett and Washburne in their 1931 study. They indicated it was safer not to try to teach children to read before they reached a mental age of 6.5 years. Morphett and Washburne's findings gained almost universal acceptance and probably influenced educational programs as much as any single research investigation. To this day, many schools subscribe to the notion that a child is not ready to begin reading until he has reached this designated level.

Singer (1978) classified historical research in reading into the following three divisions:

1. Reading research that makes a difference.
2. Reading research that should have made a difference.
3. Reading research that made a difference, but should not have.

The study by Morphett and Washburne (1931) appeared in Singer's last category. This critique will offer some insights as to why it received such rueful billing.

Long before Morphett and Washburne published their results, the concept of a precise point at which to initiate reading instruction was proffered by others. One of the earliest pronouncements regarding reading readiness appeared in Rousseau's classic, *Emile*, (1762):

> When I thus get rid of children's lessons, I get rid of the chief cause of their sorrows, namely their books. Reading is the curse of childhood, yet it is almost the only

> occupation you can find for children. Emile, at 12 years old, will hardly know what a book is. 'But,' you say, 'he must, at least, know how to read.' When reading is of use to him, I admit he must learn to read, but till then he will only find it a nuisance. (pp. 80–81)

Later (1802), the Prussian philosopher Johann H. Pestalozzi said, "To instruct man is nothing more than to help nature develop in its own way, and the art of instruction depends primarily on harmonizing our messages, and the demands we make upon the child, with his powers at the moment" (Dechant, 1970, page 164). (This idea reappeared in the twentieth century and gained great acceptance as a result of the work by Jean Piaget, Eric Erickson, and Jerome Bruner.)

An American, John Dewey (Huey, 1908) made the definitive statement regarding the appropriate time to begin reading instruction. He said, "Present physiological knowledge points to the age of about eight years as early enough for anything more than an incidental attention to visual and written language-form" (page 304).

The following year (1899) another American, G. T. W. Patrick, reviewed the entire question of when to introduce a youngster to reading and writing. In an article that appeared in *Popular Science Monthly,* he raised the issue of whether reading and writing, any more than logic, should be studied by the young child. In doing so, Professor Patrick reaffirmed Dr. Dewey's thinking:

> Our increasing knowledge of the child's mind, his muscular and nervous systems, and his special senses, points indubitably to the conclusion that reading and writing are subjects which do not belong to the early years of school life, but to a later period, and that other subjects now studied later are better adapted to this early stage of development. (p. 385)

After the First World War, the burgeoning movement toward educational assessment gained a strong foothold in the public schools. Educators throughout the United States became eager to evaluate children's achievement. Since a youngster's success in school was generally seen as dependent on early reading growth, this area received a great deal of attention. Two studies conducted in 1927 paved the way for Morphett and Washburne's research.

Both Holmes (1927) and Reed (1927) revealed shocking data that because many children were unable to grasp the essentials of early reading, large numbers failed the first grade. Reed claimed that one in every six children failed at the end of the first semester in first grade, and that one in every eight failed at the end of the second semester. Moreover, Holmes concluded that these failures occurred because children were not ready to learn to read when they entered the first grade.

Finally, Morphett, as Supervisor of Research, and Washburne, as Superintendent of Schools (1931), collaborated with the Department of Educational Counsel at Winnetka, Illinois to determine the origins of children's reading difficulties in their district. They observed:

> In several instances the children's mental ages on entering the first grade has been low and that discouragement had resulted from their first attempts to learn to read. This discouragement sometimes resulted in a mental set against reading which lasted for years and which hampered all their school work. The research department, therefore, with the aid of the primary grade teachers, set about the task of discovering the

> period in the mental developmnent of children when, as a rule, there is the best chance of their learning to read readily. (p. 496)

Not only were the conclusions of their investigation instrumental in schools postponing reading instruction until children reached an approximate mental age of 6.5 years, but these findings also established the almost nationally accepted practice that a child had to be six years old to enter first grade. For the next thirty years this study was used as the basis for reading readiness programs as well (Lapp & Flood, 1978).

While Morphett and Washburne's effort, no doubt, was prompted by serious and justifiable concern, it is interesting to note that among the British, who speak the same language, a mental age of 4.5 to 5.5 years is deemed acceptable for beginning reading and children are enrolled in school at age five. Furthermore, in view of what we know regarding the complexities of the reading readiness issue today, interpretations or generalizations should never have extended beyond what the study was, i.e., *one* measure of *one* facet of the reading process.

Even more surprising than the fact that broad, sweeping applications were made throughout the educational community on the strength of this very limited investigation, was the willingness of most people to accept the validity of the research question itself. By posing the query, "When should children begin to read?" Morphett and Washburne implied that at a specific point, all youngsters were ready to begin reading. More important, they stated, "Mental age alone showed a larger degree of correlation with reading progress than did intelligence quotient or the average of mental and chronological ages" (see page 169). By singling out a child's mental age (for which the common formula is,

$$\text{Mental Age} = \frac{\text{Intelligence quotient} \times \text{Chronological age}}{100}),$$

and using it as the determining variable for when to begin reading instruction, Morphett and Washburne assigned pivotal importance to this one factor.

Mental age (M.A.) is a measure of the level of a child's mental maturity compared to youngsters of the same chronological age; the intelligence quotient (I.Q.) (for which the usual formula is,

$$\text{Intelligence Quotient} = \frac{\text{Mental Age}}{\text{Chronological Age}} \times 100)$$

is a measure of the rate of mental growth. The more advanced the child's M.A. is in relation to his or her chronological age, the higher the I.Q. Both are related to reading readiness and reading achievement. M.A. tends to be a slightly better indicator of learning in the near future; I.Q. the better long-range predictor (Harris & Sipay, 1979).

M.A. or I.Q. tests are fairly accurate in predicting reading readiness for children whose scores reflect antipodal extremes of the normal curve. Those toward the top can be expected to encounter fewer problems learning to read than others whose performance falls well below the mean. But, even using the scores for these youngsters to predict how well they may do in beginning reading can be risky unless one can determine how well a particular child performed on each test item and whether or not the test's questions match the learning demands of the reading program in

critique

which the child is enrolled. Furthermore, these tests tell us nothing about a youngster's motivation for learning to read and the quality of instructor or instruction.

Thus, Gates (1937) claimed that by approaching beginning reading instruction using small groups and by employing diverse teaching procedures, some children with mental ages of four and a half to five years may well learn to read; however, some teachers might use methods and materials that make it difficult for students whose mental ages are seven or more. In view of Gates's testimony, one may conclude that M.A. or I.Q. tests are probably helpful in assessing what children *can* do with respect to beginning reading, but the tests *cannot* consistently predict what children *will* do.

While persuasive evidence demonstrates a correlation between M.A. or I.Q. and learning to read, the correlations vary considerably depending upon which capacity tests are employed to measure achievement. Bond and Dykstra (1967) presented findings from fifteen USOE first-grade reading studies in which the correlations between intelligence scores and first-grade reading ranged from .45 to .56 with a median of .50. Like the Morphett and Washburne (1931) study, the majority of these studies relied upon correlational procedures to establish the relationships between beginning reading readiness and mental age (although other factors such as physical, social and emotional, experiential readiness, and success in beginning reading were examined too), but no correlation proved strong enough to indicate a single factor could possibly account for the differences in readiness. More significantly, correlational data do not lend themselves to inferences of causation. Karlin (1975) warned:

> A mathematical association between conditions does not imply that one produces the other; it is entirely possible that unknown factors account for any relationship that is found to exist. Perhaps one of the significant outcomes of all this research is the realization that readiness is a complex concept—that there are no simple methods for helping young children to prepare for what is for many a difficult learning task. (p. 99)

Nevertheless, armed with the erroneous assumption that mental age is the sole determinant of success or failure in beginning reading and without formulating any written hypotheses, Morphett and Washburne (1931) proceeded with the task of identifying an optimum time for teaching all children to read.

In September of 1928 and again in February of 1929, they tested 141 Winnetka first-graders to identify their mental ages upon entering school and after one-half year of instruction. Each child was administered the *Detroit First Grade Intelligence Test* (Detroit), and the *Stanford Revision of the Binet-Simon Scale* (Stanford).

These tests were probably the best instruments available at the time for measuring mental age; however, some interesting discrepancies have been cited by various critics. According to Cattell (1938), the *Detroit* is:

> easy to administer and the directions for giving and scoring are on the whole clear. The child is frequently asked to 'look at line No. . . . (so-and-so) and put a mark. . . .' Since many entering-first-grade pupils do not know the meaning of 'number' or how to read numerals, it would probably have been better to name the first picture on the next row and ask the child to look at it rather than the numbers. (pp. 101–102)

critique

Cattell's concerns have received recent confirmation through research by, among others, Downing and Oliver (1973–74). They demonstrated that many words used freely by beginning reading instructors represent concepts that are not understood, or are understood only partially, by many children. A study by Hardy, Stennet, and Smythe (1974) also indicated that such commonly used concepts as word, letter, sound of the letter, first, last, and middle, were not well understood by children entering first grade but were understood by the end of the school year.

It is plausible that some children's performance on the *Detroit* at the beginning of first grade, in the Morphett and Washburne (1931) study, was adversely affected simply because they did not understand various terminology used in the test's directions. These same children may have demonstrated a marked "increase" in reading ability at the end of a half year because they acquired some of these concepts during that period of instruction.

Furthermore, Cattell (1938) admonished that when using the *Detroit*, one must be careful interpreting the results because:

> Mental age norms are given based on 10,000 first grade children and run from 3.5 to 9.2. How this range of mental ages was obtained is not made clear. It is not often, if ever, that children are admitted to first grade at the age of three and a half years; and if enough eight- and nine-year olds to obtain satisfactory norms were admitted, it is not likely they would be typical first-grade children. (pp. 101–102)

The literature describing the strengths and weaknesses of the *Stanford* is plentiful. Harris (1965) stated summatively:

> The usefulness of the prediction tables depends on one's framework of thinking concerning the measurement of intelligence and his understanding of the logic of probability. These tables essentially assume a conventional definition of intelligence and its measurement and will appear most useful to those who define intelligence as a relatively fixed entity or stable quality of behavior. If we believe intelligence tests are achievement tests rather than estimates of aptitude, and if we believe the course of intellectual development can be closely regulated by controlling experience input, such tables have little value. (pp. B396 1542–43)

In light of Harris's statement, if one subscribes to the idea that reading readiness is based on a series of background experiences (as most authorities do today), as opposed to the heretofore belief that it resulted because of pre-established time lines (as some authorities felt during Morphett and Washburne's day), then any attempt to ascribe a level of mental age or fixed intelligence to the development of reading readiness is unreasonable. Wilson, Fleming, Burke, and Garrison (1938) implied that reading readiness is really early reading progress.

To their credit, the following year Morphett and Washburne replicated their study using different teachers, different children, a different method of determining mental age, and a different method of determining progress whereby a whole year's work instead of a half year's was taken as the measure of achievement. This effort confirmed the experiment of the previous year. Since the research question remained the same, the results are not surprising.

As in the first study, no description was made of the reading program's approach or materials other than to say, "the method, in accordance with the Win-

critique

netka technique, was largely individual so that the slow children did not retard the fast ones" (see page 163). In both instances, reading progress was measured in "steps." Twenty-one steps took the children through the beginning reading materials. The number of these steps that the child had completed by February in the first study, and June in the second, earmarked his or her achievement. In addition to these progress steps, a sight-word score for each child was determined. By February, in the first study, according to the Winnetka teachers, a child who seemed ready for reading from the beginning of the year would have successfully completed 13 progress steps and could have recognized 37 sight words. By June, in the second study, that same child would have completed all 21 progress steps and could have recognized 137 sight words. Although the authors assured those who studied their research that the first-grade teachers all "had several years of experience with the reading materials" (p. 163), they did not attempt to describe either the teachers or the materials. Because children were assigned to different teachers but no allowance was made for the variance in quality or quantity of instruction, which would no doubt have resulted by virtue of human differential, serves to taint the findings of this study.

More disturbing is the fact that Morphett and Washburne cited no other factors that may have contributed to children's success or failure in beginning reading, such as motivation, socio-economic level, experiential background, class size or classroom atmosphere, and teacher skill among others.

In conclusion, instead of considering the question of when children should begin to read, the authors would have added greatly to our understanding of beginning reading had they weighed the more enlightening and formidable issue of, "What are specific children ready to do in reading and when are they ready to do it?" This latter question differs from the former because it examines a youngster's capacity or knowledge, at any particular time, to respond appropriately to specific instructional methods or materials.

FOR FURTHER LEARNING

Those readers who are interested in continuing to explore the topic of beginning reading would find the following references helpful:

Durkin, D. A six-year study of children who learned to read in school at the age of four. *Reading Research Quarterly,* 1974–75, *10*(1), 9–16.

Durrell, D. D., & Murphy, H. A. Reading readiness research in elementary education, reading: 1933–1963. *Journal of Education,* Dec. 1963, *146,* 3–10.

Mason, G. E., & Prater, N. J. Early reading and reading instruction. *Elementary English,* May 1966, 483–488.

Ollila, K. (Ed.) *The kindergarten child and reading.* Newark, Del.: International Reading Association, 1977.

Smith, N. B. Readiness for reading, readiness for reading and related language arts. *Research Bulletin of the National Conference on Research in English,* 1950, 3–33.

---

for further learning

REFERENCES

Bond, G. L., & Dykstra, R. *Coordinating center for first grade reading instruction programs*. Final report, U.S. Dept. of Health, Education, and Welfare (Project No. X002), Minneapolis: University of Minnesota, 1967.

Cattell, P. In O. Buros (Ed.), *The Nineteen Thirty Eight Mental Measurements Yearbook*, Highland Park, N.J., 1938, 101–102.

Dechant, Emerald V. *Improving the teaching of reading* (2nd Ed.). Englewood Cliffs, N.J.: Prentice Hall, 1970.

Dewey, J. The primary education fetish. *New York Teachers' Monographs*, Nov. 1898, 315–328.

Downing, J., & Oliver, P. The child's conception of "a word." *Reading Research Quarterly*, 1973–74, 9(4), 568–582.

Gates, A. I. The necessary mental age for beginning reading. *The Elementary School Journal*, March 1937, 497–498.

Hardy, M., Stennet, R. G., & Smythe, P. C. Development of auditory and visual language concepts and relationship to instructional strategies in kindergarten. *Elementary English*, April 1974, *51*, 523–532.

Harris, A., & Sipay, E. R. *How to teach reading*. New York: Longman Publishers, 1979, 36.

Harris, D. B. Contemporary psychology. In O. Buros (Ed.), *The Sixth Mental Measurements Yearbook*. Highland Park, N.J.: The Gryphon Press, 1965, B396 1542–1543.

Holmes, M. C. Investigation of reading readiness of first grade entrants. *Childhood Education*, January 1927, *3*, 215–221.

Huey, Edmond B. *The psychology and pedagogy of reading*. New York: The McMillan Co., 1908.

Karlin, R. *Teaching elementary reading*. New York: Harcourt Brace Jovanovich, Inc., 1975, 99.

Lapp, D., & Flood, J. *Teaching reading to every child*. New York: Macmillan Publishing Co., 1978, 55.

Morphett, M. V., & Washburne, C. When should children begin to read? *Elementary School Journal*, March 1931, *31*, 496–501.

Patrick, G. T. W. Should children under ten learn to read and write? *Popular Science Monthly*, Jan. 1899, 382–391.

Reed, M. M. *An investigation of practices in the first grade admission and promotion*. New York: Bureau of Publications, Teachers College Press, Columbia University, 1927.

Rousseau, J. J. *Emile*. New York: Dutton Publishers, 1974, 80–81.

Sheppard, W. C., & Willoughby, R. H. *Child behavior: Learning and development*. Chicago: Rand McNally Publishing Co., 1975, 367–370; 517–525.

Singer, H. Research in reading that should make a difference in classroom instruction. In S. J. Samuels (Ed.), *What research has to say about reading*. Newark, Del.: International Reading Association, 1978, 59.

Wilson, F. T., Fleming, C. W., Burke, A., & Garrison, C. G. Reading progress in kindergarten and primary grades. *Elementary School Journal*, Feb. 1938, *38*, 442–449.

A Commentary on Gentile's Critique of Morphett and Washburne's Study: When Should Children Begin to Read?

LLOYD O. OLLILA

University of Victoria

The Morphett and Washburne study (1931), "When Should Children Begin to Read?," is an important and interesting one to review because of its historical significance and impact on North American primary education. As Gentile maintains, it "probably influenced educational programs as much as any single research investigation" (see page 171), helping to establish that a child had to be six years old to be in the grade-one program. Gentile's commentary is a good complement to the study. It provides the reader with a short historical background of the events leading to the study. It rightly questions the study's reliance on one single variable—mental age—to answer the problem of when a child should begin to read. Gentile also provides an excellent description of the concept of mental age and a discussion of its importance as a correlate of reading success. Gentile's analysis of the problems involved in using the *Detroit First Grade Intelligence Test* and the *Stanford Revision of the Binet Simon Scale* to measure mental age is very much to the point.

In commenting on this well-written critique, the present author will make further reference to and expand upon some of the issues and problems raised by Gentile's article. These comments focus on three areas: (1) the statistical issues and procedures of the study; (2) changes that have occurred meanwhile in children's backgrounds; (3) relevant research on beginning reading.

STATISTICAL ISSUES AND PROCEDURES

If one considers the Morphett and Washburne study in the perspective of the time when it was performed (1930s), its design and the statistical treatment of the data were quite satisfactory. However, when one looks at the study by the research standards of today, several limitations stand out. First, the correlations which were computed are all statistically significant with an N of 141 children. However, they are also somewhat moderate and only account for 24–42% of the variance. When one poses the question, "What percent of the variance of one variable is predictable from the variance of the other variable?," the results seem much less impressive. Certainly, higher correlations should be demanded in an applied situation (i.e., the determination of policy in school districts). Moreover, Gentile strongly warns against placing too much emphasis on the use of correlational data in any case.

Part of the Morphett and Washburne study was based on children's progress in learning sight words. Morphett and Washburne may well have obtained different results for their criteria of success in naming flashcards if they had changed their procedures in identifying how well the children knew those words. The study's criterion of success consisted of 13 out of 21 "steps" successfully completed and 37 out of 139 flashcards correctly identified. Instead of classifying children as meeting or not meeting these criteria, one could have computed the mean number of steps or the mean number of cards correct for each of the several chronological age groups. Those not meeting the Morphett and Washburne criteria may have been close to them or very far from them. This alternative method of reporting means resulted in different conclusions from the study.

Morphett and Washburne, to their credit, repeated the study to check the reliability of results of their earlier experiment. In general, the statistically reliable correlations, combined with their successful replication in the same school district, argue for high internal validity. That is, these findings are probably real for the conditions under which the data were collected. Other types of replications might have been carried out, however. Furthermore, the Morphett and Washburne data provided little in terms of extending the results to other situations; that is, they provided scant evidence for the external validity of the findings. This point is clearly emphasized by the Gates study (1937) as mentioned in Gentile's critique.

Gentile's critique also noted one fault of the study—that no attempt was made to describe either its teachers or the materials. It would have been interesting to see the results of the individual teachers in the study. Did they all end up with the same results? Was there a range of differences from one class to another in the results?

CHANGES IN CHILDREN'S BACKGROUNDS

If one were to replicate this study today, would the results be the same? One could make an educated guess of "No" partly based on the changes that likely have come about in the sample population. Children of today are quite different from their counterparts of the 1920s and 1930s. They have wider backgrounds of experience and conceptual knowledge, thanks to their greater mobility and a constant barrage of audio and visual stimuli from television, radio, etc. With the wealth of books and magazines and "educational" games available to them, they have greater exposure to the printed word. A growing number of children come to elementary school as graduates of nursery-school programs, programs that often include many of the activities once assigned to kindergartens. They also have more extensive vocabularies. One beginning reading authority, Hillerich (1977), suggests "Children today are ready (for reading) about a year sooner, if vocabulary development is the criterion for instruction."

OTHER RESEARCH RELEVANT TO THE STUDY

It is interesting to look at other studies investigating factors of success in beginning reading conducted since the Morphett and Washburne study. Gentile includes Gates's study (1937) to support his view that mental age, while helpful in predicting success in reading, cannot be relied on exclusively without considering other factors. Gates compared the results of four different types of reading instruction on grade-one students. He found that, in the highest achieving group, the children were successful with a mental age of 5.0. This group had good teachers and regular textbooks, but were also given supplementary practice and "teach and test" materials specifically designed for the curriculum. In the group that needed the highest mental age of 6.5 to be successful, the instruction was by whole group, with little individualized instruction, and the materials and facilities were less than adequate. In the other two groups, the children needed mental ages of 5.5 and 6.0 to be successful. Gates's results of nearly half a century ago are interesting because they coincide with and support the current opinion of a large number of beginning reading authorities such as Downing and Thackray (1975) and Durkin (1974), who would answer the question of when to begin reading with, when there is a good match between the child and the school's instructional program. In agreement with this modern view of readiness, Gentile concludes that it may be more profitable to set aside the question "When should children begin to read?" and, instead, focus more on the youngster and his/her ability to succeed with specific methods and materials.

The Gates study (1937) was published in the same decade as the Morphett and Washburne study (1931), yet had little impact compared with the latter. It is interesting to speculate why this was so. Perhaps the Morphett and Washburne study gained quick acceptance in part due to the prestigious progressive reputation that the Winnetka Public Schools (the district where the study took place) enjoyed. It also may have been easier for educators to accept the mental age concept than to adjust their program materials to the students' needs.

A number of studies currently in the literature show some children are learning to read before and during kindergarten. Sutton (1969) taught a selected group of children to read in kindergarten and followed their reading achievement through grade three. She found that, at the end of grade three, the early readers were still achieving better than the children who were not in the early reading program. Brezeinski's study (1967) of early reading in kindergarten involved nearly 4,000 children. He found that, at the grade-five level, those early readers whose instructional programs had been adjusted scored significantly higher on tests of reading than did their counterparts who began reading in grade one. Other studies on early reading have been done by Plessas & Oakes (1964), Durkin (1966), Fowler (1971), and Clark (1976).

The children in the above studies did not have to reach a mental age of 6.5 before successfully learning to read. Some children can and want to start reading earlier. One point that comes out repeatedly in these studies is the need to individualize instruction so that the teacher can help both the early starters and those who become ready later. The teacher can help the former group make further gains in reading development and the latter group to move into their first steps in beginning reading.

Although, as Gentile points out, mental age can be one factor accounting for differences in reading readiness, other factors also must be considered. Durkin's longitudinal study (1966) with 49 children (IQ range from 91 to 161) who learned to read before entering school gives an interesting description of some of these other factors. She found that these children had parents that liked to read and read to their children, thus providing an environment for the children to learn to read at home. The children had an early interest in written language and had the opportunity to look at books and use chalkboards, pencils, and paper. She followed these children for several years in school and they maintained better achievement than a control group who had not read in kindergarten.

Gentile observes that British children begin school at age five and a mental age of 4.5 to 5.5 is deemed acceptable for beginning reading. In Japan, Sakamoto (1981) reported that 86 percent of Japanese five-year-olds can read Kanji characters before entering school. He mentions that the mothers spend much time (starting when the child reaches six months of age) reading books with their children. This, he observes, is instrumental in the children reading before they start school. If, as the Morphett and Washburne study (1931) concluded, one needs a mental age of 6.5 to learn how to read successfully, then most of the five-year-old children in Britain and Japan would have to have this mental age when they start school—a statistical impossibility!

In conclusion, the present author feels Gentile's article gives a good review of the historical background for the Morphett and Washburne study (1931). Gentile is also adept at explaining the concept of "mental age" and placing it in the proper perspective for beginning reading. This commentary has mainly expanded upon the issues and problems raised by Gentile's critique and has sought to examine the statistical procedures of the original study, discuss changes that have occurred in children since Morphett and Washburne's original research, and describe other research relevant to the study of early readers. Giving children a successful start in reading is a vital part of schooling, and it is important that educators today continue to study this problem just as Morphett and Washburne did in 1931. Moreover, healthy initial reading experience is dependent upon teachers individualizing their instruction and matching the child to the reading methods and materials.

REFERENCES

Brzeinski, J. B. *Summary report of the effectiveness of teaching reading in the Denver public schools* (Cooperative project No. 5–0371). Denver: Denver Public Schools, 1967.

Clark, M. *Young fluent readers*. London: Heinemann Educational Books, 1976.

Downing, J., & Thackray, D. Reading readiness. (2nd ed.). *IKRA Teaching of Reading Monograph,* London: Hodder and Stoughton, 1975.

Durkin, D. *Children who read early*. New York: Teacher College Press, Columbia University, 1966.

Durkin, D. A six-year study of children who learned to read in school at the age of four. *Reading Research Quarterly,* 1974–75, *10*.

Fowler, W. A developmental learning strategy for early reading in a laboratory nursery school. *Interchange,* 1971, *2*, 106–125.

references

Gates, A. I. The necessary mental age for beginning reading. *Elementary School Journal,* March 1937, 497–498.

Hillerich, R. L. *Reading fundamentals for preschool and primary children.* Columbus, Ohio: Charles E. Merrill, 1977.

Morphett, M. V., & Washburne, C. When should children begin to read? *Elementary School Journal,* March 1931, *31.*

Plessas, G. P., & Oakes, C. R. Prereading experiences of selected early readers. *Reading Teacher,* 1964, *17,* 241–245.

Sakamoto, T. Beginning reading in Japan. In L. Ollila (Ed.), *Beginning reading instruction in different countries.* Newark, Del.: International Reading Association, 1981.

Sutton, M. H. Children who learned to read in kindergarten: a longitudinal study. *Reading Teacher,* April, 1969, *22,* 595–602.

section IV

PSYCHOLINGUISTICS AND READING

RESEARCH by Kenneth S. Goodman, *A Linguistic Study of Cues and Miscues in Reading*

CRITIQUE by Jay Blanchard

FOR FURTHER LEARNING

COMMENTARY by Kenneth S. Goodman

This section introduces the reader to Goodman's classic study which has been used to support the idea that words should be introduced to the child learning to read in context instead of in isolation. Blanchard's critique argues that causal implications have been drawn from the descriptive statistics of this study. Goodman defends his research and claims that an experimental paradigm would have been inappropriate for his purposes. He claims that his study has produced new knowledge and contributed to theory as well as research methodology.

A LINGUISTIC STUDY OF CUES AND MISCUES IN READING

KENNETH S. GOODMAN

Wayne State University

This is a report of the conclusions to date of a descriptive study of the oral reading of first-, second-, and third-grade children. It is a study in applied linguistics since linguistic knowledge and insights into language and language learning were used.

ASSUMPTIONS

In this study, reading has been defined as the active reconstruction of a message from written language. Reading must involve some level of comprehension. Nothing short of this comprehension is reading. I have assumed that all reading behavior is caused. It is cued or miscued during the child's interaction with written language. Research on reading must begin at this point of interaction. Reading is a psycholinguistic process. Linguistic science has identified the cue systems within language. The child learning to read his native language has already internalized these cue systems to the point where he is responding to them without being consciously aware of the process. To understand how children learn to read, we must learn how the individual experiences and abilities of children affect their ability to use language cues. We must also become aware of the differences and similarities between understanding oral language which uses sounds as symbol-units and written language which depends on graphic symbols.

This article is based on a paper delivered at the American Educational Research Association, Chicago, February 21, 1964, and subsequently published in *Elementary English,* Vol. 42, No. 6, October 1965.

CUE SYSTEMS IN READING

Here is a partial list of the systems operating to cue and miscue the reader as he interacts with written material. Within words there are:

- Letter-sound relationships
- Shape (or word configuration)
- Known "little words" in bigger words
- Whole known words
- Recurrent spelling patterns.

In the flow of language there are:

- Patterns of words (or function order)
- Inflection and inflectional agreement (examples: The boy runs. The boys run.)
- Function words such as noun markers (the, a, that, one, *etc.*)

- Intonation (which is poorly represented in writing by punctuation)
- The referential meaning of prior and subsequent language elements and whole utterances.

Cues external to language and the reader include:

- Pictures
- Prompting by teacher or peers
- Concrete objects
- Skill charts.

Cues within the reader include:

- His language facility with the dialect of his sub-culture
- His idiolect (his own personal version of the language)
- His experiential background (the reader responds to cues in terms of his own real or vicarious experiences)
- His conceptual background and ability (a reader can't read what he can't understand)
- Those reading attack skills and learning strategies he has acquired or been taught.

PROCEDURES

The subjects of this study were 100 children in grades 1, 2, and 3 who attend the same school in an industrial suburb of Detroit. Every second child on an alphabetic list of all children in these grades was included. There were an equal number of boys and girls from each room.

For reading materials, a sequence of stories was selected from a reading series not used in the school. With the publisher's permission the stories were dittoed on work sheets. A word list from each story was also duplicated.

An assistant called each subject individually out of the classroom. The subject was given a word list for a story at about his grade level. If the child missed many words, he was given a list for an earlier story. If he missed few or none he was given a more advanced story. Each child eventually had a word list of comparable difficulty. The number of words which each child missed on the lists, then, was a controlled variable.

Next the child was asked to read orally from the book the story on which his word list was based. The assistant noted all the child's oral reading behavior on the work sheets as the child read. The assistant refrained from any behavior which might cue the reader. Finally, each subject was to close his book and retell the story as best he could. He was not given advance notice that he would be asked to do this. The reading and retelling of the story was taped. Comparison between the structure of the language in the book and in the retold stories is underway utilizing the system of the Loban and Strickland studies.[1] It is not complete and will not be reported here.

WORDS IN LISTS AND IN STORIES

One concern of the research was the relative ability of children to recognize words in the lists and read the words in the stories. The expectation was that children would read many words in sto-

[1]Walter Loban, *The Language of Elementary School Children.* Champaign; National Council of Teachers of English, 1963 and Ruth Strickland, *The Language of Elementary School Children,* Bulletin of The School of Education, Indiana University, 38, July, 1962.

RESEARCH/TABLE 1
Average words missed in list and in story

	List Average	Also Missed in Story Average	Percent	Ratio
Grade 1	9.5	3.4	38%	2.8:1
Grade 2	20.1	5.1	25%	3.9:1
Grade 3	18.8	3.4	18%	5.5:1

ries which they could not recognize in lists. I reasoned that, in lists, children had only cues *within* printed words while in stories they had the additional cues in the flow of language. I was not disappointed.

As is shown in Research/Table 1, the children in this study were able to read many words in context which they couldn't read from lists. Average first graders read almost two out of three words in the story which they missed on the list. The average second grader missed only one-fourth of the words in the story which he failed to recognize on the list. Third graders were able to get, in the stories, all but 18 percent of the words which they did not know in the list.

As Research/Table 2 shows, except for a small group of first graders and a very few second and third graders, all the children in this study could read correctly in the story at least half of the words that they could not recognize on the lists. Sixty-nine percent of first-grade children could "get" two-thirds or more of their list errors right in reading the story. Sixty-six percent of the second graders could read three-fourths or more of their errors in the story. The comparable group of third graders could get better than four out of five. The children in successive grades in this study were increasingly efficient in using cue systems outside of words.

At the same time, as Research/Table 3 shows, children in successive grades were making greater attempts to use word attack skills, here defined as responses to *cue systems within words*. About half of the listed errors of first graders were omissions. The children did not attempt to figure the words out by using any available cues. Second-grade children showed an increased tendency to try to "get" the word. This is shown by the somewhat higher percent of substitutions among the list errors of second-grade children. Third graders showed a pronounced increase in the percent of substitutions among their list errors. Children in successive grades used work

RESEARCH/TABLE 2
Ability to read words in context which were missed on list

	Less Than ½	More Than ½	More Than ⅔	More Than ¾	More Than ⅘	N
Grade 1	11%	89%*	69%	49%	26%	35
Grade 2	3%	97%	81%	66%	50%	32
Grade 3	6%	94%	91%	76%	67%	33

*Cumulative percents of subjects

RESEARCH/TABLE 3
Total errors and substitution errors on lists

	List Errors Average	Included Substitutions Average	Percent	Ratio
Grade 1	9.5	4.9	52%	1.9:1
Grade 2	20.1	11.5	57%	1.3:1
Grade 3	18.1	14.3	79%	1.3:1

attack skills with increased frequency though not necessarily with increased efficiency.

There was no instance of a child getting a word right on the list but missing it consistently in the story. But often children made an incorrect substitution in the reading of the story in individual occurrences of known words. As Research/Table 4 indicates, second and third graders made more than twice as many one-time substitutions per line read as first graders. Third graders made more substitutions per line than second graders. Three possible causes of these one-time substitutions may be (1) overuse of cues within words to the exclusion of other cues, (2) miscuing by book language which differs from the language as the child knows it, and (3) ineffective use of language cues.

REGRESSIONS IN READING

This study also was concerned with regressions in reading, that is repeating one or more words. No statistics are needed to support one observation: virtually every regression which the children in this study made was for the purpose of correcting previous reading.

When a child missed a word on a list, unless he corrected it immediately he seldom ever went back. In reading the story, however, children frequently repeated words or groups of words, almost always to make a correction. Regressions themselves, then, were not errors but attempts (usually but not always successfully) to correct prior errors.

If regressions are divided into two groups, word regressions—those which involve one word immediately repeated—and phrase regressions—those which include repeating two or more words—the two types each represent almost exactly half the regressions at each of the grade levels. (See Research/Table 5)

Regressions seem to function in children's reading about like this: if the child makes an error in reading which he realizes is inconsistent with prior cues, he reevaluates the cues and corrects his error before continuing. Otherwise, he

RESEARCH/TABLE 4
One-time substitutions for known words in stories

	Average Substitutions	Average Lines Read	Substitutions Per Line Read
Grade 1	3.7	50.2	.074
Grade 2	14.9	126.2	.118
Grade 3	16.9	118.7	.142

RESEARCH/TABLE 5
Regressions in reading

	First Grade		Second Grade		Third Grade	
	Per Child	Per Line Read	Per Child	Per Line Read	Per Child	Per Line Read
Word Only						
To correct word	2.40	.048	10.11	.090	10.30	.087
To correct intonation on word	.09	.002	.49	.004	1.42	.012
Total	2.49	.050	10.60	.094	11.72	.099
*Phrase**						
To correct word by repeating phrase	1.54	.031	5.77	.052	7.54	.061
To rephrase	.29	.006	1.97	.018	1.03	.009
To change intonation	.52	.011	2.83	.026	2.76	.023
Total	2.35	.048	10.57	.096	11.33	.093

*For these purposes a phrase is considered *any* two or more consecutive words.

reads on encountering more cues which are inconsistent with his errors. Eventually he becomes aware that the cues cannot be reconciled and retraces his footsteps to find the source of the inconsistency. Thus, regressions in reading are due to redundant cues in language. They are self-corrections which play a vital role in children's learning to read. In two cases errors go uncorrected: (1) if the error makes no difference to the meaning of the passage, and (2) if the reader is relying so heavily on analytical techniques using only cues within words that he has lost the meaning altogether.

A PRELIMINARY LINGUISTIC TAXONOMY

In a third phase of the study I categorized all errors of the subjects according to linguistic terminology. This analysis produced the *Preliminary Linguistic Taxonomy of Cues and Miscues in Reading*. The Taxonomy will be published in a separate article.

It should be noted that the 100 subjects of this study, though all attend the same school and have learned to read with a fairly consistent methodology, exhibited virtually every kind of reading difficulty and deviation which I could predict linguistically.

IMPLICATIONS OF THIS STUDY

There are several implications to be drawn from the description of the oral reading of these children. Some practices in the teaching of reading are made suspect.

1. Introducing new words out of context before new stories are introduced to children does not appear to be necessary or desirable.
2. Prompting children or correcting them when they read orally also appears to

be unnecessary and undesirable in view of the self-correction which language cues in children.

3. Our fixation on eye fixations and our mania for devices which eliminate regressions in reading seem to be due to a lamentable failure to recognize what was obvious in this study: that regressions are the means by which the child corrects himself and learns.

4. Shotgun teaching of so-called phonic skills to whole classes or groups at the same time seems highly questionable in view of the extreme diversity of the difficulties children displayed in this study. No single difficulty seemed general enough to warrant this approach. In fact, it is most likely that at least as many children are suffering from difficulties caused by overusing particular learning strategies in reading as are suffering from a lack of such strategies.

5. The children in this study found it harder to recognize words than to read them in stories. Eventually I believe we must abandon our concentration on words in teaching reading and develop a theory of reading and a methodology which puts the focus where it belongs: on language.

A Critique of Kenneth Goodman's: A Linguistic Study of Cues and Miscues in Reading

JAY BLANCHARD

Texas Tech University

INTRODUCTION

K. S. Goodman's 1965 study investigating the cue systems surrounding printed language in context and isolation through linguistic analysis has become a classic in the field of reading research (Pearson, 1978). It was first presented at the American Educational Research Association in Chicago, 1964, and subsequently appeared in *Elementary English* (Vol. 42, No. 6, pp. 639–643). At the time of the study, many linguists, psycholinguists, reading theorists, and practitioners seemed to have embraced Goodman's indictments of certain aspects of phonics instruction as well as the commonly held reading practice of introducing new words in isolation before a story. The study clearly supported, within its experimental framework, the overwhelming contribution of contextual semantics in word pronunciation with beginning readers. Since that time, Goodman's research has been widely cited:

> Goodman's (1965) contextual hypothesis suggests that if words are presented outside meaningful context, children are not given the opportunity to use the syntactic and semantic cues available in language to anticipate unfamiliar words and are forced to rely only on visual cues within the word itself (Hughes, 1977).
>
> First-, second-, and third-grade children could read many more words in prose passages than the same words in lists, and this ability increased with grade level. (Gibson and Levin, 1975)
>
> . . . beginning readers were able to recognize words in running text that they were unable to recognize in a word list. (Wood, 1976)
>
> . . . formulated a linguistic or context hypothesis based on his demonstration that contextual contents facilitated identification of words children could not recognize when the words were presented in isolation. He explained that performance on the novel words improved because syntactic and semantic constraints of the sentences provided cues for anticipating the unknown words. (Singer, Samuels, and Spiroff, 1976)
>
> Goodman's work on reading cues and miscues shows that children recognize more words in context than in isolation. (Hall, Ribovich, and Ramig, 1979)
>
> Goodman's study showed that primary school children may be unable to decode words in isolation but are able to read the same words successfully in a running

This paper was first published in *Reading Psychology,* 1979, *1*(1), 67–72, and is reprinted by permission of the publisher.

> context. When given a list of words to learn, children were "calling names," a procedure more difficult than reading. (Athey, 1971)
>
> Goodman . . . has shown that although children may be unable to decode words in isolation, they deal successfully with the same words in a running context. (Ruddell, 1969)
>
> . . . young readers were less accurate in reading words presented in a list than when the same words were incorporated into stories. (Weber, 1970)

These are but a few of the many possible citations one finds with reference to Goodman's work. However, in this writer's opinion, no research effort, whether theoretical or instructional, investigating the role of decoding skill in isolation and its transformation to context should be without it. But, as can be seen, there exists some variation in just the few comments cited above regarding Goodman's original study. Whether this "freedom of interpretation" has contributed to this study's widespread popularity is anyone's guess. However, the unfortunate outcome remains: readers make personal interpretations from citations, not the original research, and each generation of readers gets further from the truth. Therefore, a review of Goodman's procedures, findings, and implications would seem pertinent.

STUDY PROCEDURES

Subjects

Goodman's study used 100 elementary school children, (from one elementary school), in an industrial suburb of Detroit. This included 35 first-, 32 second-, and 33 third-graders that "exhibited virtually every kind of reading difficulty and deviation which I could predict linguistically . . . and had learned to read with a fairly consistent methodology."

Subjects were randomly selected in alternation (every second child) from alphabetic class lists. There were equal numbers of boys and girls selected from each classroom. Subjects on a one-to-one basis with a research assistant read a word list (orally), read a story (orally) and retold the story as best they could.

Materials

At each grade level a "sequence of stories was selected from a reading series not used in the school." From each story a word list was made. Each subject was given a word list "for a story at about his grade level."

Method

A subject, with a research assistant listening and recording oral reading errors, read a word list. "If a child missed many words, he was given a list for an earlier story.

If he missed a few or none he was given a more advanced story. Each child eventually had a word list of comparable difficulty." The subject then read (orally) a story upon which the last word list (or perhaps only word list read) was based. Each subject then retold the story, without prior instructions and without the story to aid recall.

Study Findings

There would seem to be an error in Critique/Table 1 in the Grade 1 figures. If the *list average* and *also missed in story average* are correct, *percent* should be 36 instead of 38.

CRITIQUE/TABLE 1
Average words missed in list and in story

		Also Missed in Story		
	Average	Average	Percent	Ratio
Grade 1	9.5	3.4	38%	2.8:1
Grade 2	20.1	5.1	25%	3.9:1
Grade 3	18.8	3.4	18%	5.5:1

Critique/Tables 1 through 5 used with permission from "Linguistic Study of Cues and Miscues in Reading" by K. S. Goodman. Originally appeared in *Elementary English, Vol. 42, No. 6, October 1965*. National Council of Teachers of English, Urbana, Ill.

Goodman concluded from the findings in the first table: Average first graders could read almost two out of three words in the story they missed on the list. The average second grader missed only one-fourth of the words in the story which s/he failed to recognize on the list. Third graders were able to get, in the stories, all but 18 pecent of the words which they did not know in the list (see p. 190).

CRITIQUE/TABLE 2
Ability to read words in context which were missed on list

	Less Than ½	More Than ½	More Than ⅔	More Than ¾	More Than ⅘	N
Grade 1	11%	89%*	69%	49%	26%	35
Grade 2	3%	97%	81%	66%	50%	32
Grade 3	6%	94%	91%	76%	67%	33

*Cumulative percents of subjects.

Goodman concluded from the findings in the second table: Except for a small group of first graders and a very few second and third graders, all the children . . . could read correctly in the story at least half of the words they did not recognize on the lists (see p. 190).

CRITIQUE/TABLE 3
Total errors and substitution errors on lists

	List Errors Average	Included Substitutions Average	Percent	Ratio
Grade 1	9.5	4.9	52%	1.9:1
Grade 2	20.1	11.5	57%	1.3:1
Grade 3	18.1	14.3	79%	1.3:1

There would seem to be an error in Critique/Table 3. In grade 3, *list errors average*, 18.1 should be 18.8 and if this is the case, *included substitutions percent* should be 76.

Goodman concluded from the findings in the third table: Children in successive grades were making greater attempts to use word attack skills . . . About half of the listed errors of first graders were omissions. The children did not attempt to figure the words out by using any available cues. Second-grade children showed an increased tendency to try to "get" the words. This is shown by a somewhat higher percent of substitutions among the list errors of second-grade children. Third graders showed a pronounced increase in the percent of substitutions among their list errors (see p. 190).

CRITIQUE/TABLE 4
One-time substitutions for known words in stories

	Average Substitutions	Average Lines Read	Substitutions Per Line Read
Grade 1	3.7	50.2	.074
Grade 2	14.9	126.2	.118
Grade 3	16.9	118.7	.142

Goodman concluded from the findings in the fourth table: . . . second and third graders made more than twice as many one-time substitutions per line read as first graders. Third graders made more substitutions per line than second graders (see p. 190). Goodman also felt it important to note:

There was no instance of a child getting a word right on the list but missing it consistently in the story. But often children made an incorrect substitution in the reading of the story in individual occurrences of known words (see p. 190).

Goodman concluded from the findings in the fifth table:

. . . virtually every regression which the children in this study made was for the purpose of correcting previous reading (see p. 190).

Goodman did not feel this was the case when a subject missed a word on a list; there "seldom" was a regression on a word list.

In reading the story, however, children frequently repeated words or groups of words, almost always to make a correction. Regressions themselves, then, were not errors but attempts (usually but not always successful) to correct prior errors (see p. 190).

CRITIQUE/TABLE 5
Regressions in Reading

	First Grade		Second Grade		Third Grade	
	Per Child	Per Line Read	Per Child	Per Line Read	Per Child	Per Line Read
Words Only						
To correct word	2.40	.048	10.11	.090	10.30	.087
To correct intonation on word	.09	.002	.49	.004	1.42	.012
Total	2.49	.050	10.60	.094	11.72	.099
*Phrase**						
To correct word by repeating phrase	1.54	.031	5.77	.052	7.54	.061
To rephrase	.29	.006	1.97	.018	1.03	.009
To change intonation	.52	.011	2.83	.026	2.76	.023
Total	2.35	.048	10.57	.096	11.33	.093

*For these purposes a phrase is considered any two or more consecutive words. Regression in the study represented a child repeating one or more words.

> Goodman noted that if the regressions were divided into two types: . . . those which involve one word immediately repeated and phrase regressions—those which include repeating two or more words—the two types represent almost exactly half the regressions at each grade level (see p. 190).

STUDY IMPLICATIONS

Based on the procedures and findings of the study, Goodman drew the following implications:

1. Introducing new words out of context before new stories are introduced to children does not appear to be necessary or desirable.
2. Prompting children or correcting them when they read orally also appears to be unnecessary and undesirable in view of the self-correction which language cues in children.
3. . . . regressions are the means by which the child corrects himself and learns.
4. Shotgun teaching of so-called phonic skills to whole classes or groups at the same time seems highly questionable in view of the extreme diversity of the difficulties children displayed in this study.
5. The children in this study found it harder to recognize words than to read them in stories.

It is doubtful that Goodman intended or envisioned "classic" status for his research. Nevertheless, the implications have gained a wide and captive audience among educational theorists and practitioners. This comes as somewhat of a surprise when one scrutinizes the ability of the research to support Goodman's implications. For example, a number of causal implications have been drawn from descriptive statistics. A more robust verification of the findings and the causal implications might be possible if sufficient methodological information had been provided in the article; it was not. (This is probably the reason why attempts to replicate the findings have been unsuccessful. Pearson, 1978) In addition, the study's only measure of reading or linguistic achievement is oral reading fluency. There were no other measures of achievement (i.e., comprehension tests) that might have provided a clearer picture of the effects of introducing new words in isolation rather than in context. Furthermore, there were no control groups or other training groups besides the ones receiving words in isolation training. There were no groups that received training on new words in context. Goodman thus failed to support his most echoed implication: Subjects would "learn" better as a result of encountering new words in context. In conclusion, the only implication that seems to have empirical support is that children found it harder to recognize words (i.e., in isolation) than to read them in stories.

Goodman's study offers some answers to many of the more puzzling questions concerning the role of context in linguistic awareness and reading instructional theory. At best, these answers emanate from a seminal research effort which has fostered an abundance of additional research based on an unwavering belief in the veracity of Goodman's answers. At their worst, these answers are based on what seems to be unreliable and invalid research findings. The truth probably lies somewhere between these two views. Undoubtedly, a substantial number of those who support Goodman's findings and his implications do so for intuitive rather than empirical reasons: perhaps this is why the study has gained "classic" status.

FOR FURTHER LEARNING

Those readers who are interested in continuing to explore the topic of psycholinguistics would find the following references helpful:

Barr, R. The influence of instructional condition on word recognition errors. *Reading Research Quarterly,* 1972, *7,* 509–529.

Barr, R. The effect of instruction on pupil reading strategies. *Reading Research Quarterly,* 1975, *10,* 555–582.

Biemiller, A. The development of the use of graphic and contextual information as children learn to read. *Reading Research Quarterly,* 1970, *6,* 75–96.

Goodman, K. S. The psycholinguistic nature of the reading process. In K. S. Goodman (Ed.) *The psycholinguistic nature of the reading process.* Detroit: Wayne State University Press, 1968, 15–26.

Goodman, K. S. Words and morphemes in reading. In K. S. Goodman & J. T. Fleming (Eds.), *Psycholinguistics and the teaching of reading.* Newark, Del.: International Reading Association, 1969, 25–33.

Goodman, K. S. Reading: A psycholinguistic guessing game. In H. Singer & R. Ruddell (Eds.), *Theoretical models and processes of reading.* Newark, Del.: International Reading Association, 1970, 259–271.

Goodman, K. S. Analysis of oral reading miscues: Applied psycholinguistics. In F. Smith (Ed.), *Psycholinguistics and reading.* Toronto: Holt, Rinehart, & Winston, 1973a, 158–176.

Goodman, K. S. Miscues: Windows on the reading process. In K. S. Goodman (Ed.), *Miscue analysis.* Urbana, Ill.: ERIC Clearinghouse, 1973b, 3–14.

Goodman, K. S. Do you have to be smart to read? Do you have to read to be smart? *Reading Teacher,* 1975, *28,* 625–632.

Goodman, K. S., & Burke, C. L. *Theoretically based studies of patterns of miscues in oral reading performance.* (Final Report). Washington, D.C.: Office of Education, 1973. (ERIC: Document Reproduction Service No. ED 079 708).

Goodman, Y. M. A psycholinguistic description of observed oral reading phenomena in selected young beginning readers. (Doctoral dissertation, Wayne State University, 1967). *Dissertation Abstracts International,* 1968, *29,* 1A-350A. (University Microfilms No. 68–9961).

Goodman, Y. M., & Burke, C. L. *Reading miscue inventory.* New York: Macmillan, 1972.

Kolers, P. A. Reading is only incidentally visual. In K. S. Goodman & J. T. Fleming (Eds.), *Psycholinguistics and the teaching of reading.* Newark, Del.: International Reading Association, 1969, 8–16.

Menosky, D. M. A psycholinguistic description of oral reading miscues generated during the reading of varying portions of text by selected readers from grades two, four, six, and eight. (Doctoral dissertation, Wayne State University, 1971). *Dissertation Abstracts International,* 1972, *32* (11), 6108–A. (University Microfilms No. 72–14, 600).

Perfetti, C. A., & Hogabaum, T. H. Relationship between single word decoding and reading comprehension skill. *Journal of Educational Psychology,* 1975, *67,* 461–469.

Shankweiler, D., & Liberman, I. Y. Misreading: A search for cues. In J. F. Kavanaugh & I. G. Mattingly (Eds.), *Language by ear and by eye: The relationship between speech and reading.* Cambridge, Mass.: MIT Press, 1972, 293–317.

Smith, F. *Understanding reading.* Toronto: Holt, Rinehart, & Winston, 1971.

Smith, F. *Psycholinguistics and reading.* Toronto: Holt, Rinehart, & Winston, 1973.

Smith, F. *Comprehension and learning.* Toronto: Holt, Rinehart, & Winston, 1975.

Wiener, M., & Cromer, W. Reading and reading difficulty: A conceptual analysis. *Harvard Educational Review,* 1967, *37,* 620–643.

REFERENCES

Athey, I. J. Language models and reading. In F. B. Davis (Ed.), *The literature of research in reading with emphasis on models.* New Brunswick, N.J.: Graduate School of Education, Rutgers State University, 1971.

Gibson, E. J., & Levin, H. *The psychology of reading.* Cambridge, Mass.: The MIT Press, 1971.

Goodman, K. A linguistic study of cues and miscues in reading. *Elementary English,* 1965, *42*(6), 631–643.

Hall, M. A., Ribovich, J. R., & Ramig, C. J. *Reading and the elementary school child* (2nd ed.). New York: D. Van Nostrand, 1979.

Highes, M. A. *Word identification and comprehension in learning to read.* Unpublished doctoral dissertation, University of Toronto, 1977.

Pearson, P. D. On bridging gaps and spanning chasms. *Curriculum Inquiry,* 1978, *8,* 353–362.

Ruddell, R. R. Psycholinguistic implications for a systems of communication model. In K. S. Goodman and J. T. Fleming (Eds.), *Psycholinguistics and the teaching of reading.* Newark, Del.: International Reading Association, 1969.

Singer, H., Samuels, S. J., & Spiroff, J. The effects of pictures and contextual conditions on learning responses to printed words. In H. Singer & R. B. Ruddell (Eds.), *Theoretical models and processes of reading.* Newark, Del.: International Reading Association, 1976.

Weber, R. M. First graders' use of grammatical context in reading. In H. Levin & J. P. Williams (Eds.), *Basic studies in reading,* New York: Basic Books, 1970.

Wood, M. N. *A multivariate analysis of beginning readers' recognition of taught words in four contextual settings.* Unpublished doctoral dissertation, Texas Woman's University, 1976.

A Commentary on Blanchard's Critique of Goodman's: A Linguistic Study of Cues and Miscues in Reading

KENNETH S. GOODMAN

The University of Arizona

I feel obliged to comment on, and in effect critique, the recent critique of the report on my 1963–64 study in the 1965 volume of *Elementary English*.

First a little background. The report Dr. Blanchard discussed deals with some (but not all) aspects of a larger descriptive study of the reading of 100 first, second, and third grade readers. That study was the beginning of my miscue research. It lead to an early crude version of the taxonomy of oral reading miscues, and this report was in fact the first time I used the term "miscue" in print. Neither this study nor any part of it used an experimental paradigm; that would have been inappropriate for the goals. But, since the same subjects were asked to perform several tasks, a comparison of their performances on these tasks could be considered an experiment.

The study was not funded except for a few hundred dollars of seed money provided by Wayne State University. Dr. Blanchard is quite right. Not even in my wildest yearning as a fledgling researcher and underpaid assistant professor did I foresee that anyone would come to consider this study and particularly the aspects in the report as classic. Many teachers were at that time aware that children read words more easily in continuous text than in isolation. I felt that my data demonstrated that and supported a linguistic explanation (not quite yet a theory) of why it happened. At the time of the report, the general reaction was "we know that."

Dr. Blanchard has carefully and fairly represented my data and my findings. Those findings were indeed overwhelming. Of 35 first graders, only four could read less than half the words they'd missed in isolation in the story. Only one second grader of 32 and two third graders of 33 fell short of that criterion.

Those results were so overwhelming that I never again included a word list as a task in research.

Dr. Blanchard does not dispute these findings, nor does anyone he cites including Pearson, whose attempted replication produced results consistent with mine though their trend was more moderate. The studies of Wood and Hughes whom he cites and Hudelson-López (1977, see references) whom he doesn't cite all produced results which were consistent with mine. The Huddelson study (1977) did so with readers of Spanish.

This paper was first published in *Reading Psychology*, 1980, *1*(3), 192–194, and is reprinted by permission of the publisher.

Dr. Blanchard does have negative criticisms of the methodology and implicitly of the support for the findings. He confuses these criticisms, however, by relating them to the implications I draw from the research. Implications are not findings; rather they are *always* attempts to suggest what the findings might mean.

He says, "The only implication that seems to have empirical support is children found it harder to recognize words (i.e., in isolation) than to read them in stories." That's not an implication; that's a finding. One of my *implications* from that finding *and* from the developing theoretical base that underlies the study is that "introducing new words out of context before new stories are introduced to children does not appear to be necessary or desirable." Such an implication is consistent with the findings but it goes further, using logic to infer that it does not make sense to use a hard task to prepare for an easy one, particularly since the goal of reading instruction is reading connected discourse, not word lists. Another implication is that the focus in instruction and research should shift from words to language. After 18 years, that seems to have become a reality in research.

Blanchard's confusion over what research implications are can be seen in this statement: "A number of causal implications have been drawn from descriptive statistics." The five implications he cites, with the exception of the finding he's mislabeled, are all based not only on the descriptive findings but also on logic and theory. Furthermore, nothing about them is "causal." Perhaps he meant to say I have implied causal relationship. I have, since I relate the findings to the theory arguing that the causes are in the more abundant cues provided in connected discourse not present in isolated words. He does not, however, reject that implication.

What Blanchard seems to find most objectionable is my methodology. He says, "The study's only measures of reading or linguistic achievement is oral reading fluency." He believes other measures of achievement (i.e., comprehension tests) might have helped. I did use story retelling to study comprehension. These findings were not reported in the article because they were not pertinent to the issue the article focused on. There were, he says, no control groups or training groups other than those "receiving words in isolation training." There were actually no training groups. There was no training. I suppose Dr. Blanchard is implying that by asking pupils to read a word list first, they've somehow been trained on the words and that shows in better story performance. How that could be is hard to imagine. We gave no help in either task. We supplied no words, made no positive or negative comments. Our theory told us that seeing a word once on a list with no researcher aid or feedback would have little effect on the story reading but if subjects read the story first and encountered some words ten or more times in different syntactic and semantic contexts there certainly would have been an influence on list response. As for control groups, Dr. Blanchard has apparently assumed that all research must use an experimental design paradigm or perhaps he is unaware of non-experimental research paradigms.

Most puzzling is his complaint that I did not provide sufficient methodological information. My methodology was quite simple, as he himself reported. Neither in the research procedures nor in the statistical treatment of the data is anything unreported. The latter are simple frequencies, percentages, means and ratios, befitting a descriptive study. My sample was half of the whole population randomly selected. Each child responded to a word list and read a whole story at an appropriate level of difficulty. How any more information would make a verification more "robust" (whatever that could mean in this context) Dr. Blanchard doesn't indicate.

This study must be understood as a non-experimental attempt to study the full scope of what readers do when they read a complete story. To my knowledge, it was the first such attempt. The use of an experimental paradigm would have been inappropriate to this goal. Experimental studies can only at best confirm what we know. This study produced new knowledge and contributed to theory and to research methodology.

Blanchard states, "Goodman thus failed to support his most echoed implication: 'Subjects would learn better as a result of encountering new words in context.' " I submit that he has built no case to challenge either the findings or the implication. Furthermore, this report did not deal with how pupils learn. It dealt with what they do when they are asked to read lists and connected discourse.

Blanchard refers to "a wide and captive audience among educational theorists and practitioners" who have accepted my implications. If he'll tell me where they are being held captive, I'll be glad to join a campaign for their liberation.

Meanwhile, I'd like to suggest why the article is so widely cited and why its findings and implications have gained such wide acceptance:

1. The report offered both data and theory to support its conclusions.
2. It dealt with a rather simple but basic aspect of the reading process: the relationship of words to connected discourse.
3. It broke new ground methodologically and theoretically. It was among the first studies based on scientific linguistics.
4. Subsequent research and practice has supported the validity of the findings.
5. There has been a growing awareness during the eighteen years since this was published that the implications are valid, that they are important, and that they represent the early beginning of a scientific attempt to understand the reading process.

REFERENCE

Hudelson-López, Sarah. Children's use of contextual clues in reading Spanish. *The Reading Teacher*, Vol. *30*, No. 7, April, 1977, pp. 735–740.

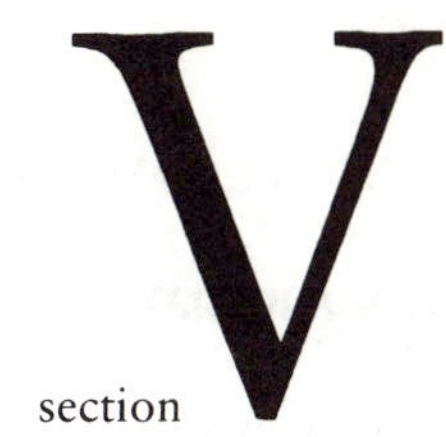

section V

READING COMPREHENSION

RESEARCH by Edward Thorndike, *Reading as Reasoning: A Study of Mistakes in Paragraph Reading*

CRITIQUE by Tom Nicholson

FOR FURTHER LEARNING

COMMENTARY by Richard L. Allington

RESEARCH by Fredrick B. Davis, *Fundamental Factors of Comprehension in Reading*

CRITIQUE by Dale D. Johnson, Susan Toms-Bronowski and Ray R. Buss

FOR FURTHER LEARNING

COMMENTARY by Camille L. Z. Blachowicz

RESEARCH by F. J. Guszak, *Teacher Questioning and Reading*

CRITIQUE by P. David Pearson

FOR FURTHER LEARNING

COMMENTARY by F. J. Guszak

RESEARCH by Dolores Durkin, *What Classroom Observations Reveal About Reading Comprehension Instruction*, and, *Reading Comprehension Instruction in Five Basal Reader Series*

CRITIQUE by Walter H. McGinitie

FOR FURTHER LEARNING

COMMENTARY by Dolores Durkin

This section introduces the reader to studies by Thorndike, Davis, Guszak and Durkin in the area of comprehension. Nicholson critiques Thorndike's classic study and offers a summary of this work as well. He feels the study has suffered in translation from theory to practice. According to Nicholson many educators have concluded from the results of Thorndike's research that asking questions about written passages is the way to determine students' comprehension. He claims this is what Thorndike said, but probably not what he meant. Allington comments that Thorndike's study has had a significant impact on educational philosophy and pedagogy. He feels we can still use his research profitably, especially in the area of teacher education. Allington claims that by extending Thorndike's analysis of responses to text we can develop a sensitivity to the complexity of the process referred to as reading comprehension. In summary, Allington recognizes that recent research has advanced our understanding of reading but we still understand little about the comprehension of text or the role of questions in developing such competence.

Johnson, Toms-Bronowski, and Buss critique Davis's classic study, *Fundamental Factors of Comprehension in Reading*. These authors focus on a discussion of the data analysis procedures and the underlying substantive assumptions Davis employed that reinforced a components skill view of reading comprehension. Implications to researchers and practitioners alike regarding the components view is also discussed in this critique with respect to the impact this view had previously and continues to have today on the field of reading. Blachowicz comments on subskills research from a historical perspective. She claims that because the issue of separable components to comprehension has been the subject of long-term analyses and reanalyses, it provides many windows through which to view the various ways research questions are formulated and the studies carried out.

Pearson critiques Guszak's study, *Teacher Questioning and Reading* and presents an analysis of the following 3 questions which Guszak's research sought to answer: 1) What kinds of thinking questions do teachers ask about reading assignments in selected second, fourth, and sixth grade classrooms? 2) How frequently are teacher questions about reading assignments met with congruent or correct student responses? 3) Do teachers employ certain questioning strategies as they question students about reading assignments? Guszak comments that it is interesting to review his original research on teacher questioning through the eyes of Pearson. He shares Pearson's interest concerning some important new directions for replicating his study. But, he cautions, such replication should take into account teacher background variables, the type and level of content, the effects of grouping, the possible sources of questions, and the instructional effects of questioning per se.

McGinitie critiques two currently important studies of comprehension instruction by Dolores Durkin. His intention is to provide a context in which Durkin's findings can be understood and used as a basis for improving instruction. His critique evaluates the evidence Durkin presents and describes some of the influences that he believes lie behind her findings. McGinitie interprets her criticisms of current practices and materials as implying her acceptance of a particular model of instruction and suggests that, although her findings clearly demonstrate the need for change, the change should be guided by a different model of comprehension instruction. Durkin's comments are an attempt to explain and defend various aspects of her research that have tended to be misinterpreted in the literature. She lauds McGinitie's critique of her work and claims that if she had access to his remarks before the reports of her studies were published, the reports would be better than they are.

READING AS REASONING: A STUDY OF MISTAKES IN PARAGRAPH READING

EDWARD L. THORNDIKE

Teachers College, Columbia University

It seems to be a common opinion that reading (understanding the meaning of printed words) is a rather simple compounding of habits. Each word or phrase is supposed, if known to the reader, to call up its sound and meaning and the series of word or phrase meanings is supposed to be, or be easily transmuted into, the total thought. It is perhaps more exact to say that little attention has been paid to the dynamics whereby a series of words whose meanings are known singly produces knowledge of the meaning of a sentence or paragraph.

It will be the aim of this article to show that reading is a very elaborate procedure, involving a weighing of each of many elements in a sentence, their organization in the proper relations one to another, the selection of certain of their connotations and the rejection of others, and the coöperation of many forces to determine final response. In fact we shall find that the act of answering simple questions about a simple paragraph like the one shown below includes all the features characteristic of typical reasonings.

J

Read this and then write the answers to 1, 2, 3, 4, 5, 6, and 7. Read it again as often as you need to.

In Franklin, attendance upon school is required of every child between the ages of seven and fourteen on every day when school is in session unless the child is so ill as to be unable to go to school, or some person in his house is ill with a contagious disease, or the roads are impassable.

1. What is the general topic of the paragraph?

   ....

2. On what day would a ten-year-old girl not be expected to attend school?

   ....

3. Between what years is attendance upon school compulsory in Franklin?

   ....

4. How many causes are stated which make absence excusable?

   ....

5. What kind of illness may permit a boy to stay away from school, even though he is not sick himself?

   ....

6. What condition in a pupil would justify his non-attendance?

   ....

7. At what age may a boy leave school to go to work in Franklin?

   ....

Consider first the following responses which were found among those

From *The Journal of Educational Psychology*, Vol. VIII, No. 6. June 1917, pp. 323–32.

made to Questions 1, 2, 5 and 6 above by two hundred pupils in Grade 6. (All are quoted exactly save that capitals are used at the beginning here regardless of whether the pupils used them.)

		Percents	No. per thousand
J1.	Unanswered	18	180
	Franklin	4½	45
	In Franklin	1	10
	Franklin attendance	1	10
	Franklin School	1½	15
	Franklin attending school	1	10
	Days of Franklin	½	5
	School days of Franklin	½	5
	Doings at Franklin	1	10
	Pupils in Franklin	½	5
	Franklin attends to his school	½	5
	It is about a boy going to Franklin	½	5
	It was a great inventor	½	5
	Because its a great invention	½	5
	The attendance of the children	½	5
	The attendance in Franklin	½	5
	School	7½	75
	To tell about school	½	5
	About school	4	40
	What the school did when the boy was ill	½	5
	What the child should take	½	5
	If the child is ill	2	20
	How old a child should be	½	5
	If the child is sick or contagious disease	½	5
	Illness	1	10
	On diseases	½	5
	Very ill	3	30
	An excuse	2	20
	The roads are impassable.	1	10
	Even rods are impossible.	½	5
	A few sentences	½	5
	Made of complete sentences	½	5
	A sentence that made sense	½	5
	A group of sentences making sense	½	5
	A group of sentences	3	30
	Subject and predicate	½	5
	Subject	½	5
	The sentence	½	5
	A letter	½	5
	Capital	5½	55
	A capital letter	½	5
	To begin with a capital	2	20
	The first word	½	5
	A general topic	½	5
	Good topic	½	5
	Leave half an inch space	2½	25
	The heading	½	5
	Period	½	5
	An inch and a half	½	5
	An inch and a half capital letter	½	5
	The topic is civics	½	5
	The answer	½	5
J2.	Unanswered	6	60
	Unless the child is so ill as to be unable to go to school	41	410
	Unless the child is unable to go to school	½	5
	Unless she is ill or the roads are impassable	1	10
	Roads are impassable	1	10
	When his baby or brother have some kind of disease	1	10
	When a parent is ill	½	5
	If her father or mother died	½	5
	On her birthday	6½	65
	On her fourteenth birthday	½	5
	On every day	4	40
	On any day	½	5
	Expected every day	1½	15
	On Monday and for 5 days a week	½	5
	On Monday	1	10
	On Friday	1	10
	When school is in session.	1	10
	The beginning of the term	½	5
	Fourteen year	½	5
	Age 11	½	5
	She is allowed to go to school when 6 years	½	5

	Per-cents	No. per thous-and
A very bad throat	½	5
When better	½	5
J5. Unanswered	2	20
If mother is ill	5½	55
Headache, ill	½	5
A sore neck	½	5
Headache, toothache or earache	½	5
When a baby is sick	½	5
Playing sickness	½	5
Serious	½	5
When the roads cannot be used	½	5
Contagious disease, roads impassable	1½	15
He cannot pass the hall	½	5
A note	½	5
J6. Unanswered	15	150
Ill with a contagious disease	5	50
Seven years old	½	5
By bringing a note	6	60
When going with his mother to his cousin	½	5
Is to go his mother	½	5
When he is well and strong	½	5
To have a certificate from a doctor that the disease is all over	½	5
Somebody else must have a bad disease	½	5
Torn shoes	½	5
Neat attendance	½	5
When he acts as if he is innocent	½	5
Being good	½	5
By being early	½	5
Get up early	½	5
Come to school	1½	15
Be at school every day	½	5
If he lost his lessons	½	5
Illness lateness or truancy	½	5
A bad boy	½	5
By not going to school	½	5
None	½	5
Not sick no condition and mother not ill	½	5
Not very good	½	5
When you come you get your attendance marked	½	5
Of being absent	½	5

	Per-cents	No. per thous-and
His attendance was fair	½	5
Truant	1	10
If some one at his house has a contagious disease	6½	65
When roads	½	5
If he was excused	½	5
Not smart	½	5
If his father or mother died	½	5
By not staying home or playing hookey	½	5

In general in this and all similar tests of reading, the responses do not fall into a few clearly defined groups—correct, unanswered, error No. 1, error No. 2, and so on. On the contrary they show a variety that threatens to baffle any explanation. We can, however, progress toward an explanation, by using the following facts and principles:

In correct reading (1) each word produces a correct meaning, (2) each such element of meaning is given a correct weight in comparison with the others, and (3) the resulting ideas are examined and validated to make sure that they satisfy the mental set or adjustment or purpose for whose sake the reading was done. Reading may be wrong or inadequate (1) because of wrong connections with the words singly, (2) because of over-potency or under-potency of elements, or (3) because of failure to treat the ideas produced by the reading as provisional, and so to inspect and welcome or reject them as they appear.

Everybody of course, understands that (1) plays a part but it is not so clearly understood that a word may produce all degrees of erroneous meaning for a given context, from a slight inadequacy to an extreme perversion.

Thus *Franklin* in the paragraph quoted (J) varies from its exact meaning as a local unit through degrees of vagueness to meaning a man's name (as in "Franklin attends to his school" as a response to question 1), or to meaning a particular personage (as in "It was a great inventor" as a response to question 1). Thus *Contagious* in paragraph J permits responses to question 5 (What kind of illness may permit a boy to stay away from school, even though he is not sick himself?) ranging from "Scarlet fever, chicken pox, measles or diphtheria," through "Scarlet fever," "Headache," "Serious," "Hay fever," "Pimple," to "Contagious or roads impassable," and "All kinds of disease." Thus *Paragraph* in J 1 when over-potent produces responses ranging from "A group of sentences making sense" through "A group of sentences," and "A few sentences," to "The sentence," "Subject and predicate," "Begin with a capital," "A letter," and "Commas and periods."

In particular, the relational words, such as pronouns, conjunctions and prepositions, have meanings of many degrees of exactitude. They also vary in different individuals in the amount of force they exert. A pupil may know exactly what *though* means, but he may treat a sentence containing it much as he would treat the same sentence with *and* or *or* or *if* in place of the *though*.

The importance of the correct weighting of each element is less appreciated. It is very great, a very large percentage of the mistakes made being due to the over-potency of certain elements or the under-potency of others.

Consider first the over-potency of elements in the questions. The first question about paragraph J was, "What is the general topic of the paragraph?" A large group of answers show over-potency of *paragraph*. Such are those quoted above to show variation in the understanding of the word. We also find an over-potency of *top* (in topic) combined with that of paragraph, resulting in such responses as: "Leave a half-inch space," "An inch and a half," "An inch and a half capital letter," "The topic of paragraph is one inch in."

The second question was: "On what day would a ten-year-old girl not be expected to attend school?" We find under-potency of *not* resulting in answers like "When school is in session" or "Five days a week." We find under-potency of *day* resulting in responses like "She is allowed to go to school when 6 years," "Age 11," and "Fourteen years."

We find over-potency of *day* shown by "Monday," "Wednesday," and "Friday"; of *ten-year-old girl* in "The ten-year-old girl will be 5 a."

Ten-year-old is over-potent in an interesting way, namely, in the very large number of responses of "On her birthday." Over-potency of *Attend school* seems to be one part of the causation of "To attendance with Franklin," "Every morning at half past 8," "She should," and "Because he did learn."

Consider next over- and under-potency of the words or phrases in the paragraph. The following list of responses shows that each of ten words taken from the paragraph is over-potent so as to appear clearly influential in the response to each of the first three questions (and in seven of the cases to the fourth question as well). These occur within five hundred responses made by children within grades 5 to 8. Cases of under-potency would be still easier to collect.

The questions, I may remind the reader, were as follows:

1. What is the general topic of the paragraph?
2. On what day would a ten-year-old girl not be expected to attend school?

3. Between what years is attendance upon school compulsory in Franklin?
4. How many causes are stated which make absence excusable?

(The numbers refer to the question to which the words were the response.)

Franklin	1. Franklin. 1. Franklin and the diseases. 1. Franklin topic. 2. Franklin. 3. Because it is a small city. 3. Franklin was in school 141 years.
attendance	1. Attendance. 2. To attendance with Franklin. 3. In Franklin attendance upon school is required. Attending school 130 days.
school	1. School. 1. They must know their lessons. 2. In the beginning of school. 3. School in session. 3. In the years of school.
seven	1. Seven and fourteen. 1. How old a child should be. 2. He should attend school at 7 years. 2. Between seven and fourteen. 3. Seven years. 4. Under seven.
fourteen	1. Every child between seven and fourteen. In Franklin how old they are. 2. Fourteenth of every day. 2. Fourteen years. 3. Fourteen years. 3. Fourteen. 4. 7 to 14.
every	1. Every child. 2. Expected every day. 2. On every day. 3. Every year. 3. Every child between fourteen or thirteen. 4. Every day.
ill	1. Illness. 1. Very ill. 1. If the child is ill. 2. Ill. 2. A very bad throat. 3. He cannot go to school unless ill. 4. When child is ill. 4. Must be sick.
contagious	1. Contagious disease. 2. If she is sick or has a contagious disease. 3. Contagious disease. 4. Contagious disease.
disease	1. Fever. 1. About disease. 2. Often sick. 3. Unless ill or contagious disease 3. Disease. 4. A terrible disease going out. 4. Because when a boy has disease.
impassable	1. The roads are impassable. 1. Snow. 2. When roads are impassable. 3. Seven to fourteen years or the roads are impassable. 4. Or the roads are impassable.

To make a long story short, inspection of the mistakes shows that the potency of any word or word group in a question may be far above or far below its proper amount in relation to the rest of the question. The same holds for any word or word group in the paragraph. Understanding a paragraph implies keeping these respective weights in proper proportion from the start or varying their proportions until they together evoke a response which satisfies the purpose of the reading.

Understanding a paragraph is like solving a problem in mathematics. It consists in selecting the right elements of the situation and putting them together in the right relations, and also with the right amount of weight or influence or force for each. The mind is assailed as it were by every word in the paragraph. It must select, repress, soften, emphasize, correlate and organize, all under the influence of the right mental set or purpose or demand.

Consider the complexity of the task in even a very simple case such as answering question 6 on paragraph D, in the case of children of grades 6, 7 and 8 who well understand the question itself.

> John had two brothers who were both tall. Their names were Will and Fred. John's sister, who was short, was named Mary. John liked Fred better than either of the others. All of these children except Will had red hair. He had brown hair.
>
> 6. Who had red hair?

The mind has to suppress a strong tendency for *Will had red hair* to act irrespective of the *except* which precedes it. It has to suppress a tendency for *all these children . . . had red hair* to act irrespective of the *except Will.* It has to suppress weaker tendencies for *John, Fred, Mary, John and Fred, Mary and Fred, Mary and Will, Mary Fred and Will,* and every other combination that could be a "*Who,*" to act irrespective of the satisfying of the requirement "had red hair according to the paragraph." It has to suppress tendencies for John and Will or brown and red to exchange places in memory, for irrelevant ideas like *nobody* or *brothers* or *children* to arise. That it has to suppress them is shown by the failures to do so which occur. The *Will had red hair* in fact causes one-fifth of children in grades 6, 7 and 8 to answer wrongly,* and about two-fifths of children in grades 3, 4 and 5. Insufficient potency of *except Will** makes about one child in twenty in grades 6, 7 and 8 answer wrongly with "all the children," "all," or "Will Fred Mary and John."

Reading may be wrong or inadequate because of failure to treat the responses made as provisional and to inspect, welcome and reject them as they appear. Many of the very pupils who gave wrong responses to the questions would respond correctly if confronted with them in the following form:

> Is this foolish or is it not?
>
> The day when a girl should *not* go to school is the day when school is in session.
> The day when a girl should not go to school is the beginning of the term.
> The day etc. . . . is Monday.
> The day is fourteen years.
> The day is age eleven.
> The day is a very bad throat.
> Impassable roads are a kind of illness.
> He cannot pass the ball is a kind of illness.

They do not, however, of their own accord test their responses by thinking out their subtler or more remote implications. Even very gross violations against common sense are occasionally passed, such as letting Mary give Tom a blue dog, or giving "Thought the man fat out" as an answer to I 1. Usually, however, the irrelevance or inconsistency concerns something in the question or the paragraph and the failure to heed it is closely akin to the under-potency of certain elements.

> I.
>
> Nearly fifteen thousand of the city's workers joined in the parade on September seventh, and passed before two hundred thousand cheering spectators. There were workers of both sexes in the parade, though the men far out-numbered the women.
>
> 1. What is said about the number of persons who marched in the parade?

It thus appears that reading an explanatory or argumentative paragraph in his text-books on geography or history

*Some of these errors are due to essential ignorance of "except," though that should not be common in pupils of grade 6 or higher.

or civics and (though to a less degree) reading a narrative or description, involves the same sort of organization and analytic action of ideas as occur in thinking of supposedly higher sorts. This view is supported by the high correlations between such reading and verbal completion tests, Binet-Simon tests, analogies tests and the like. These correlations, when corrected for attenuation, are probably, for children of the same age, as high as +.80.

It appears likely, therefore, that many children fail in certain features of these subjects not because they have understood and remembered the facts and principles but have been unable to organize and use them; or because they have understood them but have been unable to remember them; but because they never understood them.

It appears likely also that a pupil may read fluently and feel that the series of words are arousing appropriate thoughts without really understanding the paragraph. Many of the children who made notable mistakes would probably have said that they understood the paragraph and, upon reading the questions on it, would have said that they understood them. In such cases the reader finds satisfying solutions of those problems which he does raise and so feels mentally adequate; but he raises only a few of the problems which should be raised and makes only a few of the judgments which he should make. Thus one may read paragraph I with something like the following actual judgments:

> *Fifteen thousand did something—there was a parade—September seventh was the day—there were two hundred thousand something—there was cheering—workers were in the parade—both sexes in the parade—the men outnumbered the women.*

Contrast these with the following which may be in the mind of the expert reader:

> *Nearly fifteen thousand—not quite, but nearly—of the city's workers—people who worked for a living—joined in the parade—a big parade of nearly 15,000—on September seventh—the parade was in the fall—they passed before two thousand hundred cheering spectators—two hundred thousand saw the parade—they cheered it—there were workers of both sexes—there were men workers and women workers in the parade—the men far outnumbered the women. Many more men than women were in the parade.*

In educational theory, then, we should not consider the reading of a textbook or reference as a mechanical, passive, undiscriminating task, on a totally different level from the task of evaluating or using what is read. While the work of judging and applying doubtless demands a more elaborate and inventive organization and control of mental connections, the demands of mere reading are also for the active selection which is typical of thought. It is not a small or unworthy task to learn "what the book says."

In school practice it appears likely that exercises in silent reading to find the answers to given questions, or to give a summary of the matter read, or to list the questions which it answers, should in large measure replace oral reading. The vice of the poor reader is to say the words to himself without actively making judgments concerning what they reveal. Reading aloud or listening to one reading aloud may leave this vice unaltered or even encouraged. Perhaps it is in their outside reading of stories and in their study of geography, history, and the like, that many school children really learn to read.

A Critique of Edward Thorndike's Study: Reading as Reasoning—A Study of Mistakes in Paragraph Reading

TOM NICHOLSON

University of Waikato

RATIONALE: WHY THIS IS A CLASSIC STUDY

Why critique this study? After all, it was first published some 65 years ago. Well, one reason is that Thorndike's analysis of the question-answering process is still regarded as significant. In fact, the reprinting of "Reading as Reasoning" (Thorndike, 1917) in the *Reading Research Quarterly* in Summer 1971 is an indication of its seminal quality.

Another reason to look at Thorndike's work again is that it seems to have suffered in translation from theory to practice. Many schools apparently concluded that asking questions about texts *was* comprehension. This was what Thorndike said, but probably not what he meant.

In fact, some students still think that answering questions about texts *is* comprehension.[1]

> Interviewer: Why do you have to answer questions about the story?
> Pupil: To make you understand it.

THORNDIKE'S STUDY: A SUMMARY

Yet was this what Thorndike intended? To find out, we really need to review the study. According to Thorndike, the purpose of the study was to show us that

> reading is a very elaborate procedure, involving a weighing of each of many elements in a sentence, their organization in the proper relations one to another, the selection of certain of their connotations and the rejection of others, and the cooperation of many forces to determine final response (see page 209).

[1]I am grateful to Beverly Bell for this extract from an interview with a 13-year-old secondary student. The Thorndike passage and questions were readministered for me by John Coutts and Hank Popping.

To convince us that reading was "a very elaborate procedure," he analyzed the answers given by some 200 eleven-year-olds to questions which he asked about a brief passage:

> In Franklin, attendance upon school is required of every child between the ages of seven and fourteen on every day when school is in session unless the child is so ill as to be unable to go to school or some person in his house is ill with a contagious disease or the roads are impassable.

(The pupils answered seven questions in all, although Thorndike only analyzed in detail the following questions.)

1. What is the general topic of the paragraph?
2. On what day would a ten-year-old girl not be expected to attend school?
5. What kind of illness may permit a boy to stay away from school even though he is not sick himself?
6. What condition in a pupil would justify his non-attendance? (See page 209.)

THORNDIKE'S ANALYSIS OF THE CHILDREN'S ANSWERS

Thorndike was struck by the variety of responses given to the questions. He decided that three factors caused the "errors." First, some pupils did not make the word associations that the writer intended. Instead, the children attached their own meanings to these words. For example, the word "Franklin" was sometimes interpreted as the name of a pupil, or even as the name of the inventor, Benjamin Franklin.

Question: What was the general topic of the paragraph?
Answers: It was a great inventor.
Franklin attending school.

A second reason for the variety of responses was that some words or phrases exerted too much or too little influence on the pupils' understanding of the paragraph. Thorndike described this as "over-potency" or "under-potency" in a word. For example, the word "paragraph" in question 1 seemed to get considerable attention from some pupils and their answers focused on this part of the question.

Question: What is the general topic of the paragraph?
Answers: Made of complete sentences.
A group of sentences making sense.
Subject and predicate.
To begin with a capital.
Period.

The third factor was the reader's failure to treat ideas as provisional. For example, some of the responses did not make much sense. Thorndike argued that

critique

the pupils themselves would respond correctly if the ideas were presented again. For example:

> *Question:* On what day would a ten-year-old girl not be expected to attend school?
> *Answers:* The day . . . is Monday.
> The day . . . is the day when school is in session.
> The day is age eleven.
> The day is a very bad throat.

Thorndike argued that some pupils thought they understood a text because they read the words accurately. Yet very often the meaning that the reader constructed was not the meaning that the writer was trying to convey.

> In such cases the reader finds satisfying solutions to those problems which he does raise and so feels mentally adequate, but he raises only a few of the problems which should be raised and makes only a few of the judgements which he should make. (See page 215.)

What was the point of this analysis of question answering? What did it say about the comprehension process? Thorndike felt that his analysis did highlight the complexity of text comprehension, and the important role of the text itself.

> The mind is assailed, as it were, by every word in the paragraph. It must select, repress, soften, emphasize, correlate, and organize, all under the influence of the right mental set or purpose or demand. (See page 214.)

CRITIQUE OF THE STUDY

Text and task difficulty. Not everyone would agree with Thorndike that "the mind is assailed" by every word in the text. His data could be simply a result of text difficulty—the harder the text, the more need to look at every word. After all, the "Franklin" text was grammatically complex. It consisted of just one sentence, some 56 words. Moreover, the complexity of some of the questions could have influenced the results, particularly those questions that probed conditional causes in the text.

If, for example, we examine the answers to question 6, some pupils did seem to misread either the question or the text (See Critique/Table 1 for the questions and a summary of the pupils' responses). The following answers suggest that the word "non-attendance" in the question was actually read as "attendance."

> *Question:* What condition in a pupil would justify his non-attendance?
> *Answers:* Not sick, no condition and mother not ill.
> When you come and get your attendance marked.

Other pupils probably misread words in the text, which would not have helped them with their answers. Thorndike noted that one pupil misread the word "impassable" and gave the response "pass the ball is a kind of illness." Another pupil misread "roads are impassable" as "rods are impossible."

Some pupils read the words correctly but misunderstood them. For example, some pupils may have misunderstood the word "condition" (p. 209 this volume) so that for them the question meant "What kind of pupil would be a non-attender?" Hence the following responses.

> *Answers:* A bad boy.
> Truant.
> By not staying home or playing hookey.
> Not smart.

Other responses suggest that the word "condition" was interpreted as "personal characteristics." As a result, some pupils may have thought that an answer to the question required the possible personal characteristics of a non-attender who would be above suspicion as to motives for being away from school.

> *Answers:* When he acts as if he is innocent.
> Be at school every day.
> By being early.
> Being good.

Finally, some pupils may have made sense of the question by applying their own "deletion rule" to some of the wording. Rather than make sense of "condition in a pupil," they may have deleted the reference to "pupil" and created a more general question, such as "under what *normal* conditions is non-attendance justified?" If this was what the question meant to them, then the following responses make sense:

> *Answers:* If his mother or father died.
> If he was excused.
> By bringing a note.
> Torn shoes.
> When roads (are impassable).

Perhaps Thorndike dismissed too easily the impact of factors such as text and task difficulty on question-answering behaviors. He regarded the text and the questions as "simple." Yet the text is a tightly reasoned statement on school attendance, something that becomes obvious as soon as an attempt is made to rewrite it. Thorndike also did not consider that some pupils received incomplete information, such as "pass the hall" and "pass the ball" instead of "impassable." When this happened, some words exerted more influence than others as the mind tried to make sense of the text.

Thorndike's questions also required considerable inferencing on the part of the reader, not only to understand them but also to find answers. Thorndike was aware of this complexity.

> We should not consider the reading of a textbook or reference as a mechanical, passive, undiscriminating task . . . (See page 215.)

Yet he does not show clearly what the reader has to do to answer some of his questions. Thorndike's analysis, in this respect, is "text based." He focuses on the reader's need to arbitrate between plausible but competing ideas within the text itself. However, he does not explain how the reader achieves this.

critique

CRITIQUE/TABLE 1

A Summary of the pupils' responses to the "Franklin" story and questions 1, 2, 5 and 6 in Edward Thorndike's original 1917 study

1. What is the general topic of this paragraph?

RESPONSES

Franklin. Franklin attendance.
Franklin school.
Franklin attending school.
School days of Franklin.
Pupils at Franklin.
It is about a boy going to Franklin.
It was a great inventor.
What the school did when the boy was ill.
If the child is ill.
How old a child should be.
If the child is sick or contagious disease.
On diseases. An excuse.
The roads are impassable.
Even rods are impossible.
A few sentences.
A group of sentences making sense.
Subject and predicate.
A letter. Capital.
Good topic.
Leave half an inch space.
The topic is civics.
The answer.

2. On what day would a 10-year-old girl not be expected to attend school?

RESPONSES

Unless the child is so ill as to be unable to go to school.
Roads are impassable.
When a parent is ill.
If her father or mother died.
On her birthday.
On her fourteenth birthday.
On every day.
On any day.
On Monday.
On Friday.
When school is in session.
Age 11.
She is allowed to go to school when 6 years.
A very bad throat.
When better.

5. What kind of illness may permit a boy to stay away from school, even though he is not sick himself?

RESPONSES

If mother is ill.
Headache, ill.
A sore neck.
Headache, toothache or earache.
When a baby is sick.
Playing sickness.
Serious.
When the roads cannot be used.
Contagious disease, roads impassable.
He cannot pass the hall.
A note.

6. What condition in a pupil would justify his non-attendance?

RESPONSES

Unanswered. Seven years old.
Ill with a contagious disease.
By bringing a note. Torn shoes.
When going with his mother to his cousin.
When he is well and strong.
To have a certificate from a doctor that the disease is all over.
Neat attendance. Is to go his mother.
Somebody else must have a bad disease.
Being good. By being early.
Get up early. Come to school.
Be at school every day.
If he lost his lessons.
Illness lateness or truancy.

CRITIQUE/TABLE 1 (continued)

RESPONSES	RESPONSES
	A bad boy. None.
	By not going to school.
	Not sick no condition and mother not ill.
	Not very good. Of being absent.
	When you come you get your attendance marked.
	Truant. When roads.
	Hiss attendance was fair.
	If some one at his house has a contagious disease.
	If he was excused. Not smart.
	If his father or mother died.
	By not staying home or playing hookey.

A replication study: The reader in 1917 and 1981. To find out more about the role of the reader in answering these questions, a replication study was carried out. I reasoned that a comparison of 1917 and 1981 "answers" would provide more insight into the knowledge these readers brought to the text.

Since Thorndike only provided data for questions 1, 2, 5, and 6 in his original study, only these questions were used in the replication. The procedures were simple. The text and questions were given to some 87 eleven-year-olds in a Hamilton intermediate school. The pupils were asked to read the original "Franklin" passage and then answer the four questions (see Critique/Table 2 for a summary of their responses). Most of the answers to question 1 were similar to the following:

Question: What is the general topic of the paragraph?
Answers: School.
Rules of school.
Illness.
School attendance.

Some of these responses, however, reflected the changes that have taken place in schooling.

Answers: A school that has stricked rules.
Children should attend school unless they are on their last legs.

Why was it, in the 1981 study, that pupils did not confuse the word "Franklin" with the famous American inventor? The most plausible explanation is that New Zealand pupils, although somewhat familiar with American history, are not likely to know much about Ben Franklin. Yet the pupils questioned by Thorndike had this prior knowledge.

Some of the answers to question 2 in the 1981 replication also illustrate the effects of prior knowledge (see Critique/Table 2). In fact, they raise another issue not discussed by Thorndike—namely, where to find the answer.

For question 2, the "answer" is not explicitly stated in the text. The reader has to use prior experience of schooling, as well as text information, to make the expected inference.

Question: On what day would a ten-year-old girl not be expected to attend school?
Answers: (1981)
When her mother is not home and she has to look after the family.
Sometimes because of personle problem such as period for the first time.
Wednesday.

It is clear, from the above responses, that pupils in the 1981 replication tended to rely on their own "theories of the world," or "schemata" (see Rumelhart, 1981, for a discussion of schema theory and comprehension).

From the reader's point of view, such "errors" are understandable. The reader had to reconstruct the writer's intended meaning from a limited set of text cues. The reader was dealing with a text that was only partially "mapped"—that is, certain text cues were given, but basically the writer was relying on the reader to make the necessary inferences.

When we look back at the pupils' responses in the 1917 study, a similar pattern exists. Thorndike argued that these answers were a result of "word potency" or were "provisional." What may have actually happened was that some words in the text simply fitted in with the reader's own "schema." For example:

Answers: (1917)
On her 14th birthday
When a parent is ill.
A very bad throat.
On Monday.
On Friday.

A similar situation for the reader occurs with question 5, where the text "answer" is not clearly linked with the question.

Question: What kind of illness may permit a boy to stay away from school, even though he is not sick himself?

In this case, the "answer" appears to be explicitly stated in the text—that is, "if some person in his house is ill with a contagious disease." When you examine closely the responses given in the 1981 replication, however, it seems that, again, some pupils have gone "beyond the text." In other words, they have tried to translate the text information into real-life examples.

Answers: (1981)
Measles, chicken poks, tonsilous, etc.
The cold.
A bad case of the flu.

When we go back to the 1917 study, we see a similar set of responses:

Answers: (1917)
Headache.
A sore neck.
If mother is ill.
When a baby is sick.

In summary, Thorndike may have discovered two types of reader in his original 1917 study. The first type tended to have a "text-based" approach to question

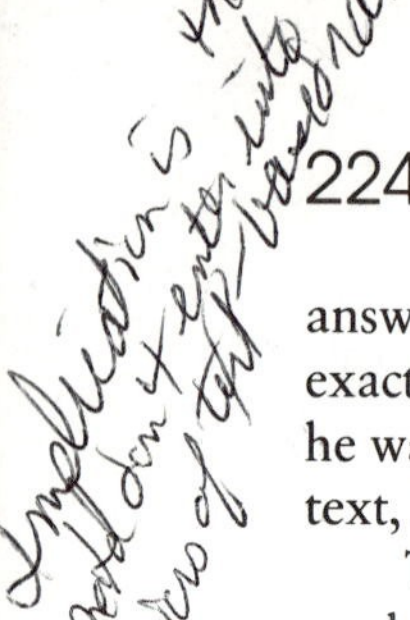

answering. This reader paid close attention to text details and tried to find out exactly what the writer intended. Thorndike applauded this kind of reader, although he was quick to point out that sometimes this type of reader got too hung up on the text, "without thinking out their subtler implications."

The second type of reader tended to have a "schema-based" approach. This reader attended to the overall meaning without getting bogged down in text details. Thorndike tried to categorize these kinds of readers. In his opinion, they were just not paying enough attention to the text.

But Thorndike might have been a bit too hard on some of these "schema-based" readers. After all, some of his questions required complex inferencing to get the "answer" embedded in the text. In fact, some of the pupils' answers showed that they could translate the text information into "real world" situations. For example:

Question: What condition in a pupil would justify his non-attendance?
Text: "if the child is so ill as to be unable to go to school."
Answer: The trots.

Most of us would agree, however, that some of these "schema-based" responses seemed to ignore the text altogether. For example:

Answer: (1917) By not staying home or playing hookey.
Answer: (1981) Playing space invaders in school time. Wagging.

CRITIQUE/TABLE 2
A summary of pupils' responses to the "Franklin" story and questions 1, 2, 5, and 6 in the 1981 replication

1. What is the general topic of this paragraph?

RESPONSES

It is mainly about school children.
School. Illnesses.
About people who are ill between 7 and 14.
That every child should go to school unless sick or has a contagious disease.
About people been ill.
About children going to school at 7 to 14 years old.
The laws concerning attendance upon school in Franklin.
School attendance.
Children must attend school unless it is impossible.
A school that has stricked rules.

2. On what day would a ten-year-old girl not be expected to attend school?

RESPONSES

When she is ill or with a disease.
Saturday. Every day.
When her road is unpassable or she has a dease.
Holiday, sick, can't get there.
If she is ill or the roads are unpassable to pass or a contages diseas in the family.
When roads are blocked.
When ill there is your mother there to help you.
When school is in session.
Wednesday.
If she is so ill or playing hooky.
Sometimes because of personle problems such as period for the first time.

CRITIQUE/TABLE 2 (continued)

RESPONSES

Every child has to go to school.
There is no real excuse of school.
Rule to say you have to attend school and why.
What children can stay away for.
Children should attend school unless they are on their last legs.

RESPONSES

This girl will not going to school because her ages is not 14 years.
When her mother is not at home or she has to look after her family.
On public holidays.

5. What kind of illness may permit a boy to stay away from school, even though he is not sick himself?

RESPONSES

Measles, chicken poks, tonsilous, etc.
Contaguous disease.
The cold.
Working too hard.
No illness.
Roads are impassable.
A bad case of the flu.
Fever.
Having a dease.
Contagious disease, roads are closed.
When he has to go to a doctor.
There might be a test and he doesn't want to sit the test.
I think his not very sick it only just a sure foot.
If the boy is waging.
When his mother or father someone in the family is sick and they want your company.
If a parent or close relation dies and he is emotionally sick.

6. What condition in a pupil would justify his non-attendance?

RESPONSES

They would properly have a disease so they can't go outside be cause it is contagious.
Some person in family was sick.
When roads are impassable.
When he was not sick.
When he or she has a dease and has passed it on to someone in his family.
The trots.
If somebody died in his family and he went to the funeral.
If he was younger than seven.
Feverous face, hot and sweaty, tired, weary.
A sickness. Illness.
To young. To old.
He would have the flu Broken leg or Arm.
TB. If he has fever.
When he is not feeling very good.
Playing space envaders in school time—wagging.
Possible reason could be messels, throat infection, person problems, death in family etc.
Not going to school because they don't like the work—going to town.
Chicken pox measles brocken limbs infections mumpins.
When he has a note expecially writen reason for his absences away from school.

CONCLUDING STATEMENT

Thorndike's analysis of children's question-answering behaviors, although written more than 60 years ago, is still remarkably current—and certainly compatible with recent research in this area (Pearson & Nicholson, 1976; Trabasso, 1981; Nicholson & Imlach, 1981).

What is disturbing is that Throndike's insights as to how children answer questions were not translated into classroom practice. Teachers somehow got turned in the direction of comprehension testing and away from understanding—yet understanding was what his study was all about.

To me, the most interesting aspect of Thorndike's study is that he analyzed and synthesized his data with no computer and virtually no statistical procedures, yet was very insightful. This is why the study is so deceptively powerful but well worth the effort of criticism.

FOR FURTHER LEARNING

Those readers who are interested in continuing to explore the topic of question-answering and comprehension would find the following references helpful:

Introductory (selected chapters)

Nicholson, T. *An anatomy of reading: A guide to understanding reading problems* (2nd ed.). Sydney: Horwitz-Grahame, 1982, Chap. 20.

Pearson, P. D., & Johnson, D. *Teaching reading comprehension.* New York: Holt, Rinehart, & Winston, 1978, Chap. 8.

Advanced

Lehnert, W. *The process of question answering.* Hillsdale, N.J.: Lawrence Erlbaum Associates, 1978. (See chapters on "focus establishment" and "finding the best answer.")

Loftus, E. *Human memory: The processing of information.* Hillsdale, N.J.: Lawrence Erlbaum Associates, 1976, 159–162.

Loftus, E. Leading questions and the eye-witness report. *Cognitive Psychology,* 1975, *7,* 560–572.

Minsky, M. A framework for representing knowledge. In P. H. Winston (Ed.), *The psychology of computer vision.* New York: McGraw-Hill, 1975.

REFERENCES

Nicholson, T., & Imlach, R. Where do their answers come from? A study of the inferences which children make when answering questions about narrative stories. *Journal of Reading Behavior,* 1981, *13*(2), 111–130.

Pearson, P. D., & Nicholson, T. Scripts and texts and questions. Paper presented at National Reading Conference, Atlanta, 1976.

Rumelhart, D. Schemata: The building blocks of cognition. In J. D. Guthrie (Ed.), *Comprehen-*

references

sion and teaching: Research reviews. Newark, Del.: International Reading Association, 1981.

Thorndike, E. Reading as reasoning: A study of mistakes in paragraph reading. *Journal of Educational Psychology*, 1917, *8*(6), 323–332.

Trabasso, T. On the making of inferences during reading and their assessment. In J. D. Guthrie (Ed.), *Comprehension and teaching: Research reviews*. Newark, Del.: International Reading Association, 1981.

A Commentary on Nicholson's Critique of Thorndike's: Reading as Reasoning—A Study of Mistakes in Paragraph Reading

RICHARD L. ALLINGTON

State University of New York at Albany

AN HISTORICAL PERSPECTIVE

Thorndike's study, it seems to me, had a greater impact on pedagogy than Nicholson suggests. Implicit in the original paper is the argument that reading is more than the correct pronunciation of the words. While this point is nearly universally accepted today (though some suggest that incorrect pronunciation is the major, if not the only, obstacle to comprehension [see Flesch, 1980]), in Thorndike's era reading was, by definition, accurate oral production of text. That is, silent reading instruction was not a normal instructional activity (Allington, in press; Mathews, 1968; Smith, 1965). Several years after the publication of the Thorndike study, the National Society for the Study of Education (1921) devoted most of its annual yearbook to arguments for an increased role for silent reading instruction and practice. Likewise, Nila Banton Smith published her text *One hundred ways to teach silent reading* (1925), which offered classroom teachers pedagogical techniques for implementing silent reading instruction.

From this perspective, Thorndike's work can be viewed as highly influential in terms of pedagogical change. His argument that the overriding concern for accurate pronunciation produced readers who were failing to access meaning was well received, and shaped, or at least buttressed, the arguments of others attempting to achieve a balance between oral and silent reading instruction. His study was one of a very few available in the effort to reshape the definition of reading from accurate oral reproduction to understanding after oral or silent reading.

Nicholson correctly notes that, from another perspective, Thorndike's study suffered in translation from theory to practice. Questions alone, of course, are not necessarily comprehension instruction. Some, such as Durkin (1978), have classified questions primarily as assessment activities, though Heap (1981) has severely criticized such limited categorization. Questions after reading can serve several functions beyond assessing recall or understanding (which, of course, are in themselves two different entities). From our observations of reading groups, it seems questions can also be posed in an attempt to maintain student attention. In poor reader groups where off-task behavior is evident, the teacher often directs questions to students who are off-task, students they feel will not be able to respond. The lack of a correct response supports issuing a reprimand for inattention. It is relatively less common for poor readers to be asked questions for reading comprehension assessment—if only due to the overwhelming use of round-robin oral reading with such groups. Rarely does the teacher ask the reader a question—rather, other students who were supposed to be listening or following the oral rendition of another, are questioned. Such questions do not truly tap reading comprehension of any sort, since most often the student responding has not read the material.

Questions can also be posed in a manner that attempts to guide student thinking. For instance, it is not uncommon to see question sequences similar to the following:

T: Where was Jack in this story?

S: At the creek.

T: What did he hear?

S: A splash.

T: What do you suppose caused that splash?

S: ———

Without the text for reference, we cannot say exactly from where the teacher expects the answer to come, but we must surely accept that the teacher has attempted to guide the student's thinking. A problem with virtually all of the research on teacher questions can be seen in this dialogue. That is, questions are typically examined in isolation from the larger conversational sequence. Thus, some categorization schemes would treat this dialogue as, say, two literal and one inferential question without regard for the potential role of the two preceding questions to the latter. Nicholson, of course, is in part correct when he argues that questions are not comprehension instruction, and that questions are not always instructional nor is the teacher's intention in asking questions always instructional. However, some questioning sequences and some teachers' intentions when posing question sequences are instructional. I am not sure that much of this argument is directly relevant to Thorndike's study. Thorndike set out to demonstrate that "reading is a very elaborate procedure . . .," (see page 209) and to that end he accomplished his goal. Faulting Thorndike for not preventing questions from becoming the raison d'etre for reading is a bit unfair, particularly as he achieved his stated goal.

Along a similar line of reasoning, it is unfair for Nicholson (see page 220) to criticize Thorndike because "he does not show clearly what the reader has to do in order to answer some of his questions." Unfair primarily because few, if any, of the studies completed since Thorndike's have attained that goal. The most frequently noted studies of questions or questioning after reading have focused on describing teacher questions (Guszak, 1967; Durkin, 1978), the development of taxonomies for questions (Barrett, 1976; Bloom, 1956), and on the effect of questions inserted in text (Frase, 1968). The move away from "test-based" analyses of questions is a recent trend, not widely accepted for a half-century after Thorndike's work was published. Even more recent is the concern for analyses of student responses and the attention to questions and responses in the larger context of the complete interactional sequences that occur as the teacher-student dialogue ensues (Heap, 1980).

Another development in terms of questioning is the framework provided by Pearson and Johnson (1978). Their three-category taxonomy proposes a system for examining the relationship between the question and the information in the text and the information that the student brings to the reading from previous experience or learning. They offer the following three classifications: *Text explicit* questions in which the response expected is explicitly stated in the text (Text: The wagon is red. Question: What color is the wagon?). *Text implicit* questions in which the expected response requires an inference that integrates information across sentences or larger text segments (Text: They decided to play a game. They got the two things they really needed—the bat and the ball. Question: What game were they going to play?). *Scriptally implicit* questions in which the expected response is based upon an "inference drawn from prior experience or knowledge" (Text: Yesterday John was sent home from school. Question: Why was John sent home from school?). While this three-part classification scheme provides an encompassing framework and acknowledges that answers can come from sources other than the text, it too fails to account for teacher intention in asking questions. The classification scheme, from our attempts at using it, is also far from foolproof since raters often disagree as to the appropriate classifications for questions. These disagreements may stem from the fact that one really needs to present both the question and the desired response to classify many questions. The disagreements might also be caused by the absence of knowledge of the intention in asking the questions (which may or may not be related to the response derived). Another problem is that virtually all "adult-like post-reading questions" fall in the scriptally implicit category, though this is an inadequate label, at best. In our analyses of teacher-student post-reading interactions, we have discovered that when working with better readers, teachers often ask questions similar to the following:

Q 1: How would you have felt . . .

Q 2: Did you think Danny would . . .

Q 3: Have you ever . . .

Q 4: What part did you like best about . . .

These questions are similar in many respects to the types of queries adults often pose to one another about material both have read—that is, when two adults discuss a novel they have both read, the first question invariably is a variation on "Did you like it?" followed by a "why" or "why not" query and finally, more specific questions similar to those above. We do not hear one adult ask another (except in university-based classes) something like "what was the name of Garp's wife's lover?" or "what color was the pick-up truck Garp chased?"

Several points can be made here. First, while Thorndike did not "show clearly what the reader has to do," (see page 220) few have attempted such a goal and none has been completely successful. We do have a better framework for examining questions and responses today, but we have advanced only modestly beyond Thorndike's analysis. Second, while we have acknowledged the role of the reader's prior experience and knowledge, we have yet to deal with "adult-like" post-reading interactions and analyze readers' affective/emotional responses to literature (see Holland, 1975, for an in-depth study), which are surely part and parcel of reading comprehension. Finally, while we have a three-part classification scheme, can we really argue that we have developed a framework for questions that will be useful in instructional situations? I think not. One can easily generate trivial textually explicit, textually implicit, or scriptally implicit questions. Currently, we know very little about questioning as a pedagogical strategy and have yet to advance significantly beyond Thorndike.

AN OVERLOOKED ASPECT

From a personal perspective, I find the most powerful aspect of Thorndike's work lies in its replicability. As Nicholson notes, Thorndike was able to present a thoroughly convincing argument without complex statistical analyses. Probably no better way exists to demonstrate that reading is a complex cognitive activity than to use Thorndike's methodology. As a training tool for teachers, replication of the Thorndike methodology (using perhaps different texts) and even replication of his analysis would go a long way in developing sensitivity to the cognitive processes and potential sources of interference. Extending his analysis along the lines suggested by Nicholson would further enhance such understanding. One might ask teachers to classify questions into the categories proposed by Pearson and Johnson (1978). Then one could provide target responses and have the teachers reclassify based upon the question-developer's expected response. Teachers could analyze incorrect responses and attempt to locate the source of these errors, in a way similar to Nicholson's analysis of responses to Thorndike's questions. Although he does not provide a listing for sources of errors, Nicholson does identify several. Upon reflection, the following seem to be potential sources for incorrect answers:

Word pronunciation difficulty. While a word does not have to be correctly pronounced to be understood (e.g., *aminal* for *animal*), mispronunciation or deliberate omission can affect understanding.

Word meaning difficulty. Correctly pronouncing a word does not ensure that word meaning, particularly a specific word meaning, is assessed (e.g., *legend* has quite different meanings in literature and geography).

Sentence complexity. There are various forms of grammatical complexity that can impinge upon comprehension, ranging from relatively less frequent constructions such as passive voice (e.g., The girl was hit by John), to embeddings (e.g., Yesterday after he got home from school, where he is the best reader in fourth grade, John sat down and wrote a list of what he had to do), to anaphoric referent (e.g., The boy went to visit friends at *their* house). These examples only touch upon the potential sources of difficulties the reader may encounter at the sentence level.

Text ambiguity. Unfortunately, not all authors write clearly (e.g., The boys visited with friends at *their* house). Thus, the reader may encounter difficulty in disambiguating text even if all other sources of difficulty are nonexistent.

Inadequate prior knowledge. Authors assume a certain level of prior knowledge exists in the intended audience. Difficulties arise if a reader's prior knowledge is more limited than the author assumed.

Inappropriate utilization of prior knowledge. As Nicholson points out, in reference to the errant responses concerning Franklin, prior knowledge has the potential to interfere with comprehension. In scriptally implicit questions, the student may respond correctly based upon prior knowledge but produce a response considered incorrect or inadequate by the teacher (e.g., Question: Why did the policeman come to the door? Response: He wanted to hit on people).

Inability to call up prior knowledge. In some cases, the learner seems to have the necessary prior experience or knowledge but seems unable to access this knowledge. Often teachers are aware of this and rephrase questions to address an experience the child has had that will facilitate response.

Lack of motivation. Even skilled readers can read a text, then fail to recall details (often even critical details such as character names) because they had no intention or motivation to remember. Think of all the textual material the average skilled reader has read and the amount of information forgotten. (Or ask yourself: Who were the four authors cited as developers of question taxonomies?) Similarly, all readers can read material but fail to adequately recall, due primarily to a lack of motivation or intention to store the information processed.

Inappropriate text-processing strategies. First among these is the lack of syntactic parsing (Schreiber, 1980) resulting in word-by-word reading. This processing, common among disabled readers, interferes with understanding.

These sources of difficulty are not exhaustive, but rather demonstrate that recall or understanding can be negatively affected by a variety of factors. Too often educators feel that difficulty in recall or understanding is due to either word level problems or a lack of intellectual ability. Attempting to track the sources of answers as Nicholson suggests may prove to be a most powerful strategy for illuminating other sources of difficulty.

SUMMARY

Thorndike produced a simple but compelling study that indicated reading was more complex than the pronunciation of a string of words. His study had a significant impact upon the instructional practices in classrooms. However, Nicholson raises an important issue as well, the need to address the source of responses to questions. We have available recent schemes for classifying questions and expected responses, but even these are lacking in many respects. While the method used by Thorndike and the analyses proposed by Nicholson will aid development of a better understanding of the reading process and the role of questions after reading, we are still ignorant about most pedagogical facets of this activity. Future research needs a broader perspective than that employed thus far. Questions do not just occur in isolation, and they do not simply occur whenever text is present. Rather, questioning as practiced in reading instruction and reading assessment occurs in a social setting, and this setting may be ultimately more critical than either the question type or the text base.

REFERENCES

Allington, R. L. Oral reading. In P. D. Pearson (Ed.), *Handbook of reading research.* New York: Longmans (in press).

Barrett, T. C. Taxonomy of reading comprehension. In R. Smith and T. C. Barrett (Eds.), *Teaching reading in the middle grades.* Reading, Mass.: Addison-Wesley, 1976.

Bloom, B. *Taxonomy of educational objectives.* New York: David McKay Co., 1956.

Durkin, D. What classroom observations reveal about reading comprehension instruction. *Reading Research Quarterly,* 1978, *14,* 481–533.

Flesch, R. *Why Johnny still can't read.* New York: Harper and Row, 1980.

Frase, L. Questions as aids to reading: Some research and theory. *American Educational Research Journal,* 1968, *5,* 319–332.

Guszak, F. Teacher questioning and reading. *Reading Teacher,* 1967, *21,* 227–234.

Heap, J. What counts in reading: Limits to certainty in assessment. *Curriculum Inquiry,* 1980, *10,* 265–292.

Heap, J. Understanding classroom events: A critique of Durkin with an alternative. Paper presented at the State of the Art Conference, S.U.N.Y. at Albany, Albany, New York, 1981.

Holland, N. *5 readers reading.* New Haven: Yale University Press, 1975.

Mathews, M. *Teaching to read: Historically considered.* Chicago: University of Chicago Press, 1968.

Pearson, P. D., & Johnson, D. *Teaching reading comprehension.* New York: Holt, Rinehart, and Winston, 1978.

National Society for the Study of Education. *Report of the society's committee on silent reading: Twentieth yearbook* (Part II). Chicago: NSSE, 1921.

Schreiber, P. On the acquisition of reading fluency. *Journal of Reading Behavior,* 1980, *12,* 177–186.

Smith, N. B. *One hundred ways to teach silent reading.* Yonkers: World Books Company, 1925.

Smith, N. B. *American reading instruction.* Newark, Del.: International Reading Association, 1965.

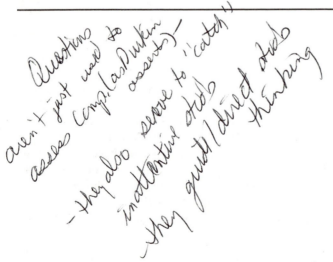

---

references

FUNDAMENTAL FACTORS OF COMPREHENSION IN READING

FREDERICK B. DAVIS

*Cooperative Test Service of the American Council on Education**

A survey of the literature was made to determine the skills involved in reading comprehension that are deemed most important by authorities. Multiple-choice test items were constructed to measure each of nine skills thus identified as basic. The intercorrelations of the nine skill scores were factored, each skill being weighted in the initial matrix roughly in proportion to its importance in reading comprehension, as judged by authorities. The principal components were rather readily interpretable in terms of the initial variables. Individual scores in components I and II are sufficiently reliable to warrant their use for practical purposes, and useful measures of other components could be provided by constructing the required number of additional items. The results also indicate need for workbooks to aid in improving students' use of basic reading skills. The study provides more detailed information regarding the skills measured by the *Cooperative Reading Comprehension Tests* than has heretofore been provided regarding the skills actually measured by any other widely used reading test. Statistical techniques for estimating the reliability coefficients of individual scores in principal-axes components, for determining whether component variances are greater than would be yielded by chance, and for calculating the significance of the differences between successive component variances are illustrated.

The application of techniques of factorial analysis to the investigation of reading has been attempted several times. Feder (11), Gans (12), and Langsam (23) have published studies that employed Thurstone's centroid method, and unpublished studies have been made by Bedell and Pankaskie. So far as the writer is aware, the study reported here is the first to make use of tests especially constructed to measure the mental skills in reading comprehension that are considered of greatest importance by authorities in the field.**

The most important step in a study that employs factorial procedures for the investigation of reading comprehension is the selection of the tests the scores of which are to be factored. Unless these tests provide reasonably valid measures of the most important mental skills that have to be performed during the process of reading, the application of the most rigorous statistical procedures can not yield meaningful and significant results. The importance of this point can hardly be overstated.

As the first step in the present study, a careful survey was made of the literature to identify the comprehension skills that are deemed most important by authorities in the field of reading. A list of several hundred specific skills was com-

*On leave for military service.

**For a detailed presentation of the basic data of this study, see (8).

From *Psychometrika,* 9(3), 1944, pp. 185–97. Reprinted with permission.

piled, many of them overlapping. This list of skills was studied intensively by the writer in order to group together those that seemed to require the exercise of the same, or closely related, mental skills. The objective was to obtain several groups of skills, each one of which would constitute a cluster having relatively high intercorrelations and relatively low correlations with other clusters of skills.

Nine groups of skills were sorted out and labeled. For the purposes of this study, they are regarded as the nine skills basic to comprehension in reading. Included within them is the multitude of specific skills considered important by the authorities consulted. These nine basic skills are as follows:

1. Knowledge of word meanings
2. Ability to select the appropriate meaning for a word or phrase in the light of its particular contextual setting
3. Ability to follow the organization of a passage and to identify antecedents and references in it
4. Ability to select the main thought of a passage
5. Ability to answer questions that are specifically answered in a passage
6. Ability to answer questions that are answered in a passage but not in the words in which the question is asked
7. Ability to draw inferences from a passage about its contents
8. Ability to recognize the literary devices used in a passage and to determine its tone and mood
9. Ability to determine a writer's purpose, intent, and point of view, i.e., to draw inferences about a writer

To provide a measure of each one of these nine basic skills, a large number of five-choice objective test items were constructed. All possible care was taken to obtain items that measured only one rather than several of the nine skills. However, it was recognized that skill 1 (knowledge of word meanings) is basic to the measurement of all the other skills, since to read at all one has to recognize words and understand their meanings, and that some overlapping of skills 2–9 is inevitable.

Since the final forms of the reading-comprehension tests used in this study were to be the published forms of Tests C1 and C2 of Form Q of the *Cooperative Reading Comprehension Tests*, practical considerations [notably the requirements of the procedure for obtaining three equivalent "scales" in the tests (6)] determined in some measure the number of items testing each basic skill that could be used. An effort was made, however, to include the proportion of items testing each one of skills 2–9 that conformed to the judgments of authorities in the field of reading.

To obtain the intercorrelations of scores in the nine basic reading skills selected for measurement, 240 multiple-choice items were administered to a large number of freshmen in several teachers colleges.* The students were told to mark every item and were allowed an unlimited amount of time. By this means, the influence of speed of reading was removed and the effects of mechanical difficulties in word perception were minimized. Of the 541 students tested, 421 actually answered every item, and, when proof was obtained that this group

*Every freshman in all of the teachers colleges of the State of Connecticut and every freshman in two of the Massachusetts State Teachers Colleges comprised the sample tested. The testing was done about a month after the beginning of the school year.

RESEARCH/TABLE 1

Intercorrelations, means, and standard deviations of raw scores in the nine basic reading skills, and their relationships with sex (N = 421)

Skill	1	2	3	4	5	6	7	8	9	Sex*	Mean	σ
1		.72	.41	.28	.52	.71	.68	.51	.68	.03	23.77	11.61
2			.34	.36	.53	.71	.68	.52	.68	−.07	12.70	3.25
3				.16	.34	.43	.42	.28	.41	−.01	4.20	1.73
4					.30	.36	.35	.29	.36	−.03	2.97	1.10
5						.64	.55	.45	.55	−.04	18.10	2.46
6							.76	.57	.76	−.01	25.67	5.67
7								.59	.68	.06	28.46	5.81
8									.58	−.05	6.75	1.86
9										−.05	15.19	4.07

*A positive coefficient in this column indicates that the men obtained a higher mean score than the women.

constituted a representative sample of the entire 541 students tested, the scores of only these 421 pupils were used in the factorial analysis. In addition to the intercorrelations of the scores, the correlations between sex and scores in each of the nine skills were computed. As would have been expected, the correlations with sex were all insignificantly different from zero. This being so, there was no need to partial out the influence of sex before making a factorial analysis.

Research/Table 1 shows the intercorrelations of the scores in the nine basic reading skills, and their relationships with sex.

The intercorrelations of the nine basic skills range from .16 to .76, the values reflecting in part their true relationships and in part the differences in their reliability. The reliability coefficients of the scores in the nine skills are shown in Research/Table 2.

As would be expected in view of the widely different lengths of the tests used to measure the nine basic reading skills, their reliability coefficients differ considerably. For even the least reliable, however, the reliability coefficient is substantially and significantly greater than zero.

Subjective judgment had forecast relatively high correlations between skill 1 and each of skills 2–9. Inspection of Research/Table 1 in the light of the data

RESEARCH/TABLE 2

Reliability coefficients of raw scores in each of the nine basic reading skills*

Skill	r_{11}	N	Number of Items
1	.90	100	60
2	.56	100	20
3	.44	100	9
4	.18	421	5
5	.55	100	22
6	.77	100	42
7	.63	100	43
8	.64	100	10
9	.71	100	27

*The division of each test into two halves was accomplished in this case by arranging the items in order of difficulty and assigning alternate items to each half. It will be recalled that speed had no influence on these scores. The reliability coefficient for skill 4 is based on 421 cases; the reliability coefficients for the other skills are based on a representative sample of 100 cases drawn from the 421 available.

RESEARCH/TABLE 3
Partial correlation coefficients among skills 2–9, skill 1 being held constant ($N = 421$)

Skill	3	4	5	6	7	8	9
2	.09	.23	.26	.40	.38	.26	.37
3		.05	.16	.22	.22	.09	.20
4			.19	.23	.22	.17	.24
5				.45	.32	.26	.32
6					.53	.33	.53
7						.38	.40
8							.38

in Research/Table 2 reveals this to be so. It is apparent that skill 1 constitutes the largest element common to all of the other initial variables; hence, it may be of interest to study the intercorrelations of skills 2–9 when skill 1 is held constant. These partial coefficients are shown in Research/Table 3.

Perhaps the most surprising feature of the data in Research/Table 3 is the small size of the coefficients. After making due allowance for the attenuation

RESEARCH/TABLE 4
Initial matrix of variances and covariances*

Variable	x_1	x_2	x_3	x_4	x_5	x_6	x_7	x_8	x_9
x_1	134.70	27.01	8.16	3.65	14.77	46.88	45.78	11.04	32.07
x_2		10.56	1.94	1.29	4.22	13.03	12.90	3.17	8.93
x_3			3.01	0.31	1.44	4.24	4.24	0.90	2.91
x_4				1.22	0.82	2.25	2.25	0.59	1.63
x_5					6.05	8.93	7.85	2.07	5.53
x_6						32.17	24.89	5.96	17.42
x_7							33.75	6.33	16.00
x_8								3.46	4.42
x_9									16.54

*Variances are shown in the diagonal cells. The Kelley method would be equally applicable if the scores in variables 1–9 were transformed into standard measures. In this case, the variance in each diagonal cell would be 1 and the covariances would be identical with the intercorrelations shown in Research/Table 1. The resulting matrix would undoubtedly present a more familiar appearance to many students. Each one of the basic reading skills would then have been weighted equally for purposes of factorial analysis. However, authorities in the field of reading quite reasonably do not judge each one of the basic skills to be of equal importance in the process of reading comprehension. Of the many possible factorial analyses (using different weights), that analysis which appears to have unique merit is a principal-axes solution based on a matrix of variances and covariances in which the initial test variances are weighted to correspond with their relative importance in the process of reading, as determined by the pooled judgment of authorities. That is the type of factorial analysis that it was intended should be performed in the present study, but practical considerations resulted in some modifications in the relative weights of the nine initial variables.

For purposes of comparison, the Kelley method was used to perform a factorial analysis of the correlation matrix shown in Research/Table 1 (excluding sex) with unit variances in the diagonals. A comparison of the factor loadings derived from the two principal-axes analyses and from a centroid analysis of the same data is now in preparation.

RESEARCH/TABLE 5
Coefficients of each of the initial variables that yield scores in the nine independent components (factor loadings of skills 1–9 in components I–IX)

Components	I	II	III	IV	V	VI	VII	VIII	IX	
Variance	192.270	22.824	8.657	5.282	3.828	3.306	2.327	1.956	1.006	
Skills										Variance
1	.813	−.571	−.064	−.033	−.082	.006	−.016	.001	.011	134.699
2	.184	.124	−.005	−.003	.971	−.019	−.017	−.028	−.076	10.563
3	.057	.054	−.001	.000	−.000	.000	.997	.000	−.004	3.009
4	.027	.048	−.000	.000	.067	.000	.000	.000	.996	1.220
5	.107	.149	.152	−.003	−.022	.970	−.014	−.024	−.012	6.050
6	.341	.469	.567	−.531	−.129	−.204	−.044	−.001	−.023	32.169
7	.336	.580	−.719	.008	−.147	−.020	−.051	−.091	−.028	33.752
8	.078	.105	−.001	.141	−.000	.000	−.010	.981	−.007	3.456
9	.233	.253	.366	.835	−.080	−.126	−.027	−.166	−.013	16.540

resulting from the comparatively low reliability coefficients of some of the variables, it is apparent that reading comprehension, as measured by the nine basic reading skills, is not a unitary ability. From the correlations it appears probable that a mental ability present to the greatest extent in skills 6, 7, and 9 is second most important in producing the intercorrelations shown in Research/Table 1. To explore this matter, a factorial analysis was undertaken, using the method described by T. L. Kelley (22).*

The initial matrix of variances and covariances used in the factorial analysis is presented in Research/Table 4.

In Research/Table 5 are presented the coefficients of each of the initial variables (the nine basic reading skills) that yield the nine independent components obtained by factorial analysis. The design shown in Research/Table 5 is one of the most interesting that has been obtained by factorial techniques.

The subjective judgment exercised in constructing the tests of the nine reading skills is reflected in the surprising extent to which several of the tests appear to be moderately "pure" factor measures. A word of caution must, however, be injected. Because some of the skills were judged to be more important than others in the reading process and because practical considerations governed to some extent the number of items used to measure each of the nine reading skills, the standard deviations of the initial variables differed considerably. And, since the initial matrix of variances and covariances used for the analysis reflected those differences, the coefficients in Research/Table 5 must be interpreted with due regard for the magnitudes of the standard deviations of the nine initial skills. Scores in skill 1, for example, have a large standard deviation in comparison with the standard deviations of scores in the other skills. So a small component loading in skill 1 may be found to have more weight in a regression equation for obtaining scores in any one of the components than

*For this study it was desirable to obtain the factor loadings of all significant components rather than the loadings for only the two or three largest components; hence a fairly large number of subjects was tested and Kelley's method was selected as being most suitable for use.

would be expected from an inspection of Research/Table 5 alone.*

A study of the values in Research/Table 5 (making due allowance for the magnitudes of the standard deviations of the initial variables) reveals that the nine components are rather readily identifiable in terms of the original nine reading skills. Component I is clearly word knowledge (skill 1). Its positive loadings in each of the nine basic reading skills reflect the fact that to read at all it is necessary to recognize words and to recall their meanings.

It is clear that word knowledge plays a very important part in reading comprehension and that any program of remedial teaching designed to improve the ability of students to understand what they read must include provision for vocabulary building. When one combines the evidence that word knowledge is so important an element in reading with the fact that the development of an individual's vocabulary is in large measure dependent on his interests and his background of experience, the relatively low correlations between reading tests in different subject-matter fields are understandable.* There is, however, no necessity to conclude that all of the fundamental factors of comprehension in reading are *not* involved in reading materials in various subject-matter fields.

Component II has been termed a measure of reasoning in reading. It has its highest positive loadings in the two reading skills that demand ability to infer meanings and to weave together several statements. It may seem puzzling at first that this component should have a strong negative loading in skill 1 (word knowledge), but consideration of the psychological meaning of components I and II indicates that this should be expected. The explanation undoubtedly lies in the fact that individuals who know accurately the meanings of a great many words are thereby given a head start toward getting the meaning of what they read. Therefore, if we are to measure reasoning in reading independently of word knowledge, we must give individuals who are deficient in word knowledge a "handicap" and then see how well they reason when they are placed on equal terms with their fellows in word knowledge. Component II apparently measures the ability to see the relationships of ideas.

*Readers who are most familiar with the centroid method of factorial analysis have sometimes questioned this statement. A principal-axes analysis makes it possible to obtain very readily a given individual's score in any one of the components for which regression coefficients (or factor loadings) have been determined. For example, individual scores in component I may be obtained from the following regression equation:

$$\begin{aligned} C_I = .813(X_1) &+ .184(X_2) + .057(X_3) \\ &+ .027(X_4) + .107(X_5) \\ &+ .341(X_6) + .336(X_7) \\ &+ .078(X_8) + .233(X_9). \end{aligned}$$

In this equation, variables 6 and 7 have nearly identical regression coefficients, but we know that the standard deviation of variable 6 is 5.67 while that of variable 7 is 5.81. Therefore, variable 7 will have a slightly greater weight in determining an individual's score in component I than will variable 6 despite the fact that the factor loadings of variables 6 and 7 in component I are almost the same.

A simple and convenient aid in interpreting the regression coefficients with proper regard for the sizes of the standard deviations of the initial variables is to construct a table containing each regression coefficient multiplied by the appropriate standard deviation of an initial variable. For example, the factor loading of skill 1 in component I (.813) would be multiplied by the standard deviation of skill 1 (11.61), yielding 9.4; the factor loading of skill 2 in component I (.184) would be multiplied by the standard deviation of skill 2 (3.25), yielding .6; and so on.

*For data on this point see (5).

Component III is not so readily interpretable as most of the others, but it is clear that individuals who obtain high scores in this component focus their attention on a writer's explicit statements almost to the exclusion of their implications. Component IV measures chiefly the ability to identify a writer's intent, purpose, or point of view (skill 9). Individuals who obtain high scores in this component are less concerned with *what* a writer says than with *why* he says it. Such individuals should presumably be better able to detect bias and propaganda than individuals who obtain low scores in this component. Component V is composed principally of ability to figure out from the context the meaning of an unfamiliar word or to determine which one of several known meanings of a word is most appropriate in its particular contextual setting (skill 2). It is reasonable that it should be essentially unrelated to skill 1, which measures memory for isolated word meanings. The slight negative loadings of skills 6 and 7 in component V may result from the fact that the latter measures deductive reasoning, while skills 6 and 7 measure inductive processes.

Judging by its very high loading in skill 5, component VI seems to be largely a measure of ability to grasp the detailed statements in a passage. It is probably a fairly direct measure of the ability to get what I. A. Richards has called "the literal sense meaning" of a passage. Skill 5 was originally intended to measure this ability and the results of the analysis suggest that this ability is more than a name; it appears to be a real psychological entity distinct from other mental skills involved in reading. Component VII seems to be a measure principally of skill 3 (ability to follow the organization of a passage and to identify antecedents and references in it). The variance of this component consists of about 77% of the original variance of skill 3.

Component VIII measures specific knowledge of literary devices and techniques, and probably reflects the influence of training in English more than the other components do. Component IX is composed largely of ability to select the main thought of a passage; it may be considered a measure of ability in the synthesis of meaning. The variance of component IX comprises approximately 82% of the original variance of skill 4 (ability to select the main thought of a passage). Students who make high scores in component IX are presumably those who would be most capable of writing adequate summaries and précis of what they read.

Of the nine components described, all except components II, III, and IV can, for practical purposes, probably be measured satisfactorily by means of raw scores in one of the nine basic reading skills selected initially. Components V through IX account for only a small fraction of the total variance, but their variances are significantly different.* A number of the skills considered most important by authorities in the field of

*The writer is indebted to Professor T. L. Kelley for the development of a precise test of the variance ratios of components obtained by his iterative process. This test is described in the article by Professor Kelley that immediately follows.

The differences between the variances of successive components are all significant at the one-per-cent level with the exception of the differences between the variances of components V and VI, and VII and VIII; those differences are significant approximately at the five-per-cent level.

It should be noted that the variance-ratio test of the significance of the difference between component variances is permitted by the Kelley method but is not permitted by other methods of factorial analysis that are frequently employed.

Whether the variance of component IX (the smallest component) is significantly greater than

RESEARCH/TABLE 6
Variance ratios of successive components

Component	Degrees of Freedom	Variance	F
I	406	192.270	
			8.280
II	399	22.824	
			2.663
III	403	8.657	
			1.622
IV	399	5.282	
			1.387
V	401	3.828	
			1.158
VI	401	3.306	
			1.428
VII	403	2.327	
			1.181
VIII	400	1.956	
			1.944
IX	400	1.006	

reading include independent elements that should be taught separately. It is not enough to assign learning exercises in reading that consist of passages followed by factual questions to be answered. Such exercises will not necessarily call the student's attention to the separate and essentially unrelated reading skills that he ought to master or give him sufficient practice in each one of them.

Because individual scores in each of the independent components defined above can readily be estimated by using appropriate regression equations (Cf. ante, footnote following Research/Table

RESEARCH/TABLE 7
Reliability coefficients, means, and standard deviations of the six independent components having reliability coefficients substantially greater than zero

Component	r_{11}	Mean	Standard Deviation
I	.94	46.30	13.87
II	.48	24.14	4.78
III	.28	.81	2.94
IV	.17	−.62	2.30
VII	.33	.27	1.53
VIII	.29	.70	1.40

5), the reliability coefficients of scores in the nine components have been determined empirically, using the same sample of 100 cases for which odd and even scores in each variable were obtained in computing the reliability coefficients of the nine initial variables.

Inspection of Research/Table 7 reveals that only components I and II are measured with sufficient reliability to warrant their use for practical purposes. However, when the significance of the reliability coefficient of each one of the nine components is tested,* it becomes evident that useful measures of at least three additional components could certainly be provided by constructing the required number of additional items of the appropriate types. Since several of the components may be satisfactorily measured, for practical purposes, by raw scores in appropriate types of test items, construction of a large number of the indicated types of items has already been started. It is believed that these may be usefulfor instructional as well as for

would be yielded by chance may be determined by noting whether the reliability coefficient of component IX is significantly greater than zero. This is not established by the data. It is highly likely, however, that the variance of the next largest component is significantly greater than would be yielded by chance.

*The standard error of a split-half reliability coefficient, corrected by the Spearman-Brown formula, may be obtained by using Shen's formula,

$$\sigma_{r_{11}} = \frac{2(1 - r_{11})}{\sqrt{N}}.$$

measurement purposes when they are employedin combination with other workbook materials.

Since useful measures of components I and II are already available, a profile chart for making a graphic record of scores in these two components has been prepared and is described in considerable detail elsewhere (9).

The correlations of components I and II with the Q and L scores derived from the *American Council on Education Psychological Examination* and with the total score on the *Nelson-Denny Reading Test* have also been reported in the literature (9, 370–371). It is hoped that the relationships between components I and II and other well-known reading tests can be obtained, for if components I and II are regarded as fundamental abilities in reading it is of paramount importance to determine the extent to which the reading tests now commonly used in high schools and colleges actually measure each of these abilities.

The study reported here has explored one means of investigating the psychological nature of reading ability. It has suggested a means of determining the validity of tests of comprehension in reading. The results indicate that there is need for reliable tests to measure several of the nine basic skills that have been defined and for workbooks to aid in improving students' abilities in them. The need for correlating scores in existing reading tests with scores in several of the principal components seems obvious. And, not least, the study provides more detailed information regarding the skills measured by the *Cooperative Reading Comprehension Tests* than has heretofore been provided regarding the skills actually measured by any other widely used reading test.*

Finally, it is hoped that the data presented will draw attention to the importance of the mental skills involved in reading and act as a stimulus to further research in the fundamental factors of comprehension.

*Frederick B. Davis, et al., *The Cooperative Reading Comprehension Tests, Lower and Higher Levels, Forms Q, R, S,* and *T.* Eight separate 40-minute reading tests are now available and are distributed by the Cooperative Test Service, 15 Amsterdam Avenue, New York, N.Y., a nonprofit agency of the American Council on Education.

REFERENCES

1. Adler, M. J. How to read a book. New York: Simon & Schuster, 1940.
2. Alderman, G. H. Improving comprehension in reading. *J. educ. Res.*, 1926, 13, 11–21.
3. Berry, B. T. Improving freshman reading habits. *Engl. J.*, College Edition, 1931, 20, 824–828.
4. Carroll, R. P. An experimental study of comprehension in reading. New York: Teachers College, Columbia University, 1927.
5. The Cooperative General Achievement Tests (Revised Series): Information concerning their construction, interpretation, and use. New York: Cooperative Test Service, 1940.
6. The Cooperative Reading Comprehension Tests: Information concerning their construction, interpretation, and use. New York: Cooperative Test Service, 1940.
7. The Cooperative Reading Comprehension Tests, Lower and Higher Levels; Forms Q, R, S, and T. New York: Cooperative Test Service.

8. Davis, Frederick B. Fundamental factors of comprehension in reading. Unpublished doctor's thesis on file at Harvard University Library, Cambridge, Massachusetts, 1941.

9. Davis, Frederick B. Two new measures of reading ability. *J. educ. Psychol.*, 1942, 33, 365–372.

10. Dewey, J. C. The acquisition of facts as a measure of reading comprehension. *Elem. Sch. J.*, 1935, 35, 346–348.

11. Feder, D. D. Comprehension maturity tests—a new technique in mental measurement. *J. educ. Psychol.*, 1938, 29, 597–606.

12. Gans, R. A study of critical reading comprehension in the intermediate grades. New York: Teachers College, Columbia University, 1940.

13. Gates, A. I. Methods of constructing and validating the Gates Reading Tests. *Teach. Coll. Rec.*, 1927, 29, 148–159.

14. Gates, A. I. The improvement of reading. New York: Macmillan Company, 1935. Ch. III and VII.

15. Gates, A. I. and Van Alstyne, D. General and specific effects of training in reading with observations on the experimental technique. *Teach. Coll. Rec.*, 1924, 25, 98–123.

16. Gray, W. S. Principles of method in teaching reading as derived from scientific investigation. National Society for the Study of Education, *Yearbook 18, Part II.* Bloomington, Illinois: Public School Publishing Company, 1919, 26–51.

17. Gray, W. S. The nature and types of reading. National Society for the Study of Education, *Yearbook 26, Part I.* Bloomington, Illinois: Public School Publishing Co., 1937, 23–40.

18. Gray, W. S. and Leary, B. E. What makes a book readable. Chicago: Univ. Chicago Press, 1935.

19. Hildreth, G. H. Learning the three R's. Minneapolis: Educational Publishers, Inc., 1936. Ch. III.

20. Hilliard, G. H. Probable types of difficulties underlying low scores in comprehension tests. *Univ. Iowa Studies in Education, II, No. 6.* Princeton, N.J.: Psychological Review Co., 1924.

21. Irion, T. W. H. Comprehension difficulties of ninth-grade students in the study of literature. New York: Teachers College, Columbia University, 1925.

22. Kelley, T. L. Essential traits of mental life. Cambridge, Massachusetts: Harvard Univ. Press, 1935.

23. Langsam, R. S. A factorial analysis of reading ability. *J. exp. Educ.*, 1941, 10, 57–63.

24. McCallister, J. M. Determining the types of reading in studying content subjects. *Sch. Rev.*, 1932, 40, 115–123.

25. Murphy, P. G. The role of the concept in reading ability. *Univ. Iowa Studies in Psychology,* XVII. Princeton, N.J.: Psychological Review Co., 1933, 21–73.

26. Pressey, L. W. and Pressey, S. L. A critical study of the concept of silent reading. *J. educ. Psychol.*, 1921, 12, 25–31.

27. Richards, I. A. Practical criticism. New York: Harcourt Brace, 1929.

28. Richards, I. A. How to read a page. New York: Harcourt Brace, 1942.

29. Richards, I. A. Interpretation in teaching. New York: Harcourt Brace, 1938.

30. Sangren, P.V. The improvement of reading through the use of tests. Lansing, Mich.: De Kleine, 1931.

31. Shank, S. Student responses in the measurement of reading comprehension. Cincinnati: C. A. Gregory, 1929.

32. Strang, R. Problems in the improvement of reading in high school and college. Lancaster, Pa.: Science Press Publishing Co., 1938. Chapter II.

33. Thorndike, E. L. The psychology of thinking in the case of reading. *Psychol. Rev.*, 1917, 24, 220–234.

34. Thorndike, E. L. Reading as reasoning: A study of mistakes in paragraph reading. *J. educ. Psychol.*, 1917, 8, 323–332.

35. Thorndike, E. L. The understanding of sentences. *Elem. Sch. J.*, 1917, 18, 98–114.

36. Touton, F. C. and Berry, B. T. Reading comprehension at the junior college level. *Calif. Quarterly sec. Educ.*, 1931, 6, 245–251.

37. Tyler, R. W. Measuring the ability to infer. *Educ. Res. Bull.*, 1930, 9, 475–480.

38. Woody, C. Measurement of a new phase of reading. *J. educ. Res.*, 1923, 8, 315–316.

39. Wyman, J. B. and Wendle, M. What is reading ability? *J. educ. Psychol.*, 1921, 12, 518–531.

40. Yoakum, G. A. Reading and study. New York: Macmillan Co., 1928. Ch. II.

41. Zahner, L. C. The testing of comprehension. *Educ. Rec.* Supplement No. 13, 1940, 21, 71–89.

42. Zahner, L. C. An approach to reading through meanings. Ch. IV in Reading in General Education. Washington, D.C.: American Council on Education, 1940.

A Critique of Frederick B. Davis's Study: Fundamental Factors of Comprehension in Reading

DALE D. JOHNSON

University of Wisconsin

SUSAN TOMS-BRONOWSKI

Wisconsin Center for Education Research

RAY R. BUSS

Louisiana State University

This paper examines the historical development of the "component skills view" of reading comprehension with special emphasis given to the work of Frederick B. Davis. Davis, an educational researcher interested in reading, was one of the first to examine the component skills involved in reading comprehension. In his initial study, Davis (1942) did a factor analysis of nine reading comprehension subskills, and discerned two *primary* reading skill components. He concluded that comprehension consisted largely of "word knowledge" or vocabulary and "reasoning in reading."

Among reading educators (Barrett, 1968; Davis, 1942, 1944, 1968, 1972; Otto & Askov, 1974; Rosenshine, 1980; Spearritt, 1972), the idea that reading comprehension is based on a number of underlying components or subskills is widely accepted. See Thorndike (1973–1974) and Thurstone (1946) for opposing views. Although the number and the degree of specificity of the subskills varies from researcher to researcher, they generally agree about the type of component skills involved in reading comprehension.

Early work by Feder (1938) and Langsam (1941) indicated that reading comprehension ability consisted of a number of factors. As a result, the construction of new objective measures to further examine these reading skill components became an important research area in the late 1930s and early 1940s (Davis, 1942, 1944; Feder, 1938; Langsam, 1941).

In 1939, Davis began research aimed at establishing the validity of the Cooperative Reading Comprehension Tests published by the Test Service of the American Council on Education. A survey of the literature in the field of reading determined which reading skills, as reported by authorities in the field, were considered the most important elements in reading comprehension. From a compilation of several hundred skills, Davis selected nine clusters of testable skills for inclusion in the new Form Q of the reading tests. They were:

1. Knowledge of word meanings.
2. Ability to select the appropriate meaning for a word or phrase in the light of its particular contextual setting.
3. Ability to follow the organization of a passage and to identify antecedents and references in it.
4. Ability to select the main thought of a passage.
5. Ability to answer questions that are directly answered in a passage.
6. Ability to answer questions that are answered in a passage but not in the words in which the question is asked.
7. Ability to draw inferences from a passage about its contents.
8. Ability to recognize literary devices used in a passage and to get its tone and mood.
9. Ability to determine a writer's purpose, intent, and point of view, i.e., to draw inferences about a writer (Davis, 1942, pp. 367–368)

The intent of the diagnostic test was that it "ought to provide reliable measures of the most important *independent mental abilities* and *specific skills* that are required in understanding the kinds of materials that students commonly have to read" (italics added, Davis, 1942, p. 365). Five choice, objective test items were constructed for each of the skill areas so that each item tested only one skill area. The number of items for each skill was determined proportionally and based "on the judgments of authorities in the field of reading concerning the importance of each skill in reading comprehension" (p. 368). Thus, for example, Skill 1: Knowledge of Word Meanings, represented what was considered by authorities in reading as the most important skill, and, therefore, it had the most test times (60). The number of items for each skill area are listed in Critique/Table 1.

After Form Q was published, the test was administered to 421 college freshmen enrolled at teachers' colleges in Connecticut and Massachusetts. The first step in the data analysis determined the intercorrelations of the nine scores. As the diagnostic test was designed to represent independent abilities (skills), it was anticipated that there would be low correlations among the skills. Critique/Table 2 shows the intercorrelations of the scores in the nine basic reading skills.

Contrary to the anticipated results, the intercorrelations of the items in Critique/Table 2 indicate that the items show a fair amount of relationship to one another. Subsequently, the data was factor-analyzed using Kelley's (1935) principal axes method. This method assumes that the factors obtained are orthogonal, i.e., uncorrelated with one another. Davis presented the nine principal components and their respective factor loadings in a subsequent article (1944); they are shown in Critique/Table 3. "The nine principal components that were obtained were remarkably clear-cut and lent themselves to ready interpretation," according to Davis (1942, p. 368). Davis noted that two components accounted for 89% of the variance. He interpreted these components as: (1) Word Knowledge, and (2) Reasoning in Reading. A closer examination of column 1 in Critique/Table 3 shows that component 1, Word Knowledge, is primarily attributable to Skill 1, Knowledge of Word Meanings. On the other hand, it appears that component 2, Reasoning in

CRITIQUE/TABLE 1
Number of items for each skill

Skill	Number of Items
1. Knowledge of word meanings.	60
2. Ability to select the appropriate meaning for a word or phrase in the light of its particular contextual setting.	20
3. Ability to follow the organization of a passage and to identify antecedents and references in it.	9
4. Ability to select the main thought of a passage.	5
5. Ability to answer questions that are directly answered in a passage.	22
6. Ability to answer questions that are answered in a passage but not in the words in which the question is asked.	42
7. Ability to draw inferences from a passage about its contents.	43
8. Ability to recognize the literary devices used in a passage and to get its tone and mood.	10
9. Ability to determine a writer's purpose, intent, and point of view, i.e., to draw inferences about a writer.	27

Reading, consists of two reading skills, Skills 6 and 7 (paraphrase and inference: see column 2 of Critique/Table 6), if we follow Davis's interpretations of his data.

In a subsequent paper, Davis interprets the nine component skills of reading comprehension as being relatively independent skills when he states, "the nine components are readily identifiable in terms of the original nine reading skills" (1944; see p. 240 of this volume). Davis (1944) notes that the same two primary components are present—i.e., (1) Word Meaning and (2) Reading as Reasoning, but he identified other components of reading comprehension in addition. Some of these

CRITIQUE/TABLE 2
Intercorrelations, means, and standard deviations of raw scores in the nine basic reading skills (N = 421)

Skill	1	2	3	4	5	6	7	8	9	Mean	σ
1		.72	.41	.28	.52	.71	.68	.51	.68	23.77	11.61
2			.34	.36	.53	.71	.68	.52	.68	12.70	3.25
3				.16	.34	.43	.42	.28	.41	4.20	1.73
4					.30	.36	.35	.29	.36	2.97	1.10
5						.64	.55	.45	.55	18.10	2.46
6							.76	.57	.76	25.67	5.67
7								.59	.68	28.46	5.81
8									.58	6.75	1.86
9										15.19	4.07

Adapted from Table 1, Davis, 1944, p. 187.

CRITIQUE/TABLE 3
Coefficients of each of the initial variables that yield scores in the nine independent components (factor loadings of skills 1–9 in components I–IX)

Compo-nents	I	II	III	IV	V	VI	VII	VIII	IX	
Variance	192.270	22.824	8.657	5.282	3.828	3.306	2.327	1.956	1.006	
Skills										Variance
1	.813	−.571	−.064	−.033	−.082	.006	−.016	.001	.011	134.699
2	.184	.124	−.005	−.003	.971	−.019	−.017	−.028	−.076	10.563
3	.057	.054	−.001	.000	−.000	.000	.997	.000	−.004	3.009
4	.027	.048	−.000	.000	.067	.000	.000	.000	.996	1.220
5	.107	.149	.152	−.003	−.022	.970	−.014	−.024	−.012	6.050
6	.341	.469	.567	−.531	−.129	−.204	−.044	−.001	−.023	32.169
7	.336	.580	−.719	.008	−.147	−.020	−.051	−.091	−.028	33.752
8	.078	.105	−.001	.141	−.000	.000	−.010	.981	−.007	3.456
9	.233	.253	.366	.835	−.080	−.126	−.027	−.166	−.013	16.540

Adapted from Table 5, Davis, 1944, p. 190.

"other" components were: Identification of Writer's Intent, Purpose, or Point of View (Skill 9); Selection of Appropriate Meaning of a Word or Phrase from Context (Skill 2); Grasping the Detailed Statements in a Passage (Skill 5); Selection of the Main Thought of a Passage (Skill 4); etc.

These two hallmark studies are the basis for the "component skills view" of reading comprehension. Davis felt reading comprehension could be divided into relatively independent component skills and that these separate skills could and should be taught depending on the individual students' needs. For instance, Davis (1942, p. 371) concluded, "In clinical use, the two independent scores (i.e., Word Knowledge and Reasoning in Reading) . . . may prove of value in determining whether a given individual would benefit most from learning exercises designed to increase his vocabulary level or his ability to relate the elements of a reading passage and make inferences therefrom." Moreover, Davis (1944; see p. 243 of this volume) further advocates the development of "workbooks to aid in improving students' abilities in them (the nine component skills)." These last two viewpoints have not gone unnoticed. Both individual reading exercises for particular students, which are often called "skill building" or "remedial work," and the design of workbook exercises which cover particular skills areas attest to Davis's influence on school reading programs and, it seems, the design of reading programs and reading research.

In critically examining Davis's (1942, 1944) results, three issues must be considered. First, the principal axes method used by Davis will extract as many components as there are skills. As Thurstone notes:

> Davis made a principal axes solution with nine factors; hence his interpretation has as many factors as there are tests. To use the principal axes solution imposes the condition that the nine factors shall be orthogonal, i.e., uncorrelated. From the point of view of psychology and education, it is a curious restriction to impose the condition that all of the nine abilities in the list of reading functions must be uncorrelated.

> Furthermore, the principal axes solution automatically imposes this restrictions (1946, p. 186)

In a seldom cited study, Thurstone (1946) reanalyzed Davis's data using Spearman's techniques and found only one factor, which he appropriately called reading ability. Our own re-analysis of Davis's data using both principal-component and factor-analysis procedures and both varimax and oblique rotation also indicate that only one factor was present.

This leads directly to our second point. In factor analysis, one usually analyzes items. Davis, however, analyzed subtests of items. The results and interpretations of his factor analysis may, therefore, be appreciably affected.

The third point deals with the subtests themselves. Since unequal numbers of items comprised the various subtests, we would expect more variation in those subtests with more items in them. It is not mere happenstance that Word Meaning with 60 items is the first reading-skill factor derived from the factor analysis, since a factor-analysis solution attempts to find those variables that have the most variance associated with them. Note that the second reading-skill factor, which consists of Skills 6 and 7, has the next highest numbers of items, 42 and 43, respectively. Thus, the number of factors and the order in which they are extracted may be greatly affected in Davis's original studies.

Despite these shortcomings, Davis's work has had a justifiably profound influence on reading from both a pedagogical point of view and a theoretical research perspective. Like it or not, many theoretical and educational perspectives are initially based on intuition as well as pragmatic and functional consideration. That certainly appears to be the case here. Therefore, Davis's interpretations of his data must also be considered within this type of educational framework. Based on subjective judgments or intuitions, authorities in the field of reading believed several things about reading comprehension. The first was that knowing words was crucial—a vocabulary was necessary. In fact, the more words a person knew, the better their text comprehension would be.

The second major belief was that reading comprehension was a thinking activity. Davis's term for his second component reflects this attitude: "Reasoning in Reading." The influence of E. L. Thorndike on Davis's coined phrase appears rather direct (Thorndike, 1917a: "The Psychology of Thinking in the Case of Reading" or 1917b: "Reading as Reasoning: A Study of Mistakes in Paragraph Reading"). According to Thorndike,

> Each word or phrase is supposed, if known to the reader, to call up its sound and meaning and the series of word or phrase meanings is supposed to be, or be easily transmuted into, the total thought. It is perhaps more exact to say that little attention has been paid to the dynamics whereby a series of words whose meanings are known singly produces knowledge of the meaning of a sentence or paragraph . . . reading is a very elaborate procedure, involving a weighing of each of many elements in a sentence, their organization in the proper relations one to another, the selection of certain of their connotations and the rejection of others, and the cooperation of many forces to determine final response. (Thorndike, 1917b, p. 323; see p. 209 of this volume)

Assuming that Davis was only peripherally influenced by Thorndike, it is not surprising that in the original test construction Skill 1 (Knowledge of Word Meanings),

Skill 6 (Ability to answer questions that are answered in a passage but not in the words in which the question is asked) and Skill 7 (Ability to draw inferences from a passage about its contents) were "weighted" through inclusion of more test items for each. Neither is it surprising that these three skills formed Davis's two major components in reading: Word Knowledge (Skill 1) and Reasoning in Reading (Skills 6 and 7). Whether one views Davis's two components of reading comprehension as a direct result of the original test construction, as his particular interpretation of his data, or as a curious empirical verification of the way comprehension was viewed, Davis's early work reinforced a "component skills view" of reading comprehension.

The early work of Davis led other researchers to investigate the component skills underlying reading comprehension. These investigators, who used a variety of techniques, obtained mixed findings. Harris (1948) obtained only one general comprehension skill when he factor-analyzed seven measures of comprehension. Hunt (1957) concluded that two reading comprehension abilities, i.e., word knowledge and a general reading-comprehension factor, were present in the Cooperative Reading Comprehension Tests after he did a differential item analysis on 204 of the 233 items used by Davis (1942, 1944). Alshan (1964, cited in Davis, 1968) factor-analyzed the first 40 items in form 2A of the Davis Reading Test (Davis & Davis, 1962) but he was unable to obtain five different component skills represented by the different items.

Davis (1968) conducted a systematic examination of eight reading comprehension skills. He carefully included an equal number of items for each of the eight comprehension skills and constructed two parallel forms of the test. After pilot testing, Davis administered the 320-item measure to 988 twelfth-grade students. Davis (1968) then performed uniqueness analyses on subtest scores for the eight skills on the two forms of the test. Davis (1968, p. 499) concluded "Surprisingly large percentages of unique non-chance variance were found, especially in scores measuring memory for word meanings and drawing inferences from content. It is clear that reading comprehension among mature readers is not a unitary trait." Critique/Table 4 presents the results of the uniqueness analyses. Note that about 35% of the non-error variance for Recalling Word Meanings (Skill 1) was unique to this skill in the set of eight comprehension skills. Moreover, 23% of the non-error variance for Drawing Inferences from the Content (Skill 5) was unique to this skill in the set of eight skills. These results indicate that reading comprehension is composed of a number of component skills. This evidence also supports the earlier claims by Davis (1942, 1944) that a number of component skills play a prominent role in reading comprehension.

Subsequent factor analyses of Davis's (1968) data were carried out by Davis (1972) and Spearritt (1972). These analyses confirmed that a number of components were required to account for Davis's data. Since Davis (1972) and Spearritt (1972) used different factor-analytic procedures and analyzed different populations, they obtained slightly different results and interpretations. For example, Davis examined the two subpopulations separately and "observed" the following four basic factors: (1) Recalling Word Meanings (Skill 1); (2) Drawing Inferences from the Content (Skill 5); (3) a combination of Finding Answers to Questions Answered Explicitly

CRITIQUE/TABLE 4
Summary of percentages of unique variance in the non-error variance of eight reading skills (N = 988)

Skill	Cross validation by	
	Items and day (Within-day Matrix)	Items (Across-day Matrix)
1. Recalling word meanings	35	29
2. Drawing inferences about the meaning of a word from context	−1	8
3. Finding answers to questions answered explicitly or in paraphrase	13	7
4. Weaving together ideas in the content	5	5
5. Drawing inferences from the content	23	18
6. Recognizing a writer's purpose, attitude, tone, and mood	14	8
7. Identifying a writer's techniques	8	3
8. Following the structure of a passage	15	12

Adapted from Table 19, Davis, 1968, p. 541.

or in Paraphrase (Skill 3) and Weaving Together Ideas in the Content (Skill 4); and (4) Drawing Inferences about the Meaning of a Word from Context (Skill 2). A fifth factor was not interpreted as readily since it was composed of different skills in the two different subpopulations. For one population, the fifth factor was a combination of Identifying a Writer's Techniques (Skill 7) and Following the Structure of the Passage (Skill 8), while the fifth factor in the second population was Recognizing a Writer's Purpose, Attitude, Tone, and Mood (Skill 6). By comparison, Spearritt (1972) combined the two Davis populations and found four factors: (1) Recalling Word Meanings (Skill 1); (2) Drawing Inferences from the Content (Skill 5); (3) Recognizing a Writer's Purpose, Attitude, Tone, and Mood (Skill 6); and (4) Following the Structure of a Passage (Skill 8). Thus, there is a fair amount of agreement in terms of the kinds of skills that Davis's (1968) previous study examined.

More important, these factor analyses indicate that a "component skills view" of reading comprehension is a plausible perspective. In particular, both Davis's (1972) and Spearritt's (1972) analyses highlight the importance of word knowledge and the ability to draw inferences. The view that word knowledge is an important and discrete comprehension skill appears in the literature today within the instrumentalist or aptitude hypotheses of vocabulary acquisition and development (Anderson & Freebody, 1979). It is also considered a discrete skill area within a knowledge hypothesis (Johnson & Pearson, 1978). The view that comprehension as reflective of reasoning with inferencing is highly important is seen in much comprehension literature today, including that literature concerned with textually explicit, textually implicit, and schema implicit models (Pearson & Johnson, 1978). For example, in a recent review of teaching reading comprehension in the middle grades, Jenkins and Pany (1980) demonstrated quite forcefully that certain reading programs and series teach the specific reading-comprehension component skills we have considered in this paper.

Apparently, Davis has had quite an influence on the theory, research, and practice of reading comprehension. However, much remains to be determined about the comprehension process during reading—and Davis's "component skills view" of this process should provide us with further insights for examining the reading-comprehension domain.

Further investigation of the critical skills of comprehension is sorely needed, especially at the elementary-school level. Nonetheless, the works reviewed here indicate that vocabulary knowledge *is* critical to comprehension. If you don't know the words, you're not going to understand the passage.

FOR FURTHER LEARNING

Those readers who are interested in continuing to explore the topic of comprehension would find the following references helpful:

Anderson, R. C., & Freebody, P. *Vocabulary knowledge and reading.* (Reading Education Report No. 11). Urbana-Champaign, Ill.: Center for the Study of Reading, 1979.

Barrett, T. C. Taxonomy of cognitive and affective dimensions of reading comprehension. In T. Clymer (Ed.), *What is "reading?": Some current concepts.* Chicago: University of Chicago Press, 1968.

Davis, F. B. Research in comprehension in reading. *Reading Research Quarterly,* 1968, *3*(4), 499–544.

Davis, F. B. Psychometric research on comprehension in reading. *Reading Research Quarterly,* 1972, *7*(4), 628–678.

Hunt, C. L., Jr. Can we measure specific factors associated with reading comprehension? *Journal of Educational Research,* 1957, *51,* 161–171.

Johnson, D. D., & Pearson, P. D. *Teaching reading vocabulary.* New York: Holt, Rinehart, & Winston, 1978.

Pearson, P. D., & Johnson, D. D. *Teaching reading comprehension.* New York: Holt, Rinehart, & Winston, 1978.

Spearritt, D. Identification of subskills of reading comprehension by maximum likelihood factor analysis. *Reading Research Quarterly,* 1972, *8,* 92–111.

Thorndike, R. L. Reading as reasoning. *Reading Research Quarterly,* 1973–1974, *9*(2), 135–147.

---

for further learning

REFERENCES

Alshan, L. M. *A factor-analytic study of items used in the measurement of some fundamental factors of reading comprehension.* Unpublished doctoral dissertation, Teachers College, Columbia University, 1964. Cited in Davis, F. B. Research in comprehension in reading. *Reading Research Quarterly,* 1968, *4,* 499–545.

Anderson, R. C., & Freebody, P. *Vocabulary knowledge and reading.* (Reading Education Report No. 11.) Urbana-Champaign, Ill.: Center for the Study of Reading, 1979.

Barrett, T. C. Taxonomy of cognitive and affective dimensions of reading comprehension. In T. Clymer (Ed.), *What is "reading?": Some current concepts.* Chicago: University of Chicago Press, 1968.

Davis, F. B. Two new measures of reading ability. *Journal of Educational Psychology,* 1942, *33,* 365–372.

Davis, F. B. Fundamental factors of comprehension in reading. *Psychometrika,* 1944, 9(3), 185–197.

Davis, F. B. Research in comprehension in reading. *Reading Research Quarterly,* 1968, *3*(4), 499–544.

Davis, F. B. Psychometric research on comprehension in reading. *Reading Research Quarterly,* 1972, 7(4), 628–678.

Davis, F. B., & Davis, C. C. *The Davis Reading Tests, Series 1 and 2, Forms A, B, C, D.* New York: Psychological Corporation, 1962.

Feder, D. D. Comprehension maturity tests—A new technique in mental measurement. *The Journal of Educational Psychology,* 1938, *29,* 597–606.

Harris, C. W. Measurement of comprehension in literature. *The School Review,* 1948, *56,* pp. 280–289; 332–342.

Hunt, C. L., Jr. Can we measure specific factors associated with reading comprehension? *Journal of Educational Research,* 1957, *51,* 161–171.

Jenkins, J. R., & Pany, D. Teaching reading comprehension in the middle grades. In R. J. Spiro, B. C. Bruce, & W. F. Brewer (Eds.), *Theoretical issues in reading comprehension.* Hillsdale, N.J.: Lawrence Erlbaum Associates, 1980.

Johnson, D. D., & Pearson, P. D. *Teaching reading vocabulary.* New York: Holt, Rinehart, & Winston, 1978.

Kelley, T. L. *Essential traits of mental life.* Cambridge, Mass.: Harvard University Press, 1935.

Langsam, R. S. A factorial analysis of reading ability. *Journal of Experimental Education,* 1941, *10*(1), 57–63.

Otto, W., & Askov, E. *Rationale and guidelines: The Wisconsin design for reading skill development.* Minneapolis: National Computer Systems, 1974.

Pearson, P. D., & Johnson, D. D. *Teaching reading comprehension.* New York: Holt, Rinehart, & Winston, 1978.

Rosenshine, B. Skill hierarchies in reading comprehension. In R. J. Spiro, B. C. Bruce, & W. F. Brewer (Eds.), *Theoretical issues in reading comprehension.* Hillsdale, N.J.: Lawrence Erlbaum Associates, 1980.

Spearritt, D. Identification of subskills of reading comprehension by maximum likelihood factor analysis. *Reading Research Quarterly,* 1972, *8,* 92–111.

Thorndike, E. L. The psychology of thinking in the case of reading. *Psychological Review,* 1971a, *24,* 220–234.

Thorndike, E. L. Reading as reasoning: A study of mistakes in paragraph reading. *The Journal of Educational Psychology,* 1917b, *8*(6), 323–332.

Thorndike, R. L. Reading as reasoning. *Reading Research Quarterly,* 1973–1974, 9(2), 135–147.

Thurstone, L. L. Note on a reanalysis of Davis's reading tests. *Psychometrika,* 1946, *11*(3), 185–188.

A Commentary on Johnson, Toms-Bronowski, and Buss's Critique of Davis's Study: Fundamental Factors of Comprehension in Reading

CAMILLE L. Z. BLACHOWICZ

National College of Education

Any survey of research monographs, reading texts, and theoretical discussions of comprehension would find the research of F. B. Davis frequently analyzed and cited, even by authors who disagree most strongly with his theses and conclusions. The body of studies beginning with and stemming from his work constitutes a fascinating watershed both in the analysis of comprehension and in the history of reading research. As such, it can be read on many levels.

Students of reading can survey this group of carefully conceived and executed studies for support for a separable subskills view of reading comprehension, one posited well before Davis's work (Gray, 1937) and one still implied in the construction of diagnostic and pedagogical materials. From a historical/philosophical perspective, the interested reader will also find that these ongoing analyses of a single question provide many windows from which to view the ways research questions are formulated and pursued. These last are the points of focus for this commentary, whereas the preceding critique deals with the former concerns.

Taking the first road, Johnson, Toms-Bronowski, and Buss provide an excellent critical summary of studies centering on the question of separable components in reading comprehension. Following Davis's meticulous and careful format, this war has been waged with the weapons of ever more refined statistical analyses, from "uniqueness analysis" (Davis, 1944), to his own revised factor analyses (Davis, 1968, 1972), to "maximum likelihood" factor analysis (Spearritt, 1972), to methods of analyzing reliability coefficients (Thorndike, 1973–74).

What remained essentially the same in all these investigations was the manner in which the items were formulated and the data collected; indeed, several of the studies were reanalyses of earlier data. What varied, in the aforementioned and other similar investigations (Hall and Robinson, 1945; Hunt, 1957; Schreiner, Hieronymus, and Forsyth, 1969; Thurstone, 1944), were the results. No clear evidence emerged across the studies in favor of unique and separable comprehension skills beyond the designation of vocabulary knowledge and the elusive "something else." For the former, it is not clear whether vocabulary knowledge is a reflection of a reading skill or of general aptitude (Anderson & Freebody, 1979). With respect to "something else," best consensus suggests one to three other possible skills concerning getting explicit facts and then relating them, but even this guarded statement is open to criticism (MacGinitie, 1973; Thorndike, 1973).

The less than conclusive nature of such a concerted effort suggests that such studies no longer be carried out (Rosenshine, 1980), and one could question their inclusion in a contemporary collection of research. Although equivocal on separate subskills in comprehension, this strand of research illuminates the practice of research and provides insights and caveats for students and comprehension researchers engaged in very different tasks.

Read for this purpose, one impression that emerges very strongly is that, as research is completed and disseminated, it takes on a life of its own. Davis's formulation of the question and the methodology for investigating it formed the touchstone for later researchers and remained relatively unexamined. Those interested in the issue of separable subskills concentrated on the procedures for data analysis. In formulating the question and drawing conclusions, the question of what could be meant by a "separable" component of comprehension was addressed only in a statistical sense. There the discussion of separability centered on the independence of the variables to be measured. Johnson, Toms-Bronowski, and Buss comment upon the way in which the items were assured independence (in that each was related to a different reading selection) and they raise the question of the statistical appropriateness of such a definition.

What remained unclear, and unexamined, was what this would mean in terms of one comprehension skill being independent of another in the act of comprehending. Even if the data collection and analysis procedures could isolate one skill at a time, this would not necessitate that the skill ever functioned other than in concert with other components of comprehension. Work in metacognition (Flavell and Wellman, 1977) and schema activation (Spiro, 1980) suggests that experimental means for tapping skills may not give us a true picture of their functioning in real life.

Another way in which the initial research premises remained unexamined and unchanged was in the design of the data collection items. This is especially intriguing because Davis raised the most pointed question on this topic in his own study when he noted:

> It should be emphasized that the results of the present study depend basically on the appropriateness of the items used. No satisfactory manipulation of data resulting from the use of items lacking intrinsic validity can make up for their fundamental inadequacy. This fact cannot be overemphasized; basically, this study stands or falls on the psychological insight and ingenuity that characterized the items used. (Davis, 1968, pp. 512–513)

Examination of just one of the items he provides as an exemplar could (and did, in an informal meeting of colleagues) provoke some interesting discussion:

> *Weaving ideas in the content*
>
> One early April I visited a man who had an outdoor swimming pool. The first night my host asked, "Are you a morning plunger?"
>
> Thinking he referred to a tub plunge in a warm bathroom, I glowed and said, "You bet!"
>
> "I'll call for you at seven, then, and we'll go out to the pool."

It was evidently his morning custom, and I wasn't going to have it said that a middle-aged man could outdo me. My visit lasted five days, and I later learned from one to whom my host confided that they were the worst five days he had ever gone through. "But I couldn't be outdone by a mere stripling," he said, "and the boy surely enjoyed it."

The writer and his host both:

A liked to swim

B disliked swimming

C were amused by the other's behavior

D misunderstood the other's real feelings

(Davis, 1968, p. 511)

While D may be the preferred answer, it is not possible to rule out A, B, or C without some discussion or greater knowledge of the context. Indeed, a study using reading education graduate students as evaluators of responses to the Davis Reading Test found that among these evaluators, agreement was extremely low (Macola, 1981).

Given the type of analyses of textual and situational variables being done currently, a look at the items themselves would be called for if such data were to be reanalyzed today. This lack of examination of items in earlier comprehension research speaks to the time: the quantitative mode, rather than qualitative investigation, was the model of the day. Both of these observations, the assumptions inherent in the definition of the problem and the focus of reanalysis on statistical rather than, or even to the exclusion of, qualitative analysis relate to a more general comment on research.

While statistical battles may wax or wane, depending upon the formulation of more sensitive tools and improved methods of qualitative analysis, research must continue dealing with the issue of the bias inherent in one's frame of reference. In these subskill-analysis studies, the initial conceptualization of comprehension categories depended upon the judgements of "experts" about the importance of factors in reading comprehension. The designations of the skills to be looked at came from theorized skills models of the day and their modes of assessment reflected the burgeoning interest and faith in standardized testing and statistical analysis. These particular emphases were reflected in the data analyses and conclusions.

Johnson, Toms-Bronowski, and Buss allude to the "intuitions" about comprehension so strongly reflected in the works they surveyed; often the researcher's summations reflected this initial stance rather than the data. Davis's tenacity in retaining his nine originally postulated skills when only two or three seemed verified by the data is a good example of what might be called a "theoretical override." Similarly, drawing teaching implications for school-age children from studies of adult, fluent readers speaks to the questionable tendency to generalize beyond one's original purpose and population based on one's intuitions about comprehension.

Viewed from these diverse perspectives, there are several reasons why the work of F. B. Davis will continue to have value for the students of reading research. First, his work set a new standard for careful and meticulous research, one frequently not met in analyses of reading. He presented a problem in a detailed and thoughtful way so that others interested in the same questions could build on his studies. Though this question is no longer being pursued in the same manner, the ability to go beyond it was made possible by a degree of specificity in research which allowed for replication, productive interchange, re-evaluation, and reflection.

Further, his work and that which followed substantiated the importance of vocabulary knowledge to comprehension. Johnson, Toms-Bronowski, and Buss's ending comment, "If you don't know the words, you're not going to understand the passage" (see page 254) may sound obvious, but perhaps it has not been sufficiently appreciated. Whether "In the beginning was the word," remains to be argued, but the importance of vocabulary as a component of comprehension is essential to keep in mind when so much of current research and theory building deals with larger areas of text, context, and pragmatic variables.

Lastly, a survey of this line of research serves as a reminder of the ways in which theoretical paradigms shape experimental efforts and findings. The terms in which initial work is explained (consider "schema," "distinctive feature analyzer," "data driven," "bottom-up") become reified by the frequency of their use and inform the ways in which research is planned, structured, and evaluated for publication. The separable comprehension subskills research can serve as a reminder that the growth of knowledge about reading can best take place when all facets of research, from theoretical frameworks to statistical procedures, are held up to scrutiny and find open forums of expression.

REFERENCES

Anderson, R. C., & Freebody, P. *Vocabulary knowledge and reading.* (Reading Education Report No. 11.) Urbana-Champaign, Illinois: Center for the Study of Reading, 1979.

Davis, F. B. Fundamental factors of comprehension in reading. *Psychometrika,* 1944, 9(3), 185–197.

Davis, F. B. Research in comprehension in reading. *Reading Research Quarterly,* 1968, *3*(4), 499–544.

Davis, F. B. Psychometric research on comprehension in reading. *Reading Research Quarterly,* 1972, 7(4), 628–678.

Flavell, J. H., & Wellman, H. M. Metamemory. In R. V. Kail & J. W. Hagen (Eds.), *Perspectives on the development of memory and cognition.* Hillsdale, N.J.: Lawrence Erlbaum Associates, 1977.

Gray, W. S. The teaching of reading: A second report. *36th Yearbook of the National Society for the Study of Education.* Bloomington, Ill.: Public School Publishing, 1937.

Hall, W. E., & Robinson, F. P. An analytical approach to the study of reading skills. *Journal of Educational Psychology,* 1945, *36,* 429–442.

Hunt, L. C., Jr. Can we measure specific factors associated with reading comprehension? *Journal of Educational Research,* 1957, *51,* 161–171.

MacGinitie, W. H. What are we testing? In W. H. MacGinitie (Ed.), *Assessment problems in reading.* Newark, Del.: International Reading Association, 1973.

Macola, C. *The relationship between cartoon comprehension and the Davis reading test.* Unpublished master's thesis, University of Illinois at Chicago Circle, 1981.

Rosenshine, B. Skill hierarchies in reading comprehension. In R. J. Spiro, B. C. Bruce, & W. F. Brewer (Eds.), *Theoretical issues in reading comprehension.* Hillsdale, N.J.: Lawrence Erlbaum Associates, 1980.

Schreiner, R. B., Hieronymus, A. N., & Forsyth, R. Differential measurement of reading abilities at the elementary school level. *Reading Research Quarterly,* 1969, *5,* 84–99.

Spearritt, D. Identification of subskills of reading comprehension by maximum likelihood factor analysis. *Reading Research Quarterly,* 1972, *8,* 92–111.

Spiro, R. Constructive processes in prose comprehension and recall. In R. J. Spiro, B. C. Bruce, & W. F. Brewer (Eds.), *Theoretical issues in reading comprehension.* Hillsdale, N.J.: Lawrence Erlbaum Associates, 1980.

Thorndike, R. L. Reading as reasoning. *Reading Research Quarterly,* 1973–1974, 9(2), 135–147.

Thurstone, L. L. Note on a reanalysis of Davis's reading tests. *Psychometrika,* 1946, *11*(3), 185–188.

TEACHER QUESTIONING AND READING

FRANK J. GUSZAK

University of Texas

In 1917, Thorndike outlined a classic definition of reading in three words when he said, "Reading is thinking." Fifty years later, the conversation on the reading scene is still concerned with reading as thinking with regard to how varied reading-thinking skills can be developed within the classroom. Despite the numerous treatments of such reading-thinking skills as "critical reading skills" in the professional press, contentions abound that classroom teachers are doing little to develop a variety of reading-thinking skills. Rather, according to Austin and Morrison (1964) and Henry (1963), teachers appear to equate reading-thinking skills with the most narrow of literal comprehension skills.

Because standardized reading tests tend to measure literal comprehension skills, it is difficult to make wide assessments of pupils' abilities in various reading-thinking areas. In the absence of such test results, it seems advisable to examine the interaction between teachers and students in the reading circle as they engage in the development of read-thinking skills. Thus, the current study was initiated in an effort to make determinations about the state of reading-thinking skills development as it occurred in the context of the reading group in the elementary grades. Observation and study were guided by the following questions:

1. What kinds of thinking questions do teachers ask about reading assignments in selected second, fourth, and sixth grade classrooms? In what frequencies do the various question types occur?

2. How frequently are teacher questions about reading assignments met with congruent or correct student responses?

3. Do teachers employ certain questioning strategies as they question students about reading assignments? If so, what are the characteristics of these strategies?

SUBJECTS AND PROCEDURES

From a population of 106 second, fourth, and sixth grade teachers in a public school system in Texas, a sample of four teachers (and their respective students) at each of these grade levels was randomly selected for the study. The mean class size of the three grades was as follows: second grade, 29.7; fourth grade, 24.7; and sixth grade, 28.5. Three reading-group structures were operant in all of the second and fourth grade classrooms while such a functional structure was found in only one of the sixth grade classrooms.

From *The Reading Teacher,* Vol. 21, No. 3, December 1967, pp. 227–34. Reprinted with permission of the author and the International Reading Association.

Each reading group in the twelve classrooms was observed and recorded over a three day period (an average of approximately five hours per classroom). The taped recordings were subsequently transcribed to written protocols and analyzed in accordance with the research questions.

RESULTS

Results of the study are discussed in accordance with the three basic question areas. Because each set of results is based upon a conceptual framework, the initial part of each discussion will deal with these frameworks which were subsequently utilized in the measurement process.

Question 1 The initial study task was one of making a determination of what kinds of questions teachers ask about reading assignments. An extensive survey was made of the following: reading-thinking skills as identified in basal series, reading-thinking skills as identified by reading authors, and representative thinking models. From these sources, the most pertinent conceptualizations of reading-thinking skills were synthesized into the model that subsequently was called the Reading Comprehension Question-Response Inventory. After repeated testing, the instrument was found to possess face validity and reliability when applied to teacher questions and student responses in a pilot study.

READING COMPREHENSION QUESTION-RESPONSE INVENTORY

RECOGNITION These questions call upon the students to utilize their literal comprehension skills in the task of locating information from reading context. Frequently, such questions are employed in the guided reading portion of a story, i.e. Find what Little Red Ridinghood says to the wolf.

RECALL Recall questions, like recognition questions, concern literal comprehension. The recall question calls upon the student to demonstrate his comprehension by recalling factual material previously read. Generally, such activity is primarily concerned with the retrieval of small pieces of factual material, but the size of the pieces may vary greatly. An example of a recall question would be the following where the answer to the question is clearly printed in the text, i.e. What was Little Red Ridinghood carrying in the basket?

TRANSLATION Translation questions require the student to render an objective, part-for-part rendering of a communication. As such, the behavior is characterized by literal understanding in that the translator does not have to discover intricate relationships, implications, or subtle meanings. Translation questions frequently call upon students to change words, ideas, and pictures into different symbolic form as is illustrated in the following from Bloom (1956).

Translation from one level of abstraction to another; abstract to concrete, lengthy to brief communication, i.e. Briefly re-tell the story of Little Red Ridinghood.

Translation from one symbolic form to another, i.e. Draw a picture of the first meeting between Little Red Ridinghood and the wolf.

Translation from one verbal form to another; non-literal statements to ordinary English (metaphor, symbolism).

CONJECTURE These questions call for a "cognitive leap" on the part of the student as to what will happen or what might happen. As such, the conjecture is an anticipatory thought and not a rationale, i.e. What do you think that Little Red Ridinghood will do in the future when she meets a wolf in the forest?

EXPLANATION Explanation questions, like conjecture questions, are inferential in nature. However, the inference involved in the explanation situations calls upon the student to supply a rationale. The rationale must be inferred by the student from the context developed or go beyond it if the situation is data-poor in terms of providing a rationale. Instances of explanatory behaviors are found in the following: explanations of value positions, i.e. Explain why you like Little Red Ridinghood best?; conclusions, i.e. Explain why the wolf wanted to eat Little Red Ridinghood.; main ideas, What is the main idea of this story?

EVALUATION Evaluation questions deal with matters of value rather than matters of fact or inference and are thus characterized by their judgmental quality (worth, acceptability, probability, etc.). The following components of this category are adapted from a classification scheme by Aschner and Gallagher (1965).

- Questions calling for a rating (good, bad, true, etc.) on some item (idea, person, etc.) in terms of some scale of values provided by the teacher, i.e. Do you think that this was a good or bad story?
- Questions calling for a value judgment on a dimension set up by the teacher. Generally, these are "yes" or "no" responses following questions such as "Would you have liked Tom for a brother?"
- Questions that develop from conjectural questions when the question is qualified by probability statements such as "most likely." "Do you think that it is most likely or least likely?"
- Questions that present the pupil with a choice of two or more alternatives and require a choice, i.e. "Who did the better job in your opinion, Mary or Susan?"

With the determination of the categories of the Reading Comprehension Question-Response Inventory the first question concerning the kinds of questions asked by teachers was answered. Comparative frequency of the six question types is reported in Research/Table 1.

Total questions recorded numbered 1857—878 in grade two; 725, grade four, 254, grade six. The teachers spent the greatest portion of their questions on the literal comprehension realms of "recall" and "recognition." Seemingly, the observations tend to support the contention that elementary reading teachers dwell on literal comprehension. It should be added that "dwell" is imprecise as is any determination about what percentage of

RESEARCH/TABLE 1
Percentages of each question type in grades two, four, and six

Grade	Recog.	Recall	Transl.	Conjec.	Explan.	Evalua.
	%	%	%	%	%	%
Two	12.3	66.5	.2	5.7	3.8	11.5
Four	16.3	48.4	.6	6.9	7.4	20.4
Six	10.2	47.6	2.4	7.9	8.1	13.8
Total	13.5	56.9	.6	6.5	7.2	15.3

questions should be asked in each category.

Although 15.3 per cent of the teachers' questions were spent on evaluation questions, there seems to be some legitimate doubt about the thinking depth they required. A close inspection of the questions in this category revealed that nearly all called for a simple "yes" or "no" response. Thus, the measure of higher level thinking seemed to be the incidence of questions in the inferential categories of "conjecture" and "explanation." These combined categories accounted for 13.7 per cent of the teachers' questions.

The old adage that "children learn to read in the primary grades and read to learn in the intermediate grades" seems to be borne out if one interprets an increase in inferential questioning as an increase in "reading to learn." There was a pattern of decrease in literal questioning as children reach the higher grade levels. The supplementary observations of the researchers indicated that second grade teachers spent many questions upon the minute, developing details of most story sequences. This close comprehension check is further evidenced by the greater frequency of questioning in the lower grades.

Question 2 A study exclusively devoted to teacher question types would indicate little about the effect of such questions upon students. Therefore, an effort was made to check the student responses against the teacher questions that initiated such responses. If responses satisfied the substantive intents of the teacher-initiated questions, these question-response sequences were said to be congruent or correct. If the responses failed in some way (incomplete, inaccurate) to meet the intent of the teachers' questions, they were termed incongruent. Thus, congruence was a measure of the reciprocity between questions and responses. It should be pointed out that whereas response patterns were very narrow in terms of literal comprehension questions they were very loose in terms of inferential questions that allowed for numerous responses. Patterns of question-response congruence in the three grades are illustrated in Research/Table 2.

Possibly one of the most interesting observations relating to the congruence patterns is that the highest incidence of congruence was found in the second grade. A close inspection of the category frequencies reveals that the total congruence percentages are the result of the congruence percentages in the recall category. Second grade teachers obviously had higher percentages of congruence at the recall level than did their fourth and sixth grade counterparts. As indicated

RESEARCH/TABLE 2
Percentages of question-response congruence in grades two, four, and six

Grade	Recog.	Recall	Transl.	Conjec.	Explan.
	%	%	%	%	%
Two	94.6	92.5	100.0	95.1	80.0
Four	91.9	88.1	50.0	91.5	86.0
Six	100.0	84.4	80.0	100.0	88.1
Total	93.9	90.3	75.0	94.2	85.5

previously, the second grade teachers tended to question more precisely than did the upper grade teachers in that they questioned frequently about the factual material on a given page. While the upper grade teachers seemed to question specific factual bits also, it appeared that they lacked the control over the story details because of the difficulty of the memory task created by the greater quantity of words. Consequently, this factual questioning mode resulted in several situations wherein the upper grade teachers accepted as congruent certain responses which were indeed incongruent. The second grade teachers had no such problem because of the readily apparent answers in the simple reading materials.

Question 3 Many hours of observation revealed that teachers employ two basic kinds of strategies as they question children about reading assignments. First, they control the nature of the exchange relative to each question. Second, they may pattern such individual question-response exchanges into larger wholes.

In order to describe the strategy elements involved in the single question the concept of the Question-Response Unit (QRU) was developed. The QRU represented the boundaries wherein the anatomy of an exchange could be illustrated. As such, it contained the following elements: the teacher's initiating question; any subsequent remarks on the part of the teacher that might serve to extend, clarify, or cue subsequent student response; the referent in the reading materials for the question; the way in which the student subsequently dealt with the question; and finally the phase wherein attention was shifted away from the initiating question.

Conceivably, every initiating question can be met by a congruent response on the first response attempt. However, such is not always the case. In some instances, the teacher may move the focus before a student can respond. In other instances, response time may be allowed, but none may be forthcoming. In this case, the teacher may drop the unit or invoke a sustaining statement that will either clarify the question or offer some cues as to the correct response. These examples represent a very small number of alternatives that may happen in the context of a QRU.

Many QRU patterns were identified. Because so many were seen in only one or two instances, the decision was made to focus upon those which occurred in at least three instances. Research/Table 3 presents a frequency report of such patterns. The following symbols are used to identify the patterns:

Q—teacher's initiating question
R—student response
/—a clarifying, extending, or cueing remark by teacher
+—congruent response
−—an incongruent response
(−)—response allowed but only silence heard
(O)—teacher did not allow time for student response
|—separate responses

A question followed by a single congruent response (SR+) was the dominant pattern of interaction. Furthermore, observation indicates that the pattern tends to be closely associated with "recall" questions. Because "recall" questions were most abundant in the second grade classes, the SR+ pattern was likewise most prominent in the second grade.

A second focus relative to teacher questioning strategies was the concept of the Question-Response Episode. The Question-Response Episode represented a combination of two or more Question-

RESEARCH/TABLE 3
Frequencies of question-response unit patterns

Patterns	Recog.	Recall	Transl.	Conjec.	Explan.	Evalua.	Total
SR+	74	681	4	56	50	189	1054
S(O)/R+	5	34	0	1	4	2	46
SR−	4	41	0	0	1	0	46
SR−/R+	6	15	0	4	1	1	27
SR+/R+	0	5	0	3	3	4	15
SR+|R+	1	1	0	2	0	6	10
S(−)	0	6	1	0	1	1	9
S(−)/R+	0	5	0	0	0	0	5
S(O)/(O)/R+	1	2	0	0	1	0	4
SR+|R−	0	4	0	0	0	0	4
S(O)/R−/R+	1	2	0	0	0	0	3
S(O)/(−)	1	1	0	0	1	0	3
Total	93	797	5	66	62	203	1226

Response Units which tended to be related in the following ways:

SETTING PURPOSE FOLLOW-UP These episodes occur when a teacher follows-up a "setting purpose" question (S(O)) with a parallel question calling for a response. The teacher asks the first question as a guide for the students and then repeats the question in a manner that calls for response.

VERIFICATION Verification episodes involve questions wherein congruence can be verified by referring to the text. As such, it is the reverse of the previous episode type. In verification episodes, the teacher follows up a student response with a question that calls for the verification or finding of the referent for the response to the previous question.

JUSTIFICATION These episodes appear when a teacher calls upon a student to justify his own or somebody else's previous response by the use of explanation. This explanation most frequently follows a judgmental or conjectural response to a previous question.

JUDGMENTAL These episodes occur in situations wherein a teacher asks for an evaluation of the student response to the preceding question. Thus, judgmental episodes constitute a reversal of the order employed in the justification episodes.

Of the 142 Question-Response Episodes tallied (Research/Table 4), sixty-seven were "setting purpose follow-up" episodes. "Judgmental" episodes represented the least observed type.

CONCLUSIONS AND IMPLICATIONS

Although the following conclusions and the implications based upon them are aimed specifically at the sample teachers, it is the feeling of the researcher that these items may be keenly appropriate to a much wider group of teachers.

1. Conceivably, the expenditure of nearly seventy of a hundred questions in the literal comprehension areas may be justified. Unjustifiable, however, is the involvement of these so-called literal comprehension questions with retrieval of the trivial factual makeup of stories. In real life reading situations, readers seldom approach reading with the purpose

RESEARCH/TABLE 4
Frequencies of question-response episodes in grades two, four, and six

Grade	SP Follow-up	Verification	Justification	Judgmental	Total
Two	26	11	11	3	51
Four	35	14	23	2	74
Six	6	8	2	1	17
Totals	67	33	36	6	142

of trying to commit all the minute facts to memory. Rather, the reader is more interested in getting broad understandings of the material, finding out specific things commensurate with his interests or other needs, etc. It would appear, then that much of the recall questioning actually leads the students away from basic literal understandings of story plots, events, and sequences. It seems quite possible that students in these recall situations may miss the literal understanding of the broad text in their effort to satisfy the trivial fact questions of the teachers. Seemingly, if teachers want to get at utilitarian aspects of literal understanding, they would offer many situations (rather than the few evidenced) for translational activities wherein they could really determine the extent to which children were understanding the literal elements. Of course, before teachers can employ more comprehensive questioning patterns, they must be aware of such. Thus, reading series should clearly spell out their comprehension structures in such a way that classroom teachers can have some clear insights into their task in comprehension development.

2. Students invariably are sensitive to "what teachers want" and generally do a good job of supplying it. This appears very evident with regard to questions about reading when one notes that over 90 per cent of all literal comprehension questions are met with congruent responses on the first student try. Presumably, the programmed learning buff would comment that this is the way it should be. However, inspection of the makeup of the questions proves the folly of such a notion. About the only thing that appears to be programmed into the students is the nearly flawless ability to anticipate the trivial nature of teachers' literal questions. As evidenced by the high congruence of immediate responses, the students have learned quite well to parrot back an endless recollection of trivia. It would be interesting to measure the same students' understandings of the story via a translational question.

3. If educators want to condition students for irresponsible citizenship, it seems quite appropriate to ask children for unsupported value statements, a practice which is very frequent in the reading circle according to this study. It seems imperative that teachers pattern the all-important "why" questions after students take positions. Until such is the common practice it seems that teachers will condition students to take value positions without the vital weighing of evidence that seems to separate the thinking individual from the mob member. Perhaps the use of a tape recorder would indicate to teachers their patterning practices with regard to such potentially dangerous questioning practices.

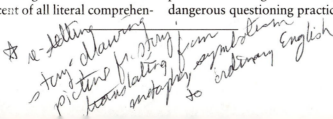

REFERENCES

Aschner, Mary June, Gallagher, J. J., Perry, Joyce M., Afsar, Sibel S., Jenne, W., and Farr, Helen. A system for classifying thought processes in the context of classroom verbal interaction. Champaign, Illinois: Institute for Research on Exceptional Children, 1965.

Austin, Mary C., and Morrison, C. The first R: the Harvard report on reading in elementary schools. New York: Macmillan, 1964.

Bloom, B. S. (Ed.) Taxonomy of educational objectives: handbook 1: cognitive domain. New York: McKay, 1956.

Henry, J. Reading for what? *Teachers College Record*, 1963, *65*.

Thorndike, E. L. Reading as reasoning: a study of mistakes in paragraph reading. *Journal of Educational Research*, 1917, *8*, 323–332.

A Critique of F. J. Guszak's Study: Teacher Questioning and Reading

P. DAVID PEARSON

University of Illinois at Urbana-Champaign

In 1967, Frank Guszak reported the findings of a larger study (Guszak, 1966) in which he observed, over a period of three days, the kinds of questions that second-, fourth-, and sixth-grade teachers asked their students as they discussed their basal reading stories. For some reason, Guszak's research had relatively little impact on the reading community during the late 1960s and early 1970s. In contrast, his work is cited more frequently during the late 1970s and early 1980s. Perhaps this difference reflects little more than increased concern for comprehension and comprehension instruction over the last decade. Whatever the reasons, the increased interest in Guszak's work creates an opportune situation in which to revisit and review his original work. This is especially true given the recent surge of interest in comprehension-instruction practices motivated by the work of Durkin (1978–79, 1981) and the expanding perspective on role of questions in instruction stemming from the mathemagenic tradition (Anderson & Biddle, 1975), the teacher effectiveness tradition (Duffy & McIntyre, 1980), and instructional work in reading education (for example, Brown & Palincsar, in press; Hansen, 1981; Hansen & Pearson, 1982; Raphael, 1980; Raphael, Winograd, & Pearson, 1980).

THE CRITIQUE

The Facts of the Case

Guszak randomly selected four classroom teachers in each of grades two, four, and six. All of the second and fourth and one of the sixth-grade teachers used a traditional three-group instructional organization (presumably the other three sixth-grade teachers used whole-class instruction). Guszak recorded the reading lessons of each teacher over a period of three days (M = five hours per teacher); the tapes of the lessons were subsequently transcribed to written protocols, and the written protocols became the data for subsequent analyses.

Guszak used these data to try to answer the following three questions:

1. What kinds of thinking questions do teachers ask about reading assignments in selected second, fourth, and sixth-grade classrooms? In what frequencies do the various question types occur?

2. How frequently are teacher questions about reading assignments met with congruent or correct student responses?

3. Do teachers employ certain questioning strategies as they question students about reading assignments? If so, what are the characteristics of these strategies?

To answer question one, Guszak developed and validated a taxonomy called the Reading Comprehension Question-Response Inventory, which could be applied to the teacher questions and the student responses. While Guszak is silent (at least in the shorter report of these data) about the source of the categories in the taxonomy, the influence of Bloom (1956) (whom he cites to explicate one category—translation) and Barrett (1976) (who developed his taxonomy about this time and was Guszak's advisor at Wisconsin) seems evident. While space does not permit a full description of the subcategories within each category, I will exemplify each of the main categories, paraphrasing liberally from Guszak.

Recognition. Frequently employed during guided reading, these questions require students to use "literal comprehension skills" to locate information in the text: "Find out what Little Red Ridinghood says to the wolf."

Recall. These questions also concern literal comprehension and require students "to retrieve small pieces of factual material . . . clearly printed in the text": "What was Little Red Ridinghood carrying in the basket?"

Translation. These questions require paraphrase of different chunks of literally stated information into a different symbolic code: Retell a story (where length of communication is shortened), draw a picture (verbal to pictorial representation), tell what X means (where X might be a word or a phrase—particularly a figure of speech).

Conjecture. This category is defined almost identically to what we most often call predicting outcomes, what will happen next or what might happen in the future.

Explanation. Like conjecture, these questions are inferential in nature, and require students to offer "rationales," presumably for character actions. They focus on character motivations, with one exception: Guszak chose to include all main idea questions in this category.

Evaluation. These questions require judgments of "worth, acceptability or probability" often satisfied by a simple yes or no or a forced choice response: Was it a good or bad story? Would you have liked Tom for a brother? Do you think event X or Y is more likely? Who did a better job, X or Y?

Each teacher question was unambiguously classified into one of these six categories. The data are reported in Critique/Table 1, taken directly from the Guszak (1967) article.

While studying the data, Guszak noted a trend toward decreasing frequency of questions across grades (2 = 878, 4 = 725, 6 = 254), an overall emphasis on the

CRITIQUE/TABLE 1
Percentages of each question type in grades two, four, and six

Grade	Recog.	Recall	Transl.	Conjec.	Explan.	Evalua.
	%	%	%	%	%	%
Two	12.3	66.5	.2	5.7	3.8	11.5
Four	16.3	48.4	.6	6.9	7.4	20.4
Six	10.2	47.6	2.4	7.9	18.1	13.8
Total	13.5	56.9	.6	6.5	7.2	15.3

literal end of the continuum, tendency for evaluation questions to require little more than yes–no responses without any follow-up justification for the choice selected, and a bit of a trend toward switching from literal to inferential across grades.

The data for question two regarding student responses were generated by judging whether or not the responses given by the students were congruent (congruent = correct; incongruent = incomplete or inaccurate) with the teachers' questions. Guszak admits that congruency criteria were exacting and narrow for literal questions, and loose for inferential questions. Critique/Table 2 provides Guszak's data for response congruence.

Guszak notes the highest incidence of congruence for grade-two teachers and attributes this difference to recall category differences. This, he reasoned, probably occurred because second-grade teachers tended to question more precisely than the other teachers (i.e., about the factual material on a given page) *and* because the memory task in the upper level stories, created by the sheer increase in number of words in a story, interfered with recall for older students. In short, second-grade stories were easier, less complex, and less cluttered with detail, making it easier for the students either to locate or retrieve (it is not clear which Guszak intends) factual details.

The data for the third question, concerning teachers' questioning strategies, will not be dealt with in this revisit (parsimony, not lack of interest for what is a very rich data set, is the motive). Suffice it to say that Guszak defined strategies in terms

CRITIQUE/TABLE 2
Percentages of question-response congruence in grades two, four, and six

Grade	Recog.	Recall	Transl.	Conjec.	Explan.
	%	%	%	%	%
Two	94.6	92.5	100.0	95.1	80.0
Four	91.9	88.1	50.0	91.5	86.0
Six	100.0	84.4	80.0	100.0	88.1
Total	93.9	90.3	75.0	94.2	85.5

of Question-Response Units that mapped the interactive flow between teacher questions and student responses. Note that one category (question followed by correct response) accounted for 57% of all QRUs (actually 86% of those QRUs had at least three classifiable examples). These data are, of course, not surprising given the high congruence rates in Critique/Table 2.

In his discussion, Guszak admits that the literal comprehension focus he found "may be justified" but bemoaned the emphasis on what he called questions invoking "retrieval of the trivial factual make-up of stories" (see page 268). He would have preferred more emphasis on translation questions (remember they call for a paraphrase from one level of abstraction to another). He also emphasized the congruence finding: "Students invariably are sensitive to what teachers want and generally do a good job of supplying it" (see page 269). Given the emphasis upon "an endless recollection of trivia" (see page 269), he questioned the virtue of this finding. Finally, he expressed concern that so few value-oriented questions were followed up by asking students to justify the judgments they had made, fearing that the failure to require support might foster irresponsible citizenship.

Critiquing the Facts

One can critique a piece of research at various levels; for example, issue relevance, methodology, data analysis, data presentation, and interpretation of the findings. In any critique, however, one must remember the context in which the study was conducted: the tenor and dominant issues of the times, the sophistication of the available research technology, and the purpose of the research. In this spirit, I will stipulate at the outset that Guszak's study was exemplary and pioneering within the reading field. While there was already an observational research tradition within education as a whole (e.g., Flanders, 1967), only the work of Harris and Serwer (1966) was a contemporary match in level of detail about aspects of reading instruction. It was pioneering because it addressed issues of comprehension in a period when concern for beginning reading, especially decoding instruction, dominated the field. This was a time, remember, when the First-Grade Studies (Bond & Dykstra, 1967) and "The Great Debate" (Chall, 1967) were on our minds. Nonetheless, at a more specific level of detail, there are many questions about the work of Harris and Serwer.

The Taxonomy

Guszak's work is closely acquainted with Bloom's taxonomy of the cognitive domain (1956) and with Barrett's (1976) subsequent extrapolation of Bloom for reading comprehension. And it suffers from the same problem as its predecessors: it allows classification of a question without respect to a critical contextual variable; namely, the information available to the students when they are asked to answer it.

Pearson and Johnson (1978), building on the work of Nicholson and Pearson (1976) and Lehnert (1978), became acutely aware of this problem when trying to build their three-level taxonomy. The problem of varied quality responses to what they thought were straightforward literal recall or recognition questions (that is, information seemed readily available in the text to answer the question) caused them to move from a question taxonomy to a taxonomy of question-answer relationships (QARs). In so doing, the issue of whether a student has engaged, for example, in literal or inferential processing, depends not solely upon the question probe, but also upon the information available in the text and the apparent source of the student's response.

The example responses (actual responses given by students in the Bormuth, Manning, Carr, and Pearson, 1971 study) given to questions derived from paragraph (1) illustrate the problem.

(1) When items made of rubber first came out, customers were not happy with them. They turned glue-like in the hot summer and rock-hard in the cold of winter. Storekeepers who had purchased such items had to bury piles and piles of their goods. Because they lost a lot of money, storekeepers became fed up with rubber products.
(2) **Why did storekeepers become fed up with rubber products?**
(3) Because they lost a lot of money.
(4) Because no one would buy them.
(5) Because they couldn't sell them.
(6) Because they had to bury so many.
(7) Because customers didn't like them.
(8) They turned like glue and rocks.
(9) **Why did rubber products turn glue-like in the hot summer?**
(10) They were too soft.
(11) They didn't add sulphur yet.
(12) **Why weren't customers happy with items made of rubber at first?**

Notice that question (2) permits a straightforward literal response from the same sentence that generated question (2); (3) illustrates such a literal response. But how does one classify perfectly sensible responses such as (4) or (5)? They are clearly related to the text, perhaps even pragmatically implied by it (the most common way for a storekeeper to lose money is not being able to sell stock, implying, of course, that customers do not buy it). But the responses do not come from the text; they come, instead, from students' prior knowledge about how and why storekeepers lose money.

To distinguish between such QARs, Pearson and Johnson (1978) coined the terms text-explicit (TE) to characterize responses like (2) to questions like (1), and script-implicit (SI—the term script denotes prior knowledge; the term implicit suggests an inferential leap). But what about responses like (6), (7), and (8), which come from the text? Do they exemplify literal, i.e., text-explicit, comprehension? Not really, because the students generating such responses had to establish a causal link between becoming fed up and each of the responses. Pearson and Johnson used the term text-implicit (TI) to characterize such responses—responses that derive from the text but require a linking (or text-connecting) inference on the part of the reader.

In fairness to Guszak, one must concede that at least his taxonomy implies that recall and recognition questions have answers available in the text. However, the taxonomy has great difficulty dealing with variant responses such as (3)–(8), which

critique

do not match the obvious response expectation. On the other hand, the QAR system simply recognizes that a single question stimulus can elicit different sorts of responses, all plausible. One other point: Guszak's system does not distinguish between text-explicit and text-implicit comprehension—any question with a plausible answer in the text is regarded as a literal recognition or recall question even though, as examples (6)–(8) illustrate, task demands vary dramatically between the two. In fact, recent work by Raphael (1980) and Raphael, Winograd, and Pearson (1980) suggest that questions that invite a text-implicit (TI) response, but preclude a text-explicit (TE) question-answer relationship (QAR) such as (12), are more difficult than those inviting either TE or SI QARs. Just because an answer is available in a text does not mean that a question will be easy to answer.

The final word on taxonomies of questions, especially questions constrained by the linguistic, textual, and situational contexts in which they appear, is not in. The Pearson and Johnson (1978) scheme has taken but one of many steps necessary to ferret out the role and influence of questions. While that taxonomy is a valid model for examining differential response strategies to questions (Raphael, Winograd, and Pearson, 1980), scoring recall protocols (Wixson, 1980), and providing strategy instruction (Raphael, 1980), it falls woefully short of its mark on a number of counts.

First, it has trouble dealing with evaluative QARs. The simple text/script, explicit/implicit dichotomies cannot handle questions like (13), (14), or (15).

(13) Why do you think this author doesn't know very much about mushrooms?
(14) Why was Jenny justified in quitting the play?
(15) Is that a statement of fact or opinion? Why?

It is not clear just how much text versus script (head) knowledge is used to generate answers to such questions, nor is it clear what the source of the question is. The system is just too simplistic to handle such murky matters.

Second, the system should be expanded to handle some other kinds of questions that teachers use in discussions. For example, Kamil and Davis (1980) have suggested a script-explicit (SE) category to handle questions that, while related to the general topic of the text, are almost incidental to the text. Question (16), for example, in the context of passage (1), represents such a probe.

(16) By the way, who was it that discovered the vulcanization process?
(This would be a sensible probe after a response like (1).)
(17) How do you suppose the storekeepers felt toward the rubber manufacturers?

Or how about the very common practice of asking for a definition of a term in the selection, such as Question (18)?

(18) What is meant by the term product?

Third, some questions are the logical complement of script-implicit (SI) QARs; that is, the question stems from prior knowledge but the answer comes from the text; furthermore, such probes seem eminently reasonable, especially as follow-ups to earlier QARs. Consider, for example, question (19) and response (20), perhaps as a follow-up to a response from question (17).

critique

(19) What makes you believe they were angry with the rubber manufacturers?
(20) Well, it says that they got fed up with rubber and manufacturers were the ones who made the rubber stuff they had to bury.

In general, citing textual evidence to support a conclusion only implied by the text requires this script-text type of strategy. I am hard pressed even to find a label for such a response.

Fourth, the system has grave difficulty with paraphrase responses. Suppose in response to question (2), asking for reasons to explain getting "fed up with rubber," a student gives a response like (21) or (22).

(21) Their profit margins disappeared.
(22) It wasn't sufficiently elastic.

Clearly neither (21) nor (22) uses the specific language of the text, but each seems to be a sophisticated paraphrase of a text segment. Should such responses be coded as text-based or script-based? Perhaps some other category is needed, one suggesting that the student has integrated text information into his/her knowledge structure and pulled out the superordinate category from memory as a response. Indeed, Raphael (1980) found that students often provided such superordinate (as well as subordinate and coordinate) paraphrases to questions that allowed, and even invited, a clear-cut text-explicit question-answer response.

Finally, the whole system makes sense only if and when one can assume that the text is available to search when students are responding to questions. If the students cannot look back, or if they listen to the content, then what difference does it make where questions and responses come from? Whatever has seeped into memory from the written or orally presented text becomes amalgamated (hopefully) with what the reader already knows about the topic. Either the student does or does not retrieve the requisite information. In a sense, all QARs are "script-explicit" in such a situation.

One can, in this no-access-to-text circumstance, continue to search for responses that are verbatim, paraphrased, or entailed (logically implied) reconstructions of information that was in the text; however, one cannot infer unambiguously that the text was the source of such a response since it is logically possible that the student already possessed the information—perhaps even in verbatim form—in a store of prior knowledge.

At present, I have no simple recommendations for solving these thorny problems presented by a taxonomy that I claim solves a couple of other problems raised by the taxonomy put forth by Guszak. My goal has been, quite simply, to raise issues that future researchers need to address.

Data Analysis

As one examines Guszak's data, one is tempted to ask for some way of determining how much faith to place in his claims about the relative differences among question types across grade levels, etc. Granted, an "interocular test of significance" (hits you between the eyeballs) will tell us Critique/Table 1 has more recall questions than any other type; however, Guszak's claims about the increase in the frequency of evaluation questions across grades seems less impressive. As a first approximation to some evidence establishing a degree of faith, I decided to subject the data in Critique/Table 1 to a simple χ^2 test of association to determine whether the relative incidence of question type was influenced by grade level. I did this by converting percentages back into row frequencies and applying the $\Sigma(F_o - F_e)^2$ formula. About this same time, I discussed my reanalysis and this paper with Guszak. He volunteered to send me his dissertation (Guszak, 1966), the original work upon which the article in *Reading Teacher* was based. Upon receiving his dissertation, I discovered that he had already conducted the omnibus χ^2 tests. And, indeed, there is a strong relationship between question type and grade level, $\chi^2 = 155.38, p < .001$. Resorting once more to "interocular tests," the major difference appears to stem from the relatively higher incidence of recall questions in grade two and the relatively lower incidence of "higher level" questions (sum of conjecture + explanation + evaluation) in grade two. By grades four and six, a sizeable proportion of recall questions were replaced with these higher-level questions.

I also found, when I studied the dissertation, that he did something I was surprised not to find in the article—examine the relative incidence of question type by reading ability levels. Since these data have never been reported in the research literature, I report them here, with Guszak's permission. To allow a clearer picture of the patterns across grade and ability level, I have summed across recognition and recall categories to create a literal emphasis score and, across the other categories, to create a non-literal emphasis score. When Guszak originally did the complete ability level χ question type (with all six question types) analysis for each grade level, the χ^2 statistics proved significant for each grade level, indicating that teachers emphasized different types of questions with students of differing ability levels. The summed data, reported in Critique/Table 3, indicate a somewhat different pattern.

The data indicate that second-grade teachers tend not to differentiate among students of differing ability in the general emphasis of the questions they ask; to the contrary, intermediate-grade teachers tend to separate students into two groups: average and above-average students get higher proportions of non-literal questions than do low-ability students. Examined from the perspective of a student progressing through the grade levels in a school, whereas a high or average-ability student can look forward to a progressively changing diet of questions, a low-ability student can look forward to more of the same. For comparison with the overall (grade level)

CRITIQUE/TABLE 3
Question emphasis by grade and ability level (reported as percentages of total)

	Literal Emphasis			Non-literal Emphasis		
Grade Ability	2	4	6	2	4	6
High	74	59	49	26	41	51
Average	83	60		17	40	
Low	77	80	71	23	20	29

data in Critique/Table 1 (see page 273), I performed a similar summation across my literal and non-literal categories; the percentage of literal drops from 79% in grade two, to 65% in grde four, to 58% in grade six. Clearly, most (not all) of this overall drop is attributable to changing patterns for high-ability students only. One wonders what we would find today if we replicated Guszak's original study. I think it unfortunate that Guszak did not report these ability data in the 1967 article. Alas! The rigors of space constraints!

These regrouped analyses suggest a criticism of his original data analysis plan that I mention only in passing. There were very few observations in some of the cells (0 in a few cases). We have all been apprised of the danger of empty or low *N* cells in χ^2; one wonders whether, for example, the grade two ability χ question-type analysis would have proved significant with the kind of regrouping that I did with two, rather than six, categories.

WHERE SHOULD WE GO FROM HERE?

I have already suggested, at least by implication, directions that we might pursue regarding question taxonomies. Let me summarize those briefly (from the section entitled The Taxonomy) and then suggest some further empirical and descriptive plans.

Regarding taxonomies, I have suggested that while the Pearson and Johnson (1978) work extends Guszak's study, much amplification of the Pearson-Johnson Taxonomy is still needed. We need to expand that work to explain issues surrounding evaluative skills, information dealing with the topic but not the text, the "what's your evidence" kind of interaction for paraphrase responses, and the critical variable of presence or absence of text during question-answering time.

Regarding the general line of research on questions, I make these recommendations:

1. Right now, we need to replicate Guszak's work to see if, overall, anything has changed in the last 15 to 20 years. We may want to add some twists on his original data-collection procedures, but we need a broad-scale view of what is going on today. As for modifications, it would be interesting to know whether teacher questions vary as a function of (a) teacher experience (do more experienced teachers ask different sorts of questions?), (b) philosophy about reading (does the teacher who has a meaning-emphasis question differently from the teacher with a code-emphasis—or maybe the distinction is between getting the facts of the text straight versus interpreting the text in light of prior knowledge), (c) type of content (stories versus content area material), to name but a few candidates. Surely, we must take a hard look at reading ability group as a variable, as did Guszak.
2. Another question that needs to be addressed is, Where do teachers' questions come from? Do they rely on manuals? Do they use some a priori self-generated perception of what is important in a selection? Or do they have their own

internalized (perhaps even externalized) scheme for kinds of questions that should be asked and in what proportion?

3. We also need to know whether questions can be "instructive." By that, I mean that if students are exposed to a particular type of question emphasis over a long period of time, do they get better at answering that kind of question, perhaps at the expense of their ability to answer other kinds of questions? In other words, does practice have any transfer value?

These are but a few of many questions that deserve some answers. Personally, I am grateful to Guszak for laying the important groundwork in this area. We are remiss in not examining the import of his work earlier than we did. Believing, however, that it is never too late for a "renaissance," I hope this critique will stimulate some new work on a topic that most certainly deserves our attention. Here are, I think, some questions we cannot afford not to answer.

FOR FURTHER LEARNING

Those readers who are interested in continuing to explore the topic of comprehension would find the following references helpful:

Pearson, P. D., & Johnson, D. D. *Teaching reading comprehension.* New York: Holt, Rinehart, & Winston, 1978.

Lehnert, W. G. *The process of question answering.* Hillsdale, N.J.: Lawrence Erlbaum Associates, 1978.

REFERENCES

Anderson, R. C., & Biddle, W. B. On asking people questions about what they are reading. In G. Bower (Ed.), *Psychology of learning and motivation* (Vol. 9). New York: Academic Press, Inc., 1975.

Barrett, T. C. Taxonomy of reading comprehension. In R. Smith & T. C. Barrett (Eds.), *Teaching reading in the middle grades.* Reading, Mass.: Addison-Wesley, 1976.

Bloom, B. (Ed.). *Taxonomy of educational objectives.* New York: McKay Company, 1956.

Bond, G. L., & Dykstra, R. The cooperative research program in first grade reading. *Reading Research Quarterly,* 1967, 2.

Bormuth, J. R., Manning, J. C., Carr, J. W., & Pearson, P. D. Children's comprehension of between- and within-sentence syntactic structures. *Journal of Educational Psychology,* 1971, *61,* 349–357.

Brown, A. L., & Palincsar, A. S. Inducing strategic learning from texts by means of informed, self control training. *Topics in learning and learning disabilities,* in press.

Chall, J. S. *Learning to read: The great debate.* New York: McGraw-Hill, 1967.

Duffy, G., & McIntyre, L. *A qualitative analysis of how various primary grade teachers employ the structured learning component of the direct instruction model when teaching reading* (Research Series No. 80). Institute for Research on Teaching, Michigan State University, June 1980.

Durkin, D. What classroom observations reveal about reading comprehension instruction. *Reading Research Quarterly,* 1978–79, *14,* 481–533.

Durkin, D. Reading comprehension instruction in five basal reading series. *Reading Research Quarterly*, 1981, *16*, 515–544.

Flanders, N. Teacher influence in the classroom. In E. Amidon & J. Hough (Eds.), *Interaction analysis: Theory, research, and application*. Reading, Mass.: Addison-Wesley, 1967.

Guszak, F. J. *A study of teacher solicitation and student response interaction about reading content in selected second, fourth, and sixth grades*. Unpublished doctoral dissertation, University of Wisconsin, 1966.

Guszak, F. J. Teacher questioning and reading. *The Reading Teacher*, 1967, *21*, 227–234.

Hansen, J. The effects of inference training and practice on young children's comprehension. *Reading Research Quarterly*, 1981, *16*, 391–417.

Hansen, J., & Pearson, P. D. *An instructional study: Improving the inferential comprehension of fourth grade good and poor readers* (Technical Report No. 235). Urbana: University of Illinois, Center for the Study of Reading, March 1982.

Harris, A. J., & Serwer, B. L. The CRAFT Project: Instructional time in reading research. *Reading Research Quarterly*, 1966, *2*, 27–56.

Kamil, M. L., & Davis, C. A. Old and new perspectives on teaching reading comprehension. *Directions in Reading: Promoting Literacy*, 1980, *2*, 1–18.

Lehnert, W. G. *The process of question answering*. Hillsdale, N.J.: Lawrence Erlbaum Associates, 1978.

Nicholson, T., & Pearson, P. D. Scripts, texts, and questions. Paper delivered at the National Reading Conference, Atlanta, 1976.

Pearson, P. D., & Johnson, D. D. *Teaching reading comprehension*. New York: Holt, Rinehart, & Winston, 1978.

Raphael, T. E. *The effects of metacognitive strategy awareness training on students' question answering behavior*. Unpublished doctoral dissertation, University of Illinois, 1980.

Raphael, T. E., Winograd, P., & Pearson, P. D. Strategies children use when answering questions. In M. L. Kamil & A. J. Moe (Eds.), *Perspectives on reading research and instruction*. Washington, D.C.: National Reading Conference, Inc., 1980.

Wixson, K. *The effects of postreading questions on children's discourse comprehension and knowledge acquisition*. Unpublished doctoral dissertation, Syracuse University, August 1980.

Commentary on Pearson's Critique of Guszak's Study: Teacher Questioning and Reading

FRANK. J. GUSZAK

University of Texas at Austin

Dave Pearson's sojourn into history to review my study of teacher questioning as reported in the December 1967 issue of the *Reading Teacher* stirred a lot of old memories and kindled some new excitement. Because he delved deeper than the single article did and looked in detail at the more involved research of the dissertation, I would like to partition my commentary in terms of (1) the critique of the *Reading Teacher* article, (2) the new information from the dissertation, and (3) possible directions for a replication.

Pearson's initial concern about the sources of my taxonomy (if it can be called such) seems understandable and his speculation partially correct. While Barrett was my major professor and the real stimulus for the entire study, he had not, as yet, done his taxonomy of reading questions. In fact, I first saw Barrett's after it was published in the N.S.S.E. Yearbook. Rather, we both looked to Bloom (1956) and to adaptions of Bloom's work by Sanders (1964). Sanders found problems with the scope of Bloom's comprehension category which included the following subunits: comprehension, translation, interpretation, and extrapolation. While Sanders's attempts to use a modified structure proved useful to him and some others, the structure lacked specificity for describing the outcomes of the textual reading task. Further perusal of some of the interaction studies of the day involving questioning (Smith, 1962; Bellack & Davitz, 1963; Aschner & Gallagher, 1965) provided some valuable inputs. However, in the final analysis, I decided to go with Spache's (1963) rationale of examining the products of reading comprehension and sought to use a model developed by Letton (1958). The Letton model appeared capable of tagging the thinking products of teacher questions about reading. At first, the categories seemed to be extensive, mutually exclusive, and inclusive of the components of the models of Guilford (1959), Smith (1962), and Russell (1961) (important contributors to the scene at this point in time). A pilot study indicated problems of identification, which resulted in the development of the final set of categories that were subsequently represented in the dissertation (summarized by Pearson in the preceding pages).

The study sought to describe teacher-pupil questioning in the context of the basal reading group (which appeared to be the dominant theme of elementary reading instruction at that time as well as now). Consequently, the temporal considerations of "guided silent reading" and "after the fact questioning" were primary concerns to be tapped by *recognition* and *recall* questions. To me, such distinctions are important regardless of whether such questions are *textually explicit* or *textually implicit*.

Pearson and Johnson's (1978) contribution of the QAR is certainly a valuable one in that it recognizes the (1) teacher probe, (2) intervening text, and (3) student response. Although I analyzed all three, I did not analyze the second one in the same fashion. Pearson and Johnson's system is a further development, yet Pearson cheerfully acknowledges that the system has further needs!

> we have adopted a question taxonomy with only three categories. As such, it hardly qualifies as a taxonomy. In our estimation its greatest value is its ability to capture the relationship between information presented in a text and information that has to come from a reader's store of prior knowledge (scripts and schema).
>
> (Pearson and Johnson, 1978, p. 157)

Hopefully, a more comprehensive system will be developed for the much-hoped-for future research. Such a system surely needs to probe the thorny issues raised by Pearson in his insightful discussion of that group of skills referred to as evaluation.

In the data-analysis section, I was gratified to see Pearson's statistical analysis of the relationships between question types and grade levels was similar to mine. Yes, the "interocular tests" suggested that higher level questions occurred less frequently in the lower grade levels where I sensed the teachers were holding texts in hand and pursuing sequential bits of information. Memories of the classroom observations I made while taping the interactions still remain vivid. As students reached the higher grade levels, it appeared that the press of time and greater content amounts (more pages per story) meant the teachers changed their modus operandi considerably. Consequently, there was a tendency to ask higher level questions dealing with overall story concerns.

THE NEW INFORMATION FROM THE DISSERTATION

While Pearson charitably suggests that spatial limitations prevented me from reporting the differences between ability groups in my *Reading Teacher* article, such was not the case. Rather, I just did not recognize the significance at the time. Consequently, I am indebted to Pearson for rediscovering what I had previously discovered and forgotten—namely, that teachers tended to operate differently with different reading groups (high, middle, and low) in terms of questioning.

While my X^2 analysis indicated that teachers at each grade level emphasized different types of questions with differing reading groups, Pearson's re-analysis (combining literal elements versus inferential elements) indicated that the real differences occurred in the middle grades rather than the primary (second) grade. While I am pleased that he extended the analysis (including the assimilation of empty cells), I still have some concerns about the patterns of grouping that emerged as we went into the higher grades (sixth grades frequently saw only one or two groups). The question is certainly an important one (where varied groups exist within classes) and should be the focus of further research of this type.

POSSIBLE DIRECTIONS FOR REPLICATION

That Pearson sees value in replicating the 17-year-old study is gratifying. Although I have not done so, I, too, have wondered if the effects today might not be similar. Reports over the interim have suggested that the high frequencies of literal questions have not changed (Lalik, 1982). Nevertheless, the study has not been replicated in its original form, and such a project would offer a unique basis for comparison.

In closing, I would like to comment on the following modifications suggested for a replication:

1) **Determine the effects of teacher experience and/or philosophy upon teaching questioning behavior.** This worthy suggestion was attempted at the outset of the present study. The dissertation was part of a larger study I did that sought to determine the relationship between teachers' theoretical knowledge about reading comprehension and their subsequent questioning practices. Unfortunately, the tests of theoretical knowledge would not discriminate between neophytes and so-called professional teachers. Hopefully, more sensitive descriptions of teacher knowledge and practice will be made so that we might make some basic distinctions between theoretical underpinnings and practices.

2) **Determine the effect of the type of content on the questions that were asked.** Since my research was restricted to narrative selections, I would like very much to see some classifications of materials into discourse categories such as reference, persuasive, literary, and expressive (Kinneavy, 1971).

3) **Determine the effects of ability grouping.** Conceivably, such research could include the within-class groupings as typically found in high, middle, and low group arrangement, as well as the between-class groupings for teachers who teach different ability sections (an organizational arrangement that appears to be occurring earlier and earlier in the elementary school).

4) **Determine the source of teacher questions.** I am tempted to analyze the old protocols and teacher manuals to see what type of match-ups were apparent. For the future, however, we must go deeper and seek, through introspective analysis, the "whys" of certain questions.

5) **Determine whether questions are instructive.** While studies (Pearson's included) have tackled this area, it seems most promising for researchers from varied disciplines (especially those willing to invest some time in longer studies).

My thanks go to Dave Pearson for scraping off the cobwebs and challenging us to continue our thinking about the implications of teacher questioning.

REFERENCES

Aschner, M. J.; Gallagher, J. J.; Perry, J. M.; Apser, S. S.; Jenne, W.; and Farr, H. *A system for classifying thought processes in the context of classroom verbal interaction*. Champaign, Ill.: Institute for Research on Exceptional Children, 1965.

Bellack, A., and Davitz, J. R., *The language of the classroom, part two*. New York: Institute of Psychological Research, Teachers College, Columbia University, 1963.

Bloom, B. (Ed.). *Taxonomy of educational objectives. Handbook 1: Cognitive domain*. New York: David McKay Co., 1956.

Guilford, J. Three faces of intellect. *American Psychologist,* 1959, *14,* 469–479.

Kinneavy, J. *A theory of discourse*. Englewood Cliffs, N.J.: Prentice-Hall, 1971.

Lalik, R. (An oral report on her dissertation findings at Syracuse University.) Presented to doctoral seminar at the University of Texas at Austin, March 17, 1982.

Letton, M. Evaluating the effectiveness of teaching reading. Evaluation of Reading. Supplementary Educational Monographs, No. 88. Chicago: University of Chicago Press, 1958.

Pearson, D., & Johnson, D. *Teaching reading comprehension*. New York: Holt, Rinehart, and Winston, 1978.

Russell, D. *Children learn to read*. Boston: Ginn and Co., 1961.

Sanders, N. The taxonomy of classroom questions. Unpublished report. Manitowoc, Wis., 1964. (To appear as a published book.)

Smith, B., et. al. *A study of the logic of teaching*. Urbana, Ill.: Bureau of Educational Research, 1962 (mimeographed).

Spache, G. *Toward better reading*. Champaign, Ill.: Garrard Publ. Co., 1963.

WHAT CLASSROOM OBSERVATIONS REVEAL ABOUT READING COMPREHENSION INSTRUCTION

DOLORES DURKIN

University of Illinois

Examines through classroom observations of reading and social studies whether elementary schools provide comprehension instruction. Social studies was included on the assumption that comprehension instruction is required by the difficulty of social studies textbooks. Grades 3 through 6 were selected for the observations on the assumption that more comprehension instruction exists there than in grades 1 and 2. Major findings included the fact that almost no comprehension instruction was found. The attention that did go to comprehension focused on assessment, which was carried on through teacher questions. Instruction other than that for comprehension was also rare. It could not be concluded, therefore, that teachers neglect comprehension because they are busy teaching phonics, structural analysis, or word meanings. What they do attend to are written assignments. As a result, time spent on giving, completing, and checking assignments consumed a large part of the observed periods. Sizeable amounts of time also went to activities categorized as "Transition" and "Non-instruction." Other findings indicated that none of the observed teachers view social studies as a time to help with reading comprehension. Rather, they see their responsibility as covering content and having children master facts.

This research was supported by the National Institute of Education under Contract No. US-NIE-C-400-76-0116. From *Reading Research Quarterly,* (XIV)4, 1978–79, pp. 481–533. Reprinted with permission of the author and the International Reading Association.

On April 1, 1976, the National Institute of Education issued a Request for Proposal (RFP) describing the need for a Center for the Study of Reading whose central concern would be comprehension. Why the Center seemed essential was described in the RFP as follows:

> A considerable, though not entirely adequate body of facts has been assembled about decoding but much less is known about the process of understanding written text. Researchers and practitioners, accordingly, have strongly urged the NIE to focus its attention and that of the field upon the problems of reading comprehension. (p. 2)

The RFP outlined application responsibilities this way:

> *Application*—The Center will identify and implement means by which knowledge gained from research relevant to reading can be utilized in developing and improving practices for informal and formal reading instruction. The Center will also be involved in identifying means by which basic research on reading and linguistic communication can be made

> more relevant to practical problems in improving the level of reading comprehension. (p. 5)

Apparent in the RFP were 3 assumptions that are especially pertinent for teacher education:

1. Reading comprehension can be taught.
2. Reading comprehension is being taught.
3. What is done to teach it is not as effective as comprehension instruction needs to be if reading problems are to be reduced.

As a veteran observer of elementary school classrooms, I was especially struck by the second assumption because my frequent visits to schools have revealed almost no comprehension instruction. Two facts could have accounted for this, however. First, comprehension instruction never was the preselected focus for an observation and, second, the bulk of the observing was in primary grades. In one 4-year study, however, grades 1, 2, 3, and 4 were observed. Comparisons of the last 2 grades with the first 2 prompted such conclusions as these:

> Classroom observations during the third grade year revealed a few other changes—none of a kind that would foster greater progress in reading. To cite an example, the amount of time given to reading instruction appeared to decrease, whereas the amount of time spent on written assignments increased. This was especially true for the best readers, who were now being given lengthy assignments. (Durkin, 1974–1975, pp. 34–35)
>
> In summary, it could be said that the fourth-grade reading program continued to have basal readers, workbooks, and worksheets as its core. In addition, instruction continued to be deemphasized in the sense that less time was spent on teacher-directed lessons, whereas written assignments continued to grow longer and to become more numerous. (Durkin, 1974–1975, p. 42)

When the NIE contract for the Center for the Study of Reading was awarded to the University of Illinois, I decided to see what conclusions would be reached if middle- and upper-grade classrooms were observed for the purpose of finding, describing, and timing comprehension instruction. Such a study seemed central to the mission of the Center, since it is impossible to improve instruction until what goes on now, and with what frequency, is known.

PILOT STUDY

The earlier classroom observations suggested categories for describing what teachers might do in the time scheduled for reading instruction. To find out whether these categories were realistic and exhaustive, a pilot study was undertaken during the 1976–1977 school year (Durkin, 1977). Since "teaching comprehension" was both an essential and important category, great care was taken to define it.

Review of the Literature

To begin, the literature was searched in order to see whether it provided guidelines for a definition, or included studies by others who had observed in classrooms to learn about comprehension instruction. Only 1 such study was found: Quirk, Trismen, Weinberg, and Nalin, 1973; Quirk, Weinberg, and Nalin, 1973; Quirk, Trismen, Nalin, and Weinberg,

1975; Quirk, Trismen, Weinberg, and Nalin, 1976. Called "The Classroom Behavior of Teachers and Students during Compensatory Reading Instruction," the study involved 46 observers, 135 teachers (divided among grades 2, 4, and 6), 34 schools, and 21 cities. Although each class was visited 9 times, only 15 minutes of coding took place per visit. With that kind of sampling, the researchers (Quirk *et al.*, 1975, p. 191) found that teachers used the largest amounts of time in the following ways:

	Percent of Time
Management Instruction	30
Pronunciation and Word Recognition Activities	26
Comprehension Activities	12
Spelling	9
Non-reading Instruction	4

In concluding their report, the researchers say:

> Content categories could be combined in a number of ways to determine the percent of time that teachers spent in reading activities. If Content categories 1–4 (Comprehension, Pronunciation and Word Recognition, Language Structure, Reading Silently) are combined, this would indicate that the teachers spent 43 percent of their time in reading instruction activities. If Content categories 5 (Spelling) and 6 (Listening) are also included, the teachers spent 56 percent of their time in reading and reading-related activities. (Quirk *et al.*, 1975, p. 191)

Although this report appears to tell about instruction, the researchers' definitions of categories are not consistently confined to that focus. Further, because teachers and children are considered together, the definitions are often flawed by a lack of clarity. To illustrate, when "instructional activities" are discussed, comprehension is singled out as "those instances in which the teacher, students, or others in the classroom demonstrate understanding of what the students have read. It includes questions, statements, or actions such as defining a word, giving the meaning of a sentence, or interpreting a story." (Quirk, Trismen, Weinberg, and Nalin, 1973, p. 7.) When examples of "comprehension activities" are cited in another report of the same study (Quirk, Weinberg, and Nalin, 1973, p. 21), they include:

> Teacher asks for meaning of *bluff*.
>
> Teacher asks: "What words in the story helped you to see how the farm looked?"
>
> Teacher asks children to use *parliament* in a sentence.

All in all, the report helped neither with definitions nor with clearly stated information about classroom practices.

Another publication whose title suggested a comprehension-instruction focus was the report of the international study directed by Thorndike (1973). It was called *Reading Comprehension Education in Fifteen Countries*. In spite of the title, it is a comparison of comprehension test scores that led to such conclusions as "It must be confessed that the results of the study provide little guidance for the improvement of the educational enterprise." (Thorndike, 1973, p. 99)

A few of the many other publications that promised more help than they provided will be cited in order to show that efforts to locate a definition of comprehension instruction in the literature were fruitless.

In a chapter entitled "An Operational Definition of Comprehension Instruction," Bormuth (1969) makes interesting comments but offers no definition that is useful for classroom observations. Under the heading "General Definition of Comprehension," he says, ". . . comprehension ability is thought to be a set of generalized knowledge-acquisition skills which permit people to acquire and exhibit information gained as a consequence of reading printed language." (p. 50) He continues, "Consequently, the content of comprehension instruction might be said to be the rules describing how the language system works to transmit information; and the tasks of research in reading comprehension instruction are 1) to enumerate these rules, 2) to develop teaching tasks for shaping children's behaviors in the manners described by these rules, and 3) to organize them into a systematic sequence for instruction by determining their relative complexities." (p. 50) Offering no evidence to support the claim, Bormuth still maintains that "Comprehension is both one of the most important and one of the weakest areas of instruction." (p. 48)

Another publication that sounded promising also omitted a useful definition. This was a chapter by Wardhaugh called "The Teaching of Phonics and Comprehension: A Linguistic Evaluation." (1969) Initially, Wardhaugh discusses problems related to definitions of reading (too vague, too all-inclusive, and so on); then he goes on to assert that "no matter what else a definition of reading includes, it must recognize that there is a connection between English orthography and the phonological system of English; and, second, sentences have meanings that can be accounted for in terms of syntactic and semantic rules. The first of these claims will be discussed in connection with phonics instruction and the second, in connection with the teaching of comprehension." (p. 80) Wardhaugh covers the latter in 2 pages, primarily through an analysis of sentences in order to show that "a reader must be able to relate . . . the deep structure of a sentence . . . to its surface structure. . . ." (p. 86)

Journals for teachers were not overlooked in the search for a definition of comprehension instruction. The last example that will be cited of the many articles that offered more hope than help appeared in *The Reading Teacher* and was called "Improving Children's Comprehension Abilities." (Tovey, 1976) Without wasting many words, this article eliminated any chance of offering a definition by taking the position that "It appears that comprehension cannot be taught directly, but situations can be provided to facilitate and encourage the processing of print into meaning." (p. 289) The situations are described in the form of 10 examples of "practical suggestions for involving children in successful reading experiences." (p. 289) They include a) Help children select books they can read; b) help children develop an understanding of the purpose and nature of reading; and c) encourage children to read high interest material. Almost all the suggestions can be summarized with the last one mentioned: "Motivate children to read, read, read!" (p. 291)

The *Dictionary of Education* (Good, 1973) was consulted next, but it has no entry for "comprehension instruction." Although one for "instruction" *was* found, it hardly provided clarification. The entry reads, "In a precise sense, [instruction is] the kind of teaching that obligates the instructor to furnish the learner with some lasting direction and is accountable for pupil performances commensurate with precise statements of educational objectives." (p. 304)

The final attempt to get help from others was a letter to the IRA Committee responsible for developing a Dictionary of Reading Terms; but again, the effort was non-productive. And so it was necessary to reason out the definition of comprehension instruction that would be used in the observational research.

Definition of Comprehension Instruction

Working out a definition of *comprehension instruction* can move in at least 2 directions. The first starts by equating comprehending with reading; it thus concludes by accepting as comprehension instruction anything that is done to help children acquire reading ability. Within this very broad framework, instruction concerned with such things as whole word identification, word meanings, and phonic and structural analyses belongs under the umbrella called *comprehension instruction.* And this seems logical. After all, if the identification or meaning of too many individual words is unknown, problems with comprehension follow.

Although seeming to be logical, equating comprehension instruction with anything that helps children become readers has 1 obvious drawback. It makes comprehension instruction so global and all inclusive that it no longer is a separate entity. That is, as it becomes everything, it becomes nothing in particular. The loss of identity suggests another path for arriving at the definition. This one bypasses single, isolated words and puts comprehension instruction into a framework that only includes efforts a) to teach children the meaning of a unit that is larger than a word, or b) to teach them how to work out the meaning of such units.

Subsequent to arriving at a definition, I found a report by Golinkoff (1975–1976) in which she discusses "the components of reading comprehension," which she lists as being:

> *Decoding*—Identifying individual words
> *Lexical access*—Having "a meaning for the printed word in semantic memory"
> *Text organization*—Extracting "meaning from units larger than the single word, such as phrases, sentences, and paragraphs (p. 633)

As can be seen below, the definition of comprehension instruction selected for the observations is similar to what Golinkoff calls "text organization":

> *Comprehension: instruction*—Teacher does/says something to help children understand or work out the meaning of more than a single, isolated word.

Ideally, comprehension instruction has transfer value; thus it will help children cope with the meaning of connected text not used in the instruction. This suggested another category for classifying what teachers might be expected to do:

> *Comprehension: application*—Teacher does/says something in order to learn whether previous instruction enables children to understand the meaning of connected text not used in that instruction.

An example of application follows:

> Subsequent to instruction that shows how experiences help readers to comprehend, the teacher has children tell which of 2 events mentioned in sentences occurred first, based on their own experiences (*e.g.,* Annie hurt her knee when she fell. They ate too much candy and got sick.)

research

Examples of Comprehension Instruction

Before additional categories for teacher behavior are mentioned, examples of what would be classified as *comprehension: instruction* will be listed. (The ease with which they could be described briefly was the main criterion used in selecting them.) They are given in order to clarify the definition still further. Such clarification is important since the value of the data to be reported is affected by the degree to which the definition is acceptable.

The first series of examples focuses on individual words but in the context of a sentence or more. With explanations and sample sentences, the teacher:

helps children understand the difference in the meaning of *and* and *or*.

calls children's attention to the meaning and importance of key words in written directions *(e.g., each, if, all, underline, match)*.

helps children understand that certain words signal sequence *(e.g., first, before, at the same time, later, meanwhile, ultimately)*.

Other comprehension instruction might focus on extracting meaning from single sentences or pairs of sentences. For instance:

Using a sentence like *The little kindergarten boy was crying,* teacher asks children to name everything it tells about the boy. Each fact is written on the board. Teacher next asks what the sentence does not tell about the boy.

Using pairs of sentences, teacher has children compare their content to see whether it is the same. Pairs might be something like:

Once home, she changed into her old clothes.
She changed clothes after she got home.

He was killed by the train at the crossing.
It was at the crossing that the train killed him.

With the help of suitable sentences, teacher explains the meaning of *appositive;* shows how appositives are set apart from the rest of a sentence with commas; and illustrates how they assist with the meaning of words.

Comprehension instruction with paragraphs (or more) might use procedures like the following:

Using a paragraph that describes a person, teacher asks children to read it and, as they do, to try to get a mental picture of the person. Once the person is discussed, the paragraph is reread in order to decide what details were omitted. Using additional paragraphs in a similar fashion, teacher encourages children to picture what is described whenever they read.

Asking a question that may or may not be answered in a given paragraph, teacher directs children to read it until they get to the answer. Children who think they found it are asked to give the answer and to tell why they think it does answer the question. Answers are also analyzed to see whether they can be shortened and still be correct.

Using a paragraph that contains a main idea embellished with supporting details, teacher asks children to read it in order to be able to state in a very few words what the paragraph is about. Responses are compared and discussed in order to select the best, which is written on the board. The children are then asked to reread the paragraph, this time to find all the details that have to do with the main idea. These are written below the main idea in outline form. Once a number of paragraphs are analyzed in this way, teacher discusses the meaning of "main idea" and "supporting detail." Finally, other paragraphs are analyzed, some of which contain a main idea and supporting details, others of which only relate a series of details. Comparisons are then made between the 2 kinds of paragraphs.

Questions and Comprehension Instruction

Because of the close association between comprehension and question-asking, a few comments about the way teacher questions would be classified are in order.

If what a teacher did with questions and answers were likely to advance children's comprehension abilities, it would be classified as *comprehension: instruction*. Some of the examples of instruction just listed include questioning of this type. On the other hand, if a teacher asked questions and did nothing with children's answers except, perhaps, to say they were right or wrong, that questioning would be *comprehension: assessment*, which is described below.

> *Comprehension: assessment*—Teacher does/says something in order to learn whether what was read was comprehended. Efforts could take a variety of forms—for instance, orally posed questions; written exercises; request for picture of unpictured character in a story.

Admittedly, the distinction being made between interrogation that is instruction and interrogation that is assessment is not what everyone would call "clearly apparent." This researcher's worries about possible vagueness ceased once classroom visitation began because observed questioning was very routine. Rarely, for example, was anything done with wrong answers except to say that they were wrong. Never did children have to prove or show why they thought an answer was correct. Frequently, in fact, the emphasis seemed to be on guessing what the teacher's answer was rather than on recalling what had been read. All these characteristics explain why only 6 question-answer sessions were classified in the study as *comprehension: instruction*. All the rest were *comprehension: assessment*.

Additional Categories for Teacher Behavior Related to Comprehension

Thus far, 3 categories for comprehension have been discussed: instruction, assessment, and application. The latter category, it will be recalled, is for practice carried on under a teacher's supervision. Practice in the form of written assignments was classified differently:

> *Comprehension: assignment*—Teacher gives written assignment concerned with comprehension.

Earlier classroom observations indicated the need for a related category:

> *Comprehension: helps with assignment*—Teacher helps one or more children with comprehension assignment.

If a teacher provided comprehension instruction, it was possible that she or he might review it later. This suggested another classification:

> *Comprehension: review of instruction*—Teacher goes over earlier comprehension instruction.

Prior observations also pointed up the need for:

> *Comprehension: preparation for reading*—Teacher does/says something in order to prepare children to read a given selection—for instance, identifies or has children identify new words; poses ques-

tions; relates children's experiences to selection; discusses meanings of words in selection.

The final category concerned with comprehension was identified during the pilot study when an observed teacher stopped children before they came to the end of a story in order to have them predict what the ending might be. In one sense, the teacher's behavior was *comprehension: assessment* because the children's predictions reflected either comprehension or non-comprehension of what they had read. On the other hand, it could also be viewed as *comprehension: preparation for reading* since the discussion of predictions was preparation for reading the final part of the story. Rather than force the behavior into an existing category, an additional one was established:

Comprehension: prediction—Teacher asks for prediction based on what was read.

To sum up, 8 categories were used to classify teacher behavior in relation to reading comprehension:

Comprehension: instruction
Comprehension: review of instruction
Comprehension: application
Comprehension: assignment
Comprehension: help with assignment
Comprehension: preparation for reading
Comprehension: assessment
Comprehension: prediction

Categories for Other Kinds of Instruction

Even though the central concern of the research was comprehension, other facets of instructional programs were also to be classified and timed. If it turned out that little was being done with comprehension, the additional data could show how teachers do spend their time.

It was assumed that some teacher time would go to phonics and structural analysis. Following the pattern used for comprehension, 6 more classifications were created:

Phonics: instruction
Phonics: review of instruction
Phonics: application
Structural Analysis: instruction
Structural Analysis: review of instruction
Structural Analysis: application

The category *Comprehension: preparation for reading* covers time given to word meanings prior to the reading of a given selection; however, it was thought that middle- and upper-grade teachers would plan additional instruction with meanings because of their obvious significance for comprehension. To describe their efforts, the following categories were selected:

Word Meanings: instruction
Word Meanings: review of instruction
Word Meanings: application

Because prior observations showed that beyond the primary grades, teachers give numerous written assignments and often at rapid rates, another decision was to deal with all assignments (with the exception of those for comprehension and study skills) under more general categories:

Assignment: gives
Assignment: helps with
Assignment: checks

The close connection between comprehension and study skills (for example, outlining, paraphrasing an encyclopedia article, and so on) seemed to require separate categories for the latter:

Study Skills: instruction
Study Skills: review of instruction
Study Skills: application
Study Skills: assignment

Some Additional Categories

Almost immediately, the pilot study identified the need to account for the time when one activity shifts to another, when a teacher moves from working with one group to another, and so on. The selected category is described below:

> *Transition*—Time required for changing from one activity to another or from one classroom to another; for waiting for children to get to the reading table; for waiting for them to get a book or find a page; and so on.

Equally clear was the need for:

> *Non-instruction*—Time given to chastisement; to waiting while children do assignments; to checking papers at desk while children do an assignment; to non-instructional conversation with one or more children, and so on.

Other categories not yet mentioned are in the total list that comprises Appendix A. Directions for using the categories (rather than definitions) are given in order to facilitate use of them by other researchers who may want to replicate the present study.

THE STUDY

The primary reason for the observational study was to learn whether elementary school classrooms provide comprehension instruction and, if they do, to find out what amount of time is allotted to it. On the assumption that there is less of it in the primary grades because of the concern there for decoding skills, middle and upper grades were selected for the observations.

Originally, only the reading period was to be observed. However, because the pilot study (Durkin, 1977) revealed such a dearth of comprehension instruction, a decision was made to observe during social studies, too. This decision was based on the assumption that even if teachers gave little time to comprehension during reading, they could be expected to work on it during social studies, since children's problems with content subject textbooks are both major and well known. One further decision was to use for both reading and social studies the same list of categories for describing teachers' behavior. If it was insufficient for social studies (or for the reading period), the necessary categories could be added.

Three-prong Focus

In order to look at comprehension instruction from a variety of perspectives, 3 sub-studies were done. One concentrated on fourth grade because it is commonly believed that at that level a switch is made from *learning to read* to *reading to learn*. It is also at that level that content subjects begin to be taken seriously. These 2 factors, it was thought, made fourth grade a likely place to find comprehension instruction.

The second part of the research was a study of schools. In this case, grades 3 through 6 were observed in order to see whether individual schools differ in the amount of time they give to comprehension instruction, and whether various grade levels show differences.

The third sub-study concentrated on individual children in an attempt to see what instructional programs look like from a child's perspective.

In all 3 sub-studies, each classroom was visited on 3 successive days. This procedure was followed to allow for continuity and also to reduce the likelihood that teachers would only be seen on an atypical day. On the assumption that both the content and the quality of instruction varies on different days of the week, the 3-day visits were scheduled so that all 5 days of the week would be included with equal frequency by the time the research terminated. On the assumption that the quality of an instructional program also varies at different times in the school year, observations began in early September and continued until mid-May.

Still more facets of the research were common to the 3 sub-studies. For instance, all the teachers knew beforehand that they were to be visited; more likely than not, therefore, at least some put forth their best efforts. Although each was asked to do exactly what she or he would do were there no visitor in the room, evidence exists that in at least 1 case the request was not followed. A teacher who was observed by this writer, and who had forgotten about the observation, was found at her desk working on report cards while the children were filling out workbook pages and ditto sheets. With the arrival of the visitor, she circulated around the room offering help to the children.

To be noted, too, is that whenever an administrator was contacted about the possibility of observing, a request was made to see the best teachers. While there is no guarantee that the best (which would have different meaning for different administrators) were seen, it is likely that the worst were not seen. Although each teacher knew about the observer's interest in reading, the special interest in comprehension instruction was never mentioned.

In many ways, then, what was seen should have allowed for a positive account of reading programs. In addition to asking to observe the best teachers on a faculty and letting them know they were to be observed, the researchers started recording and timing behavior not when an official schedule indicated a period was to begin but, rather, when it actually began. Since starting on time was uncommon, the selected procedure resulted in less time being assigned to *non-instruction* than would have been the case had the recording adhered to the official schedule.[1]

Another relevant fact needs to be mentioned. Because observations could only be made with a teacher's permission, times when instruction might be reduced both in quality and in quantity were omitted from the observation schedule. Teachers and/or administrators did not permit visiting, for example, at the very beginning of the school year, or at the very end. Nor were teachers willing to be observed during the weeks that preceded Thanksgiving and Christmas. Even days like Halloween and Valentine's Day had to be omitted. All this is to say that what was seen should have been examples of fairly good instructional programs.

[1]The common and sometimes large discrepancies between the amount of time officially scheduled for reading and the time spent on it indicate that researchers who are interested in examining the relationship between instructional time and reading performance must make certain that they deal with actual schedules, not paper ones.

Observers

All the observations were made by this researcher and 2 assistants, who had been prepared to be observers in a number of ways. To begin, both had had elementary school teaching experience; both had also taken reading methodology courses with this writer and had themselves taught an undergraduate course in reading. Before the observations started, time was spent on descriptions and illustrations of each category; directions for recording what was observed were carefully outlined, too.

When a teacher was the focus, recording sheets had the following headings:

Time	Activity	Audience	Source

The time that each different activity began and ended was noted in the first column, which was also used to indicate how an activity was classified. The second column was for descriptions of each activity. Who was with the teacher at the time of an activity was named in the third column (for example, whole class, small group, single child, principal, etc.) The fourth column allowed for information about the source of an activity—for instance, a workbook or manual. Only the headings "Time" and "Activity" were used when a child was being observed.

Careful preparation may account for the identical classifications of activities by the observers during 4 trial observations. Two problems were identified, however. With 1 observer, a consistent error in timing activities occurred during the first trial observation because, instead of marking the starting time of an activity to correspond with the concluding time of the previous activity, she skipped a minute. For example, if the categories *transition* and *comprehension: preparation* described 2 successive activities of a teacher, the first of which ended at 9:06, she erroneously noted the second as starting at 9:07 instead of 9:06.

Another observer's reporting was unnecessarily detailed in its accounts of behavior. To remedy that, distinctions had to be made between what was essential and, in contrast, what could be recorded *if* time permitted.

Originally, a minute was considered the basic unit of time. However, as the observations proceeded, some activities were so brief as to require descriptions that used half minutes.

For all 3 sub-studies, every description and classification was checked by this researcher. Unclear descriptions or questionable classifications were discussed with the observer. Questionable classifications, which were uncommon, were resolved through discussions of the given behavior or—and this occurred more frequently—through the addition of categories. All added categories were used infrequently; they included: *sustained silent reading* (both teacher and children are engaged in silent reading); *diagnosis: checks* (teacher looks over sheet on which notes about problems are written); *diagnosis: writes* (teacher makes a notation about a problem or need).

SUB-STUDY 1: FOURTH GRADE

In the study of fourth grades, reading was observed for 4,469 minutes; social studies, for 2,775 minutes. The 24 classrooms that were visited were in 13 different school systems in central Illinois. All the classes were taught by women, 7

RESEARCH/TABLE 1
Percentage of teacher time spent on comprehension and study skills during the reading period

Behavioral Categories		Percentage of 4,469 Minutes
Comprehension: instruction		0.63
Comprehension: review of instruction		N.O.[a]
Comprehension: application		N.O.
Comprehension: assignment		2.13
Comprehension: help with assignment		5.46
Comprehension: preparation for reading		5.53
Comprehension: assessment		17.65
Comprehension: prediction		0.25
Study skills: instruction		N.O.
Study skills: review of instruction		N.O.
Study skills: application		0.43
Study skills: assignment		0.16
	Total	32.24

[a]N.O. = not observed

of whom had aides. Six of the 24 classes were third-fourth grade combinations.

Class size in the observed rooms ranged from 11 to 32 children with a mean of 22.7. In 8 schools, interclass groupings were used when reading was taught; the remaining 16 had self-contained rooms. Only 1 school used interclass groups for social studies.

Findings for the Reading Period

The amount of time the 24 observed teachers spent during the reading period on instruction and activities concerned with comprehension and study skills is summarized in Research/Table 1. As the table shows, less than 1 percent (28 minutes) went to comprehension instruction. At no time was study skills instruction seen. The observed comprehension instruction, found in 5 different classrooms, is described below.

Language of poets (1 min.): Teacher read aloud a page in a basal reader that dealt with the way poets use language in a special way—a "rich" way. The page pointed out that instead of saying something like "an apartment that is 150 feet high," the poet might say "an apartment halfway up the sky."

Main idea (7 min.)[2]: Children and teacher listened to a tape that explained a main idea as "what a story is mostly about." Narrator talked about titles as being main ideas. Directed by the tape, children read aloud a poem from cards in order to see whether they could tell what its main idea was. Teacher stopped the tape, and children told what they thought the main idea was.

Meaning of common expression (2 min.): Questioning the children about a

[2]All this instruction was from a tape. The teacher just listened. Ordinarily, her listening would have been classified as "Listens." However, since the tape dealt with comprehension instruction, her behavior was categorized as *comprehension: instruction.*

story they just read, teacher asked, "What does 'Two wrongs don't make a right' mean?" One child gave vague explanation, so teacher added a better one. Further examples were mentioned by the children.

Extracting the main idea from facts (14 min.): Children were unable to tell in a few words what a series of facts in a basal reader selection was telling them, so teacher explained "main idea." She next posed questions about the 5 pages on which the facts had been related. Her questions and directions included: Why did the author put the ideas on pp. 116–130 in this story? What did we learn from those pages? What was the author showing us? Think about what you learned from those pages. Let's see if we can group the facts together and give them a name. That will be the main idea in all the facts.

Analysis of compound sentence (4 min.): Guided by a page in a basal reader, teacher mentioned that *and* and *but* are "connecting words." Said they often connect words to make long sentences. Teacher then wrote on the board *Pollywog sat in Mrs. Weaver's class and looked out the window and prayed for rain.* Had children read the sentence aloud. Asked whether someone could say what one short sentence in the long sentence said. Child offered, "Pollywog sat in Mrs. Weaver's class." Teacher then asked for another short sentence. When a child offered. "Looked out the window," teacher reminded him to start with "Pollywog." Same reminder had to be given to another child when he suggested, "Prayed for rain" as being the third short sentence in the long one.

Even though each of the above episodes meets the requirements of *comprehension: instruction,* it should be noted that what was done (with the exception of the 14-minute episode) was not likely to be instructive for comprehension. Take the last episode as an illustration. In some ways, it had the greatest potential, but the teacher failed to relate what she was doing either to additional sentences or to comprehending in general. Instead, she followed the book, did neither more nor less than what it covered, then shifted to something else. Quick, unexplained shifts were exceedingly common in all the classrooms and may explain why the category *comprehension: application* was not needed for the fourth grade observations.

Used with noticeable frequency, on the other hand, was the category *comprehension: assessment* (17.65 percent; see Research/Table 1). Teacher's questions dominated here. Only the questions depicted in the *comprehension: instruction* episodes just described, however, had the potential to be instructive. With the rest, the concern was to see whether children's answers were right or wrong. Although no attempt was made to count or classify questions, a generous use of literal ones was very apparent. Most questions were taken from basal manuals.

Except for questions, manuals were rarely used. How little manuals appeared to affect instructional programs is reflected in the small amount of time spent on preparing children to read something (5.53 percent). The typical preview consisted of brief attention to new vocabulary followed by the posing of 2 or 3 questions that were never written. This meant that the children could not refer to them before, during, or after they read. It also meant that they may have been forgotten not only by the children but also by the teacher. This is suggested by the fact that questions raised before a story was read were not repeated when the story was discussed.

While it is true that manuals were visible with surprising rarity, workbooks and ditto sheets appeared everywhere

research

in great numbers. This omnipresence is reflected in the amount of time teachers spent on activities connected with assignments, which is summarized in Research/Table 2. *Comprehension: assessment* appears in Research/Table 2 because the assessment was of assigned reading.

The category *assignment,* it will be recalled, covers all assignments excluding those for comprehension and study skills. As Research/Table 2 shows, the 3 dimensions of the category account for 14.35 percent of the teachers' time.

Inspection of Research/Table 2 may raise a question about the possibility that *comprehension: help with assignment* and *assignment: help with* obscure assistance that was instruction. If so, the answer is "no." The help in both cases was with the mechanics or directions for an assignment, not with features that could be instructive. Mechanics and directions caused problems for children because, all too often, numerous assignments were given at the same time, the preparation for doing them was insufficient, or the directions were unclear.

Data in Research/Table 3 show that the observed neglect of comprehension instruction was not the result of teachers being too busy teaching other things.

Prior to the study, it had been assumed that, by fourth grade, fairly sizeable amounts of time go to structural analysis instruction because, by then, complicated-looking derived and inflected words appear frequently in materials. It was also assumed that word meanings receive special attention because the same materials show generous use of words not likely to be in fourth graders' listening-speaking vocabularies. Research/Table 3 points up that neither assumption was correct.

To describe how the observed teachers did spend their time, Research/Table 4 lists all the categories showing total percentages of 4 or more. Three categories in Research/Table 4 have not yet been mentioned but, combined, they consumed almost 31 percent of the teachers' time. The 3 are *non-instruction, transition,* and *listens: to oral reading.*

Non-instruction describes the times when a teacher was doing such things as chastising, talking about something that had no academic value (*e.g.*, a bus schedule), doing nothing while the children worked on assignments, or correcting papers at her desk. The largest contributor to the 10.72 percentage figure shown for *non-instruction* was "correcting pa-

RESEARCH/TABLE 2
Percentage of teacher time spent during the reading period on activities connected with assignments

Behavioral Categories	Percentage of 4,469 Minutes
Comprehension: assignment	2.13
Comprehension: help with assignment	5.46
Comprehension: assessment	17.65
Study skills: assignment	0.16
Assignment: gives	4.72
Assignment: helps with	6.94
Assignment: checks	2.69
Total	39.75

RESEARCH/TABLE 3
Percentage of teacher time spent during the reading period on various types of reading instruction, review, and application excluding comprehension and study skills

Behavioral Categories		Percentage of 4,469 Minutes
Oral reading: instruction		Not observed
Oral reading: application		0.43
Phonics: instruction		0.36
Phonics: review		0.18
Phonics: application		2.17
Structural analysis: instruction		0.20
Structural analysis: review		0.18
Structural analysis: application:		2.44
Word meanings: instruction		0.43
Word meanings: review		0.09
Word meanings: application		2.10
	Total	8.58

pers at desk." Frequently they were math papers. While this writer was surprised at the frequency with which teachers were willing to sit at their desks correcting papers while an observer was in the room, it is possible that they would have been there with even greater frequency if a visitor had not been present. This is suggested by the fact that more correcting went on when the research assistants were observing than when this writer was the observer.

The category *transition* accounts for time required to get ready for or to end an activity. From the teacher's perspective, it refers to waiting. (If something other than waiting was observed, the teacher's behavior was not called *transition.*) From the children's perspective, transition time went to finding a book, walking to or from the reading table, finding a given page, and so on. One of the things that became noticeable in the course of observing is that schools with interclass groupings for reading are noticeably inefficient. That is, large amounts of time are consumed by waiting, getting attention, and settling down.

The other category in Research/Table 4 that has not yet been mentioned is *listens: to oral reading.* This covers time spent on "round robin" reading. Although this writer's earlier observations in primary grades showed it to be much more common at those levels, the 9.76 percent figure in Research/Table 4 indicates that it persists into fourth grade. That round robin reading is also used when social studies is taught will be shown when the social studies data are reported.

Social Studies Programs

Earlier visits to classrooms had established both general and specific expectations for what would be found when reading was observed. In contrast, the lack of prior observations of social studies allowed for nothing more than conjecture. The following assumptions about what might be observed seemed logical:

RESEARCH/TABLE 4
Categories for the reading period with largest percentages of time allotted to them

Behavioral Categories	Percentage of 4,469 Minutes
Comprehension: assessment	17.65
Non-instruction	10.72
Transition	10.47
Listens: to oral reading	9.76
Assignment: help with	6.94
Comprehension: preparation for reading	5.53
Comprehension: help with assignment	5.46
Assignment: gives	4.72

1) The reading ability of some children is sufficiently poor that they cannot read social studies textbooks; 2) because of these deficiencies, teachers supplement the prescribed textbook with easier materials; and 3) social studies periods are viewed not only as a time to cover content but also as an opportunity a) to teach children how to read expository materials and b) to teach such study skills as outlining, scanning, and varying rate of reading to suit purpose.

The one assumption that turned out to be correct is the first. The others were naive or, at best, unrealistic for such reasons as the following: *All* the observed teachers saw the social studies period as a time to cover content—as a time to have children "master the facts." Nothing that was observed indicated that distinctions were made between important facts and trivia. If it was in the book, it was important.

Concurrently, *no* teacher saw the social studies period as a time to help with reading. Children who could not read the textbook were expected to learn the content from round robin reading of the text by better readers, and from films and filmstrips.

Just as few provisions were made for poor readers, so too was very little done to challenge able ones. Instead, social studies was a time for whole class work. As was true of the reading period, considerable time went to written assignments, many of which caused major problems for poor readers. Although workbooks were less common for social studies than they were for reading, ditto sheets were equally common. Prepared by the teachers themselves, many of the sheets were difficult to read because the material was overly crowded or the ink was too light. Both flaws account for some of the time assigned to *assignment: helps with*.

The more specific data that will be reported for social studies both support and amplify these more general observations. They are based on 2,775 minutes of observing.

Findings for the Social Studies Period

Data in Research/Table 5 single out categories pertaining to comprehension and study skills. Especially surprising is the little time that went to preparing children to read a chapter. Before the observations, it had been taken for granted that teachers spend considerable time preparing children by giving attention to

RESEARCH/TABLE 5
Percentage of teacher time spent on comprehension and study skills during the social studies period

Behavioral Categories		Percentage of 2,775 Minutes
Comprehension: instruction		N.O.[a]
Comprehension: review of instruction		N.O.
Comprehension: application		N.O.
Comprehension: assignment		0.86
Comprehension: help with assignment		1.77
Comprehension: preparation for reading		1.73
Comprehension: assessment		8.25
Comprehension: prediction		N.O.
Study skills: instruction		N.O.
Study skills: review of instruction		0.50
Study skills: application		0.32
Study skills: assignment		0.18
	Total	13.61

[a]N.O. = not observed

terms whose meanings and pronunciations are likely to cause problems, by sketching what a chapter will cover, and by posing questions designed both to motivate and to guide the reading. The 48 minutes (1.73 percent) recorded for *comprehension: preparation for reading* gives evidence that this was another unrealistic assumption.

Questions posed for assessment purposes were common during the social studies period. This is reflected in the 8.25 percent figure listed in Research/Table 5 for *comprehension: assessment*. The vast majority of the questions focused on facts, many of which were trivial, some of which are no longer "facts." That social studies, as it was being taught, has little to do with children's current lives was underscored in practically all the classrooms.

Research/Table 6 lists categories with the largest percentages of time allotted to them. The list reinforces the importance of assignments—as this is measured by the amount of time spent on them. As has been mentioned, problems with assignments explain the sizeable amount of time (11.5 percent, or 318 minutes) shown for *assignment: help with*.

The amount of time for *listens* (almost 11 percent) is largely accounted for by the use of films and filmstrips to cover content. Whenever a teacher listened to such aids, her behavior was described as *listens*. Since one reason for the films and filmstrips was to help slower children, 2 other categories ought to be in Research/Table 6, but the little time consumed by them do not warrant their inclusion: *Listening: preparation* took 0.86 percent of the time observed and *listening: check*, 2.64 percent. If a teacher did something to prepare children for a film or filmstrip, her behavior was called *listening: preparation*. If a subsequent effort was made to find out what children learned from the aid, it was called *listening: check*. Because so much of the narration for the films and filmstrips moved quickly and included many terms not likely to be familiar to the children, the little time spent in preparation was both surprising and disappointing. Even more disappointing was the time spent watching films whose content was either obsolete or no longer relevant to what was being studied.

RESEARCH/TABLE 6
Categories for the social studies period with largest percentages of time allotted to them

Behavioral Categories	Percentages of 2,775 Minutes
Assignment: help with	11.50
Transition	11.21
Listens	10.95
Comprehension: assessment	8.25
Discussion	7.89
Listens: to oral reading	7.75
Non-instruction	7.71
Review: oral	5.44
Assignment: gives	3.64
Assignment: checks	3.39

SUB-STUDY 2: GRADES 3–6

The second part of the research focused on schools, grades 3–6. In each of the 3 schools that participated, 4 classes covering the grade 3–6 range were observed. None of the fourth grades was in Sub-study 1.

The observed teachers included 10 women and 2 men. (In all the discussion, teachers will be referred to as *she* in order to minimize the possibility of identifying anyone.) Two teachers had aides, but only for reading. All 3 schools, however, had remedial reading and learning disability teachers; in all 3, therefore, considerable traffic in and out of classrooms was common.

Class size ranged from 17 to 28 children, with a mean of 21.9. In 3 rooms (grades 3, 4, and 6) social studies was not being taught when the observations took place, so science was observed instead. In 3 rooms, interclass groupings were used for social studies; in 4, they were used for reading. Reading was observed for 2,174 minutes; social studies and science, for 1,119 minutes.

The 3 schools in Sub-study 2 were in central Illinois and were selected for the following reasons. One was very traditional; the second had the reputation of being "open"; and the third was in a school system that had made a special effort to improve its reading program during the year prior to the observations. The choices, it was thought, offered the possibility that both good *and* varied instructional programs would be found. Such was not the case.

Prophetic Findings

The first class observed for Sub-study 2 was a fourth grade. What was seen and heard turned out to be strikingly similar to what was observed in all subsequent classrooms. Some of the details of the 3 days of observing will provide a background for the report of the data concerned with how the grade 3-6 teachers spent their time.

The fourth grade teacher was clearly an assignment giver, not an instructor. It was in her classroom that the first of many examples of "mentioning" (as opposed to instructing) was seen. One minute of her time went to contractions, followed by 2 minutes for the sounds that 3 digraphs record. At first, the brevity and also the abrupt, unexplained shift in focus were puzzling. Quickly, though, an explanation was forthcoming in the form of workbook assignments dealing with contractions and the 3 digraphs. (The most apparent example of "mentioning" occurred later in a third grade. In 22 minutes—again this preceded workbook and worksheet assignments—the teacher attended to bats, syllabication, various sounds for *ea*, limericks, new vocabulary, homographs, syllabication (again), and the suffix *-teen*.)

Although "mentioning" seemed designed to allow children to complete written assignments, it was often insufficiently thorough to achieve that end. This is why the category *assignment: help with* was used with some regularity, why *non-instruction* often had to do with chastisement, and why many interruptions occurred when a teacher was with a sub-group of the class.

The importance of completing assignments was also apparent in all the classrooms visited. With the fourth grade teacher, it first became noticeable when she skimmed over several topics, the last of which was prefixes. The children seemed puzzled about them; however, instead of amplifying what she had said, the teacher suggested, "Do this first [referring to the prefix ditto sheet] while they're still fresh in your mind."

In all the observed rooms, completing assignments and getting right answers seemed much more significant than concerns like *Do the children understand this?* and *Will what I'm assigning contribute to reading ability?* Lack of attention to the second concern must have been exceedingly common because a large number of assignments had little or no significance for reading. With the fourth grade teacher, the lack of attention may have accounted for her altering an assignment in a way that made it less significant than it originally was. The assignment was a workbook page that listed a number of sentences, all taken directly from a basal story that the children were about to read. The task was to number the sentences in an order that matched the sequence of events in the story. When making the assignment, the teacher suggested to the children that they copy the number of the page on which they found each sentence; then the page numbers would show the sequence. "That way," she commented, "you'll be sure to get the page right."

Making certain that there was enough time for written assignments (regardless of their value) also affected what the teachers did. This became apparent during the first observation when the teacher was working with the poorest readers. What she was doing (attending to new words, discussing the meanings of some, posing questions about the story that was to be read) seemed essential. Nonetheless, she rushed. Why she hurried was explained with her own comment: "I want all of you to get 2 workbook pages done by 10 o'clock." And while the children completed them, the teacher just waited. Waiting while a class worked on assignments was common in the observed classroom and accounted for some of the time called *non-instruction*.

While the reading period in the fourth grade was closely similar to what was to be seen in other classrooms, what took place when social studies was taught turned out to be an even better predictor of what was to come.

The fourth grade teacher used 1 social studies textbook with the entire class. Again, round robin reading by the more able children was used to communicate the content of a chapter to the less able readers. As in other classrooms, the oral reading was often poor. Children stumbled over hard-to-pronounce terms, read in a monotone, and were often difficult to hear.

Intermittently, what was read was discussed. Frequently, the focus of a discussion was the meaning of a word:

Teacher: Who can tell us what a continent is?
Child: A really big place with states and countries and stuff.
Teacher: Could anybody give us another description?
Child: It's a large land mass.
Teacher: Fine. Good.

How seriously teachers take textbook definitions (even when children do not understand them) was displayed many times but never as graphically as in the fourth grade classroom. In this case, the word was *group*. The teacher asked for an example of a group, so one child proposed, "A fight."

"When we find out the 4 reasons that make a group," the teacher responded, "you'll see that a fight isn't a group."

The next volunteer was more successful; he offered, "When you're on a bus in Chicago."

Now the response was, "Once we read about the rules of a group, that will fit."

Supplementing discussions like these were written assignments that posed large numbers of literal questions about a chapter. As in Sub-study 1, the children who could not read the text could not read the dittoed questions not only because the words were difficult but also because the teacher's cursive writing was hard to decipher or—as was also true in Sub-study 1—the ink was too light.

With a program like the one just depicted, the potential for discipline problems is great. In the fourth grade being described, the teacher was strict; thus her room was generally quiet. But in others, noise was both frequent and loud and accounted for frequent use of the category *non-instruction* to describe chastisement.

How all the categories were (or were not) used when grades 3–6 were observed will be reported next.

Findings for the Reading Period

Sub-study 2 was done to see whether attention given to comprehension instruction might vary from school to school, or from grade to grade.

When data from the 3 participating schools are compared, similarities rather then differences emerge because, as Research/Table 7 points up, 2 schools gave no time to comprehension instruction while the third spent a total of 4 minutes on it. The 4 minutes of instruction were found in 1 fourth grade and occurred on 2 different days. Descriptions of what this teacher did will explain why the category *comprehension: application* was never used. They will also illustrate the sudden, unexplained shifts in focus that were referred to earlier and that were so characteristic of all the observed classrooms.

> *Similes—grade 4* (2 min.): Teacher asked child to read top part of page in basal reader, which told how it is possible to describe something by comparing it to something else. Teacher explained that a comparison is called a simile, and wrote *simile* on the chalkboard. On the same page, examples of similes were listed (*e.g.*, "The skinny old cat looked like a stringy, wet mop.") Three children took turns reading one aloud. (This was followed by a sudden shift to new vocabulary in a story the children were about to read.)

Homographs—grade 4 (2 min.): Using a basal reader manual, teacher wrote *lead, wind, record,* and *close* on the chalkboard. Pointed to *lead* and said, "The pencil has lead in it. Lead me to school. Sometimes it says *lead* and sometimes *lead.*" Used same procedures with the other 3 words; then commented, "These are called homographs. You have to look at the rest of the sentence to know how to pronounce these words." (This was followed by a sudden shift to syllabication in words like *part-parted,* and *clean-cleaned.*)

As with the teachers in Sub-study 1, those in Sub-study 2 rarely used manuals except for the post-reading interrogation that was heard everywhere. (See Research/Table 7.) While the teacher just referred to was an exception in her use of manuals, she appeared to use them without ever asking *What is the purpose of this?* The result was brief and shallow instruction.

Shallowness also characterized procedures used to review comprehension instruction. One such procedure occurred in the same fourth grade that provided the 2 samples of comprehension instruction; the other was in a third grade. Both are described below.

Figurative language—grade 4 (1 min.): Using a basal reader manual, teacher asked children, "What does *Blind as a bat* mean?" Child explained. Teacher commented, "Remember? We call that figurative language. What does *strong as an ox* mean?" Child responded. (This was followed by sudden shift to the use of alphabetical order with encyclopedias.)

Literal/figurative meanings—grade 3 (2 min.): Teacher and children were discussing story in basal reader. Teacher called their attention to the words *drew near to the edge.* Asked, "What is the figurative meaning of those words? We've talked about figurative meanings before." Child explained. Teacher then asked, "What about its literal meaning?

RESEARCH/TABLE 7
Percentage of teacher time spent on comprehension and study skills during the reading period

Behavioral Categories	School No. 1 (694 min.)	School No. 2 (670 min.)	School No. 3 (810 min.)
Comprehension			
instruction	N.O.[a]	0.60	N.O.
review of instruction	N.O.	0.15	0.25
application	N.O.	N.O.	N.O.
assignment	2.74	3.13	0.99
help with assignment	N.O.	2.54	1.11
preparation	2.89	4.78	0.86
assessment	7.06	16.87	17.28
prediction	N.O.	N.O.	N.O.
Study skills			
instruction	N.O.	N.O.	N.O.
review of instruction	N.O.	0.60	1.11
application	N.O.	N.O.	0.37
assignment	N.O.	N.O.	N.O.

[a]N.O. = not observed

What do those words mean just as they are? Remember, that's the literal meaning." Child explained. (Teacher left reading table to write names of mischievous children on chalkboard. Upon returning, asked questions about the story.)

The assignments that dealt with comprehension (see Research/Table 7) generally focused on cloze exercises or on questions that pertained to content that was as short as a paragraph or as long as a workbook page; this means they looked very much like items in standardized reading tests. Other assignments categorized as *comprehension* were connected with basal reader selections. With these, children did such things as answer questions, match partial sentences on one side of a workbook page with partial sentences listed on the other side, arrange sentences in sequential order, match items, explain the meanings of idiomatic expressions, and so on.

Since, as Research/Table 7 demonstrates, not much was done with comprehension or study skills (except to interrogate and give assignments), a logical question is *How* did *the teachers spend their time*?

To answer this, all the categories were ranked according to the percent of time assigned to them. The 16 most frequently used for each school were compared in order to see whether any appeared on all 3 lists. Four categories did, and they are listed in alphabetical order in Research/Table 8. The introductory comments for the report of Sub-study 2 explain why these 4 qualify for such a listing.

Combined, the data in Research/Tables 7 and 8 prompt the question *Whatever happened to instruction*? To answer, data concerned with instruction are listed in Research/Table 9. While some of the percentages in Research/Table 9 are surprising, others are not. Data for the 3 dimensions of *assignment,* for instance, are hardly unexpected; for, from the beginning of the observations until they ended in May, the central role played by assignments was obvious everywhere. In this respect, third grade classes seemed more like fourth grades than like the second grades that have been visited for other research (Durkin, 1974–1975). If this is correct, it suggests the possibility that teachers teach in grades 1 and 2; then, when children are able to do some independent reading, they switch to assignment giving and interrogation.

One of the reasons for Sub-study 2, it will be recalled, was to see whether changes occurred from grade to grade insofar as comprehension instruction is concerned. Since such instruction was

RESEARCH/TABLE 8
Percentage of teacher time spent during the reading period on 4 types of behavior frequently found in all 3 schools

Behavioral Categories	School No. 1 (694 min.)	School No. 2 (670 min.)	School No. 3 (810 min.)
Assignment: help with	12.39	11.49	22.22
Comprehension: assessment	7.06	16.87	17.28
Non-instruction	34.87	16.12	13.70
Transition	7.92	10.75	8.27

RESEARCH/TABLE 9
Percentage of teacher time spent during the reading period on various types of reading instruction, review, application, and assignments

Behavioral Categories	School No. 1 (694 min.)	School No. 2 (670 min.)	School No. 3 (810 min.)
Phonics			
instruction	N.O.[a]	0.45	N.O.
review of instruction	N.O.	N.O.	0.12
application	3.31	0.15	0.62
Structural analysis			
instruction	N.O.	1.04	N.O.
review of instruction	N.O.	N.O.	N.O.
application	1.73	2.39	1.11
Word meanings			
instruction	1.01	1.19	N.O.
review of instruction	N.O.	N.O.	N.O.
application	0.15	N.O.	N.O.
Assignment			
gives	8.21	5.22	1.85
helps with	12.39	11.49	22.22
checks	9.08	2.84	5.93

[a]N.O. = not observed

practically non-existent, no meaningful comparison is possible.

What was found when social studies was observed in the 3 schools will be reported next.

Findings for the Social Studies Period

As was mentioned before, in 3 of the 12 classrooms (grades 3, 4, and 6) social studies was not being taught when the observations took place; thus, science was observed instead. As it happened, in all 3 of the classrooms, science time was spent on experiments followed by discussions. Because reading did not enter into any of the activities, only what was seen and heard during social studies will be reported.

Research/Table 10 summarizes what was observed insofar as comprehension is concerned. If nothing else, the data—or the lack of data—require attention to the question *What was going on during social studies?*

To answer this question, the procedure followed for the reading-period data was repeated. That is, all the categories were ranked according to the percent of time assigned to them. The 6 most frequently used for each school were compared to see whether any appeared on all 3 lists. In this case, only 2 categories did: *non-instruction* (which was at the top of all 3 lists), and *transition* (which was close to the top on all 3). Three categories appeared on 2 of the lists:

RESEARCH/TABLE 10
Percentage of teacher time spent on comprehension and study skills during the social studies period

Behavioral Categories	School No. 1 (458 min.)	School No. 2 (274 min.)[a]	School No. 3 (243 min.)[b]
Comprehension			
instruction	N.O.[c]	N.O.	N.O.
review of instruction	N.O.	N.O.	N.O.
application	N.O.	N.O.	N.O.
assignment	1.97	4.00	N.O.
help with assignment	N.O.	6.93	N.O.
preparation	N.O.	N.O.	N.O.
assessment	4.59	44.89	N.O.
prediction	N.O.	N.O.	N.O.
Study skills			
instruction	N.O.	N.O.	N.O.
review of instruction	N.O.	N.O.	N.O.
application	N.O.	N.O.	N.O.
assignment	N.O.	N.O.	N.O.

[a]In this school, time is reduced for 2 reasons. Following the first observation, teacher informed the observer that nothing else was going to be done with social studies "for a while." Science was taught in another room, which further reduces the time shown in the table.
[b]Two of the 4 classrooms in this school were teaching science rather than social studies. This accounts for the reduced time shown in the table.
[c]N.O. = not observed

assignments: helps with; discussion; and *listens.*

While data for social studies are based on a smaller amount of observation time and show less of a pattern than did data for the reading period, they still indicate that teachers in grades 3–6 do not perceive social studies as a time to add to reading comprehension abilities even though some children in every classroom cannot read the assigned textbook.

SUB-STUDY 3: INDIVIDUAL CHILDREN

How teachers spend their time during the reading and social studies periods was the concern of Sub-study 1 and Sub-study 2. In contrast, Sub-study 3 examined what individual children do. As with the 2 other studies, the primary purpose of Sub-study 3 was to learn whether time is spent on activities likely to add to reading comprehension abilities.

Only 3 children were observed in Sub-study 3 in order to allow for extensive data on each one. They were in grades 3, 5, and 6. Fourth grade was skipped, since it was the sole focus of Sub-study 1.

Criteria for selecting subjects reflected the interest in collecting data from fairly good instructional programs. They also reflect what has been learned over the years during visits to classrooms: a) Instructional programs in reading are geared to children reading on grade level, and b) girls, as a group, seem more interested in school activities than boys, as a group. Consideration of all these factors accounted for the decision to observe average readers, 2 of whom would be girls. The 3 subjects were selected arbitrarily from average readers during trial observations in their classrooms. The girls were in grades 3 and 6; the boy was in grade 5. Neither the subjects nor their teachers (all of whom were described by administrators as being among the best on their faculties) knew that individual children were being studied. This meant that an observer spent time in a room even when she learned upon arrival that a subject was absent. (Such time, however, does not enter into any of the reported data.) To do otherwise might have revealed the nature of the study and, in turn, prompted the teacher to be more consciously aware of the subject than would have been the case under normal circumstances.

All other aspects of Sub-study 3 were like Sub-study 2 and Sub-study 1. Each child's classroom was visited approximately every 3 weeks on 3 successive days; the days were selected to cover all 5 days of the week with equal frequency; and the observations went on from September until May.

None of the 3 classrooms in Sub-study 3 was in the other 2 studies. Each was in a different city, all located in central Illinois.

Categories for Describing Children's Behavior

Once decisions were made about categories for describing a teacher's behavior in Sub-study 1 and Sub-study 2, most categories for a child's behavior followed automatically. For instance, the 12 categories pertaining to comprehension and study skills were as follows:

Answers aloud: comprehension assessment
Listens to: comprehension instruction
comprehension instruction review
comprehension application
comprehension preparation
comprehension assessment
Listens to: study skills instruction
study skills instruction review
study skills application
Writes: comprehension assessment
comprehension assignment
study skills assignment

Writes: comprehension assessment refers to times when a child is writing something as a result of the teacher's interest in learning whether assigned reading was comprehended. The same classification also refers to the many times that subjects were observed using SRA Reading Laboratory materials and specifically to when they were writing answers to comprehension questions about material they had just read. The category *writes: comprehension assignment* was used whenever a subject was engaged in a written exercise that depended upon comprehension—for instance, filling in blanks in a cloze exercise, pairing strings of words to make sentences, and so on.

All other categories for Sub-study 3 are in Appendix B. Again, directions for using them (rather than definitions) are given in order to facilitate replications of the study.

Instructional Programs for Reading

To make the data that will be presented more meaningful, thumbnail sketches of the 3 classrooms will be given first.

The third grade had 24 children who were divided into 5 groups for reading. For some of the observations, a student teacher was present. During the year, the third-grade subject used 2 third-grade basal readers. The teacher's work with her group was very traditional: Basal stories were read and discussed, and written assignments from workbooks and ditto sheets followed. A sizeable number of written assignments had to do with cursive writing. In fact, 10.27 per cent of the time, the subject was observed practicing cursive writing.

The fifth-grade subject was in a grade 4–5 classroom and worked in a fifth-grade basal reader. His class, numbering 25 children, also had 5 reading groups. The teacher met with each twice a week, at which times she made numerous assignments; typically these included some for spelling. Thus, 16.35 per cent of the time the fifth grader was observed was spent on spelling assignments that were of 2 types: a) writing words a given number of times followed by writing sentences that included the words, and b) completing pages in a spelling workbook that gave as much attention to phonics as it did to spelling. Children in this room were also expected to complete specified numbers of SRA Reading Laboratory exercises as part of their written work.

The school attended by the sixth-grade subject used interclass, "homogeneous" groups for reading. These, according to the teacher, eliminated the need for further grouping when reading was taught. During the reading period, therefore, whole class ($N = 22$) work dominated, much of it written assignments. (In this school, a "clerical assistant" was available to run off ditto sheets.) While the children did assignments, the teacher sometimes worked at her desk correcting papers and recording grades. Some of the work done by the children was SRA Reading Laboratory exercises, which were unpopular. The teacher knew this but said that the one year she eliminated them, standardized reading test scores dropped.

Findings for the Reading Period

A quick glance at all the data for the 3 subjects marks them first as being listeners and second as being doers of written assignments. The more detailed analysis presented in Research/Table 11 supports the initial impression; it also indicates that very little reading went on except for that which was required to do assignments. As can be seen in Research/Table 11, adding the categories *non-instruction* and *transition* accounts for the bulk of the time the subjects were observed. (*Non-instruction* was used when subjects walked aimlessly about the room, sharpened their pencils, stared out the window, chatted with another child, were chastised, and so on.) The sizeable amount of time assigned to *non-instruction* for the fifth-grade subject correctly reflects his lack of interest in doing written assignments. Although he seemed to like reading books (see Research/Table 11), he did whatever he could to avoid assignments. His "delaying tactics" resulted in chastisement, which helps to account for the large amount of time assigned to *non-instruction* for him.

In contrast, the girls in third and sixth grades started assignments promptly and saw them through to completion. At times, the sixth grader almost seemed compulsive about getting assignments done. While others in her class took advantage of "free reading," she would work on assignments that were not due for several days.

Research/Table 12 singles out data for comprehension and study skills. As is shown there, comprehension assess-

RESEARCH/TABLE 11
Behavioral categories that consumed large percentages of the time spent observing 3 subjects during the reading period

Behavioral Categories	Third Grader (1,548 min.)	Fifth Grader (1,957 min.)	Sixth Grader (1,439 min.)
Listens	27.77	11.85	24.25
Writes	32.75	43.33	39.05
Reads:			
follows another's oral reading	3.04	1.69	8.83
aloud	0.71	0.77	0.35
silently	8.91	12.01	3.75
Non-instruction	9.24	21.00	11.40
Transition	4.07	4.75	4.24
Totals	86.49	95.40	91.87

RESEARCH/TABLE 12
Percentage of 3 subjects' time spent on comprehension and study skills during the reading period

Behavioral Categories	Third Grader (1,548 min.)	Fifth Grader (1,957 min.)	Sixth Grader (1,439 min.)
Answers aloud:			
comprehension assessment	0.26	0.15	0.07
Listens to:			
comprehension instruction	0.58	0.15	0.07
comprehension instruction review	N.O.[a]	N.O.	N.O.
comprehension application	N.O.	N.O.	N.O.
comprehension preparation	N.O.	N.O.	N.O.
comprehension assessment	7.04	1.84	1.39
Writes:			
comprehension assessment	4.65	5.42	8.55
comprehension assignment	8.91	7.56	9.03
Listens to:			
study skills instruction	1.42	N.O.	0.35
study skills instruction review	2.39	N.O.	N.O.
study skills application	N.O.	N.O.	N.O.
Writes:			
study skills assignment	0.90	0.87	N.O.

[a]N.O. = not observed

ment continues to loom large; comprehension instruction remains insignificant. What was done with the 13 minutes spent on comprehension instruction is described below.

Idiomatic expression—grade 3 (1 min.): During round robin reading, teacher stopped oral reader to ask about the meaning of *Take me or leave me.* Child who responded said it meant, "You can take me with you or leave me here. I don't care which." Teacher then commented about the fact that "some expressions just don't mean what they sound like word by word." Told children what the expression meant. Asked whether that meaning made sense in what was being read aloud. Children said it did. (Round robin reading continued.)

Interrogative sentences—grade 3 (8 min.): To prepare the entire class for a ditto-sheet assignment, teacher stated that certain words at the beginning of a sentence mean a definite answer is expected. Said 2 such words are *where* and *when.* Asked class for another example. One child suggested *who.* Teacher then asked if anyone could name still more. *What* and *why* were volunteered. Teacher asked, "What about *how*?" Class discussed *how.* Next, teacher listed on the board the following words, commenting that they mean a "yes" or "no" answer is required: *can, is, does, do,* and *are.* Teacher reminded class to watch for all these words in their reading, and to think about what they ask for. (Directions for completing the ditto sheet followed.)

Skimming to find key words—grade 5 (2 min.): One child read aloud a paragraph from a basal reader that discussed skimming as a way to find "key words." Following that, teacher mentioned that by glancing down a page, one can pick up key words. Directed children to look at the next page in their books and asked, "What key words tell you that the mountain men were in constant danger?" Individuals named the words; teacher praised them. (Round robin reading resumed.)

Inferential questions—grade 5 (1 min.): After directing children to read a story in a basal reader and to write answers to the questions at the end of it, teacher asked children to look at the questions. Said that not all the answers would be found directly in the story, and that this meant they would have to think about what they read because not all the answers were given right on a page. (Silent reading of the story came next.)

Meaning of stage directions—grade 6 (1 min.): In preparation for reading a play and, later, performing it, teacher asked class if they could figure out the meaning of the directions given for various sound effects. Asked what *evil theme, up and under, out* might mean. Nobody answered. Teacher next asked for meaning of *evil theme.* One child explained. Teacher said that *up and under, out* meant "it gets louder, then fades away." Teacher added that putting the 2 meanings together would give a meaning for the whole thing. One child explained what the directions meant. (Assignments for reading the play followed.)

Inspection of Research/Table 12 shows that 2 of the 3 subjects in Substudy 3 spent a little time listening to study skills instruction (27 min.), and to a review of it (37 min.). As the table points up, most of the listening was done by the third-grade subject. In the third grade, both the instruction and the review were concerned with use of the glossary that was in the children's basal readers. In the sixth grade, the study skills instruction was preparation for a workbook assignment and focused on using the card catalogue in a library.

On the assumption that the 3 subjects would be listening to still other kinds of reading instruction, categories had been

RESEARCH/TABLE 13
Percentage of 3 subjects' time spent in the reading period listening to various kinds of instruction excluding comprehension and study skills

Behavioral Categories	Third Grader (1,548 min.)	Fifth Grader (1,957 min.)	Sixth Grader (1,439 min.)
Phonics			
instruction	N.O.[a]	N.O.	N.O.
review of instruction	N.O.	N.O.	N.O.
application	0.39	N.O.	N.O.
Structural analysis			
instruction	0.13	0.41	N.O.
review of instruction	N.O.	N.O.	N.O.
application	N.O.	N.O.	N.O.
Word meanings			
instruction	2.20	1.89	0.07
review of instruction	N.O.	N.O.	N.O.
application	N.O.	N.O.	N.O.

[a]N.O. = not observed

selected for phonics, structural analysis, and word meanings that parallel those used to describe teacher behavior in Sub-study 1 and Sub-study 2. Data for these categories are listed in Research/Table 13. The paucity of data shown there again points out that comprehension and study skills instruction were not being neglected in favor of other kinds.

Time spent on written assignments for phonics, structural analysis, and word meanings is listed in Research/Table 14. Because practically all observed assignments came directly from commercially prepared materials, the best explanation for data concerned with assignments is "That's what came next in the book." That diagnostic teaching exists in read-

RESEARCH/TABLE 14
Percentage of 3 subjects' time spent in the reading period or written assignments concerned with phonics, structural analysis, and word meanings

Behavioral Categories	Third Grader (1,548 min.)	Fifth Grader (1,957 min.)	Sixth Grader (1,439 min.)
Writes			
phonics	0.84	1.58[a]	N.O.[b]
structural analysis	1.10	0.36	N.O.
word meanings	2.45	5.42	8.62

[a]This figure underestimates written assignments for phonics because the spelling workbook, used during the reading period, had a phonics orientation.
[b]N.O. = not observed

ing was not verified in this or the other 2 sub-studies.

Instructional Programs for Social Studies and Science

The total time spent observing social studies in the third grade was only 547 minutes. The brevity reflects the short period set aside for it (30 minutes), which, on occasion, was shortened still more or omitted entirely.

Social studies in third grade proceeded primarily through whole-class discussions that were highly effective because of the teacher's skill in leading them. Themes came from the textbook, of which there were 10 copies. The 10 were used only for their pictures and diagrams. Supplementary materials entered into special reports given by individual children.

The dominant role played by discussions is reflected in the 319 minutes (58.32 percent of the observed time) assigned to the category *listens to: discussion*. It also helps explain why the third-grade subject spent so little time reading.

In the fourth–fifth grade room, science was taught in the first semester; social studies, in the second. Science topics, suggested by the textbook, were developed through experiments, discussions, good films, and written reports by children, some of which were read aloud. The oral reading, combined with the film presentations, accounted for 201 minutes (17.34 percent of the observed time) being assigned to the category *listens to: oral reading*. (Whenever a subject watched a film, his or her behavior was called *listens to: oral reading*.) Round robin reading of the science textbook was observed, too. (A child's participation in round robin reading was labeled *follows oral reading*.

Many supplementary materials were in the fourth–fifth grade classroom for both science and social studies. For the latter, the teacher and the school librarian worked together to match materials with the children's reading abilities. In social studies, supplementary materials were used primarily for writing reports and answering questions distributed by the teacher.

The sixth-grade teacher often expressed negative feelings about the prescribed textbook, and this may explain why the social studies period in her room rarely began on time and why, on occasion, it was shortened or omitted in favor of something else. The routine for social studies was round robin reading of a chapter followed by the distribution of questions—as many as 40 or more—that were composed by the teacher and called "Study Guide." Written answers were required because "writing answers helps them remember the important details." The children were also expected to write summaries of newspaper articles that were of interest.

For the sixth-grade subject in Substudy 3, 36.01 percent of the observed time was spent on some kind of writing activity. While she and others wrote, the teacher often sat at her desk correcting papers, recording grades, and helping individuals who came to her with questions about an assignment.

As can be deduced from the 3 brief overviews of programs, none of the teachers in Sub-study 3 saw social studies or science as a time for helping with reading. Again, covering content was the goal. For the most part, 2 of the 3 covered it in ways that seemed to be of interest to the children. All 3 teachers worked hard. At times, however, they seemed to work at the wrong things. This was especially characteristic of the sixth-grade teacher.

Findings for the Social Studies and Science Periods

Since teaching children to be better readers of content subject textbooks never entered into any of the observed activities, the data in Research/Table 15 are not unexpected. The 16 minutes that went to study skills instruction in the third grade wascarried on in the school library during the social studies period and concentrated on how to find a book in the-catalogue and on the shelves. In the fourth–fifth grade classroom, study skills instruction included 6 minutes of attention on how to take notes from reference materials in preparation for writing a science report, which was followed the next day by 3 minutes of review and 4 minutes of application practice. Later in the year, when social studies was being taught, the fifth-grade subject received 2 minutes of individual instruction in how to use an index to learn where information about American Indians might be found.

RESEARCH/TABLE 15
Percentage of 3 subjects' time spent on comprehension and study skills during the social studies and science periods

Behavioral Categories	Third Grader (547 min.)	Fifth Grader[a] (1,159 min.)	Sixth Grader (810 min.)
Answers aloud:			
comprehension assessment	N.O.[b]	N.O.	N.O.
Listens to:			
comprehension instruction	N.O.	N.O.	N.O.
comprehension instruction review	N.O.	N.O.	N.O.
comprehension application	N.O.	N.O.	N.O.
comprehension preparation	N.O.	N.O.	N.O.
comprehension assessment	0.91	4.92	1.85
Writes:			
comprehension assessment	N.O.	4.83	10.49
comprehension assignment	0.91	3.97	4.20
Listens to:			
study skills instruction	2.93	0.69	N.O.
study skills instruction review	N.O.	0.26	N.O.
study skills application	N.O.	0.35	N.O.
Writes:			
study skills assignment	N.O.	N.O.	N.O.

[a]This time divides between science and social studies. For the other 2 subjects, all the time is social studies.
[b]N.O. = not observed

A SUMMARY

The primary reason for the research described here was to learn through classroom observations of reading and social studies whether elementary schools provide comprehension instruction. Social studies was included on the assumption that comprehension instruction is required by the difficulty of social studies textbooks. Grades 3–6 were selected for the observations on the assumption that more comprehension instruction would be found there than in grades 1 and 2.

Major findings of the research are listed below.

1. Practically no comprehension instruction was seen. Comprehension assessment, carried on for the most part through interrogation, was common. Whether children's answers were right or wrong was the big concern.

2. Other kinds of reading instruction were not seen with any frequency either. It cannot be said, therefore, that the teachers neglected comprehension because they were too busy teaching phonics, structural analysis, or word meanings.

3. In addition to being interrogators, teachers also turned out to be assignment-givers. As a result, time spent on giving, completing, and checking assignments consumed a large part of the observed periods. Sizeable amount of time also went to activities categorized as *transition* and *non-instruction*.

4. None of the observed teachers saw the social studies period as a time to improve children's comprehension abilities. Instead, all were concerned about covering content and with having children master facts.

Before the data are discussed, limitations of the research will be recognized.

LIMITATIONS OF THE RESEARCH

One possible limitation lies with the amount of time spent observing. For the 3 sub-studies for both reading and social studies, the total time was 17,997 minutes or 299.95 hours. Of the total, 175.62 hours focused on teachers, while 124.33 hours went to the study of individual children. Whether this amount of time is enough to produce an accurate picture of classroom practices is debatable. What can be stated with certainty is that it was the maximum allowed by funds supporting the research.

With that limitation, observation time still could have been spent differently. Less time in each classroom, for instance, would have allowed for a larger number of different classrooms. Or, instead of focusing on both teachers and children, all the time could have gone to teachers. The problem is that every variation has its own limitations. Since the observed classrooms were so strikingly similar, however, it is possible that all such variations would yield data very much like what have been reported.

Admittedly, the similarity of classrooms may relate to the fact that all the participating schools were in central Illinois, which raises a question about the possibility of 1 location allowing for a representative sample of classrooms. Based on consulting work in a great variety of locations, the contention is made here that the classrooms in the research are more like than different from classrooms in other parts of the country. Only future research can confirm or deny such a contention. Meanwhile, confirmation comes from some existing reports, only a few of which will be mentioned.

research

Austin and Morrison (1963) reported on their extensive contacts with schools in *The First R*. Among what they call "undesirable trends" are the following:

> . . . comprehension drills which scarcely begin to probe into the child's understanding of factual information; the absence of any sustained teaching of reading skills appropriate for children in the intermediate grades; . . . reading skills in the content areas neglected or never taught. (p. 3)

In *Behind the Classroom Door*, Goodlad and Klein (1970) made the following observations:

> We are forced to conclude that the vast majority of teachers in our sample [158 classrooms in 67 schools in 26 school districts] was oriented more to a drive for coverage of certain material than to a reasonably clear perception of behavior sought in their pupils. (p. 78)
>
> . . . classroom programs were remarkably similar from school to school, regardless of location and local realities. (p. 78)
>
> . . . telling and questioning were the predominant characteristics of instruction in our sample of classrooms. (p. 79)
>
> . . . we were struck with the dullness, abstractness, and lack of variety in the learning fare. (p. 80)
>
> Textbooks and workbooks dominated the teaching-learning process. (p. 81)
>
> Seatwork assignments were common to large numbers of children . . . , the slow hardly ever completing the assignment. (p. 82)

Goodlad and Klein also raise a question, one that the research being reported in this article frequently prompted:

> Is some stereotype of schooling built into our culture that it virtually shapes the entire enterprise, discouraging or even destroying deviations from it? (p. 91)

One more report will be mentioned, this from the Educational Products Information Exchange Institute (1977), better known as EPIE. In addition to pointing out that 95 per cent of what is done in classrooms can be attributed to commercially prepared materials, the report also makes such comments as:

> There is a sameness about the most-used materials and a diversity about less widely used materials. (p. 22)
>
> Virtually no relationship existed between a teacher's willingness or lack of willingness to reuse the materials and that teacher's perception of how well students performed with the materials. (p. 23)

One more possible limitation of the present study will be mentioned—one that plagues any researcher who attempts an observational study, for it pertains to questions like: Were all activities accounted for? Were they described accurately and categorized correctly? Was the categorization consistent over time? If different individuals had been the observers, would the data be the same? In response, all that can be said is what was mentioned earlier: Every effort was made to ensure that all such questions would have a positive answer.

DISCUSSION

Before the present study was undertaken, it had been assumed that at least some of the time they are teaching reading, teachers adhere to a sequence like the following: instruction, application, practice. The data that were collected, however, do anything but support that assumption. Instead, they portray teachers as being "mentioners," assignment givers and checkers, and interrogators. They further show that mentioning and assignment giving and checking are characteristic whether the concern is for comprehension or something else. Just as comprehension instruction was slighted, therefore, so too were all other kinds.

Another assumption not supported by the research pertains to basal reader manuals. Since prior observations by this researcher in grades 1 and 2 showed teachers using manuals almost as if they were scripts for teaching, it had been assumed that teachers in the present study would use them with considerable frequency. That was not the case. Instead, manuals were usually consulted only when a teacher wanted to learn what the new vocabulary for a story was and, secondly, when questions were needed after the story was read.

When attention did go to new vocabulary, it was brief. Typically, each word was identified once, and the meanings of some were mentioned. That the skimpy attention created problems for poor readers was verified whenever round robin reading followed because when these children read, new words were rarely recalled.

Once a story was read, manuals were consulted again—this time for questions. Whether the type of interrogation that was observed closely mirrored manual suggestions is not known. If it did, manuals need to be altered in ways that will encourage teachers to carry on the kind of probing that not only tests comprehension but also develops it.

Whereas the influence of manuals was less than what had been expected, the overwhelming influence of workbooks and other assignment sheets was *un*expected. As was mentioned, it had been taken for granted prior to the study that there would be—in fact, should be—some written assignments to provide for practice. But the thought that they would constitute almost the whole of instructional programs was never entertained. Nonetheless, that was the case.

In 1 room in particular, ditto sheets literally ran the program. It was there that the vast number of ditto masters supplied by basal reader publishers was revealed. If even some had been selected as a means for remedying a problem or providing needed challenge, the abundant number of assignments would have been easier to accept. What was observed, however, pointed to indiscriminant use that resulted in what has to be called "busy work." Unfortunately, a concomitant result is the equation of reading with doing exercises.

In every classroom, certain children did the busy work promptly—in fact, in very business-like ways. Meanwhile, others did whatever they could to avoid it. Whether a lack of interest or a lack of ability accounted for their resistance could not be discerned. What *could* be identified were the discipline problems and chastisement that ensued.

Still another point must be made about assignments because it pertains to comprehension. It is the fact that their sizeable number often meant that several days intervened between the time a story was read by children and the time their teachers queried them about it. With the delay, it was impossible to ascertain whether the questions were assessing the ability to comprehend or the ability to recall what had been comprehended.

Since what was observed both for reading and for social studies was very different from what is recommended in such sources as reading methodology textbooks, it is only natural to wonder what influenced the observed teachers to do what they did. Apparently, some source of influence is both great and widespread because of the close similarity of their procedures.

The heavy reliance on workbooks and ditto sheets forces consideration of the possibility that "Do what is easy" is a significant source of influence. Still, it has to be assumed that some of the observed teachers were conscientious professionals who did what they did because they think that is the way to conduct school. Ask such teachers what they do and they would say "Instruct."

Other conscientious teachers may have done what they did because they think that is what is expected of them. That there may be some administrators and parents who believe that the quality of an instructional program is directly related to the number of completed assignment sheets cannot be overlooked. After all, isn't this evidence of "back to basics"?

Knowing what *does* influence teachers is mandatory, if their behavior is to be changed. And everything uncovered in this research indicates that it must be changed if only to reduce the boredom and irrelevance that were so pervasive when classrooms were observed. Even if what was seen produces good readers—or at least successful testtakers—change still would be recommended to overcome the monotony of observed practices.

Since class size in the observed rooms averaged 23 children, small classes do not seem to be an automatic solution. The fourth grade with an enrollment of 11 students demonstrated this as the teacher went about doing what others did who had 28 or 29 students. More specifically, she used 1 basal reader with 2 sub-groups who read it in round robin fashion. While both groups completed workbook assignments, she corrected spelling and math papers. The social studies period showed whole-class work that relied on round robin reading of the textbook.

Providing teacher aides is not an automatic solution either—at least it wasn't in the 7 observed classrooms that had aides. Instead of using them in ways that would facilitate individualized instruction and practice, the teachers often had them doing things like correcting workbooks. The result was more checking, not better teaching.

It also seems clear from the research that adding to teachers' knowledge of what constitutes good instruction will not be sufficient to bring about change. Take the case of comprehension instruction as an example. Admittedly, not nearly enough is known about it. It still is a fact, nonetheless, that many of the procedures likely to improve comprehension and that are mentioned in all the reading methodology textbooks (and probably in all the reading methods courses) were never seen. Nor were what some consider to be procedures taken-for-granted for preparing children to read chapters in content subject textbooks. Since it seems safe to say, then, that the observed teachers knew more than they used, teaching them still more is not apt to alter how they spend their time when, presumably, they are teaching reading.

SUGGESTIONS FOR FUTURE RESEARCH

To say that more needs to be learned about reading programs is not meant to exaggerate what is presently known. As

Goodlad (1977) correctly observes, "There is only one honest answer to the question, 'What goes on in our schools?' It is that our knowledge is exceedingly limited." (p. 3) According to a review of research by Rosenshine (1978), augmenting that knowledge will not be accomplished by asking teachers what they do because "teacher reports are never significantly correlated with systematic observer data on the same behavior." (p. 167)

Even though all this points directly at the need for more observational studies, such a recommendation is made with hesitation because it never seems to be taken seriously. Several years ago, for example, an editorial in *Reading Research Quarterly* by Farr and Weintraub (1975–1976) also confirmed the need to know more about "the classroom realities of teaching reading"; but that hardly led to teachers' being beseiged with requests from researchers to study their programs. The present study suggests that more than just researchers ought to be making such requests. Clearly in need of accurate information about "the realities of teaching reading" are authors and publishers of basal reader materials, authors of reading methodology textbooks, and professors of reading methods courses.

If observational studies are done and reveal classroom practices like those described in this report, identifying what influences teachers to do what they do becomes crucially important. However, even if the added portrayals of classrooms are more positive, such identification still is important if the better practices are ever to become common practices.

Not to be forgotten are other problems and questions raised by the present research. One has to do with the fact that in every observed classroom, there were children who were good readers. If their teachers are not teaching, how did such children acquire their ability? And this raises an even more fundamental question: Is reading comprehension teachable? Or, to phrase it differently, if the observed teachers had been found giving time to procedures that we think represent comprehension instruction, would their students be better comprehenders than they are now? We don't know.

Nor, apparently, do we know how to help children who are not making it insofar as reading is concerned because they, too, were seen in every observed room. Since reading ability still is a requirement for full participation in classroom activities, such children are "outsiders" as early as third and fourth grade. To see them was disquieting. In schools where Title I, learning disability, and reading remedial teachers were almost tripping over each other, it was also puzzling.

While public criticism of our schools is often exaggerated or even unfounded, anyone willing to spend time in classrooms will come away convinced both that problems exist and that solutions are neither obvious nor simple.

REFERENCES

Austin, Mary C., & Morrison, Coleman. *The first r*. New York: The Macmillan Company, 1963.

Bormuth, John R. An operational definition of comprehension instruction. In Kenneth S. Goodman & James T. Fleming (Eds.). *Psycholinguistics and the teaching of reading.* Newark, Delaware: International Reading Association, 1969. Pp. 48–60.

Durkin, Dolores. A six year study of children who learned to read in school at the age of four. *Reading Research Quarterly,* 1974–1975, *10* (*1*), 9–61.

Durkin, Dolores. *Comprehension instruction—Where are you?* Reading Education Report No. 1, Center for the Study of Reading. University of Illinois, Urbana, October, 1977.

EPIE Institute. *Report on a national study of the nature and the quality of instructional materials most used by teachers and learners.* No. 76. New York: EPIE Institute, 1977.

Farr, Roger, & Weintraub, Samuel. Practitioners should play a role in developing new methodologies. *Reading Research Quarterly,* 1975–1976, *11* (2), 123–135.

Golinkoff, Roberta M. A comparison of reading comprehension processes in good and poor comprehenders. *Reading Research Quarterly,* 1975–1976, *11* (4), 623–659.

Good, Carter V. (Ed.). *Dictionary of education* (3d Ed.). New York: McGraw-Hill Book Company, 1973.

Goodlad, John I. What goes on in our schools? *Educational Researcher,* 1977, *6,* 3–6.

Goodlad, John I., & Klein, M. Frances. *Behind the classroom door.* Worthington, Ohio: Charles A. Jones Publishing Company, 1970.

Quirk, Thomas J.; Trismen, Donald A.; Weinberg, Susan F.; & Nalin, Katherine B. *The classroom behavior of teachers and students during compensatory reading instruction, project report.* Princeton, N.J.: Educational Testing Service, 1973.

Quirk, Thomas J.; Weinberg, Susan F., & Nalin, Katherine B. *The development of a student observation instrument for reading instruction, project report.* Princeton, N.J.: Educational Testing Service, 1973.

Quirk, Thomas J.; Trismen, Donald A.; Nalin, Katherine B.; & Weinberg, Susan F. The classroom behavior of teachers during compensatory reading instruction. *Journal of Educational Research,* 1975, *68,* 185–192.

Quirk, Thomas J.; Trismen, Donald A.; Weinberg, Susan F.; & Nalin, Katherine B. Attending behavior during reading instruction. *The Reading Teacher,* 1976, *29,* 640–646.

Rosenshine, Barak V. Review of teaching styles and pupil progress. *American Educational Research Journal,* 1978, *15,* 163–169.

Thorndike, Robert L. *Reading comprehension education in fifteen countries.* New York: Halsted Press, 1973.

Tovey, Duane. Improving children's comprehension abilities. *The Reading Teacher,* 1976, *30,* 288–292.

Wardhaugh, Ronald. The teaching of phonics and comprehension; a linguistic evaluation. In Kenneth S. Goodman and James T. Fleming (Eds.). *Psycholinguistics and the teaching of reading.* Newark, Delaware: International Reading Association, 1969. Pp. 79–90.

APPENDIX A

Categories for a Teacher's Behavior: Directions

Assignment: checks—If a teacher spends time with 1 or more children in order to check answers connected with an assignment, use this description for her/his behavior. (If a teacher checks papers while the children do something else, use the description *non-instruction.*)

Assignment: gives—All reading assignments get this description except those dealing with comprehension or study skills.

Assignment: helps with—If teacher assists 1 or more children with an assignment that does not focus on comprehension of connected text or on study skills, use this category.

Collects materials—This category should be used when a teacher collects something—for instance, art supplies or completed assignment sheets.

Comprehension: application—If the teacher does or says something in order to learn whether comprehension instruction enables children to understand connected text, use this description.

Comprehension: assessment—This is like the category *Assignment: checks* (reread that description) except that it is assessment related to comprehension. It includes questioning children about something they have read. (Anything concerned with comprehension must be described in detail in the time-accounts.)

Comprehension: assignment—If teacher gives assignment that requires the comprehension of connected text (e.g., a cloze exercise), the behavior goes here. (Note: If list of questions about material to be read is given *before* the reading begins, list the activity as *Comprehension: preparation.* If a teacher says something like, "After you read the story, answer the questions at the end," it goes under *Comprehension: assignment.*)

Comprehension: helps with assignment—If a group or individual is having problems with a comprehension assignment and the teacher helps (raises questions; suggests certain parts be read again; asks what something means "in your own words," etc.), the teacher's behavior is *Comprehension: helps with assignment.*

Comprehension: instruction—Use this category whenever a teacher does/says something to help one or more children understand or work out the meaning of more than a single word.

Comprehension: prediction—If a teacher says something like, "Now that you've read the first part of the story, what do you think is likely to happen in the next part?" the behavior goes here.

Comprehension: preparation—This includes everything a teacher does to prepare for reading *before* it begins. The category thus covers attention to new vocabulary. Often, attention will also go to the meanings of words. (Only if special and separate attention goes to meanings does the activity belong under the category *Word meanings: instruction.*) Preparation might also include questions or attempts to motivate the children, or to provide them with background information.

Comprehension: review of instruction—If teacher offered earlier comprehension instruction and now takes the time to review or repeat it, use this category.

Demonstrates—Teacher shows something—for instance, a special book, a diagram, or how to manipulate something. (If child shows and discusses something, the teacher's behavior is *Listens.*)

Diagnosis: checks information—If teacher checks written information pertaining to diagnosis of instructional needs, use this category.

Diagnosis: writes—Use this category if the teacher writes something that pertains to an instructional need.

Discussion: teacher directed—Whenever this category is used, specify what is being discussed. (If the discussion is an effort to find out whether children comprehended something they read, use *Comprehension: assessment.* If the discussion is clearly non-instructional (e.g., deals with lost property, revised bus schedule), describe the teacher's behavior as *Non-instruction.* If the discus-

research

sion has instructional potential but the teacher is listening rather than directing the discussion, list her/his behavior as *Listens.*)

Distributes materials—If a teacher takes time to give materials to individuals (for example, for an assignment), the activity goes here.

Listening: check—This will be used whenever a teacher attempts to find out what was comprehended in a listening activity—for instance, in a film that was shown.

Listening: preparation—If the teacher does something prior to the start of a listening activity that is meant to help children comprehend, the activity is described with this label.

Listens—If a teacher is listening to something other than oral reading, the activity is assigned to this category. (If s/he is listening to children's answers to assess their correctness, the activity is *Assignment: checks* or *Comprehension: assessment.*) Listening to a movie or to a record is *Listens.*

Listens: to oral reading—If a teacher spends time listening to individuals or a group read aloud, the activity goes under this category. (If s/he is having the children read aloud in order to check on responses, the activity goes under *Assignment: checks* or under *Comprehension: assessment.*) Reserve the above category for the round-robin type of reading, or for something like listening to a child read a definition from a dictionary.

Map making—If a teacher does something like sketch a coastline or draw the shape of a sea, use this category.

Map reading—This category is for teacher-directed activities related to maps that do not involve reading any text. (If reading is involved, the activity ought to be classified differently.)

Non-instruction—This heading is to be used whenever a teacher spends time doing something that is not instructing anybody in reading—for instance: checks papers at desk, chastises child, records grades, waits while children do assignments, participates in non-instructional discussion with 1 or more children.

Oral reading: application—If a teacher directs 1 or more children to put into practice what s/he has been stressing about good oral reading and s/he guides the practice, the activity is put here.

Oral reading: instruction—If a teacher spends time on ways to improve the oral delivery of written material, use this description.

Phonics: application—If the teacher has children practice (use) what has been taught, the effort goes here. (If the practice is being done *under the supervision of the teacher,* this is where to put the activity. If the practice is an assignment that the children will do on their own, the activity is classified as *Assignment: gives.*)

Phonics: instruction—If a teacher provides instruction in some aspect of phonics, the activity is classified under this category. (*Phonics instruction* is concerned with roots, whereas *Structural analysis* deals with derived and inflected words, compounds, and contractions.)

Phonics: review of instruction—This is for times when a teacher goes over previous phonics instruction.

Reads aloud—If the teacher reads aloud to 1 or more children, use this category.

Review: oral—If a teacher directs an oral review of what was done or studied earlier (e.g., in a previous social studies chapter), put the behavior here.

Silent reading: children—The individual or group with whom the teacher is working is reading silently, *and the teacher waits.* (If s/he does something *while* they read, what s/he does should be classified under another heading.)

Structural analysis: application—If the teacher is directing an activity in which 1 or more children are using or applying what was taught earlier about word structure, it is put under this heading. (If the use or application is an assignment that will be done by the children working independently, classify it as *Assignment: gives.*)

Structural analysis: instruction—If something about the structure of derived, inflected, or compound words is taught, use this category to describe the teacher's efforts. Attention to contractions goes here, too.

Structural analysis: review of instruction—If the teacher goes over something taught previously, use this category.

Study skills: application—If the teacher is directing an activity in which 1 or more children are using or applying what was taught earlier about a study skill, use this description.

Study skills: assignment—If the teacher gives an assignment in study skills (*e.g.*, an exercise in skimming, one that requires paraphrasing, or one that deals with guide words in a dictionary), use this description for her/his behavior.

Study skills: instruction—If the teacher gives instruction in a study skill (*e.g.*, outlining; use of SQ3R, skimming, varying rate to suit purpose and difficulty of material), use this category.

Study skills: review—If earlier instruction about a study skill was given and the teacher repeats or reviews it, put the activity under this category.

Sustained silent reading—If both teacher and children read silently, the activity is *Sustained silent reading.* (Change to another category when the teacher stops reading.)

Tests—Use this description if the teacher is engaged in an effort to test in a formal way—a written, end-of-the-week test, for example. If teacher does something else while the children take the test, describe and time the *other* activity. Use this category only when s/he waits while the test is in progress.

Transition—When what is necessarily done as one activity shifts to another, the time for the shift is *Transition.* Often, this heading will have the teacher *waiting* while the children do such necessary things as move from one room to another or to the reading area in a room, find books, find pages. The category also deals with those times when the teacher writes on the board in preparation for an activity.

Word identification: practice—If teacher directs activity concerned with word practice, use this category.

Word meanings: application—Use this category if what was taught about word meanings is being used by children under the supervision of the teacher.

Word meanings: review of instruction—Use this description if teacher repeats or goes over earlier instruction with word meanings.

APPENDIX B

Categories for a Child's Behavior: Directions

Absent—This is for times when subject leaves room for such reasons as to go to library, office, or lavatory. (If subject goes to library with other children, the researcher should accompany group.)

Answers question aloud—If subject answers question that is not related to reading comprehension assessment, use this category. If it *is* related, use the next category.

Answers aloud: comprehension assessment—If subject responds aloud when teacher is assessing reading comprehension, use this category.

Draws—Use this category whenever subject is engaged in art activity (assigned or aimless doodling) that has nothing to do with reading. (If child is asked to draw picture of *un*pictured character in a story, activity is *Writes: comprehension assessment.*)

Follows oral reading—This covers times when subject is participating in round-robin reading. (The important detail is that subject appears to be silently following what someone else is reading aloud.)

Listens—This broad, unspecified description should be used only when subject is listening to something noninstructional.

Listens: to answers—This is for times when subject is listening to answers that do not pertain to comprehension assessment.

Listens: to comprehension application—If teacher or other children are using or applying (aloud) what has been taught, and subject appears to be listening, use this category.

Listens: to comprehension assessment—This category is used whenever subject is listening to something (e.g., answers, discussion) that relates to teacher's effort to assess whether a piece of connected text was comprehended.

Listens: to comprehension instruction—If teacher (or tape) provides oral instruction in comprehension, the child's listening is put here. (Since the instruction deals with comprehension, it must be specified *in detail* in the time accounts.)

Listens: to comprehension preparation—Whenever subject listens to teacher preparing group (including subject) for reading a selection, this category should be used. (Preparation includes attention to new vocabulary.)

Listens: to comprehension review—If it appears that teacher offered comprehension instruction earlier and is now repeating it, the child's listening goes here. (Be sure to describe in the final accounts what is being reviewed.)

Listens: to directions—If directions are for academic assignment, put the listening here. If they deal with something like directions for a bus schedule, use the broad category *Listens.*

Listens: to discussion—Use this category only when subject is listening to something academic. (If subject is listening to child tell what s/he did yesterday after school, behavior is classified as *Listens.*) If subject participates in the academic discussion, categorize that part of his/her behavior as *Participates: in discussion.* (Remember: if discussion is teacher's attempt to find out what children comprehended, the subject's behavior is *Listens: to comprehension assessment.*)

Listens: to oral reading—If subject appears to be listening to child, teacher, or narrator of a film read something, put the listening here. On the other hand, if subject is listening *and* following (round-robin), the behavior is *Follows oral reading.*

Listens: to phonics application—Application, in contrast to instruction, covers times when subject is listening to someone (teacher or child) *use* or *apply* what has been taught.

Listens: to phonics instruction—If teacher provides oral instruction in some aspect of phonics and subject appears to be listening, use this category.

Listens: to phonics review—This category is used when subject is listening to a review of something taught earlier.

Listens: to structural analysis application—If teacher or other children are applying (aloud) something that was taught earlier about word structure, and subject appears to be listening, the behavior goes here.

Listens: to structural analysis instruction—If teacher provides oral instruction in some aspect of structural analysis, use this category. (Phonics is concerned with roots; structural analysis with derivatives, inflected words, contractions, and compound words.)

Listens: to structural analysis review—This category is used whenever subject listens to a review of something that was taught earlier about word structure.

Listens: to study skills application—This is for times when child is listening to the teacher or another child use what was taught about a study skill.

Listens: to study skills review—This category is for times when teacher reviews or offers reminders about a study skill.

Listens: to word-meaning instruction—If teacher is carrying out a special lesson with word meanings and subject appears to be attending to it, use this category.

Listens: to word meanings—If subject is listening to someone tell or read the meaning of one or more single words, put the behavior here.

Map reading—Whenever subject spends time with a map, put his/her behavior here.

Non-instruction—Use this category whenever subject spends time with something that has no instructional value. The category fits when subject blows nose, chats with neighbor, does nothing, stares, looks out window, sharpens pencil, etc.

Participates: in discussion—If something academic is being discussed (but it does not pertain to comprehension assessment), and subject contributes to discussion, put the behavior under this category. (If s/he responds when the activity pertains to comprehension assessment, the correct description is *Answers aloud: comprehension assessment.*)

Reads: aloud—This heading is for time spent by subject reading aloud. In the time-account, specify what is being read.

Reads: silently—This category is used whenever subject appears to be reading silently. In the time descriptions, indicate what is being read.

Requests help—Following the colon, specify the request. For instance, if child asks for help with the identification of a word, the description is *Requests help: word identification.* If directions for an assignment are not understood, the label is *Requests help: directions.*

Self-check: answers—This is for times when subject checks his/her own answers; for instance, from an answer sheet. (If the exercise focuses on comprehension of connected text, the correct description is *Self-check: comprehension answers.*)

Self-check: comprehension answers—If the self-checking pertains to comprehension, use this category and describe activity in time-accounts.

Studies—This covers times when subject is preparing for something like a test; that is, when the goal is to try to *remember* (as opposed to *comprehend*). Following the colon, specify what is being studied—for instance, word meanings, social studies chapter, state capitals, spelling, etc.

Transition—This heading is for activities that are non-instructional, yet necessary for the logistics of instruction; for example: subject takes materials out of desk, looks for certain pages, walks to reading area, distributes papers to other children.

Writes—This non-specific category will be used whenever subject spends time composing something like a letter or a story, or when s/he copies material from the board. It also is used for penmanship practice.

Writes: comprehension assessment—If subject is writing in response to a teacher's effort to learn whether something has been comprehended (*e.g.*, gives children a test on the meanings of certain idioms, or has children write answers to comprehension questions), subject's writing goes here. Activity must be described in detail in time-accounts since it deals with comprehension.

Writes: comprehension assignment—If subject is doing something like filling out a workbook page that concentrates on comprehending connected text, use this category. One example: using context to select appropriate word for blank in sentence. Specify activity in detail in time-account.

Writes: grammar assignment—This includes such exercises as capitalizing proper nouns, inserting apostrophes where needed, etc.

Writes: phonics assignment—Use this category whenever subject is filling out something like a workbook page or ditto that requires use or application of what has been taught in phonics.

Writes: spelling assignment—If subject is doing something like writing a word 3 times for spelling, the activity goes here.

Writes: structural analysis assignment—This category covers written exercises designed to give practice in using or applying what has been taught about word structure.

Writes: study skills assignment—This category is for written work dealing with such things as using alphabetical order, using a dictionary's guide words, outlining, etc.

Writes: test—Some of the testing activities in social studies or science may pertain to comprehension assessment; but many will be an assessment of what can be recalled or of what was memorized. The latter go under this heading. (If the assessment is of comprehension, the activity is classified as *Writes: comprehension assessment.*)

Writes: word-meaning assignment—If child is filling out a workbook page (or something else requiring writing) that has to do with the meanings of single words, put the activity under this category. Writing a definition of a word, for instance, or pairing synonyms belongs here. (If the focus is the meaning of a phrase or more, use the category *Writes: comprehension practice.*)

READING COMPREHENSION INSTRUCTION IN FIVE BASAL READER SERIES

DOLORES DURKIN

University of Illinois

The manuals of five basal reader programs, kindergarten through grade six, were examined in order to learn what they suggest for comprehension instruction. This was done to see whether what they offer and what was found in an earlier classroom-observation study might be similar. In the latter study, almost no comprehension instruction was seen when grade 3–6 classrooms were visited. On the other hand, considerable time went to comprehension assessment and written exercises. Like the teachers, the manuals give far more attention to assessment and practice than to direct, explicit instruction. When procedures for teaching children how to comprehend *are* provided, they tend to be brief. Such brevity is not unlike what was referred to in the report of the classroom-observation study as "mentioning." This was the tendency of the observed teachers to say just enough about a topic to allow for a written assignment related to it. Other features of manuals that are similar to the teachers' behavior are discussed, and recommendations for change in these teaching guides are made.

Presumably, a classroom is a place where instruction is offered and received. However, in a classroom-observation study of the kind and amount of reading comprehension instruction that grades 3–6 provide, a different picture emerged (Durkin, 1978–1979). Instead of being instructors, the 39 observed teachers tended to be questioners and assignment givers. Since almost all their questions were an attempt to learn whether the children had comprehended a given selection or chapter, the teachers seemed more intent on testing comprehension than on teaching it. They were also "mentioners," saying just enough about a topic (e.g., unstated conclusions) to allow for a written assignment related to it.

With findings like these, it was only natural to wonder why something as important as comprehension instruction was slighted. Since basal reader materials are thought to exert a strong influence on elementary school practices, a decision was made to examine basal reader manuals, kindergarten through grade six, in order to see what they recommend for teaching children how to comprehend and, in the process, to learn if a match existed between what was seen in classrooms and what is in the manuals. Basal programs published by Allyn and Bacon, Inc. (*Pathfinder,* 1978), Ginn and Company (*Reading 720,* 1979), Harcourt Brace Jovanovich, Inc. (*Bookmark*

From *Reading Research Quarterly,* (XVI)4, 1981, pp. 515–44. Reprinted with permission of the author and the International Reading Association.

Reading Program, 1979), Houghton Mifflin Company (*Houghton Mifflin Reading Series,* 1979), and Scott, Foresman and Company (*Basics in Reading,* 1978) were chosen for the analysis because each had a current copyright date and, in addition, each met at least one of the two following criteria: (a) a leading seller, and (b) widely promoted.

REVIEW OF THE LITERATURE

Both before and after the manuals were analyzed, efforts were made to locate other studies of comprehension instruction in basal materials. Little was found, however. The best known analysis of basal reader programs has been done by Chall (1967) but, unlike the present study, hers concentrated on beginning methodology. So, too, did an examination of eight commercial programs by Beck and McCaslin (1978). Their aim was "to study how instruction is arranged in the first two grades of elementary school for teaching beginning readers to break the code . . ." (p. 5).

Only four reports dealing with both basal programs and comprehension were located. Davidson's master's thesis (1972) considered how three series teach inferential comprehension in grades 4–6. One conclusion of the study was that inferential skills are sometimes defined but not taught, or are taught but not defined. Whether defined or taught, inferential skills are always practiced through teacher-directed questions and short exercises.

The second report was another master's thesis (Allcock, 1972). Three basal reader series (grades 4–6) were studied in order to see what they do to teach critical reading skills. According to this analysis, the selected series define terms, ask questions, and provide exercises. The author concluded that the manuals overemphasize some skills with definitions and exercises even though others are slighted or omitted.

In one part of another report, Jenkins and Pany (1978) described findings after looking at three series. "Specifically examined were the third and sixth grade level student workbooks and the teacher manual recommendations for teaching main idea and overall story comprehension" (p. 10). Results showed that "the dominant instructional procedure for reading comprehension is questioning. Thus, in basal series 'instruction for' and 'testing for' comprehension appear to be closely aligned" (p. 12). The authors continue, "It is tempting to conclude that comprehension instruction consists primarily of repeated testing with feedback" (p. 12).

The fourth study that was found, "Instructional Dimensions That May Affect Reading Comprehension," was reported by Beck, McKeown, McCaslin, and Burkes (1979). Although the purpose of their research was to identify in the lessons of two basal programs what is "facilitative or problematic for comprehension," findings and conclusions highlight what may be problematic. The researchers question the little attention that goes to new vocabulary, the unwarranted assumptions made about children's knowledge of the world, and the types of questions that are proposed for postreading discussions. Selections in the readers and the illustrations that accompany them are criticized, too.

To sum up, then, the three studies that have been done to learn what basal manuals do with comprehension foster the conclusion that they are generous in providing definitions, assessment questions, and practice exercises but very limited in what they propose for instruction. The one study that looked at the components of basal reader lessons supported the conclusion that all is not well in what basal programs do to teach children how to be proficient comprehenders of print.

DEFINITIONS FOR THE PRESENT STUDY

As was indicated in the report of the study of classrooms (Durkin, 1978–1979), articles and books concerned with teaching comprehension provide no definition for "comprehension instruction." The survey of the literature done for the present study reached the same conclusion. Even in the three studies just referred to, in which the aim was to locate comprehension instruction in manuals, definitions are missing.

Definition of Comprehension Instruction

The definition of comprehension instruction underlying the earlier study of classrooms was used in the present research, since findings from the two were to be compared. The definition, revised for manuals, is:

> A manual suggests that a teacher do or say something that ought to help children acquire the ability to understand, or work out, the meaning of connected text.

The "doing" and "saying" referred to in the definition are assumed to be some combination of definitions, explanations, descriptions, illustrations, demonstrations, and questions. With the latter, only those that deal with the *process* of comprehending meet the demands of the definition; questions focusing on its *products* are catalogued as being assessment. Questions thought to be instructive for a topic like intersentence relationships might include: "What do you need to know to understand that last sentence? . . . Read the whole paragraph to see what 'Because of that' means. . . . Where did you find what *that* means? . . ." On the other hand, if "Why didn't the birds return?" is all that is suggested, that question is thought to be assessment.

While the indisputable significance of vocabulary knowledge for comprehension is recognized, the focus of the instruction to which the definition refers is connected text, with the following exceptions:

1. Function words, homonyms, and homographs treated as text-dependent words.

2. Signal words treated as offering cues about phenomena (e.g., sequence, cause-effect relationship) that are revealed in connected text.

Also to be noted is that the definition pertains to efforts to teach children how to comprehend, not to factors that facilitate comprehension (e.g., world knowledge, motivation). Nor does it try to impose any theory of comprehension on the data, since the purpose of the study was simply to describe what exists.

In order to specify still further the parameters of "instruction," a few manuals were examined in a somewhat cursory manner before the formal analysis got under way. Four more guidelines for classifying manual suggestions resulted:

1. Headings for manual segments (e.g., Comprehension Instruction) will not be considered in classifying them.

2. Although definitions can be expected to enter into comprehension instruction, in and of themselves they do not constitute such instruction. More specifically, if *fact* and *opinion* are defined, but nothing is done either immediately or later to show how knowing the difference between the two should affect how something like an ad is read, the attention is not thought to be comprehension instruction.

3. If a manual suggestion focuses on what writers do and why they do it, but fails to deal with the significance of this for understanding written text, it is not considered to be comprehension instruction.

4. Whenever a manual provides comprehension instruction about a topic that was covered earlier but adds something new that is judged to be significant for understanding connected text, it will be called "elaboration" (not review) and will be counted as an additional instance of comprehension instruction.

Other Definitions

Before the manuals were analyzed, it was assumed that suggestions for comprehension instruction would be supplemented with others for application and practice. Also assumed was that at least some of the instruction would be reviewed. This called for three more definitions, which parallel those used in the earlier classroom-observation study:

Application
A manual suggests a procedure that allows for the use of what was featured in instruction. This is carried out under a teacher's supervision.

Practice
A manual suggests a procedure that allows for the use of what was featured in instruction. This is carried out by the children working independently.

Review of Instruction
A manual suggests that a teacher do or say something for the purpose of going over comprehension instruction that was offered previously.

It was also assumed that two other activities concerned with comprehension would be in the manuals:

Preparation
A manual suggests that a teacher do or say something that will prepare children to read a selection. Such preparation may include attention to new vocabulary, word meanings, background knowledge, and prereading questions.

Assessment
A manual suggests that a teacher do or say something for the purpose of learning whether a selection was comprehended.

The close connection between comprehension and study skills pointed up the need to identify the study skills instruction that manuals offer. It also created the need for another definition that corresponds to one used in the earlier study of classrooms:

Study Skills Instruction
A manual has a teacher do or say something that ought to help children understand content subject textbooks.

While whatever is done to teach children how to comprehend connected text should help with content subject textbooks, study skills instruction was conceived for this research as being more specialized; that is, as attending to topics like interpreting graphs and diagrams, varying rate in accordance with the reader's purpose, and skimming and scanning. Omitted from consideration, on the other hand, is attention to locational skills because the research was not focusing on what is done to teach children how to find information but, rather, on what is done to teach them how to process it. Review, application, and practice for study skills were defined in ways that parallel the definitions used for comprehension.

PROCEDURE FOR ANALYZING THE MANUALS

Every page in each manual of the five basal programs was read for the purpose of identifying and recording recommendations that matched any of the six definitions related to comprehension and to any of the four for study skills. (Although manuals were the focus of the examination, readers, workbooks, and ditto masters entered into the analysis whenever suggestions for using them appeared in a manual.) Following the analysis of a manual, a second examiner checked all the examples of comprehension instruction, comprehension review, study skills instruction, and study skills review in order to see whether each met the requirements of the definitions. The few differences in judgments were resolved through discussion, which served to specify even more the parameters of the definitions.

As a further check, the second examiner went through each manual, randomly selecting pages to see if any procedure that should have been recorded as being instruction or review had been overlooked. For the same purpose, the second examiner randomly selected from each series one manual in the grade 3–6 range and read that page by page. The grade 3–6 range was chosen on the assumption that middle- and upper-grade manuals offer more comprehension instruction than do those for the earlier grades, making it easier to overlook relevant activities in the advanced materials.

The analyses just described took eight months. After they were completed, the first examiner read each manual in each series once more, this time looking only for comprehension instruction, comprehension review, study skills instruction, and study skills review. What was found was checked by the second examiner; it was also checked against what had been identified in the initial examination. Now 100% agreement was found for all the judgments.

In spite of the agreement, the study admittedly suffers from all the limitations of research that must rely on judgments rather than well-established facts. This needs to be kept in mind as findings are reported.

FINDINGS: FREQUENCY DATA

The frequency of manual suggestions for the six categories concerned with comprehension (instruction, review, application, practice, preparation, and assessment) is listed in Research/Table 1. To give meaning to the frequency data and, in particular, to show that doing more is not the same as doing better, comments about each category follow.

Instruction

Both across the five series and within each one, what was considered to be a procedure for comprehension instruction varied substantially in length. More

RESEARCH/TABLE 1
Number of procedures related to comprehension and study skills in five basal reader series, kindergarten—grade six

	COMPREHENSION						STUDY SKILLS			
	Inst.	Rev.	Appl.	Prac.	Prep.	Assess.	Inst.	Rev.	Appl.	Prac.
Series A	128	346	436	693	328	328	13	31	39	61
Series B	122	158	253	746	429	393	9	23	22	42
Series C	98	418	538	832	335	335	8	29	34	27
Series D	92	121	303	662	491	437	15	15	51	33
Series E	60	85	111	495	346	346	13	11	33	59

specifically, a suggestion that was one sentence long and, in contrast, one that was well developed were each counted as one example.

In examining the frequency data for instruction, it should also be remembered that certain recommendations were called comprehension instruction even when what teachers were to do was unclear. For example, what *is* the meaning of manual directives like: Lead the children to generalize that. . . . Guide the pupils to conclude that. . . . Help the students to understand that. . . .? Or, what are teachers supposed to do or say when, in preparation for work with main ideas, a manual directs them to "Introduce the word *idea*"?

All this suggests what was common in the five series: They offered very precise help (e.g., obvious answers to assessment questions) when it was needed, but they were obscure or silent when specific help was likely to be required. Even some of the specific help is of questionable value. For instance, first-grade teachers who say to children exactly what manuals tell them to say would use such advanced language as *literal meaning, logical, infer, main idea, pause momentarily, evident, situation, refer to,* and *prepositional phrase.* This may indicate that some authors of manuals are out of touch with younger children.

Review

Typically, suggestions for review in all the series were one sentence in length; consequently, they were also nonspecific (e.g., "Remind pupils that authors sometimes give clues to when things happen" or "Review that a comma suggests the reader should pause"). When how to review *was* specified, the suggested procedure merely repeated what had been recommended earlier for instruction. This was true even of the series that explicitly promised "alternative lessons."

Important to note, too, is that the frequency with which topics or skills were reviewed appeared to have no connection with their difficulty or their relevance for comprehension. Instead, the amount of review in all the series seemed more like the product of random behavior than of a pre-established plan. In one series, for example, the use of commas to set off the person addressed was reviewed 20 times, whereas the need for a reader to vary rate to suit his or her purpose was not reviewed at all.

How review is spaced throughout a manual also seemed to be the product of random decisions. Sometimes a topic was covered, then reviewed with great frequency. At other times, a topic was introduced, then forgotten either for a long while or forever. Like its amount, then, the timing of review did not suggest a carefully constructed, predetermined plan for developing the manuals.

Application

Before the manuals were analyzed, it was assumed that a suggestion for comprehension instruction would be followed by one for application. In fact, such an assumption is made explicit in the definition of application referred to earlier. While this did not rule out the possibility of there being more than one instance of application for each instance of instruction, the large discrepancy actually found between the frequency of instruction and the frequency of application was unexpected (see Research/Table 1).

The large discrepancy stemmed from the tendency of all the examined manuals to teach by implication rather than with direct, explicit instruction. This means that if an objective had to do with drawing conclusions that were not stated by an author, manuals were not likely to offer an instructional procedure designed to teach children *how* to reach unstated conclusions. Rather, they were apt to provide teacher-supervised exercises (that is, application) in which the concern was to see *whether* they could arrive at them. If children are unable to do the exercises, all that is offered is more exercises.

Another example of application replacing instruction was on a page that urged teachers to read a certain paragraph aloud, after which the children were to be questioned about the sequence of events that it described. Even though the paragraph contained signal words like *first* and *after that,* they were never referred to in the suggestions. (Nor is instruction about them offered earlier.) Instead, only assessment questions were provided—for example, "What did Mark do first when he made the kite?" Nonetheless, the activity is explicitly described in the manual as "instruction for following a sequence." This example shows, then, not only how application replaces instruction but also why headings in manuals were ignored.

Since application is a type of assessment, it is important to note that the frequency data shown in Research/Table 1 for application point to one possible reason why the teachers observed in the earlier research spent so much time assessing. The same data might also help account for the frequency of what that study called "mentioning": saying just enough about a skill to allow for an assignment related to it. Another possible explanation for the mentioning is the brevity of some of the manual suggestions for instruction.

Practice

As Research/Table 1 shows, suggestions for written practice were even more numerous than those for application. Again, this reflects what seems to be the underlying assumption of the manuals: Children come to understand by doing, not by receiving, direct, explicit instruction that is complemented with application and practice.

One characteristic of the many suggestions for practice was the use of brief pieces of text even when what was to be practiced seemed to call for larger units of discourse. This characteristic means that if the concern is for something like making predictions while reading fiction, practice is likely to be with sentences, not stories. Consequently, the job for the children might be to connect sentences listed in one column ("Suzie was cold") with sentences listed in a second column ("Suzie went inside"). Although such practice might help clarify the meaning of "making a prediction," its value for making predictions while reading a story has to be questioned, especially since the manuals did not urge teachers to point up the relationship—if one existed—between the practice exercise and reading a story in which sequence was important.

In addition to the use of brief pieces of text for practice, manual descriptions of practice were also brief. Typically, too, one brief reference to practice was followed by another for more practice that focused on something entirely different. The result is a large number of manual pages that flit from one topic to another. To illustrate, one page deals in quick succession with: word meanings based on context; finding titles in the Table of Contents that include a person's name; classifying given words under the categories "fruit" and "meats"; telling whether specified words have the same vowel sound; and writing a story using listed words. In still another series, one manual page refers to: identifying words using contexts and sounds; distinguishing between main idea and supporting details; recognizing time order; interpreting figurative language; recognizing descriptive words; using dictionary skills; and getting information from diagrams. Ditto-sheet practice exercises are supplied for all the topics with the exception of the descriptive words. Why none was included for that was not explained.

Preparation

Traditionally, a basal manual offers suggestions to prepare children for each selection in the reader, which usually pertain to new vocabulary, background knowledge, and motivation. Since what is done is meant to facilitate comprehension, the limited attention given new vocabulary, especially in the middle- and upper-grade manuals, was unexpected.

The series that offered the least amount of help explicitly assured teachers that, by fourth grade, students who have been using its materials will be able to figure out the pronunciation and meaning of all the new words with the help of contextual and graphophonic cues. To check out the likelihood of such independence, some new words were randomly selected and the sentences in which children would first encounter them were examined. That the series displayed unrealistic optimism was the only conclusion that could be reached, since contexts were not always helpful and spellings were not always regular. Compounding the problem is the fact that many of the new words are not likely to be in the children's oral vocabularies. That manuals and teachers may need to do much more with new words before children attempt to read a selection is something that merits serious consideration.

Assessment

Before the present study got under way, it was taken for granted that manuals list comprehension assessment questions and, at the primary-grade levels, that they provide page-by-page assessment questions for every selection. Unknown at the time was that questions appearing elsewhere in manuals also deal with assessment even though headings and subheadings suggest something else.

Based on the incomplete knowledge, a pre-analysis decision was to count the questions at the end of a selection plus any that might be offered for individual pages as a single example of comprehension assessment. This meant that no selection could be credited with more than one example of assessment. It also meant that the data in Research/Table 1 seriously underestimate the large amount of comprehension assessment that is in the manuals. Had each assessment question been counted, Jenkins and Pany's (1978) observation that "the dominant procedure for comprehension is questioning" would have been abundantly reinforced.

FREQUENCY DATA BY GRADE LEVEL

As was mentioned earlier, it was assumed prior to the study that grade 4–6 manuals offer more comprehension instruction than do those for kindergarten through grade 3. To show why that was an erroneous assumption, Research/Table 2 organizes frequency data for instruction and review by grade level.

One reason for the sparse amount of instruction in the more advanced manuals is that their authors give frequent attention to location skills—how to find something in a dictionary, a glossary, an index, a library card catalog, and so on. They also use many pages to review topics introduced in prior manuals and to provide assessment questions. Authors of K–3 manuals, on the other hand, use a generous amount of space to teach phonics, to promote highly expressive oral reading, and to provide large numbers of assessment questions, some of which—as both Chall (1967) and Beck et al. (1979) correctly suggest—can be answered by examining the numerous illustrations that are in beginning readers.

FURTHER DISCUSSION OF THE FREQUENCY DATA

Since the present study was prompted by an earlier one in which classroom observations were used to learn what is done to provide for comprehension instruction, it is relevant to ask, "Is there a correspondence between what the observed teachers did and what is in the manuals of five basal reader series?"

Although the frequency data reported in Research/Table 1 cannot explain why the observed teachers spent their time the way they did, the data *are* able to point to a close match between the teachers' behavior and the examined manuals. Both, for example, give considerable time (or space) to assessment and practice but very little to direct instruction. Since most manual recommendations for instruction are brief, a match also exists between that brevity and the teachers'"mentioning."

Because only five basal series were analyzed, a question might be raised about the correspondences just referred to, especially since the observed teachers used more than those five. Here it is relevant to refer to three of the studies reviewed earlier (Allcock, 1972: Davidson, 1972; Jenkins & Pany, 1978). All focused on comprehension instruction in basal manuals, but none used the same materials that figured in the present study. Nonetheless, their findings were similar. All three uncovered little instruction but considerable amounts of practice and assessment.

RESEARCH/TABLE 2
Number of procedures for comprehension instruction and review, and for study skills instruction and review, in five basal reader series

	COMPREHENSION											STUDY SKILLS									
	Series											Series									
	A		B		C		D		E			A		B		C		D		E	
Grades	I	R	I	R	I	R	I	R	I	R	Grades	I	R	I	R	I	R	I	R	I	R
K–III	79	271	88	106	53	157	65	71	27	38	K–III	6	14	6	10	0	0	14	5	3	1
IV–VI	49	75	34	52	45	261	27	50	33	47	IV–VI	7	17	3	13	8	29	1	10	10	10
K–VI	128	346	122	158	98	418	92	121	60	85	K–VI	13	31	9	23	8	29	15	15	13	11

Until other research with basal reader manuals is done, it will be assumed that what characterizes the five series examined for this study describes other basal programs. Until further research is done, it will also be assumed that basal reader manuals help to account for the fact that little comprehension instruction was seen when classroom teachers were observed.

FINDINGS: CONTENT ANALYSIS

Anyone interested in remedying flaws in basal reader manuals insofar as comprehension is concerned needs to know more than the frequency of instruction. Of equal importance is what the instruction covers. For that reason, the topics dealt with when manual segments were judged to be providing comprehension and study skills instruction will now be reported.

For purposes of reporting, topics are divided into 17 categories that were established after the analyses were completed. Since not all the categories are marked by totally distinct boundaries, some topics could be (but were not) assigned to more than one category.

Eight of the categories are listed in Research/Table 3. The number of different topics covered by the five programs taken together is shown under each category. Also shown in Research/Table 3 is the number of topics that each program dealt with. For instance, Series A

RESEARCH/TABLE 3
Categories of topics for which comprehension instruction is provided, and the number of attended to by five series

Categories and Number of Topics for Each	Basal		Reader		Series
	A	B	C	D	E
Graphic Signals (N = 41)	17	13	18	10	11
Signal Words (N = 19)	12	10	5	5	4
Language Functions (N = 14)	10	8	9	6	3
Possession (N = 5)	3	3	3	5	1
Anaphora (N = 5)	3	1	3	1	2
Less Than A Sentence (N = 20)	13	8	9	11	5
Sentence (N = 28)	13	15	7	8	1
More Than A Sentence (N = 14)	10	9	5	4	3

provided what was judged to be instruction for 17 of the 41 topics that pertain to graphic signals.

Data for each of the eight categories will be discussed now. The remaining nine will be considered afterwards.

Graphic Signals

Written English is characterized by certain visual properties that offer information that is helpful and even necessary for comprehending connected text. As Research/Table 3 indicates, 41 topics covered by the manuals were classified as relating to these graphic signals. Sample topics were:

Exclamation mark suggests emotion or excitement.
Indentation signals new paragraph.
Stress indicated by underlining may alter meaning.

Lest anyone think that the judgments made for this study were based on excessively demanding criteria, it can be pointed out here that many manual recommendations for graphic signals (and for other categories as well) that were called comprehension instructions were one sentence in length. To be more specific, if a manual recommended that a period be described as something that shows where a sentence ends, that was called comprehension instruction. Although lean, the directive was judged to be both relevant and instructive since children do need to know how to tell where sentences end if they are to comprehend them. However, *prior to* being told about this function of periods, they need to be helped to understand what a sentence is. Manual authors overlooked this. That children need to have some understanding of what a question is before they are ready to learn about the question mark was not recognized either.

All this is to say that what was counted as an instance of instruction about a graphic signal was not always dealt with in a way or in a sequence that made sense. Is it sensible, for instance, to offer instruction about an ellipsis (in this case, three dots) as early as grade one (as did two of the five series) or as early as grade two (as did two others), and then review that instruction 24 times? Or, for example, does it make sense to explain the function of italics *after* a selection is read in which italicized words appear? (Providing instruction after it would have been useful in comprehending a selection was characteristic of all the series. If what was taught was then applied in the subsequent selection, the sequence would be more acceptable. That was not the practice, however. Instead, something else usually got attention in the next selection.)

Why graphic signals received so much attention in all the primary-grade manuals has to do with the great concern for stories in grades 1–3. Going along with that concern is a constant stress on expression, sometimes treated as an end in itself. This is exemplified by the special attention given to the comma as something that signals a pause, not as something that keeps thought units together. Expression treated as an end in itself is also exemplified by the frequent recommendations in manuals to have children read aloud a given piece of dialogue in order to show how it would sound if spoken with an emotion specified by the teacher—excitement, for example. While knowing how a character says something is, at times, important for comprehension, readers generally have to learn how it was said from information in the text (or from their knowledge of human behavior), not from a teacher and, commonly, not from such special graphic signals as italics, all capitals, or underlining.

The amount of attention given graphic signals in the framework of expressive oral reading raised other questions. For example, do we want children to actually pause for a comma or to actually stress an underlined word when they are reading silently? Or, to the contrary, do we want them only to be aware of what graphic signals mean so that they can respond to them mentally in a way that enhances comprehension? If it is the latter response that is desirable, then what seems to be taken-for-granted practice in primary-grade basal materials (*much* prolonged attention to expressive oral reading) needs to be reexamined.

So, too, does the taken-for-granted practice of dwelling on stories with beginners, which obligates manuals to attend to a number of graphic signals almost immediately (e.g., quotation marks, comma to set off person addressed). As a result, it immediately burdens children with trying to remember not only what all the signals mean but also what they are called. This prompts the question, Would attempts to learn to read be easier and more successful than they now are for some children if the silent reading of simple, factual material took up at least some of the time that currently goes to reading stories aloud with much expression?

Signal Words

Like punctuation, certain words offer readers cues that can assist with the comprehension of connected text. Nineteen topics dealing with such words were dealt with in the examined manuals in a way that was judged to be instruction. To illustrate the kinds of topics that were assigned to signal words, three are listed below:

Or indicates an appostive or an alternative.
As and *like* suggest a comparison.
For that reason refers to a previously mentioned idea or event.

One example of what was judged to be instruction with a signal word allows for an observation that is pertinent not just for signal words but for the research as a whole: A manual procedure may be called comprehension instruction, yet not be instructive. To illustrate, one series dealt with the linking function of *and* in a first-grade manual by recommending that children be told that *and* is used to connect two words. Following that, a list is to be put on the chalkboard so that children can name the words being connected with *and* (e.g., "Mary and John," "up and down").[1]

Although this recommendation was thought to fulfill the requirements of the definition of comprehension instruction, it is highly unlikely that first graders can grasp the intended meaning of "connect." It is possible, therefore, that all they would derive from the recommended procedure is word identification practice.

Language Functions

In addition to offering what may be too difficult (or unnecessary), authors of manuals appear to forget that reading, not writing, is the concern. This is suggested by the number of comments in manuals that are more relevant for writers than for readers, some of which were about language functions.

Perhaps the best way to define language functions is to list some of the 14 topics that were classified under that heading:

> Details are for the purpose of communicating clear idea or picture.
> Caption aids in understanding illustration or picture.
> Sarcasm may serve to provide humor or insult.

Why what manuals said about the functions of language was not always viewed as being instructive for readers (or as being correct) can be illustrated with the series that recommended telling children that whatever is at the beginning or end of a sentence attracts attention. Elsewhere, the same series teaches that variety in sentence structure serves to keep a reader's attention. With another series, instructors would teach that short sentences can function to convey excitement. In still another, time goes to explaining that descriptive details make sentences more interesting. What is important to note is that in none of these instances was anything done with the possible significance for reading (if there is any) of what was being discussed.

Possession

Knowing how possession is signaled (e.g., with *of*) is relevant for comprehending connected text; therefore, manual recommendations for any apsect of possession made up some of the comprehension instruction in the five basal reader series. As Research/Table 3 shows, five topics were assigned to that category, one of which was the difference between the apostrophe of possession and the apostrophe in contractions.

As it happened, contrast used as a method for clarifying was rarely found in the manuals. (Teaching the meaning of *and,* for example, in contrast with the meaning of *or* seems like a highly desirable way to clarify the meaning of both; yet that was never done.) Also noticeable by their *in*frequent appearance in manuals were periodic reviews in which related material (e.g., different ways to show possession) is brought together so that the whole can be seen. Instead, the generous amount of review found in all the manuals tended to be of isolated learnings.

Anaphora

Comprehending connected text requires knowing the referents for whatever anaphora authors choose to use. As Research/Table 3 points out, only five topics that pertain to anaphora were covered; and none of the series dealt with all five even though anaphoric devices cause comprehension problems. What two of the series did with pronoun referents will be described because it exemplified a frequently occurring pattern in all the series no matter what the topic was.

In several manuals, the two series suggested that teachers use one or two sentences to point out that pronouns refer to other, previously mentioned words. This was immediately followed by application. That is, teachers were directed to use additional sentences that included pronouns in order to see if the children could name their referents. And that was all that was done. No suggestions were made for what to do if children were unable to name the referents, nor were teachers encouraged to link what was being done with reading. Specifically, they were never directed to explain that understanding a sentence may require knowing who or what a referent is; and that if a mental substitution cannot be made for pronouns or for certain adverbs, rereading may be necessary. Instead, the recommendation constituted a brief, isolated event in which a means (finding the referent) is treated as an end in itself.

The frequency of such events in *all* the manuals suggests the possibility that those responsible for preparing them do not believe it is necessary to explain to children exactly and explicitly how what is done during the reading period relates to reading. Nor do they seem to think it is necessary to offer alternative teaching procedures, should the recommended one not succeed. Instead, the assumption seems to be that *more* (more of the same teaching or more practice or more assessment) will eventually get the job done. Perhaps these are assumptions that need to be re-evaluated.

Less Than a Sentence

Since all the categories discussed thus far have to do with understanding less than a sentence, some of the 20 topics placed under this particular heading might be the best way to define it:

Difference between simile and metaphor explained.
Expression may have both literal and figurative meaning.
Differently worded phrases may have the same meaning.

One topic assigned to this category, contextual help for word meaning, allows for attention to two other questionable patterns in all the manuals: They offer too little specifically informative instruction, and, second, they do not encourage probing. In the case of contextual help for word meanings, only once did any of the five series recommend instruction that was specific. (In this instance, a manual dealt with the possibility that a familiar synonym or antonym may define an unfamiliar word occurring in the same sentence.) At other times, attention to contextual help was as vague and circular as: The meaning of a word is sometimes suggested by the context. The context sometimes suggests what a word means. Following this comes application and practice. Thus, teachers are to list sentences and have the children tell the meanings of specified words. All the while the concern is for right and wrong answers; consequently, teachers are not directed to probe with questions like: How do you know it means that? What words in the sentence tell you what it means? Why couldn't it mean ________ in this sentence?

Whether nonspecific instruction and too little probing prevent manual procedures from helping children when they are reading on their own is something that those who prepare manuals need to consider.

Sentence

As is shown in Research/Table 3, 28 topics were assigned to the sentence category. Sample topics were:

Adding *not* to a sentence gives it opposite meaning.
Placement of comma in sentence can alter meaning.
Adjectives and phrases make kernel of sentence more descriptive.

What is done with sentences prompts more questions about some of the characteristic practices of manuals. One characteristic referred to earlier is their failure to relate what is done to reading. The neglect is further illustrated in what one series did with the grammar of sentences. What it did at the start related very directly to how-to-read, for it dealt with topics like:

> Finding subject may help in comprehending sentence.
> Appositive adds information about the subject.

As the grammar instruction became more advanced, however, explicit attention to the link between sentence structure and sentence meaning was absent. Instead of continuing to relate what was being taught to how to comprehend, manual passages switched to a technical treatment of grammar treated as an end in itself. In this case, turning a means into an end in itself—a *very* common practice in all the series no matter what the topic—not only deprived children of information that was relevant for working out the meaning of complicated sentences but also required them to learn new terms pertaining to grammar. This might be unwise, especially for children who have to struggle to become readers even when a reading program stays on target.

Other topics assigned to the sentence category also call for comment. For instance, one described as "Gerund construction at end of sentence refers to subject" has to do with a well-developed instructional procedure designed to assist children in processing a type of sentence structure that appeared in a selection just read and that might cause problems. This manual passage was not only thorough and directly related to reading but also unusual. That is, even though the structure of sentences in basal reader selections provided natural subject matter for comprehension instruction, it almost never received explicit, careful attention. This was the case in spite of the fact that, starting at grade 2, some sentences in all the readers were complex and probably different from what children had heard in spoken language.

Two other topics also call for comment:

> Placement of phrase may affect meaning of sentence.
> Placement of phrase does not usually alter meaning.

One manual in a series teaches about the first topic shown above; later, another manual in the same series focuses on the second. What is important to note is that nowhere were the two opposite conclusions brought together and compared so that children could see when a change affects meaning and when it does not. As was mentioned before, one flaw in the examined manuals is an insufficient amount of review that allows for such syntheses. Perhaps another is an insufficient amount of coordination among the separate manuals that make up a series.

More Than a Sentence

Together, as Research/Table 3 shows, the five basal programs dealt with 14 topics in the more than a sentence category. Some examples were:

> A cause and its effect may be in separate sentences.
> Elliptical sentence requires reference to previous sentence to be understood.
> First sentence in paragraph may express its main idea.

That seven of the 14 pertained to main ideas hardly communicates the popularity of this topic, starting in grade 1, because most of the attention given to main ideas was judged to be application, not instruction. Why this was the case (and why what is done is of questionable value) can be explained with an illustration.

The early attention that all the series give to main ideas makes use of what they call "stories." One such story follows:

> Vincent asked Anne to take care of Blackie while he was gone. He asked his father to watch out for the gerbils. His mother would feed the canary.

Instead of asking children to state what they thought the main idea was, several possibilities were presented. With the story above, three were offered:

> Vincent is going away on a vacation.
> Vincent is coming back from camp.
> All the pets are leaving.

What this single example points out is what mars much of what was done with main ideas:

1. What is said to have a main idea does not always have one.
2. What is said to be the main idea is not always correct.
3. The multiple-choice answers provided are such that only one stands a chance of being correct.
4. Stories rather than expository text are often used even though main ideas are much more characteristic of the latter than of the former.

Unquestionably, what is done with main ideas gives further support to what has already been identified as flaws: Basal manuals sometimes offer incorrect information; more frequently, they turn means into ends in themselves by not relating what is being done to how-to-read. In the case of main ideas, only two of the five series ever suggested telling children that attending to main ideas helps readers remember content.

Expository Discourse

Even though expository selections are more numerous in basal readers than they once were, the next table, Research/Table 4, makes it clear that the literary side of reading is still the dominant focus.

Topics for expository discourse for which instruction was provided included:

> Nature of expository material.
> Persuasive techniques.
> Authors' explanations of the words they use.

Three of the five basal programs placed some of their instruction about expository material in the children's readers, not the teachers' manuals. Whenever instruction did appear in a reader, it offered guidelines and advice about a given comprehension task—for instance, following the sequence of an explanation or being alert to an author's assumptions. Manual recommendations for reader-based instruction suggested that children read it either silently, or silently and then orally. Teacher interrogation was to follow, with assessment questions coming from the manual, the children's reader, or both.

Often, comprehension instruction in the readers is far superior to many of the teacher procedures in manuals. For the most part, for example, the content is both specific and directly related to how-to-read. Sometimes, too, helpful pictures supplement the text. In spite of the good pedagogy, however, the content is often dense; much is covered quickly. This suggests the possibility that only the children who already read well will profit from the reader-based instruction unless

RESEARCH/TABLE 4
Categories of topics for which comprehension instruction is provided, and the number attended to by five series

Categories and Number of Topics for Each	Basal	Reader	Series		
	A	B	C	D	E
Expository Discourse (*N* = 21)	13	3	7	6	5
Study Skills (*N* = 33)	13	9	8	15	13
Procedural Discourse (*N* = 5)	4	3	3	2	3
Narrative Discourse (*N* = 75)	23	38	25	26	19
Poetry (*N* = 9)	4	4	0	5	1
Plays (*N* = 6)	3	4	4	3	2

teachers do more than just ask questions about the content.

Why some instruction was placed in readers and, second, how decisions were made about which topics would be covered there, was not explained in any of the three programs.

Study Skills

Illustrative topics assigned to the study skills category are shown below:

Headings show organization of ideas.
Rate of reading should reflect purpose.
Interpreting a circle graph.
Skimming: attending to titles, subtitles, and illustrations in order to preview/review material.
Scanning: finding something quickly.

Although each of the five programs dealt with skimming and scanning, inconsistency characterized their use of the terms. More specifically, three used skimming to describe both kinds of rapid reading. The fourth series, on the other hand, defined skimming and scanning in its sixth-grade manual as they are defined above even though, at an earlier level, skimming was used for what is later called scanning. The fifth series did the opposite. It began with definitions that corresponded to those listed above but, subsequently, used skimming for what had been called scanning earlier.

It is possible that the above confusion merely reflects confusion about these terms in the reading profession at large. Even if that is the case, a series should at least be consistent with its own definitions. The lack of consistency points out again that the separate manuals that make up each series do not always combine into a well-coordinated whole.

Procedural Discourse

What the five series did to teach children how to comprehend directions was assigned to the procedural discourse category. As is shown in Research/Table 4, procedural discourse received very little attention even though reading directions is a common need that can cause problems. Topics covered included:

Directions provide sequence and basic details.
Directions should be read through first to see what is to be done.
Following directions requires attention to sequence.

For whatever reason, the frequent need to make inferences when following directions (e.g., a recipe) went unrecognized in all five programs.

Narrative Discourse

Topics related to narrative discourse were so numerous that nine subcategories were established to get them organized. Sample topics for each of the nine are listed below. The total number of different topics for each subcategory is indicated, too.

1. Dialogue: ($N = 7$)
   New paragraph for each speaker.
   Who is saying something may not be noted directly.
2. Characters: ($N = 14$)
   Author may tell about characters directly with adjectives.
   How a reader would feel were s/he the character helps reveal how character felt.
3. Plot: ($N = 21$)
   Events may be told out of order.
   What is happening may come from clues rather than direct explanations.
4. Setting: ($N = 6$)
   Setting may or may not be important to plot.
   Setting and character's behavior may be related.
5. Mood: ($N = 3$)
   Mood affected by setting, characters' appearance and behavior, and descriptive words.
   Mood may change.
6. Perspective: ($N = 4$)
   First-person narration revealed through use of *I* or *we*.
   Third-person narration revealed through use of *they, she,* and *he*.
7. Structure: ($N = 6$)
   Story has characters, plot, and setting.
   Story is a problem, an attempt to solve it, and a resolution.
   Subtitles divide story into parts.
8. Kinds: ($N = 13$)
   Fable has animal characters, teaches a lesson, and is very old.
   Tall tale is humorous through exaggeration.
   Real and make-believe stories contrasted.
9. Author: ($N = 1$)
   Knowing author's motive for writing may aid in understanding story.

Although opportunities existed in all the series to show how fiction should be read in comparison with what expository text requires, almost none were taken advantage of. One series that did attempt a comparison did so by saying that stories can be read more quickly and only once, whereas study reading has to be done slowly and, perhaps, repeated. While this is praiseworthy, the advice contradicts what all five series did routinely:

encouraged teachers to analyze fiction with *numerous* questions, and, second, recommended that some stories be read as many as three times.

Unfortunately, when the manuals did give attention to subject matter that should help children learn how to comprehend narrative discourse, their suggestions were not always suitable for the target population. In one second-grade manual, for example, plot conflicts were treated in an excessively mature way, since seven-year-olds are not apt to understand, or be interested in, some of the struggles discussed: between characters and their environment, between values, within an individual. Nor are second graders likely to understand, or be interested in, subtle distinctions between a topic and a main idea, or between the subject of a selection and its theme. While none of these observations are meant to deny the value of literary appreciation, they are intended to suggest that some of the time given to quite sophisticated aspects of various literary genres might be better spent on other concerns that include new vocabulary, word meanings, and ways for working out what long, complicated sentences say.

Poetry

The number of poems in the examined series ranged from 38 in one to 155 in another. As Research/Table 4 points up, comprehension instruction for poetry was lacking or almost lacking in two of the five series. One of the two explicitly recognized the scant attention and explained it by saying that excessive analysis and discussion hinder children from appreciating poetry. If this consequence is correct, it prompts the question, Why does this series, like the other four, analyze and discuss prose in such minute detail even when its content is thin and obvious?

Plays

Earlier in the report, a question was raised about the routine use of stories with beginners since that obligates manuals to deal fairly quickly with a wide variety of graphic signals. For the same reason, introducing plays as early as first grade is questioned because they, too, have physical features that require explanations. Since relatively few people read plays, it was surprising to find (see Research/Table 4) that three of the five series provided more instruction for plays than for procedural discourse.

Additional Categories

The three remaining manual passages that were thought to offer comprehension instruction had to do with the categories autobiography, biography, and diary. One of them directed teachers to explain that an autobiography is written from one perspective, which needs to be kept in mind when an autobiography is read. The second passage thought to be instructive for comprehension had to do with the possibility that parts of biographies may be fiction used to make the account more interesting. The other example of comprehension instruction focused on diaries. While what was suggested came close to being nothing more than a definition, it was still thought that what was said (e.g., that diaries contain emotional reactions as well as thoughts and observations) might assist children on those very rare occasions when they find themselves reading someone's diary.

FURTHER DISCUSSION OF TOPICS

One of the many questions for which authors of basal readers provide no answer has to do with the way they decide what will be covered in manuals. The lack of an answer makes it natural to wonder why so little (sometimes nothing) is done with certain topics whereas others are overemphasized.

In the early grades, for instance, all five programs assigned great importance to expressive oral reading even though it is possible that the persistent attention may encourage children to conclude that reading is a performing art, not a thought-getting process. Main idea was another popular topic with all five series even when the selection under consideration did not appear to have one.

In contrast, when all the anaphoric devices that authors use are kept in mind (Nash-Webber, 1977), it has to be concluded that anaphora were among the neglected topics. Why only one of the five series even recognized, for instance, that adverbs are anaphora, is puzzling. Equally puzzling is why a topic that has as much practical value as procedural discourse won no more attention than did one like the reading of plays.

Placed alongside the classroom-observation research that prompted the present study, data about the examined manuals also make it necessary to ask, *When* do children get the help they need if they are to be successful with expository texts? In the earlier research, 106 hours of the observing was of social studies, during which time not a single instance of comprehension instruction was seen. Since, as Research/Table 4 showed, not a great deal was done with expository discourse in basal reader programs, it may be only natural that a large number of children have considerable difficulty trying to cope with content subject textbooks.

SOME CONCLUDING COMMENTS

Even though the data that are reported in Research/Tables 1–4 suggest variation rather than similarity among the five basal programs, analyzing their manuals did foster the *impression* that they are very much alike. Such a reaction is probably rooted in the fact that all five series share certain characteristics. Because what they share may keep them from doing better than they now do with comprehension, a brief review of some common features seems like an appropriate conclusion.

Unquestionably, one common characteristic is the tendency to offer numerous application and practice exercises instead of direct, explicit instruction. When instruction does appear in manuals, the connection between what is being taught and how to read is either minimized or entirely overlooked. As a result, identifying referents for pronouns, reading with "a big voice," distinguishing between facts and opinions, finding topic sentences—all these activities become ends in themselves. One possible consequence is that the children receiving the instruction never do see the relationship between what is done with reading in school and what they should do when they read on their own. The very large number of written exercises supplied by all the programs may also mean that they will not want to read on their own.

What writers do is significant for readers; however, another characteristic of the five programs is the tendency to treat what writers do in a way that fails to pinpoint the significance. In this case, the characteristic means that instruction often stops short of being instructive for reading comprehension.

Even though anyone who is concerned about comprehension has an obligation to deal with its assessment, all five series seem to take this responsibility too seriously. Since all five also use assessment questions when what is really needed is explicitly informative instruction, the result is an amount of questioning in all the manuals that does seem excessive. Noticeable by its absence, on the other hand, are attempts to explain what it means to answer a question, and, second, what the possible strategies are for getting it answered.

Whereas all five programs are exceedingly generous with questions, not one provides an answer about the way their authors arrived at priorities insofar as comprehension is concerned. It now seems important to know exactly how decisions are reached about (a) what will be taught and when, (b) how each selected topic will be taught, (c) how often and when each will be reviewed, and (d) how much practice and what kind will be provided. Why some comprehension instruction is in the children's readers, why suggestions for reviewing a topic are usually identical to what is recommended for teaching it, and why manuals rely much more on application and practice to teach than on direct instruction are still other questions that deserve answers.

NOTES

This research was supported by the National Institute of Education under Contract No. US-NIE-C-400-76-0166. The opinions expressed do not necessarily reflect the position or policy of the National Institute of Education, and no official endorsement should be inferred.

1. The wording of the examples has been altered to avoid identifying the series, but the essence of the recommended procedure remains intact. This is the case throughout the report whenever illustrations are given.

REFERENCES

Allcock, Gail C. *An analysis of three basal reader programs to determine the critical reading skills taught, the extent to which they are taught, and the methods for teaching them.* Unpublished master's thesis, National College of Education, 1972.

Basics in Reading. Glenview, IL: Scott, Foresman and Company, 1978.

Beck, I. L. & McCaslin, E. S. *An analysis of dimensions that affect the development of code-breaking ability in eight beginning reading programs.* Learning Research and Development Center, University of Pittsburgh, 1978.

Beck, I. L. McKeown, M. G., McCaslin, E. S., & Burkes, A. M. *Instructional dimensions that may affect reading comprehension: Examples from two commercial reading programs.* Learning Research and Development Center, University of Pittsburgh, 1979.

Bookmark Reading Program. New York: Harcourt Brace Jovanovich, 1979.

references

Chall, J. *Learning to read: The great debate.* New York: McGraw-Hill Book Company, 1967.

Davidson, L. E. *An analysis of three basal reading programs to determine the inferential reading skills taught, the extent to which they are taught, and the methods used in teaching them.* Unpublished master's thesis, National College of Education, 1972.

Durkin, D. What classroom observations reveal about reading comprehension instruction. *Reading Research Quarterly,* 1978-79, *XIV* (4), 481–533.

Houghton Mifflin Reading Series. Boston: Houghton Mifflin Company, 1979.

Jenkins, J. R. & Pany, D. *Teaching reading comprehension in the middle grades* (Reading Education Report No. 4). Urbana: Center for the Study of Reading, University of Illinois, January 1978.

Nash-Webber, B. L. *Anaphora: A cross-disciplinary survey* (Tech. Rep. No. 31). Urbana: Center for the Study of Reading, University of Illinois, April 1977.

Pathfinder. Boston: Allyn and Bacon, Inc., 1978.

Reading 720, Rainbow Edition, Lexington, Mass.: Ginn and Company, 1979.

A Critique of What Classroom Observations Reveal About Reading Comprehension Instruction and Reading Comprehension Instruction in Five Basal Reader Series: Durkin's Contribution to Our Understanding of Current Practice

WALTER H. MACGINITIE

University of Victoria

The two articles discussed here are an integral pair. Each makes an important contribution in its own right, but together they tell what is perhaps the most important story about reading instruction in present-day North America. The gist of the story is that instruction in reading comprehension is unintentionally but systematically neglected, both in the classroom and in instructional materials. Most teachers and most people who prepare instructional materials regard comprehension as the critical outcome of reading. They would say that without comprehension there is no reading in any meaningful sense. How is it that teachers and developers of instructional materials recognize the centrality of comprehension but provide almost no instruction in it? This paradox deepens when one realizes that many teachers and developers of instructional materials believe they *are* providing instruction in reading comprehension. Durkin's two articles do not tell the whole story behind this paradox, but they present one aspect of it clearly, and one can read much of the rest of the story between the lines. The aim of this article is to examine what Durkin's work does tell us, trace the part of the story that is only implied, and try to fill in what is missing.

It is certainly worth the effort to think carefully about Durkin's articles, for the way in which the articles are interpreted will strongly influence the direction of change in reading-comprehension instruction in the years ahead. For this reason, I welcome the opportunity to critique the Durkin articles, for I hope that we will be wise enough to seize on the useful information they give us and to reject the impulse to rectify the current situation by instituting a new regimen in which instruction *about* reading comprehension takes the place of reading.

The first of Durkin's articles, "What Classroom Observations Reveal About Reading Comprehension Instruction," shows—if the data are generalizable—that teachers do not give children much help in learning how to comprehend written texts. The second of Durkin's articles, "Reading Comprehension Instruction in Five Basal Reader Series," shows that basal reader programs do not help the teachers help children learn how to comprehend. I wish that the two articles had been published in the reverse order, so they would show cause and effect more clearly. It is my opinion that Durkin found the teachers giving almost no comprehension instruction because teachers were mainly following a model of instruction provided by the basal reader series. The only thing missing to document the chain of influence is a study of the influence of basal reader materials and manuals on the teachers' instructional practices.

Although the main direction of influence appears to be from the materials to the teachers to teaching practice, it is inaccurate to conclude that the causal relationships are that simple. Teachers themselves have a strong influence on publishers; publishers are sensitive to the needs of teachers as they understand those needs. Publishers are particularly cautious about making changes that will make more work for teachers, or be confusing to them. Oftentimes, when teachers complain about the nature of the materials that publishers provide, they are in fact complaining about materials that were devised by, or demanded by, fellow teachers. Publishers are responsive to the demands of textbook selection committees, and teachers are often the dominant voice on such committees. It is a mistake to believe that textbook and materials characteristics are determined only by a few large states with state adoption policies. The reactions of textbook selection committees, even in small school districts, make their way to the editorial offices of publishers, and, collectively, these reactions are a very strong influence on the nature of textbooks and other materials.

Most selection committees will not choose a basal series with a copyright more than a few years old. Publishers therefore impose on themselves a requirement that a basal series be revised about every five years. One result is that, as Durkin says, "the separate manuals that make up each series do not always combine into a well-coordinated whole" (see page 348). The enormous number of words, pictures, procedures, exercises, analyses, evaluations, and promotional steps that must go into the many components and levels of a basal reader series almost precludes producing a "well-coordinated whole" at a reasonable cost in a period of five years. If textbook selection committees would select the good in favor of the new, and, particularly, if they would encourage partial revisions that would incorporate improvements but leave the best features unchanged, the basal series could evolve more rationally. The publishers aggravate this problem, of course, by promoting newness, flashiness, and ease of teaching as values in their materials.

In addition to the influence of instructional materials, a second major influence on the way teachers teach is the training they are given. Faculties of education both train teachers in instructional methods and enunciate principles to guide the development of instructional materials. Professors of education produce methods textbooks, write journal articles concerning reading instructional methods, guide teachers in their initial training, and provide much of the professional training. It would be useful to know the mutual influences among teacher trainers, publishers, and teachers.

Durkin's first study, "What Classroom Observations Reveal About Reading Comprehension Instruction," has been criticized primarily for the definition of comprehension instruction that Durkin used (e.g., Hodges, 1980). One complaint is that the definition is too narrow and excludes many activities that would, in fact, help

critique

students learn to understand what they read. It is, of course, true that just reading, or listening to something being read, is likely to help students learn to comprehend better. In fact, if the materials are appropriate, these may be two of the best ways of improving reading comprehension for most students.

The main concern with Durkin's definition, however, has been that it excludes what most basal reader series include under the label of reading comprehension: it excludes asking children questions to see if they have understood what they have read, unless those questions are accompanied by other procedures to help the child understand the text. It seems likely that children can learn something about reading comprehension from hearing another child answer a question and may learn from simply being asked a question that calls attention to something of importance in the text. Considering the reliance placed on questioning in the name of instruction, what children *do* learn from hearing other children give correct answers should be studied.

While it is clear that simply asking questions and getting answers from the students does not fit Durkin's definition of comprehension instruction, it is not entirely clear from her examples what *would* constitute comprehension instruction. Her examples include sequences of activities, such as trying to get a mental picture of a described person while reading, then discussing the person, then rereading the paragraph to decide what details were omitted, then using additional paragraphs in a similar fashion. In another example, children are asked to read a paragraph and give a brief summary of it (the main idea); after that, the responses are compared and discussed and the best is selected. The best is written on the board, then the children reread the paragraph to find details that have to do with the main idea. These details are written on the board below the main idea, then the concepts of "main idea" and "supporting detail" are discussed. Finally, other paragraphs are analyzed, some of which lack a main idea statement. How many of the activities included in each of these examples must be carried out for the activities to be classed as "comprehension instruction"?

Some of the activities mentioned under the definition of *Comprehension: Helps with assignment* (see page 324) sound like comprehension instruction ("raises questions; suggests certain parts be read again; asks what something means 'in your own words' "). Durkin insists, however, that "The help . . . was with the mechanics or directions for an assignment, not with features that could be instructive" (see page 300). This description does not specify whether she excluded helping children understand written directions for assignments from the classification *Comprehension: Instruction*. Finally, many teachers regard asking children to read something with expression (*Oral reading: Application* and *Oral reading: Instruction*, page 324) as a good way to help them understand what they are reading.

Of course, to classify any activity as comprehension instruction, Durkin had to assume that the activity would or did "help children understand or work out the meaning of more than a single, isolated word" (see page 291). Yet, as Durkin herself puts it at the end of her article, "if the observed teachers had been found giving time to procedures that we think represent comprehension instruction, would their students be better comprehenders than they are now? We don't know" (see page 322).

critique

Having complained a bit about Durkin's definition of reading-comprehension instruction, I should emphasize two points. First, defining reading-comprehension instruction is a difficult task, and Durkin's definition and implementation of it seem to be generally useful for her purposes. Second, the questions I have raised about her definition are not of a sort that would be likely to influence Durkin's findings in any major way. It seems clear that Durkin found teachers doing very little to help children understand what they read.[1] Durkin is justified in saying that teachers need to learn how to be more effective in giving reading-comprehension instruction.

Durkin points out that we are not sure if reading comprehension is teachable or that we know *how* to teach it. Well, we will not know if it is teachable until we try, and, according to Durkin's findings, we have not really tried yet. The question then becomes, what *should* the teacher do to try to help children learn to understand what they read?

Several statements in Durkin's first article indicate what Durkin thinks is appropriate reading-comprehension instruction. She deplores the heavy use of workbooks and ditto sheets, noting that the result is "the equation of reading with doing exercises" (see page 320). Good comprehension instruction will surely avoid this equation of reading with doing exercises. It will also avoid equating reading with lessons or lectures *about* reading.

Some of the activities that Durkin uses to illustrate comprehension instruction sound, however, much like separate lessons, detached from the child's engagement in meaningful reading. For example, her illustrations of comprehension instruction include helping "children understand the difference in the meaning of *and* and *or,*" helping children "understand that certain words signal sequence (e.g., first, before, later)," and using pairs of sentences to show the same idea expressed in different ways. The fact that Durkin finds sudden shifts in the focus of instruction undesirable also leads me to worry that the comprehension instruction she sees as desirable would take the form of "lessons." In fact, if instruction is based on what the child is reading (or has just read), sudden shifts in the focus of instruction would quite naturally and appropriately occur, for the text will typically present a variety of different kinds of problems. Similarly, Durkin's assumption that teachers would teach the application of what they have taught does not readily fit with a model of instruction that bases help with comprehension on the child's active engagement in reading. One type of application that would fit the model would be returning, after instruction, to the text the child was reading. If the teacher devises a linguistic analog—uses familiar content in the same structure as a difficult text segment (MacGinitie, in press)—to help children understand, the analog could be classed as instruction and the re-examination of the text as application.

The second of Durkin's articles, "Reading Comprehension Instruction in Five Basal Reader Series," is an analysis of what appears to be a major source of the teachers' patterns of reading instruction. Durkin noted in her first article that the

[1]Substudy 1 showed so little instruction as to preclude much variation among schools. There was little hope, therefore, that Substudy 2 would show any interesting differences, and indeed it did not. More variation might have been found at the level of individual teachers. It would be useful to document what a teacher who seems to be effective in teaching reading comprehension (and I believe I have seen several) actually does.

teachers' manuals for basal reader series were used infrequently, except to obtain the list of new vocabulary for a story or as a source of questions to ask about the story.[2] However, since so much of the observed lesson time involved the teacher asking the children questions, the pattern of questioning may have been stimulated and reinforced by the content of the teachers' manuals.

Durkin studied five basal reader programs, primarily the teachers' manuals, to see what the nature and amount of reading-comprehension instruction might be. Durkin states that, "Although manuals were the focus of the examination, readers, workbooks, and ditto masters entered into the analysis whenever suggestions for using them appeared in the manual" (see page 335). This division of attention between manuals and related materials occasion some ambiguity, for, although Durkin notes that "Three of the five basal programs placed some of their instruction about expository material in the children's readers" (see page 335). The main data table lists "the frequency of *manual* suggestions for the six categories . . . (instruction, review)." It is probably safe to assume that presence or absence of the procedures in the children's readers would not alter the main pattern of findings. The definition of comprehension instruction used in the second study is a logical extension of the definition used in the first study, and similar questions about judgments required in categorizing what was found are pertinent.

In the first study, the unit of data collection and analysis was a natural one—the time (in minutes) devoted to each activity. In the second study, the unit of analysis is what Durkin refers to as a "procedure," probably also a natural unit of analysis, if we could be sure what she meant by this term. In spite of Durkin's obvious concern for clear and meaningful definitions, this basic unit for the second study is virtually undefined. One can obtain an intuitive notion of what a "procedure" might be from such indications as "A manual suggests that a teacher do or say something" (see page 333), "the 'doing' and 'saying' referred to . . . are assumed to be some combination of definitions, explanations, descriptions, illustrations, demonstrations, and questions" (see page 333). "Each manual . . . was read for the purpose of identifying . . . recommendations," "the frequency of manual suggestions," and "what was considered to be a procedure . . . varied substantially in length" (see page 335). One hopes that essentially the same criteria for what constituted a single procedure were used for all of the categories into which the manual's content was divided.

Durkin's categorization of procedures into Preparation, Instruction, Application, Practice, Review, Assessment, and Study Skills Instruction, is a scheme best suited for the analysis of instruction that takes the form of "lessons." There is little doubt that, had one of the manuals suggested that a teacher casually point out the significance of some conventional usage (such as an idiom or an appositive), Durkin would have included that suggestion as a "comprehension instruction procedure." However, her categorization scheme is not well suited to the concept of comprehension instruction as something that might frequently accompany purposeful reading.

[2]We should not assume that, because the teacher's manual was not widely used for other purposes at the fourth-grade level, it is not commonly used more extensively as a guide to methodology in earlier grades.

Also, the categorization was sometimes stretched to fit the content of the manual. For example, although Durkin says an instance of *application* occurs when "a manual suggests a procedure that allows for the use of what was featured in instruction" (see page 334), she gives an example of *application* (see page 333) that was not preceded by relevant instruction.

In site of these quarrels with Durkin's definitions, I would argue, as with the classroom observations study, that problems of definition are not a major influence on the findings. Durkin attempted to make the definitions as clear as possible while making them relevant to what goes on in the classrooms. The study gains, rather than loses, from this choice.

Here I must admit that my own extensive but undocumented classroom observations bias me toward accepting Durkin's results and conclusions at face value. If one assumes that reading-comprehension instruction involves helping a student understand something the student is reading, and if this help involves something beyond naming or defining words, one will find very little of this type of instruction in the majority of classrooms, and almost no suggestion to encourage it in any basal reader manual. Anyone can easily verify this statement as far as the manuals are concerned. Any of the manuals contains hundreds of questions for the teacher to ask the students to see if they understood what they read. If these assessment questions are meaningful, one must assume they will frequently reveal a lack of student understanding. How do the manuals deal with this most obvious opportunity for comprehension instruction? Little or nothing appears in any of the manuals in the way of suggestions about what to do when a child demonstrates that he or she does not understand.

I will assume at this point that Durkin's conclusions are essentially correct—that many teachers, and certainly most basal reader programs, give little direct instruction to help the child who does not understand what he or she reads. I will further assume that such help would be desirable, and that children *can* be helped to learn to understand what they read. Again, the question is, what kind of help should we give? If we really taught reading comprehension, what would we do? In her report on basal reader series, Durkin presents a number of criticisms of the basal reader manuals and thereby indicates what she believes comprehension instruction should be like. I shall comment on some of these criticisms, for, while they often seem unwarranted, they seem to be based on a model of instruction that consists of formal lessons. While formal lessons may have a place in comprehension instruction—even an important place—I would like to promote an alternate view in which comprehension instruction is given in response to student needs generated by purposeful reading.

Durkin criticizes one manual, for example, for not instructing children concerning what a question is before instructing them about the use of question marks. While there are many complex linguistic formulations of questions, most children of school age have a very good intuitive notion of what a question is, and I would hope that not all the children in a class would have to sit through such a lesson before being told what a question mark is for.

In criticism of one manual, Durkin asks if it makes sense "to explain the function of italics *after* a selection is read in which italicized words appear" (see page 342). Good teachers often let students read through a selection first and then go back and give help with parts that may have been difficult to understand, or they may use the reading to make instruction about some convention of language meaningful. Again, the implicit assumption that instruction should always be in the form of a lesson followed by application is questionable.

Durkin gives some good examples of a confused focus in some manuals that suggest talking to the children about something they are reading as if they are writing it. However, in introducing these examples with the complaint that authors of "manuals appear to forget that reading, not writing, is the concern" (see page 343). Durkin denies a place in reading instruction to the process of writing. Most teachers assume that children can learn about reading from writing and that an integrated language arts program contains important values.

On the other hand, Durkin notes that "even though the structure of sentences in basal reader selections provided natural subject matter for comprehension instruction, it almost never received explicit, careful attention" (see page 346). This comment indicates that Durkin recognizes the value of basing some instruction on what the child is actually engaged in reading. Her comment here seems inconsistent with her earlier criticisms.

I wish to call special attention to Durkin's finding that the basal reader series gave very little attention to helping children understand written directions ("procedural discourse"). She wonders why a topic with as much practical value as this was not given more attention. To the extent that basal reader series reflect teachers' methodological preferences, it is not surprising that instruction in the comprehension of written directions was slighted. Many teachers appear to avoid helping children learn how to read directions because it is a difficult and frustrating task (MacGinitie, in press).

Finally, Durkin criticizes the manuals for failing to use the better instructional procedures recommended by methods texts. It is not my impression that most reading methods textbooks, except when dealing with study skills, generally offer strong alternatives to the common procedure that Durkin found, in which evaluation of comprehension is substituted for instruction in comprehension. It would be interesting to find out whether even the methods textbooks suggest, apart from study skills, very many procedures that fit Durkin's definition of reading-comprehension instruction.

Having found many shortcomings in the basal reader series, Durkin questions the nature of the priorities followed by the authors of the series, and concludes that "it now seems important to know exactly how decisions are reached about (a) what will be taught and when, (b) how each selected topic will be taught, (c) how often and when each will be viewed, and (d) how much practice and what kind will be provided" (see page 352). The demand for this kind of model—this kind of organization—for reading-*comprehension* instruction seems misplaced and out of keeping with what the student must learn. I believe that it is not desirable to teach comprehension with the kind of formal lessons and structure that Durkin's request implies. Again, if one views comprehension instruction as helping a child learn to understand what he or she would not otherwise understand, one has to ask what a child would not understand. One surely cannot answer that question with broad categories such as "anaphora," or "story grammar." Such categories cover enormous ranges of difficulty and include examples with an infinitude of contexts, contents, and intents. The difficulty of transferring learnings from formal lessons to real uses of language is well known. Beyond the mechanics of reading, at least, it may be better for a child to learn to understand written language by reading it and by receiving help when needed.

This does not mean that direct instruction cannot be effective, simply that it is most effective when it helps a learner solve a problem. I believe that effective reading-comprehension instruction should be guided by two basic principles: (1) If a child does not know something that is important, and if the occasion is right, then the child should be helped to learn. (2) The occasion is more likely to be right for reading-comprehension instruction if it involves an ongoing reading experience that is significant and meaningful to the child.

We have not trained teachers to give this kind of reading comprehension instruction. Basal reader series give little help with it. Most teachers do not do it. It is time we tried to incorporate this kind of instruction into teacher training, teachers' manuals, and classroom practice. It would be unfortunate if what we see in response to Durkin's work turns out to be new lessons and exercises on cohesive ties, idioms, story grammars, and discourse structures . . . and less reading.

FOR FURTHER LEARNING

Those readers who are interested in continuing to explore the topic of comprehension instruction would find the following references helpful:

Adams, M. J., Anderson, R. C., & Durkin, D. Beginning reading: Theory and practice. *Language Arts,* 1978, *55,* 19–25.

Anderson, R. C., & Biddle, W. B. On asking people questions about what they are reading. In G. Bower (Ed.), *Psychology of learning and motivation* (Vol. 9). New York: Academic Press, 1975.

Ausubel, D. P. *The psychology of meaningful verbal learning.* New York: Grune & Stratton, 1963.

Bartlett, F. C. *Remembering.* Cambridge: Cambridge University Press, 1932.

Bruce, B. What makes a good story? *Language Arts,* 1978, *55,* 460–466.

Chall, J. S. *Learning to read: The great debate.* New York: McGraw-Hill, 1967.

Durkin, D. The little things make a difference. *The Reading Teacher,* 1975, *28,* 473–477.

Frase, L. T. Purpose in reading. In J. T. Guthrie (Ed.), *Cognition, curriculum, and comprehension.* Newark, Del.: International Reading Association, 1977.

LaBerge, D., & Samuels, S. J. Toward a theory of automatic information processing in reading. *Cognitive Psychology,* 1974, *6,* 293–323.

Rothkopf, E. Z. Learning from written instructive materials: An exploration of the control of inspection behavior by test-like events. *American Educational Research Journal,* 1966, *3,* 241–249.

for further learning

Rumelhart, D. E. *Toward an interactive model of reading* (CHIP Report No. 56). San Diego: University of California, Center for Human Information Processing, March 1976.

Smith, F. *Understanding Reading*. New York: Holt, Rinehart, & Winston, 1971.

Stauffer, R. S. *Teaching reading as a thinking process*. New York: Harper & Row, 1969.

Wilson, M. M. The effects of question types in varying placements on the reading comprehension of upper elementary students. *Reading Psychology*, 1980, *1*, 93–102.

REFERENCES

Hodges, C. A. Toward a broader definition of comprehension instruction. *Reading Research Quarterly*, 1980, *15*, 299–306.

MacGinitie, W. H. Readability as a solution adds to the problem. In R. C. Anderson, J. Osborn, & R. J. Tierney (Eds.), *Learning to read in American schools: Basal readers and content texts*. Hillsdale, N.J.: Laurence Erlbaum Associates, in press.

A Commentary on MacGinitie's Critique of Durkin's Studies: What Classroom Observations Reveal About Reading Comprehension Instruction and Reading Comprehension Instruction in Five Basal Reader Series

DOLORES DURKIN

University of Illinois

When I learned that Professor MacGinitie would be reviewing the two reports of my studies, I could not have been more pleased, for I knew his critique would be informative. Since his reactions support the prediction, this commentary will be brief.

To begin, even though the reports suggest to Professor MacGinitie that I confine "teaching" to formal lessons (some of which might even deal with what children already know), that is hardly the case. Anyone familiar with my reading methodology textbooks (Durkin, 1978, 1980) knows that, for a number of years, I have been urging teachers to take advantage of unexpected opportunities to teach what is significant for reading. Readers of my textbooks are also aware of my saying repeatedly that teaching that originates in the unplanned event may be not only more interesting for students, but also more instructive than what originates in commercially prepared materials or a teacher's carefully planned lesson. As it happens, use of the unexpected—and the "unexpected" includes problems that children might encounter in what Professor MacGinitie calls "meaningful reading" and, at another place, "purposeful reading"—was never seen during the classroom observation study. Had it been, it would be classified "comprehension instruction" if what was done met the criteria laid down by my definition. Like Professor MacGinitie, then, I believe that comprehension instruction comes in many different forms and can originate in many different sources. *Unlike* Professor MacGinitie, I do not see how my proposed definition confines it to lessons of a type that he portrays as being excessively formal and disconnected from real reading.

Why Professor MacGinitie confined references to published reactions to my research to the one that is critical (Hodges, 1980) is also puzzling, since three other reactions that also appeared in *Reading Research Quarterly* (Cloer, 1980; Shannon, 1980; Viti, 1980) are positive and even complimentary. One, in fact, begins by observing, "Hodges has marched majestically backwards . . . Instead of offering insights as to how instructors might more effectively employ instructional techniques, Hodges has only made an attempt to justify what is currently used as 'instruction' in reading comprehension" (Cloer, pp. 566–567).

Personally, the most disquieting point made by Professor MacGinitie is that my studies may lead to even less reading—if that is possible—than now goes on in classrooms, because instruction about reading comprehension could take the place of reading. Again, I do not know what in the reports prompted such a concern since, among other things, I suggested that the best application of what is taught comes not by having children do exercises but by having them read a selection in which what was taught will help them comprehend it.

In contrast, I *do* understand why Professor MacGinitie wondered whether the comprehension instruction found in some basal readers was included in what he calls "the main data table." It *was,* because references to it, along with directions for how to use it, were in the manuals.

I must make two final points. The first is that I am now engaged in the kind of research that Professor MacGinitie refers to when he writes: "The only thing missing to document the chain of influence is a study of the influence of basal reader materials and manuals on teachers' instructional practices" (see page 356). The other point is that if I had had Professor MacGinitie's reactions before the reports of my studies were published, the reports would be better than they are.

REFERENCES

Cloer, C. T. Letters to the editors. *Reading Research Quarterly,* 1980, *15,* 566–568.

Durkin, D. *Teaching them to read* (3rd ed.). Boston: Allyn and Bacon, Inc., 1978.

Durkin, D. *Teaching young children to read* (3rd ed.). Boston: Allyn and Bacon, Inc., 1980.

Hodges, C. Toward a broader definition of comprehension instruction. *Reading Research Quarterly,* 1980, *15,* 299–306.

Shannon, P. Letters to the editors. *Reading Research Quarterly,* 1980, *15,* 565.

Viti, R. Letters to the editors. *Reading Research Quarterly,* 1980, *15,* 566.

section VI

READING PREFERENCES AND INTERESTS

RESEARCH by George W. Norvell, *The Challenge of Periodicals in Education*

CRITIQUE by Sam Weintraub

FOR FURTHER LEARNING

COMMENTARY by Lyndon W. Searfoss

SUMMARY by Karla Hawkins-Wendelin, of *Children's Reading*

CRITIQUE by Karla Hawkins-Wendelin

FOR FURTHER LEARNING

COMMENTARY by Judith W. Irwin and Jill P. May

This section introduces the reader to Norvell's study, *The Challenge of Periodicals in Education,* and Terman and Lima's classic research, *Children's Reading.* Weintraub critiques Norvell's study and offers a sharp historical perspective on reading preferences and interests among children in the United States. While he pinpoints areas of weakness in the research that has been done by Norvell and others in this area, he commends Norvell's additive approach, i.e., he combined new data to his previous base and compared or contrasted reading preferences and interests over a 40-year time period. Searfoss's comments focus on the evolution of the way we view research on reading preferences. He suggests that studying reading preferences in the 1980s involves defining new elements that affect human behavior and borrowing or developing more effective research tools for use in this area. His commentary argues for data which is collected through ecologically valid studies.

Hawkins-Wendelin summarizes and critiques Terman and Lima's expansive study, *Children's Reading.* She critiques the two areas of reading interest stressed in this study: differences with regard to mental ability and differences with regard to sex. Hawkins-Wendelin is critical of the authors' unsophisticated research methods and statistical analyses. However, she claims that the Terman-Lima study did provide a basis from which to discuss and explore the developmental nature of children's reading interests. Irwin and May comment further on the methodological problems of the Terman-Lima study, stressing those that continue to cause problems today. They focus on the reliability and validity of the data, the sampling procedure, and the conclusions. Moreover, Irwin and May illuminate problems inherent in comparing sex differences in literary preferences and the issues surrounding professional censorship.

THE CHALLENGE OF PERIODICALS IN EDUCATION

GEORGE W. NORVELL

Mr. Norvell, now retired from his position as Supervisor of English in the New York State Department of Education, resides in Albany, New York.

An investigation of periodical reading in grades 3 to 6 was made recently by the writer in nine school systems in Connecticut, Illinois, Massachusetts, and Ohio. A total of 6,000 children equally divided between boys and girls participated (147 classes in grades 4 to 6; 123 classes in grade 3). The data for grade 3 were tabulated separately, making possible the noting of certain changes of interest from grade 3 to the elementary grades.

Each pupil was given a list of magazines and asked to indicate his degree of interest in each one with which he was acquainted, by checking in the appropriate column. The total replies for a particular magazine were then expressed by formula as an interest score.*

The study adds to the evidence that periodicals are important both in the education and the recreation of children. The data show that boys and girls nine to twelve are acquainted with an average of ten magazines, and that not more than one or two children in a hundred are entirely unacquainted with this reading field.

ORDER OF POPULARITY

Research/Table 1 lists thirty-one magazines in their order of popularity with boys, with girls, and with both boys and girls in grades 4 to 6. In each instance the number of reports and the interest score are given. On the boys' list, three of the four most popular *(National Geographic, Popular Science,* and *Popular Mechanics)* are edited for adults. Seven of the top fifteen are adult magazines. Among the four highest on the girls' list, only one *(National Geographic)* is primarily for adults. Among the fifteen best liked, however, six are published for adults.

The boys' favorite is *Boys' Life,* but by only one-tenth of a point over *National Geographic.* With girls *National Geographic* ranks a half point higher than *American Girl.* On the combined list, *Boys' Life* ranks second, while *American Girl* is eighteenth. The explanation for the low ranking of *American Girl* com-

From *Elementary English,* April 1966.

*A detailed description of the form of the questionnaire and the procedures may be found in *The Reading Interests of Young People* (Heath), and *What Boys and Girls Like to Read* (Silver Burdett).

RESEARCH/TABLE 1

The interests of boys and girls, grades 4 to 6, in 31 magazines listed in the order of popularity (1962)*

	Boys			Girls			Boys and Girls	
Magazine	No.	Score	Magazine	No.	Score	Magazine	No.	Score
Boys' Life	1263	89.3	National Geographic	760	86.5	National Geographic	1655	87.9
National Geographic	895	89.2	American Girl	706	86.0	Boys' Life	1519	80.1
Popular Science	591	86.7	Calling All Girls	834	84.2	Junior Scholastic	1043	79.7
Popular Mechanics	640	85.9	Seventeen	433	84.1	Junior Natural History	320	79.3
Hot Rod	669	85.4	Junior Scholastic	518	80.2	Scouting	570	78.4
Junior Natural History	208	81.7	Modern Screen	98	79.1	Explorer	475	75.7
Scouting	453	81.6	Junior Natural History	112	76.8	Saturday Evening Post	1421	74.2
Model Airplane News	227	80.1	McCall's	1062	75.9	Life	2731	73.6
Explorer	319	79.9	Scouting	117	75.2	Hot Rod	773	73.5
Junior Scholastic	525	79.1	Saturday Evening Post	649	74.8	Popular Science	735	73.2
Saturday Evening Post	772	73.6	Life	1354	74.4	Modern Screen	174	72.5
Life	1377	72.8	Children's Digest	1029	72.7	Reader's Digest	2107	71.5
Reader's Digest	1049	70.9	Reader's Digest	1058	72.1	Current Events	338	70.0
Newsweek	472	69.0	Photoplay	111	71.6	Children's Digest	1934	69.9
Current Events	201	68.4	Current Events	137	71.5	Look	2339	68.9
Children's Digest	905	67.0	Explorer	156	71.5	Popular Mechanics	788	68.8
Look	1172	66.9	Junior Red Cross News	221	71.0	Newsweek	801	68.2
My Weekly Reader	1336	66.5	Boys' Life	256	70.9	American Girl	756	67.0
Modern Screen	76	65.8	Look	1167	70.9	My Weekly Reader	2666	67.0
Time	739	65.7	Children's Activities	169	69.8	Junior Red Cross News	414	66.9
Junior Red Cross News	193	62.7	My Weekly Reader	1330	67.5	Seventeen	560	66.9
Children's Activities	122	61.7	Newsweek	329	67.3	Calling All Girls	902	66.0
Child Life	211	60.4	True Confessions	100	67.0	Photoplay	199	65.9
Photoplay	88	60.2	Child Life	264	66.7	Children's Activities	291	65.8
True Confessions	102	52.9	Better Homes & Gardens	650	62.6	Model Airplane News	251	65.1
Seventeen	127	49.6	Good Housekeeping	595	61.6	Child Life	475	63.6
American Girl	50	48.0	Hot Rod	104	61.5	Time	1398	62.9
Calling All Girls	68	47.8	Time	659	60.0	McCall's	1662	61.8
McCall's	600	47.6	Popular Science	144	59.7	True Confessions	202	60.0
Better Homes & Gardens	411	44.0	Popular Mechanics	148	51.7	Better Homes & Gardens	1061	53.3
Good Housekeeping	355	39.4	Model Airplane News	24	50.0	Good Housekeeping	950	50.5

*The questionnaire was submitted to approximately 3,280 children (half boys and half girls).

pared with *Boys' Life* on the combined list is the tolerance of girls for reading materials intended for boys and men, a tolerance illustrated repeatedly when boys' and girls' interests in the various reading fields are compared. It is worth noting also that at this level, in almost every instance, children's magazines intended for both boys and girls are scored higher by girls than by boys: *Child Life, Children's Activities, Children's Digest, Current Events,* and *My Weekly Reader.*

That in important areas boys and girls eight to twelve years old have markedly different interests is emphasized by the contrast in placement of certain of the magazines. While *Popular Mechanics, Popular Science, Hot Rod,* and *Modern Airplane News* place near the top of the boys' list, they are placed near the end by girls. Conversely, *American Girl, Calling All Girls, Seventeen,* and *McCall's* rank high with girls, but are found near the bottom of the boys' list.

RESEARCH/TABLE 2
The interests of boys and of girls in grade 3 in 12 magazines listed in the order of popularity (1962)*

Magazine	Boys No.	Boys Score	Magazine	Girls No.	Girls Score	Magazine	Boys and Girls No.	Boys and Girls Score
Popular Science	185	88.1	My Weekly Reader	970	85.3	National Geographic	501	85.5
National Geographic	275	86.0	National Geographic	226	85.0	My Weekly Reader	2015	83.9
Popular Mechanics	148	84.1	Jack and Jill	908	82.8	Popular Science	256	81.8
Children's Activities	134	82.5	Children's Digest	439	79.0	Junior Natural history	179	79.6
My Weekly Reader	1045	82.4	Humpty Dumpty	834	77.5	Children's Activities	257	79.5
Junior Natural History	110	82.3	Junior Natural History	69	76.8	Children's Digest	841	77.7
Children's Digest	402	76.4	Children's Activities	123	76.4	Jack and Jill	1657	76.0
Child Life	195	76.2	Popular Science	71	75.4	Popular Mechanics	191	75.8
Humpty Dumpty	715	73.2	Child Life	221	73.5	Humpty Dumpty	1549	75.4
Jack and Jill	749	69.1	Look	401	67.5	Child Life	416	74.9
Life	591	69.1	Popular Mechanics	43	67.4	Life	1131	66.3
Look	494	63.0	Life	540	63.5	Look	895	65.3

*The questionnaire was submitted to approximately 2,720 children (half boys and half girls).

THIRD-GRADE PREFERENCES

Let us now look at the ranks given by third-grade children (Research/Table 2) who average eight years of age. Even here, the boys place adult magazines in the first three places: *Popular Science, National Geographic,* and *Popular Mechanics.* The girls enter *National Geographic* in second place, but include no other adult magazine among the first seven. The two men's magazines, *Popular Science* and *Popular Mechanics,* which boys place so high, are far lower by the girls' ratings. Unfortunately, there are no magazines planned primarily for girls or women on the list tested with the third grade. Of the seven children's periodicals edited for both boys and girls, the boys prefer three, and the girls four.

It is significant that at eight years of age boys give three adult magazines a much higher average rating (86.1) than they give to the seven planned specifically for children (av. 77.4). Eight-year-old girls give *National Geographic* a score of 85.0, and the seven children's magazines an average of 78.8.

A comparison of the breadth of familiarity of children in grades 4 to 6 with adult magazines and with children's magazines is revealing. When the thirty-one magazines of Research/Table 1 were rearranged to show frequency of acquaintance instead of degree of popularity, it was found that seven of the ten most widely known were adult magazines. *Life* ranked first, followed by *My Weekly Reader, Look,* and *Reader's Digest.* This pattern of acquaintance is explained in part by the frequency with which adult magazines are found in the children's homes.

AMOUNT OF READING

The use of an equal number of girls and of boys in the study made possible a comparison of the amount of reading by the two groups in the magazine field. Research/Table 3 presents the data. Since

RESEARCH/TABLE 3
Comparison of the amount of boys' and girls' magazine reading in grades 4 to 6, grades 7 to 9, and 10 to 12 expressed as the percentage girls' reading is of boys' reading, using only magazines edited for both boys and girls, or for both men and women* (1962)

Grade Level	No. of Magazines	Total Reports Boys and Girls	Percentage Girls' Reading Is of Boys' Reading
Grades 4 to 6	16	16,028	95.8
Grades 7 to 9**	17	15,176	108.6
Grades 10 to 12**	19	22,852	123.6

*The number of boys and of girls questioned were equal.
**The magazines used at the different grade levels were the same only in part. However, since four widely-read adult magazines *(Life, Reader's Digest, Saturday Evening Post,* and *Time)* were used at all three levels, additional computations were made for the four only. For this group, girls' percentages of boys' reading were: for grades 4 to 6, 94.5; for grades 7 to 9, 100.7; and for grades 10 to 12, 113.2.

studies of magazines by the same procedures were made for grades 7 to 9, and for grades 10 to 12, comparable data for these levels are included. Only magazines edited for both boys and girls, or both men and women are used. The numbers of magazines (16, 17, and 19), and the totals of reports at each level (16,028 for grades 4 to 6; 15,176 for grades 7 to 9; and 22,852 for grades 10 to 12) strongly suggest that for magazines planned to appeal to both sexes, girls' reading in grades 4 to 6 is less extensive than boys' reading (95.8%); in junior high school, girls' reading is greater than boys' (108.6%); and in senior high school, girls' reading is still greater, comparatively, than boys' reading (123.6%). As recorded in the footnote of the table, when the data for four widely-read, adult magazines only are considered, the tendency for girls to gain on boys in amount of magazine reading with advancing age is again illustrated, though the gain in percentage points is smaller than with the wider list.

This finding that girls' reading gradually increases with age compared with boys' reading conforms with the evidence of an unpublished study of adult reading by the writer—that women read four books for every three read by men.

PREFERENCES IN 1936

A quarter of a century preceding the current investigation, the writer made a study of periodicals which employed the same procedures. Research/Table 4 lists the tested magazines in the order of popularity with boys and with girls in grades 4 to 6. Since a number of the same magazines were used in the two studies, comparisons are possible. *Popular Mechanics* and *Boys' Life* are ranked very high on both lists by boys. *American Girl* places high on both girls' lists. *National Geographic* is today highest on the girls' list, and second on the boys' list. In 1936 this magazine was sixth in popularity with boys, and seventh with girls. However, on the combined list it ranked second. This is explained by the fact that on the boys' list the magazines in first, second, third, and fourth places ranked very low with girls; while five of the first six choices by girls were placed low by boys. Con-

RESEARCH/TABLE 4
Magazines ranked in the order of popularity by children in grades 4 to 6 in 1936*

Boys	Girls	Boys and Girls
Popular Mechanics	Child Life	My Weekly Reader
Boys' Life	Children's Playmate	National Geographic
Open Road for Boys	American Girl	Child Life
Popular Science	Wee Wisdom	Popular Mechanics
American Boy	My Weekly Reader	Popular Science
My Weekly Reader	Tiny Tower	Tiny Tower
National Geographic	National Geographic	Wee Wisdom
Tiny Tower	St. Nicholas	Boys' Life
Child Life	Nature	St. Nicholas
Nature	Popular Science	American Boy
Wee Wisdom	Popular Mechanics	Nature
St. Nicholas	Boys' Life	Open Road for Boys
Children's Playmate	American Boy	Children's Playmate
American Girl	Open Road for Boys	American Girl

*The average number of reports for this list of magazines was 518.

sequently, *National Geographic,* given a moderately good rating by both boys and girls, had an average that placed it second.

One finding was surprising. An examination of the scores for the six magazines tested in both studies showed that the average interest score for the six was 3.8 points lower in the current study than the average score for the same magazines in the earlier study.

The limited number of magazines jointly tested raises a question as to the significance of this finding. That the finding may be significant, however, is suggested by the data obtained in corresponding studies in grades 7 to 9, and 10 to 12 made at the same time. The data permit a comparison of scores by boys and girls for twelve magazines in junior high school, and for twenty-three in senior high school. In both comparisons the average loss of interest during the quarter-century was greater than the loss shown in grades 4 to 6. Of the twelve comparisons at the junior high school level, only one showed a gain in interest. At the senior high school level, only three of twenty-three showed gains. It seems germane to mention that there has been a loss of interest in books during the same period. The evidence does not suggest, however, that total reading by children has declined.

Usually, curriculum materials in reading and literature for children in grades 3 to 6 are chosen on the assumption that the reading interests of boys and girls vary little before adolescence. To test the validity of this assumption as to magazines, a correlation using the rank

RESEARCH/TABLE 5
Correlations of rankings given by boys and by girls in grade 3, and by boys and by girls in grades 4 to 6 (using the rank-difference method)

Grade Level	Number of Magazines	Coefficient of Correlation
Grade 3	12	+0.241
Grades 4-6	31	−0.091

RESEARCH/TABLE 6
Comparisons of the interests of children of three age levels in the daily newspaper (1936)

	Grades 4 to 6			Grades 7 to 9			Grades 10 to 12		
Type of Paper	No. of Papers	No. of Reports	Int. Score	No. of Papers	No. of Reports	Int. Score	No. of Papers	No. of Reports	Int. Score
Large City Daily	8	416	89.6	18	2475	81.4	19	3441	81.3
Small City Daily	6	128	89.3	14	379	81.2	14	369	75.5

difference method was run between boys' and girls' interest scores for the thirty-one magazines used in grades 4 to 6, and a similar correlation at the third-grade level with twelve magazines (Research/Table 5).

Of the magazines tested in grades 4 to 6, five were edited for boys or men, six for girls or women, and twenty for both sexes. Of the third-grade list, *Popular Science* and *Popular Mechanics* are planned for men, while the ten remaining magazines aim to attract both boys and girls or both men and women. For the third grade, the correlation was 0.241, and for grades 4 to 6, even lower: −0.091. The strong opposition between boys and girls in interests shown by both correlations clearly mandates the use of all available information in choosing periodicals for children as early as age eight.

NEWSPAPER READING

That newspaper reading is a major influence in the lives of boys and girls is indicated by the fact that they spend more time with it than they do with magazines or in the voluntary reading of books. Further, in grades 4 to 6, children are more interested in the daily paper than they will be in later years, though interest in the medium remains high throughout life. This is shown by Research/Table 6 which presents data gathered by identical methods for three age levels in 1936.* The average score for 416 boys and girls in grades 4 to 6 (av. age, 11) was 89.6; for 2,475 boys and girls in grades 7 to 9, it was 81.4; for 3,441 young people in grades 10 to 12, it was 81.3.

Research/Table 7 compares the interests of boys and girls in newspapers, and in *My Weekly Reader* in 1936, and contrasts the data on *My Weekly Reader* for 1936, and for 1962. Further, the interest scores of boys and girls obtained in 1962 are given for *Current Events, Newsweek,* and *Time.* These data suggest that elementary school boys enjoy the daily newspaper somewhat better than girls, and that *My Weekly Reader* appeals slightly more to girls than to boys. Girls at this age also rate *Current Events* higher than boys. By contrast, boys are more interested than girls in *Newsweek* and *Time.*

SIGNIFICANT CHANGES

The most notable contrast presented by this table is the change in interest for both boys and girls in *My Weekly Reader* in the twenty-six years from 1936 to

*The investigation in grades 4 to 6 in 1962 did not include the daily paper.

RESEARCH/TABLE 7

Interest scores for daily newspapers in 1936, and for *My Weekly Reader* in 1936 and 1962, and for *Current Events*, *Newsweek*, and *Time* in 1962 by children in grades 4 to 6

		Boys		Girls		Boys and Girls	
Periodicals	Date	No. of Reports	Score	No. of Reports	Score	No. of Reports	Score
14 Dailies	1936	316	92.6	278	87.8	594	90.2
8 Large City Dailies	1936	209	90.9	207	82.2	416	89.6
My Weekly Reader	1936	764	84.4	780	85.5	1544	85.0
My Weekly Reader	1962	1336	66.5	1339	67.5	2666	67.0
Current Events	1962	201	68.4	317	71.5	338	70.0
Newsweek	1962	472	69.0	329	67.3	801	68.2
Time	1962	739	65.7	659	60.0	1398	62.9

1962. The many pupils reporting, and the number and variety of schools represented force the conclusion that the quarter of a century has compassed a great change in children's assessment of what is interesting. Reading materials rated at 85.0 (the score given *My Weekly Reader* in 1936) are in the highest quartile in interest; those ranked at 67.0 (the score in 1962) are below the mid-point in interest.

That children's reading interests have been modified in twenty-six years is confirmed by results for grades 7 to 9, and grades 10 to 12. Further, changes in interest are not confined to newspapers. A decline in interest has occurred for magazines, and for stories and poems, at all age levels.

What has produced this startling change? The reply might be: the increased sophistication of the population observable at all levels. This answer would be facile, but vague. Modern life and thought are being changed by many factors. Especially influential is television. That children, particularly young children, are fascinated (or bewitched) by this new mode of communication is not only obvious to parents; it is verified by the astonishing time youngsters devote to it, an average of three hours daily, and by the premier rating they give it. On reflection, does it not appear inevitable that news, formalized and relayed through inanimate print, should pale in children's eyes compared with the drama of life in action?

SUMMARY

Careful studies of periodical reading by many investigators justify the following:

1. Reading magazines and newspapers is popular at all age levels beginning with the primary grades.
2. For every adult reader of books, there are two readers of magazines.
3. Two of three adults read magazines, 95 percent read newspapers, and fewer than half read books.
4. Adult readers with an eighth-grade education spend more than four-fold as much time on periodicals as on books.
5. Of the thousands of magazines published, children and adults alike are largely uninformed as to which could serve them best.
6. Aside from radio and TV, periodicals are for the vast majority the principal sources of information about the world, from the local community to the Congo.
7. Following school days, periodicals provide the most important means of lifetime education for American citizens.
8. There are important values in periodicals of which the majority of readers are unaware.
9. Classroom instruction can improve taste and promote independent judgment respecting periodicals.
10. Very few adults have developed plans for the efficient reading of newspapers.
11. Certain quality magazines published for adults are as well liked by children eight to ten years old as the most popular children's magazines.
12. Too often the magazines recommended by professional educators are not read willingly by children.
13. Schools generally have made little effort to guide the newspaper reading of girls and boys.

IMPLICATIONS

The implications of these findings seem clear. Schools should accept responsibility for regular, carefully-planned instruction in the use of periodicals, beginning in the primary grades; provide suitable juvenile and adult magazines that children thoroughly enjoy; and help children develop effective standards in choosing magazines, and efficient plans for reading them.

Children of the elementary grades place the reading of their favorite magazines and newspapers near the top of enjoyable pursuits, and will continue to do this throughout their lives—if they follow their elders. The time they devote to periodicals will dwarf that given to books; more than half, including some college graduates, will discontinue book reading after they leave school.

In summary: If we are to adequately prepare our children for life now and in the future, our schools must give much greater time to regular, carefully-planned (not occasional and haphazard) preparation for useful activities most will perform every day of their lives.

A Critique of Reading Preferences with Special Reference to Norvell's Study: The Challenge of Periodicals in Education

SAM WEINTRAUB

State University of New York at Buffalo

Few aspects of reading have received more attention in the research literature than that dealing with reading preferences/interests.[1] The importance of interest as a factor in motivation and as a basis for selecting books has been long recognized. One of the earliest published reading research reports in the United States focused on what children were reading (True, 1889). The state of the art has not progressed a century's worth since True wrote about the children in his classroom.

Norvell's article, reprinted in these pages from *Elementary English*, is of interest for several reasons. First, Norvell pursued his study of this area over a period of about 40 years. In addition, his work was done in an additive manner; i.e., he combined new data to his previous data base and/or compared and contrasted preferences over time periods. Such efforts are most commendable. It is relatively rare to find a researcher concentrating in one area over such an extended period of time.

Second, the sheer magnitude of Norvell's sample sizes warrants attention. He collected data from great numbers of subjects. The data base for one 1950 publication, for example, included over 50,000 pupils and 1,590,000 individual opinions by these subjects on from 10 to 40 or 50 selections (Norvell, 1950).

Third, the reprinted article exemplifies in a shortened version the procedures followed in Norvell's longer reports, all of which appeared in book form. Norvell himself states that the questionnaires and procedures reported in the article are the same as those used in previous investigations. In his last book, published posthumously, the same procedures are followed (Norwell, 1973). Norvell's work is not dissimilar from that of other studies on reading preferences in general. Indeed, in some respects it represents a more rigorous attempt to determine reading preferences than do many other studies. Therefore, many of the criticisms stated in this analysis

[1]The terms "reading interests" and "reading preferences" are frequently confused in the research literature. In *A Dictionary of Reading and Related Terms,* a distinction is made between the two. Reading preference is defined as what people read when offered a choice; interests refer to those things "about which a person not only shows a desire to read but does read," thereby indicating an active disposition toward a specific goal (Harris & Hodges, 1981). It is preferences which are investigated in most of the research in reading. The Norvell article referred to most frequently in this critique assesses more a feeling towards a material than it does either preferences or interests. However, because it appears closer to the one than the other, and because most of the reported research deals with preferences, that is the term used throughout this article.

apply not just to the *Elementary English* reprint but to Norvell's work as a whole and even to much of the research in reading preferences and interests, in general.

There is yet another sense in which Norvell's work is important to evaluate. Because of the large samples employed, because the research appeared in book form rather than as brief journal articles, and because of the long time period over which his investigations appeared (1936–73), Norvell's work is frequently cited and, it would appear, has had some impact. We really have no gauge that validly assesses the impact of a piece of research. Mere reference to a work and a listing in a bibliography is not even a guarantee that a study has been read, let alone that it has been influential in changing thinking. Therefore a citation count is not a particularly valid criterion for determining impact and importance, but it is one of the few readily accessible objective measures available.

In this analysis, Norvell's work is viewed from several aspects—first the design, including the instruments and procedures, is discussed and commented upon; second, the findings, conclusions, and implications are critiqued. Although this analysis focuses on Norvell's contributions, another dimension presents some questions about research into reading interests/preferences generally and discusses some of the issues and problems in that area.

DESIGN

Even though no explicitly stated purpose for the study is stated in *Elementary English,* one or more can be inferred. The general purpose would appear to be to continue his (Norvell's) research into reading preferences, this time by adding to and updating the information on the periodical reading choices of elementary school children. A secondary purpose noted and compared the changes in the periodical reading choices of third-graders with those of upper elementary grade children. Additional purposes include noting developmental changes by viewing choices among even older students and also contrasting choices made in the early 1960s with choices made by children in 1936. Thus the study covers a considerable amount of territory in terms of the intent.

The procedures and type of instrument Norvell used throughout his studies remained very much the same. In the journal article research, each pupil was given a simple form with a list of magazines. Beside each periodical the children were to check one of three columns: Very Interesting, Fairly Interesting, or Uninteresting. To obtain an interest score on each of the 31 periodicals, Norvell totaled the number of "Very Interesting" responses and half the number of "Fairly Interesting" ones. He then divided this number by the total number of pupils reporting on a given journal. This figure became the interest score. He made tabulations for boys and girls separately, as well as for the whole group.

In his other studies, Norvell only included data on a selection if he had a minimum of 300 pupil reports on it. In the *Elementary English* article, 5 periodicals fall below that number in grades four to six and 3 of the 12 periodicals on the grade-three list also do not meet that standard. When reporting on interest scores of

critique

books, Norvell used a score of 70 and up as one considered suitable for the classroom. One can only assume that he would apply the same criterion level for periodicals as for books.

Research/Table 1 of Norvell's article presents the list of magazines preferred by children in grades four to six. Interestingly, *National Geographic* appears high on the lists for both boys and girls and is top-ranked when sexes are combined. Given that finding plus the number of adult magazines on the list, one wonders whether the children are responding merely to familiarity and/or to magazines with pictures. How many nine-to-twelve-year-old boys actually read *National Geographic, Popular Science,* and *Popular Mechanics?* These same three periodicals are also top listed by eight-year-old boys. When the magazines were listed in order of frequency of acquaintance rather than frequency of popularity at grades four to six, seven of the ten were found to be written for adults. Norvell explains the frequency of acquaintance with adult magazines as a function of what is found in the home. However, it is quite possible that children (and Norvell, too) have equated familiarity with popularity.

Although Norvell did not, as many preference studies have, ask for a choice between two alternatives, his instrument does have other weaknesses. Primarily, it reflects a limited list of magazines. Many, if not most, are adult periodicals and quite likely do reflect what children have seen in their homes. To draw conclusions about preferences based on such an instrument would be somewhat "iffy." Moreover, to build a curriculum incorporating such data would be most inappropriate.

Even though Norvell does not discuss the reliability of his instrument in the *Elementary English* article, he does report in other works on the standard deviation of his interest score for varying totals of pupil reports (Norvell, 1973). He assumed that an interest score based upon 4,000 to 5,000 reports was close to a true score. He then used his assumed true score to test scores obtained from samples of 100, 300, and 800 reports. To do this, Norvell obtained 58 samples of 800 reports from eight different selections, each of which had between 4800 and 6700 reports on it. He determined the standard deviation of these 58 scores to be 2.31. Norvell felt that about two-thirds of interest scores based on a minimum of 800 pupil reports would fall within 2.31 points of the assumed true score. After additional calculations, he established that 1.5 standard deviations represented an appropriate error limit to indicate the probable range within which the true score would fall (Norvell, 1973). He then computed standard deviation values for smaller sample sizes.

It must be noted again that Norvell did not present reliability data for the periodicals discussed in his *Elementary English* article. One must assume that he followed the same procedures in the article as he did in his other studies, as they relied on similar procedures. Perhaps he made no attempt to establish reliability for his study of magazines.

The attempt to establish reliability, although different from the manner in which we ordinarily determine it, is commendable. All too frequently in interest/preference research reports, no attempt is made to establish either validity or reliability. Even so, there are serious problems with the instrument.

How might Norvell have designed an instrument that might have been better? Perhaps he could have begun with the children themselves. Direct questioning of

critique

children, logs or records maintained by children over time, and reports of journal usage from school and public libraries could have been the basis for a more appropriate list of journals. There is no information about the list's origin or development. In some of Norvell's earlier reports, data are based on literary works read or studied in classes (Norvell, 1950, 1958). Obviously the list of journals was not obtained by such means. A review of the list suggests that Norvell may have included some of the more popular adult magazines. Possibly he obtained the information from circulation figures. The dozen or so children's periodicals may have been based also on popularity as determined by numbers printed or sold. Because specific information on the development of the list is not available, it is not possible to determine the source with any degree of confidence. Thus the development of the instrument is a major weakness.

One supportable approach would be to establish the list by circulation figures. However, that procedure has inherent problems. While it is possible to obtain an indication of familiarity based on such an approach, it is also true that the journals most widely sold would tend to be most familiar. However, they might not be the most appealing. A more rigorous determination of the development of the instrument is called for. As done, the list offers no opportunity for children to add magazines they really liked.

FINDINGS AND INTERPRETATIONS

If the instrument by which data are collected is questionable, so, too, must be the findings and interpretations based on it. Some of these have been questioned already; i.e., does Norvell have merely a ranking of familiarity and not one of true preference? In addition, others need to be considered.

In grades four to six, *American Girl* is ranked by girls as second in popularity. It was identified by 706 girls and received an interest score of 86.0. Only 50 boys rated the same magazine as familiar, and the interest score for boys was 48.0, placing it near the bottom of the boys' lists. When the combined ranking for both sexes is reported, American Girl receives an interest score of 67.0, just slightly below the 70.0 cutoff Norvell considered suitable for usage in the classroom. Norvell does not indicate how he determined the combined sex ranking, but the mean of 86 and 48 is 67. Thus, the interest ranking based on 706 girls and that based on responses from 50 boys received equal weight in establishing a composite listing. Such a procedure appears odd at the very least. Indeed, with findings of such sharp discrepancies between boys' choices and girls' choices, it is not particularly reasonable to combine the two to achieve a joint list.

Another collection of data relates to the amount of magazine reading done at grades four to six, seven to nine, and ten to twelve. Norvell does not describe how he determined amount of reading. There is only an indication of the numbers of subjects reporting, the number of magazines reported on (16, 17, and 19 at the three grade level groupings, respectively), and the percentage girls' reading is of boys' reading for those periodicals. From the information given, it seems that amount of

critique

reading is equivalent to the totals of subjects reporting on the familiarity/interest scale. If such is indeed the case, the findings are even more confused.

In still another section of the *Elementary English* article, Norvell makes a comparison of the data obtained in 1962 with those collected in 1936. While such comparisons are useful, it is regretable that Norvell diverged from what appeared to be his major interest in this article. Again, the discussion of the differences in the two time periods assumes that his procedures and instrument are useful and valid. Further, data for newspaper reading collected in the 1936 study only are presented and interpreted as if they were relevant for the early 1960s. Contrasts in the interest scores of *My Weekly Reader*, the one constant in the newspaper area over the two time periods, show differences between 1936 and 1962. The change in the interest rating of *My Weekly Reader* and other materials is attributed primarily to the influence of television. Quite possibly other, more interesting informational materials were available. The high interest scores given to newspapers in 1936 and the comparatively lower rankings given to adult news magazines (*Newsweek, Time*) in 1962, in combination with the drop in *My Weekly Reader* interest ratings from 1936 to 1962, leads Norvell to conclude there was a decline in interest in such materials. Norvell's statements on this information are confusing. He comments, "Further, changes in interest are not confined to newspapers. A decline in interest has occurred for magazines, and for stories and poems at all levels" (see page 376). Yet when he summarizes findings from other sources, he writes, "Reading magazines and newspapers is popular at all levels beginning with the primary grades" (see page 376).

Norvell does not include a bibliography or support his summary statements in any manner. They are merely attributed to "careful studies of periodical reading by many investigators" (see p. 376).

The final list of implications of his study needs to be dealt with. Like motherhood and apple pie, there is nothing in the list with which one cannot agree. However, the implications do not all seem to grow out of the findings of the research reported in the article. Indeed, they are recommendations that could and ought to be made without any basis in research, for they represent the implementation of worthwhile instructional objectives.

OTHER CONSIDERATIONS

This "revisit" is not intended as a diatribe against Norvell's article in particular. Indeed, as stated earlier, his work is not unrepresentative of research into reading interests/preferences in general. When taken as a whole, Norvell's work represents some contributions which researchers in this area might well heed. Foremost among these is his effort to collect data in one area systematically over an extended period of time, using comparable instruments and procedures. In addition, Norvell tried to establish reliability on his instruments. The employment of large numbers of subjects is also useful in this type of study. It places greater credence in the findings than in similar research where 30 pupils may have been the total population.

The area of interests/preferences in reading is not known for rigor of design. We must deal with issues in the research into reading interests/preferences if our knowledge base in this important area is to advance. Primary among the needs in research is the necessity to go beyond the mere listing of titles and topics as the basis for our information. In-depth analyses of the factors in materials contributing to preferences must be collected. We need to know not just what children prefer but what it is about the material that contributes to their like or dislike. These data have to go beyond mere surface generalizations to the effect that children like action or that children like stories about animals. All action stories are not liked, all stories about animals are not preferred. What are the elements that differentiate those that are liked from those that are not? What is it about one periodical that makes it more enjoyable to children than another periodical which, on the surface, looks similar? The answers are not easy. We must be careful not to find pat responses.

Even more important, in this author's opinion, is the need to investigate the factors that contribute to interests, tastes, and preferences. In this area, too, we need to delve deeper into more areas than relatively surface factors as age, sex, and intelligence. It is important to address with thought, care, and perceptive intelligence some of the questions raised by Norvell in his last publication (1973). In addition to the effect of the three factors mentioned, he notes the need to look at literary qualities, artistry, writing style, the influence of teaching, and of home and family.

Such research will not be easy. The simplistic approaches of prior years will not do. We need to look for unique approaches to assess reading preferences and interests and to further our knowledge with long-term studies on the topics. Until we do some rethinking of how to investigate these areas, we will probably not move much beyond Mr. True and his century-old report.

FOR FURTHER LEARNING

Those readers who are interested in continuing to explore the topic of reading preferences and interests would find the following references helpful:

Belloni, L. F., & Jongsma, E. A. The effects of interest on reading comprehension of low-achieving students. *Journal of Reading,* Nov. 1978, *22*(2), 106–109.

Bernstein, M. R. Relationship between interest and reading comprehension. *Journal of Educational Research,* 1955, *49,* 283–288.

Estes, T., & Vaughn, J. Reading interest and comprehension: Implication. *The Reading Teacher,* Nov. 1973, *27*(2), 149–153.

Kline, L. Market research: What young people read. *The Journal of Reading,* Dec. 1980, *24*(3), 284–286.

Pank, W. The interest level—That's the thing. *Journal of Reading,* March 1973, *16*(6), 459–461.

---

for further learning

REFERENCES

Harris, T. L. & Hodges, R. E. (Eds.), *A dictionary of reading and related terms.* Newark, Del.: International Reading Association, 1981.

Norvell, G. W. *The reading interests of young people.* Boston: D. C. Heath, 1950.

Norvell, G. W. *What boys and girls like to read.* Morristown, N.J.: Silver Burdett Company, 1958.

Norvell, G. W. *The reading interests of young people.* East Lansing, Michigan: Michigan State University Press, 1973.

True, M. B. C. What my pupils read. *Education,* 1889, *10,* 42–45.

A Commentary on Weintraub's Critique of Norvell's Study: The Challenge of Periodicals in Education

LYNDON W. SEARFOSS

Arizona State University

Weintraub lists four reasons why Norvell's work should be of interest today: the longitudinal, additive nature of the data collection; magnitude of the sample sizes; use of similar procedures in the 1936 and 1962 studies; and, the frequent citation of Norvell's work by other authors. Weintraub does a thorough job of balancing his comments, both positive and negative, as he discusses each of the above reasons. He also mentions a number of factors that seriously affect the validity of conclusions drawn from the data Norvell collected. These include the lack of an explicitly stated purpose for the studies, accuracy of children responding to a list containing adult magazines above their reading levels, use of newspaper data from 1936 as if it were relevant for the early 1960s, and the use of an adult-generated list for children to rank.

The Norvell studies are basically simple, forced-choice ones in which children were given a predetermined list of 31 periodicals and asked to indicate their reading preferences. The raw data from these lists were transformed to derived scores and displayed as interest scores to draw implications and conclusions regarding the preferences of children for the 31 periodicals.

After re-reading Norvell's study in *Elementary English* and analyzing Weintraub's critique, three factors deserve additional expansion. First, the list of periodicals used by Norvell was generated by adults. The use of this type of list to measure the reading preferences of young readers assumes that adults are able to predict what young readers prefer to read. Observation of children's reading preferences in general, however, reveals this is a faulty assumption—faulty in 1936, 1962, or in 1982. Popularity with adults has never guaranteed popularity with younger readers. Some research also supports this observation. In a systematic study of the books most highly acclaimed by critics during a 25-year period from 1950 through 1975, Nilsen, Peterson, and Searfoss (1980) found a *negative* correlation between the praise of respected adult critics and the reaction of the majority of younger readers. This study indicated that younger readers make decisions about what books they prefer to read and these decisions may bear little comparison to adult preferences. If a book does not hold their attention, they put it down. The same conclusion can easily be extended to the periodical reading preferences of that same group of readers.

A second factor that deserves additional discussion is the rather superficial conclusions Norvell draws regarding the sex differences in the periodical reading preferences of younger readers. He reports that seven of the top fifteen (7/15) periodicals on the boys' list are adult magazines and that six of the top fifteen (6/15) on the girls' list are adult magazines. Norvell then states:

> The explanation for the low ranking of *American Girl* compared with *Boys' Life* on the combined list is the tolerance of girls for reading materials intended for boys and men, a tolerance illustrated repeatedly when boys' and girls' interests in the various reading fields are compared. It is worth noting also that this level, in almost every instance, children's magazines intended for both boys and girls are scored higher by girls than by boys. (See pages 369–70 of this volume.)

Could this be explained because boys' magazines are more interesting, in general, than magazines designed exclusively for girls? Are girls' magazines simply dull, whether you are old, young, a girl, or a boy? Is the quality of writing for younger readers equally important to them as the personal interest they have in topics? These questions are unanswered by Norvell's work. One final note on this factor of sex differences. A recent check of several public libraries concerning *Boy's Life* and *American Girl* by the author revealed one librarian who stopped purchasing *American Girl* several years ago but quickly added that the library found *Boys' Life* still very popular. Two other librarians informed the author that *American Girl* was probably out of print.

The third and last factor worth additional comment is the distinct disadvantage the reader has when not familiar with the longer works of Norvell. Weintraub mentioned that Norvell's studies were in book form, providing much greater detail than found in the *Elementary English* article. Without this detail, the implications and conclusions stated by Norvell in his article cannot be supported. This is the major, obvious flaw in his work, but one deserving some degree of forgiveness until the longer works are considered by people analyzing Norvell's 1936 and 1962 studies.

The negative comments in Weintraub's critique or those made thus far in this commentary are not meant to denigrate Norvell's work. However, the value of his research to us in the 1980s should come not from his design, procedures, implications, or conclusions. Its value lies in what it leads us to do differently in conducting research to explore the reading preferences of younger readers. Weintraub succinctly foreshadows the future of this research at the end of his critique. He concludes:

> Such research will not be easy. The simplistic approaches of prior years will not do. We need to look for unique approaches to assess reading preferences and interests and to further our knowledge with long-term studies on the topics. Until we do some rethinking of how to investigate these areas, we will probably not move much beyond Mr. True and his century-old report. (See page 384 of this volume.)

Weintraub concludes the search for unique approaches to assess reading preferences is necessary because future research will lead reading researchers away from their traditional literature and body of research designs or data analyses. They will need to turn to the work of researchers such as Bronfenbrenner (1976), who examines the ecology of educational research and argues for ecologically valid inquiry. He asserts that most of our research focuses on outcomes or products of human behavior rather than on underlying processes. This research enables us to predict the "concomitants of certain combinations of conditions, but not to understand the causal connections that produce the observed effects" (page 159). Applied to Norvell's studies, we can observe that periodical preferences vary as a function of sex, but do we really know why after examining the data? Bronfenbrenner rather cynically defines most educational research as "dustbowl empiricism" and the "science of the strange behavior of children in strange situations with strange adults for the briefest possible periods of time" (page 138).

What is ecologically valid research? Quite simply, it is research that views human behavior as part of a network or system. Thus, when a researcher studies one aspect of behavior, e.g., reading preferences, a prerequisite to designing and conducting a study is the careful definition of the network or system, of which reading preferences is one element. The term "radical contextualist" has been applied to the study of human language functioning with the same underlying mandate. To study reading preferences, then, is to study all the elements involved in the simple act of a young reader selecting a book or magazine and choosing or not choosing to read it. Among the factors we can identify as affecting a young reader's choice are some obvious ones such as the availability of print in the home and school, grade level, sex, parental reading patterns, and peer or sibling behaviors. These and others have been and continue to be investigated. There are, however, some less obvious factors that must be added to the list. These include the library-use policy of the school (open versus closed), teacher's attitude toward reading, principal's attitude toward reading, cooperative or non-cooperative environment of the classroom, purchasing policies of public and school libraries, community censorship—the list goes on and on.

Crucial to developing unique approaches is the definition of the elements involved in the network or system that affects the young reader's choice of reading materials. Moreover, to continue to study each new element we define in isolation, as has been the pattern of previous research efforts, will lead only to more information but little new knowledge. The study of the combined effects of elements in a network or system is a second prerequisite to conducting ecologically valid research. This will require not more complicated statistical procedures, but new or borrowed methods of collecting data. Some of these new tools will come from ethnomethodology—participant observation, interviews, records or logs, and unobtrusive observation (Spradley, 1980). Anthropologists have used these tools with great success for many years to collect ecologically valid data related to human cultures and their functioning.

The task, then, of studying reading preferences with the unique approaches suggested by Weintraub is not simple. It involves a change in the way we view and conduct research. It involves defining new elements that affect human behavior. It involves developing or borrowing research tools now unfamiliar to most reading researchers. But, in the final analysis, studying reading preferences with an expanded viewpoint and new tools signals the beginning of our truly understanding why young readers choose to read what they do.

REFERENCES

Bronfenbrenner, U. The experimental ecology of education. *Teachers College Record,* Dec. 1976, *78*(2), 157–204.

Nilsen, A. P., Peterson, R. P., & Searfoss, L. W. The adult as critic vs. the child as reader. *Language Arts,* May 1980, *57*(5), 530–539.

Spradley, J. P. *Participant observation.* New York: Holt, Rinehart, and Winston, 1980.

references

A SUMMARY OF LEWIS TERMAN AND MARGARET LIMA'S STUDY: CHILDREN'S READING

KARLA HAWKINS-WENDELIN

University of Texas at San Antonio

As stated in the "Preface to the First Edition," *Children's Reading* was "based on an experimental study of the qualitative and quantitative aspects of children's reading, with special reference to individual differences caused by age, sex, intelligence and special interests" (p. vi). The study was rather broad in scope, reporting information collected from parents, teachers, and individual groups of children, and using several data-gathering instruments. Results obtained from the various groups of subjects were combined to form the basis of *Children's Reading*.

The original research by Terman and Lima was published in 1925, updated in 1926, and a second edition was published in 1931. The first part of *Children's Reading* is a report of the research; the second part is an extensive list of recommended books for children. The major portion of the revisions in the later editions concentrated on the authors' recommendations of books and in their changing views toward literature.

Terman and Lima's viewpoints on using literature with children provide the introduction to the report of their various findings on interests. According to the authors, an appreciation of good literature and the formation of good reading habits must be *taught* to children. Steps toward these goals include: mastery of reading skills, extensive supply of good books; avoidance of "objectionable or worthless" books, and discussion of literature in the home.

CHILDREN'S INTERESTS

According to Terman and Lima, what books children read usually depends as much on what is presented to them as on their own interests. In *Children's Reading*, however, they discuss "certain well defined tendencies in reading interests that change as the child's experience grows" (p. 31). A summary of children's reading interests, by age, follows:

Before five	—interest in jingles and nursery rhymes, simple fairy tales, and talking-beast animal stories.
Six & seven	—high interest in nature stories. Children enjoy fairy tales. Books must

Terman, L. & Lima, M. *Children's Reading* (2nd Ed.), New York: Appleton, 1931.

summary

be profusely illustrated.

Eight —greatest interest is in fairy tales. Children start to appreciate realistic stories.

Nine —interest in stories of real life. Changes in boys' and girls' interests emerge. Children begin to read much more on their own.

Ten —travel books and stories of other lands, myths, and legends are popular. Interest in simple biographies emerge.

Eleven —boys turn to adventure and mystery; girls, to stories of home and school life.

Twelve —this is the age of hero worship. Boys enjoy biography, history, and adventure. Girls read stories of home and school life, but are acquiring an interest in adult fiction.

Thirteen —boys' interests intensify rather than change. Particularly popular are high adventure stories with an element of wish-fulfillment. Girls read adult fiction, classics, and poetry.

Fourteen–Sixteen—interests become more specialized. Boys read more non-fiction. Girls' interests turn to sentimental fiction. Adult reading tastes are fairly well formed.

Age is only one factor influencing children's reading interests. Others, according to Terman and Lima, include physical development (maturity), health, school environment, socio-economic status, home training, and personality. The two influences on reading interests that the authors chose to investigate in *Children's Reading* were differences by sex and mental ability. Data regarding amount of reading was also collected.

SUBJECTS AND PROCEDURES

Differences in Mental Ability

Approximately 2,000 children in California, ranging in age from 6 to 14, kept reading records. Half the children were identified as the gifted group, based on the Stanford-Binet Intelligence Test. The control group comprised all the remaining children from every classroom included in the study. For a period of two months, the subjects recorded the titles of all books they read and their opinions regarding the books.

summary

Difference by Sex

The reading records of the 2,000 children supplied the majority of the data regarding the influence of differences by sex on interests. Two supplementary studies provided further information. A group of 100 graduate students in education at Stanford University were asked to recall ten books they had read as children. In the second study, 1,827 children in grades one to eight listed books they had recently read.

Amount of Reading

Data on amount of reading came from the reading records of the 2,000 subjects. Parents and teachers of these children also supplied information on the amount of reading by the subjects as they perceived it. Teachers were asked to compare the reading habits of each child with the "average child" to determine if the child read "very much, more than average, an average amount, less than average, or very little." Estimates of the number of hours per week that the child spent reading were obtained from the parents of the gifted group. Data were not available from the parents of the control group. Additional findings regarding the amount of reading were based on reading records kept by a group of 808 children in California, age 6 to 16.

CONCLUSIONS

Terman and Lima drew the following conclusions from their analysis of the research data:

1. Reading interests of the gifted and control groups were substantially different with regard to the number of books read and the age at which they were read.
2. Very bright children read on an average three to four times as many books as children of average intelligence.
3. General intelligence influences quality and range of literature read.
4. Girls show more homogeneity in reading taste than do boys.
5. Girls reread books with much greater frequency than do boys.
6. The differences in reading interests of boys and girls becomes greater as they increase in age.
7. Girls tend to read "boys' books;" however, boys show almost no interest in "girls' books."
8. The number of books read by children increases gradually as they grow older, peaking at about age 14.

REFERENCES

Terman, L., and Lima, M. *Children's Reading* (2nd ed.). New York: Appleton, 1931.

Terman, L. and Lima, M. *Childrens' Reading,* A Guide for Parents and Teachers, New York, London, D. Appleton & Co., 1926.

A Critique of Lewis Terman and Margaret Lima's Study: Children's Reading

KARLA HAWKINS-WENDELIN

University of Texas at San Antonio

Terman and Lima's investigation of children's reading interests was termed a "classic" by Russell (1961) in his discussion of ten research studies which he felt most influenced reading education. According to Russell, *Children's Reading* examined reading interests at various age levels and provided some basis for the selection of books for children, thus contributing to the evolution of developmental reading.

The subject of reading interests is not a new one. Numerous studies were conducted before Terman and Lima's time, and the topic has been actively researched in the intervening years. According to Carter (1978), the early attempts to assess reading interests have influenced the procedures of subsequent research. She also observed that generalizations regarding reading interests have remained fairly consistent over the years. According to the literature, however, research into reading interests has been plagued with difficulties. One problem was that a clear definition of "interest" seemed impossible from study to study (Purves & Beach, 1972; Harris & Sipay, 1980). Other difficulties related to a lack of specificity with regard to methodology and the questionable reliability of data-gathering instruments (Purves & Beach, 1972; Weintraub, 1977).

Keeping these points in mind and considering the apparent influence of early studies of children's reading interests on later research, the Terman and Lima investigation seems worthy of re-examination.

STUDY PROCEDURES

Terman and Lima combined several studies in the report on children's interests. They provided methodology and results for research on amount of children's reading and the influences of mental ability and differences by sex on interests.

Subjects

Varying numbers of subjects participated in the separate studies. Findings regarding the "amount of reading" were based on reading records kept by 808 children age 6 to 16 in three small California cities.

The specific number of subjects involved in the study on "mental ability" and "differences by sex" on interests was not cited. As stated in the text of the report, nearly 2,000 children age 6 to 14 from "larger cities" in California kept reading records. Approximately 1,000 of the children were identified as the gifted group, based on the Stanford-Binet Intelligence Test. (A score of 135 was designated as the criterion for giftedness.) A control group contained all the remaining children from every classroom included in the study. Additional data on amount of reading was obtained from these reading records. Parents and teachers also completed surveys regarding amount of students' reading, although there was no mention of how many were actually included in the report of the findings.

Two supplementary studies provided further data regarding the influence of differences by sex on interests. A group of 100 graduate students in education and psychology (equal numbers of men and women) at Stanford University were asked to recall ten books they had read as children. In the second study, 1,827 school children in grades one to eight in three small California cities listed books they read recently.

Methods and Materials

The major portion of the findings from the Terman and Lima investigation was based on the reading records kept by the 2,000 subjects. For a period of two months, the children recorded the titles of all books they had read and their opinions regarding the books. A sample of the record booklet is shown in Critique/Table 1.

Additional information was secured from questionnaires administered to university students during regular class periods. The students were requested to: (1) name ten books they had read in childhood (ages 5 to 16), and (2) indicate those they would presently recommend for children's reading.

CRITIQUE/TABLE 1
Sample page of the record booklet

Title of book________________

Name of author________________

Date when you finished it, if you did finish it: Month_____ Day_____

If you did not finish it, tell why________________

Below, make a cross before the statement that tells how well you liked it.
(Give your real opinion, no matter what others think about the book.)
_____"One of the best I ever read."
_____"Liked it very well—better than most books."
_____"Liked it fairly well."
_____"Did not care much for it."
_____"Did not like it at all."

Had you ever read this book before?________________

How many times before this time?________________

Do you think you will want to read it again?________________

Teachers and parents supplied information regarding amount of reading. The subjects' teachers were asked to respond to the following question: "As compared with the average child of the same age, does this child read (1) very much, (2) more than average, (3) an average amount, (4) less than average, or (5) very little?" (Terman & Lima, 1931, p. 52). Estimates of the number of hours per week which the child spent reading were obtained from the parents of the gifted subjects. The questions to which the parents responded are shown in Critique/Table 2.

CRITIQUE/TABLE 2
Parent information blanks

(a) Did the child learn to read before starting to school? At what age?

(b) Give kind and amount of home reading by the child at various ages, not including school studies.

Age	Hours weekly	Sample of books or magazines read at each age
Before 5		
Ages 5 and 6		
Ages 7 and 8		
Ages 9 and 10		
Ages 11 and 12		
13 or above		

(c) Jot down a rough estimate of the number of books in the home library.

Data were not available from the parents of the children in the control group.

STUDY FINDINGS

Amount of Reading

Terman and Lima discussed, rather generally, the amount of reading done by children based on reading records kept by the 808 children. The data, in terms of book reading, are reported in Critique/Table 3.

CRITIQUE/TABLE 3
Average reading of children 6 to 16 years of age

Age of Child, in Years	Number of Cases	Average Number of Books per Month
6 to 8	32	0
8 to 10	163	1.5
10 to 12	286	2
12 to 14	230	3
14 to 16	97	2.5

The authors commented that these figures were probably high because the communities in which the children lived were rather affluent with good libraries.

Differences with Regard to Mental Ability

After analyzing the data collected from the reading records kept by the gifted and control groups, Terman and Lima found that the differences in reading interests were "very great with respect to number of books read and the age at which they were read" (1931, p. 52). With regard to the type of literature being read by both groups, the differences were "somewhat less extreme but were nevertheless very significant" (p. 52). Use of the term "significant" is unclear in the report of the results. In the "Preface to the First Edition," Terman and Lima stated that the data in the study were "statistically treated." However, there is no mention in the text of the statistical methods used, other than the percentages that reported the findings.

The validity of an IQ test as a measure of intelligence (to determine who was or was not gifted), or "mental ability," as referred to in this study, is questionable. Furthermore, one must also question the arbitrary selection of 135 as the score that determined placement in the gifted group.

With regard to amount of reading, the information from the teachers is tabulated in Critique/Table 4.

CRITIQUE/TABLE 4
Teachers' estimates of reading for gifted and control groups

Percent Reading More Than Average			Percent Reading Less Than Average		
Age	Gifted, Percent	Control, Percent	Age	Gifted, Percent	Control, Percent
8	79	30	8	00	23
9	90	43	9	00	18
10	91	34	10	00	17
11	91	31	11	00	20
12	88	40	12	00	28
13	79	21	13	00	26
14	88	38	14	00	22

The percentages presented in this table can be considered only in very general terms. The criterion, the amount of reading done by the "average child," cannot be identified. In addition, teachers had limited information regarding children's recreational reading to use in making their comparisons. Further, teachers may have expected gifted children to read more, thus they were more aware of their reading. Terman and Lima conceded that it could not be assumed that teachers' responses were "always accurate." However, they did comment that when working with large groups, fairly accurate general trends could be shown. The authors stated that the

validity of the teachers' estimates was borne out by the data from the subjects' daily reading records. The average number of books read by both groups for the two-month period that the records were kept is shown in Critique/Table 5.

CRITIQUE/TABLE 5
Average reading for two months by groups

Age	Gifted Group	Control Group
6 and 7	10.2	0
8 and 9	13.7	3
10 and 11	15	4
12 and 13	14.6	6
14 and 15		5

One must consider the questionable reliability of such records. According to Terman and Lima, the results from this part of the study were "as reliable as data of this kind could well be" (1931, p. 55). The authors concluded that "exceptionally bright children read on an average three or four times as many books as children of average intelligence read" (1931, p. 56).

The average number of hours per week spent reading by boys and girls in different age groups, as furnished by the parents, is shown in Critique/Table 6.

CRITIQUE/TABLE 6
Parents' estimates of average reading hours per week of gifted children

Age	5 and 6	7 and 8	9 and 10	11 and 12	13 and up
Gifted Boys	2.9	7.2	9.6	10.44	12.5
Gifted Girls	2.9	6.16	8.29	9.97	12.9

As estimated by the parents, boys spent slightly more time reading than did girls. This finding, however, was not in keeping with the data from the reading records of the children. Terman and Lima accounted for this discrepancy by proposing that perhaps boys read other types of reading material in addition to books, that girls might have read more rapidly, or that girls might have read books of shorter length.

Variation in length is certainly noteworthy when discussing amount of time spent reading. In addition, when amount is measured in terms of hours, extent of concentration and attention to the task merit consideration.

The existence of other influencing factors besides intelligence must be considered in a discussion of amount of reading. The general attitude of the teachers and parents toward recreational reading certainly affects the amount of time children would choose to spend reading. Availability of books, in terms of library facilities and personally owned books, is another important factor. Terman and Lima discussed some of the extraordinary amounts of time that individual subjects spent reading (a few indicated as much as 30 hours per week). These large amounts are likely a reflection of the time at which this study was conducted. In the 1920s, distracting media influences and sophisticated toys and games were not in existence to draw children away from reading as a recreational activity to the extent that they have in subsequent years.

According to Terman and Lima, intelligence influences not only amount of reading but also the quality and variety of literature read.

In the reading records, the gifted and control groups combined reported over 10,000 book readings. The books read were classified as to type of literature, and percentages were calculated by sex for both gifted and control groups for each type (see Critique/Table 7).

Terman and Lima concluded that reading by gifted children was of "better average quality" than that by the control group. They pointed out that differences between the two groups "stand out very clearly."

> The (control group) set a standard of excellence which we should encourage all children to approximate as far as possible. We may not entirely succeed in this, but our efforts will have been worthwhile if they result in any appreciable shift of reading interest from emotional fiction and stories of wild adventure to the fields of history, biography, travel, science, poetry, and classical fiction (1931, p. 62).

Closer examination of the table, however, reveals that the gifted group actually read very little in the categories of science, poetry and drama, encyclopedias, and history,

CRITIQUE/TABLE 7
Percentage of books read by types

	Gifted Boys, percent	Control Boys, percent	Gifted Girls, percent	Control Girls, percent
Fairy Tales, Folk Tales, and Legends	8	5	12	5
Nature and Animal Stories	9	4	6	6
History, Biography, and Travel	6	3	6	2
Science	4	0.5	1	0.2
Stories of Adventure or Mystery (mostly boys' juvenile and series books)	49	63	15	22
Stories of Home and School Life (mostly girls' books)	2	3	31	33
Poetry and Drama	1	0.1	1	0.2
Children's Encyclopedias	1	0.1	1	0.1
Informational Fiction, Including the Classics	19	11	14	9
Emotional Fiction (the popular novel and love story)	1	6	11	19

biography, and travel. In fact, the gifted children read more of the type of literature that the authors would consider undesirable than anything else. That they read more in the other categories than the control group may be attributed to the greater amount of reading they did in general.

Any discussion of type of literature read (or preferred) is hampered by broad interpretations of the various literary categories. A particular book may be classified into more than one category. For example, *Call of the Wild* was listed as a book enjoyed by both boys and girls. Is it an "adventure" or a "nature" story? In addition, many different types of stories may be subsumed by one category heading. An "adventure" story might be one of high action, suspense, personal courage, or other interpretations.

Differences with Regard to Sex

According to Purves and Beach (1972) in their review of studies on reading interests, sex is the most important determinant of differences in what children read. Terman and Lima found quite a disparity between boys and girls in their interests, and the differences became greater as the children grew older. The authors drew their conclusions from different groups of subjects. A group of 100 graduate students was asked to list ten books they remembered reading as children. Women students were fairly consistent in their selections in that they tended to list the same titles. The men's lists, however, showed a greater variety, "indicating a wider range of interests and more individualized tastes" (1931, p. 70). This finding was borne out by the children's reading records of books they had read more than once. Girls re-read books with much greater frequency than boys.

The reading records also showed sex differences in reading interests. These results are summarized in Critique/Table 8.

CRITIQUE/TABLE 8
Types of books read by boys and girls

	Boys, percent	Girls, percent
Fairy Tales, Folk Tales, and Legends	7	10
Nature and Animal Stories	7	6
History, Biography, and Travel	5	4
Science	3	1
Stories of Adventure or Mystery (mostly boys' juvenile and series books)	56	18
Stories of Home and School Life (mostly girls' books)	2.5	32
Poetry and Drama	0.4	1
Children's Encyclopedias	0.5	0.4
Informational Fiction, Including the Classics	15	11
Emotional Fiction (the popular novel and love story)	3.5	16

Terman and Lima concluded from these findings that:

> Animal stories are enjoyed by both boys and girls, but, as a rule, girls prefer stories of animal pets while boys prefer stories of wild animals. . . . Boys read much more nonfiction than do girls. They read more science, slightly more history, and far more encyclopedia material (1931, p. 71).

As with the interests reflected by the differences in mental ability, the comparisons between boys and girls revealed in Critique/Table 8 do not appear to be as great in the above mentioned areas as Terman and Lima imply.

The authors also noted that "although boys show practically no interest in girls' books, girls show a most decided interest in boys' books" (1931, p. 72). Assuming from the discussion in this study that a "boys' book" is one which features a male protagonist involved in an exciting adventure and that a "girls' book" portrays a female main character in a home or school situation, one must again consider the importance of availability of books. Had there been, at the time of Terman and Lima's study, more books available in which boys *and* girls were involved in a variety of settings and plot situations, both groups might have chosen other reading material.

Another division of the study, involving 1,827 children, corroborated the findings from the reading records as to the type of literature preferred. Subjects listed four or five books that they had enjoyed reading during the previous year. The 20 most-liked books by boys and girls were tallied. Comparison of the two lists revealed that one-fourth of the books (five titles) were read by both boys and girls. (Terman and Lima reported in error that four titles appeared on both lists.)

The authors gave passing mention to the influence of society upon the roles of men and women and commented that "such long-continued and pervading suggestion" in all likelihood affected reading interests. The pervasive influence of traditional sex roles on many facets of life, as well as reading interests, has become an accepted notion in recent years. It is a goal of educators today to present a wide variety of non-sexist literature to children.

Development of Reading Interests

Terman and Lima included in their report an extensive discussion of children's reading interests at various ages. The authors did not make it clear where the data in this section originated. It is assumed that some of the information came from the reading records kept by the subjects in the study. In the Appendix to *Children's Reading,* Terman and Lima included all the data-gathering instruments used in their investigation. One such instrument was the "Interest Blank" (see Critique/Table 9).

Again, it is assumed that a portion of the discussion on reading interests originated from the Interest Blanks. However, this form (except for item "b") is never referred to in the report of the findings. Data from item "b," in which children were asked to name four or five books that they had enjoyed reading during the previous year, were secured from a different group of subjects than those who kept reading records. It is possible that the chapter devoted to reading interests is a compilation of all the sources used in the study.

CRITIQUE/TABLE 9
Interest blank

(a) Put "x" before each of the following kinds of reading you like.
Put "xx" before each kind you like very much.

Fairy stories	Book of Knowledge
Love stories	Encyclopedias
Stories of home life	Bible
Adventure stories	Poetry
Travel stories	Plays
Biographies	Essays
Detective stories	Current events
Housekeeping books	History
Garden books	Politics
Inventions	Business
Electricity	Nature Study
Machinery	

(b) Name four or five books you have most enjoyed reading in the last year.

(c) Name the magazines you read.

IMPLICATIONS OF THE STUDY

Russell (1961) praised his ten pieces of reading research that "made a difference" for their simplicity of design and statistical analysis. The Terman and Lima study is not sophisticated with regard to its methodology nor its statistics. In keeping with the difficulties noted by Purves and Beach (1972) and Weintraub (1977), this study might be questioned regarding the validity of the information obtained from the various instruments used to gather data. One over-all problem with *Children's Reading* is the somewhat convoluted report of the findings. This difficulty may be a direct result of the amount and variety of data obtained in the study. The authors' analysis of the results was often difficult to follow, particularly with regard to the instruments from which the different data came. However, the results did provide a framework for discussion on the developmental nature of children's reading interests.

The Terman and Lima study offers an interesting historical perspective to children's literature. The authors devoted a great deal of attention to the importance of developing good reading habits in children (e.g., keeping them away from "objectionable or worthless books"). They stressed providing children with a variety of *good* literature at home and at school, thus lessening the chances that they would turn to "insipid" juvenile novels. Terman and Lima assumed somewhat of an elitist attitude. They deplored the "sensational adventure" that boys often read and the "sentimental trash" that appealed to girls. Their attitude is reflected in a quotation in the text from a teacher with whom the authors had worked: "It's better not to read anything than to read poor books" (1931, p. 66). Many reading teachers would take issue with such a statement. One wonders how Terman and Lima would react to the contemporary realistic fiction prevalent today and to the popularity of such authors as Judy Blume.

In spite of the passage of time since the research was conducted for *Children's Reading,* Terman and Lima (1931) presented some implications that still have relevance for teachers and parents:

"Home training is more important than any other single educational force in forming good reading habits in the child" (p. 48).

"Individual differences are so great that what will interest one child will hold no appeal for another" (p. 46).

"It is important that parents, teachers, and librarians recognize the wide variations of children's interests and strive to provide reading that will satisfy every need" (p. 46).

FOR FURTHER LEARNING

Those readers who are interested in continuing to explore the topic of reading preferences and interests would find the following references helpful:

Carter, S. M. *Interpreting interest and reading interests of pupils in grades one through three.* Unpublished doctoral dissertation, University of Georgia, 1976.

Ford, R., & Koplay, J. Children's story preferences. *The Reading Teacher,* 1968, *22,* 233–237.

Johnson, B. L. Children's reading interests as related to sex and grade in school. *School Review,* 1932, *40,* 258–272.

Kirsch, D. From athletes to zebras—young children want to read about them. *Elementary English,* 1975, *52,* 73–78.

Kirsch, D., Pehrsson, R., & Robinson, H. A. Expressed reading interests of young children: An international study. In J. E. Merritt (Ed.), *New horizons in reading.* Newark, Del.: International Reading Association, 1976.

Kujoth, J. S. (Ed.). *Reading interests of children and young adults.* Metuchen, N.J.: Scarecrow Press, 1970.

McKay, J. *A summary of scientific research and professional literature on reading interest.* Unpublished doctoral dissertation, University of Pittsburgh, 1968.

Norvell, G. *The reading interests of young people.* Boston: Heath, 1950.

Norvell, G. *What boys and girls like to read.* Morristown, N.J.: Silver Burdett, 1958.

for further learning

Norvell, G. *The reading interests of young people.* East Lansing, Mich.: Michigan State University Press, 1973.

Robinson, H., & Weintraub, S. Research related to children's interests and to developmental values of reading. *Library Trends,* 1973, *22,* 81–108.

Rogers, H., & Robinson, H. A. Reading interests of first graders, *Elementary English,* 1963, *40,* 707–711.

Stanchfield, J. Boys' reading interests as revealed through personal conferences. *The Reading Teacher,* 1962, *16,* 41–44.

Weintraub, S., Robinson, H., Smith, H. K., Pleassas, G. P., & Rowls, M. Reading Interests. *Reading Research Quarterly,* 1975, *10,* 427–434.

Witty, P., Coomer, A., & McBean, D. Children's choices of favorite books: A study conducted in ten elementary schools. *Journal of Educational Psychology,* 1946, *46,* 266–278.

Zimet, S. Children's interests and story preferences. *Elementary School Journal,* 1966, *67,* 122–130.

Zimet, S., & Camp, B. W. A comparison between the content of preferred school library book selections made by inner-city and suburban first grade students. *Elementary English,* 1974, *51,* 1004–1006.

REFERENCES

Carter, S. M. Interests and reading. *Journal of Research and Development in Education,* 1978, *11,* 61–68.

Harris, A. J., & Sipay, E. R. *How to increase reading ability* (7th ed.). New York: Longman, 1980.

Purves, A. C., & Beach, R. *Literature and the reader: Research in response to literature, reading interests, and the teaching of literature.* Urbana, Ill.: National Council of Teachers of English, 1972.

Russell, D. H. Reading research that makes a difference. *Elementary English,* 1961, *38,* 74–78.

Terman, L., & Lima, M. *Children's reading* (2nd ed.). New York: Appleton, 1931.

Weintraub, S. Two significant trends in reading research. In H. A. Robinson (Ed.), *Reading and writing instruction in the United States.* Newark, Del.: International Reading Association, 1977.

A Commentary on Hawkins-Wendelin's Critique of Terman and Lima's Study: Children's Reading

JUDITH WESTPHAL IRWIN

Loyola University

JILL P. MAY

Purdue University

The Wendelin critique of *Children's Reading* by Terman and Lima provides a useful overview of that work and of the general criticisms that should immediately be made. In this discussion, therefore, we would like to focus on some of the critical methodological problems in the Terman and Lima study, some of which continue to be problems in research today.

First, several methodological points made by Wendelin deserve added emphasis. For instance, the questionable reliability of the teachers' estimates with regard to amount of reading cannot be overstressed. Teacher expectations, quality of teacher-student communication, and amount of information available to the teacher all undoubtedly influenced these reports. Similarly, the questionable reliability of the students' records must also be examined. Gifted children are more inclined to achieve. Gifted students might also be more willing and/or able to increase their amount of reading in response to the demands of the situation than were the students in the "control" group. (Terman and Lima address this by noting that many booklets were accompanied by letters from the parents saying that the amount was typical. No mention is made of the exact numbers or of the reliability of parental testimony.) Finally, Wendelin quite appropriately points out that the source of the data on developmental interests is unclear and that the related statistical procedures are entirely unstated. Certainly, these are not minor points when one is examining one of the "classics" that "most influenced education" (Russell, 1961 cited by Wendelin; on page 395 of this volume).

One important aspect of this study that Wendelin does not address is the questionable sampling procedure and the resultant external validity problem. One thousand gifted children from the "larger cities" in California were identified. The selection of the "control" group is unspecified except that whole classrooms in various schools were used. We do not feel that Terman and Lima clearly explain whether these classrooms were the same classrooms which contained the gifted students. The resultant group comparisons on subjects like socio-economic status are also never explained.

Moreover, we hope that many contemporary readers find results such as these inapplicable in many situations. Today, we are aware of the pluralistic nature of our society. Unanswered questions include the following: Are the reading interests the same for children from country homes? What about children with ethnic backgrounds? Are these results specific to middle-class city children? Would the interests of low-income city children be the same? McKay (1971) found a difference in the reading interests of middle-class white suburban and lower-class Black urban children. Terman and Lima mention many individual difference variables in Chapter 6, but their sampling and statistical procedures do not reflect this awareness.

Yet another problem with this study was that the sources of the books chosen and the question of free choice were unexplained and uncontrolled. Perhaps peer pressure affected choices. Perhaps one group selected from a large community library or from home libraries more often than the other did. Perhaps children in the control group were limited to classroom libraries or were guided by teachers into "easier" books. These questions also remain unanswered.

Another problem that Wendelin does not completely address is the possible interaction between and/or among amount of reading, rate of reading, and depth of comprehension. Perhaps gifted students read more books simply because they read faster. Perhaps "amount of time" was the same for the groups. Perhaps gifted students read superficially for quantity while the control group continued to read thoroughly, though slowly. Clearly, data on amount of reading that simultaneously considered rate and comprehension would be much more meaningful.

Moreover, Terman and Lima conclude that intelligence "influences" amount and quality of reading. Even if one ignores the questionable reliability of their data and accepts that there is a correlation between intelligence and amount and quality of reading, one simply cannot conclude that there is a causal relationship. There are too many other rival hypotheses.

Similarly, Terman and Lima conclude, as have many others since then, that a reading program based on their developmental interest findings will be more effective than one in which stories are chosen in another way. Again, this conclusion needs experimental verification. (Authorities in the field of children's literature today claim that a literature program based upon developmental needs and interests will create sensitive readers—Huck, 1976; Sutherland, 1981; and others. To our knowledge, none of the authorities has either carefully defined how the literature they suggest fits into a developmental pattern or experimentally tested their hypotheses.)

Furthermore, as Wendelin acknowledges, investigating sex differences in literary preferences has inherent methodological problems. Although Terman and Lima noted real differences in story categories, they did not carefully define boys' literature as opposed to girls' literature. The four titles listed by Terman and Lima as favorably cited by both boys and girls were *Ivanhoe, Treasure Island, Call of the Wild,* and *Tale of Two Cities.* To explain this, Terman and Lima simply state that girls frequently read boys' books. Yet a close look at the books could result in other conclusions. It has been widely accepted that both sexes prefer fast-moving plots with straightforward action to descriptive literary masterpieces. In all four cases, although the books are well written, they also have exciting plots which are easily followed. Although *Ivanhoe* can be considered a boys' story because of setting and characterization, it must also be considered a love story and a family story. *Call of the Wild* is an animal story, above sex stereotypes. *Tale of Two Cities* is the dramatic story of a people's revolution, while *Treasure Island* is a story purposely written to entertain with its adventure. (Terman and Lima omitted noting that boys and girls both also chose *The Three Musketeers*.)

In addition, conclusions like "boys read much more non-fiction than do girls" (Terman & Lima, 1931, p. 71) can only be interpreted in the light of the non-fiction available. A quick perusal of standard lists of available non-fiction shows that male topics far outweigh female ones. For instance, in the 1925 list of suggested biography titles, Terman and Lima named 15 books about females. In contrast, 53 titles concerned males. Many of these are well-known U.S. heroes such as Benjamin Franklin, Abraham Lincoln, and Davy Crockett. Some are public service citizens such as mounted police. Of the 15 biographies with female heroines, most were dissident choices. Thus, Joan of Arc is the main character of four of the titles. Abigail Adams and an early suffragette, Ann Howard Shaw, are others.

Wendelin suggests that if more books had been available in which both sexes were represented, "both groups might have chosen other reading material" (see page 402). This situation still exists today and should be considered when interpreting all of the current research comparing boys' and girls' reading interests. For instance, in Charlotte Huck's third edition of her children's literature text (1976), she lists 139 recommended biographies; only 32 of these are about women (pp. 582–85). A closer examination shows that the men represented are largely well-known U.S. adventurers, statesmen, and sports figures, but that boys can also find books about men who were composers, artists, and authors. Most men chosen were heroes in their lifetimes. Of the women included on the list, 15 were from racial minorities, 6 were authors, and 2 were important only because they were relatives of famous U.S. presidents. Only four books discuss women leaders in government, and two of these are biographies of Shirley Chisholm. Only one sports figure, Billy Jean King, is included; two women adventurers who traveled through Africa are on the list. Only one woman scientist, Rachel Carson, is included. Four of the six authors covered wrote for children; the remaining two authors were early U.S. poets. Thus, the women in currently recommended biographies are, in the main, ones who were involved in minority struggles in society. Their voices were met with skepticism or anger from many of their contemporaries. Only the women authors represented in these biographies depict females acclaimed during their lifetimes, and, of these, three were semi-reclusive, anti-social women. If biography, which represents the broad spectrum of those who have succeeded in various fields of study, is an example, then young girls are often forced either to read minority literature or to read about famous men. It seems logical that they would turn to fiction.

A close examination of children's literature, however, also indicates that comparing boys' and girls' choices of fiction may be a questionable procedure in light of the nature of the "quality" fiction available. The much respected Newbery Award began in 1922, three years before Terman and Lima's results were first published. The award is given to the author whose book has been selected as the most distinguished in the field of children's literature during the year. Since authors must have a permanent residence in the U.S., these are books available to and used by U.S.

children. Not one book depicting a girl as the main heroine was selected until 1930. That book, *Hitty, Her First Hundred Years,* was a doll story. In 1934, *Invincable Louisa* won the award; it has been the only book about a real woman to win thus far. Moreover, a recent study of 12 randomly selected Newbery Award books indicates that the male protagonists in these books resolve all dilemmas at higher moral stages than the female protagonists, according to Kohlberg's (1968) stages of moral development (Rihn, 1980). Perhaps girls' choices are related to factors in "girls' " and "boys' " books which have yet to be described.

Finally, we would strongly agree with Wendelin's suggestion that some of Terman and Lima's statements reveal "somewhat of an elitist attitude" (see page 404). Terman and Lima stress that good reading will occur if the child masters the mechanics of reading, is supplied with good books, and is kept away from "objectionable or worthless books" (1931, p. 5). They conclude that a child who has been exposed to good literature, but who turns to "cheap and sensational books" (p. 6) needs special attention. They argue that "if the child is left to browse in a library that contains many worthless and harmful books, his reading taste is likely to become perverted" (p. 8), then conclude that this will "warp his whole life" (p. 8). Further, their choices for suitable books are not based upon children's interests, the supposed topic of study, but upon what they feel best for children to read. When evaluating the five books popular to both girls and boys, Terman and Lima only rated two as exceptionally good choices: the classics *Treasure Island* and *Tale of Two Cities* were considered more worthwhile than *Call of the Wild, Ivanhoe,* and *The Three Musketeers.* For the last title, their suggested reading list included an abridged edition that left out a few of the objectionable features in the original. Moreover, an examination of the books they cited as most worthwhile reveals that they tended to choose moralistic stories over well-written literature. This is a clear example of a kind of professional censorship that continues today. We would strongly recommend that if this practice is to continue, then the advisability of controlling children's reading according to professional judgments of quality should be carefully tested in experimental situations.

REFERENCES

Huck, C. *Children's literature in the elementary school* (3rd ed.). New York: Holt, Rinehart, and Winston, 1976.

Kohlberg, L. Stage and sequence: The cognitive-developmental approach to socialization. In D. A. Goslin (Ed.), *Handbook of socialization theory and research.* Chicago: Rand McNally, 1968, 347–480.

McKay, M. A. G. *The expressed reading interests of intermediate grade students from selected schools in the metropolitan Pittsburgh area.* Unpublished doctoral dissertation, University of Pittsburgh, 1971.

Rihn, B. A. Kohlberg level of moral reasoning of protagonists in Newbery Awards winning fiction. *Reading Research Quarterly,* 1980, *15,* 377–398.

Sutherland, Z., et al. Sixth edition. Glenview, Ill.: Scott, Foresman & Co., 1981.

Terman, L., and Lima, M. *Children's reading* (2nd ed.). New York: Appleton, 1931.

references

section VII

TEACHER EFFECTIVENESS IN READING INSTRUCTION

SUMMARY by Timothy R. Blair and William H. Rupley, of *Improving Instruction in Reading: An Experimental Study*

RESEARCH by Arthur I. Gates, *The Necessary Mental Age For Beginning Reading*

CRITIQUE by Timothy R. Blair and William H. Rupley

FOR FURTHER LEARNING

COMMENTARY by Gerald G. Duffy

This section introduces the reader to a summary of William S. Gray's study, *Improving Instruction in Reading: An Experimental Study* and the original work of Arthur I. Gates, *The Necessary Mental Age For Beginning Reading.* Both of these studies investigated and reported on key elements of teacher effectiveness in reading instruction. Blair and Rupley's critique of this research is informative and provides a deeper understanding of several features of teacher behavior that influence reading achievement. However, the authors feel that while the results of Gray's and Gates's research have provided a core of common factors associated with effective reading teachers, these studies lacked the specificity that allows teachers to make use of the results in a way which would positively affect their classroom instruction. Duffy's comments support Blair and Rupley's conclusions and expose several significant questions regarding process-product research: What have we learned about teacher effectiveness?, What do we have yet to learn about teacher effectiveness?, What are some of the classroom complexities concerning teacher effectiveness?, What constitutes teaching?, and Is teacher effectiveness universal?

SUMMARY: WILLIAM S. GRAY, IMPROVING INSTRUCTION IN READING: AN EXPERIMENTAL STUDY

TIMOTHY R. BLAIR and WILLIAM H. RUPLEY

Texas A & M University

In 1925 the members of the Educational Research Committee reviewed the progress made in the scientific study of school subjects and considered at length those problems that merited further investigation. As a result, two important conclusions were reached: first, research relating to curriculum and learning problems was going forward far more rapidly than were efforts to apply the results in improving school practices; and second, there was urgent need for a detailed study of the problems involved in reorganizing and improving teaching in harmony with results of scientific studies. William S. Gray was commissioned to conduct an intensive study of ways and means of applying the results of reading research in improving both the content and the methods of teaching.

The chief purposes of the study were:

1. To determine ways and means of reorganizing and improving the teaching of reading in harmony with the results of scientific studies.
2. To study the character of the administrative, supervisory, and teaching difficulties encountered in a supervisory campaign planned to improve instruction in reading.
3. To determine the effect, if any, on the achievement of pupils that accompanies and follows vigorous efforts to improve teaching.

Gray, William S. *Improving Instruction in Reading: An Experimental Study*. Chicago: University of Chicago Press, 1933.

The study was conducted at the elementary school level and involved three groups of schools. The first group included 16 schools that differed widely in size and in the type of supervision provided. The second group included 5 schools representing widely different racial, social, and economic conditions. The third group included 5 schools of widely different conditions that served as control schools.

The study lasted five years and was divided into three main parts. The first was an initial survey to determine the status of reading in the schools, the nature of the reading activities provided, the amount and the character of the free reading of the pupils, and the achievement of the pupils near the close of the school year. The second part involved effecting changes and improvements in teaching reading. The pupils were tested at the beginning of the school year to determine their achievement and needs in reading. The teachers then made desirable changes in the content and the methods of teaching reading. The teachers were aided by a study of the professional literature and demonstrations and conferences with supervisors. At the close of the year, the pupils were retested to determine progress. The third part of the study entailed a determination of the permanency of the constructive effort as measured by the effort of the teachers and supervisors and pupil achievement. Pupil achievement was assessed by using a variety of standardized word recognition tests, oral reading paragraph tests, and silent reading tests.

The results of this study indicated that all the schools that attacked the problem seriously made distinct progress in increasing the achievement of pupils in reading. The study concluded that notable progress can be made in improving teaching through the study and the application of the results of scientific investigations related to reading. Among the reasons cited for success were intelligent planning, persistent effort, and teacher knowledge of important research results and their application to the classroom. The improvement in teaching resulted from a cooperative enterprise involving teachers and supervisory staff. A further condition for success beyond a high level of competency of both teachers and supervisory personnel was the time needed to effect significant changes. The schools that made the greatest improvement continued their efforts for two or more years after the experiment terminated. The study's recommendations for fostering change in faculty and supervisor attitudes toward reading improvement are excellent and are applicable in our schools today.

---

summary

THE NECESSARY MENTAL AGE FOR BEGINNING READING

ARTHUR I. GATES

Teachers College, Columbia University

For some time the problem of determining the optimum or necessary mental-age level at which reading can be successfully introduced has been under investigation. Recently statements have been made, in books written primarily for professional workers, which imply that this problem is fairly well solved. For example, Harrison states, "It has been found that in order to make any progress in reading a child must have attained a mental age of at least six years and that a mental age of six and one-half years more nearly insures success."[1] Betts also states, "An analysis of reading-readiness or aptitude tests shows the following factors to be significant for success with the typical first-grade reading program: (*a*) a mental age of at least six and one-half years. . . ."[2]

These statements and most others appearing in professional books imply, more specifically, that success with *typical* first-grade reading programs requires a stipulated mental age, six and a half years being the age usually given. These statements may be correct, although a critical analysis of some of the experiments would cause some persons to doubt the validity of stipulating so definite a level. The fact remains, however, that it has by no means been proved as yet that a mental age of six and a half years is a proper minimum to prescribe for learning to read by *all* school methods, or organizations, or *all* types of teaching skill and procedures. It is quite conceivable—indeed the evidence in general tends now definitely to show—that the crucial mental-age level will vary with the materials; the type of teaching; the skill of the teacher; the size of the class; the amount of preceding preparatory work; the thoroughness of examination; the frequency and the treatment of special difficulties, such as visual defects of the pupil; and other factors. For example, in a study by Gates and Bond,[3] a mental age of six and a half years did not appear to be a critical level.

In the present article are assembled data on the relations between mental age and success in learning to read in Grade I in a number of different groups which were taught by appreciably different methods and materials. The particular

[1]M. Lucile Harrison, *Reading Readiness,* p. 6. Boston: Houghton Mifflin Co., 1936.

[2]Emmett Albert Betts, *The Prevention and Correction of Reading Difficulties,* pp. 24–25. Evanston, Illinois: Row, Peterson & Co., 1936.

For most of the statistical work involved in this article the author is indebted to the services of workers in United States Works Progress Administration Project No. 6063–C.

Reprinted from *The Elementary School Journal,* 1937, pp. 497–508, by permission of the University of Chicago Press.

[3]Arthur I. Gates and Guy L. Bond, "Reading Readiness," *Teachers College Record,* XXXVII (May, 1936), 679–85.

classes selected for this report are taken from a somewhat larger number that were analyzed to illustrate the facts related to certain issues.

FIRST GROUP

The first illustrations are taken from the results of the work in first-grade classes in which the teaching was done under the supervision of Miss Florence W. Raguse, of the State Teachers College at Indiana, Pennsylvania.[4] The pupils were divided into two classes of forty-one and thirty-seven pupils, respectively. The average intelligence quotient of the former class was higher than that of the latter. Full details concerning the pupils and the methods of instruction are given in Miss Raguse's article. It will be sufficient to state here that, in addition to the usual equipment of books, these teachers were provided with a considerable amount of supplementary practice and teach-and-test materials made up for the purpose. Not only was the teaching rather closely supervised, but the teachers had a larger amount of easy reading and self-diagnostic material than usual. For the present purposes, the pupils of these two classes have been combined into one group. The reading attainments were measured more than a month before the end of the school year with the three Gates Primary Silent Reading Tests. As a measure of success in reading, the results of these three tests were averaged. The teachers also kept a record of the total number of books read prior to the time that the achievement tests were given.

[4]Florence W. Raguse, "Qualitative and Quantitative Achievements in First Grade Reading," *Teachers College Record,* XXXII (February, 1931), 424–36.

In the group of seventy-eight pupils the correlation between mental age and average reading grade was .62 ± .05. This figure, it will be noted, is rather high in comparison with the correlations usually obtained in similar studies. The correlation between chronological age and average reading grade was .10 ± .08. The correlation between average reading grade and the number of books read was .84 ± .02.

As an illustration of the procedure, the records of the individual pupils for mental age, chronological age, average reading grade, and number of books read are given in Research/Table 1, in rank order from the highest to the lowest mental age. As a means of locating a possible critical mental age for success in beginning reading, these pupils were grouped according to mental age by six-month steps beginning with a step containing pupils from the lowest in the list to 5.0 years, inclusive; then from 5.0 to 5.5, inclusive; and so on to the highest. In these classes was a range of mental age from 53 months to 102 months, or approximately 2 to 1. The lowest mental age was four years and five months, and the highest eight years and six months, a difference of four years and one month. It will be noted that practically half the members of the class had a mental age of less than six years on entering. An inspection of these several groups will show that practically all the near-failures fell in the group with a mental age below five years.

The method of determining the minimum mental age desirable for introducing a child to reading involves certain problems. For example, what reading ability should a pupil have acquired by the end of the year to have achieved a status which may be described as a successful reading experience? Since this

RESEARCH/TABLE 1

Reading achievement of 78 pupils in Raguse's study distributed according to mental age

Mental Age (in Months)	Chronological Age (in Months)	Average Reading Grade	Number of Books Read	Mental Age (in Months)	Chronological Age (in Months)	Average Reading Grade	Number of Books Read
102	90	3.23	31	73	76	3.48	37
102	77	3.02	27	73	75	2.88	15
95	113	2.20	14	71	79	2.08	14
92	71	3.25	26	71	79	2.18	19
92	71	3.25	26	71	88	2.21	20
91	69	3.28	31	71	79	2.52	22
90	77	3.18	24	70	75	2.53	18
90	76	3.32	27	70	70	2.60	24
88	87	3.28	36	70	74	2.34	17
88	80	3.47	28	70	68	1.95	8
87	85	2.75	23	69	77	2.90	24
85	83	2.88	18	69	77	2.03	9
84	74	2.80	21	68	76	2.03	16
84	69	2.90	21	68	76	2.57	20
83	77	3.22	31	68	72	2.87	19
83	78	3.15	22	67	80	2.83	26
83	75	2.45	20	67	87	2.50	21
83	79	2.90	19	67	68	2.23	14
83	79	2.57	17	66	82	1.97	8
82	73	2.32	22	66	72	2.23	21
81	74	2.53	24	66	89	2.90	30
80	83	3.00	23	65	74	2.43	31
80	81	3.18	25	65	76	2.82	23
80	87	2.93	26	65	75	1.91	3
80	77	2.26	9	64	73	2.05	9
79	80	2.67	19	64	73	1.85	9
79	72	2.57	23	64	77	2.68	22
77	73	2.73	21	62	76	2.50	21
76	78	2.75	20	62	81	1.98	8
76	78	2.52	20	61	80	1.73	4
75	68	2.62	22	61	70	3.07	27
75	78	3.25	21	60	72	1.90	4
75	88	2.62	20	59	72	0.40	0
75	77	1.65	4	58	90	1.55	2
74	73	2.55	15	55	70	2.58	21
74	73	2.73	22	55	77	1.68	3
73	73	2.73	21	54	71	1.85	8
73	72	3.20	18	54	68	0.00	0
73	72	2.37	14	53	66	0.47	0

matter is one on which opinions may differ, the data from these pupils have been computed on three bases: (1) the percentage of pupils who in the final test achieved a reading-grade score of 1.50 or higher, (2) the percentage achieving a reading-grade score of 1.75 or higher, and (3) the percentage equaling or exceeding 1.95. The last figure represents substantially the norm on the Gates test for the end of Grade I. It should be noted that in the population at large approximately 45 percent of the pupils would have fallen below a reading grade of 1.95 at the end of Grade I. Research/Table 1 shows that every pupil achieving a reading grade of 1.95 or higher is credited with having read a considerable number of books during the year; that, of those who reached or exceeded a grade of 1.75, none failed to read a number of books; and that, of those reaching a reading grade of 1.50 or lower, none had a record of extensive successful reading.

From Research/Table 1 the data in Research/Table 2 have been assembled, showing the percentages of pupils in the group with stipulated beginning mental age, such as 5.0 or higher, who failed to exceed a reading grade of 1.50, 1.75, and 1.95, respectively. Thus, of all the pupils who had a mental age of 5.0 or higher at the beginning of the year, none made a reading grade at the end of the year below 1.50, 3 percent made a reading score below 1.75, and 7 percent made a score below 1.95. Of the children who had a mental age of 5.5 or higher at the beginning of the year, none fell below a reading grade of 1.50, 2 percent fell below 1.75, and 2 percent fell below 1.95. Of the children having a mental age of 6.0 years or higher at the beginning of the year, none fell below a reading grade of 1.50, 2 percent fell below 1.75, and 2 percent below 1.95. Of those having a mental age of 6.5 or higher, none made a reading grade below 1.95.

As already stated, decision concerning the level of achievement in reading which should be considered optimum or satisfactory is arbitrary. If we assume that a program is, under practical conditions, highly satisfactory when no more than 10 percent of the pupils fall below a reading grade of 1.95, it appears that in the case of this group a mental age of 5.0 is satisfactory. Only 7 percent of the pupils with a beginning mental age of 5.0 or higher fell below a final reading grade of 1.95. Since defects in vision and in hearing, poor previous training, illness, absence from school, and many other factors, as well as inadequate mental age, are known to result in inferior reading attainments, it will be obvious that the record in this class was remarkably good. Since substantially all the seriously backward cases fell in the group with a mental age of five years or less at the beginning of the year and since very few of the seriously backward pupils appeared among the higher mental ages, the writer considers it entirely justifiable to say that a mental age of 5.0 at the beginning of the year, other things being satisfactory, is sufficient for learning to read satisfactorily. It should be noted that the achievement of this class as a whole, indeed the achievement of the half of the class with the lowest mental ages, was superior to the attainment of average pupils in typical American schools.

SECOND GROUP

A second group of pupils was taught in a New York City school by teachers who were judged to be more expert than the average and who used a considerable

RESEARCH/TABLE 2
Percentages of pupils in Raguse's study who failed to achieve reading grades of 1.50, 1.75, and 1.95, distributed according to mental age

Mental Age	Percentage of Pupils with Reading Grades		
	Below 1.50	Below 1.75	Below 1.95
5.0 or above......	0	3	7
5.5 or above......	0	2	2
6.0 or above......	0	2	2
6.5 or above......	0	0	0

body of experimental materials developed by the writer and his colleagues. These materials consisted of various types of practice and seatwork, teach-and-test materials, and supplementary easy reading material, largely limited to the vocabulary used in the basal books. The class consisted of forty-eight pupils, for forty-five of whom complete records were obtained. A summary of the pertinent data is contained in Research/Table 3. The first part of the table gives a summary of the data for the pupils arranged in a mental-age hierarchy by half-year units. The second part of the table is a summary identical in form with that presented in Research/Table 2. In this class pupils with a mental age of less than five

RESEARCH/TABLE 3
New York pupils taught with specially prepared materials who failed to achieve reading grades of 1.50, 1.75, and 1.95, distributed according to mental age

Mental Age	Number of Pupils	Reading Grade Below 1.50	Reading Grade Below 1.75	Reading Grade Below 1.95
		Number of Pupils		
7.5–8.0	2	0	0	0
7.0–7.4	3	0	0	0
6.5–6.9	8	0	1	1
6.0–6.4	9	1	1	1
5.5–5.9	10	0	1	2
5.0–5.4	8	0	1	3
4.5–4.9	5	1	2	3
		Percentage of Pupils		
5.5 or above ...	32	3	9	12
6.0 or above ...	22	5	9	9
6.5 or above ...	13	0	8	8
7.0 or above ...	5	0	0	0

years were not so successful as in the class reported by Raguse. One out of five fell below a reading grade of 1.50, two fell below 1.75, and three below 1.95. When all the pupils who began with a mental age of 5.5 or higher are considered, it is found that only 3 percent fell below 1.50, 9 per cent below 1.75, and 12 percent below 1.95. The records for the pupils with a minimum mental age of 6.0 are similar. To the writer it appears reasonable to state that this program was satisfactorily adjusted—some allowance being made for the practical limitations due to absence from school, uncorrected defects, and other constitutional limitations—to pupils with a mental age of 5.5 or higher. In other words, it is a program which represents a difficulty level about one-half year higher than that employed for the first group.

In this group the correlation between mental age and reading grade was .55, somewhat lower than the .62 found for the Raguse group.

THIRD GROUP

A third group consisted of forty-three pupils in a rather superior urban public school. In this class very good teaching was conducted with a better-than-average amount of typical classroom reading matter and other equipment, but the teacher did not have any large amount of the specially prepared types of teach-and-test material employed in the two groups previously considered. Research/Table 4 gives a summary of the data for forty pupils in the same form as that employed in Research/Table 3. In this case poor reading appeared among the pupils with mental ages below 6.0. For the entire group with mental ages of 5.5 or above, 14 percent earned a reading grade

RESEARCH/TABLE 4

Urban pupils in superior public school taught without large amount of specially prepared materials who failed to achieve reading grades of 1.50, 1.75, and 1.95 distributed according to mental age

Mental Age	Number of Pupils	Reading Grade Below 1.50	Reading Grade Below 1.75	Reading Grade Below 1.95
		Number of Pupils		
7.5–8.0	1	0	0	1
7.0–7.4	3	0	0	0
6.5–6.9	7	0	1	1
6.0–6.4	9	1	1	2
5.5–5.9	9	1	2	4
5.0–5.4	7	1	3	5
4.5–4.9	4	2	3	4
		Percentage of Pupils		
5.5 or above	29	7	14	27
6.0 or above	20	5	10	20
6.5 or above	11	0	9	18
7.0 or above	4	0	0	25

research

below 1.75 and 27 percent below 1.95. When the group is restricted to those with mental ages of 6.0 or higher, only 5 percent fell below a reading grade of 1.50, 10 percent below 1.75, and 20 percent below 1.95. Figures for the higher mental-age groups were greatly affected by two pupils in the upper mental ages who fell below the average reading score. These represent instances of special factors contributing to reading difficulty which may, and do, appear at all levels. If some allowance is made for this possibility, it is reasonable to say that the program in this case was fairly well suited for all pupils with a beginning mental age of six years or higher. In other words, the program used with this group requires a mental age a full year in advance of that used in the Raguse group and a half-year in advance of that used in the New York City group.

The correlation between mental age and reading grade in this group was .44. It will be noted that, thus far, the better the program is suited to the pupils of lower mental age, the higher the correlation between mental age and reading ability at the end of the year.

FOURTH GROUP

The fourth group comprises eighty pupils from two public-school classes in a metropolitan area. Both classes were large; the teachers were judged to be somewhat below the average of those in the system; and the reading materials and other equipment were inferior. The classes were taught largely by mass methods, with much oral instruction and little individual or self-manageable work. There was less attempt than usual to adjust instruction to individual needs.

The data in Research/Table 5 indicate that in this group a larger proportion of the pupils fell below reading grades of 1.50 and 1.75 than in the other groups. It will be noted also that some pupils from all the mental-age categories except the two highest fell below a reading grade of 1.50. Of the pupils with a mental age above 6.5, 8 percent achieved a reading grade below 1.50, 16 percent below 1.75, and 36 percent below 1.95. Of those having a mental age of 7.0 or higher, however, only 9 percent fell below 1.75, although 36 percent fell below 1.95. It is, of course, difficult to designate a satisfactory mental-age level for instruction which was apparently of rather unsatisfactory general character. If a reading grade of 1.75 is set up as a reasonably satisfactory achievement at the end of the year, 84 percent of the pupils with a mental age above 6.5 would have been rated as successful and 91 percent of those with a mental age above 7.0. In other words, it would appear that on this rather conservative basis a mental age of somewhere between 6.5 and 7.0 would be necessary for a reasonable assurance of success in reading.

The correlation between mental age and reading grade in this group was .34.

CONCLUSIONS

These representative data point rather convincingly to certain conclusions concerning the relation between mental age and success in beginning reading. In the first place, they indicate clearly that statements concerning the necessary mental age at which a pupil can be intrusted to learn to read are essentially meaningless. The age for learning to read under one program or with the method employed by one teacher may be entirely

RESEARCH/TABLE 5
Pupils in metropolitan schools taught with inferior materials who failed to achieve reading grades of 1.50, 1.75, and 1.95, distributed according to mental age

Mental Age	Number of Pupils	Reading Grade Below 1.50	Reading Grade Below 1.75	Reading Grade Below 1.95
		Number of Pupils		
8.0–8.4	1	0	0	0
7.5–7.9	3	0	0	1
7.0–7.4	7	1	1	3
6.5–6.9	14	1	3	5
6.0–6.4	17	3	5	8
5.5–5.9	17	2	4	9
5.0–5.4	13	4	6	11
4.5–4.9	8	3	5	8
		Percentage of Pupils		
5.5 or above	59	12	22	44
6.0 or above	42	12	21	40
6.5 or above	25	8	16	36
7.0 or above	11	9	9	36

different from that required under other circumstances. In the first of the groups compared, in which modern and effective instruction, well adjusted to individual differences, was provided, a mental age of 5.0 appears to be sufficient. Of the children equaling or exceeding a mental age of five years in this group, none appeared to be seriously retarded and only 7 percent fell below a reading grade of 1.95, which is the average reading achievement for pupils in America at large at the time in the school year that the measurement was made. A second group was found in which the minimum reading age was about a half-year higher. A third group required a mental age of about 6.0 years, or one full year higher. In a fourth group, representing the opposite extreme of the first, children with a mental age of 6.5 fared none too well, and some of those with mental ages of 7.0 or above had difficulty. Of the latter, 36 percent failed to exceed the national norms. Obviously, therefore, general statements that any given mental age should be achieved by a pupil before he begins to learn to read are misleading. The question must be asked: How and what is the pupil to begin to read?

The foregoing conclusion should not be interpreted to imply that mental age is of no significance in learning to read. In the several groups considered in this article, the correlations between mental age and reading grade were .62, .55, .44, and .34, respectively. These coefficients show, as do the more detailed data given in the tables, a substantial but variable relation between mental age and reading achievement. The most significant finding is the fact that the correlations between mental age and reading achievement were highest in the classes in which the best instruction was done and the lowest in those in which the poorest instruction was provided. More specifically, the magnitude of the correlation seems to vary directly with the effectiveness of the provision for individual differences in the classroom. When the teacher uses a mass method, with little or no provision for helping individuals in their special needs, with a program which would appear to be pointed to those with a certain equipment and background, these pupils seem to get on rather well but others encounter difficulty. It should be noted that in this case factors other than mental age play a considerable role, since pupils with relatively high mental ages fail occasionally to learn to read especially well. In such a group the correlation apparently is low partly for the reason that the instruction fails to give each pupil an opportunity to apply his mentality most effectively. If he is to be enabled to do so, attention must be given to his particular difficulties and limitations as well as his special aptitudes and interests.

The preceding discussion, furthermore, should not be considered as antagonistic to the plan of attempting to determine the mental-age level or other characteristics of the pupil needed for making a successful beginning in reading. The study reveals the necessity of determining these factors in relation to the particular program into which the pupils are to be introduced. The writer believes, in fact, that this consideration is not only an important but a necessary phase of normal instruction. That is to say, he believes that it is necessary for each teacher to understand the mental age and other qualifications required for successful pursuance of the program that she will put into effect. One of the reasons for the success of the programs used with the first two groups is the fact that the abundant use of individualized, self-diagnostic materials enabled the teacher to discover the particular needs of the individual pupils and to make adjustments to them, whereas in the fourth group the use of the mass method resulted in a disregard of all sorts of individual aptitudes, difficulties, failures, absence from school, and other factors which determine achievement. The study shows that the determination of the optimum mental age and other factors in reading readiness is not so simple as some recent pronouncements seem to imply. It is impossible to set up, once and for all, a stipulated list of particular requirements for successful work in beginning reading in general. Reading is begun by very different materials, methods, and general procedures, some of which a pupil can master at the mental age of five with reasonable ease, others of which would give him difficulty at the mental age of seven. It is necessary for each teacher to determine exactly what mental age, what background of previous experience, what special aptitudes her particular program requires.

Finally, it should be made clear that the results presented in this report do not answer the question: At what age is it best to introduce reading to pupils? Although the data seem to indicate that it is *possible* to organize materials and methods to teach children to learn to read at a mental age of 5.0 or higher, they do not, in any way, imply that it is *desirable* to do so. Decision on the optimum time of introducing reading to pupils must be based upon investigations of the value of this activity at different stages of development. It would be necessary to determine the general educational, personal, and social effects of introducing reading at different stages by methods so well adjusted to the pupils that they would all learn to read successfully.

A Critique of William S. Gray and Arthur I. Gates's Studies of Teacher Effectiveness in Reading Instruction: Early Efforts to Present A Focus

TIMOTHY R. BLAIR
and
WILLIAM H. RUPLEY

Texas A & M University

The importance of empirically specifying those teaching behaviors associated with effective classroom reading instruction has long been recognized by researchers as a major means to improve the quality of such instruction. Several major research efforts over the past fifty or more years have focused on teachers' instruction in relation to pupils' success in reading. Two investigators who conducted research in the early portion of this time period were William S. Gray and Arthur I. Gates.

Gray's study (1933): (1) identified procedures based on the results of scientific studies to recognize and improve reading instruction; (2) studied the difficulties that administrators, supervisors, and teachers encounter in a campaign aimed at improved instruction in reading; and (3) determined the effect of efforts to improve reading instruction in relation to pupils' achievement in reading.

Gray's investigation spanned a five-year period, from 1925 to 1930, and was divided into three major parts. Part one was conducted during the 1925–26 school year and was aimed primarily at "determining the status of reading in the schools, the nature of the reading activities provided, the amount and the character of the free reading of pupils, and the achievement of the pupils near the close of the school year" (Gray, 1933, p. 5). Additional efforts were undertaken to stimulate in both supervisors and teachers an inquiring attitude regarding reading problems and to motivate them to improve both the content and the methods of teaching.

Part two of the investigation was carried out during the 1926–27 school year. The focus of this part was to effect changes and improvements in reading instruction in each of the four school units and five experimental schools that participated. The basic steps involved pretesting pupils at the beginning of the school year to identify their achievement and reading needs. Based on this pretesting, teachers then made necessary changes and adjustments to the content and the methods of teaching reading. Several procedures were employed to assist teachers in making such adjustments, which included studying recent professional reading literature, discussing results of scientific studies of reading, and attending demonstrations and conferences with supervisors. Gray noted that, "paralleling such steps, detailed studies were made of the administrative, the supervisory, and the teaching problems encountered and of the methods which could be used to advantage in overcoming the difficulties" (1933, p. 5). Pupils were post-tested at the end of the school year with duplicate forms of the pretest to assess their progress during the year.

The third part of the investigation spanned almost three years, from September 1926 to June 1930. Part three attempted to ascertain the lasting effects of the program initiated in 1926–27. These effects were measured in terms of the efforts of school officials and teachers' reading test results. Due to attrition, however, only pupils' progress in three school units was available in June 1928, and two school units in June 1930.

Gray felt that the results of his study were both enlightening and suggestive. In his summary, he noted that, "The evidence is conclusive that notable progress can be made in improving teaching through the study and the application of the results of scientific investigation relating to reading. All the schools included in this investigation which attacked the problem seriously made distinct progress in increasing the achievement of pupils in reading" (1933, p. 208). In this section, Gray also identified several major concerns related to effective reading instruction. Two concerns that addressed effective teaching were *principles that underlie good procedure* and *conditions essential to success.*

Principles that underlie good procedure—These were principles that warranted careful attention in any effort to effect significant changes in reading instruction.

1. The improvement of teaching should be conceived as a cooperative enterprise.
2. The specific duties and responsibilities of each type of school officer and teacher should be clearly defined and fully understood.
3. Constructive effort should begin at the level of current practice and should lead gradually to improved types of teaching.
4. All who aid in the improvement of teaching should cooperate actively in critical studies of current practice, the results of related scientific investigations, and the recommendations of qualified experts.
5. Desirable changes and readjustments should be defined clearly and illustrated concretely in order that they may be attacked intelligently.
6. Constructive steps should be recommended as rapidly as they can be introduced without placing undue burden on the staff or without distracting attention from other legitimate phases of the school's program.
7. As teachers endeavor to make significant changes, continuous help and guidance should be provided for those teachers who need it.
8. Continuous study should be made of the progress achieved and of the difficulties encountered in effecting desirable reforms.
9. Teachers should be stimulated at all times to take interest in raising instruction to successively higher levels in harmony with progressive trends and the results of research.

critique

10. The more capable teachers of a staff should be encouraged to assume leadership in the study of problems, in the selection or development of new materials in instruction, and in various types of service research that may be needed.

11. The work undertaken during any year should lay the foundation for continuous effort to improve teaching.

12. Types of recognition that stimulate and inspire should be given to members of the staff for valuable service rendered or for unusual progress in improving teaching (Gray, 1933, pp. 209–10).

Conditions essential to success—These were conditions deemed essential in effecting desirable changes in teaching reading.

1. Capable leadership within the schools. The evidence is conclusive that capable leadership within the school is essential if constructive changes are to be made in teaching. Wherever such leadership was provided, rapid progress was made in improving teaching. Furthermore, a foundation was laid for constructive work which continued over a period of years.

2. A competent and professionally minded staff. In each of the schools which made distinct progress, the members of the staff were either reasonably well trained and prepared to cooperate intelligently or were capable and willing to learn. The fact that a staff with limited training but with appropriate professional attitudes can revise its practices in the light of progressive trends was demonstrated in all schools directed by stimulated informed leaders.

3. Familiarity with current trends and the results of scientific studies. Substantial progress in improving teaching depends to a considerable extent on familiarity with progressive trends and the results of scientific studies. The evidence is conclusive that instruction rises to high levels only as school officers and teachers make continuous studies of their problems through the use of professional literature, including reports of scientific studies.

4. The need of continued research. The experiences gained in this study show clearly that research of at least two types should accompany most efforts to improve the teaching of reading. The first of these involves the study of fundamental problems about which little or no scientific evidence is available. The second type of research grows out of the fact that laboratory studies often deal with fundamental issues only and fail to translate their findings into terms that can be readily used by teachers. As a consequence, many types of service research are essential in any constructive effort to improve teaching.

5. The importance of time. The study shows clearly that much time is required to effect significant changes in a reading program. The schools which made the greatest improvement continued their efforts for two or more years after the experiment terminated (Gray, 1933, pp. 216–19).

Although the majority of Gray's conclusions did not specify the use of distinct instructional process variables associated with pupils' reading achievement, they did

critique

point out the importance of the teacher and addressed several major generic areas of an effective reading program. His major purpose was to support the need for scientific study of reading that has application in the classroom. Arthur I. Gates's study in 1937, which investigated the necessary mental age required for success in beginning reading, is one such scientific effort that has had widespread and decisive influence, not only on beginning reading, but on the importance of effective reading instruction.

In the mid-1930s, most educators felt that success in first-grade reading programs required a stipulated mental age (generally 6.5). Gates (1937) disagreed with this popular concept and felt that success in reading depended greatly upon the type and quality of instruction. His purpose was to determine the relation between mental age and success in reading of four groups of first-graders. Each group was taught by a different teacher, using different methods and materials.

Group one consisted of 78 pupils divided into two groups, who were instructed by teachers deemed extremely competent. A considerable amount of supplementary practice and teach-and-test materials, diagnostic materials, and an abundance of easy reading books were provided to the teachers. Reading achievement was measured by three Gates Primary Silent Reading Tests administered more than a month before the end of the year. Each teacher gathered additional data on the total number of books read prior to the administration of the achievement tests.

The correlation between mental age and average reading grade for this first group was 0.62. To locate a possible critical mental age for success in reading, pupils were grouped according to mental age. Commenting on the results of the first group, Gates stated:

> If we assume that a program is, under practical conditions, highly satisfactory when no more than ten percent of the pupils fall below a reading grade of 1.95, it appears that in the case of this group a mental age of 5.0 is satisfactory. Only seven percent of the pupils with a beginning mental age of 5.0 or higher fell below a final reading grade of 1.95. (See page 417 of this volume.)

Forty-eight first graders in group two were taught by teachers judged more expert than average educators. They used a variety of experimental materials—practice and seatwork activities, teach-and-test materials, and various easy reading books. Unlike the first group, these pupils required a mental age of 5.5 to meet the success criterion. The correlation between mental age and reading grade was 0.55. Gates concluded:

> To the writer it appears reasonable to state that this program was satisfactorily adjusted—some allowance being made for the practical limitations due to absence from school, uncorrected defects, and other constitutional limitations—to pupils with a mental age of 5.5 or higher. In other words, it is a program which represents a difficulty level about one-half year higher than that employed for the first group. (See page 420 of this volume.)

The third group consisted of 43 first-graders in a superior urban school. The teachers used the regular reading instruction materials but lacked specially prepared types of teach-and-test material of the first two groups. The correlation between mental age and reading grade was 0.44.

critique

Discussing the results of group three, Gates stated:

> Figures for the higher mental age groups were greatly affected by two pupils in the upper mental ages who fell below the average reading score. These represent instances of special factors contributing to reading difficulty which may, and do, appear at all levels. If some allowance is made for this possibility, it is reasonable to say that the program in this case was fairly well suited for all pupils with a beginning mental age of six years or higher. (See page 421 of this volume.)

Group four contained two large classes with a total of 80 children. The teachers were adjudged below average in teaching ability and used inferior reading materials and equipment. The teachers were also characterized as not adjusting instruction to meet pupils' needs. The correlation between mental age and reading grade was 0.34. Reflecting on the obvious inadequate instruction provided in group four, Gates rather conservatively decided that a mental age of somewhere between 6.5 and 7.0 would be required to be successful in learning to read.

In viewing the findings on all four groups, Gates stated:

> The most significant finding is the fact that the correlations between mental age and reading achievement were highest in the classes in which the best instruction was done and the lowest in those in which the poorest instruction was provided. More specifically, the magnitude of the correlation seems to vary directly with the effectiveness of the provision for individual differences in the classroom. (See pages 422–23 of this volume.)

Gates's research turned attention away from the individual child to the importance of the teacher in effective reading instruction. Unfortunately, this study was largely ignored at the time of its publication. Yet today, Gates is continually cited for his work. Although cause-and-effect relationships cannot be stated from a correlational study, Gates's study is a significant landmark in reading teacher effectiveness research.

Although the two aforementioned research projects were not the only ones conducted during the early history of effective reading instruction research, they do represent two of the major efforts that led to a strong belief that teacher quality determines the effectiveness of reading instruction. The research interest in this area has increased greatly during the last several decades. A general overview of the progress and focus of this research since the classic studies of Gray and Gates is presented below.

From the mid-1950s into the early 1970s, the majority of research in reading teacher effectiveness focused on instructional materials and methods, teacher characteristics, and universal traits. In the early portion of this time span, many researchers focused on identifying the best methods or materials to teach reading. They were, in a sense, trying to identify teacher-proof methods and materials. These earlier studies implied that if a general method or material could be identified as successful for teaching all children to read, then the teacher's role would simply be to serve the demands of the methods or materials. The results of such investigations were not very promising, and neither a best method nor a best set of materials was identified for pupil reading achievement gains across various classroom settings.

A large number of studies in the 1960s investigated characteristics of effective reading teachers, such as teachers' personalities, sex, education, years of experience, race, and so forth in terms of their effects on pupils' reading achievement. Results of this research were not very optimistic (Rupley & Blair, 1978). For example, results on personality variables supported the notion that effective reading teachers and teachers in general were good, decent individuals. The results indicated that these teachers possessed characteristics associated with most well-adjusted people regardless of their occupations. A major problem of research in characteristics of effective reading teachers is that such variables are not readily receptive to change. Little information is available that can be put into application in classroom reading instruction and few guidelines are available for planning programs of teacher education (Artley, 1969).

Although this type of research has resulted in the identification of a core of common factors associated with effective reading teachers, much of this research lacked the specificity that would allow teachers to use such information and expect similar results in their classrooms.

In general, much of the early research in reading teacher effectiveness did not produce many clear-cut guidelines for improving classroom reading instruction. Earlier research did, however, contribute significantly to the direction that later research took. Some of this earlier research provided instructional implication for effective teaching of reading that became more credible when coupled with other investigations over a longer period of time. This early research highlighted time and time again the importance of the teacher in effective reading instruction. It showed us that the role of the teacher is extremely important and turned researchers' focus toward process-product dimensions of effective teaching of reading.

During the late 1960s and into the 1970s, researchers attended more to teachers' instructional activities and how these afffected pupils' achievement. Actual teaching activities were referred to as process variables. Process variables included behaviors that could be observed or reported on in classroom settings, for example, teacher-initiated talk, pupil-initiated talk, time spent on an instructional task, and so forth (Cruickshank, 1976). Another way of conceptualizing process variables is looking at how a teacher behaves when actually teaching (Medley, 1977).

The product dimension in process-product research in teacher effectiveness most often refers to pupils' achievement gain. Pupil achievement gain focuses specifically on an important feature of any instruction, that is, how much pupils learned from the teacher's reading instruction. For major researchers interested in identifying teaching behaviors related to pupil achievment, the focus had been on either achievement gains (Brophy, 1979; Good, 1979; Rosenshine, 1976) or actual achievement versus expected or predicted achievement (Blair, 1975; Rupley, 1977; Rupley & McNamara, 1979). Admittedly, this product is not the only outcome measure that teachers should be concerned with in teaching; however, it is a major thrust of public education and clearly within the domain of edcuators' primary responsibilities.

Today, a new focus is developing in teacher effectiveness research. Researchers are investigating not only the behavior of the teacher, but student variables as well. Many student variables fall within the domain of direct teacher influence and control; however, the trend is not to specify teacher behaviors based on research outcomes (Rosenshine, 1977). For example, two variables of interest that pertain to

critique

students are *content covered* and *academic engaged time.* Content covered refers to whether or not pupils had an opportunity to learn the information or skills that were measured to determine their level of achievement. Academic engaged time is the time that students interact with pertinent academic materials at a moderate level of difficulty (Berliner, Fisher, Filby, & Marliene, 1976).

The basic areas of interest and developmental characteristics of teacher effectiveness in reading instruction presented above identify some of the research thrusts over the last 40 or 50 years. Essentially, the research focus has shifted from broad, difficult-to-define variables to those that deal specifically with the process of teaching as it relates to pupils' achievement.

Many of the effective teaching attributes proposed by Gray (1933) and Gates (1937), such as adjusting one's program to pupil needs, diagnosing pupil strengths and weaknesses, providing a balance between instructional and independent reading in the classroom, and allowing for meaningful practice of reading skills to ensure transfer, are now being underscored as important to pupil achievement in recent studies on teacher effectiveness.

Although research in reading teacher effectiveness has received considerable attention in the last decade, instructional guidelines that *cause pupil learning* can not yet be specified accurately. The results of this research are, perhaps, best viewed as having a positive effect on pupils' reading achievement. As Medley indicated in his extensive review of 289 teacher effectiveness research investigations:

> Suppose we examine them to see what they tell us about how the day-to-day practices of competent teachers differ from the day-to-day practices of less competent teachers. Does it not seem reasonable to expect that a novice teacher can benefit from learning the best current practices of competent teachers? (1977, p. 6)

We feel strongly that reading teachers and researchers can benefit from knowing about practices of competent teachers. Results of process-product research hold considerable promise for advancing our knowledge of effective teaching of reading.

FOR FURTHER LEARNING

Those readers who are interested in continuing to explore the topic of teacher effectiveness in reading instruction would find the following references helpful:

Anderson, L., Everston, C., & Brophy, J. An experimental study of effective teaching in first-grade reading groups. *Elementary School journal,* 1979, *79,* 193–222.

Duffy, G. G. Teacher effectiveness research: Implications for the reading profession. In M. Kamil (Ed.), *Directions in reading: Research and instruction.* Clemson, S.C.: National Reading Conference, 1981, 113–136.

Gage, N. L., & Giaconia, R. Teaching practices and student achievement; Causal connections. *New York University Education Quarterly,* Spring 1981, 2–9.

Guthrie, J. T., Martuza, V., & Seifert, M. *Impacts of instructional time in reading.* Newark, Del.: International Reading Association, 1976.

McDonald, F. J. *Summary report: Beginning teacher evaluation study—phase II, 1973–74*. Princeton: Educational Testing Service, 1976.

Peterson, P. L. Direct instruction: Effective for what and for whom? *Educational Leadership,* October 1979, *37*, 46–48.

Rosenshine, B. V. Content time and direct instruction. In H. Walberg and P. Peterson (Eds.), *Research on teaching: Concepts, findings and implications.* Berkeley; McCutchen Publishing Company, 1979.

Rupley, W. H., & Blair, T. R. Specification of reading instructional practices associated with pupil achievement gain. *Educational and Psychological Research,* 1981, *1,* 161–169.

Schneider, E. J. Researchers discover formula for success in student learning. *Educational R & D Report,* Fall 1979, *2*, 1–6.

Stallings, J., Needels, M., & Stayrook, N. *The teaching of basic reading skills in secondary schools—phase I and phase III.* Menlo Park, Calif.: SRI International, 1979.

REFERENCES

Artley, A. The teacher variables in the teaching of reading. *The Reading Teacher,* 1969, *23,* 239–248.

Berliner, D. C., Fisher, C. W., Filby, N., & Marliene, R. *Proposal for phase III of beginning teacher evaluation study.* San Francisco: Far West Laboratory for Educational Research and Development, 1976.

Blair, T. R. *Relationships of teacher effort and student achievement in reading.* Unpublished doctoral dissertation, University of Illinois at Urbana-Champaign, 1975.

Brophy, J. E. Teacher behavior and student learning. *Educational Leadership,* 1979, *37,* 33–38.

Cruickshank, D. R. Syntheses of selected, recent research on teacher effects. *Journal of Teacher Education,* Spring 1976, *27,* 57–60.

Gates, A. I. The necessary age for beginning reading. *Elementary School Journal,* 1937, *37,* 497–508.

Good, T. L. Teacher effectiveness in the elementary school. *Journal of Teacher Education,* March–April 1979, *30,* 52–64.

Gray, W. S. *Improving Instruction in Reading: An Experimental Study.* Chicago: University of Chicago, 1933.

Medley, D. M. *Teacher competence and teacher effectiveness: A review of process-product research.* Washington, D.C.: American Association of Colleges for Teacher Education, 1977.

Rosenshine, B. V. Recent research on teaching behaviors and student achievement. *Journal of Teacher Education,* 1976, *27,* 61–64.

Rosenshine, B. V. *Academic engaged time, content covered, and direct instruction.* Paper presented at the American Educational Research Association Annual Meeting, New York, 1977.

Rupley, W. H. Teacher instructional emphases and pupil achievement in reading. *Peabody Journal of Education,* 1977, *54,* 286–291.

Rupley, W. H., & Blair, T. R. Characteristics of effective reading instruction. *Educational Leadership,* 1978, *36,* 171–173.

Rupley, W. H., & McNamara, J. F. Effects of instructional emphases and pupil engaged time in reading achievement. In M. L. Kamil and A. P. Moe (Eds.), *Reading research: Studies and application.* Clemson, S. C.: National Reading Conference, Inc., 1979, 199–203.

references

Commentary on Rupley and Blair's Critique of Gray and Gates's Studies of Teacher Effectiveness in Reading Instruction: A Mere Beginning

GERALD G. DUFFY

Michigan State University

Rupley and Blair nicely illustrate how the work of Gray in the 1920s and of Gates in the 1930s represents the "roots" of teacher effectiveness research, especially as it relates to the process-product work done in the 1970s. They quite correctly point out that recent advances are significant and that, after decades of research that proved to be of little assistance, we are finally obtaining teacher effectiveness findings that suggest useful guidelines for instructional practice.

However, one must also point out that the process-product findings themselves are not enough. What we know from such research, while important, is but a mere beginning to our understanding the nature of teacher effectiveness.

WHAT HAVE WE LEARNED ABOUT TEACHER EFFECTIVENESS?

The process-product studies have focused almost exclusively on the teaching of basic skills (mostly reading and mathematics) in primary grade settings where academic achievement has been traditionally at or below national norms. Within this context, the numerous findings substantiate Carroll's (1967) "opportunity to learn" principle in that time has been established to be of crucial importance. Hence, teachers are most effective when they allocate more time to reading; ensure that their pupils are engaged in the academic reading activity for high proportions of this time; closely monitor pupil efforts to ensure continued engagement; use the time to call for frequent repetition, to drill to overlearning, and to provide corrective feedback; establish efficient management routines to minimize time wastage; set positive expectations so that students are psychologically able to make maximum use of the instructional time, and ensure high student success levels so that this psychological condition can be maintained (Duffy, 1981a; Rosenshine, 1976, 1979, 1980; Brophy, Note 1; Good, Note 2).

While these findings can be summarized in terms of the single concept of opportunity to learn, they are nevertheless significant. They legitimatize the intuitively sensible notions that (1) a student who spends more time on a task will learn more than one who spends less time; and (2) that instruction that is direct and intentional in creating certain outcomes will be more effective than indirect or incidental instruction. As such, the findings support the concept that quality teachers are those who are academically oriented, efficient, and business-like in teaching basic reading skills. Further, while Rupley and Blair indicate that these instructional guidelines do not *cause* pupil learning, the experimental studies reported by Anderson, Evertson, and Brophy (1979) and by Good and Grouws (1979) suggest otherwise.

WHAT DO WE HAVE YET TO LEARN ABOUT TEACHER EFFECTIVENESS?

Process-product research has produced useful information about the nature of teacher effectiveness and the realization that we have just scratched the surface in our efforts to understand what makes an effective teacher. Three examples illustrate.

Classroom complexities and teacher effectiveness. Descriptive research has contributed the understanding that the classroom is a complex workplace. The implicit and explicit rule systems that govern classroom social interactions (McDermott, 1977; Seiler, Note 3), the complexities of efficiently organizing and managing the classroom (Brophy, 1979, Brophy & Putnam, 1979), the difficulties of equitably distributing instructional time among 25 or 30 children (Shulman, Note 4), the implicit and explicit mandates teachers must deal with (Schwille, Porter, & Gant, 1980), and the multiple roles they must play (Shulman, Note 4), all make the classroom a difficult place to work.

These complexities affect how teachers go about their work. It had long been assumed that teachers act as rational decision-makers following relatively clear-cut models in carrying out classroom reading instruction (Borko, Shavelson, & Stern, 1981; Cunningham, 1977; Harste & Burke, 1977; Kamil & Pearson, 1979). However, descriptive studies of planning (Clark & Yinger, 1979), of interactive instructional decision-making (Buike, 1980; Marland, 1979), of classroom instructional practice (Duffy & McIntyre, 1980; Durkin, 1979; Morine-Dershimer, 1979), and of teacher conceptions of reading (Bawden, Buike, & Duffy, 1979; Buike, Burke, & Duffy, Note 5; Duffy, 1981b), all indicate that the complexities of the workplace force teachers to be more like technicians who use basal textbooks to maintain a smooth activity flow than like decision-makers who select from among instructional alternatives.

When combined with process-product research, the above findings suggest an intriguing question. Are effective teachers of basic skills technicians rather than decision makers? It would seem so. While the process-product studies indicate that effective teachers use time efficiently by creating high engagement rates, careful monitoring and drill, descriptive studies suggest that such practices may not be the result of conscious decision-making, but the reflection of a pervasive concern for activity flow and management, which is caused by the complexities of the classroom. Obviously, before we can further progress regarding teacher effectiveness, we must learn more about what "triggers" effective teaching behavior and the relative roles played by abstract conceptions and the complexities of practice.

What constitutes teaching? Descriptive research also relates to the absence of direct explanation, explication, and demonstration among elementary school teachers of reading (Brophy, Note 6; Duffy & Roehler, Note 7). The pervasive model of teaching appears to be one of "repeated exposure," in which it is assumed that pupils will learn to read if exposed to reading enough and that instruction is the process of providing such exposure. Such instruction focuses on monitoring the practice activities assigned to pupils, with the teacher providing guidance through the reactive insertion of "correctives" after a pupil errs.

Again, the image of the teacher as a technician emerges. Further, since process-product findings indicate that "repeated exposure" produces desired achievement, perhaps a teacher only needs to be a technician. However, just as we intuitively sense that instructional decision-makers will be more effective than technicians, we also sense that teachers who assist pupils in learning by explicating the crucial features and components of doing a task successfully will be more effective than technicians who emphasize only practice activities. This, then, is another dimension of teacher effectiveness that needs to be explored.

Is effectiveness universal? A final consideration concerns the universality of teacher effectiveness findings. As previously noted, nearly all the process-product studies were conducted in primary grades and focused on basic skills (which, rightly or wrongly, refers mostly to decoding). Leading researchers of teaching, however, argue strongly that teacher effectiveness is context bound (Good, Note 2; Brophy, Note 6).

Several contextual conditions are particularly important. First, effective teaching with very young children in the primary grades may very well be ineffective for intermediate-grade or middle-grade school pupils. Second, effective teaching for decoding may not be effective teaching for comprehension. Third, effective instruction for developing love and appreciation for reading will be qualitatively different from effective instruction of skill competence or other important reading outcomes.

This list, of course, can be extended to include additional contextual variables. The point, however, is that what is effective in one situation may not be effective in another. Determining the components of effectiveness for various contexts is another aspect of teacher effectiveness to be learned.

CONCLUSION

While it is true, as Rupley and Blair state, that the results of process-product research hold promise for advancing our knowledge of effective teaching of reading, it is equally true that these results represent a rudimentary beginning. While it is important to point to the results we do have, it is equally important to note that additional, more sophisticated research must be conducted to enrich those findings and to provide more specific guidelines regarding what triggers and governs teacher behavior, what constitutes teaching, and what elements are appropriate in some contexts but not in others. These and other concerns will occupy researchers interested in the effectiveness of classroom teachers of reading in the foreseeable future.

NOTES

1. Brophy, J. *Teachers' cognitive activities and overt behaviors.* Paper presented at the Conference of Basic Components in the Education and Mathematics Teachers, Rieste, West Germany, April 1980.
2. Good, T. Research on teaching. Paper presented at the American Educational Research Association, Boston, April 1980.
3. Seiler, H. *Social relations and interactions as they affect time allowed to learn: Comparisons of high and low ability reading groups in one first grade classroom.* Doctoral dissertation in progress, Michigan State University.
4. Shulman, L. *Reflections on individual differences and the study of teaching.* Unpublished paper, Michigan State University, 1980.
5. Buike, S., Burke, E., & Duffy, G. *Teacher conceptions of reading as they influence instructional decision and pupil outcomes.* Paper presented at the Annual Conference of the International Reading Association, St. Louis, 1980.
6. Brophy, J. *Potential policy implications of recent research on teaching.* Paper presented at the Summer Institute on Learning and Motivation in the Classroom, University of Michigan, Ann Arbor, June 1981.
7. Duffy, G., & Roehler, L. *The illusion of instruction.* Unpublished paper, Michigan State University, 1981.

REFERENCES

Anderson, L., Evertson, C., & Brophy, J. An experimental study of effective teaching in first grade reading groups. *Elementary School Journal,* 1979, *79,* 193–222.

Bawden, R., Buike, S., & Duffy, G. *Teachers' conceptions of reading and their impact on instructional behavior* (Research Series No. 47). Michigan State University: Institute for Research on Teaching, 1979.

Borko, H., Shavelson, R., & Stern, P. Teachers' decisions in the planning of reading instruction. *Reading Research Quarterly,* 1981, *16,* 449–466.

Brophy, J. *Teacher behavior and its effects* (Occasional paper no. 25). Michigan State University: Institute for Research on Teaching, Sept. 1979.

Brophy, J., & Putnam, J. Classroom management in the elementary grades. In D. Duke (Ed.), *Classroom management.* (Seventy-eighth yearbook of the National Society for the Study of Education). Chicago: University of Chicago Press, 1979.

Buike, S. *Teacher decision making in reading instruction* (Research Series No. 79). Michigan State University, May 1980.

Carroll, J. A model for school learning. *Teacher's College Record,* 1967, *64,* 723–733.

Clark, C., & Yinger, R. *Three studies of teacher planning* (Research Series No. 55). Michigan

State University: Institute for Research on Teaching, 1979.

Cunningham, P. Match informal evaluation to your teaching practices. *The Reading Teacher*, 1977, *31*, 51–56.

Duffy, G. *Teacher effectiveness research: Implications for reading education* (Occasional paper no. 45). Michigan State University, 1981a.

Duffy, G. *Theory to practice: How it works in real classrooms* (Research Series No. 98), Michigan State University, 1981b.

Duffy, G., & McIntyre, L. *A qualitative analysis of how various primary grade teachers employ the structured learning component of the direct instruction model when teaching reading.* (Research Series No. 80). Michigan State University, 1980.

Durkin, D. What classroom observations reveal about reading comprehension instruction. *Reading Research Quarterly*, 1979, *14*, 481–533.

Good, T., & Grouws, D. The Missouri mathematics effectiveness project: An experimental study in fourth grade classrooms. *Journal of Educational Psychology*, 1979, *71*, 355–362.

Harste, J. C., & Burke, C. L. A new hypothesis for reading teacher research: Both teaching and learning of reading are theoretically based. In P. D. Pearson (Ed.), *Reading: Theory, research and practice.* Twenty-sixth Yearbook of the National Reading Conference, Clemson, S.C., 1977.

Kamil, M., & Pearson, P. Theory and practice in teaching reading. *New York University Educational Quarterly*, 1979, 10–16.

Marland, P. W. *A study of teachers' interactive thoughts.* Unpublished doctoral dissertation, University of Alberta, 1978.

McDermott, R. *Kids make sense: An ethnographic account of the interactional management of success and failure in one first grade classroom.* Unpublished doctoral dissertation, Stanford University, 1977.

Morine-Dershimer, G. *Teacher plans and classroom reality: The South Bay Study, Part IV* (Research Series No. 60). Michigan State University, 1979.

Rosenshine, B. Classroom instruction. In N. L. Gage (Ed.), *The psychology of teaching methods*, 75th Yearbook of the National Society for the Study of Education, Part I. Chicago: University of Chicago Press, 1976.

Rosenshine, B. Content, time and direct instruction. In A. Walberg & P. Peterson (Eds.), *Research on teaching: Concepts, findings and implications.* Berkeley: McCutchan Publishing, 1979.

Rosenshine, B. How time is spent in elementary classrooms. In C. Denham & A. Lieberman (Eds.), *Time to learn.* Washington, D.C.: National Institute of Education, May 1980.

Schwille, J., Porter, A., & Gant, M. *Content decision making and the politics of education* (Research Series No. 52). Michigan State University, 1980.

section VIII

READING IN THE CONTENT AREAS

RESEARCH by A. Sterl Artley, *A Study of Certain Relationships Existing Between General Reading Comprehension and Reading Comprehension in a Specific Subject-Matter Area*

CRITIQUE by John E. Readence

FOR FURTHER LEARNING

COMMENTARY by Larry Mikulecky

This section introduces the reader to the original study by Artley that investigated the extent to which general reading comprehension factors were related to factors involved in social studies comprehension. Readence does a thorough job of critiquing this study and claims that Artley's research is significant because he sought to more clearly define the role of reading teachers and content area teachers in teaching comprehension. He focuses intensively on the study itself and discusses the validity of its findings and the educational implications drawn from them. Mikulecky praises Readence's critique and adds to it by presenting the meaning and significance of this study to educators in general, and, in particular to readers separated from the study by four decades. He proposes that research need not be dismissed simply because additional qualifications need to be made to an author's original investigation.

A STUDY OF CERTAIN RELATIONSHIPS EXISTING BETWEEN GENERAL READING COMPREHENSION AND READING COMPREHENSION IN A SPECIFIC SUBJECT MATTER AREA

A. STERL ARTLEY

Stephens College, Columbia, Missouri

Editor's note: A problem of considerable practical and theoretical importance, particularly at the secondary school level, is that of the general and specific character of reading comprehension. The author finds evidence of both general and specific factors in reading.

THE PROBLEM

In spite of the increased attention being directed by research workers and school practitioners to the nature and extent of the reading problem on the secondary school level, responsibilities for the development of an effective reading program have not been clearly allocated. This is due, in part, to the fact that the very nature of reading comprehension itself has not been clearly described.

In general, school policies in relation to the provision made for reading instruction have varied between two points of view. The first point of view, based upon the assumption that the factors that make for reading comprehension are "general" and, as such, are applicable to several areas of instruction, places a premium upon the development of general reading comprehension under the guidance of the English teacher or special reading teacher. The second point of view, in contradistinction to the first, emphasizes the development of reading comprehension under the instruction of the "subject" or "content area" teacher, on the assumption that reading comprehension is composed of a pattern of abilities that vary as to the content area studied, as well as to the purpose for which one reads within that content area. Between these two somewhat extreme points of view is the one that conceives of the responsibility for the development of the skills and abilities that make for adequate comprehension as belonging to both the English or reading teacher and the "content area" teacher. The proponents of this viewpoint base their belief on the assumption that reading comprehension involves both general and specific factors. Hence, the reading teacher furnishes the nucleus around which basic training is given, while the other teachers apply these basic learnings to their par-

From *Journal of Educational Research,* 1944, *37,* pp. 464–73.

ticular instructional area, as well as develop those other skills and abilities that appear uniquely related to their own content field.

Related to this basic problem are several others of no less importance. First, that of determining the extent to which the factors of general and specific reading comprehension enter into achievement in a particular content area. A solution to this problem is essential if the responsibilities of each teacher in relation to reading instruction are to be clearly defined. Second, that of determining the relative order of importance to comprehension in each subject-matter area of certain skills and abilities presumed to be the components of reading comprehension. Finally, that of investigating the semantic implications of vocabulary and facts in reading comprehension, since an adequate understanding of the printed page is dependent upon the interrelation of both language and content.

Essentially then, the study reported here grows out of the need for a more adequate appraisal of the nature of reading comprehension and the factors that comprise it. With objective data at hand there will be available a basis for allocating the responsibilities related to the development of effective reading and study abilities in the secondary school.

PURPOSES OF THE STUDY

The problems discussed above relative to the nature of reading comprehension are translated into four specific purposes as follows:

1. To determine the relationship between scores on tests purporting to measure abilities related to comprehension in a specific subject-matter area and scores on a test designed to measure a more general type of reading comprehension.
2. To determine the extent to which reading comprehension of both the general and specific types enters into an informational type of achievement in a specific subject-matter area.
3. To determine the relative importance of certain factors assumed to be components of reading comprehension in a specific subject-matter area.
4. To determine the extent to which a knowledge of certain facts and a command of the vocabulary employed in utilizing those facts enter into comprehension in a specific subject-matter area.

CONTENT AREA AND POPULATION SELECTED FOR STUDY

Specific reading comprehension referred to throughout this report is that type of comprehension appraised by tests in the general area of the social studies. This field was selected because it is such a vital one in general education, and because more nearly adequate research instruments appeared to be available for the purpose of the investigation. The test population consisted of eleventh grade pupils.

DEFINITION OF TERMS

For the purpose of this study general reading comprehension is defined as the type appraised by the Cooperative Test

Service. *Test of Reading Comprehension, C1.* Specific reading comprehension is defined as the type appraised by the Cooperative Test Service, *Social Studies Abilities Test* and the Progressive Education Association, *Application of Principles Test 1.5.*

SUMMARY OF RELATED LITERATURE

With only a few exceptions, reading comprehension in the past was considered an undifferentiated ability with the assumption that the factors that made for successful comprehension in one area were the same as those that entered into understanding and evaluation in another. On this basis one reading test might suffice to appraise achievement in several instructional areas. However, investigations of reading tests conducted by such research workers as Wrightstone (21), Shank (14), Betts (2), Tinker (19), and Strang (16) show a general lack of consistency among several tests purporting to appraise certain factors involved in comprehension. Hence, the common conclusion appears to be that the various reading tests seem to measure different aspects of reading comprehension, and that similarities among tests purporting to measure the same thing exist in name only.

More closely related to the problem under investigation is a series of research aiming to study the relationships between the ability to read various types of material. Among these studies are those of Ritter and Lofland (12), Tyler (20), Bedell (1), Dewey (3), Grimm (6), and Gans (40). Quite consistently do these investigators conclude that the ability to engage successfully in one type of reading activity has a low relationship to the ability to engage successfully in another type of reading activity. Shores (19), and Swenson (17), while finding closer relationships between the abilities involved in reading various types of material than the group mentioned above, conclude, nevertheless, that each of the various types of reading materials has its own "individual peculiarities."

Additional light is thrown upon this study by those who have attempted to determine the amenability to training of certain factors involved in reading comprehension. The findings of these investigators, however, are somewhat at variance concerning the effect of reading instruction upon scholastic attainment. On the whole, it might be concluded that the results of reading instruction of a general nature upon performance in a specific subject-matter area have been quite uniformly disappointing. Such is the finding of Jacobson (7, 8), and McCullough (9). Salisbury (13), though, found that training in outlining based on general materials "tended to improve the mastery of content subjects." Whether there would have been the same or greater improvement in school performance had training been given in the particular area in which improvement was appraised, is a question left unanswered.

PROCEDURES

The data for this study were secured by means of a series of tests appraising achievement in general reading comprehension, certain aspects of reading comprehension in the social studies, informational achievement in the social studies, and non-verbal intelligence. After an extensive investigation of available tests in relation to certain preestablished criteria, final selection resulted in the following tests for the various categories listed:

I. General reading comprehension.
   Cooperative Test Service, *English Test C1: Reading Comprehension,* Form Q, purporting to measure:
   1. General vocabulary.
   2. Speed of comprehension.
   3. Level of comprehension.

II. Certain aspects of reading comprehension in the social studies.
   Progressive Education Association *Application of Principles in Social Studies 1.5,* purporting to measure:
   1. Ability to see logical relations.
   2. Ability to evaluate arguments.

   Cooperative Test Service, *Test of Social Studies Abilities,* Experimental Form Q, purporting to appraise:
   1. Knowledge of sources.
   2. Ability to organize.
   3. Ability to interpret.
   4. Ability to apply generalizations.

   Cooperative Test Service, *Test of General Proficiency in the Field of Social Studies, Form QR* (Terms and concepts subtest only)

III. Informational achievement in the social studies.
   Cooperative Test Service, *Survey Test in the Social Studies,* Form O, purporting to measure "achievement of a topical content nature in the several social studies areas."

IV. Non-verbal intelligence.
   Chicago Non-Verbal Examination.

These tests, requiring a total testing time of approximately five hours, were administered to 242 eleventh grade pupils in the Williamsport High School, Williamsport, Pennsylvania. All tests were administered by the investigator. As far as is known there were no irregularities in the test procedure. The data obtained made possible all computations on the basis of 200 cases. All raw test data were transferred to Hollerith cards and the necessary "makings" for correlations, regression equations, etc., were obtained through the use of International Business Machines.

SUMMARY OF FINDINGS

The findings are summarized in relation to the purposes as established in a preceding section.

1. To determine the relationship between scores on a test purporting to measure abilities related to comprehension in a specific subject-matter area and scores on a test designed to measure a more general type of reading comprehension.
   a. A coefficient of correlation of .79 was found to exist between the measures of reading comprehension of a specific nature (social studies) and general reading comprehension.
   b. The relation between measures of reading comprehension of a specific nature and general reading comprehension was increased to .86 when the test scores were corrected for attenuation.
   c. The relation between measures of specific reading comprehension and general reading comprehension was reduced to .75 when the effect of intelligence was partialled out.

2. To determine the extent to which reading comprehension of both the general and specific types enters into information achievement in social studies.

The intercorrelations and correlations furnishing the basis for all of the beta weights are presented in the two following tables:

The contributions to informational achievement in the social studies of a team composed of the tests of general and specific reading comprehension are indicated in the partial regression equation in standard score form.

$\bar{Z}_{\eta}$—$.410_{z_1} + .401_{z_2}$ where

$\bar{Z}_0$—informational achievement in the social studies

z_1—general reading comprehension

z_2—specific reading comprehension

3. To determine the relative importance of certain factors assumed to be components of reading comprehension in a specific subject-matter area (social studies).

a. The relative weights of the specialized and general vocabulary tests taken as a team in predicting the criterion measure of reading comprehension in the social studies are

RESEARCH/TABLE 1

Intercorrelations between measures of the several factors presumed to be components of reading comprehension in the social studies (N = 200)

Factor	1	2	3	4	5	6	7	8
1. Ability to Obtain Facts	....	.400	.471	.523	.367	.351	.484	.499
2. Ability to Organize	....	....	.600	.499	.433	.309	.608	.608
3. Ability to Interpret	....	....	....	.553	.466	.447	.669	.647
4. Ability to Apply Generalizations	....	....	....	....	.383	.275	.564	.603
5. Ability to Perceive Logical Relations	....	....	....	....	....	.387	.536	.501
6. Ability to Evaluate Arguments	....	....	....	....	....	....	.317	.347
7. Command of General Reading Vocabulary	....	....	....	....	....	....	....	.785
8. Command of Social Studies Vocabulary	....	....	....	....	....	....	....	....

RESEARCH/TABLE 2

Correlations between measures of the several components of reading comprehension and the criterion measure of reading comprehension in the social studies ($N = 200$)

Factor	r
1. Ability to Obtain Facts	.732
2. Ability to Organize	.772
3. Ability to Interpret	.827
4. Ability to Generalize	.729
5. Ability to Perceive Logical Relations	.691
6. Ability to Evaluate Arguments	.576
7. Command of General Reading Vocabulary	.735
8. Command of Social Studies Vocabulary	.741

shown in the following partial regression equation in standard score form.

$\bar{Z}_0 = .396_{z_1} + .432_{z_2}$ where
$\bar{Z}_0$ = reading comprehension in the social studies
z_1 = general reading vocabulary
z_2 = social studies vocabulary

b. The contributions to reading comprehension in the social studies of a team composed of the six original components of the criterion measure are shown in the following partial regression equation in standard score form.

$\bar{Z}_0 = .277_{z_1} + .274_{z_2} + .277_{z_3} + .166_{z_4} + .228_{z_5} + .127_{z_6}$ where
$\bar{Z}_0$ = reading comprehension in the social studies
z_1 = ability to obtain facts
z_2 = ability to organize
z_3 = ability to interpret
z_4 = ability to apply generalizations
z_5 = ability to perceive logical relations
z_6 = ability to evaluate arguments

4. To determine the extent to which a knowledge of specialized facts and a command of the specialized vocabulary employed in dealing with the facts enter into comprehension in a specific subject-matter area (social studies).

The contributions of measures of knowledge of social studies facts and a command of social studies vocabulary to reading comprehension in the social studies are indicated in the multiple regression equation in standard score form presented below:

$\bar{Z}_0 = .456_{z_1} + .385_{z_2}$ where
$\bar{Z}_0$ = reading comprehension in the social studies
z_1 = command of social studies vocabulary
z_2 = knowledge of social studies facts

CONCLUSIONS

Within the limitations of the study the following conclusions appear to be valid:

1. The extent of the relationship that exists between tests of general reading comprehension and reading comprehension in the social studies makes it appear that, *in general,* ability to read material of a general informative type is associated with ability to read a type of material more specifically related to the social studies area.

2. The absence of a perfect correlation between measures of general and specific reading comprehension provides evidence that there exists a high degree of specificity in the factors relating to reading comprehension in the social studies.
3. A measure of non-verbal intelligence appears to exert only a slight influence upon the relationship between tests of general reading comprehension and reading comprehension in the social studies.
4. It appears that an adequate measure of comprehension in the social studies area may be made with a test of general reading comprehension. That is, the tests of general and specific comprehension correlate as high as do two tests of general reading ability.
5. The abilities measured by tests of general and specific reading comprehension appear to be present to an equal extent on an informative test of achievement in the social studies.
6. If measures of general and technical vocabulary were the only two factors involved in predicting scores in reading comprehension in the social studies, it would appear that though both measures contribute substantially to adequate comprehension, the test of the vocabulary unique to the particular area being studied would have slightly more weight than the test of the vocabulary of a general nature.
7. Of the measures of the several components presumed to contribute to comprehension of social studies material, tests of the ability to interpret, to obtain facts, and to organize appear to contribute most to the prediction of scores on a test of the ability to comprehend in this area.
8. Though tests measuring the knowledge of facts in the social studies, as well as the command of the vocabulary to use those facts, weigh heavily in predicting scores on a test purporting to appraise the ability to comprehend social studies material, a command of the specialized vocabulary is at least as important as a knowledge of social studies facts.

EDUCATIONAL IMPLICATIONS

While testing techniques furnished the data for this study, the implications that are inherent relate to instruction as well as to appraisal. They are stated as follows:

1. The English teacher or the teacher invested with the responsibility of caring for the reading needs of the pupils in the secondary school can make a material contribution toward giving a type of training that will operate in a functional manner in the social studies.
2. The social studies teacher who develops effectively the skills essential to adequate comprehension in his area, probably will note a general improvement in other content fields.
3. Every classroom teacher has the direct responsibility for developing those reading skills and abilities essential for adequate comprehension within his particular area of instruction, as well as for applying to his content field and making functional those skills and abilities being developed by teachers in other areas of instruction.

4. The fact that an adequate measure of comprehension in the social studies may be made with a test of general reading comprehension, makes less important the necessity of developing specialized tests for this area. Hence, a good test of general reading comprehension administered at the beginning of the school year should serve adequately for the purpose of informing the teacher of history, civics, or problems of democracy of the relative status of the various pupils in the ability to comprehend.

5. The classroom teacher should direct much more than casual attention to the development of a general vocabulary as well as to the development of the vocabulary directly related to the area in which he is giving instruction. Moreover, for adequate comprehension, the development of a specialized vocabulary should receive equal attention to that given to the development of the facts of the course. This vocabulary, however, should be developed in a functional manner in connection with the development of other reading skills rather than as an isolated perfunctory drill on words. In short, each teacher is dealing with the development of language-fact relationships. Therefore, in developing adequate comprehension he must be careful to maintain the proper balance between facts, on one hand, and language, on the other.

A SELECTED BIBLIOGRAPHY

1. Bedell, Ralph. *The Relationship Between the Ability to Recall and the Ability to Infer in Specific Learning Situation.* Bulletin of Northeast Missouri State Teachers College. Vol. 34, No. 9. Kirksville, Missouri: December, 1934.
2. Betts, E. A., "Reading Problems at the Intermediate Grade-Level," *Elementary School Journal,* XL (June, 1940). Pp. 737–46.
3. Dewey, Joseph, "The Acquisition of Facts as a Measure of Reading Comprehension," *Elementary School Journal,* XXXV (January, 1935). Pp. 346–48.
4. Gans, Roma, *A Study of Critical Reading Comprehension in the Intermediate Grades.* New York: Teachers College, Columbia University Contributions to Education, No. 811, 1940.
5. Gray, W. S. (chairman), *Reading in General Education.* Washington, D.C.: American Council on Education, 1940.
6. Grimm, Paul, "Interpretation of Data and Reading Ability in the Social Studies," *Educational Research Bulletin,* XIX (September, 1940). Pp. 372–74.
7. Jacobson, Paul B., *Two Experiments with Work-Type Reading Exercises in Ninth Grade.* Iowa City: University of Iowa Studies in Education, Vol. VIII, No. 5, 1933.
8. ———, "The Effect of Work-Type Reading Instruction Given in Ninth Grade," *School Review,* XL (April, 1932). Pp. 273–81.
9. McCullough, Constance, "Improving Reading Comprehension in Grade IX," *School Review,* XLV (April, 1937). Pp. 266–73.
10. Peters, C. C., and W. R. VanVoorhis, *Statistical Procedures and Their Mathematical Bases.* New York: McGraw-Hill, 1940.
11. *Reading Instruction in Secondary Schools.* National Education Research Bulletin, Vol. XX, No. 1. Washington, D.C.: National Education Association, January, 1942.
12. Ritter, B. T., and W. T. Lofland, "The Relation Between Reading Ability as Measured by Certain Standardized Tests and

bibliography

the Ability Required in the Interpretation of Printed Matter Involving Reason," *Elementary School Journal,* XXIV (March, 1924). Pp. 529–46.

13. Salisbury, Rachel, "A Study of the Transfer Effects of Training in Logical Organization," *Journal of Educational Research,* XXVIII (December, 1934). Pp. 241–54.
14. Shank, Spencer, "Student Responses in the Measurement of Reading Comprehension," *Journal of Educational Research,* XXII (September, 1930). Pp. 119–29.
15. Shores, James H., *The Ability to Read Historical Materials as Related to Eighth-Grade Achievement and General Reading Ability.* Unpublished Master's thesis, University of Minnesota, 1938.
16. Strang, Ruth, "An Evaluation of Reading Tests for College Students," *The Role of Research in Educational Progress,* Official Report of American Education Research Association, Washington, D.C.: American Educational Research Association, 1937.
17. Swenson, Esther, *The Relation of Ability to Read Material of the Type Used in Studying Science to Eighth Grade Achievement.* Unpublished Master's thesis, University of Minnesota, 1938.
18. *Thirty-Sixth Yearbook of the National Society for the Study of Education.* Part I, The Teaching of Reading: A Second Report. Bloomington, Illinois: Public School Publishing Company, 1937.
19. Tinker, Miles, "The Relation of Speed to Comprehension in Reading," *School and Society,* XXXVI (July 30, 1932). Pp. 158–60.
20. Tyler, Ralph, "Measuring the Ability to Infer," *Educational Research Bulletin,* IX (November 19, 1930). Pp. 475–80.
21. Wrightstone, Wayne J., "Newer Appraisal Techniques in Language," *Elementary English Review,* XVIII (November, 1941). Pp. 243–49.

A Critique of A. Sterl Artley's: A Study of Certain Relationships Existing Between General Reading Comprehension and Reading Comprehension in a Specific Subject-Matter Area

JOHN E. READENCE

Louisiana State University

The research to be critiqued in this paper was originally conducted by Artley in August, 1942, at the Pennsylvania State University under the guidance of Emmett A. Betts and subsequently published in the *Journal of Educational Research* in 1944. Some historical perspective is necessary to give readers an idea of the rationale for this study. The beginning of interest in reading comprehension is usually credited to Thorndike (1917) who focused researchers' attention on the reasoning aspects of reading (see pages 209–27 of this volume). Shortly thereafter, attention in reading research and instruction shifted away from word recognition and oral reading to comprehension and silent reading. Subjective analyses of the component abilities of comprehension were undertaken (e.g., Gray, 1919). Factor-analytic studies, attempting to isolate important factors of reading comprehension by investigating students' performances on various reading tests, were also made (e.g., Davis, 1941, 1944; see pages 235–45 of this volume). Another area of research related to comprehension, central to the rationale for Artley's study, was whether comprehension abilities were general (i.e., applicable to all materials regardless of content area) or specific to particular fields.

At issue here was the role of content teachers in teaching reading comprehension and the belief that different subject-matter areas required different skills for readers to comprehend adequately. Gray (1952) stated, "The importance of guidance in reading in all curriculum areas was first emphasized on a national scale in the 1925 report of the National Committee on Reading" (p. 6). Later, the slogan "Every teacher a teacher of reading," was adopted by the National Committee in its annual report (1937). This slogan gained popularity with professionals in reading education and is still used today. To its advantage, the slogan was intended to sensitize all teachers of subject-matter areas to the demands of reading in content areas and to make them aware of their responsibility for providing guidance for reading. To its disadvantage, it tended to create opposition on the part of many teachers rather than elicit their support (Dishner and Readence, 1978). There was no clear delineation as to what "responsibility" in teaching reading in content areas was and why it should be done.

Adding controversy to this issue was previous research which examined the teachers' attempts to cope with the concepts in the text, and to deal with any new vocabulary they determined was significant to comprehension in various content areas. Ritter and Lofland (1924) investigated the relation between general reading ability and the ability required in reading material which entailed reasoning. They refuted the assumption that reading was a singular ability and that a single type of training in reading was invalid. Rather, they found "interpreting one type of content is probably very different from that required in another. It is as much the duty of the school to teach the reading technique which underlies the interpretation of history or geography as it is to teach such a technique for literature" (p. 546).

McCallister (1930, 1932) examined the types of reading required in studying content subjects. In these studies, McCallister found that the type of reading activities required in different subjects varied accordingly. Additionally, he concluded that "guidance in reading should be recognized as a function of every instructor" (1930, p. 200), and that "each subject has its own purposes, forms, and applications of reading" (1932, p. 123). Such studies led McCallister (1936) to write the first textbook containing a separate section of five chapters and dealing with the problems of providing instructional guidance in reading material related to history, mathematics, and science.

Wagner (1938) investigated the relation between various reading skills and the achievement of ninth-graders in content areas. She concluded that the reading abilities essential to achievement in various content areas differed. On the other hand, it was also found that a general comprehension ability was a "highly significant factor in composite ninth grade achievement" (p. 56).

Artley viewed decisions made concerning reading instruction as varying between two extreme points of view. One point of view was based upon the assumption that the factors which comprised reading comprehension were "general" in nature and, therefore, applicable to several instructional areas. Thus, under this viewpoint, responsibility for the development of reading comprehension would fall under the auspices of the reading teacher or, if this position did not exist, the English teacher. The opposing point of view assumed that reading comprehension was composed of discrete abilities which varied according to the content area studied. This viewpoint emphasized, then, that reading comprehension was best developed under the auspices of teachers in the separate content areas.

Artley posed a middle position between these two extremes. This entailed responsibility for comprehension instruction as belonging to both the reading or English teacher and content teachers. This viewpoint assumed that comprehension involved both general and specific factors, with the reading teacher providing instruction in the basics of comprehension, and content teachers applying the basics to their own subject areas and providing instruction in comprehension abilities unique to their content fields. Thus, Artley saw a need to discover the extent to which the common factors and the differentiating factors of comprehension were present in the reading materials in the various subjects. To accomplish this, Artley chose social studies as the subject area to be investigated.

This writer subscribes to the notion that some general comprehension abilities are necessary and endemic to learning from text, regardless of the content area being studied. Each content area requires students to draw upon their previous experience to associate new information with known information, to use their reasoning pow-

critique

various demands placed on students in comprehending text material in different encounter. And, as Singer (1979) found, it is the responsibility of every teacher to help students read and learn from text. To say that it is only the responsibility of reading teachers or content teachers is hardly supportable.

At the same time, the notion that comprehension and learning from text are generic does not deny the notion that specific skills are useful in specific content areas. Certainly it is necessary to deal with the literary devices peculiar to English or the word problems and numerical skills peculiar to mathematics to be successful in those texts. Thus, this writer is in agreement with the findings of this study but feels the conclusions, as posed by Artley, are not strong enough with regard to the importance of a general comprehension factor.

At the same time, it is important to review such research because this is as much a topic of concern now as it was then. One would only have to explore the recent literature (e.g., O'Mara, 1981; Santa and Hayes, 1981) or recent conference programs (e.g., College Reading Association, International Reading Association) to see that investigations into the factors that comprise comprehension in various content areas are still an issue. Perhaps the research findings of Artley as well as those of Shores (1938), Swenson (1938), and others should be considered when undertaking additional studies in this area.

PURPOSES OF THE STUDY

Four specific questions were addressed in this study:

1. What was the relationship between scores on tests purporting to measure abilities to comprehend in social studies and scores on tests designed to measure general comprehension?
2. To what extent did reading comprehension of both the general and specific natures enter into an informational type of achievement in social studies?
3. What was the relative importance of factors assumed to be components of reading comprehension in social studies?
4. To what extent did factual knowledge and the command of vocabulary employed in using that knowledge enter into comprehension of social studies?

CONTENT AREA AND SAMPLE

Social studies was selected for the study for two reasons: 1) it was essential for general education, and 2) adequate research instruments which fit the purposes of the study appeared to be available. Therefore, it might be inferred that the second reason was more prominent in selecting social studies as the subject to be studied.

The sample selected for the study consisted of eleventh-grade students. This was all the information that was provided about the subjects. One could hardly call this an adequate description of the sample studied. The reader had no idea of the achievement levels of these students in either reading or social studies, their socioeconomic status, or any other information which might be pertinent to the generalization of any of the findings of this study.

DEFINITION OF TERMS

Comprehension of both a general and a specific nature was defined and, interestingly, was defined only in terms of the type of tests used. This is a severe limitation of the study as comprehension is defined in terms of the dependent measures. Obviously, different dependent measures might measure different comprehension skills as Artley pointed out in his review of related research.

SUMMARY OF RELATED LITERATURE

The review of related literature was broken down into three areas: 1) investigations of reading tests purporting to measure reading comprehension, 2) investigations into the relationship between abilities to read in various content areas, and 3) investigations into the possibility of training subjects in factors involving reading comprehension.

In Part One of the review, Artley was seemingly setting the stage for the types of tests used in his research. If comprehension in one content area were the same as that of another, then one reading test could have been used to evaluate achievement in several content areas. His review pointed out that this was not the case; the research cited showed that reading tests seemed to be measuring different factors of comprehension, and that any similarities between tests existed in name only. It might be inferred, then, that this was the reason Artley used tests for social studies comprehension and a test for general reading comprehension instead of two general reading comprehension tests.

Part Two of the review found that low relationships seemingly existed between subjects' ability to comprehend successfully in different types of reading activities. "Reading activities" were not defined, but it probably can be assumed that they meant comprehending in various types of subject-matter materials. This should have been spelled out more clearly. Artley, to his credit, pointed out some research (Shores, 1938; Swenson, 1938) which contradicted the above finding. Conspicuously missing, however, were the research and writing of Wagner (1938) and that of McCallister (1930, 1932, 1936), cited previously.

The final part of the review examined the effect of transfer of instruction in general comprehension to subjects' performance in comprehending content area material. With one exception, Artley cited literature which concluded that such transfer effects were negligible. Even given the fact that this section of the review dealt with the problem of general versus specific factors of comprehension, it remains that Artley's study was *not* a training study, and it leaves one wondering about the necessity of this section. The additional light thrown upon his study by this part of the review is lacking; therefore, the reason for its inclusion is questionable.

PROCEDURES

In this section readers are first told how the data were to be secured. Included in securing the data were tests of general comprehension, social studies comprehension, non-verbal intelligence, and informational achievement in social studies. Next, readers are told the tests were selected after an "extensive investigation" of available tests by using "certain pre-established criteria." Since these "pre-established criteria" are not specified, critical readers might speculate that test selection was made because of availability and familiarity rather than objectivity.

Next, the tests were listed under the various categories mentioned earlier. Artley used the term "purport to measure." This was a key issue in his study; thus, a general comment is warranted here. No reliability and validity data on these tests were provided. The question is, "Do these tests actually measure what they said they did?" Artley's previous conclusion in his review that general comprehension tests showed a lack of consistency might also be applicable here.

Specific questions readers may have about these tests bring to mind a comment made earlier concerning the definition of terms. It would be advantageous to know what the subtests are measuring. For this, a look into the tests themselves is necessary. For instance, in the *Test of Social Studies Abilities,* Part I was labelled "Obtaining facts"; Artley labelled this as "Knowledge of Sources." This entailed using charts, graphs, maps, and index material to answer questions. "Ability to organize" dealt with subsuming information under its proper heading and recognizing the hierarchical arrangement of material. "Ability to interpret" and "ability to apply generalizations" both used passage comprehension, similar to that found in general reading comprehension tests, to measure the ability to make logical inferences and the ability to apply general statements to specific paragraphs, respectively.

The *Test of General Proficiency in the Field of Social Studies* (Terms and Concepts subtest) turns out to be mainly a social studies vocabulary test. The combination of this subtest with the passage comprehension subtests of those mentioned above made this part of the assessment very similar to general reading tests. Finally, information achievement in social studies as measured by the *Survey Test in the Social Studies* entailed factual knowledge in numerous social studies areas including ancient history, European history, American history, medieval history, civics, economics, and sociology. This test is closely akin to what may be described as a "social studies IQ" test. Knowledge of this information would help readers of this research understand the interpretation of the data that followed.

The concluding paragraph in the procedures dealt with the administration of the tests and the transfer of data for calculation. All tests were administered by Artley, thus eliminating any special problems that could have arisen in administration with multiple examiners. Data were obtained, however, on only 200 of the 242 subjects involved in the research. The loss of subjects is not explained, and the possibility of a biased sample arises.

critique

SUMMARY OF FINDINGS

Findings were summarized according to the purposes presented earlier in the research. Artley found a correlation coefficient of .79 to exist between measures of general comprehension and social studies comprehension. Given the similarity of the tests, one would expect such a high correlation. It should be mentioned that when given a general reading test, approximately 62% of the variance can be accounted for by knowing the subjects' score on the social studies test, thus presenting a powerful relationship between general comprehension and social studies comprehension. Correcting for attenuation, or measurement error, the correlation increased to .86, accounting for 74% of the variance. Finally, the correlation was reduced to .75 when IQ was partialled out.

Research/Tables 1 and 2 were provided to give readers an idea of the extent to which general comprehension and social studies comprehension entered into informational achievement in social studies. In Research/Table 1, Factor #1, "Ability to Obtain Facts," was the terminology used in the testing instrument, but *not* by Artley. This corresponded to what was labelled in the study as "Knowledge of Sources," as mentioned earlier in this paper. Though this may be considered minor, not knowing of the terminology change in the study could lead readers to have problems in interpreting Research/Table 1. Likewise, Factor #8, "Command of Social Studies Vocabulary," referred to the "Terms and Concepts" subtest of the *Test of General Proficiency in the Field of Social Studies*. Again, without previous knowledge, readers would have to interpret this on their own.

An examination of Research/Table 1 reveals the relative strength of relationships between all factors taken two at a time. Such correlations should not have been unexpected, given the similarity of the tests. In Research/Table 2 it should be noticed that the highest correlations, outside of command of vocabulary, existed in the first 3 factors, i.e., ability to obtain facts, ability to organize, and ability to interpret.

To conclude his second overall finding, Artley used a partial regression equation in standard score form. Kerlinger (1973) has stated that "multiple regression analysis is a method for studying the effects and the magnitudes of the effects of more than one independent variable on one dependent variable using principles of correlation and regression" (p. 603). Partial regression "means that the effects of variables other than one to which the weight applies are held constant" (Kerlinger, 1973, p. 624). When using multiple regression analysis, the examination of the relative weights of each factor gives readers an indication of the importance of the respective factors, in this case, to informational achievement in social studies. Thus, it can be said that both general comprehension and social studies comprehension were important contributors to informational achievement.

Partial regression equations were also used to determine the relative importance of factors assumed to be components of comprehension in social studies. The 8 factors in Research/Table 2 were divided into 2 groups to ascertain the relative contributions of vocabulary versus comprehension in predicting social studies comprehension. As would be expected, both general vocabulary and social studies vocabulary were important contributors in predicting social studies comprehension, with a slight advantage to social studies vocabulary.

critique

In examining the relative weights of the 6 comprehension factors in predicting social studies comprehension, it can be seen that the largest weights rested in the ability to obtain facts, ability to organize, and ability to interpret. This would be expected, as pointed out earlier, by an examination of the resultant correlations in Research/Table 2. It should be pointed out that a "law of diminishing returns" (Kerlinger, 1973) was in operation with this particular regression equation. Essentially, the addition of numerous variables in a regression equation, in effect, resulted in redundancy after the first three variables were presented. Thus, the addition of the ability to apply generalizations, the ability to perceive logical relations, and the ability to evaluate arguments to this regression equation was unnecessary.

Finally, in determining the extent to which social studies facts and social studies vocabulary entered into social studies comprehension, the resultant regression equation revealed substantial weights for both social studies vocabulary and social studies facts, with a higher weight resulting for vocabulary. Certainly, it would be expected that prior knowledge of a subject greatly influenced comprehension of that subject.

CONCLUSIONS

The first conclusion that, in general, social studies comprehension was associated with general comprehension seems to be an understatement of that relationship. Given the findings of Salisbury (1934), Shores (1938), Swenson (1938), and Wagner (1938) and the common sense notion that comprehension is comprehension no matter what the material, there was sufficient evidence to say that there *was* a relationship between general comprehension and social studies comprehension. Added to this is Artley's finding that approximately 62% of the variance on a general comprehension score can be accounted for by knowing the subjects' social studies comprehension score; thus, a stronger statement seems warranted.

The second conclusion that the "absence of a perfect correlation" between general comprehension and social studies comprehension indicated a "high degree of specificity" in factors related to social studies comprehension seems to be overstated. With 62% of the variance accounted for, how can there exist a "high" degree of specificity in the factors related to social studies comprehension? Artley did, however, give credence to the middle position of responsibility described in the introduction to his study: reading comprehension instruction should not be the sole domain of either the reading teachers or content teachers; both types of teachers have a vested interest in teaching comprehension.

The third conclusion that non-verbal intelligence appeared to exert little influence upon test performance was valid simply because one would not expect a non-verbal intelligence measure to exert a great influence on verbal measures. The fourth conclusion that a general comprehension test appeared to be an adequate measure of social studies was valid. The fifth conclusion that the abilities measured by the general comprehension test and the social studies test appeared to be equally influencing informational achievement in social studies was predictable, given the similarities of general and specific measures of comprehension. The sixth conclusion that a social studies vocabulary test would have more weight than a general vocabulary test in predicting social studies comprehension was valid. The seventh conclusion that the abilities to interpret, to obtain facts, and to organize, contributed most to predicting social studies comprehension is valid given the data found in Research/Table 2 of the study. The last conclusion, that a command of social studies vocabulary is at least as important as knowing social studies facts in predicting comprehension, was valid, although the conclusion should probably have been worded more positively to stress the importance of social studies vocabulary over facts.

EDUCATIONAL IMPLICATIONS

Artley stated that the implications for education to be made related to "instruction as well as appraisal." It probably would be better stated as "instruction as well as *prediction*."

The first implication that the reading teacher can contribute toward giving training in social studies comprehension was valid, but probably too general. The reading teacher can make a material contribution toward reading comprehension that will operate in a functional manner *if* it is specific to the vocabulary and skill needs of students.

The second implication that social studies teachers can contribute to improvement in general comprehension by developing social studies skills was unwarranted. A general comprehension factor was found to exist in social studies comprehension *only*. No other content area was investigated in this study. Jacobson (1932) lent support to the idea that one should not expect to give training in one content area and have that ability transfer directly to another.

The third implication that all teachers can contribute to comprehension improvement in their instructional areas as well as to teach those comprehension skills being developed by other content teachers was partially valid, given the confines of this research. Again, there is no support in this research for recommending anything to teachers in content fields other than social studies.

The fourth implication that giving a general comprehension test would serve adequately to measure social studies comprehension and eliminate the need for multiple tests was valid.

The last implication needs to be addressed at some length. It is true that classroom teachers should direct their attention to the vocabulary of their subject (Johnson and Pearson, 1978), but there was no support in this research for the development of general vocabulary by classroom teachers. Needless to say, this may occur naturally during instruction. Given the results of this study, the development of specialized vocabulary should receive more—not equal—attention than the development of facts. At the same time the results of this study can only recommend this to social studies teachers. Additionally, there was no justification for stating that vocabulary should be developed in a functional manner rather than in isolated drill. That was outside the confines of the research. (Many reading professionals would agree with that belief!) The final statements that teachers were dealing with the development of "language-fact relationships," though probably valid, was unwarranted given the confines of the research.

critique

SUMMARY

Artley's study validated the middle position he posed as part of the rationale for this study. Responsibility for comprehension instruction rests with all teachers, regardless of content area. Additionally, the reading teacher is also responsible for comprehension instruction. Assuming that comprehension instruction fell under the auspices of *either* reading teachers *or* content teachers ignored the needs of students.

Today we can examine the literature on teaching reading in the content areas and see diverse approaches to reading and learning. Some educators emphasize discrete skills in each content area as the means to teach subject information (e.g., Burmeister, 1978; Shepherd, 1978). Others stress more general comprehension abilities across content areas (e.g., Herber, 1978). Certainly, Artley's findings might be interpreted differently depending on one's educational and philosophical orientation.

Nevertheless, it is unfortunate that today this main finding of Artley is not altogether heeded. Imposing the notion that "every teacher is a teacher of reading" rather than stating that every teacher helps students learn from text material has apparently camouflaged the importance of the findings of this study.

FOR FURTHER LEARNING

Those readers who are interested in continuing to explore the topic of reading in content areas would find the following references helpful:

Hall, W. E., & Robinson, F. P. An analytical approach to the study of reading skills. *Journal of Educational Psychology,* 1945, *36,* 429–442.

Jacobson, P. B. The effect of work-type reading instruction given in ninth grade. *School Review,* 1932, *40,* 273–281.

McCallister, J. M. Reading difficulties in studying content subjects. *Elementary School Journal,* 1930, *31,* 191–201.

McCallister, J. M. Determining the types of reading in studying content subjects. *School Review,* 1932, *40,* 115–123.

Ritter, B. T., & Lofland, W. T. The relation between reading ability as measured by certain standardized tests and the ability required in the interpretation of printed matter involving reason. *Elementary School Journal,* 1924, *24,* 529–546.

Salisbury, R. A study of the transfer effects of training in logical organization. *Journal of Educational Research,* 1934, *28,* 241–254.

Shores, J. H. Skills related to the ability to read history and science. *Journal of Educational Research,* 1943, *36,* 584–593.

Wagner, E. (Bond). *Reading and ninth grade achievement.* Columbia University Contributions to Education, No. 756. New York: Teachers College Press, 1938.

---

for further learning

REFERENCES

Burmeister, L. E. *Reading strategies for middle and secondary school teachers* (2nd ed.). Reading, Mass.: Addison-Wesley, 1978.

Davis, F. B. *Fundamental factors of comprehension in reading.* Unpublished doctoral dissertation, Harvard University, 1941.

Davis, F. B. Fundamental factors of comprehension in reading. *Psychometrika,* 1944, *9,* 185–197.

Dishner, E. K., & Readence, J. E. Content reading: Past. Present! Future? *Reading Horizons,* 1978, *19,* 78–81.

Gray, W. S. Principles in method in teaching reading as derived from scientific investigation. *Eighteenth Yearbook of the National Society for the Study of Education,* Part 2. Bloomington, Ill.: Public School Publ. Co., 1919, 26–51.

Gray, W. S. Progress achieved and the tasks faced in improving reading in various curriculum areas. In Gray, W. S. (Ed.), *Improving reading in all curriculum areas.* Supplementary Educational Monographs No. 76, 1952, 6–11.

Herber, H. L. *Teaching reading in content areas* (2nd ed.). Englewood Cliffs, N.J.: Prentice-Hall, 1978.

Jacobson, P. B. The effect of work-type reading instruction given in ninth grade. *School Review,* 1932, *40,* 273–281.

Johnson, D. D., & Pearson, P. D. *Teaching reading vocabulary.* New York: Holt, Rinehart and Winston, 1978.

Kerlinger, F. N. *Foundations of behavioral research* (2nd ed.). New York: Holt, Rinehart and Winston, 1973.

McCallister, J. M. Reading difficulties in studying content subjects. *Elementary School Journal,* 1930, *31,* 191–201.

McCallister, J. M. Determining the types of reading in studying content subjects. *School Review,* 1932, *40,* 115–123.

McCallister, J. M. *Remedial and corrective instruction in reading: A program for the upper grades and high school.* New York: Appleton-Century, 1936.

O'Mara, D. A. The process of reading mathematics. *Journal of Reading,* 1981, *25,* 22–30.

Ritter, B. T., & Lofland, W. T. The relation between reading ability as measured by certain standard tests and the ability required in the interpretation of printed matter involving reason. *Elementary School Journal,* 1924, *24,* 529–546.

Salisbury, R. A study of the transfer effects of training in logical organization, *Journal of Educational Research,* 1934, *28,* 241–254.

Santa, C. M., & Hayes, B. L. (Eds.). *Children's prose comprehension: Research and practice.* Newark, Del.: International Reading Association, 1981.

Shepherd, D. L. *Comprehensive high school reading methods* (2nd ed.). Columbus, Ohio: Charles Merrill, 1978.

Shores, J. H. *The ability to read historical materials as related to eighth-grade achievement and general reading ability.* Unpublished master's thesis, University of Minnesota, 1938.

Singer, H. Attitudes toward reading and learning from text. In Kamil, M. L., & Moe, A. J. (Eds.), *Reading research: Studies and application.* Twenty-eighth Yearbook of the National Reading Conference, 1979, 254–260.

Swenson, E. *The relation of ability to read material of the type used in studying science to eighth grade achievement.* Unpublished master's thesis, University of Minnesota, 1938.

Thorndike, E. L. Reading as reasoning: A study of mistakes in paragraph reasoning. *Elementary School Journal,* 1917, *8,* 98–114.

Wagner, E. (Bond). *Reading and ninth grade achievement.* Columbia University Contributions to Education, No. 756. New York: Teachers College Press, 1938.

Whipple, G. W. (Ed.). *The teaching of reading: A second report.* Thirty-sixth Yearbook of the National Society for the Study of Education, Part I. Bloomington, Ill.: Public School Publ. Co., 1937.

A Commentary on Readence's Critique of Artley's Study of Certain Relationships Existing Between General Reading Comprehension and Reading Comprehension in a Specific Subject-Matter Area

LARRY MIKULECKY

Indiana University at Bloomington

Readence's critique is a thorough examination of Artley's study from a viewpoint of research methodology. He systematically examines inadequacies in population description, instrument validity, and procedures. Readence even does the reader the service of providing a much-needed historical perspective of what previous research had been available for Artley to draw upon before performing his 1944 study. The methodological perspective provided by the Readence critique is useful and informative.

Rather than react to Readence's observations and comments in a point-by-point fashion, I'd like to comment on the work of both Artley and Readence from another perspective. Since Readence has done such an effective job of critiquing the methodological aspects of the Artley study, my comments will focus on the meaning and significance of such work to educators in general and, in particular, to readers separated from the study by four decades.

CONCLUSIONS BASED UPON CORRELATIONAL DATA

An initial point of departure for commenting on Artley's study ought to be, "What, exactly, should the reader make of Artley's statistical results?" Artley has chosen to use regression analysis to determine how much overlap or "correlation" exists between performance on one test and performance on a different test. In the case of this study, the tests are the several subsections of a general reading test (i.e., ability to obtain facts, ability to interpret, etc.) and one's performance on a reading test focusing on reading specialized social studies material. The logic behind such a study is that if there is a great deal of overlap between general reading test scores and social studies reading performance, then general abilities have transferred. If there is only a small correlation or overlap, then the researcher presumes that the abilities are separate to some degree.

It is important to consider this major assumption on which Artley's entire study is built. Would high correlations between general reading test scores and social studies reading test scores indicate that the abilities transfer? If the assumption is invalid, the technical perfection or technical flaws of the study are irrelevant. Research of the last few years has brought into question the assumption that Artley's research technique is built upon—especially in relation to reading test score correlations.

Let me provide a few specific examples. High correlations between one test score and another can be indicative of several things other than transfer of abilities. John Carroll, in his invited remarks to the 1981 International Reading Association convention, commented upon correlations between one reading subskill and another. Some researchers have assumed that since correlations between subskills are high, one must assume the skills are inseparable. Abilities, it is often assumed, have transferred or blended, or are really simply one general ability. Carroll cautions that the assumption based on correlational data may be invalid. The high correlation between reading subskill scores can be accounted for using another explanation. Good students are absent less frequently than poor students and tend to learn several different reading subskills at about the same time, according to Carroll. The result is that good students perform well on most tests; average students, who are absent more, perform less well; and poor students, who are absent a great deal, tend to perform poorly on most subskills tests. The result is that when students learn to read in school, the correlations are high. Good students tend to do well in nearly everything and poor students do poorly in nearly everything.

There is some evidence to support Carroll's observations. Sylvia Scribner and Michael Cole have studied literacy among the Yai people in Liberia (Scribner and Cole, 1978). In this culture, literacy is separate from schooling. Children go to school and are trained in how to perform in their society, but training in reading and writing comes later, individually, and often on the job as it is needed. Unlike western schooling in literacy, everyone doesn't learn at the same time. School attendance patterns do not cloud the degree of correlation or overlap between one skill and another. Scribner and Cole conclude that "the effects of literacy and perhaps of schooling as well are restricted . . . generalized only to closely related practices" (1978, p. 457). Sticht (1980, p. 303) makes similar comments about the transferability of reading skills. He notes that special training in how to handle job-related reading material has been effective. He states:

> Job reading gains were much larger than general reading. This is important because it indicates that people are learning what they are being taught. Clearly the present results show that reading is not altogether a generic skill assessable by any test of general reading. (p. 303)

The whole point of this discussion is that recent research has brought into question the validity of using correlational data to comment upon separability of one reading subskill from another, especially when the individuals involved have learned literacy in a controlled lock-step fashion. The correlation may not be saying much about reading abilities. It may be, rather, a reflection of school attendance patterns.

commentary

EDUCATIONAL SIGNIFICANCE

A second perspective from which to examine the work of both Artley and Readence is that of educational significance. If one can accept the findings of Artley's study to some extent, what do those findings mean for education as it exists today?

Readence provided a short research history lesson to let the reader know what Artley knew before doing his study. It is also important to be aware of what we've learned and what has changed since Artley did his study. Results from 1944 may lose significance in the educational sense as the decades pass.

One change that has occurred since the Artley study is the make up of student population in high school social studies classes. In the early 1940s less than 50% of the population stayed in school for 12 full years (Digest of Educational Statistics, 1979). It is highly likely that the students Artley had in high school classrooms were, for the most part, from the top half of 1944 seventeen-year-olds. Over 50% of the class would have dropped out of school and it is likely that a high percentage of the dropouts would be from the low end of the reading ability curve. Currently, high schools can plan on about 80% of seventeen-year-olds staying in school for 12 years. This means that simply comprehending a social studies text would be a problem for a significant proportion of today's students. Differences between Artley's students and current students make application of his results questionable.

In the last few years, researchers have more closely examined what students read in school and how much time they spend doing it. In a sense, this sort of research might be looked upon as an attempt to touch base with current reality. Wolf and Greenwald (1980) have videotaped secondary school classes in an attempt to determine what sorts of reading and writing activities students perform in a range of secondary school subjects. Results from their study indicate that students read less than 80 minutes a day in school. Only about half that time is spent in actually reading textbooks as opposed to reading handouts, transparencies on screens, or the chalkboard. Mikulecky (1982) found similar amounts of time being spent on reading by students. High school juniors averaged only 98 minutes daily for school-related reading including homework. Artley's 1944 concern about general reading ability and specialized subject area reading ability may be a moot point superseded by a more pressing concern about students not reading much of anything in schools. The key question may be, "How can we structure school experiences to make sure students read something and gain some proficiency?" rather than "Does general reading proficiency transfer to specialized reading materials and demands?"

Still other recent research has examined the way adults handle reading demands outside of school. Shirley Brice-Heath (1982) has determined that much out-of-school reading is a social act in the sense that an individual reads something, asks questions of other people about what has been read, perhaps tries to apply the information and then re-reads. In an isolated situation, strategies needed for daily functional reading differ significantly from strategies used in mastering textbook chapters. Mikulecky (1981), in a study of the reading patterns of 150 workers and 100 students, found similar results. Workers on the job ask questions about what they have read and discuss alternative explanations on the order of 2 to 3 times more often than students do in school. The whole point of making these observations about current research is to call into question what "social studies reading" might mean and how important it might be to research a student's ability to do "social studies reading" from out of a textbook in an isolated test situation.

USEFULNESS OF RESEARCH

After reading the comments made by Readence and by this author, there is a tendency to presume that Artley's research is of no use. Readence has identified methodological shortcomings; this commentary has questioned basic assumptions of Artley's study and pointed out the difficulty of generalizing work over four decades. New readers of research tend to dismiss that research once flaws become apparent. Such blanket dismissal is not warranted.

No research, except the most simple and artificially controlled, is free of flaws and safe from criticism. Little research in education can be generalized from one situation to another, let alone from one decade to another, without a good deal of qualification. Artley's research ought not to be dismissed because of its imperfections, or even because it was not designed with the pressing questions of our own decade in mind.

Consumers of research need to weigh and balance results against qualifications and place research results into a larger pattern which includes everything that is known about a particular subject. For example, when all is said and done, Artley did test some 200 students with different types of material and he did examine how well students performed with these different materials. His work and results can be valuable, even if his conclusions are no longer accurate and the students tested may not greatly resemble today's students.

Readence has commented on the study's shortcomings in population description and in instrument validity. One can concede these points and move onward. We aren't exactly sure what Artley's students were like, but it is reasonable to assume that they differed somewhat from today's students. So let us not try to generalize Artley's results to a full-range high school class of our own decade. Artley found that his students (probably about 49% of seventeen-year-olds) had a relatively high degree of overlap or intercorrelation between general reading subskill scores and social studies reading scores. These intercorrelations ranged from $r = .34$ to $r = .64$ (see Research/Table 1, page 445). This suggests an overlap of variance of from about 12% to 41%. Given Carroll's comments about inflated correlations when reading is learned in a lock-step fashion, one might mentally lower the overlap reported by Artley. An overlap of 10% to 25% between general reading skills and specific abilities with specialized materials seems to fit within the pattern suggested by the more recent work of Scribner and Cole (1978) and of Sticht (1980). It is possible to separate the results of research from the conclusions of the author. As a matter of fact, as new information is published and new explanations are offered, the consumer of research ought to re-examine results in terms of new frameworks and new conclusions.

The efforts of researchers do not need to be dismissed simply because their hypotheses are no longer of high interest or their assumptions and conclusions are questionable. If the consumer of research is able to keep qualifications in mind, data from the past can be reanalyzed and reinterpreted in the light of new information. This is as it should be.

REFERENCES

Artley, A. S. A study of certain relationships existing between general reading comprehension in a specific subject matter area. *Journal of Educational Research,* Feb. 1944, *37*(6), 464–473.

Brice-Heath, S. Protean shapes in literacy events: Ever-shifting oral and literate tradition. In D. Tannen (Ed.), *Spoken and written language.*

Carroll, J. B. *Analyses of reading test data.* Invited research presentation, International Reading Association Convention, New Orleans, May 1, 1981.

Digest of Educational Statistics, 1979. U.S. Department of Health, Education and Welfare, National Center for Educational Statistics, 1979, pp. 14; 63; 93.

Mikulecky, L. J. *Job literacy: The relationship between school preparation and workplace actuality.* Final report, Feb. 1981. (Washington, D.C.: National Institute of Education #NIE-G-79-0168.)

Mikulecky, L. J. *Job literacy: The relationship between school preparation and workplace actuality. Reading Research Quarterly,* Spring 1982, *17*(3).

Scribner, S., & Cole, M. Literacy without schooling: Testing for intellectual effects. *Harvard Education Review,* 1978, *48*(4), 448–461.

Sticht, T. G. Comprehending reading at work. In Just, M. A., & Carpenter, P. A. (Eds.), *Cognitive processes in comprehension.* Hillsdale, N.J.: Lawrence Erlbaum Associates, 1980.

Wolf, A., & Greenwald, J. *Frequency of reading in secondary content areas: A follow-up observation study.* Paper presented at the National Reading Conference, San Diego, Calif., Dec. 3–6, 1980.

section IX

READING DISABILITY

SUMMARY by Jules C. Abrams, of *Reading Difficulty and Personality Organization*

CRITIQUE by Jules C. Abrams

FOR FURTHER LEARNING

COMMENTARY by Merna M. McMillan and Lance M. Gentile

This section introduces the reader to Edith Gann's pioneer study, *Reading Difficulty and Personality Organization.* Abrams summarizes and critiques this study and promulgates insights regarding its innovative methods. He notes that Gann was the first researcher to use the Rorschach projective test as a means of analyzing reading disabilities. He claims, however, that this study did not pay enough attention to cause and effect and, unfortunately, this led to some unwise emphasis on psychogenic etiologies of reading disorders. Abrams states that currently the pendulum has shifted to neurological factors related to reading problems. He feels there is a continued need to ascertain the role of optimal emotional development in children's ability to learn to read. McMillan and Gentile's commentary is supportive of Abram's position but suggests it is time for a precise review and synthesis of what is already known in relation to emotional problems and reading difficulties. These authors claim that without organizing and interpreting this body of knowledge, future investigators will continue to perpetuate repetitive research.

SUMMARY OF E. GANN'S STUDY: READING DIFFICULTY AND PERSONALITY ORGANIZATION

JULES C. ABRAMS

Hahnemann Medical College

PROBLEM

The study of reading difficulties or disabilities in terms of the organization of the personality as it adapts itself to the reading situation.

HYPOTHESIS

Dynamic processes in the personality organization that determine its means or types of adaptations are related to and influential in the reading experience. These processes are associated with or may be responsible for the difficulties or retardations. Are there actual (reliable) differences in the personality dynamic (the way in which the personality approaches, organizes, or adapts itself to stimulating situations) between unsuccessful readers and average or very successful ones?

THEORETICAL FORMULATIONS SERVING AS BASES

1. "Intellectual processes . . . do not function in isolation but are related to the affective processes."
2. "The affective aspects of the personality are organizing media in relation to behavior and activity."
3. Social environments provide a "framework of attitudes, interests, wishes, and ideas and patterns of behavior with which [the person] approaches situations."
4. "Physical factors . . . play a relatively minor role in contributing to disabilities in reading."
5. "Apparent failure . . . is caused less by inefficient teaching, trivial reading materials, or lack of diagnostic and check techniques than by certain detrimental patterns of behavior, attitudes, resistances and lack of interest and motivation."

POPULATION

The population consisted of three matched groups of boys and girls in grades 3–6. The three groups were labeled "retarded readers," "average readers," and "good readers." Each group had 34 members; a total then of 102 in the sample.

Gann, Edith, *Reading Difficulty and Personality Organization*. Morningside Heights, N.Y.: King's Crown Press, 1945,

INSTRUMENTATION

To Appraise Intelligence:

• *Kulmann-Anderson Tests,* 4th edition for grades 3, 4, 5, and 6.

• *Kohs-Block Design Test,* a performance scale, involving the manipulation of materials in graded series of increasing complexity. Raw scores are translated to Mental Ages.

• *Vocabulary Test from Revised Stanford-Binet Scale,* Form L.

To Evaluate Reading:

• *Gates Reading Survey from Grades 3 to 10.*

• *Standardized Oral Reading Paragraphs* by William S. Gray.

Check List of Difficulties—Oral Reading

• *Visual Perception Test,* adapted from *Gates Reading Diagnosis Test* used to "appraise the reversal tendency" observed in retarded readers.

To Study Personality Processes:

• *The Rorschach Test* (The scoring symbols used were largely those included in the "Record Blank for the Rorschach Method of Personality Diagnosis," by Klopfer and Davidson.)

• *Aspects of Personality,* an inventory sampling three aspects of personality:

Ascendance–Submission
Extroversion–Introversion
Emotionality

The items of the inventory are designed to eliminate the possibility of the subjects answering with acceptable responses, merely because he wants to make a favorable impression.

• *Personality Rating Scale.* The writer designed this five-point scale, a sample given below. The writer checked items characteristic of the subject as he took the *Kohs-Block* Test.

Concentration

1. Distracted by many stimuli
2. Rather easily distracted
3. Working at surface of task
4. Working interestedly at task
5. Deeply absorbed in task

• *Interest in Reading,* an attitude inventory with 85 items. Each item has two parts, one reflecting a positive attitude and one reflecting a negative attitude toward reading.

• *Reading Interests,* a scale of the rank order type where the subjects were asked to rank the types of reading materials they preferred on a scale from 1 (most preferred) to 10 (least preferred).

• *Teacher-Pupil Information Blank* (Teacher). The teacher commented on:

1. Child's work
2. Home background
3. Personality of the child
4. Teacher-pupil rapport

• *Teacher-Pupil Information Blank* (Pupil), Children were asked to respond to 20 items describing his teacher. The list was headed "How I feel about my teacher." Each item contained one positive and one negative part describing the same characteristic. Example: kind – strict

PROCEDURE

Selection of the population: This sample was selected from a group of 714 youngsters who were given the *Kuhlmann-Anderson Tests* and the *Gates Reading Survey* for grades 3–10. To determine the groups, the MA obtained on the *Kulmann-Anderson* was used and the total reading age from the *Gates Survey* was used. The criteria then were as follows:

1. Retarded Group—Mental Age–Total Reading Age = −1 or more
2. Average Group—Mental Age–Total Reading Age = 0
3. Good Group—Mental Age–Total Reading Age = +1 or more

The retarded group was selected on the basis of the above difference being greater than or equal to −1, and on evidence provided by the teacher or principal. The two control groups were then selected by matching with the retarded group on the following:

- chronological age
- mental age
- intelligence quotient (Kuhlmann-Anderson)
- school experience
- sex

No further indication of procedure is given. Evidently each instrument was administered to each subject. The scoring of the Rorschach was checked by an expert, and the tests were scored without knowledge of group assignment.

RESULTS

1. **Pertaining to Intelligence:** Although the groups were matched for intelligence using the *Kuhlmann-Anderson,* a significant difference was found between groups 1 and 2 and groups 1 and 3, on Mental Ages derived from the *Kuhlmann-Anderson.* There was no significant difference between any of the groups on the *Kohs-Block Design Test.* Significant differences were found between the groups on the vocabulary score from the *Binet.*
2. **Pertaining to Reading:** Significant differences were found between the groups on Total Reading Age, Vocabulary Age, Comprehension Age, and Speed Age on the *Gates Survey,* and on the Oral Reading Age from *Gray's Oral Reading Paragraphs.*

   Differences were also noted on the check list and the Visual Perception Test. In both cases, the retarded readers showed greater difficulty in coping with the task.
3. **Personality Organization:**

The Rorschach Analysis

A. The mean number of "Evidences of Adjustment" was calculated for each group. Significant differences were found between groups 1 and 2 and groups 1 and 3, but not between groups 2 and 3.

B. The mean number of "Indicators of maladjustment" is small for all groups; however, group 1 has the greater number and shows a reliable difference from groups 2 and 3. There is not a reliable difference between groups 2 and 3.

Aspects of Personality

- ASCENDANCE – SUBMISSION: no reliable difference between groups.
- EXTROVERSION – INTROVERSION: Group 1 differs reliably from 2 and 3 in the direction of introversion.

summary

• EMOTIONALITY: Group 2 differs reliably from 1 and 3.

• **Rating Scale** (in conjunction with *Kohs-Block Design*)

Group 3 was reliably superior to 1 and 2 except in impulsiveness.

• **Interest in Reading**

Groups 2 and 3 were reliably different from Group 1 in the direction of favorable attitudes toward reading.

CONCLUSIONS

Conclusions are given throughout the results. In general, these conclusions are reached:

1. "Group 1 is in a less fortunate position than Groups 2 or 3."
2. "The bulk of experimental material substantiates the hypotheses to a great extent, and reflects personalities less able (for retarded readers) than successful readers to cope with intellectual (specifically, in this case, reading) and social situations that confront them."

   The retarded reader is "emotionally less well adjusted and less stable," "insecure and fearful in relation to emotionally challenging situations," and "socially less adaptable in relation to the group."
3. "The retarded reader is resistant rather than friendly toward reading experiences."
4. "Retarded readers reflect less of an interest in and occupation with reading."
5. "Retarded readers, both from their own point of view and from their teachers' are experiencing difficulty in adjustment, as well as in learning."
6. "It is the writer's opinion, however, that a secure and stable person will, with the usual school arrangements, learn along with others to read at least with average success."

IMPLICATIONS

1. "The writer suggests that [the personality difficulties] have originated in the home situation, and that the insecurity and instability have resulted from unfortunate parent and sibling relationships."
2. Further study might include:
   A. Family case study of retarded readers.
   B. An interpretation analysis of fantasy material from retarded, average, and good readers to identify emotional conflicts and feeling in relationship to others.
3. The retarded reader should be considered as a personality problem as well as a learning problem by school personnel.

A Critique of E. Ganns' Study: Reading Difficulty and Personality Organization

JULES C. ABRAMS

Hahnemann Medical College

Psychologists have long recognized that emotional and personality maladjustment occur in conjunction with reading difficulty. Much of the controversy in this area has raged around the "chicken or the egg" proposition over which is cause and which is effect. Although many mental health professionals have taken the view that social-emotional maladjustment is a primary cause of reading disability, many other investigators are of the opinion that the disturbed and deviate behavior of many children suffering with reading problems stems directly from the tensions, failures, and conflicts associated with the disability.

In 1945, Edith Gann submitted her research on reading difficulty and personality organization in partial fulfillment of the requirements for the degree of Doctor of Philosophy, in the Faculty of Philosophy, Columbia University. It is doubtful that she could have anticipated the impact of her research on both the psychological and educational communities. Gann had been a teacher in the elementary school, a psychologist and administrator. She had been interested for a long time in application of psychological principles to educational situations and problems, and in the conduct of psycho-educational research. Despite her interest in the two related fields, it is hardly likely that she truly recognized the significance of her dissertation, particularly in the climate of the times.

There is no question that Gann's research triggered a wave of interest in the emotional factors that could cause reading disability. Her study would have to be considered a major contribution if only for the fact that she introduced the Rorschach as an invaluable tool for exploring the relationship between reading difficulty and personality organization. But her work had even greater impact than that. Unfortunately, as I will show, some prejudice in her research, and especially the interpretations of that research by many in the professional community, created serious problems that have just begun to abate.

This certainly is not meant to imply that there was little interest in the relationship of personality factors to reading prior to Gann's research. In the early 1930s, Blanchard (1928, 1935, 1936) had presented the intriguing psychoanalytic thesis that there is a need on the part of the retarded reader to inflict self punishment in order to relieve anxiety and guilt feelings. In many instances, the reading disability is a disguised expression of hidden motives, satisfying the need for punishment and relieving guilt by exposing the child to a situation of failure in school and to criticism. Blanchard elaborated on her point still further, attributing many reading disabilities to difficulties in establishing masculine identification and in handling aggressive impulses, together with excessive anxiety and guilt over destructive, hostile, and sadistic feelings. The signs of emotional conflict appear chiefly in the educational disability and overactive fantasy life.

Sylvester and Kunst (1943) also had investigated the psychodynamic aspects of reading problems. They viewed the factor of anxiety as being very important in conditioning the learning process. Anxiety in a specific situation may be generated by (1) inadequate capacity for mastery; (2) fear of loss of love; and (3) the child's destructive threat toward the persons on whom he depends. The reading disability thus becomes a defense against anxiety which may be stimulated by curiosity. Sylvester and Kunst conclude that "the disturbances in reading are disturbances of the exploratory function, and that symptomatic treatment by pedagogical methods is not enough. . . . Where tutoring succeeds, it does so because the tutor intuitively has met some of the emotional requirements presented by the child" (p. 70).

In still earlier research, Ladd (1933) studied 315 children in the elementary grades and found no marked relationships existing between reading ability and gross scores on socio-economic status of the home, play interests, and general personality adjustment. However, she did uncover a slight tendency for good reading achievement to be associated with such desirable traits or conditions as better socioeconomic status, absence of foreign language in the home, and better personality adjustment. Ladd concludes that the teacher or psychologist cannot interpret an unfavorable score on a personality test as being a valid indication of the cause of a reading problem.

Preston (1939) found that many of the emotional problems in cases of reading disability have their source in the home relationships. Preston especially was interested in the reactions of parents to children's reading failure. She found that often parents make disagreeable comparisons, remove privileges, and, at times, resort to physical punishment. These parents are characteristically worried, tense, and concerned, all of which certainly do not contribute to the security of the child. It is not surprising then that many of these children come to the reading situation with a great deal of anxiety and apprehension.

McCallister (1930), Bell (1945), and Jastak (1934) are among many others who had investigated the relationship of emotional factors to reading prior to Gann's classic research. What must be emphasized, however, is that no previous study had utilized projective techniques to any extent, and *none* had employed the Rorschach technique (1942) as one of the major assessment instruments. This is rather astonishing since in the early 1940s projective testing was well established as a viable method of exploring the dynamic, interactive aspects of the individual's psyche rather than accumulating an aggregate of discrete personality traits. Essentially the rationale behind the use of a projective test is simple. The individual is presented with a relatively unstructured stimulus. In the course of responding to this stimulus, the person must project his own ideas, wishes, needs, feelings, and experiences onto the stimulus. Thus a projection of the individual personality's private world is elicited because he has to organize the field, interpret the material and react affectively to it. What is obtained amounts to a kind of x-ray of the personality.

critique

Given the advantages of projective tests in comparison to the self-report and rating scales utilized in 1945, it is incredible that the Rorschach had not previously been employed in personality-reading research. It is almost certain that the technique was used widely by clinical psychologists in their individual assessment of children. Gann herself points out that the Rorschach was chosen as the projective technique and "is so widely known at this time, that minute description of the test seems unnecessary" (p. 49). We can only speculate that projective tests, and specifically the Rorschach, were considered to be the tools of the clinical psychologist and were to be used to investigate psychopathology in children, not learning problems. On the other hand, Gann, as a psychologist *and* educator, viewed the reading process essentially as a complex but unitary psychological function, "a type of behavior or experience of an interactive character, in which reader and writer are in communication with each other and which produces changes in the reader, if he has at all responded to the meanings expressed by the writer. This implies a response of the whole personality, comprising ideational, emotional, attitudinal or motor aspects as they organize themselves to respond" (p. 4). In other words, Gann strongly believed that "if the whole personality is involved in reading behavior, and there is a dynamic relation between the reader and the meanings he derives, evidences of difficulty should also be sought in the organization or adjustment of the personality in relation to reading" (p. 9). It is no wonder then that she chose to "break ground" and use the Rorschach as it had never been used before.

If there were a need to speculate on why projective tests had not been used more extensively to explore reading behavior prior to Gann, indeed we know that her pioneer effort detonated a veritable explosion of research investigating personality and reading via the medium of projectives. One of the first to follow-up on Gann's research was Vorhaus (1946) in a study in which two groups of non-readers, differing in their adjustment, were compared. Vorhaus translated the non-reading syndrome which she developed into Rorschach terms, and then she examined the actual Rorschach records for substantiation of her hypothetical picture. She concluded that non-reading is an expression of resistance—that reading is perceived by the child as a symbol of conforming to an accepted pattern of growing up and fitting into a straight jacket.

Stewart (1950) used projective techniques to evaluate personality adjustment and concluded from his data that there is no single personality trait characteristic of all superior or all inferior readers. Siegal (1951), primarily utilizing the Rorschach, attempted to study the range of personality structures in known cases of reading disability and to compare these personalities with those of children who read adequately but present other clinical problems. Siegal concluded that there is a range of personality structures, rather than any particular personality type within a population of reading disabilities. Probably the most comprehensive study following Gann was the one carried out by Vorhaus (1952) in which she attempted to discover certain Rorschach configurations associated with reading disability. Employing a population of 309 cases of retarded readers (never adequately defined), she assumed that emotional factors play an important role in cases in which mentally normal individuals suffer from extreme and long continued reading retardation. Emphasis is placed on intrapersonal dynamics and on the evidence, offered by the Rorschach, that different individuals, reacting to the same environmentally conditioned disturbance, have worked out various kinds of adaptations.

One might suspect that, following Gann's study, the interest in the psychogenic etiology of reading disability, and the use of projective techniques in particular, for the assessment of emotional status, might have been intense but short-lived, but this was hardly the case. Indeed the emphasis on emotional factors continued for at least twenty years. If anything, the projective hypothesis was expanded to encompass the aspects of personality that could be derived from an exploration of the relationships among the subtests of the Wechsler Intelligence Scale for children (1949). Graham (1952) made a study of 96 unsuccessful readers and found that they manifested a definite superiority in favor of performance items over verbal items. It was also discovered that the subtests of Arithmetic, Digit Span, Information, Digit Symbol, and Vocabulary averaged below the mean. Object Assembly, Picture Completion, Picture Arrangement, Block Design, Comprehension, and Similarities averaged above the mean. Graham attributed these differences to emotional factors related to stress. Abrams (1955) attempted to discover whether significant differences existed in the personality characteristics of non-readers and achieving readers. Utilizing the Wechsler, the Rorschach, and a number of objective tests of personality, he found that non-readers experience difficulty in maintaining sustained abstract attention probably as a result of feelings of anxiety. They are acutely aware of their difficulties which are reflected in symptoms of insecurity, irritability, and poor home and school adjustment. They are decidedly more impulsive and less able to respond appropriately to emotional stimuli. "These personality traits bear particular relevance to the non-readers' incapacity for adequate means of expression and effective control of emotions under the stress of reading failure" (p. 79).

It must be emphasized that Gann was interested in demonstrating a *causal* relationship between personality organization and failure in reading. She very clearly states her point of view in carrying out her research: "Reading difficulties and disabilities are part of a larger organization, 'the total personality,' and should therefore be studied in this relationship. The definition, herein submitted is that the personality is a functioning unit—a totality—patterned of part processes which have relationships one to the other, and which influence each other in significant and demonstrable ways. These processes include the organic, affective, volitional, and intellectual life of the person. With a specific situation as a focus, all of these processes will organize themselves and will inevitably operate, influencing each other in ways determined by the structure and maturity of the organism, as well as characteristically by the particular past experiences and present situation of the learner" (p. 35).

Gann's hypothesis logically emerges from the above orientation. "Dynamic processes in the personality organization which determine its means or types of adaptations are related to, and influential in the reading experience. These processes are associated with, or *may be responsible* for the difficulties or retardations" (p. 37, italics mine). The problem, therefore, as she proposes in her investigation, is the study of reading difficulties or disabilities in terms of the organization of the personality as it adapts itself to the reading situation. Again it should be noted that

critique

the Rorschach can be extremely helpful in reflecting the organization of the personality, providing varied patterns of the inadequately or poorly adjusted personality, ranging from mild insecurities or instabilities to the pathologies of the extremely abnormal.

Gann's most important findings are those emanating from her analysis of the Rorschach patterns. Through the use of this technique, she is able to attend to various modes of intellectual functioning as well as specified tendencies to react in characteristic ways emotionally. As she states: "One of the major emphases in the Rorschach materials is the relation between efficient intellectual functioning and the quality of the emotional adjustment. This aspect is especially useful to this study, which is primarily concerned with the effect of the emotional system upon the intellectual one" (p. 66).

Gann indicates that her experimental material substantiates her hypothesis and reflects personalities less able than successful readers to cope with intellectual and social situations that confront them. More specifically, she finds the retarded reader to be emotionally less well-adjusted and less stable, insecure and fearful in relation to emotionally challenging situations, and socially less adaptable in relation to the group. Gann also stresses the retarded readers' apparent inability to make efficient utilization of their potential mental capability. She points out that retarded readers "are not interested in the abstract or theoretical aspects of experience, but prefer the practical and the tangible. Since reading by its nature is more abstract than it is concrete, [retarded readers] would be less inclined to show a prime interest in it" (p. 136). Gann recognizes that this inclination should not prevent retarded readers from achieving at least average success. She points out that their lack of even average success can be explained by "a strong tendency to concern themselves with the small, detailed, and unimportant aspects of a situation. . . . They are inclined to escape from facing the full situation, and will be so affected as to occupy themselves with the unusual or important aspects of a situation" (p. 136). The retarded reader is therefore less efficient in coping with the full implications of a problem. "This tendency would indeed be a limiting influence on a process like reading, which requires comprehension both through abstraction and through appreciation of total meaning" (p. 136).

There is no argument here with Gann's conclusions. Certainly they are supported by the results of her study, specifically the data from the Rorschach analyses. But somewhere along the way, the fact that relationship does *not* necessarily indicate causation has been forgotten. It will be recalled that Gann herself stated that personality processes *may be* responsible for reading difficulties. In her summary, she states: "Though treatment of the data *cannot claim to demonstrate a cause and effect relationship*, the findings are relevant enough to point to possible explanations for the reading difficulty" (p. 136, italics mine). Unfortunately Gann appears to have been anxious to isolate a unique personality structure characteristic of the disabled reader—a type of personality functioning that would lead inevitably to reading failure. Early in her study she points out that previous research had been content to report mainly symptoms of inadequate adaptation or adjustment. "The present investigation attempts an exploration of relationships, patterns, and processes within the personality out of which symptoms may have grown" (p. 37).

critique

If Gann was perhaps overly zealous in her interpretation of her results, she was at least aware of the possible limitations (witness her statement regarding cause and effect). Nevertheless, her conclusions provided a foundation for a variety of clinical practices wherein all too many youngsters experiencing reading disabilities and concomitant emotional problems were shuttled off to a psychotherapist. Unfortunately, all too often, after two or three years in therapy, the children would be discharged with some of their problems resolved but their reading disability still intact. Psychotherapy may be helpful to some youngsters whose reading difficulties are directly the result of emotional disturbance, but most frequently the emotional symptoms are the result of learning failure, not the cause.

There is little doubt that youngsters who have suffered with reading disability over any sustained period of time are going to have serious questions about themselves and their abilities. Constantly frustrated, besieged with intense feelings of defectiveness, it is no wonder that they often react with hostility and various forms of acting out behavior. Is it any wonder that retarded readers are "emotionally less well-adjusted and less stable; and insecure and fearful in relation to emotionally challenging situations?" Many of these children must feel helpless in the face of their inability to learn to read. And when they feel this way, they become even more frightened and anxious. As a result, they tend to become either more aggressive, more hostile, or, sometimes, withdrawn. Gann also points to the lack of interest on the part of the retarded readers in the abstract and theoretical aspects of experience, and their tendency to escape from facing a total situation. I would suspect that any child in danger of further wounding to his narcissism or already hurt pride would beat a hasty retreat. The child must leave the situation because any possibility of failure represents a severe threat to self-esteem. This is basically a type of failure—avoidant behavior, but the extremes to which the child will go to retreat from challenge are remarkable (Abrams, 1980).

As so frequently happens, once the professionals became disenchanted with the results of the psychogenic emphasis, there was a strong shift of the pendulum to the physiologic basis. Terms such as minimal cerebral dysfunction, specific learning disability, dyslexia, and others provided a niche, a label, for children who had puzzled and defeated physicians, parents, and educators for a long time. Disillusioned by what the therapist had been able to accomplish, educators viewed with optimism a treatment which was described as remarkably effective and which consisted of environmental manipulation and specialized education. In other words, the clinical situation had been reversed; neurological factors overpowered functional factors and emerged as the most common cause of learning disabilities in childhood. This, too, is unfortunate because this type of orientation often tends to give short shrift to a very important aspect of the child—his personality. From the psychodynamic view, the child's feelings in relation to himself and feelings about those in the environment greatly influence the motivation for learning. This is in no way meant to minimize the cognitive realm but to reinforce what Gann did stress accurately—that cognition is very much intertwined with the affective sphere.

In conclusion, Gann's study undoubtedly made a significant contribution to our understanding of the intricate relationships between personality development and reading disability. Although her attempt to structure a unique personality characteristic of the disabled reader was unwise, it did elicit a number of research studies that revealed much about the emotional status of youngsters suffering with learning problems. As I have pointed out repeatedly, her willingness to use the Rorschach as it had not been used before, stimulated many studies employing projective tests. Today, despite the continuing controversy over neurological vs. psychogenic causation, there seems to be increasing agreement concerning the need to consider the child's personality. The time-honored question of cause and effect remains the major enigma. The field is in dire need of some carefully constructed experimental studies to investigate some of the problems which have been the subject for argumentation over a great many years. At the present time we may only conclude that emotional and personality maladjustments may operate as a cause of reading disability, as an effect of reading failure, or as both cause and effect.

FOR FURTHER LEARNING

Those readers who are interested in continuing to explore the topic of reading disability would find the following references helpful:

Abrams, J. A psychodynamic understanding of the emotional aspects of learning disorders. In B. K. Koegh (Ed.), *Advances in Special Education*. Greenwich, Conn.: JAI Press, Inc., 1980.

Abrams, J., & Kaslow, F. Learning disability and family dynamics: A mutual interaction. *Journal of Clinical Child Psychology*, 1976, *5*, 35–40.

Blanchard, P. Psychoanalytic contributions to the problems of reading disability. *Psychoanalytic Study of the Child*, 1946, *2*, 163–187.

Gever, B. Failure and learning disability. *The Reading Teacher*, 1970, *23*, 311–317.

Harris, I. *Emotional blocks to learning*. New York: Free Press, 1961.

Pearson, G. H. J. *Psychoanalysis and the education of the child*. New York: W. W. Norton, 1954.

REFERENCES

Abrams, J. *A study of certain personality characteristics of non-readers and achieving readers*. Unpublished doctoral dissertation, Temple University, 1955.

Abrams, J. A psychodynamic understanding of the emotional aspects of learning disorders. In Barbara K. Keogh (Ed.), *Advances in Special Education*. Greenwich, Conn.: JAI Press, Inc., 1980.

Bell, J. E. Emotional factors in the treatment of reading difficulties. *Journal of Consulting Psychology*, 1945, *9*, 128–131.

Blanchard, P. Reading disabilities in relation to maladjustment. *Mental Hygiene*, 1928, *12*, 772–778.

Blanchard, P. Attitudes and emotional disabilities. *Mental Hygiene*, 1929, *13*, 550–563.

Blanchard, P. Psychogenic factors in some cases of reading disability. *American Journal of Orthopsychiatry*, 1935, *5*, 361–374.

Grahan, E. Wechsler-Bellevue and WISC scattergrams of unsuccessful readers. *Journal of Consulting Psychology*, 1952, *16*, 235–241.

Jastak, J. Interferences in reading. *Psychological Bulletin,* 1934, *31*(4), 244–272.

Ladd, M. *The relation of social, economic and personal characteristics to reading ability.* New York: Teachers College, Columbia University, Bureau of Publications, 1933.

McCallister, J. M. Character and causes of retardation in reading among pupils of the seventh and eighth grades. *Elementary School Journal,* 1930, *31,* 35–43.

Preston, M. The reaction of parents to reading failure. *Child Development,* 1939, *10,* 173–179.

Rorschach, H. *Psychodiagnostics.* New York: Grune and Stratton, 1942.

Siegal, M. *The personality structure of children with reading disabilities as compared with children presenting other clinical problems.* Unpublished doctoral dissertation, New York University, 1951.

Stewart, R. Personality maladjustment and reading achievement. *American Journal of Orthopsychiatry,* 1950, *20,* 410–417.

Sylvester, E., and Kunst, M. Psychodynamic aspects of the reading problem. *American Journal of Orthopsychiatry,* 1943, *13,* 69–76.

Vorhaus, P. Non-reading as an expression of resistance. *Rorschach Research Exchange,* 1946, *10,* 60–69.

Vorhaus, P. Rorschach configurations associated with reading disability. *Journal of Projective Techniques,* 1952, *16,* 1–19.

Wechsler, D. *Wechsler Intelligence Scale for Children.* New York: Psychological Corporation, 1949.

A Commentary on Abrams' Critique of Gann's Study: Reading Difficulty and Personality Organization

MERNA M. McMILLAN

Santa Barbara County Mental Health Services

LANCE M. GENTILE

North Texas State University

In his critique of Edith Gann's study, Abrams succinctly describes why he believes the work has historical significance, the controversial issues highlighted by the study, and the unresolved dilemma of precisely defining the etiology of reading difficulties. The continuing concern over the relationship between reading problems and emotional maladjustment is presented in an historical context that aids in understanding the focus and methods of this particular study and subsequent research. In his critique Abrams makes the significant point that conclusive answers are still not available after all these years.

However, according to Abrams, Edith Gann's research did make an unprecedented "impact on the psychological and educational communities." More emphatically he states, "it is hardly likely that she truly recognized the significance of her dissertation, particularly in the climate of the times." Unfortunately, he does not present the evidence to support these claims. Abrams does acknowledge research prior to Gann's, but before she examined the relationship between personality and reading many other prominent researchers documented their findings in this area (Gray, 1925; Hincks, 1925; E. K. Rosen, 1925; Bird, 1927; Strachey, 1930; Newell, 1931; Dolch, 1931; Klein, 1931; Monroe, 1932; Durrell, 1932). Support for this documentation was presented by Natchez (1959). She said:

> Between 1924 and 1933 the first concentrated attention was paid to the relationship of attitudes and personality traits in educational achievement. Widespread use of standardized intelligence and achievement tests had drawn attention to the fact that there was often a high discrepancy between them (usually between 30 and 60 percent). Increasing interest turned to the scientific study of personality in relation to reading. In these studies two prominent hypotheses were advanced. One stated that emotional maladjustment causes poor reading and the other claimed that poor reading causes emotional maladjustment. (p. 9)

Abrams contends, "Gann's research triggered a wave of interest in the emotional factors that could cause reading disability." However, it appears the trigger was pulled 20 years earlier.

What Gann did, and Abrams addresses this directly, is introduce the Rorschach as a testing instrument exploring personality organization and reading problems. Abrams describes Gann's major contribution as encouraging the use of projective tests for examining the relationship between emotional problems and reading. He states that this in itself is reason enough to accord her study high significance. This assertion can be challenged, since there is disagreement among psychologists and educators as to the amount of credence given to the findings of projective instruments. Howes (1981) claimed:

> It is somewhat of a paradox that in the beginning the theory and practice of projective techniques was largely a reaction to the objective (and seemingly dehumanizing) psychometric approach to personality assessment. It is now this apparent lack of objectivity and absence of rigid adherence to psychometric standards which has catalyzed much of the criticism of the projective techniques (Anastasia, 1968; Arthur, 1969; Cleveland, 1976; Cohen, 1973; Davids, 1973; Harrower, 1976; Ivnik, 1977; Moore, Bobbitt, and Wildman, 1968; and others). (p. 339)

Although other researchers have recognized Gann's study as being important (Bond, Tinker, and Wasser, 1979; Sampson, 1968; etc.) they have considered the thrust and results of her research, i.e., to obtain evidence on the question of whether or not reading disorders are an aspect of the total personality to be more significant than the fact that she first used the Rorschach to measure these variables. Natchez (1959), for example, in addition to describing the findings noted by Abrams, writes:

> She took great pains in evaluating personality dynamics through the Rorschach test and other instruments. The traits of "persistence," "concentration," and "impulsiveness" were measured. Results indicated that superior readers appear to be reliably better than average and poor readers in every characteristic save "impulsiveness." Average and poor readers do not differ except in "persistence." In this trait, the three groups are reliably different from each other, becoming increasingly persistent as the groups improve in reading. (p. 10)

Other authors note Gann's use of the Rorschach as well as other tests, but they do not single it out as a noteworthy aspect of her study.

The fact that Gann was the first person to use the Rorschach for this purpose is unquestionably innovative but critics of projective instruments might question how much significance this innovation warrants. It is very likely that they would not perceive the establishment of this trend as positive and would believe the information could be obtained by more objective and reliable methods. Among the reasons for these conflicting opinions is evidence that indicates using the Rorschach to pinpoint emotional disturbances and reading problems may actually induce unwarranted anxiety or stress in younger students with reading difficulties. This could lead to invalid results and erroneous conclusions. Dana (1978) cautioned:

> Examiner bias and expectancy effects are undisputed components of Rorschach experience. Nonetheless, the specific effects upon data and interpretation are only beginning to be described. For example transient stress, specific verbal reinforcement and sex and experience of the examiner affect Rorschach protocols. The anxiety-stimulating potential of the Rorschach itself can affect the entire procedure. The Rorschach is thus an experience for the examinee that is almost inevitably stressful.

> Examiner characteristics, examiner behavior, order of administration, and reasons for assessment, all contribute to unknown situation-specific exacerbations that may lead to over interpretation of the data. (pp. 1041–42)

For some youngsters who have had a history of reading problems, asking them to interpret ambiguous ink blots only mirrors the frustrating experiences they have encountered with reading. In essence, they once again are being required to respond to unintelligible marks on paper. The level of stress may rise in this testing situation because even though students are led to believe there are no right or wrong answers on the Rorschach, their responses are being scored both in terms of quantity (number) and quality (content).

Without inferring cause, the effects of emotional instability or anxiety on performance cannot be discounted in testing or reading. Abrams states, "Psychotherapy may be helpful to some youngsters whose reading difficulties are directly the result of emotional disturbance, but most frequently the emotional symptoms are the result of learning failure, not the cause." Yet there is evidence to the contrary. For some children, attending to the emotional aspects may improve reading performance. Roswell (1954) found that "remedial teaching carried on by a well-qualified tutor with psychological orientation can have therapeutic effects." Natchez (1959) expanded Roswell's statement: "Tutoring which incorporates both educational and psycho-therapeutic techniques may afford the child with reading difficulty a more realistic opportunity to work through his problems." Earlier research by Tinker (1934) led him to conclude: "Emotional maladjustment is primary: prognosis for successful remediation of reading disability is poor until the emotional problem is treated."

A recent study was conducted by Gentile (1981) comparing the gains in reading (comprehension and vocabulary) and self esteem among 52 students enrolled in remedial reading instruction (Group 1), counseling (Group 2), or remedial reading/counseling (Group 3). Over a treatment period of approximately one year, the students enrolled in just counseling (Group 2) showed significant gains in comprehension when compared to the other two groups. Students enrolled in just remedial reading (Group 1) showed a significant decrease in self esteem. No significant differences occurred in comprehension, vocabulary, or self esteem for students enrolled in remedial reading/counseling (Group 3) when compared to students in Groups 1 or 2.

In Gentile's study counselors employed the Minuchin Family Systems counseling methods, which attempt to reduce the amount of conflict/stress within a family that may be blocking a particular member's healthy emotional adjustment. In contrast to Dr. Abrams who claims, "Most frequently the emotional symptoms are the result of learning failure, not the cause," Gentile's findings indicate that if an individual experiences a reduction in the amount of stress or conflict in his/her home life, that person may then be freed from some of the emotional barriers that inhibit the ability to concentrate on and make sense of written text.

Resistance to using the Rorschach and other projective tests has intensified over the years as conflicting theories, new therapies, and additional research findings have emerged. Moreover, today there is much less emphasis on individual assessment than at the time Edith Gann undertook her research. This is a function of both time and circumstance. The factors contributing to this trend include economic considerations, criticism of testing in general and the public demand for "objective" criteria in diagnosing and placing students. Furthermore, during the intervening years since Gann's study, the Rorschach has continued to be the most controversial, most studied, and yet most widely used projective instrument.

Abrams describes the Rorschach as being comparable to an "x-ray of the personality." Extending this analogy, one could argue that gross abuse and misuse of x-rays as diagnostic tools have occurred. Ethical considerations must be invoked in the use of any diagnostic procedure, whether for physical or psychological purposes. First it is essential to question if the information can be obtained by less intrusive, damaging, or stressful means. The final decision should be based on the quality or utility of the information to be gained. Can or will the results be used to ameliorate the identified disorder? The same questions should be applied to repetitive research. At some point practical application should be required. The process of assessing a person's private world with projective instruments may ultimately adhere to the phenomenon described by Adam Smith (1975) as "never easy to explain and impossible to photograph."

Abrams terminates his critique of Gann's study with the acknowledgement, "At the present time we may conclude that emotional or personality maladjustment may operate as a cause of reading disability, as an effect of reading failure, or as both cause and effect." He suggests more research is needed to investigate these issues which have been the source of intense debate for many years. We would suggest it is time for a precise review and synthesis of what is already known in relation to emotional problems and reading difficulties. Without organizing and interpreting this body of knowledge, future investigators will continue to generate repetitive research that leads to more "cataloging" of children's emotional and reading difficulties but fails to provide applicable solutions. It is time not only to "catalogue the Augean stable, but to cleanse it."

REFERENCES

Anastasia, A. *Psychological Testing.* New York: Macmillan, 1968.

Arthur, A. Diagnostic testing and the new alternatives. *Psychological Bulletin,* 1969, *72,* 182–192.

Bird, G. Personality factors in learning. *The Personnel Journal,* 1927, *6,* 56–59.

Bond, S. L., Tinker, M. A., & Wasson, B. *Reading difficulties: Their diagnosis and correction* (4th ed.). Englewood Cliffs, N.J.: Prentice-Hall, 1979, p. 99.

Cleveland, S. Reflections on the rise and fall of psychodiagnosis. *Professional Psychology,* 1976, *7,* 309–318.

Cohen, D. Transient stress, rater bias, and Rorschach interpretation. *Journal of Clinical Psychology,* 1973, *29,* 345–347.

Dana, R. H. Tests and reviews: Personality. In O. Buros, (Ed.), *The eighth mental measurements yearbook.* Highland Park, N.J.: Gryphon Press, 1978, 1041–1042.

Davids, A. Projective testing: Some issues facing academicians and practitioners. *Professional Psychology,* 1973, *4,* 445–453.

Dolch, E. W. *The psychology and teaching of reading.* Boston: Ginn and Co., 1931.

Durrell, D. D. Confusions in learning. *Education,* February 1932, *52,* 330–331.

Gentile, L. M. *The effects of remedial reading, counseling and remedial reading/counseling on students' development of comprehension, vocabulary, and self esteem.* Paper presented at 31st annual National Reading Conference, Dallas, Texas, December 5, 1981.

Gray, W. S. Summary of investigations relating to reading. *Supplementary Educational Monographs,* 1925, (No. 28).

Harrower, M. Rorschach records of the Nazi war criminals: An experimental study after 30 years. *Journal of Personality Assessment,* 1976, *40,* 341–357.

Hincks, E. M. Disability in reading and its relation to personality. *Harvard Monographs in Education,* 1925 (No. 7).

Howes, R. J. The Rorschach: Does it have a future? *Journal of Personality Assessment,* 1981, *45*(4), 339.

Ivnik, R. Uncertain status of psychological tests in clinical psychology. *Professional Psychology,* 1977, *8,* 206–213.

Klein, M. A contribution to the theory of intellectual inhibition. *International Journal of Psychoanalysis,* 1931, *12.*

Monroe, M. *Children who cannot read.* Chicago: University of Chicago Press, 1932.

Moore, G., Bobbitt, W., & Wildman, R. Psychiatric impressions of psychological reports. *Journal of Clinical Psychology,* 1968, *24,* 373–376.

Natchez, G. *Personality patterns and oral reading: A study of overt behavior.* Unpublished doctoral dissertation, New York University, 1959.

Newell, N. For non-readers in distress. *Elementary School Journal,* Nov. 1931, *32,* 183–195.

Rosen, E. K. *The intellectual and educational status of neurotic children.* (Contributions to Education, No. 188) New York: Teachers College Columbia University, 1925.

Sampson, O. Reading and adjustment: A review of the literature. In L. M. Schell & P. Burns (Eds.), *Remedial reading: An anthology of sources.* Boston: Allyn and Bacon, 1968, p. 65.

Smith, A. Powers of Mind, New York: Ballantine Books, 1975, p. 8.

Strachey, J. Some unconscious factors in reading. *The International Journal of Psychoanalysis,* 1930, *11,* pp. 321–31.

Tinker, M. Remedial methods for non-readers. *School and Society,* 1934, *40,* 526.

GENDER-RELATED ISSUES AND READING

SUMMARIES by Patricia L. Anders, of *Sexism and Reading: A Critical Review of the Literature,* and *Adolescent Reading Preferences for Type of Theme and Sex of Character*

RESEARCH by Phillip Goldberg, *Are Women Prejudiced Against Women?*

CRITIQUE by Patricia L. Anders

FOR FURTHER LEARNING

COMMENTARY by Kathleen S. Jongsma, Margaret Griffin, and Lance M. Gentile

This section introduces the reader to studies of gender-related issues and reading. Two of the studies are summarized by Anders and the third is reprinted in its entirety. Anders critiques all three. The focus of her critique, of the first study, *Sexism and Reading: A Critical Review of the Literature,* concerns the lack of sufficient and appropriate criteria used by the authors to conduct and evaluate their reviews. The second study, *Adolescent Reading Preferences for Type of Theme and Sex of Character,* is criticized by Anders for certain aspects of the authors' design and implications. Anders' critique of the third study, *Are Women Prejudiced Against Women?,* takes the position that the author has made an inadequate presentation of the data. Jongsma, Griffin, and Gentile's commentary suggests that gender-related concerns should be secondary to the broader issue of the manner in which reading affects a person's values and beliefs. These authors express concern for the quality of the materials students are assigned to read and the way that readers are portrayed in these materials. Finally, Jongsma, Griffin, and Gentile suggest that future research should stress the overall effects of reading on human behavior instead of simply gender-related issues.

SUMMARY OF A. J. KINGSTON AND T. LOVELACE'S STUDY: SEXISM AND READING: A CRITICAL REVIEW

PATRICIA L. ANDERS

The University of Arizona

This review reports on the findings of 78 studies "which presume to investigate sexism in basal readers, textbooks, and children's literature" (p. 135). A majority of the studies reviewed appear to be of the descriptive type; for example, researchers calculated and reported ratios of males to females mentioned in materials read by children, others calculated ratios of male to female authors cited, and still others reported the number of illustrations which portrayed women in instructional materials. In addition to the descriptive studies, approximately ten of the citations were attributed to publishers' and educators' opinions regarding guidelines for avoiding sexism in educational materials and other publications. The other types of studies reviewed included two empirical studies, one "systematic analysis and interpretation of a massive body of reported research" (p. 174), two opinion polls, and eight essays or reviews "based largely upon the works of others" (p. 152). Kingston and Lovelace report and organize the review data into 11 categories and three tables.

As a result of their review, Kingston and Lovelace raise a number of questions and issues. For example, they resurrect the question of whether schools should "reflect society or should educators, through their curricula and instruction, guide and lead society in order to reform it?" (p. 156). They question also if publishers' guidelines are not really regulations and standards, as those articles "not conforming to these 'guidelines' are returned to authors for revision" (p. 153). In addition, the issue of censorship is discussed. Kingston and Lovelace suggest that "perhaps the time has come for a *bona fide* debate concerning the degree to which such policies and guidelines actually may hinder learning by presenting an unreal, artificial life to school children" (p. 155). Further, the authors ask researchers to "ascertain how grave the problem of sexism and sex role stereotyping actually is" (p. 157). In addition to these educational and social questions, the authors conclude their review with five suggestions for future investigators of this topic.

SUMMARY OF K. C. BEYARD-TYLER AND H. J. SULLIVAN'S STUDY: ADOLESCENT READING PREFERENCES FOR TYPE OF THEME AND SEX OF CHARACTER

PATRICIA L. ANDERS

The University of Arizona

The purpose of this study, as stated by the authors, was "to investigate adolescent preferences for type of theme and sex of character in story synopses derived from contemporary realistic novels for adolescents" (p. 105). Two experiments, a preference for type of theme study and a preference for sex of character study, are reported. The second experiment is discussed here.

A total of 576 subjects in grades seven, nine, and eleven participated in the study (192 subjects from each grade level). The procedures for development of the data gathering instruments and a sample item are included in the report. The data were analyzed by *T*-tests and a $3 \times 2 \times 2$ analysis of variance. The dependent variable for the two types of analyses was the number of synopses chosen with a protagonist of the same gender as the subject. *T*-tests revealed that the mean number of synopses chosen by both the boys and the girls were "significantly greater than the expected chance means of 1.0:t (287) = 4.50, $p<.001$ for girls, and t (287) = 5.59, $p<.001$ for boys" (p. 115). The ANOVA yielded no significant main effects, but

> did yield significant interactions for sex by grade level, F(2,564) = 4.12, $p<.05$, and for sex by school district, F(1,564) = 4.97, $p<.05$. . . . The sex by grade level interaction reflects an increasing preference for male protagonists among boys and a decreasing preference for female protagonists among girls as grade level increases. (p. 115)

ARE WOMEN PREJUDICED AGAINST WOMEN?

PHILIP GOLDBERG

Connecticut College

What happened when college girls evaluated the same articles half written by "John T. McKay," half by "Joan T. McKay."

"Woman," advised Aristotle, "may be said to be an inferior man."

Because he was a man, Aristotle was probably biased. But what do women themselves think? Do they, consciously or unconsciously, consider their own sex inferior? And if so, does this belief prejudice them against other women—that is, make them view women, simply because they *are* women, as less competent than men?

According to a study conductred by myself and my associates, the answer to both questions is Yes. Women *do* consider their own sex inferior. And even when the facts give no support to this belief, they will persist in downgrading the competence in particular, the intellectual and professional competence of their fellow females.

Over the years, psychologists and psychiatrists have shown that both sexes consistently value men more highly than women. Characteristics considered male are usually praised; those considered female are usually criticized. In 1957 A. C. Sheriffs and J. P. McKee noted that "women are regarded as guilty of snobbery and irrational and unpleasant emotionality." Consistent with this report, E. G. French and G. S. Lesser found in 1961 that "women who value intellectual attainment feel they must reject the woman's role"—intellectual accomplishment apparently being considered, even among intellectual women, a masculine preserve. In addition, ardent feminists like Simone de Beauvoir and Betty Friedan believe that men, in important ways, are superior to women.

Now, is this belief simply prejudice, or are the characteristics and achievements of women really inferior to those of men? In answering this question, we need to draw some careful distinctions.

DIFFERENT OR INFERIOR?

Most important, we need to recognize that there are two distinct dimensions to the issue of sex differences. The first question is whether sex differences exist at all, apart from the obvious physical ones. The answer to this question seems to be a unanimous Yes—men, women,

Published by permission of Transaction, Inc. from *Transaction,* Vol. 5, April 1968, pp. 128–30.

and social scientists agree that, psychologically and emotionally as well as physically, women *are* different from men.

But is being different the same as being inferior? It is quite possible to perceive a difference accurately but to value it inaccurately. Do women automatically view their differences from men as *deficiencies?* The evidence is that they do, and that this value judgment opens the door to anti-female prejudice. For if someone (male or female) concludes that women are inferior, his perceptions of women—their personalities, behavior, abilities, and accomplishments—will tend to be colored by his low expectations of women.

As Gordon W. Allport has pointed out in *The Nature of Prejudice,* whatever the facts about sex differences, anti-feminism—like any other prejudice—*distorts perception and experience.* What defines anti-feminism is not so much believing that women are inferior, as allowing that belief to distort one's perceptions of women. More generally, it is not the partiality itself, but the distortion born of that partiality, that defines prejudice.

Thus, an anti-Semite watching a Jew may see devious or sneaky behavior. But, in a Christian, he would regard such behavior only as quiet, reserved, or perhaps even shy. Prejudice is self-sustaining: It continually distorts the "evidence" on which the prejudiced person claims to base his beliefs. Allport makes it clear that anti-feminism, like anti-Semitism or any other prejudice, consistently twists the "evidence" of experience. We see not what is there, but what we *expect* to see.

The purpose of our study was to investigate whether there is real prejudice by women against women—whether perception itself is distorted unfavorably. Specifically, will women evaluate a professional article with a jaundiced eye when they think it is the work of a woman, but praise the same article when they think its author is a man? Our hypotheses were:

- Even when the work is identical, women value the professional work of men more highly than that of women.
- But when the professional field happens to be one traditionally reserved for women (nursing, dietetics), this tendency will be reversed, or at least greatly diminished.

Some 140 college girls, selected at random, were our subjects. One hundred were used for the preliminary work: 40 participated in the experiment proper.

To test the second hypothesis, we gave the 100 girls a list of 50 occupations and asked them to rate "the degree to which you associate the field with men or with women." We found that law and city planning were fields strongly associated with men, elementary-school teaching and dietetics were [illegible]s strongly associated with women, and two fields—linguistics and art history—were chosen as neutrals, not strongly associated with either sex.

Now we were ready for the main experiment. From the professional literature of each of these six fields, we took one article. The articles were edited and abridged to about 1500 words, then combined into two equal sets of booklets. The crucial manipulation had to do with the authors' names—the same article bore a male name in one set of booklets, a female name in the other set. An example: If, in set one, the first article bore the name John T. McKay, in set

research

two the same article would appear under the name Joan T. McKay. Each booklet contained three articles by "men" and three articles by "women."

The girls, seated together in a large lecture hall, were told to read the articles in their booklets and given these instructions.

> "In this booklet you will find excerpts of six articles, written by six different authors in six different professional fields. At the end of each article you will find several questions. . . . You are not presumed to be sophisticated or knowledgeable in all the fields. We are interested in the ability of college students to make critical evaluations. . . ."

Note that no mention at all was made of the authors' sexes. That information was contained—apparently only by coincidence—in the authors' names. The girls could not know, therefore, what we were really looking for.

At the end of each article were nine questions asking the girls to rate the articles for value, persuasiveness, and profundity—and to rate the authors for writing style, professional competence, professional status, and ability to sway the reader. On each item, the girls gave a rating of from 1 (highly favorable) to 5 (highly unfavorable).

Generally, the results were in line with our expectations—but not completely. In analyzing these results, we used three different methods: We compared the amount of anti-female bias in the different occupational fields (would men be rated as better city planners, but women as better dieticians?); we compared the amount of bias shown on the nine questions that followed each article (would men be rated as more competent, but women as more persuasive?); and we ran an overall comparison, including both fields and rating questions.

Law: A Strong Masculine Preserve

These are the total scores the college girls gave to the six pairs of articles they read. The lowest possible score—9—would be the most favorable; the highest possible score—51—the most critical. While male authors received more favorable ratings in all occupational fields, the differences were statistically significant only in city planning, linguistics, and especially—law.

	Mean	
Field of Article	Male	Female
Art History	23.35	23.10
Dietetics	22.05	23.45
Education	20.20	21.75
City Planning	23.10	27.30
Linguistics	26.95	30.70
Law	21.20	25.60

Starting with the analysis of bias by occupational field, we immediately ran into a major surprise. (See box above.) That there is a general bias by women against women, and that it is strongest in traditionally masculine fields, was clearly borne out. But in other fields the situation seemed rather confused. We had expected the anti-female trend to be reversed in traditionally feminine fields. But it appears that, even here, women consider themselves inferior to men. Women seem to think that men are better at *everything*—including elementary-school teaching and dietetics!

Scrutiny of the nine rating questions yielded similar results. On all nine questions, regardless of the author's occupational field, the girls consistently found an article more valuable—and its author more competent—when the article bore a male name. Though the articles themselves were exactly the same, the girls felt that those written by the John T. McKays were definitely more impressive, and reflected more glory on their authors, than did the mediocre offerings of the Joan T. McKays. Perhaps because the world has accepted female authors for a long time, the girls were willing to concede that the female professionals' writing styles were not *far* inferior to those of the men. But such a concession to female competence was rare indeed.

Statistical analysis confirms these impressions and makes them more definite. With a total of six articles, and with nine questions after each one, there were 54 points at which comparisons could be drawn between the male authors and the female authors. Out of these 54 comparisons, three were tied, seven favored the female authors—and the number favoring the male authors was 44!

Clearly, there is a tendency among women to downgrade the work of professionals of their own sex. But the hypotheses that this tendency would decrease as the "femaleness" of the professional field increased was not supported. Even in traditionally female fields, antifeminism holds sway.

Since the articles supposedly written by men were exactly the same as those supposedly written by women, the perception that the men's articles were superior was obviously a distortion. For reasons of their own, the female subjects were sensitive to the sex of the author, and this apparently irrelevant information biased their judgments. Both the distortion and the sensitivity that precedes it are characteristic of prejudice. Women—at least these young college women—are prejudiced against female professionals and, regardless of the actual accomplishments of these professionals, will firmly refuse to recognize them as the equals of their male colleagues.

Is the intellectual double-standard really dead? Not at all—and if the college girls in this study are typical of the educated and presumably progressive segments of the population, it may not even be dying. Whatever lip service these girls pay to modern ideas of equality between men and women, their beliefs are staunchly traditional. There real coach in the battle of the sexes is not Simone de Beauvoir or Betty Friedan. Their coach is Aristotle.

research

A Critique of A. J. Kingston and T. Lovelace, K. C. Beyard-Tyler and H. J. Sullivan, and P. Goldberg's Studies: Sexism and Reading: A Critical Review, Adolescent Reading Preferences for Type of Theme and Sex of Character, and Are Women Prejudiced Against Women?

PATRICIA L. ANDERS

University of Arizona

INTRODUCTION

Sexist . . . feminist . . . women's liberation . . . These and many other associations probably come to mind when one hears or reads the terms "sex differences" or "sexism." These two terms are the usual descriptors for scholarly investigation of gender variables as they relate to the reading process. For the purposes of this chapter the term "gender-related" is adopted because it encompasses the studies discussed without introducing the political implications of "ism" words. Moreover, "gender-related" emphasizes neither differences nor similarities between males and females.

The three articles by A. J. Kingston and T. Lovelace, K. C. Beyard-Tyler and H. J. Sullivan, and P. Goldberg address gender-related questions in different ways; however, the larger issue of reader response is the common thread which ties them together.

CRITIQUE: SEXISM AND READING: A CRITICAL REVIEW

Literature reviews are important and necessary contributions to the professional research community. However, sufficient and appropriate procedures as well as criteria for conducting and evaluating reviews have been lacking. Recently, Jackson (1980) suggests six tasks which should be followed by researchers when conducting and reporting literature reviews. These six tasks provide a model for the criticism of a literature review and are applied to this revisit of Kingston and Lovelace.

Task 1: Selection of Questions or Hypotheses. According to Jackson (p. 442), asking the right question or questions is fundamental to conducting and reporting a scholarly review. Unfortunately, the question(s) asked by Kingston and Lovelace are not reported.

Task 2: Sampling the Research to be Reviewed. Jackson (pp. 444–445) emphasizes that reviewers should report the methods used for the source search. Kingston and Lovelace reviewed 78 articles, and claim in their introductory sentence that "the literature has been filled with articles" about sexism, but do not report their methods for choosing the 78 studies. Of the studies cited in the bibliography, 10 were papers presented at conferences, one was a dissertation (the co-author's) and 46 were journal articles. The remaining 21 citations are from various textbooks, trade books, publishers' reports, newspapers, and technical reports. None of these sources are inherently inappropriate, but an explanation of procedure and reasoning should be provided.

Task 3: Representation of the Characteristics of the Primary Studies. According to Jackson (pp. 445–446), this task is analogous to the data collection step in empirical studies. Essentially, the reviewer has two responsibilities: to report procedures used to represent the studies for analysis; and to report what was done to locate missing information. Kingston and Lovelace included neither type of information in their report.

Task 4: Analyzing the Primary Studies. Jackson defines analysis as the "process by which the reviewer makes inferences from the primary studies" (p. 446). This task is usually complicated because findings can vary moderately or extensively. The variance in results may be caused by "sampling error, differences in the methodological adequacy of the studies, or differences in the phenomena that were studied" (p. 447). Kingston and Lovelace offer no evidence that these factors are considered in their review. For example, the authors discuss seven studies (pp. 145–146) which concluded that male/female social roles were presented stereotypically in materials. These studies were criticized and dismissed for lack of operational definitions and for the lack of defined criteria. Following the seven studies, however, is a report of a study which reviewers describe as "somewhat more elaborate and sophisticated" (p. 146). This study (Saario, Jackson, and Tittle, 1973) confirmed the results that were found in the less well done studies. Might this not suggest that there is some support for the contentions of the previous studies? Jackson would say so, while Kingston and Lovelace suggest that the poorly done studies are of little value.

Analysis of primary studies may also be done by using Glass' meta-analysis procedures. Interested readers should refer to the bibliography for sources of information on meta-analysis.

Task 5: Interpreting the Results. Interpretation of the results of a review should, among other possible types of conclusions, make conclusions about theory, policy, or practice and perhaps offer suggestions for future reviews (Jackson, p. 456). It is clear by their conclusions that Kingston and Lovelace were very disappointed in the

critique

studies they found. In light of their disappointment they did make recommendations for future research. They did not, however, make suggestions for future reviews.

Task 6: Reporting the Review. At a minimum, a review should describe the sampling, measurement, analyses, and findings (Jackson, p. 456). As can be concluded from the above discussion, this was done in only the most superficial sense by Kingston and Lovelace.

This critical review has made a limited contribution to gender-related research. Thorough reviews following the guidelines suggested by Jackson are needed.

CRITIQUE: ADOLESCENT READING PREFERENCES FOR TYPE OF THEME AND SEX OF CHARACTER

Beyard-Tyler and Sullivan have carried out and reported a study which responds, at least in part, to one type of research that Kingston and Lovelace called for: the study of "students' preferences for stereotyped versus non-stereotyped selections" (p. 157). Admittedly, Kingston and Lovelace would probably argue that the authors of the present study did not carry their investigation far enough, as they made no attempt to determine if the materials were stereotypic or sexist, but they did examine adolescents' preferences for sex of protagonist.

The Beyard-Tyler and Sullivan study is an example of a creative design with a logical and reasonable rationale. However, there are a few points having to do with the reporting, design, and implications of the study that merit consideration.

First, one result was that significant interactions were found for sex by school district. The authors have no explanation for this interaction. The similarities and differences of the two districts should have been more fully investigated and reported. The authors should have recommended in their report that this investigation be replicated in parts of the country other than the southwest. Given the significant interaction of sex by school district, one should question whether the subjects represent a normal population.

A second area of concern has to do with the design of the study. The authors do not report the precautions that were taken to insure that the subjects had not already read the books which were the basis of the synopses. If some subjects had read the books, they might have been inclined to select the synopsis with which they were familiar.

Another design-related concern has to do with the synopses. A comparison of the sample synopses used in the sex preference study shows very little similarity between the two passages. One synopsis has to do with the inner workings and feelings of a very confused young person, while the second synopsis seems to have more to do with peer pressure, the law, and society.

A third design question is related to the dependent variable. Subjects were asked to choose one of the synopses. To what extent does this "force choice" represent the subjects' true judgments? What if the subjects judged one synopsis only a little better than the other? The degree to which one feels strongly about a choice might affect the educational implications of this study.

The final design-related question is one of ecological validity. To what extent does subjects' choice of one 100-word synopsis over another 100-word synopsis accurately indicate a preference for books with certain characteristics? Many factors might attract a person to a book—a familiar author, the recommendation of a friend, the review of a respected columnist, the publisher's marketing strategies, or a movie based on the book. Perhaps only occasionally does one select a book based on a synopsis. How valid is it to assume, then, that subjects' choices between synopses represent their preferences for gender of protagonist?

In conclusion, the readers of this research need to be reminded that these are group results representing a small and perhaps unrepresentative sample of the adolescent population. A girl reading novels with a male protagonist should not be dissuaded from that literature on the basis of these results. Second, and this also relates to Kingston and Lovelace, what is the teacher's role? If these results are accepted, should teachers reinforce these preferences, or should they broaden students' horizons by recommending books with alternate gender protagonists?

Finally, these data and results should provide an impetus for further research. While the conclusions reached in this study are tentative, a good beginning has been made. Research investigating questions such as these will make a major contribution toward an understanding of gender-related variables and the reading process.

CRITIQUE: ARE WOMEN PREJUDICED AGAINST WOMEN?

The Goldberg study introduces a third gender variable related to the reading process: the evaluation of male authors and female authors as credible sources. One's ability to evaluate an author as competent and credible is often cited as a skill associated with critical reading (Dale, 1967; DeBoer, 1967; Ernis, 1967; Robinson, 1967; and Spache, 1973). Bettinghaus (1968) proposed that a reader's perceptions of an author's age, sex, or socio-economic status may affect the degree to which that author is judged credible.

A critical reader of Goldberg's study would find many faults. The author makes global generalities without offering much support for his claims. One might wonder, for example, in what context he found that "ardent feminists . . . believe that men . . . are superior to women" (see page 493). Or, how he can be so confident that men, women, and social scientists agree *unanimously* that women are psychologically and emotionally different from men. Scholars may forgive problems such as these but the inadequate presentation of the data is not forgivable. He reports trends in the data and statistically significant results in the same manner with no differentiation and he neglects to report a level of significance.

This study has received considerable attention. A literature search (Lawrence, 1980) revealed 11 studies which built their hypotheses on the basis of Goldberg's results. The findings of these studies were mixed: six of the studies supported Goldberg's conclusions but five found no significant differences.

critique

The Goldberg study and the others emanating from Goldberg suggest that well conceived research investigating readers' evaluations of authors needs to be conducted. Readers should be able to evaluate the competence of an author (Nesbitt and Ross, 1980); yet research in progress (Anders and Steen) suggests that very little is done instructionally to promote this ability. In all likelihood, little is done in schools because of an inadequate research base.

CONCLUSION

Three gender-related research articles have been revisted that represent the types of research being conducted on this topic. Different as these studies are from each other, they may be linked by the common thread of reader response. Researchers and educators are interested in how readers respond to reading materials: researchers because readers' responses (reactions to and evaluations of printed discourse) provide a window into the reading process, and educators because the guiding of readers' responses and the offering of viable alternative responses is a part of teaching.

One aspect of reader response is critical reading. Critical reading—evaluating and making judgments about what one reads—is a fuzzy and little understood area of reading comprehension. Despite the fuzziness connected with critical reading, these three articles, each in its own way, suggest that critical reading is a fertile field for investigation that would probably have far reaching pedagogical implications.

The research, for example, which was reviewed by Kingston and Lovelace, was carried out because the researchers believed that readers' values and belief systems are influenced by what is read. If this is so, and surely it must be true, then school people have a responsibility to portray a balanced reality through the materials they assign to students. It is important and necessary, then, for researchers to describe value-connected (i.e., race-related, gender-related, age-related, etc.) aspects of text. Tangentially, teachers should strive to provide quality materials, authored by individuals who portray their knowledge of the world the best they can, in a classroom environment where questioning and challenging of the printed word is encouraged.

The Beyard-Tyler and Sullivan article investigates readers' responses (reactions) to protagonists who vary by gender. If the conclusions made by the authors are valid, there are several implications for future research and for pedagogy which are related to critical reading. What if adolescents were made aware of their biases toward certain kinds of protagonists? Could their responses be altered? Could readers be taught to control their responses? Or, from a descriptive research angle, were there factors other than gender of protagonists in those synopses that influenced the male and female readers? These questions could all be categorized under the rubric of critical reading; in other words, what is the process of responding judgmentally to written discourse, can it be monitored, and can it be altered?

Goldberg investigated female responses to male authors and to female authors. If the conclusions of this study are to be believed, females judge male authors as more credible than they do female authors. Author credibility is also categorized under the rubric of critical reading (Robinson, 1975 and others). In light of social change and conflicting subsequent research results, more research should be done on readers' evaluations of an author as credible. Further, teachers need to provide opportunities for readers to judge the credibility of authors. This means that reading materials that contain subtle or blatant author biases need to be used in classrooms.

The critique of these articles and the discussion of reader response demonstrates that the research question of gender-related variables and the reading process is multi-faceted and complex. This is essentially uncharted territory which should provide infinite research opportunities. Future researchers investigating this topic should develop and employ creative and comprehensive research designs in order to better understand the role of gender variables and the reading process.

FOR FURTHER LEARNING

Those readers who are interested in continuing to explore the topic of gender-related issues and reading would find the following references helpful.

Anders, P. L. The relationships among status of author, sex of author, sex of reader, and sex-role-identity of reader and the evaluation of an author as credible. Unpublished doctoral dissertation, University of Wisconsin—Madison, 1976.

Frasher, R. S., & Frasher, J. M. Influence of story characters' roles on comprehension. *Reading Teacher,* 1978, *32*(2), 160.

Glass, G. V. Integrating findings: The meta-analysis of research. In L. Shulman (Ed.) *Review of research in education, 5,* Itasca, Ill.: S. E. Peacock, 1978.

Glass, G. V. Primary, secondary, and meta-analysis of research. *Educational Researcher,* 1976, *5,* 3–8.

Guthrie, J. T. Research views. *The Reading Teacher,* March 1981, *34*(6), 748–751.

Juergens-Ellsworth, J., & Stockseth, J. And did he say it, or did she? Selected gender-related variables and mature reading response. In P. L. Anders (Ed.) *Research on reading in secondary schools,* Fall, 1981, *8,* 41–49.

Key, M. R. *Male/female language: With a comprehensive bibliography.* Metuchen, N.J.: Scarecrow Press, 1975.

Light, R. J. Capitalizing on variation: How conflicting research findings can be helpful for policy. *Educational Researcher,* 1979, *8*(9), 7–14.

Light, R. J., & Smith, P. V. Accumulating evidence: procedures for resolving contradictions among different research studies. *Harvard Educational Review,* 1971, *41,* 429–471.

Maccoby, E. E., & Jacklin, C. N. *The psychology of sex differences.* Stanford, Calif.: Stanford University Press, 1974.

REFERENCES

Anders, P. L. & Steen, R. *Author credibility: Who teaches it?* Unpublished manuscript, 1982 (available from P. L. Anders, Department of Reading, College of Education, University of Arizona, Tucson, AZ, 85721).

Bettinghaus, E. *Persuasive communication.* Newark, Del.: Holt, Rinehart & Winston, 1968.

Dale, E. The critical reader. In M. King, B. Ellinger, & W. Wolf (Eds.), *Critical reading.* New York: Lippencott, 1967.

references

DeBoer, J. J. Teaching critical reading. In M. King, B. Ellinger, & W. Wolf (Eds.), *Critical reading.* New York: Lippencott, 1967.

Ernis, R. H. A definition of critical thinking. In M. King, B. Ellinger, & W. Wolf (Eds.), *Critical reading.* New York: Lippencott, 1967.

Jackson, G. B. Methods for integrative reviews. *Review of Education Research,* 1980, *50,* 438–460.

Lawrence, A. Effects of status and gender of author and sex of reader on evaluation of author credibility. Unpublished doctoral dissertation, University of Arizona, 1980.

Nesbitt, R., & Ross, L. *Human inference: Strategies and shortcomings of social judgment.* Englewood Cliffs, N.J.: Prentice-Hall, 1980.

Robinson, H. A. *Teaching reading and study strategies* (2nd ed.) Boston: Allyn and Bacon, 1978.

Robinson, H. M. Developing critical readers. In M. King, B. Ellinger, & W. Wolf (Eds.), *Critical reading.* New York: Lippencott, 1967.

Spache, G. D., & Spache, E. B. *Reading in the elementary school* (3rd ed.). Boston: Allyn and Bacon, 1973.

Mischel, H. N. Sex-bias in the evaluation of professional achievements. *Journal of Educational Psychology,* 1974, *66,* 1957–1966.

Nilson, A. P., Bosmajian, H., Gershuny, H. L., & Stanley, J. P. *Sexism and language.* Urbana, Ill.: NCTE, 1977.

Pheterson, G., Kiesler, S., & Goldberg, P. Evaluation of the performance of women as a function of their achievement and personal history. *Journal of Personality and Social Psychology,* 1974, *4,* 321–329.

Pillemar, D. B., & Light, R. J. Synthesizing outcomes: How to use research evidence from many studies. *Harvard Educational Review,* 1980, *50,* 176–195.

Saario, T. N., Jacklin, C. N., & Tittle, C. K. Sex role stereotyping in the public schools. *Harvard Educational Review,* 1973, *43,* 386–416.

Sheridan, E. M. (Ed.) *Sex stereotypes and reading: Research and strategies.* Newark, Del.: IRA, 1982.

Vygotsky, L. S. Thought and word. In P. Adams (Ed.), *Language and thinking.* Baltimore: Penguin Books, 1972.

A Commentary on Anders' Critique of A. J. Kingston and T. Lovelace, K. C. Beyard-Tyler and H. J. Sullivan, and P. Goldberg's Studies: Sexism and Reading: A Critical Review, Adolescent Reading Preferences for Type of Theme and Sex of Character, and Are Women Prejudiced Against Women?

KATHLEEN S. JONGSMA
and
MARGARET M. GRIFFIN

Texas Woman's University

LANCE M. GENTILE

North Texas State University

In her critique of these three research studies, Anders has allowed some of the concern of the sixties and seventies concerning gender-related issues in reading material to re-surface. However, it would appear that the reading profession's time and energies should be focused on the greater concerns and questions that those who have studied gender-related issues never really addressed, i.e., do reading materials really affect a reader's perceptions of social issues or, more specifically, does reading about gender-related issues influence the reader's attitudes or behavior toward gender?

While not much has been done to study the influence of reading on social issues, Beach (1976) has suggested that researchers need to devote their energies to studying the actual effect or impact of reading on individual behavior. We feel that it is this larger issue that needs to be addressed, rather than the number of text-based, gender-related issues such as male-female pronouns that a writer uses, the ratio of male-female characters portrayed, the number of women presented as working outside the home, etc.

Research has yet to prove that reading usually considered to be sexist materials promotes sexism. For this reason, Beach and others have suggested the need for more research to investigate the relationship between reading about a topic and its impact on sociological or psychological behavior. Such research could clarify once and for all whether, at this level, gender-related issues in reading merit further attention. If research shows little or no link between reading material and an individual's behavior, studies such as those critiqued by Anders should be criticized for posing erroneous or specious research questions, rather than for their design or other methodological flaws.

Prior to commenting further on Anders' critique, it seems important to raise two other important issues that she does not address. In the long run these may prompt more relevant concerns than those raised by the three studies of Kingston and Lovelace, Beyard-Tyler and Sullivan, and Goldberg.

The first concern should stress the quality of material students read, rather than the sex of the protagonist, etc. Reading teachers and classroom teachers in general need to concern themselves with putting more realistic reading material in the hands of students, rather than worrying about matching the gender of a reader with that of the author or that of various characters in a story. Some relatively recent studies (Asher & Markell, 1974; Frasher, 1977; Lovelace, 1980; Scott & Feldman-Summers, 1979; Coley, 1980; Frasher & Frasher, 1978) indicate that story content and interest may be more important than concerns about sex of character. Students will read stories about individuals of the opposite sex if the story content is interesting and motivational. Additionally, Zimet (1972) reported a series of studies demonstrating that few healthy models of readers appear in any of the reading materials used by the schools in the primary grades. Children were not exposed to positive portrayals of reading or readers in literature. In most cases, readers did not even encounter school-related activities in their reading. In a survey of the most widely used basal reading materials in Texas, Burris (1978) discovered that of all the stories portrayed in the reading materials, only two percent involved reading incidents of an explicit nature, and of that two percent, some incidents portrayed negative illustrations of reading and a student's selection of reading as a meaningful activity. Perhaps, if there is a link between reading about reading as an activity itself and/or a person fulfilling the role of a reader, Beach's observation merits further examination. It may be that we need to be more concerned with how readers and reading are portrayed in the materials students read.

Burris (1978) used interviews and her *Reading Enjoyment Scale* to explore the impact character models in stories had on readers. She found that first graders ranked themselves as liking reading more than the reading characters depicted in a story, while fifth graders ranked the reading characters in the stories they read as having more positive attitudes toward reading than themselves. Though extensive research is needed in this area, there are indications that what readers bring to the printed page in terms of attitude about reading affects their perception of the story character models. In this case, a more important question is, does what we read affect our attitudes or do our attitudes remain constant irrespective of what we read? We need this preliminary work of Burris expanded into larger studies that explore the actual effects of reading on the reader.

In light of this, it is curious that Anders chose these three research articles as representing significant gender-related concerns. We asked, why these three? Certainly they are not highly significant. If one thinks of a pivotal study as being that which is frequently cited, only Goldberg's article qualifies. Goldberg's study did spawn many others, and it is frequently cited in articles on gender-related concerns. Kingston and Lovelace, and Beyard-Tyler and Sullivan are not frequently cited, however, and therefore should not be considered in the same vein. However, even if one were only using the criterion of citation as a measure of a study's importance, it seems that Anders would more likely have included the following, any of which has received more attention in the literature: Waples, Berelson, and Bradshaw (1940); Britton and Lumpkin (1977); Zimet (1966, 1972); Women on Words and Images (1972); and Feminists on Children's Literature (1971).

If the criterion for including these three studies was not frequent citation, perhaps Anders selected what she felt to be exemplary research. Exemplification by design or conceptualization is frequently a criterion for considering studies to be significant. If this were the criterion, than all three of the studies she chose must be considered skeptically. Certainly, Goldberg's study contains several major flaws and can be criticized from the standpoint of its sample, treatment, design, and results.

Is the Beyard-Tyler-Sullivan study any better? Perhaps! But it also has some noticeable flaws, the most serious relating to validity. What students selected to read in Beyard-Tyler and Sullivan's contrived research setting may not have had any relation to what they would have chosen to read on their own, given another setting and free choice of reading materials. Of course, this indictment is not aimed at Beyard-Tyler and Sullivan alone; the same criticism applies to most of the research on reading attitudes and interests. Most of these studies are rather artificial and unrelated to free reading practices. When asked to make a decision in a forced-choice setting, students are restricted in a way that is not always representative of the outside world of reading. While Anders does address a few of these concerns, her criticism only touches a small part of the "ecological validity" issue. Nevertheless, she is correct to point out many of the flaws in this body of research.

Anders rightly faults Kingston and Lovelace for failing to address many of the issues in the research they reviewed, and for failing to report studies in enough detail for the reader to recognize their strengths or weaknesses. She suggests that meta-analysis might be a useful technique for analyzing these studies in greater depth. But, while meta-analysis is becoming popular as a technique for analyzing research, we feel there is little use in applying such a technique to gender-related issues in reading materials if the wrong questions continue to be asked.

Finally, Anders comments on Kingston and Lovelace's conclusion that readers' values and belief systems are influenced by what they read. She goes on to state, "If this is so, and surely it must be true, then school people have a responsibility to portray a balanced reality through the materials they assign to students." We question the "and surely this must be true" portion of this statement, for it appears to us that the major problem in the whole area of gender-related issues and reading is the lack of information with respect to reading's overt effects on human behavior. Future research needs to focus on this factor, rather than on text based, gender-related concerns. John Tukey's (1962) statment provides a better perspective of this matter: "The most important maxim for data analysts to heed, and one which many statisticians have shunned, is this: 'Far better an approximate answer to the right question, which is often vague, than an exact answer to the wrong question, which can always be made precise' " (pp. 13–14).

REFERENCES

Asher, S. R., & Markell, R. A. Sex differences in comprehension of high- and low-interest reading material. *Journal of Educational Psychology,* 1974, *66,* 680–687.

Beach, R. Issues of censorship and research on effects of and response to reading. *Journal of Research and Development in Education,* 1976, *9,* 3–21.

Britton, G. E., & Lumpkin, M. For sale: Subliminal bias in textbooks. *Reading Teacher,* 1977, *31,* 40–45.

Burris, N. A. P. *The portrayal of readers in selected elementary reading textbooks and trade books and an exploration of student inferred identification with these story characters.* Unpublished doctoral dissertation, Texas Women's University, 1978.

Coley, C. B. *Reader response to androgynous characterization in juvenile fiction at second, fifth, and seventh grade levels.* Unpublished doctoral dissertation, Washington State University, 1980.

Feminists on Children's Literature. A feminist look at children's books. *School Library Journal,* 1971, *17,* 19–24.

Frasher, R. S. Boys, girls, and Pippi Longstocking. *The Reading Teacher,* 1977, *30,* 860–863.

Frasher, R. S., & Frasher, J. M. Influence of story characters' role on comprehension. *The Reading Teacher,* 1978, *32,* 160–164.

Lovelace, T. Elementary readers' inferences and preferences for characteristics of protagonists in stories. In M. L. Kamil & A. J. Moe (Eds.), *Reading research: Studies and applications,* 1979, 249–253.

Scott, K. P., & Feldman-Summers, S. Children's reactions to textbook stories in which females are portrayed in traditionally male roles. *Journal of Educational Psychology,* 1979, *71,* 396–402.

Tukey, J. W. The future of data analysis. *Annals of Mathematical Statistics,* 1963, *33,* 13–14.

Waples, D., Berelson, B., & Bradshaw, F. R. *What reading does to people.* Chicago: University of Chicago Press, 1940.

Women on words and images. *Dick and Jane as victims: Sex stereotyping in children's readers.* Princeton, N.J.: National Organization for Women, 1972.

Zimet, S. G. Children's interest and story preferences; A critical review of the literature. *Elementary School Journal,* 1966, *67,* 122–130.

Zimet, S. G. (Ed.). *What children read in school.* New York: Grune and Stratton, 1972.

section XI

CULTURAL DIFFERENCES AND READING

RESEARCH by Lance M. Gentile, *Effect of Tutor Sex on Learning to Read*

CRITIQUE by Jesus Garcia and John W. Logan

FOR FURTHER LEARNING

COMMENTARY by Lance M. Gentile

RESEARCH by George Weber, *Inner-city Children Can Be Taught to Read*

CRITIQUE by Irving P. McPhail

FOR FURTHER LEARNING

COMMENTARY by Al Kingston

This section introduces the reader to studies of cultural differences and reading. Garcia and Logan critique Gentile's work, *Effect of Tutor Sex on Learning to Read.* These authors make the point that the examination of a single variable regarding reading achievement is shortsighted. They also feel that until recently there has been an attempt to ascribe ethnic learners' reading difficulties or lack of success in school to their cultural backgrounds. Garcia and Logan point to Gentile's study as one such example from the 1970s. Their critique disavows many of the findings of earlier research in the area of sex differences and reading achievement. Gentile's comments acknowledge some of Garcia and Logan's criticisms as being well founded but he presents a defense of the study from the standpoint of how it was conceived, the underlying principles that guided his thinking at that time, and what he has learned since that conflicts with or supports the findings of this original study.

McPhail critiques Weber's study, *Inner-city Children Can be Taught to Read.* His remarks concern the new thrust in research in the field of urban education which focuses on successful educational practices. He claims this movement has provided evidence to dispel the myth that urban schools are inevitably and irreparably inferior. McPhail sees Weber's work as being representative of this kind of research because it investigated identifiable school-oriented practices instead of factors related to students' socioeconomic backgrounds. Kingston agrees with McPhail's basic premise but finds his criticisms to be somewhat "gentle." He feels Weber's findings would have more impact had the critieria for determining essential or non-essential teacher behavior and pedagogical methodology been operationally defined. Kingston feels that descriptive statements in the original study force the reader to accept Weber's generalizations.

EFFECT OF TUTOR SEX ON LEARNING TO READ

LANCE M. GENTILE

Gentile teaches graduate courses in reading at Pan American University, Edinburg, Texas, where he is an associate professor. He also serves as a consultant for implementing bilingual reading programs.

It has been observed that, in general, girls establish a definite superiority in educational achievement during the elementary grades. Preston (1962) showed that American girls were better readers than American boys. Numerous studies support the observation that boys have more difficulty with reading than do girls. The interactions of the particular variables that account for this phenomenon have been difficult to isolate.

There has been an historical interest in identifying these variables. Some researchers have stressd maturational differences, particularly in emotional and intellectual development. Bentzen (1963), however, contended that boys' achievement in reading is lower because boys are slower to mature physically than girls. He noted that girls generally reach maturity about a year and a half earlier than boys.

Monroe (1932) attempted to account for the differences between boys and girls by suggesting that the incidence of certain constitutional factors that hinder progress in reading may be greater among boys. Gallagher (1948) indicated that the difference might be explained on the basis of heredity and suggested that a substantial deviation in the language mechanism may be a primary cause of reading disability.

Other researchers have intimated that girls possess a natural advantage of interest in verbal rather than mechanical or athletic activities. Sheridan (1948) suggested that girls, even those of lesser intelligence, have a superior language sense. However, Harris (1956) determined that girls' sewing and doll-playing activities may help to develop fine manual skills and improve near point vision.

Earlier it was suggested that the prevalence of women teachers may be a determining factor. Ayres (1909) concluded that schools were better fitted to the needs and natures of girls than of boys. It was his feeling that the poorer showing of the boys was the result of over-feminization. St. John (1932) agreed with Ayres and pointed out that:

> . . . the consistent inferiority of the boys in school progress and achievement is due chiefly to a maladjustment between the boys and their teachers which is the result of interest, attitudes, habits, and general behavior tendencies of the boys to which the teachers (all women) fail to adjust themselves and their school procedures as well as they do to the personality traits of girls.

From *The Reading Teacher,* May, 1975, pp. 726–30. Reprinted with permission of the author and the International Reading Association.

Betts (1957) also observed:

> First, there is some evidence to the effect that girls are promoted on lower standards of achievement than boys are. Second, girls use reading activities for recreation more often than boys do. Third, there is a need for more reading materials to challenge the interest of boys.

A related factor may be the different roles society expects of boys and girls. Smith and Dechant (1961) claimed that:

> . . . boys are supposed to be athletic and aggressive; girls are expected to be physically inactive and docile. And the non-reading boy's aggressiveness leads him to create trouble in school whereas the non-reading girl's tractability causes her to suffer in silence. Thus it may be that boys tend to be referred to clinics in greater numbers because their aggressive symptoms bring them so sharply to parent and teacher notice.

Thus the implications of the differences between the achievement of boys and girls may be influenced by the conflict boys face in trying to engage in the "passive, docile, conforming" behaviors favored by female teachers while attempting to behave in an active, "masculine" manner deemed appropriate for American males.

The Mexican-American boy is not only surrounded by this Anglo concept of maleness but is strongly affected by the cultural influence of masculinity called "machismo," a compulsive view of maleness emphasizing physical strength, sexual prowess, self-confidence, aggressiveness, and courage, which many Mexican-American men rate so highly. Aramoni (1971) attempted to crystallize the essence of this cultural phenomenon and stated that:

> Machismo is a reaction and a paradoxical behavior in which the male seeks hypermanliness to prove himself "very much a man," "very macho,"—man, more man, most man.

Silvaroli(1963) stated that:

> . . . the evidence seems to indicate that when children of different cultural backgrounds are compared, the child with the home background which is more oriented to the values reflected in the school has an advantage both in readiness for reading and for later achievement in reading.

It may be, therefore, that the Mexican-American boy is operating with an added disadvantage over his Anglo classmates in attempting to meet the expectations of two cultures not consonant with many female teachers' standards. Chilcott (1968) pointed out that the school culture for the Mexican-American student is seldom compatible with his overall cultural background. Based on the evidence reported by Chilcott, it would appear that if the Mexican-American boy misbehaves in or repudiates the school, he does so because he values rewards of his own culture more than those of the school. Mattila (1973) stated that:

> Mexican-American students are authoritarian and male-oriented in their leadership expectation. Consequently, permissiveness tends to be interpreted as weakness, and the verbal, positive leader who knows what he wants is easily accepted.

Empirical evidence supporting the efficacy of male teachers in the elementary school has been contradictory. However, Mazurkiewicz (1960) studied cultural differences that might account for the fact that boys outnumber girls by a four-to-one ratio in the retarded reading population. Based on Mazurkiewicz's study, it may be that society holds stereotyped views of what "real" boys and "real" girls are thought to be like. According to this stereotype, boys are good athletes, never show emotions, scorn such activities as music, art and reading, and are tall, strong, and forceful.

The results of Mazurkiewicz's study would indicate that in the population studied males generally view reading as a mostly feminine activity and that this attitude may exert some influence on a boy's reading ability. The hypothesis that achievement in reading is to some extent a reflection of some cultural influences appears to have been substantiated.

In light of the evidence reported thus far, it may be that if Mexican Amercian boys worked with male tutors, a compatible identity might develop with reading and intellectual pursuits. The potential for increasing reading achievement of Mexican-American boys taught by male tutors calls forth some interesting speculations. A confounding effect may occur if all tutors were members of either Anglo of Mexican-Amercian ethnic groups. It may also be necessary to use students from more than one grade level to determine whether any interactions between or among grade levels exist. In order to investigate this problem the following study was undertaken.

Method of study

A random sample of sixty Mexican-American boys from the second, third and fourth grades was drawn from the population of the Saguaro Elementary School in Casa Grande, Arizona. More than one-third of the school's enrollment was comprised of Mexican-American children, most of whom were functioning below grade level in reading. Ten male and ten female tutors were randomly drawn from the population of the Arizona Job Colleges, also located in Casa Grande, Arizona. AJC is a federally and privately funded project which trains persons who meet the national poverty guidelines in specific vocational skills so that they may qualify for future job placement. One-half of the male tutors and one-half of the female tutors were Mexican-American and the other half were Anglo. This distribution allowed the researcher to block on the possible nuisance variable of tutor ethnic group. The tutors were trained for two weeks (twenty hours) to construct and use materials from the National Reading Center's Right to Read Tutorial Program. This package contains sixty unsequenced lessons and also a problem-solving exercise booklet designed for the relatively unskilled paraprofessional tutor to teach decoding, comprehension, structural analysis, study and motivation skills, and reading in the content areas. Ongoing training to expand procedural techniques was extended throughout the experiment. One boy from each of the three grade levels was randomly assigned to each tutor.

The tutors worked with each student twice a week in one-hour sessions for a period of eight weeks. Pretest measures included Form I of the Gates-MacGinitie Reading Tests, Primary A for second and third grade. In addition, the Classroom Reading Inventory (CRI, Silvaroli) was administered to all grades. The same measures were used as posttests (Form 2 of the Gates-MacGinitie and Form B of the CRI). All tests were administered by reading specialists whose sex matched the sex of the student. The Gates-MacGinitie tests provided a vocabulary and a comprehension score, while the CRI provided a graded word list score and a comprehension score. Thus, four dependent variables were available for each subject, constituting a

Tutoring schedule

Time	Monday		Tuesday		Wednesday		Thursday		Friday
9:00 a.m.	Tutor Male	N = 5	Tutor Male	N = 5	Tutor Male	N = 5	Tutor Male	N = 5	Each week this day was set aside for the purpose of the planning and preparation of materials to be used during forthcoming tutorial sessions. The investigator as well as the tutors met for a full two hours.
	Students 2nd & 3rd	N = 10	Students 2nd & 3rd	N = 10	Students 4th	N = 5	Students 4th	N = 5	
	Tutor Female	N = 5	Tutor Female	N = 5	Tutor Female	N = 5	Tutor Female	N = 5	
	Students 2nd & 3rd	N = 10	Students 2nd & 3rd	N = 10	Students 4th	N = 5	Students 4th	N = 5	
10:00 a.m.	Tutor Male	N = 5	Tutor Male	N = 5	Tutor Male	N = 5	Tutor Male	N = 5	
	Students 2nd & 3rd	N = 10	Students 2nd & 3rd	N = 10	Students 4th	N = 5	Students 4th	N = 5	
	Tutor Female	N = 5	Tutor Female	N = 5	Tutor Female	N = 5	Tutor Female	N = 5	
	Students 2nd & 3rd	N = 10	Students 2nd & 3rd	N = 10	Students 4th	N = 5	Students 4th	N = 5	

The above chart represents a one week period in the Saguaro Elementary School. The tutors were randomly selected and assigned to students among the various grades.

four-way multivariate analysis with repeated measures. Factors in the design were tutor sex, two levels; tutor ethnic group, two levels; grade level, three levels; and trial, two levels.

The data were analyzed in three multivariate analyses. All sixty students were compared using the CRI graded word lists and comprehension scores. Second and third grade students were compared using all four dependent measures. The fourth grade students were also compared using all four dependent measures. The effects which were of interest for all three analyses were the trial effect and any interactions involving trial as a factor. That is, the researcher wanted to determine if all students changed or adjusted their reading behavior during the tutorial experiment and, perhaps more importantly, whether a particular tutor sex or tutor-sex-grade level combination was more effective than others in producing any significant differences. The level of confidence chosen was .05.

A significant trial effect for both the CRI graded word lists and comprehension scores was found for the total group. The tutor sex by trial interaction was not significant. However, the tutor sex by grade by trial interaction was significant for the CRI graded word list scores. An examination of the means showed a differential effect of tutor sex at the second and third, but not the fourth grades. For the second grade students, the female tutored group had a higher mean gain score than the male tutored group, while in the third grade the male tutored group had a higher mean gain score. The means were practically identical for the fourth grade groups. An interesting interaction that was also significant was the grade by trial interaction, where fourth grade students made the greatest gain on both measures.

A significant trial effect for all four measures was found for the second and third grade group. However, no other interactions involving the trial effect were significant, except for the previously mentioned tutor sex by trial interaction.

No trial effect interactions were significant for the fourth grade group. However, the trial main effect was significant for all four measures.

It appears that the students as a total group made a significant gain over the eight week tutoring treatment but that the different grade levels made varying amounts of gains. The "seesawing" of the tutor sex grade level means may suggest that, at the lower grades, women tutors are more effective in producing significant gains. However, starting in the upper primary grades, men tutors are either more effective or no difference exists between tutor sexes.

It is not clear why fourth grade students made a significantly greater gain than the other groups. It may be that the regular classroom reading activities at this particular level, in contrast to those at the lower grade levels, interacted positively with the tutoring activities.

The results of this study suggest that male tutors affect greater gains in the reading achievement of Mexican-American boys for at least one grade level. Further research in this area should probably investigate this effect over a broader range of grade levels and also might compare the scores of Anglo, Black, Indian, or Oriental boys tutored by males. If particular tutor sex effects are significant, a long term goal may be to analyze the male, or female, tutor's behavior in order to determine which components effect the most gain in reading achievement. Further investigation is needed to develop more appropriate testing instruments and tutorial materials that reflect the experiential background of culturally and linguistically different students. The evidence gathered in this study would indicate a need for a replication using instruments to measure self-concept or attitudinal adjustments to reading. It may be that these aspects of growth are more sensitive to change than reading achievement gains per se.

REFERENCES

Aramoni, A. "Machismo," *In the Name of Life,* B. Landis and E. S. Tauber. Eds. New York, New York, Holt, Rinehart, and Winston, 1971.

Ayres, Leonard P. *Laggards in Our Schools.* New York, New York, Russell Sage Foundation, 1909

Bentzen, Francis, "Sex Ratios in Learning and Behavior Disorders." *American Journal of Orthopsychiatry,* vol. 33 (1963), pp. 92–8.

Betts, Emmett Albert, *Foundations of Reading Instruction,* New York, New York: American Book Company, 1957.

Chilcott, J. "Some Perspectives for Teaching First Generation Mexican-Americans." *Readings in the Socio-cultural Foundations of Education.* J. H. Chilcott and others. Eds. Belmont, California. Wadsworth Publishing Co., Inc., 1968.

Gallagher, J. Roswell, "Can't Spell, Can't Read" *Atlantic Monthly,* vol. 181 (June 1948), pp. 35–9.

Harns, Albert J. *How to Increase Reading Ability,* third edition, New York, New York: Longman Green & Company, 1956.

Mattila, Ruth H. "As I See Spanish-speaking Students." *The Reading Teacher,* vol. 26, no. 6 (March 1973), pp. 605–8.

Mazurkiewicz, A. J., "Social-cultural Influences and Reading." *Journal of Developmental Reading,* vol. 1 (1960), pp. 235–40.

Monroe, Marion, *Children Who Cannot Read,* Chicago, Illinois, University of Chicago Press, 1932.

Preston, R. C., "Reading Achievement of German and American Children," *School and Society,* vol. 90 (1962), pp. 350–4.

Sheridan, Mary D., *The Child's Hearing for Speech,* London, England: Methuen & Company, Ltd., 1948.

Silvaroli, Nicholas J., Intellectual and Emotional Factors as Predictors of Children's Success in First Grade Reading. Unpublished doctoral dissertation, Syracuse University, 1963.

Smith, Henry P. and Emerald V. Dechant, *Psychology in Teaching Reading,* Englewood Cliffs, New Jersey, Prentice-Hall, Inc., 1961.

St. John, Charles W., "The Maladjustment of Boys in Certain Elementary Grades," *Educational Administration and Supervision,* vol. 18, (1932), pp. 659–72.

A Critique of L. M. Gentile's Study: Effect of Tutor Sex on Learning to Read

JESUS GARCIA AND JOHN W. LOGAN

Texas A & M University

If one is to fully appreciate the approaches employed by Gentile and others who addressed the reading needs of minority children in the 1960s and early 1970s, an historical analysis of the educational literature concerning Mexican-Americans is warranted. Until recently, the attempt has always been to look at background experiences of ethnic learners to explain their lack of success in school settings. In the early 1900s, with the influx of Mexican immigrants to the Southwest, school officials established "Mexican schools" aimed at Americanization of this population. As late as the 1950s, the Mexican-Americans were assigned to programs that ensured their subordinate positions in society. At the elementary level, learners were provided with a rudimentary education and teachers expressed little concern regarding Mexican-Americans who did not learn as well as their Anglo counterparts. Secondary schools also offered little assistance and the consensus was that a general or vocational education was in the group's best interests. Few educators questioned the rationale supporting such educational thrusts (Carter & Segura, 1979).

The 1960s resulted in a change in the status quo. Educators rediscovered Mexican-Americans and seriously attempted to rectify the inequities in schools. Unfortunately, the approaches that surfaced were extremely narrow and focused on perceived deficiencies (social, cultural, psychological) that precluded school success.

The research literature dealing with minority groups indicates that several studies in the 1960s and early 1970s described the academic difficulties of "disadvantaged" Mexican-American learners (Peterson, 1981). Several reasons were provided to explain these academic difficulties. Educators hypothesized that Mexican-Americans performed poorly because they possessed a poor self-concept. Low self-esteem was attributed to the learner's negative experiences at home and in formal school settings. Williamson indicated that "of all the areas of personality correlated with reading achievement, one factor—self-concept—seems to be particularly useful for reading teachers" (1973, p. 35).

Another explanation dealt with the fact that Mexican-American learners experience success at home and bewilderment with rejection at school. Unable to resolve differences between home and school, many of these learners left the school setting. A fourth explanation suggested that peculiar personality traits among lower-class Mexicans inevitably resulted in school failure. This theory maintained that lower-class Mexican-Americans do not join formal organizations, are more physical than verbal, are fatalistic in their beliefs, and possess other such negative characteristics.

These personality traits often clashed with school expectations, resulting in school failure.

Another suggestion was that poverty was the major variable accounting for school failure. Litsinger reports, "poverty is so prevalent among Mexican-Americans that it must be considered as an element in their characterization" (1973, pp. 36–37).

Many approaches to educating Mexican-Americans in the 1960s and early 1970s were often interpreted as being biased. The lack of school success among Mexican-American learners was attributed to group characteristics or forces closely associated with the group. This is not to suggest that researchers of the 1960s and 1970s were racially motivated. Rather, we feel the approach of "blaming the victim" is the initial tactic a social agency employs to explain its inability to provide for the targeted group. Other groups, e.g., handicapped and gifted, have experienced similar treatment.

The Gentile article is an early 1970s endeavor that describes a method of assisting elementary Mexican-American learners to enhance their reading capabilities. Gentile focused on one cultural characteristic—machismo—to explain why Mexican-Americans read poorly. The results suggested that fourth-grade Mexican-American boys in the study learned to read better when tutored by males. This conclusion reinforced a prevailing attitude that the culture was a major influence in the ability of Mexican pupils to become effective learners. Today, a less parochial view is being assumed when examining why Mexican-American learners do poorly in schools. Educators of the 1980s think in a much broader perspective that focuses on the examination of school organization and school-related practices to help the Mexican-American learner.

Educational researchers of the 1980s are also less likely to attribute the lack of school success among Mexican-American learners to single variables (i.e., machismo, poverty, language handicaps). Researchers are aware that the problems Mexican-American learners experience in public schools are extremely complex. Typically, researchers examine a number of variables such as group characteristics, societal forces, school practices, teacher behaviors, and the curriculum. These approaches in identifying why Mexican-American children do not read well may prove more productive than the more narrowly focused research of the 1960s and 1970s. Other variables specifically related to sex roles and reading achievement will be discussed more explicitly in the following section of this critique.

SEX ROLES AND READING ACHIEVEMENT

A multiplicity of variables associated with sex roles and differences, classroom instruction, and reading achievement has been studied by research investigators for several decades (e.g., Austin, Clar, & Fitchett, 1971; Ayers, 1909; Downing, 1973; Rosenberg & Sutton-Smith, 1964, 1969). Sex as a potent predictor of human behavior is a well-established belief, and several differences between achievements, attitudes, and behaviors of the sexes have been reported (Bank, Biddle, & Good,

critique

1980). Even though there is controversy regarding magnitude, causes, and implications of these differences, most investigators would agree that societal expectations do impact sex roles. Because sex roles are often markedly distinct, society often expects children to perform and behave in a fashion deemed appropriate to their sex (Bank, et al, 1980).

In the United States, one major contention is that, by and large, girls perform better in reading achievement and verbal skills than do boys (Blom, 1971). Gentile's study goes beyond substantiation of this general concern by specifically examining whether or not male tutors affect gains in the reading achievement of Mexican-American boys. Gentile speculated that Mexican-American boys are at a disadvantage in Anglo classrooms due to their perceived need to exhibit "machismo"—a behavior classroom teachers often perceive as inappropriate. Gentile hypothesized that Mexican-American boys, given the opportunity to relate more readily to a male, would exhibit significant reading achievement gains. Readers of this article need to be aware that a great deal of current literature in sex roles and reading achievement has become available since the development of the Gentile study. This information indicates that not a single variable, but rather a wide range of variables, influences reading achievement among children. Although Gentile may not have intended the specific conclusion that male tutors only can make the difference in enhancing reading achievement among Mexican-American boys, individuals who read his article and lack understanding of other considerations may arrive at this conclusion.

Based upon a review of the literature, Bank, et al. (1980) provide a rather comprehensive set of hypotheses that attempts to account for several of these variables. Their cumulative list of hypotheses is based upon several conclusions of many studies that dealt with sex roles and reading achievement. For example, physical maturation was once thought a possible explanation as to why reading achievement is higher among girls than boys. It is now considered questionable due to the contradictory data surfacing from numerous cross-cultural studies. For example, Gentile reports that in the Preston (1962) study, reading achievement among American girls was greater than their male counterparts. However, further examination of this notion indicates that on a cross-cultural scale, sex differences and reading achievement are often of little significant difference, or show evidence that boys outperform girls (e.g., Japan, Germany, Nigeria). As a result, Downing (1973) cautions researchers against making conclusions that favor one sex over the other. Other hypothetical variables that Bank, et. al. (1980) suggest include:

1. feminization of reading (the consideration that reading is a feminine activity),
2. discrimination hypothesis (the notion that teachers' expectations for appropriate pupil behaviors lead them to treat boys and girls differently due to their sexual identities),
3. differential response hypothesis (suggests that teachers notice and respond to the different behaviors and interests of pupils, rather than to sex and experiential background elements),
4. sex relevant teaching styles (views teachers as persons who hold different values of instruction that produce varying teaching styles), and

5. female teacher bias (the notion that prejudice exists toward boys in the classroom).

A recent summary of the research related to sex differences in reading suggests some findings contradictory to those suggested by Banks, et al. (1980):

1. Negative treatment—Boys appear to have more types of interaction with both male and female teachers. Female teachers do not exhibit a greater amount of negative treatment to boys.
2. Grades—There is little evidence to suggest that female teachers are biased toward giving higher grades to girls.
3. Higher achievement—No support was found for the idea that boys' achievement is higher when taught by males.
4. Alienation—It does not appear that female teachers structure their classrooms in ways that alienate boys.

(Heilman, Blair, & Rupley, 1981, (pp. 82–83)

Overall, there is insufficient evidence to suggest that female teachers negatively affect boys' reading capabilities and that, at this time, little evidence supports the notion that the sex of the teacher accounts for the difference between boys' and girls' reading achievement.

In summary, we recommend that readers of this study keep in mind the many variables that could have enhanced the reading achievement of the Mexican-American boys in this investigation. More important, we agree with Gentile's recommendation that individuals responsible for reading instruction of Mexican-American learners consider the experiential and conceptual backgrounds of these pupils when matching instructional strategies and materials for classroom reading purposes. Materials used and developed for instruction should reflect "real life," functional, and meaningful content relative to Mexican-American learners, as well as provide a rich source of purposeful reading skills.

FOR FURTHER LEARNING

Those readers who are interested in continuing to explore the topic of cultural differences and reading would find the following references helpful:

Campbell, P. B., & Wortenberg, J. How books influence children: What the research shows. *Interracial Books for Children Bulletin*, 1980, *11*(6), 3–6.

Downing, J. *Comparative reading: Cross-national studies of behavior and processes in reading and writing*. New York: Macmillan, 1973.

Entwistle, D. R. Implications of language socialization for reading models and for learning to read. *Reading Research Quarterly*, Fall 1971, 7(1), 111–167.

Finn, J. D. *Sex differences in educational outcomes: A cross national study*. Paper presented at annual meeting of the American Educational Research Association, San Francisco, April 1976.

Foshay, A., et al. *Educational achievements of 13-year-olds in 12 countries.* Hamburg: UNESCO Institute for Education, 1962.

Frasher, R. S., & Frasher, J. M. Influences of story characters' role on comprehension. *The Reading Teacher,* Nov. 1978, *32,* 160–64.

Gates, A. I. Sex differences in reading ability. *Elementary School Journal,* May 1961, *61*(8), 431–434.

Gunderson, D. V. Sex differences in language and reading. *Language Arts,* March 1976, *53*(3), 300–306.

Johnson, C. S., & Greenbaum, G. R. Are boys disabled readers due to sex role stereotyping? *Educational Leadership,* March 1980, *37,* 492–496.

Johnson, D. D. Sex differences in reading across cultures. *Reading Research Quarterly,* 1973–74, *9*(1), 67–86.

Kingston, A. J., & Lovelace, T. Sexism and reading: A critical review of the literature. *Reading Research Quarterly,* 1977–78, *13,* 133–161.

Klein, H. A. Cross-cultural studies: What do they tell about sex differences in reading? *The Reading Teacher,* May 1977, *30*(8), 880–886.

Maccoby, E., & Jacklin, C. *The psychology of sex differences.* Stanford, Calif: Stanford University Press, 1974.

Malmquist, E. *Factors related to reading disabilities in the first grade of the elementary school.* Stockholm: Almquist and Wiksell, 1958.

Orlow, M. Literacy training in West Germany and the United States. *The Reading Teacher,* Feb. 1976, *29*(5), 460–467.

Preston, R. C. Reading achievement of German and American children. *School and Society,* Oct. 1962, *90,* 350–354.

Preston, R. C. Issues raised by the Wiesbaden-Philadelphia study. *Comparative Education Review,* June 1963, *7,* 61–65.

Rupley, W. H., Garcia, J., & Longnion, B. Sex role portrayal in reading materials: Implications for the 1980s. *The Reading Teacher,* April 1981, *34*(7), 786.

Sexton, P. *The feminized male classrooms, white collars and the decline of manliness.* New York: Random House, 1969.

Stroud, J. B., & Lindquist, E. F. Sex differences in achievement in the elementary and secondary schools. *Journal of Educational Psychology,* Dec. 1942, *33,* 657–667.

Thorndike, R. L. *Reading comprehension education in 15 countries: An empirical study.* New York: Halsted Press, 1973.

Tibbetts, S. L. Wanted: Data to prove that sexist reading material has an impact on the reader. *The Reading Teacher,* Nov. 1978, *32,* 165–168.

REFERENCES

Austin, D., Clar, U., & Fitchett, G. *Reading rights for boys.* New York: Appleton-Century-Crofts, 1971.

Ayers, L. *Laggards in our schools.* New York: Russell Sage Foundation, 1909.

Bank, B., Biddle, B., & Good, T. Sex roles, classroom instruction, and reading achievement. *Journal of Educational Psychology,* 1980. 72(2), 119–132.

Blom, G. E. Sex differences in reading disability.

In E. Calkins (Ed.), *Reading forum*. Bethesda: National Institute of Neurological Disease and Stroke, 1971.

Carter, T., & Segura, R. *Mexican Americans in school: A decade of change*. Princeton: College Entrance Examination Board, 1979.

Downing, J. *Comparative reading: Cross-national studies of behavior and processes in reading and writing*. New York: Macmillan, 1973.

Heilman, A., Blair, T., & Rupley, W. *Principles and practices of teaching reading* (5th ed.). Columbus, Ohio: Charles E. Merrill, 1981.

Litsinger, D. E. Quoted in M. L. Peterson, All children bright and beautiful: But why can't they read? *Contemporary Education,* Fall 1981, *53,* 34–38.

Litsinger, D. E. *The Challenge of Teaching Mexican-American Students*. New York: American Book Company, 1973, p. 36–37.

Peterson, M. L. All children bright and beautiful: But why can't they read? *Contemporary Education*, Fall 1981, *53,* 34–38.

Preston, R. Reading achievement of German and American children. *School and Society*, 1962, *90,* 350–354.

Rosenberg, B. G., & Sutton-Smith, B. The relationship of ordinal position and sibling sex status to cognitive abilities. *Psychonomic Science,* 1964 *1*, 81–82.

Rosenberg, B. G., & Sutton-Smith, B. Sibling association, family size, and cognitive abilities. *Journal of Genetic Psychology,* 1969, *109,* 271–279.

Williamson, A. P. "Afflictive Strategies for the Special Reading Teacher." *Journal of Reading.* December 1973, *17,* 229–33.

A Commentary on Garcia and Logan's Critique of Gentile's Study: Effect of Tutor Sex on Learning to Read

LANCE M. GENTILE

North Texas State University

Generally, Garcia and Logan have done a good job of critiquing the study I carried out ten years ago. They have pointed to more recent research findings reviewed by Heilman, Blair, and Rupley (1981) that indicate little evidence to show that the sex of the teacher has any significant impact on the reading achievement of boys or girls.

I would agree with this statement, but since the research I conducted related directly to Mexican-American boys, it is helpful to understand how the study was conceived, some of the underlying principles that guided or influenced my thinking at that time, and what I have learned since that conflicts with or supports the findings of this initial investigation.

First of all, I feel any attempt to earmark teacher sex as a distinguishing characteristic of a student's success or lack of success in reading is grossly naive. Most of us would agree that gains or difficulties in reading are attributable to a number of interrelated factors. No single variable is the determinant of reading achievement.

However, it appears to me today, just as it did a decade ago, that growth and development in reading is attributable to people's ability to identify reading as an important extension or dimension of their own lives. In short, people who read see themselves as readers. In conjunction with this notion, it is fair to say that role models play an important part in our acceptance or rejection of certain activities. The tendency to imitate those we admire is a strong influence in shaping our learning. Moreover, according to Blackham and Silberman:

> If one wishes to increase imitative behavior in an observer, one must (1) specify the behavior that is desirable for the observer to learn, (2) have an appropriate model perform the desired behavior, (3) reinforce the model for performance of the desired behavior, and (4) reinforce the observer for appropriate imitation of the modeled behavior. (1980, p. 49)

My early teaching experiences with Mexican-American boys in California and Arizona, and recently in Texas, show that many of them have few male role models for reading and achievement in school. Seldom do some of these boys have the opportunity of seeing fathers, uncles, brothers, or male peers reading or benefiting from reading. Consequently, these boys fail to develop a perspective of reading as something that men do. As a result, I question what motivation could some of these Mexican-American boys have to relate to reading or "behave" like readers?

While this situation also exists in other cultures, it appears particularly important to Mexican-American boys because some of them are influenced by the Mexican cultural syndrome of "machismo" or manliness, which accentuates particular traits among males, i.e., physical strength, sexual prowess, honor, object orientation, adventurousness, courage, independence, self-confidence, aggressiveness, verbal articulation, and the predominance of "masculinity." Many of the Mexican-American boys in this study were from lower socio-economic "barrios" and believed strongly in these principles. I did not use men as tutors for these boys in reading to determine if men would be better teachers than women for them, but to emphasize the role Mexican-American men can play in developing boys' attitudes toward reading, to make these adults more comfortable in a school setting, and to get them more directly involved in their children's education. The study was also designed to provide healthy male role models for reading and learning where previously there were few or none. While there may be scant empirical evidence to demonstrate, as Garcia and Logan suggest, any measurable achievement differences between sex of the tutor and sex of the learner, it was and is my belief that in situations where boys do not interact with significant men (regardless of their cultural identity) who vigorously express and demonstrate the value of reading and learning, they may not assign serious or prolonged worth to these pursuits.

An additional concern in reference to Mexican-American boys in this study was evidence provided by Mazurkiewicz (1960) that indicated members of the male sex in the general population of the United States viewed reading as a mostly "feminine" activity. Over the years the distinctions between gender-related activities have become increasingly blurred, but at that time, and as I have pointed out with reference to the population of Mexican-American boys in this study, masculine behavior was more clearly defined. Mazurkiewicz postulated that boys' perception of reading as a feminine activity might exert some negative influence on their achievement. He determined that reading was probably a reflection of some cultural influences.

Sound support for Mazurkiewicz's contention comes from Dwyer (1973). She reviewed theories of sex differences in reading and described four types of causal explanations:

1. differentiated rate or level of maturation
2. reader content
3. negative treatment of boys by female teachers
4. cultural expectations for the male sex role

Dwyer concluded that the first three of these theories were inadequate to explain differences between boys' and girls' reading achievement but claimed the fourth category, "cultural expectations," was strongly supported by empirical evidence. Garcia and Logan have presented research findings by Banks, Biddle, and Good (1980) that support Dwyer's dismissal of the first three causal explanations as relatively insignificant to reading development among boys and girls. However, Garcia and Logan fail to discuss the impact of cultural expectations. Dwyer claimed: "Boys' perceptions of school and the reading activity as inappropriate to or in conflict with development of the male sex role may depress boys' achievement" (1973, p. 455).

Today, these perceptions are referred to as sex role standards and have been described thoroughly by Kagan (1964); Stein (1971); Stein, Pohly, and Mueller (1971); and Stein and Smithells (1968, 1969). Recently, Downing and Thomson (1977) found that the majority of elementary school, high school, and college students, as well as a random sample of adults in one Canadian city, considered reading a more appropriate activity for young girls than for young boys.

If these findings are true for the populations in the United States and Canada, I wonder what implications they may hold for some Mexican-American boys who might have strong needs to identify with activities they feel are more "masculine." This is not, however, as Garcia and Logan propose, an attempt to "blame the victim" or search for personality traits among "lower-class Mexicans" that result in reading or school failure. Teachers must be made aware of the cultural expectations that influence these boys and they must be shown how to develop and employ methods and materials with which these youngsters can identify. They can help offset or restructure Mexican-American boys' misperceptions of reading and learning in school which are fueled by more "traditional" approaches. Garcia and Logan acknowledged my intent in their critique of this study, and I must admit that nothing has occurred during the past ten years of research in reading to change my thinking. When these steps and precautions are taken, whether men or women act as tutors, most Mexican-American boys will experience long-term gains from their school-based reading instruction.

REFERENCES

Banks, B., Biddle, B., & Good, T. Sex roles, classroom instruction, and reading achievement. *Journal of Educational Psychology,* 1980, 72(2), 119–132.

Blackham, G., & Silberman, A. *Modification of child and adolescent behavior* (3rd ed.), Belmont, Calif.: Wadsworth Publ. Co., 1980, 49.

Downing, J., & Thomson, D. Sex-role stereotypes and learning to read. *Research in the Teaching of English,* 1977, *11,* 149–155.

Dwyer, C. A. Sex differences in reading. *Review of Educational Research,* 1973, *43,* 455–466.

Heilman, A., Blair, T., & Rupley, W. *Principles and practices of teaching reading* (5th ed.). Columbus: Charles E. Merrill Publ. Co., 1981, 82–83.

Kagan, J. The child's sex-role classification of school objects. *Child Development,* 1964, *35,* 1051–1056.

Mazurkiewicz, A. J. Social-cultural influences and reading. *Journal of Developmental Reading,* 1960, *1,* 235–240.

Stein, A. H. The effects of sex-role standards for achievement and sex-role preference on three determinants of achievement motivation. *Developmental Psychology,* 1971, *4,* 219–231.

Stein, A. H., Pohly, S. R., & Mueller, E. The influence of masculine, feminine, and neutral tasks on children's achievement behavior expectancies of success, and attainment values. *Child Development,* 1971, *42,* 195–207.

Stein, A. H., & Smithells, J. *The sex-role standards about achievement held by Negro and white children from father-present and father-absent homes.* Unpublished manuscript, Cornell University, 1968.

Stein, A. H., & Smithells, J. Age and sex differences in children's sex-role standards about achievement, *Developmental Psychology,* 1969, *1,* 252–259.

INNER-CITY CHILDREN CAN BE TAUGHT TO READ: FOUR SUCCESSFUL SCHOOLS

GEORGE WEBER

Council for Basic Education

INTRODUCTION

For some time before I began this project I had been intrigued by three facts. First, reading achievement in the early grades in almost all inner-city schools is both relatively and absolutely low.[1] Second, most laymen and most school people believe that such low achievement is all that can be expected. Third, I had seen for myself one inner-city school and had heard reports of several others in which reading achievement was *not* relatively low, in which it was, indeed, about the national average or better.

The first fact can be easily documented. Now that reading achievement scores by school are released to the public by many large-city school systems, the public itself can see the high correlation between these achievement scores and the average income level of the neighborhoods in which the elementary schools are located. The school officials of any large school system can easily make such an analysis for themselves. If they take the five (or ten) schools in the highest-income areas of their district, a similar number of schools in an average-income area, and a similar number of schools in the lowest-income area, they will almost certainly find that the reading achievement scores will generally distribute themselves accordingly: high for the high-income areas, more or less average for the average-income areas, low for the low-income areas. And the school officials, better than the public, will know (or should know) just how low the reading achievement is, absolutely, in the lowest-income schools. Several studies have done this correlation between reading achievement and income on an extensive basis. Possibly the best known are those by Patricia Cayo Sexton for all the elementary schools of a large Midwestern city[2] and by James S. Coleman and others for the nation as a whole.[3]

In view of the general situation and the existence of studies such as those cited

[1]By "relatively low" I mean relative to schools in other areas. By "absolutely low" I mean low in terms of the requirements of the middle grades. Many of the inner-city children who fail to learn to read in the primary grades never learn to read well. They leave school years later as functional illiterates. Moreover, during their remaining years in school they are constantly frustrated and handicapped by their reading deficiency.

Reprinted with permission of George Weber and the Council for Basic Education, 725 15th St., N.W., Washington, D.C. 20005.

[2]See *Education and Income,* Viking, 1961, pp. 25–38.

[3]See *Equality of Educational Opportunity,* U.S. Office of Education, 1966, esp. pp. 21 and 296.

above, the second fact is understandable. Laymen and school people alike are not surprised to learn that reading achievement in the inner-city schools is very poor. What varies is their explanation for this phenomenon. Mrs. Sexton, more than ten years ago, explained it by saying (and offering evidence) that inner-city schools received less money. Such an explanation would hardly do today, since for several years now the (Federal) Elementary and Secondary Education Act, charitable foundations, and local school systems themselves have frequently provided *more* resources for inner-city schools than were available for schools in higher-income areas. The Coleman Report explained it in terms of the family background of the pupils. Arthur R. Jensen explained it primarily in terms of differences in intelligence.[4] Some educators explain it by saying that we do not yet know how to teach reading to disadvantaged children.

None of the above explanations satisfied me. Even though the family background of these children is generally poor, it is no poorer than that of millions of children who had learned to read in the United States in the past. Even though in my opinion the intelligence of poor children is somewhat lower, on the average, high intelligence is not necessary to learn the relatively simple skill of beginning reading. Perhaps the best evidence of this is the fact that several foreign countries are considerably more successful in teaching beginning reading to the whole population than we are. Most of all, the third fact (the apparent existence of successful schools) suggested to me that beginning reading achievement in inner-city schools does not have to be as low as it usually is.

[4]See Arthur R. Jensen, "How Much Can We Boost IQ and Scholastic Achievement?" in *Harvard Educational Review,* Winter 1969.

Accordingly, I developed a hypothesis: that several inner-city public schools exist in the United States where reading achievement in the early grades is far higher than in most inner-city schools, specifically, is at the national average or higher. A study to investigate this hypothesis would have two purposes. If the hypothesis proved correct, the study would show that inner-city children can be taught reading well, and it might discover some common factors in the success of the good programs. In the spring of 1970, the Board of Directors of the Council for Basic Education approved my undertaking the project, and a grant was later obtained from the Victoria Foundation to cover some of the expenses.

During the school year 1970–71, I conducted the study and found the four successful schools that serve as the basis of this report. Two of them are in New York, one in Kansas City, and one in Los Angeles. The remainder of this paper describes the project as a whole, describes in some detail the four successful schools, and draws some conclusions. Appendix 1 deals with the test that was used to determine reading ability. Appendix 2 contains a comment on beginning reading achievement and income.

THE PROJECT

Definitions

The school as the unit of study was not selected by accident. I could have studied a smaller unit, the teacher and her individual class, or a larger unit, the school system. I rejected the single class because almost all teachers have their pupils only one school year, and one school year is often insufficient, even for an outstanding teacher, to teach beginning reading skills to disadvantaged young children. Moreover, even if I had documented successes on the individual class basis, they could have been attributed to the outstanding quality of the individual teachers involved. There is a limited number of outstanding individual teachers at every level of the nation's public schools, and those teachers accomplish far more, by any one of several measures, than average teachers. To have documented such successes in reading instruction would have shown that disadvantaged children can be taught beginning reading well, but it would have reduced the chances of discovering success factors other than teacher quality.

On the other hand, I rejected the school system as a unit of study because, when the project was conceived, I did not believe that any big-city public school system in the country was succeeding in beginning reading instruction in all, or even most, of its inner-city schools. (During the course of the project, I found one system that did seem to be successful, but more about that later.)

Having defined the unit to be studied, I had to work out definitions for "inner-city" and "successful reading achievement."

Definition of an inner-city school may seem an easy matter, but it did present some difficulties. I began by using the term "ghetto," with the thought that these days it conveys a rather unambiguous meaning: a fairly homogeneous area in a large city inhabited by very low-income persons belonging to a group that is "trapped" in the area not only because of its poverty but because of its ethnic or national origin. The major such groups in the United States today are the blacks, the Puerto Ricans, and the Mexican-Americans. I have decided to discard "ghetto" for several reasons. First, many people dislike it, and some school people working in these areas do not like to have the term attached to their schools. Secondly, the term "ghetto" is often associated with Negro areas only; Spanish-speaking groups prefer "barrio," and other poor groups do not like either term. Lastly, not all ghetto areas are populated by very poor people. In fact, in many large cities there are ghetto areas that are middle-class or at least not very poor. I was interested in schools attended by very poor children of whatever origin because such schools, in addition to having very low reading achievement, are generally associated with low expectations on the part of the public and school personnel. As it turned out, all of the inner-city schools I visited were attended largely by blacks, Puerto Ricans, or Mexican-Americans. This was due partly to the fact that a disproportionate number of our very poor people, particularly in our large cities, *are* members of these groups. It was due partly to happenstance; I was not successful in efforts to visit schools attended by very poor children who do not belong to any of these groups.

My final definition of an inner-city school was *a non-selective public school in the central part of a large city that is attended by very poor children.* In determining whether a school met this definition, I decided that Title I designation was a necessary but not sufficient criterion; the selection of schools for Title I funds varies considerably from large city to large city. A second criterion was a high percentage of children eligible for free lunch under the Federal program. Another criterion, which applied to New York City alone, was eligibility for the Special Service category. In New York

City, about 240 of the 600 elementary schools are so eligible on the basis of five criteria: pupil turnover, teacher turnover, percentage of pupils on free lunch, number of children with foreign language problems, and the extent of welfare and attendance problems.

Successful reading achievement also had to be defined. Since most elementary schools in very low-income areas have reading achievement medians substantially below national norms on whatever nationally standardized test is used, I thought it reasonable to require that an inner-city school, to be regarded as successful, would have to achieve a national grade norm score as a median. But it seemed desirable to require that a "successful" school meet another test: that the percentage of gross failures be low. Typically, inner-city schools not only have a low achievement median, but the number of gross reading failures—children achieving far below national norm levels—is high.

The third grade seemed to be the best level at which to test this success. In the first place, what might be called "beginning reading instruction" normally ends with the third grade. Although many children master the "mechanics" of reading by the second grade, some in the first, and a few even before coming to school, the standard reading curriculum in the United States assumes, starting with the fourth grade, that children have achieved the mechanics, and branches out into vocabulary extension, grammar, independent writing, and literature. In the second place, testing earlier than the third grade might have biased the outcome in favor of one or another reading method or approach. Today there are many different instructional methods and approaches being used, and they start out in different ways. But there comes a time, and I would submit that it is the third grade at the latest, by which the school should have taught the child the basic reading skills, whatever method or approach is used. Accordingly, reading success was examined in this project during the middle and latter part of the third grade. At that point the school, to be "successful," had to achieve a national grade-level norm or better as a median and had to have an unusually low percentage of non-readers. The non-readers, incidentally, may have been able to read some individual words but were nonetheless, for all practical purposes, unable to read.

Every effort in this project was made to avoid a bias with respect to particular instructional approaches, methods, and materials. In most cases I had no idea, before I visited the school, of the program being used. As I think will be evident to persons familiar with current reading instruction in the United States, the Council for Basic Education was determined to let the methodological chips fall where they may. At many points during the project I made this clear to school people and others. I developed an absurd illustration to emphasize the point: I said that if we found an inner-city school that achieved success in beginning reading by having the children stand on their heads for a half-hour every morning, I would write up such a school in the final report.

Getting and Winnowing the Nominations

As soon as the project was approved, in April of 1970, I began to gather names of schools that might ultimately qualify as success stories in this report. I asked specialists in the field of reading, publishers, and school officials for nominations. I did some searching of the literature. I placed a notice in the *CBE Bulletin*. I asked the superintendents of five big-city systems and central-office administrators of six others for nominations. I kept the nomination process open for over a year. The search did not have to be a complete one, however. I did not need to find *all* of the inner-city schools that were successful in beginning reading instruction. The purpose of the search was simply to find enough schools so that several reasonably representative successes could be described and analyzed in the final report. Accordingly, there are undoubtedly a number of successful schools beyond the four that are written up in the next section.

All told, about 95 schools were nominated. Of these, some obviously were not non-selective public schools in the inner-city sections of large cities. But 69 seemed to be such schools, and to each of these I wrote a letter, addressed to the principal, asking if he believed that his school met both criteria (type of school and reading success) and if he would welcome an independent evaluation of reading achievement and the reading program. This step of asking the principal for permission to visit his school took a substantial toll on the nominees. Some principals did not reply at all. Others replied that they were not inner-city schools or that they were not successful in beginning reading instruction in terms of the criteria to be used. Finally, a number of principals refused to have me visit when the nature of the independent evaluation was spelled out in detail. In the end, I visited 17 schools in seven large cities. I would have visited a few more had there been time prior to the closing of school in May and June of 1971.

Independent Evaluation of Reading Achievement

I took for granted from the outset that an independent evaluation of reading achievement would have to be made. The alternative was to accept, in most cases, results on tests that the schools had administered themselves. Although it is customary in public education to do just that—to allow schools and school systems to evaluate themselves—it is obviously unreliable and unsatisfactory. Most teachers and administrators try to administer standardized tests honestly to their pupils. But without any auditing procedure, the temptations are very great, not only for teachers and administrators, but for publishers and others with an interest in the outcome. The greater the pressure for results—and the pressure is increasing with the current trend toward greater "accountability"—the less reliable self-evaluation becomes.

The existence of "irregularities" with respect to achievement testing is common knowledge among school people but has come to public attention only recently, for example in the case of certain New York City public schools.[5] Although most irregularities take the form of coaching (excessive preparation) for the test, there are more flagrant types of misbehavior, such as teaching the particular words to appear on the test, practicing on the test itself, changing the answers before the tests are scored, giving pupils

[5]See articles in *The New York Times,* April 3, 5, 7, 9, 1971.

aid during the test, allowing additional time, and failing to test selected pupils who are expected to do poorly. (I saw evidence or heard reliable reports of all of these irregularities during my visits to the seven large cities.) The question of coaching is a particularly difficult one because New York and other school systems tell their personnel that it is permissible to prepare pupils for the tests by drilling them on similar material. Particularly in the case of young children who have had little or no experience with such tests, some such preparation does seem justified because otherwise children who are experienced in test-taking will have an advantage. Problems arise because different schools engage in different amounts of such preparation.

My first plan was to administer a nationally standardized test. I rejected this because the tests are not entirely comparable and because whatever test was used would tend to favor schools in cities that used that particular test. Moreover, such a procedure would not have avoided the differences in pupil preparation for the kind of test involved, since all of the major nationally standardized reading achievement tests for the lower grades are similar in form. Accordingly, I decided to use a test that none of the large cities used.

The test tentatively selected was the Basic Test of Reading Comprehension used by Professor S. Alan Cohen of Yeshiva University.[6] Since that test was unpublished and unavailable to me, I decided (with Professor Cohen's permission) to make up a test based on the same approach. Because I was interested in testing the ability of poor children to read words that they already understood by ear, I devised a test entirely of words that I thought they so understood. I also decided to use a test different in form from the nationally standardized reading achievement tests. The test would then evaluate not their breadth of aural vocabulary nor their ability to take tests of the multiple-choice type, but their "mechanical" ability to read simple American English. After drafting a test, I tried it out in the city of Alexandria, Virginia, through the generous cooperation of its superintendent, Dr. John C. Albohm. Alexandria has 14 elementary schools whose reading scores at third-grade level range from substantially above national norm to substantially below. I gave the test to every present third-grade child in five schools: the two schools with the lowest reading scores in the city, two schools with average scores, and the school with the top scores. I also tested the fifth grade in one of the lowest schools. In addition, I tested the vocabulary on a number of individual children. This field testing allowed me to refine the test and obtain scores which could be equated with national norm scores on nationally standardized tests.

The resulting test contained 32 items and could be administered in 15 minutes actual test time. I planned to give the test myself so as to make the administration as uniform as possible. (Further details on the test are given in Appendix 1.)

The School Visits

The 17 big-city schools in the project were visited between January and June of 1971. With one exception, the school visits lasted two or three days. (The one exception, a school that obviously did not meet the inner-city criterion, was visited only one day.)

[6]See pages 67–69 of his *Teach Them All To Read,* Random House, 1969.

There were three purposes for visiting the schools. The first was to check on whether the school met the inner-city criterion. This involved asking various questions. The second was to ascertain, through administration of the test, whether the school met the reading-success criterion. The third was to determine the nature of the beginning reading program and, in those cases where the school seemed to meet both the inner-city and reading-success criteria, the factors that seemed to account for the success. All third-grade classes were tested as early as possible in the visit. The only third-grade children not tested were those absent and those who could not speak English. The test papers were hand-scored by me as soon as possible so that the results could affect the nature of the rest of the visit. Many primary-grade classrooms were observed during reading instruction. Any remedial reading programs for primary-grade children were observed. The principal, other administrators, teachers, and reading specialists were interviewed. In some cases other personnel, such as psychologists and teachers of English as a second language, were interviewed or observed.

General Results

Six of the 17 schools that were visited and tested met the inner-city criterion but not the reading-success criterion. Seven of the schools met the reading-success criterion but not the inner-city criterion. Four met both criteria, in my opinion, beyond any doubt. First, they were nonselective public schools in the central areas of large cities that were attended by very poor children. Second, at the third-grade level, their reading achievement medians equalled or exceeded the national norm and the percentages of non-readers were unusually low for such schools. These schools were P.S. 11 in Manhattan, the John H. Finley School (P.S. 129) in Manhattan, the Woodland School in Kansas City, Missouri, and the Ann Street School in Los Angeles. The next section describes in some detail these schools and their successful beginning reading programs.

THE FOUR SUCCESSFUL SCHOOLS

In the following descriptions of the four inner-city schools that were found to be notably successful in teaching beginning reading, there will be no detailed discussion of their individual reading achievement scores. All four of them had achievements far above the typical inner-city school, and the differences among them were relatively slight. Accordingly, they are listed in an arbitrary order: first the two schools in Manhattan, arranged in numerical order, and then, moving west, the school in Kansas City and the school in Los Angeles. This arrangement does not, to repeat, indicate any order of quality; they are all outstanding in beginning reading in comparison to most inner-city schools.

To illustrate their general level of achievement, I have developed the following table.

The third line shows the four successful schools. The first figure shows the percentage of all third-graders that were not tested, either because they were absent or because they did not speak English. The remaining figures show the distribution of the third-grade children tested in terms of their national norm reading grade equivalents. Even though the "non-readers" may have known some individ-

	% of Third Grade Not Tested (absent or non-English)	Percentages of Third-Graders Tested Receiving Various Grade-Equivalent Scores				
		Non-Reader	I	II	III	IV & Up
Typical High-Income Schools (estimated)	5–15	0–5	0–5	3–10	3–10	72–92
Typical Average-Income Schools (estimated)	5–15	10–20	10–20	10–20	10–20	30–50
The Four Successful Inner-City Schools (actual)	12–20	7–14	6–12	13–23	16–21	42–46
Typical Inner-City Schools (estimated)	10–25	25–35	5–30	10–25	10–20	15–25

ual words, for all practical purposes they were unable to read. For comparison with these scores for the four successful schools, I have estimated, on the basis on my testing in 18 other schools, comparable figures for typical inner-city schools, typical average-income schools, and typical high-income schools. The table shows that the *achievement of the four successful inner-city schools is approximately that of typical average-income schools.*

The first column means that in the four successful inner-city schools, 12 to 20 percent of the third-graders enrolled were not tested. It is estimated that typical inner-city schools would be in approximately the same range. Typical average-income and high-income schools would show a lower figure, partly because they have far fewer third-graders who do not speak English, partly because their average absence rate is lower.

Turning to the reading achievement scores, the greatest visible differences, naturally, are in the two extreme achievement categories: non-readers and fourth-grade-and-higher. In the four successful inner-city schools, 7 to 14 per cent of the third-graders tested were non-readers. This is substantially better than the 25 to 35 percent that one would find in typical inner-city schools. It is approximately the result one would find in typical average-income schools, if one makes an adjustment for the higher absence rate of the successful inner-city schools. It is significantly poorer than what one would find in typical high-income schools. On the other extreme, in the four successful inner-city schools 42 to 46 percent of the third-graders tested scored fourth grade or higher on a national norm basis. This is substantially better than the 15 to 25 percent that one would find in typical inner-city schools. It is roughly what one would find in typical average-income schools (30–50%), but far below what one would find in typical high-income schools (72–92%). (For a comment on why typical high-income schools have higher achievement in beginning reading than even these successful inner-city schools, see Appendix 2.)

With this understanding of just how well the four successful inner-city schools did in beginning reading achievement, we will turn to a description of the four successful schools and their programs.

P.S. 11, MANHATTAN
320 West 21st Street
New York, New York 10011
Murray A. Goldberg, Principal

Manhattan's P.S. 11 is in Chelsea, fairly far down on the island's west side. The school area is bounded by 16th Street on the south, 26th Street on the north, the Hudson River on the west, and Fifth Avenue on the east. The school itself, on 21st Street between Eighth and Ninth Avenues, is an old building on a treeless lot among tenements, shops, and housing developments. The building, constructed in 1925, had a million-dollar renovation in 1963 which improved the interior, particularly the classrooms, but left it with black-floored, dark corridors and old steel staircases.

There are 750 pupils in pre-kindergarten through fifth grade. Ten years ago the school had 1,200, but widespread demolition and urban renewal led to a lower enrollment. With available space, P.S. 11 became one of the More Effective Schools five years ago. The More Effective Schools program, boosted by the American Federation of Teachers and initiated by its New York affiliate, has smaller classes as its key feature. Accordingly, to be chosen for the program, a school had to have the space to reorganize its pupils into a greater number of classes. Instead of the pupil-teacher ratio of 31:1 in the majority of New York's elementary schools or the 28:1 in the Special Service schools, MES schools have a ratio of 22:1. Last spring P.S. 11 had 120 pupils enrolled in its third grade. Of these, 112 were in five regular classes (a ratio of 22.4:1) and eight were in a "junior guidance" (disciplinary) class. Counting all six classes, the ratio was 20.0:1.

In addition to the smaller classes, the MES program provides the school with supplementary "cluster teachers" (a fourth teacher for every three classes), more supervisory and auxiliary personnel (for example, three assistant principals), and pre-kindergartens. The MES programs requires heterogeneous grouping. The cluster teachers visit each of their three classes for one-and-a-half hours a day. In the primary grades, this is usually during the reading period. The cluster teacher sometimes instructs the whole class, sometimes takes part of the class while the regular teacher takes the other.

The limited number of MES schools in New York City were chosen primarily on the basis of their having enough space for the smaller class sizes. Of the 27 MES schools, 24 are in disadvantaged areas and would be in the Special Service category if they were not MES. P.S. 11 is such a school. Eighty percent of its pupils qualify for free lunch. Twenty percent enter school not knowing English, and 30 percent more enter knowing English from Spanish-speaking homes. In total, about half of the pupils are Puerto Rican, 17 percent are black, and the remaining third are "other." Almost all are very poor.

P.S. 11 is a clean and orderly and business-like school. The atmosphere is purposeful and optimistic. Mr. Goldberg, who has been principal for 14 years, runs a "tight ship." He seems to know and care about everything that goes on in the school. His office is very well organized, and facts and figures are, if not in his head, usually within his arm's reach.

P.S. 11 has no single reading program. Eight or nine sets of reading materials are available in the school. The teachers have wide latitude in choosing among these and in ordering new materials, although purchases must be approved by the assistant principal responsible for the particular grade. Among the materials I saw being used in the primary grades were the Scott, Foresman basals, the Bank Street readers, the *We Are Black* series by Science Research Associates, SRA's reading laboratory, the Scholastic Library of paperbacks, the McCormick-Mathers phonics workbooks, *Phonics We Use* (published by Lyons and Carnahan), *Standard Test Lessons in Reading* by McCall and Crabbs (published by Teachers College), and various games and teacher-made materials. In addition, there was a large quantity and variety of storybooks. Every classroom had its own library of these, and in addition a large school library seemed to be extensively used. Children could take books home for a week at a time.

There is a strong emphasis on reading without its taking over the whole primary-grade curriculum. From one-and-a-half to two hours a day are spent in reading instruction in the regular classes. About 20 percent of the children in grades three, four, and five (the ones who are doing poorest in reading) spend an additional hour and a half a week (two 45-minute sessions) with a specialized reading teacher, who takes them in groups of about six. She uses a large variety of phonics materials not used in the regular classrooms. Her work, and the classroom teachers' as well, focuses on individualization. The reading specialist's individualization is formal, starting out with a careful diagnosis of where the pupil is; the classroom teachers' individualization is informal but nevertheless brings to bear an attitude that different children are at various stages of learning to read and have to be treated differently. This individualization is encouraged by the heterogeneous nature of the classes. The heterogeneous assignment is done very carefully and consciously in P.S. 11. For example, at the end of the second grade, all pupils are ranked by teachers in terms of reading achievement. Then the children are assigned to third-grade classes by random distribution of each of the various achievement groups.

Although the school does not use in the regular classrooms any basal series with a strong phonics approach, there are many phonics workbooks and supplemental materials in use. Much of the teaching and teacher-made materials center around phonics. This emphasis dates from the principal's reading, three years ago, of the book by Jeanne Chall *(Learning to Read: The Great Debate).* The book made a profound impression on him, he says, and he called his teachers together to urge them to use more phonics. Before that time, the feeling in the school was somewhat anti-phonics, to the point where some teachers felt that they had to "bootleg" the use of phonics.

In line with the MES guidelines, there are no special classes for children from Spanish-speaking homes. In fact, there is a conscious effort to mix such children into all classes. There is a "bilingual teacher" who conducts an orientation program for Spanish-speaking children and their parents. But she does not teach English.

There are four "junior guidance" classes in the school. Such classes have existed in the New York City schools for about ten years. They are made up of pupils who are disruptive in the regular classrooms. At P.S. 11, the four junior guidance classes are at the second-, third-, fourth-, and fifth-grade levels. Children are assigned to them, with parental approval, on the principal's decision, which is based on the recommendations of counselors and classroom teachers. The policy is to keep them no more than two years before they are returned to the regular classrooms, and many return sooner. The eight boys in the third-grade group were a mixture of those who "acted out" and those who were withdrawn. Their reading attainment ranged from low to high. Their teacher was a man.

Homework is given at all levels at P.S. 11. The amount varies, and the teachers have considerable latitude in its assignment, but the policy of giving it is built into the school program.

P.S. 11, being an MES school, has unusually small classes. It has also had extra personnel and pre-kindergarten for five years, which would mean that the third-graders tested had full benefit, in most cases, of these advantages. But there is more to P.S. 11's success in beginning reading than those factors. If there were not, all disadvantaged MES schools would be equally successful—and most of them are not. At P.S. 11 there is the order and purpose of a well-run school. High expectations and concern for every pupil are reflected in many things, including the atmosphere at individualization. Most of all, there is an obvious emphasis on early reading achievement and the importance given to phonics instruction.

JOHN H. FINLEY SCHOOL (P.S. 129), MANHATTAN

425 West 130th Street
New York, New York 10027
Mrs. Martha Froelich, Principal

The John H. Finley School, built in 1957, is at 130th Street and Convent Avenue in northwest Harlem, several blocks south of City College, with which it is affiliated in a demonstration, research, and teacher education program. Most new teachers at the school come from City College. The district, made up of tenements and housing projects, is bounded by 125th Street on the south and southwest, 131st Street on the north, Broadway on the northwest, and St. Nicholas Terrace on the east.

There are 980 pupils in kindergarten through sixth grade. Finley is a Special Service School, one of about 40 percent of the New York City elementary schools so categorized because they serve disadvantaged children. At Finley, the poverty of the children is evidenced by the fact that almost all of them qualify for free lunch. Seventy percent of the children are black, about 30 percent Spanish-speaking. Being a Special Service School, its pupil-teacher ratio is supposed to be no higher than 28:1. Last spring Finley had 133 pupils in five third-grade classes for a ratio of 26.6:1.

The school is orderly and has a confident and optimistic air. Mrs. Froelich, who has been principal for 11 years, is a no-nonsense leader who is also friendly and kind. Often out in the halls and dealing with individual children, she seems to be always available to children, teachers, parents, and others on school business.

The reading program through the second grade is well planned, uniform, and highly structured. It was started in 1962.[7] There is no formal reading program in the kindergarten, but there is a formal program involving the acquisition of fundamental knowledge and concepts. A checklist of 21 items is used.

[7]For an earlier account of the reading program by persons connected with the school, see "Success for Disadvantaged Children," by Martha Froelich, Florence Kaiden Blitzer, and Judith W. Greenberg, *The Reading Teacher*, October 1967.

Some of the items are "writes first name," "knows colors," "counts to ten," and "understands concept more/less." When the children enter in September, each child is checked against the list and a record made. During the year deficiencies are made up.

During the first half of the first grade, there is no achievement grouping. Reading time is devoted to work charts and experience stories. Work charts of various kinds are posted around the room to indicate the children's chores and class activities. These are read aloud during the day. The experience stories are made up from the children's talk. They are copied, and each child builds his own reader by pasting them in a hardcovered notebook. On the pages with the experience stories are homework, which begins the very first day of first grade (and continues on an every-night basis), and word patterns to teach what Mrs. Froelich calls "intrinsic phonics." Here are two examples of such patterns:

sn	eat
snake	eat
snail	beat
snack	heat
	meat
	seat
	wheat

At the beginning of the second half of the first grade, children are grouped by reading attainment. This is done by a reading coordinator as part of a systematic program of reading evaluation. The reading coordinator tests every child once a month during the first grade and every six weeks during the second grade by means of a modified Harris Test. This test consists of eight graded lists of ten words each. All testing is done on an individual basis by the reading coordinator, and the words are not known to the classroom teachers. The child reads the words aloud, starting with the easiest list. The child is placed at the level where he first fails to read more than four words out of the list of ten. (The test is also used to place new children coming into the school.) Administration of the test takes less than ten minutes per child.

During the second half of the first grade the children read for a half-hour per day in homogeneous groups determined by this placement. For this half-hour children go to another classroom, if necessary, to join their assigned groups. They read various basals with the teacher in an orthodox instructional situation. An unusual aspect of the reading program is their independent reading. Finley has organized a large number of storybooks and textbooks from pre-primers through second-grade level and higher into a sequence of difficulty that has been determined by the school's own experience. A book may be lower or higher on the school list than the publisher's designation. There are 14 books on the first pre-primer level, ten on the second pre-primer level, 17 on the third pre-primer level, seven on the primer level, and so forth. Each child reads these books at his own pace. After finishing each book, he completes a worksheet of questions on it. He may not read all the books at one level before he goes on to the next, but a prodigious amount of reading is done.

Roughly the same procedure is followed in the second grade. But at the beginning of the year, the children are assigned to classes on the basis of their progress in reading. The book reading continues, but on a class basis rather than on an individual basis. Again, the number of books covered is very large, in sharp contrast with the typical second-grade class elsewhere, which is kept to a single basal and possibly a supplemental book or two. The pace is suggested by the fact that one second-grade class I observed was asked to read an entire short storybook and study all the new words for a single night's homework. In the second grade, phonics is covered by the *Phonics We Use* workbooks, published by Lyons and Carnahan.

Going into the third grade, the children are again grouped on the basis of their progress in reading. The third-grade classes this past year were using a variety of commercially published and teacher-made materials. Many trade books were involved in individual work.

For children whose native language is Spanish, there is a bilingual teacher who works with one, two or three pupils at a time, three times a week. She had a total of 29 children last spring.

Five features of the reading program stand out: all of the pupils are started out in the same way in heterogeneous classes in the first half of the first grade; individualization and grouping on the basis of reading progress begins in the second half of the first grade; careful and frequent evaluation is done by someone outside the classroom; a very large quantity and variety of materials is used; and phonics, both implicit and explicit, is taught in the first two grades. This planned, precise reading program benefits from a general school atmosphere that includes high expectations, a concern for every child, and considerable home involvement through homework and school-home communications.

WOODLAND SCHOOL

711 Woodland Avenue
Kansas City, Missouri 64106
Don Joslin, Principal

Woodland School is a couple of miles northeast of the center of Kansas City in a black district. Built in 1921, it sits on a large lot in the middle of an urban renewal area, a lot that includes a playground, outbuildings, and a parking area. Nearby are small houses and a large, high-rise housing project.

There are about 650 pupils in kindergarten through seventh grade. Before urban renewal demolished so many buildings there had been 1,200 pupils. Ninety-nine percent of the children are black; almost all of them are very poor. About 90 percent get free or largely free lunch.

Last school year (1970–71) was the second year as principal for Don Joslin. Previously he had been principal of another Title I school. Mr. Joslin believes in the power of cooperation, and he often deals with pupils in terms of asking them for "help."

Classes are relatively large. Last spring each of the three regular third-grade classes (one was a combined class of third- and fourth-graders) had 29 pupils. A special education class for second- and third-graders had 14. Including that class, the pupil-teacher ratio for the third grade was 25.3:1.

Woodland School is part of a multi-school program, Project Uplift. The driving force behind this project is a black man, Robert R. Wheeler, area superintendent for the Division of Urban Education. Mr. Wheeler served with the Kansas City schools before he went to Oakland, California, for three years. When he returned to Kansas City in 1966, he was determined to improve the reading achievement of children in the inner city. "We began," he has said, "with the fundamental belief that inner-city pupils can learn as well as other pupils, provided the priorities are sensible, the effort intense, and the instructional approaches rational in terms of the needs of the learners. We have not accepted the myth that environmental factors develop unalterable learning depression. We believe that so-called negative environmental factors can be overcome with sensitive and responsive teaching." And so, in the fall of 1968, when the educational establishment was contending that slum children were permanently disadvantaged and, in Mr. Wheeler's words, "needed more zoo trips or didn't have enough oatmeal," he began a program that emphasized beginning reading skills.

The program included reading and speech specialists in each school, teacher aides, and a change from traditional whole-word basals to the Sullivan Programmed Reading Series, published by McGraw-Hill. In-service training of teachers was crucial because staff expectations about pupil potential had to be raised. As Mr. Wheeler put it, "The staff has to believe the pupils can and will learn before they can convince the students that they are not doomed to fail."

Project Uplift involves 11 elementary schools. I visited only one, but I was told that several other project schools had results at least as good in beginning reading. Although I will describe the beginning reading program at Woodland, that program can be understood only in terms of the spirit and objectives of the whole project.

The heart of the beginning reading program at Woodland is the Sullivan readers. These are the McGraw-Hill version (a similar Sullivan series is also published by Behavioral Research Laboratories). This series is "programmed"; that is, it is designed for use by the pupil working by himself. It consists of 21 paperbound, graded booklets, nominally intended for the first three grades. The first seven booklets are at first-grade level, the second seven at second-grade level, the last seven at third-grade level. But of course they can, and should, be used on an individualized basis. Each child begins with the first book and proceeds as fast or as slowly as he masters the material. Each page is divided into two sections. The larger one presents questions or problems in the form of statements to be completed with one answer or another. The smaller section lists the correct answers. This section is covered by the child with a cardboard "slider," which is moved down to reveal the answers one at a time. Typically, the child works by himself and has his work checked by the teacher or someone else after every page. At the end of each book he takes a test on the whole book. A major problem with such young children is to establish and maintain a routine of self-discipline so that the child actually works in the way that he is supposed to. Obviously children could cheat by working from the answers to the questions. I have been in schools where so much of this is done that the program is ineffective.

At Woodland the program seemed to be implemented quite well. There was very little cheating or racing to see who could finish his book first. Every primary-grade class had a full-time teacher aide who, of course, helped with the Sullivan work. There was a considerable spread within classes with respect to which books the children were reading, a situation which testified to the individualization of the program. From one-and-a-half to two hours per day were devoted to working with the books. From 20 to 30 minutes per day were used for group instruction on decoding skills. If a child did not finish Book 21 by the time he completed third grade, he continued with the series into the fourth grade and even into the fifth, if necessary, until he finished. Within grades, classes were

research

roughly grouped by reading attainment. The Sullivan program began in 1968–69, and so the third grade this past spring was the first third grade at the school to have begun the program in the first grade.

The Sullivan program has built into it a regular procedure of individual evaluation, the page and end-of-book checks. Even if this is implemented with only moderate competence, the resulting reading evaluation system is far superior to that typically carried out in the primary classes of our public schools.

Woodland, like other Project Uplift schools, has a full-time "speech improvement" teacher. She spends 20 to 25 minutes twice a week in each of the classes from kindergarten through fourth grade. She uses a variety of techniques, including children's plays and oral reports to class, to improve pupils' verbal facility so that youngsters can move from the neighborhood dialect to the English used in the classroom.

The school has two full-time reading specialists, one of whom is assigned to kindergarten through grade three, the other to grades four through seven. These specialists do not teach the children outside of the classroom. Their duties include in-service work with the classroom teachers, demonstrations in the classroom, and general monitoring of the reading program.

The school has a library which children visit regularly once a week. They may borrow books to take back to use in the classroom, but they may not take books home.

Woodland has a state-aided program of special education. There are three classes: one for second and third grades, one for fourth and fifth, and one for sixth and seventh. Assignment to the classes is considered for children with a Stanford-Binet score of 79 I.Q. or lower. Some children who test this low are able to keep up in regular classes and remain there. Before assignment to a special education class, parents' approval is secured. Last spring 12 third-graders were in the special education class. Although the children had worked in the Sullivan series when they were in the regular classes, in the special education class they used a whole-word basal series. Out of the ten tested third-graders who were nonreaders, seven were in the special education class.

The most important factors in Woodland's success in beginning reading instruction are the high expectations and the use of the McGraw-Hill Sullivan program. The considerable time devoted to reading is another factor. The reading and speech specialists and the teacher aides round out the picture. The special education classes are probably, on balance, a negative factor. While special education classes can benefit both the children assigned to them and the regular classes from which they come, the Woodland program does not seem to do so.

ANN STREET SCHOOL

126 East Bloom Street
Los Angeles, California 90012
Mrs. Joyce D. Zikas, Principal

Ann Street School is in a very low-income area in the center of Los Angeles, about ten blocks northeast of City Hall. The school building, erected about 1955, and its playground occupy a small block entirely surrounded by a housing project.

There are 406 pupils in kindergarten through sixth grade. Sixty-two percent of the children are Mexican-American; 38 percent are black. All of the pupils live in the William Mead Homes, a housing project of two- and three-story buildings where rent is as low as $29 per month. Out of 435 elementary schools in the Los Angeles school system, only 55 are Title I. Ann Street is one of these. All of the children are eligible for both free breakfast and free lunch. During the past year, from one-quarter to one-half of the pupils took free breakfast; all took free lunch.

Mrs. Zikas came to the school as principal four years ago. Her first problem, as she saw it, was to establish order in the building and to create a level of discipline that would facilitate learning. Having accomplished that, she turned to the curriculum.

Classes are relatively small. The nominal pupil-teacher ratio is 24:1. The school has a non-graded primary organization covering grades one through three. Of the ten primary classes last spring, three were composed entirely of pupils in their first year after kindergarten (K-plus-1), two were mixtures of K-plus-1 and K-plus-2, one was K-plus-2, one was a mixture of K-plus-2 and K-plus-3, one was K-plus-3, and two were mixtures of K-plus-3 and K-plus-4. A child may take three or four years to complete the primary-grade program.

The primary classes operate on a "divided day." Half the children in a class come to school from nine o'clock to two o'clock; the other half come from ten to three. This allows two hours a day (from nine to ten and two to three) in which only half the class is present. It is these two hours that are used for the chief reading instruction.

Beginning with the year 1969–70, no report cards have been given to primary-grade children. Instead, parent conferences are held three times a year. The idea at the time that this procedure was decided upon was that the children were doing so poorly that honest grades would discourage both them and their parents. Now that achievement has risen, report cards may be reinstituted.

In some cases teachers stay with a class more than one year. Last spring one teacher was teaching the same class for the third straight year, from kindergarten through "second grade."

The school has two classes for mentally retarded children of 15 pupils each. The children must be eight years old and test below 80 I.Q. on a Stanford-Binet or Wechsler individual intelligence test.

There are also two "opportunity classes" for disciplinary problems. Most of these children are in the upper grades. The class for fourth-, fifth-, and sixth-grade has 15 pupils. The primary class has six pupils.

A student council is very active. An unusual feature is a series of school-wide "commissioners" in addition to the councilmen who represent the various grades. Many of the 17 commissioners are for non-academic matters such as safety, but there are several commissioners in the academic fields, including handwriting, mathematics, and reading. The student Commissioner of Reading Improvement makes regular reports on reading progress to the weekly student council assembly. At the same meeting, she may well ask skill questions of the student audience. There is also a student School Improvement Committee that deals with school discipline.

The reading program at the primary level consists largely of the McGraw-Hill Sullivan series. Since this series has been described above in connection with its use at Woodland School in Kansas City, it will not be described again here. At Ann Street the Sullivan program was begun in November 1969 in the whole primary bloc. After the Sullivan pre-reading program, the pupils enter the 21-booklet series. Nominally Books 1 through 16 are covered in the primary grades, and Books 17 through 21 are used in the fourth grade and later as supplementary reading. But in practice the series is used, as it was intended, on an individualized basis, and this past spring some "third-graders" had progressed as far as Book 19 and some were as far back as Book 4. The children can take the Sullivan books home if they wish.

Each primary class has either two teachers or a teacher and an aide. With the divided-day arrangement described above, the child-adult ratio during the Sullivan instruction can be quite low.

In addition to the Sullivan series, a variety of other materials is used in the later primary period. Chief of these is the Science Research Associates reading laboratory, which is typically begun by the child when he reaches Book 10 of Sullivan. Other materials being used this past spring included *Speech-to-Print Phonics, Open Highways* (published by Scott, Foresman), storybooks and library books.

There is a full-time reading specialist provided by the state's Miller-Unruh Act. Until this past year, there were two. The specialist (Mrs. Dorothy A. Brumbaugh) works with the primary group only, both in the regular classroom and with the teachers. There is no pupil instruction outside of the classroom. The reading specialist has developed two diagnostic tests that are related to the Sullivan series, one for Books 1–7, the other for Books 8–14. These group tests are administered three times a year. The results of the tests, in the form of a chart showing the skills that each child has mastered, are posted in the classrooms.

Beginning in December 1970, the school has had a teacher who teaches English as a second language. She works with pupils in groups of 8 to 15 and has 49 pupils in all. A bilingual teacher who teaches in both English and Spanish, she meets with each group for 45 minutes every day, at a time when the children would be studying a subject other than reading in their regular classrooms. The children are grouped, whatever their age, according to their proficiency in English.

The school consciously instructs its pupils in the mechanics of test-taking. It tests the children frequently, using a variety of tests.

There are many factors, as one can see, that might account for the success in beginning reading at Ann Street. Chief among these, in my opinion, are the Sullivan series, the excellent and imaginative work of the reading specialist, the ambitious efforts of the principal, and the stress that is placed on reading achievement.

CONCLUSIONS

The hypothesis of this research project was proven. At least four inner-city public schools exist in the United States where reading achievement in the early grades is far higher than in most inner-city schools. Specifically, the four schools described in the preceding section are all non-selective public schools in the central areas of large cities and are attended by very poor children. Further, during the second half of the school year 1970–71 all four schools had reading achievement medians in third grade which equalled or exceeded the national norm and a percentage of non-readers unusually low for such schools.

The four successful schools, it should be noted, are not perfect schools, even with respect to their beginning reading programs. But they merit attention and commendation because they are doing something that very few inner-city schools do: teaching beginning reading well.

Success Factors

Now that we have found four inner-city schools that teach beginning reading well, the inevitable question arises: How do they do it? What are their secrets of success? It is not easy to be sure of the answer because schools are very complex institutions. The mere fact that a successful school is doing something different from unsuccessful schools does not mean that the different practice is the cause of success. The matter is made more complicated because successful schools always seem to do *many* things differently. Which of these different practices are responsible for the higher pupil achievement? It is, of course, impossible to be certain, but it seems reasonable to assume that when all four successful schools are following a practice not usually found in unsuccessful inner-city schools, that practice has something to do with their success. It seems reasonable, also, to conclude that different practices that exist in some of the successful schools, but not in others, are not essential to success. I will use this approach in trying to account for the success of the four inner-city schools in teaching beginning reading.

There seem to be eight factors that are common to the four successful schools that are usually not present in unsuccessful inner-city schools. These are—not, of course, in the order of their importance—strong leadership, high expectations, good atmosphere, strong emphasis on reading, additional reading personnel, use of phonics, individualization, and careful evaluation of pupil progress.

Strong leadership is not surprising. But it was striking that all four schools have clearly identifiable individuals who would be regarded as outstanding leaders by most people who are knowledgeable about our public schools. In three cases, these individuals are principals: Mr. Goldberg at P.S. 11, Mrs. Froelich at the John H. Finley School, and Mrs. Zikas at the Ann Street School. In the fourth case, the leader is Mr. Wheeler, the area superintendent responsible for Woodland and ten other schools in Kansas City. (Mr. Joslin, the principal at Woodland, appears to be an effective administrator, but he did not supply the initiative for the reading program.) In all four instances, these persons have not only been the leaders of the over-all school activity but have specifically led the beginning reading program. A new reading program, if it is to succeed, has to be inaugurated with conscious purpose but also has to be followed up to see that it keeps on a productive course.

All four schools have had high expectations with regard to the potential achievements of their inner-city children. Understandably, this is a prerequisite to success; if these schools had believed that their pupils could achieve no better in reading than inner-city children usually do, they would hardly have worked so hard for better performance. But high hopes are only a necessary, not a sufficient, condition for success. As important as the level of aspiration is, if that were all there were to it, many more schools would succeed in these days of concern for the inner-city child.

The good atmosphere of these schools is hard to describe. And yet it is difficult to escape the conviction that the order, sense of purpose, relative quiet, and pleasure in learning of these schools play a role in their achievements. Disor-

research

der, noise, tension, and confusion are found in many inner-city schools at the elementary level. I have been in schools where such conditions prevail, but, overall, the four successful schools were quite different.

It may go without saying that these schools place a strong emphasis on reading. And yet in these days of television, of many new media in the schools, and of a widespread interest in the "affective" side of learning, in many inner-city schools reading seems to be only one subject of many. While these four successful schools do not, of course, concentrate all their attention on reading, they do recognize that reading is the first concern of the primary grades. This strong emphasis on reading is reflected in many ways.

All four schools have additional reading personnel. All four schools have reading specialists working with the primary grades. In addition, P.S. 11 has the extra number of regular teachers to allow for the small class size and "cluster teachers" (a fourth teacher for every three classes) who serve primarily as reading teachers; Woodland has a full-time teacher aide for each class and a speech specialist; and the Ann Street School has a second teacher or a teacher aide for each primary class. These additional personnel serve two functions. The specialists bring expertise and concentration to the reading program. The other personnel allow the pupil-adult ratio to be reduced during reading instruction. This approach is probably more effective than using the same amount of money to reduce class size, a matter that is discussed below.

The use of phonics is important. By this time, more than three years after the publication of Jeanne Chall's book, *Learning to Read: The Great Debate*, there is a widespread recognition of the superiority of the phonics, or decoding, approach. But recognition and implementation are two different things. Many teachers are not sufficiently knowledgeable about phonics to teach it, and it requires particularly knowledgeable teachers to use the phonics approach with materials that do not have the phonics built in. Of the four schools, two use the Sullivan program, which does have the phonics approach built in. The other two schools use non-phonics readers as their basic books, but have supplemented them with extensive phonics materials. All four schools are using phonics to a much greater degree than most inner-city schools.

The seventh success factor is individualization. By this I do not mean, necessarily, individualization in the narrow sense of having each child work at a different level. I mean that there is a concern for each child's progress and a willingness to modify a child's work assignments, if necessary, to take account of his stage of learning to read and his particular learning problems. The Sullivan program, used by two of the four schools, allows and even encourages individualization. In the other two schools, individualization is achieved by other methods. At P.S. 11, the great variety of materials and the extensive use of library books facilitate individualization. At the John H. Finley School, the whole system of evaluation, assignment, and use of the large list of reading books is involved. At all four schools, individualization is, of course, partly a matter of attitude and approach.

The last factor that seems to account for these schools' success is careful evaluation of pupil progress. Here again, the Sullivan program, if properly implemented, has this evaluation built in. Each child's work is checked after each page or two and again after the end of each book. In addition, the Ann Street School has the excellent diagnostic tests developed by the school reading specialist. At P.S. 11, the heterogeneous grouping of the classes requires careful evaluation in connection with individualization and annual assignment. At the John H. Finley School, a frequent evaluation of pupil progress is made by the reading coordinator by means of the modified Harris Test. In addition, there is evaluation by means of checking on each book read and evaluation for the purpose of achievement grouping for second- and third-grade classes.

In addition to these success factors, a word should be said about the age of these successful beginning reading programs. In no case was the success achieved in a year, or even in two years. This fact should serve as a warning to schools who hope to do the job in a year. In the case of P.S. 11, the approximate age of the beginning reading program in its present form is three years. At John H. Finley, it is nine years! At Woodland, it is three years. At the Ann Street School, the Sullivan program has been used only two years, but many of the features of the beginning reading program date back four years, to the time when the principal came to the school.

Non-essential Characteristics

Turning from success factors, let us look at some characteristics often thought important to improved achievement in beginning reading that are *not* common to these four successful schools. Some of these characteristics may, indeed, be important to the success of one or more of the four schools, but they apparently are not essential to success or it is reasonable to assume that they would be present in all four.

First is small class size. P.S. 11 is the only one of the four schools that has unusually small classes, about 22. Ann Street averages about 24, John H. Finley about 27, and Woodland a relatively high 29. School systems often spend large sums of money to reduce class size, even by such small numbers as two or three pupils. This study strongly suggests that such sums, if spent at all, could be better used in other ways. One of the obvious alternatives is additional personnel, described above as one of the "success factors."

Second is achievement grouping. Although achievement grouping or grouping by presumed ability may facilitate success in beginning reading instruction, if it were necessary to such success it would be hard to account for the success at P.S. 11, where under the MES program there is an extensive effort to make all classes heterogeneous. The other three schools use some kind of homogeneous grouping.

Third is the quality of teaching. No one writing about the schools can ignore the importance of good teachers. Naturally any program is better by virtue of its being implemented by good teachers. The better the teachers, the better the chances of success. But the relevant point here is that not one of the four schools had, in the primary grades, a group of teachers all of whom were outstanding. The teachers seemed to be, on the whole, above average in competence but not strikingly so. This is an important point because outstanding teachers can teach beginning reading successfully with *any* materials and under a wide range of conditions. At the other extreme, poor teachers will fail with the best materials and procedures. The four successful schools probably were somewhat favored by the quality of their teaching, but some mediocre and even poor teaching was observed.

Fourth is the ethnic background of the principals and teachers. Today there is considerable attention being paid to the ethnic identification of school personnel. Some community groups are trying to secure teachers and principals of the same ethnic group (black, Mexican-American, etc.) as the majority of the pupils in the school. Although it cannot be denied that in some cases this effort may be of educational value, it is interesting to note that the leaders of these four schools were, in all but one case, not members of the ethnic group predominant in the school's pupil population. The one exception was Mr. Wheeler in Kansas City, who is black. But there the principal of Woodland, where almost all of the pupils are black, is a white man. A similar observation can be made about the teachers: although some of them belong to the same ethnic group as is represented in the school, many do not. This study would suggest that there are far more important matters than the ethnic background of the administrators and teachers in achieving success in beginning reading instruction.

The fifth characteristic is the existence of preschool education. Today it is often argued that early formal training is extremely important—even the key—to success in the education of inner-city children. This study does not support that argument. While the successful third grade at P.S. 11 had had, for the most part, a prekindergarten experience, almost all children in the other three schools had not. Of course, this is not to say that early training would not help inner-city children, merely that only a small minority of the children in these four successful schools had had such training.

A last characteristic worth noting has to do with physical facilities. Not one of the four schools looked like the ultramodern buildings so lauded in some of the school magazines. In fact, two of the buildings (P.S. 11 and Woodland) were noticeably old. And all of the buildings were basically what is derisively called by some people "eggcrate" in nature. Without denying that new buildings are nice, this study suggests that many other factors (some of which are far less costly) are much more important in achieving reading success in the primary grades.

Summary

Reading achievement in the early grades in almost all inner-city schools is both relatively and absolutely low. This project has identified four notable exceptions. Their success shows that the failure in beginning reading typical of inner-city schools is the fault not of the children or their background—but of the schools. None of the successes was achieved overnight; they required from three to nine years. The factors that seem to account for the success of the four schools are strong leadership, high expectations, good atmosphere, strong emphasis on reading, additional reading personnel, use of phonics, individualization, and careful evaluation of pupil progress. On the other hand, some characteristics often thought of as important to school improvement were *not* essential to the success of the four schools: small class size, achievement grouping, high quality of teaching, school personnel of the same ethnic background as the pupils', preschool education, and outstanding physical facilities.

A Critique of George Weber's Study: Inner-city Children Can Be Taught to Read: Four Successful Schools

IRVING P. McPHAIL

Johns Hopkins Center for Metropolitan Planning and Research

George Weber's (1971) study of four inner-city schools, where the majority of third-graders were reading on grade level, was a forerunner of the new thrust in research in urban education that focuses on the identification and analysis of successful inner-city schools. This classic study will be critiqued in the following areas: (1) the problem, (2) design and methodology, (3) findings, and (4) conclusions.

THE PROBLEM

The soundness of the logic underlying the identification of common factors in the reading programs of successful inner-city schools as the major focus of the study is evident in Weber's discussion of the significance of the problem. Specifically, the existence of schools that were successful in teaching low-income minority students to read suggested that beginning reading achievement in inner-city schools did not have to be as depressed as it usually is. In rejecting the rationales for failure most prevalent during the early 1970s[1]—poor family background and alleged differences in intelligence between low-income minority students and their white middle-class counterparts—Weber appears to be endorsing the "Excellence" philosophy. However, Weber stated that "even though in (his) opinion the intelligence of poor children is somewhat lower, on the average, high intelligence is not necessary to learn the relatively simple skill of beginning reading" (see page 528).

The "Excellence" philosophy, as defined by the National Association of Black Reading and Language Educators, rejects the "Deficit" and "Difference" type ideologies in favor of the belief that Black children can learn anything if taught, and seeks to propagate those persons and programs that work in teaching Black children. "Deficit" views of Blacks, e.g., that a flaw in Black genes is responsible for low reading scores for Blacks, must be rejected. Most "Difference" views of Blacks, e.g.,

[1]The issue of language differences was also advanced during this period as a primary causal factor in Black children's reading failure. The reader is referred to Baratz and Shuy, 1969; Labov, 1972; Laffey and Shuy, 1973; McPhail, 1975, 1981a; Piestrup, 1973; Tolliver-Weddington, 1979; Williams, 1970; and Williams, 1975 for discussions of this issue. In addition to the Coleman Report, the reader is referred to Moynihan (1965) for "Deficit" views on the Black family, and to Billingsley (1968) and Hill (1972) for "Excellence" views on the Black family.

that Blacks are so different in their language and culture that they cannot learn, or they require a "special" non-academic education, must also be rejected (see Hoover, 1978). Although Weber did not discuss the basis for his opinion on the intelligence of poor children, he did make reference to Jensen's (1969) controversial work, which argues in favor of a "Deficit" view of Blacks. Jensen's theory that the average lower I.Q. score for "American Negroes" (as compared to the averages for whites and American Orientals) is the result of heredity has been soundly challenged by the overwhelming evidence in support of the influence on I.Q. of social and physical environmental factors (see Senna, 1973) and the built-in bias of the I.Q. tests themselves (Ristow, 1978; Williams, 1972; Word, 1974).

By selecting the school as the unit of study, Weber rejected the teacher and the individual class, and the school system, as potential units of study. The school, in contrast to the school system or the classroom, is the basic organizational and institutional unit responsible for providing instruction. Even within school systems, schools enjoy a fairly high degree of autonomy in organizing their instructional programs. Families typically form attachments to, and develop concerns about, their neighborhood school. A child's educational experiences are organized principally around the school, with curriculum and instruction organized and sequenced by grade level within schools, and with a host of extracurricular and other non-instructional activities located in, and organized by, the school. Yet, recent trends in the effective-schools research suggest that factors that distinguish successful schools from unsuccessful schools also seem to distinguish effective classrooms and teacher behaviors from their less effective counterparts. Weber's naiveté on this point is discussed later in this article.

Having defined the school as the study unit, Weber next defined "inner-city" and "successful reading achievement." The criteria established for defining these key terms avoided one major pitfall, yet suggested another pitfall that has made much of the teacher effectiveness and effective-schools research inadequate. Most of this research uses a relative definition of effectiveness, in which schools or teachers are identified as effective if their *average* achievement level is higher than those with comparable school or classroom composition. Such a relative definition could lead to accepting achievement differences between schools and classrooms with low-income students versus those with middle-class students. Weber wisely avoided this problem by requiring that inner-city schools, to be defined as successful in reading achievement, achieve a *national* grade norm score as a median and that the percentage of gross failures be low. On the other hand, "if one accepts the definition of instructional effectiveness which includes the criterion that the relationship between pupil background and achievement, within the school, approach zero, (then) only research which treats the variance in student achievement (and especially the extent to which such variance covaries with racial, ethnic, and/or social status characteristics of individual pupils) as a topic for investigation will permit identification of alterable school and instructional factors which can reduce the correlation between pupil background and performance" (Cohen, p. 738, n.d.). In this regard, Weber can be criticized for not reporting any differences in student achievement between Black, Puerto Rican, Mexican-American and "other" students in the inner-city schools (P.S. 11, Manhattan; P.S. 129, Manhattan; Ann Street School, Los Angeles), that had more than one ethnic group represented in its student body. Weber's selection of only low-income schools avoided any difficulties arising from the covariation of student achievement and social status characteristics.

Finally, the decision to focus on the third grade was appropriate given the investigator's objective of assessing the children's mastery of the *basic* reading skills covered in the *beginning* reading program, i.e., the children's " 'mechanical' ability to read simple American English" (see page 530). Yet we know that many schools demonstrate steady growth up to grade 3 and then the achievement curve falls sharply to grade 12. School effectiveness research thus far has not examined instruction in higher level cognitive skills (comprehension, mathematical reasoning) at the elementary level, instruction in writing at the elementary and secondary levels, and instruction in reading and mathematics at the secondary level. Future research, then, needs to identify effective school and classroom instructional practices at higher grade levels, for more complex skills, and in writing, as well as reading and mathematics.

DESIGN AND METHODOLOGY

The procedures described by Weber to obtain nominations of successful inner-city schools and to secure permission to visit 17 schools that supposedly met both criteria (type of school and reading success) are clearly described. The reasons why 52 of the second sample of 69 schools selectively dropped out of the project are of particular interest.

The decision to conduct an independent evaluation of reading achievement was most appropriate given the limitations that nationally standardized test results pose in this type of research design. Adequate information pertaining to the design (see Cohen, 1969, pp. 67–68) and standardization properties of the reading test developed by Weber is provided in the text (see pages 531–32), including evidence of a preparatory validation study of the test having been conducted. However, Weber did not provide adequate statistical data about the reliability and validity of the test, i.e., correlation coefficients with standardized reading tests. We must, therefore, *assume* that the test possessed adequate reliability and validity.

The purposes for conducting the visits to 17 big city schools and the description of field procedures (observations and interviews) used to collect data are discussed. The field procedures determined the nature of the beginning reading program and, where the school met both the inner-city and reading success criteria, the factors that accounted for the success. However, had Weber been conducting the study today instead of in 1971, he might have used ethnographic monitoring in one or more of the schools that met both criteria (see Dabney, in press; Rist, 1973; Watkins, 1981; Wilson, 1977).

To summarize, Weber found four schools that met the following criteria: (1) "they were non-selective public schools in the central areas of large cities that were attended by very poor children, and (2) at the third-grade level, their reading achievement medians equalled or exceeded the national norm and the percentages of non-readers were unusually low for such schools" (see page 533).

FINDINGS

Weber assumed that when all four of the successful schools followed a practice that was not usually found in unsuccessful schools, that practice had something to do with their success. He concluded, further, that different practices that existed in some, but not all, of the successful schools were not essential to success. Based on these two propositions, Weber accounted for the success of beginning reading instruction in the four successful schools.

Eight factors common to the four successful schools and not usually present in unsuccessful inner-city schools were identified as success factors. These factors were strong leadership, high expectations, good atmosphere, strong emphasis on reading, additional reading personnel, use of phonics, individualization, and careful evaluation of pupil progress. The non-essential school-level factors were small class size, achievement grouping, high quality of teaching, school personnel of the same ethnic background as the pupils, preschool education, and outstanding physical facilities.

Weber's identification of school-level factors that seemed to account for successful beginning reading instruction in low-income minority schools carved the path for the later, more sophisticated studies in this area (see Dabney, in press; Edmonds, 1979; Hoover, 1978). Weber's analysis of success factors did, however, leave out important details about at least two of the four schools that he reported on: The Woodland School and the John H. Finley School.

Selected success factors. Silberman (1970) and Thomas (in press) found active parental involvement and strong in-service, teacher-training components were major keys in the success of Finley and Woodland, respectively. Also, at Woodland, teachers were trained to be aware of their students' use of Black English Vernacular and to accept it, as well as to teach the children to be facile in "standard" English (Thomas, in press). Weber's description of the role of the "speech improvement" teacher at Woodland did not suggest the bi-dialectal perspective operative at Woodland that Thomas revealed. Perhaps the bi-dialectal perspective runs counter to Weber's views on the issue of Black children's language. In an earlier report on one successful inner-city school in Harlem (P.S. 192), Weber (1969) observed that the school "makes no concessions to what has been called by some 'the inner-city English dialect' " (p. 4). Weber reported:

> Dr. Gang (principal) says that the school does not worry about it, uses standard English. He comments characteristically that 'the dialect problem' is important only in the educational and sociological literature. (p. 4)

Hoover (1978) found that other successful low-income minority schools put great emphasis not on exposure to Black English Vernacular but to standard Black English (Taylor, 1971), which uses standard grammar in addition to elements of Black style, speech events, and vocabulary (see Piestrup, 1973; Smitherman, 1981; Williams & Whitehead, 1978).

At the Finley School, Silberman (1970) observed that "great stress (was) placed on developing pride in children's racial and ethnic identity" (p. 111), a factor that Weber failed to mention.

critique

A somewhat different analysis of the Silberman (1970) and Thomas (in press) observation of active parental involvement in the Finley and Woodland schools argues that characteristics of successful low-income minority schools, such as strong leadership, high expectations, good atmosphere, etc., are *causally* important, but only in schools that have an adequately socialized student body. That is, there is a conditional relationship in which factors such as those identified by Weber, are important *only* if students are prepared to work in schools, but are not powerful enough to overcome the negative effects of students who are unmotivated and who do not receive adequate support and encouragement at home and in their communities. Similarly, schools with well-prepared students may still turn out to be ineffective if they are not doing the things identified in Weber's and other's work. However, evidence suggests that an inadequately socialized student body may, in fact, be re-socialized through the exercise of instructional options under the school and classroom's control.

Specifically, research has demonstrated that a "literate environment" at home produces early readers and children who experience greater reading achievement in school (Durkin, 1966; Sakamoto, 1975; Thorndike, 1973). Yet, Cohen (1968) found that inner-city second-grade students from a *non-literate* home environment advanced in their reading, language skills, and interest in reading, in a school that provided a literate classroom environment. The children in Cohen's experiment were read to daily and encouraged to take part in activities that stimulated interaction. This data was coupled with the results of three remarkable studies (Levenstein, 1975; Sprigle, 1972; Strickland, 1973) that demonstrated that low-income children who are given experiences, at school or at home, in a cognitively and affectively rich environment, get higher scores on intelligence and reading achievement tests and on measures of affective development. The findings *strongly* suggest that, regardless of socio-economic status, schools can make the difference in the education of minority children.

Weber's finding of strong leadership as a success factor is also of great interest. In three of the four schools, the strong leadership was provided by the building principal. The brief descriptions of the three principals suggest a leadership style characterized by the ability to manage the instructional program, clarify and emphasize goals, allocate and procure resources, and supervise personnel and program (Barnard & Hetzel, 1976). This view of the principal as a strong *instructional* leader runs counter to the ethnographic study of an elementary school principal by Wolcott (1973) which portrayed the principal as one responding to a multitude of complex forces, many of which had little to do with classroom instruction. Principals who view their ideal role as that of an instructional leader, in fact, seem to spend more of their time managing conflict. Perhaps successful low-income minority schools are effective precisely because they are more tightly managed and more collectively committed to basic skills instruction. This seems logical on its face, though we need to know more about *how* principals exercise instructional leadership in the face of a multitude of complex, competing forces.

Finally, Weber's identification of the use of phonics as a success factor is not surprising. No aspect of reading instruction has been investigated more than the effect of teaching sound/spelling relationships (Johns, pages 97–104 of this volume).

The major studies have concluded that systematic instruction in sound/spelling patterns increases performance on reading tests through the primary grades (Chall, 1967; Dykstra, 1968). In fact, Hoover (1978) reported that "the use of a structured approach to reading which focuses on the orthographic rules/spelling patterns of English" (p. 760) emerged as one of the *most striking* characteristics of successful low-income minority schools. However, Hoover was correct in observing that the use of phonics does not preclude the use of the language experience approach, for example, at the Woodland School. Recent psycholinguistic research and notions of reading as a language process support the organization of a reading/communication arts plan that integrates and balances activities from all four communication perspectives (reading, writing, listening, speaking) and emphasizes the search for meaning (Botel, 1977; Goodman, 1968).

Selected non-essential characteristics. Weber (1971) identified quality of teaching as a non-essential characteristic. He argued that "outstanding teachers can teach beginning reading successfully with *any* materials and under a wide range of conditions . . . poor teachers will fail with the best materials and procedures" (p. 701). Weber suggested that the four successful schools were probably favored, somewhat, by the quality of their teaching, but some mediocre and even poor teaching was evident. Weber, in the opinion of this writer, erred in his judgement that quality of teaching is not, in fact, a *primary* causal factor in the success of the four schools.

Until recently, little has been written concerning *exactly* what happens in the classrooms of successful low-income minority schools; however, a relatively well-developed research tradition has demonstrated that the teacher is the most important determinant of students' reading achievement (Bond & Dykstra, 1967; Harris & Morrison, 1969; Harris, 1978). It is not surprising, then, that factors which distinguish successful schools from unsuccessful schools also seem to distinguish effective classrooms from their less effective counterparts: strong leadership, high expectations, good atmosphere and emphasis on reading. Dabney (in press) summarized the general findings of studies of more effective teaching behavior which suggest that low-income minority children achieve more in reading when their teacher:

1. assumes the role of a strong leader, using time efficiently and keeping students engaged in task-related activities;
2. organizes students into medium to large groups for instruction;
3. monitors work while being available to answer student-initiated questions;
4. asks low-ordered questions, insuring that students experience a great amount of success and have the opportunity to learn sufficient amounts of content;
5. keeps interaction at a low level of complexity, structures lessons so that students are aware of objectives;
6. sustains a classroom environment that is warm, friendly, democratic, relatively free of disruptive behavior and tolerant of linguistic diversity (McPhail, 1979a).

critique

Clearly, there is a need to learn *what* teachers do on a day-to-day basis and *how* they make decisions on the nature of instructional activities; the nature, size and composition of instructional groups (Weber's comments on achievement grouping were most helpful in this regard); strategies for motivating and rewarding student behavior; and strategies for coping with a considerable diversity of student ability and prior performance within the classroom. Again, the research tool of ethnographic monitoring is likely to prove useful in unraveling these complex issues.

Further, we need to radically redesign pre-service teacher education programs which purport to prepare teachers for service in low-income minority schools. Pre-service programs should reflect the knowledges and skills identified as successful teacher behaviors generally and, specifically, in the teaching of reading (McPhail, 1981b).

Weber included the ethnic background of the principals and teachers in the category of non-essential characteristics. Given that the leaders of the four schools were, in all but one case, not members of the ethnic group predominant in the school's student population, Weber concluded that "there are far more important matters than the ethnic background of the administrators and teachers in achieving success in beginning reading instruction" (p. 701). To be sure, the competence, attitude and commitment of the teachers and administrators in low-income minority schools to the teaching of basic skills are more critical than their ethnic backgrounds. Yet, there are powerful reasons to suggest the need for more competent and committed Black, Puerto Rican and other minority teachers and administrators in low-income minority schools who endorse the "Excellence" perspective.

Rhody McCoy (1970), a leader of the controversial struggle for decentralization and community control of schools in Ocean Hill-Brownsville (Brooklyn, New York) in the late 1960s has argued that:

> Here in New York it's conceivable that a kid can go from first grade all the way through high school and never see a Black teacher. If all these kids coming up today still see the white principal, the white district superintendent, the white Board of Education, white State Commissioner of Education, then their only conception is that in order to be successful, and be the boss, you gotta be white. That's not so. At least we don't want these kids to believe that it's so. So we're interested in having success models. (p. 256)

Weber did not include instruction in test-wiseness as a non-essential characteristic or success factor; however, he observed that pupils at the Ann Street School were consciously instructed "in the mechanics of test-taking . . . It (the school) tests the children frequently, using a variety of tests (see page 546). The prevalence of testing in schools, particularly minimum competency testing as a prerequisite for graduation, has alerted educators to the importance of test-taking skills (Downey, 1977). Limited attention has been focused on the role of test-wiseness in the test performance of minority students (McPhail, 1979b); however, informal reports from classroom teachers who have taught test-wiseness systematically have been encouraging. This informal data, with the limited empirical data on teaching test-wiseness to minority students, suggests that these students can be taught to be test-wise and can improve their performance as a result. Future research on these hypotheses, and on which skills to teach, is a critical need (McPhail, 1981).

CONCLUSIONS

The hypothesis of Weber's research study was proven. At least four inner-city public schools existed in the United States whose achievement in beginning reading instruction was far higher than in most inner-city schools. As such, Weber confirmed that the failure of low-income minority children to learn to read is the "fault not of the children or their background—but of the schools" (see page 547). Despite the limitations of the study critiqued above, the work of George Weber will remain a classic study of the assertion that low-income minority children can learn to read if taught.

FOR FURTHER LEARNING

Those readers who are interested in continuing to explore the topic of cultural differences and reading would find the following references helpful:

Beck, M. Black Catholic school in Chicago strives where others fail. *Wall Street Journal,* October 22, 1976, 1; 18.

Black schools that work. *Newsweek,* January 1, 1973, 57–58.

Blakeslee, S. School for Blacks offers money-back guarantee. *New York Times,* June 4, 1975, 35.

Lindenmeyer, O. Found and lost. *Black history: Lost, stolen or strayed.* New York: Avon, 1970.

The Muslim way. *Newsweek,* Sept. 25, 1972, 106–107.

New York State Education Department. *Reading achievement related to educational and environmental conditions in 12 New York City elementary schools.* New York: Division of Education Evaluation, 1974.

Slater, J. Learning is an all-Black thing. *Ebony,* October 1972, 87–91.

Success in the ghetto. *Time,* November 8, 1976, 77.

REFERENCES

Baratz, J. C., & Shuy, R. W. (Eds.). *Teaching Black children to read.* Washington, D.C.: Center for Applied Linguistics, 1969.

Barnard, D. P., & Hetzel, R. W. The principal's role in reading instruction. *Reading Teacher,* 1976, *29,* 386–388.

Billingsley, A. *Black families in white America.* Englewood Cliffs, N.J.: Prentice-Hall, 1968.

Bond, G. L., & Dykstra, R. *Coordinating center for first grade reading instructional programs: Final report.* (U.S.O.E. Project No. X-001). Minneapolis: University of Minnesota, 1967.

Botel, M. *Literacy plus.* Washington, D.C.: Curriculum Development Associates, 1977.

Chall, J. S. *Learning to read: The great debate.* New York: McGraw-Hill, 1967.

references

Cohen, D. H. The effect of literature on vocabulary and reading achievement. *Elementary English,* 1968, *45,* 209–213+.

Cohen, M. *Instructionally effective schools* (Research Area Plan). Washington, D.C.: National Institute of Education, n.d.

Cohen, S. A. *Teach them all to read.* New York: Random House, 1969.

Dabney, N. *See how it runs: A successful inner-city school.* Unpublished doctoral dissertation, University of Pennsylvania, in press.

Downey, G. W. Is it time we started teaching children how to take tests? *American School Board Journal,* 1977, *164,* 27–30.

Durkin, D. *Children who read early.* New York: Teachers College Press, 1966.

Dykstra, R. Summary of the 2nd phase of the cooperative research program in primary reading instruction. *Reading Research Quarterly,* 1968, *4,* 49–70.

Edmonds, R. Effective schools for the urban poor. *Educational Leadership,* 1979, *37,* 15–24.

Friere, P. *Pedagogy of the oppressed.* New York: Seabury Press, 1970.

Goodman, K. S. The psycholinguistic nature of the reading process. In K. S. Goodman (Ed.), *The psycholinguistic nature of the reading process.* Detroit: Wayne State University Press, 1968.

Harris, A. J. *The effective teacher of reading, revisited.* Paper presented at the twenty-third annual meeting of the International Reading Association, Houston, May 1978. (ERIC Document Reproduction Service No. ED 153 193)

Harris, A. J., & Morrison, C. The CRAFT project: A final report. *Report Teacher,* 1969, *22,* 335–340.

Hill, R. B. *The strengths of Black families.* New York: Emerson Hall, 1972.

Hoover, M. R. Characteristics of Black schools at grade level. *Reading Teacher,* 1978, *31,* 757–762.

Jensen, A. R. How much can we boost I.Q. and scholastic achievement? *Harvard Educational Review,* 1969, *39,* 1–123.

Labov, W. *Language in the inner-city: Studies in the Black English Vernacular.* Philadelphia: University of Pennsylvania Press, 1972.

Laffey, J. L., & Shuy, R. (Eds.). *Language differences: Do they interfere?* Newark, Del.: International Reading Association, 1973.

Levenstein, P. *The mother-child home program.* New York: The Verbal Interaction Project, 1975.

Malcolm X. *The autobiography of Malcolm X.* New York: Grove Press, 1964.

McCoy, R. Why have an Ocean Hill-Brownsville? In N. Wright (Ed.), *What Black educators are saying.* San Francisco: Leswing Press, 1970.

McPhail, I. P. *Teaching Black children to read: A review of psycho- and sociolinguistic theories and models.* Philadalphia: University of Pennsylvania, 1975. (ERIC Document Reproduction Service No. ED 103 819)

McPhail, I. P. A study of response to literature across three social interaction patterns: A directional effort. *Reading Improvement,* 1979a, *16,* 55–61.

McPhail, I. P. Test sophistication: An important consideration in judging the standardized test performance of Black students. *Reading World,* 1979b, *18,* 227–235.

McPhail, I. P. Beyond Black English: Toward an ethnography of communication in the inner-city classroom. *Proceedings of the Retreat on the Black Child: An In-Depth Study of Those Factors Affecting Learning.* Dallas: ESAA Pilot Project, East Oak Cliff Sub-District, Dallas Independent School District, 1981a, 43–56. (ERIC Document Reproduction Service No. 172 178)

McPhail, I. P. *An agenda for urban education: Implications for teacher education from the study of successful low-income minority schools.* Keynote address at the Second Annual Conference on Urban Education, Dallas Teacher Education Center Council and Teacher Corps Project, Dallas, April 1981b.

McPhail, I. P. Why teach test-wiseness? *Journal of Reading,* 1981, *25,* 32–38.

Moynihan, D. P. *The Negro family: The case for national action.* Washington, D.C.: U. S. Department of Labor, Office of Planning and Research, 1965.

Piestrup, A. M. Black dialect interference and accommodation of reading instruction in first grade. *Monographs of the Language—Behavior Research Laboratory,* No. 4. Berkeley: University of California, 1973.

Rist, R. C. *The urban school. A factory for failure.* Cambridge, Mass.: Massachusetts: Institute of Technology Press, 1973.

Ristow, W. Larry P. versus I.Q. tests. *The Progressive,* 1978, *42,* 48–50.

Sakamoto, T. Preschool reading in Japan. *Reading Teacher,* 1975, *29,* 240–244.

Senna, C. (Ed.). *The fallacy of I.Q.* New York: The Third Press, 1973.

Silberman, C. *Crisis in the classroom: The remaking of American education.* New York: Vintage Books, 1970.

Smitherman, G. (Ed.). Black English and the education of Black children and youth. *Proceedings of the National Invitational Symposium on the King Decision.* Detroit: Center for Black Studies, Wayne State University, 1981.

Sprigle, H. *The learning to learn program: Final report.* 1972. (ERIC Document Reproduction Service No. ED 066 669).

Strickland, S. Can slum children learn? In C. Senna (Ed.), *The fallacy of I.Q.* New York: The Third Press, 1973.

Taylor, O. Response to social dialects and the field of speech. In *Sociolinguistics: A cross-disciplinary perspective.* Washington, D. C.: Center for Applied Linguistics, 1971.

Thomas, J. M. The Woodland school. In M. R. Hoover (Ed.), *Proceedings of the Conference Sponsored by the Public Committee for the Humanities.* Philadelphia: University of Pennsylvania, in press.

Thorndike, R. L. *Reading comprehension education in fifteen countries: An empirical study.* New York: John Wiley & Sons, 1973.

Tolliver-Weddington, G. (Ed.). Ebonics (Black English): Implications for education. *Journal of Black Studies,* 1979, *9,* 363–494.

Watkins, M. *Teachers' perceptions of parents' roles vs. parents' perception of their roles in children's acquisition of literacy for learning.* Unpublished manuscript, University of Pennsylvania, 1981.

Weber, G. How one ghetto school achieves success in reading. *Council for Basic Education Bulletin,* 1969, *13,* 1–4.

Wilcox, P. Education for Black humanism: A way of approaching it. In N. Wright (ed.), *What Black educators are saying.* San Francisco: Leswing Press, 1970.

Williams, F. (Ed.). *Language and poverty.* Chicago: Markham, 1970.

Williams, F., & Whitehead, J. L. Language in the classroom: Studies of the Pygmalion effect. In J. S. DeStefano (Ed.), *Language, society, and education: A profile of Black English.* Worthington, Ohio: Charles A. Jones, 1973.

Williams, R. L. Abuses and misuses in testing Black children. In R. L. Jones (ed.), *Black psychology.* New York: Harper and Row, 1972.

Williams, R. L. (Ed.). *Ebonics: The true language of Black folks.* St. Louis: The Institute of Black Studies, 1975.

Wilson, S. The use of ethnographic techniques in educational research. *Review of Educational Research,* 1977, *47,* 245–265.

Wolcott, H. *The man in the principal's office: An ethnography.* New York: Holt, Rinehart, & Winston, 1973.

Word, C. Testing: Another word for racism. *Essence,* Oct. 1974, p. 38 +.

A Commentary on McPhail's Critique of George Weber's Study: Inner-City Children Can be Taught to Read: Four Successful Schools

ALBERT J. KINGSTON

University of Georgia

McPhail's thoughtful commentary on Weber's "Four Successful Schools" updates and elaborates on the original report. Weber's original study of inner-city schools, which appeared to achieve salutary goals is, of course, widely known. McPhail, who is obviously knowledgeable about and interested in the problems of educating inner-city, culturally disadvantaged children, criticizes the study from the vantage point of a decade of additional research and opinion. Those reading McPhail's critique should recognize that in 1971, when the Weber study was made, evaluation techniques were somewhat crude and less sophisticated.

As McPhail's commentary notes, many writers in the 1970s focused on those factors that Weber concluded are either essential or non-essential in successful schools. In light of these more recent developments, Weber's study cannot be regarded as definitive in either scope or design. In fact, descriptive studies of ideal or model schools generally leave much to be desired.

McPhail devotes considerable space to discussing philosophical issues involving the problem faced by Weber. It probably would have sufficed to note that academic achievements in inner-city schools are usually somewhat less than educators hope for. McPhail, however, does discuss Weber's choice of the school as the unit for study but, in the opinion of this writer, could have explored the pros and cons of this decision at much greater length. After all, schools are not just buildings but rather involve teachers, pupils, curriculum methods, and much more. The findings in the original study may have been affected by the decision to study "schools." I agree wholeheartedly with McPhail's call for additional information concerning demographics, e.g., race, social status, etc.

McPhail might have focused on Weber's choice of third-grade achievement as the basis for judging successful and unsuccessful schools. Recent findings from the National Assessment of Educational Progress indicate that reading scores have improved at the primary grade level but not at the middle and secondary grade levels. McPhail does comment briefly on this criterion, but could have greatly expanded his criticisms. After all, few reading specialists equate word recognition skills with reading, and comprehension involves many complex reasoning and inferential factors. If Weber had used upper grade achievements, measured with a test that reflected higher level mental processes, one strongly suspects that he might have obtained a somewhat different list of essential and non-essential elements.

McPhail seems to be somewhat gentle in certain of his criticisms. I believe that the paucity of descriptive data prevents the critical reader from careful study of the results. Descriptive statements in the original report force the reader to accept Weber's generalizations. However, many of the statements in the Weber report would simply provoke "amens" from professional educators. Almost all educators, for example, believe that teacher behavior affects pupil learning. Almost all reading programs include some type of "phonics." Almost all reading supervisors plead for "strong emphasis on reading." The problem, of course, is to define any essential and non-essential factors in terms of specific classroom behavior or pedagogical methodology. In addition, McPhail quite correctly notes the lack of pertinent information about the reading test employed. Reading tests do vary considerably in reliability and validity. Weber's findings would be more helpful if the criteria deemed essential or non-essential were operationally defined. In short, one can only wonder, as McPhail seems to, where do we go from here? Can we shore up the weaknesses in Weber's study and focus more specifically on those factors that seem to be found in successful school programs?

section XII

READING MEASUREMENT

RESEARCH by P. A. Killgallon, *A Study of Relationships Among Certain Pupil Adjustments in Reading Situations*

CRITIQUE by Timothy Shanahan

FOR FURTHER LEARNING

COMMENTARY by Kenneth Ahrendt

RESEARCH by J. R. Bormuth, *Readability: A New Approach*

CRITIQUE by Eugene A. Jongsma

FOR FURTHER LEARNING

COMMENTARY by Priscilla Drum

This section introduces the reader to two studies in the area of reading measurement by P. A. Killgallon and J. R. Bormuth. Shanahan critiques Killgallon's study which is widely cited as the source of the criteria used for placing students in texts of appropriate reading difficulty. Shanahan provides the reader with information concerning the type of evidence needed to arrive at an empirically valid set of criteria for these purposes. He then suggests that Killgallon and those who have conducted subsequent investigations have failed to provide such evidence. Ahrendt's comments indicate a difference of opinion with regard to Killgallon's purposes. He feels that Killgallon set out to study individual differences among fourth grade students with respect to reading, spelling and personality adjustment. The investigation of various levels of reading achievement was of secondary concern according to Ahrendt. He claims that Killgallon was aware that any attempt to assign an accurate instructional level of reading difficulty to text materials, based on his criteria, was arbitrary.

Jongsma critiques Bormuth's study and cites four distinguishing characteristics that set this work apart from previous readability research. He claims that Bormuth's investigation marked a turning point in readability research because it called into question a number of previously accepted beliefs about readability. Jongsma explains that its true importance stems from the fact that, by using a combination of linguistic theory and cloze methodology, it provided new ways to examine the complexities of written text.

Drum's comments on Jongsma's critique reveal a concern for the limitations of using cloze procedures as a means of measuring reading comprehension. She presents a thorough examination of these limitations and suggests that any procedure or instrument used in reading assessment should be carefully examined for both its adequacies and inadequacies.

A STUDY OF RELATIONSHIPS AMONG CERTAIN PUPIL ADJUSTMENTS IN READING SITUATIONS

P. A. KILLGALLON

The chief purpose of this investigation is to study individual differences among fourth grade pupils in typical reading situations with respect to reading, spelling, and personality adjustment. The study attempts to define the problem of differentiating reading instruction at this grade level by determining the extent of variation in the factors mentioned, the incidence of retardation in reading at various levels of intelligence and of reading achievement, the relationships among reading, spelling, and personality adjustment, and the fundamental assumptions upon which teachers base their instructional practices (p. 11).

METHOD

Two hundred and six fourth grade pupils from central Pennsylvania participated in this study. The Informal Reading Inventory was administered to every fifth pupil, forty-one in all, on the rank distribution of Gates Survey reading ages. This test is an individual, diagnostic test of reading ability (p. 82).

The test was administered in an individual manner. No person, other than the subject and the examiner, was present during the administration of the test. The time required for administering the test varied from thirty minutes to one hour and fifteen minutes (p. 83).

THE INFORMAL READING INVENTORY

The test referred to in this report as "An Informal Reading Inventory" is used extensively in the Reading Clinic of The Pennsylvania State College and was employed by Dr. E. A. Betts in an investigation of reading difficulties at the intermediate grade level (Betts, 1941). Fundamentally, it is a test of reading performance in which the subject is required to read, silently and orally for definitely set-up purposes, selected passages from a graded series of readers. Inadequacies are noted on a rather detailed check-list during the performance and comprehension is checked afterward. The test enables an experienced examiner not

Unpublished doctoral dissertation, Pennsylvania State College, 1942. (Editor's Note: Because of the length and diversity of Killgallon's work, only those sections of the dissertation which dealt with the validity of the IRI criteria are reported here. These pertinent sections were selected, edited for clarity, and reorganized for inclusion in this volume by Timothy Shanahan. Page numbers at the end of each section refer to the original pagination of the Killgallon manuscript.)

only to diagnose reading difficulties but to determine the achievement level of the elementary pupil very accurately within limits of a single grade or reader level.

The fact that reading textbooks at upper elementary and junior high school levels are not characteristically well-graded in difficulty constitutes a limitation on the use of this test which should be noted. The following textbooks were chosen to provide the selections for the test because they were unfamiliar to the subjects of this study:

> *Childhood Readers,* I through VI (Grady, Klopper & Gifford, 1939)
> *Reading and Thinking,* VII through IX (Center & Persons, 1940) (p. 89)

No single series covering the full range of difficulty required by the purpose of the investigation was available. The use of two different series involves an assumption that their gradation of difficulty is strictly comparable; an assumption which may or may not be entirely valid, and which constitutes a material limitation of this study.

In choosing selections from the textbooks at each grade level ones promising to appeal to the interest of the pupils were selected. Recognition was accorded the fact that the first half of a modern reader characteristically reviews the vocabulary of the immediately-preceding level, by selecting passages appearing in the later pages of each book (p. 90).

Criteria for the Assignment of Reading Levels.

No two individuals are likely to exhibit identical syndromes of difficulties on the Informal Reading Inventory. In any event differences in the degree to which the individual symptoms are present are almost certain to appear. Furthermore, the application of the inventory, in determining the level at which reading instruction may most profitably be initiated, will be most effective when findings are considered in relation to other pertinent factors. The character, and diversity of the child's interests, his persistence, attitude toward reading, and many other physical and psychological attributes when favorable, constitute assets which will enable one pupil to function with profit at a level where another, of similar reading ability, would fail.

An informal reading inventory, of course, cannot measure such factors. It is, however, a useful instrument for diagnosing reading difficulties in highly valid materials, the reading textbooks themselves. As a guide in the observation of reading performance it constitutes, possibly, the best single available index to reading ability at the elementary school level (p. 101).

The subjectivity of the examiner's ratings, however, must be recognized as a major limitation in the use of the inventory. The extent of this limitation is reduced and the reliability of the instrument is increased in direct proportion to the degree to which results are interpreted according to valid and objective criteria. With this in mind, the criteria outlined below were established after preliminary trial of the Informal Reading Inventory and were observed in making the ratings in the present study.

The Basal Reading Level. The highest level at which *all* of the following criteria were satisfied was denoted the basal reading level.

1. A minimum comprehension score of 90 percent.

research

2. A fluent effective oral reading performance characterized by
    a. Proper phrasing and rhythm
    b. Observation of punctuation
    c. Adequate interpretation of meaning
    d. Freedom from word-perception errors
    e. Correct pronunciation and clear enunciation
3. An efficient silent reading performance characterized by
    a. Adequate rate of comprehension
    b. Freedom from pointing, excessive lateral head movement, and all forms of vocalization (p. 102)

The Probable Instructional Level. Because the Informal Reading Inventory samples many different aspects of reading ability over a wide range, the reading selections and tests of comprehension at each grade level are of necessity comparatively brief. This condition enhanced the weight and significance of individual items and required that limits imposed by the following criteria be relatively liberal.

1. A score of 50 percent in comprehension was considered minimum in assigning an instructional level. This standard was adhered to regardless of the excellence of the reading performance in other respects.
2. The maximum ratio of word-perception errors to number of running words allowed on the instructional level was one to fourteen. In other words, no pupil was assigned any level upon which his oral performance was characterized by more than 7 percent in word-recognition.
3. Excessive lateral head movement, finger pointing and the various forms of vocalization during silent reading were interpreted as indicating undue difficulty when two or more appeared in conjunction with low comprehension or high error ratio. Accordingly, no pupil exhibiting two or more such "crutches" was assigned a level upon which he failed to score 75 percent or higher in comprehension or exceeded the ratio of one word-perception error in each fifteen running words.
4. Clearly inadequate word calling is usually an expression of a lack of understanding of the material read. Oral reading performance characterized by lack of emphasis upon meaning, inadequate phrasing, or word-by-word reading was considered sufficient justification for assigning a lower instructional level unless comprehension was 75 percent or above (p. 102–103).

The Probable Reading Frustration Level. This level may be defined as one upon which the disparity between the requirements of the material read and the adequacy of the performance is recognized and deplored by the reader. The following criterion was observed in assigning this level in the present study:

> A comprehension score of 20 percent or lower in conjunction with a word-perception error ratio of one error to each ten running words was required as evidence that a wide disparity between task and performance really existed. In addition, clearly-observable tension-type behavior was required as apparent proof that the subject deplored his inadequacy (p. 104).

Treatment of Data on the Informal Inventory

The various results on the Informal Reading Inventory were used in the manner outlined below.

1. Calculation of the mean difference in grade placement between Gates Survey and Informal Reading Inventory results.

   Grade values of .3 for pre-primer level, .5 for primer level, 1.0 for first reader level, 2.0 for second reader level and corresponding values for each succeeding level through the ninth, were assigned to the probable instructional levels found on the Inventory. The average difference between these values and the Gates Survey reading grades scores for the forty-one cases to whom the Informal Inventory was administered was then computed.

   Because the unit of measurement of the informal test was a full grade level except in the case of those few pupils who scored lower than first grade ability, a second comparison was made in which the scores of the two tests were made more comparable by dropping all fractional parts of a year from Gates Survey reading grades.
2. The average percentage of word-perception errors in terms of number of errors per hundred running words was computed at both the probable reading frustration level and distributions made.
3. The average comprehension scores on the instructional and frustration levels were computed.
4. Summary analyses of symptoms of reading difficulty at the instructional and frustration levels were compiled and percentages of occurrence computed.
5. Similar summaries of overt behavior responses were made.
6. The average comprehension score was calculated for each grade level and for all grades at the instructional and frustration levels and a distribution made (p. 104–105).

ANALYSIS OF RESULTS: SUBJECTIVE DATA

The data presented in the present chapter all involve, in some measure, findings which were taken by means of the Informal Reading Inventory. The reliability and validity of the results on this test depend upon the judgment of the examiner. They involve, in other words, the element of subjectivity.

Analysis of Reading Difficulties.

By making a random sampling over the entire range of reading abilities represented it was hoped that a group representative of the total population of the investigation would be secured. There is evidence that this result was achieved in high degree (p. 156).

Research/Table 1 describes the sample group in those terms showing the mean and range at each level. The mean instructional level, 3.16, is lower by 1.44 grades than the corresponding mean on the Gates Survey. The average difference between grade placement on the Informal Inventory and on the Gates test is 1.5 grade-levels in favor of the Gates test.

research

RESEARCH/TABLE 1
Averages and ranges of the sample group at the several reading levels ($N=41$)

Reading Levels	Average	Range
Basal	.86	0–5.0
Instruction	3.16	0–9.0
Frustration ($N=38$)	6.36	4.0–9.0
Capacity	5.10	3.0–9.0

*Three pupils were not assigned frustration levels. (p. 157)

Since the Informal Inventory scores are in units of one full grade, scores on the standardized test were made comparable by dropping all fractional parts. Calculated on the basis the Informal Inventory placed the children on average 1.06 grades lower than the standardized test. The range of 0 to 9.0 on the Inventory exceeds that on the Gates Survey, 2.4 to 10.4, by one grade-level (p. 157–158).

At each of the assigned levels shown in Research/Table 1 the variability of the group is noteworthy. Ranges extend over five, six, or nine grade-levels at each reading level. The average discrepancy between basal and instructional level is 2.4 grade-levels; the frustration level is, on the average, 3.38 grade levels above the instructional level; the reading capacity level exceeds the instructional level, 1.87 grade levels. The frustration level is not reached apparently, until a pupil is well beyond his real reading ability and above the level upon which he is able to understand the materials read to him. The wide discrepancy between basal and instructional levels may be attributed largely to careless reading. In several instances, pupils read more fluently and expressively at high levels than upon levels considerably below their ability. Too few such children were observed to permit drawing the general conclusion, that children develop slovenly reading habits when materials are unchallenging in interest and difficulty. It would, however, seem to be a logical conclusion (p. 158).

A summary analysis of the difficulties characterizing reading performance on the instructional level appears as Research/Table 2.

The symptoms of difficulty exhibited at the probable reading frustration level greatly exceeded those at the instructional level in frequency of occurrence, in number of types appearing, and in the degree of severity with which they were made manifest. The percent of pupils making each response increased in some degree at this level. The greatest increase, over 50 percent, was evidenced in respect to refusals; the least, shown in connection with faulty syllabication, was less than 1 percent. An increase in guessing of over 40 percent was surpassed only by the increase in refusals. Six times as many children held their books too close at this level as on the instructional level.

Ten symptoms appeared on the frustration level which were not represented on the instructional level, namely, various forms of reversal errors and inadequate word calling, low vocal utterance, low rate, holding the book at an angle, and finger pointing.

An increase in the severity with which many of the symptoms were demonstrated was readily observed. For example, silent lip movement became whispering; whispering gave way to low vocal utterance. Guessing tended to become extremely wild and inappropriate; refusals were less frequently preceded by independent attempts to pronounce the words. Other examples might be cited at length but, of course, cannot be easily quantified (p. 160).

Research/Table 3 shows the symptoms of reading difficulty which were

RESEARCH/TABLE 2

A summary of reading difficulties at the probable instructional level ($N = 40$)

Responses	Pupils Exhibiting Number												
	P.P	P	I	II	III	IV	V	VI	VII	VIII	IX	Total	Percent
Word Perception													
Refusal			1	1		6	1					9	22.5
Guessing			1		2	7	5	1	1		1	18	45.0
Omission			3		1	1			1			6	15.0
Substitution	1		3	1	3	4	5	1	1		1	20	50.0
Insertion			3		2	3	5					13	32.5
Repetition	1		7	1	9	6	4	1	1		1	32	80.0
Initial Consonant Error					1	2	1		1			5	12.5
Final Consonant Error					1	1	1		1			4	10.0
Faulty Syllabication						1					1	2	5.0
Omission of final "s"					2	1						3	7.5
Addition of final "s"					2							2	5.0
Ignoring Punctuation (Occasional)	1		5			5	1					12	30.0
Book too Close					1	1						1	2.5
Excessive Head Movement			1	1	4	2						8	20.0
Silent Lip Movement			1	1	1	3	2					8	20.0
Whispering					1	2						3	7.5
Rate too High						1						1	2.5

(p. 163)

RESEARCH/TABLE 3
A summary of reading difficulties at the probable frustration level ($N = 38$)

Response	IV	V	VI	Pupils VII	VIII	IX	Total	Percent
Word Perception								
Refusal	6	7	2	6	6	2	29	76.3
Guessing	6	7	7	7	5	2	34	89.5
Omission	2	4	2	5	6	2	21	55.3
Substitution	3	7	5	5	6	2	28	73.7
Insertion	3	5	1	5	4	1	19	50.0
Repetition	4	6	5	7	7	2	31	81.6
Letter Reversal	0	1	0	1	0	0	2	5.2
Word Reversal	0	2	0	0	2	0	4	10.5
Partial Reversal	0	0	1	0	1	0	2	5.3
Initial Consonant Error	2	3	1	6	3	0	15	39.5
Final Consonant Error	1	3	1	0	1	0	6	15.8
Faulty Syllabication	1	0	1	0	0	0	2	5.2
Omission of final "s"	1	0	2	1	0	1	5	13.2
Addition of final "s"	2	1	2	1	0	2	8	21.1
Rate								
Too Low	3	6	6	6	3	1	25	65.8
Too High	0	0	0	0	1	0	1	2.6
Word Calling								
Inadequate Phrasing	2	3	5	5	6	1	22	57.9
Lack of Emphasis on Meaning	3	0	3	3	0	1	10	26.3
Ignoring Punctuation	3	3	6	1	4	0	17	44.7
Excessive Lateral Head Movement	3	3	6	0	2	1	15	39.5
Vocalization								
Silent Lip Movement	3	2	1	0	2		8	21.1
Whispering	0	0	3	1	2		6	15.8
Low Vocal Utterance	1	2					3	7.9
Book too Close	1	2	1	0	1	1	6	15.8
Book at Angle						1	1	2.6
Finger Pointing	1	3	2				6	15.8

(p. 163)

observed on the probable frustration level as well as the number of pupils exhibiting each response and the grade level upon which it was recorded. The percent of pupils exhibiting each symptom is also shown. In this connection it may be noted that thirty-eight of the forty-one pupils of the sample group were assigned probable frustration levels in accordance with these criteria. Three, or approximately 7 percent, did not satisfy the criteria.

The differences between the frustration and instructional reading levels noted above are supplemented in striking manner by the data on reading comprehension at the two levels. The comprehension test at both levels included questions on the material read silently as well as that read orally. Uniformly low comprehension characterized performance upon the probable reading frustration level. For the most part, this paralleled evidence of mechanical difficulty. Some pupils, however, were able to perform adequately with respect to mechanical difficulties even when comprehension was almost entirely lacking. Sheer word calling, then must be recognized as another characteristic of the probable reading frustration level.

Research/Table 4 permits comparison of the probable instructional level and the probable frustration level from the standpoint of comprehension. The mean comprehension score at the instructional level was 71 percent; at the frustration level, 11 percent. Scores on the former level ranged from 50 percent to 95 percent; on the latter level, from zero to 13 percent (p. 162).

RESEARCH/TABLE 4
Average percent comprehension on probable instructional levels and probable frustration levels

	Instructional Level ($N=40$)	Frustration Level ($N=38$)
Grand Level	Average Percent	Average Percent
Pre-Primer	79	
First	90	
Second	95	
Third	82	
Fourth	67	13
Fifth	66	12
Sixth	60	8
Seventh	55	11
Eighth		12
Ninth	50	0

(p. 164)

The percentage of errors a pupil can make and still profit maximally from instruction upon a given level, is a problem of general concern to teachers and others who use an informal reading inventory as a guide in selecting the level upon which to initiate reading instruction. Variations in pupil abilities, interests, attitudes and capacity; differences in such peripheral items as the nature of the reading program, the materials of instruction, standards of achievement and similar factors obviate the possibility of determining any criterion in this respect which will be universally applicable. But a norm, interpreted in the light of these and other limitations would have practical values.

Data regarding the ratio of word-perception errors to number of running words at the instructional level were collected with this problem in mind. They are summarized in Research/Table 5 in terms of percent. The mean percent of error was 5.1; the limits of the range, 1.2 and 6.6. In corresponding terms, pupils made approximately five word-perception errors in every hundred running words, or one in every twenty, on the average. The lowest ratio of error to running words was one to one hundred; the highest was approximately seven per one hundred, or one to sixteen. Examination of the table will, perhaps, throw some light on the possible value of the mean ratio as a guide in selecting the most appropriate level for instructional purposes. The scores of fourteen pupils, or 35 percent of the cases, actually fall upon the interval which includes the mean. Including the four at the next lower interval, which would comprise ratios within 1 percent of the mean, the maximum percent of pupils for whom the strict ap-

RESEARCH/TABLE 5
The distribution of the sample group with respect to percentage of word-recognition errors of the probable instructional level ($N = 40$)

Percent Error	PP	P	I	II	III	IV	V	VI	VII	VIII	IX	Total
6.00–6.99			1	1	6	2	2	1				13
5.00–5.99			7			4	2				1	14
4.00–4.99	2				1	1						4
3.00–3.99					2		2		1			5
2.00–2.99			1			1						2
1.00–1.99					1	1						2
Total	2	0	9	1	10	9	6	1	1	0	1	40

(p. 166)

plication of the standard can reasonably be held appropriate is approximately 55 percent. The remaining 45 percent of the pupils would be ill-served in varying degrees by rigid adherence to the standard. But since it is not suggested that any ratio shall ever dictate the assignment of the instructional level, the mean ratio determined here appears to represent the most generally suitable one for use as a point of reference or comparison. The occurrence of perception difficulties in much greater extent than that indicated by this mean ratio will undeniably operate to obstruct the pupils' comprehension, dissipate his interest, and in many ways render his instruction uneconomical at the given level (p. 165, 167).

ANALYSIS OF TENSION BEHAVIOR

The chief purpose for which the data presented under this heading were collected was to discover and summarize the kinds of tension behavior exhibited by children at their probable reading instructional levels and at their probable reading frustration levels. The assumption is neither made nor implied here that such behavior is entirely attributable to the difficulties encountered in the reading. Several factors may conceivably cause such behavior: the conditioning of earlier failure or maladjustment; the disturbing influence of a too-exacting or unsympathetic teacher; the fear of ridicule, a nervous disability, organic or functional; and, doubtless, many others. But when tension behavior is observed to appear only after the difficulty of the reading material has been increased, or to appear with substantially greater frequency, and severity, and in additional forms following such an increase, it seems reasonable to assume that difficulty is the chief cause of the behavior.

On the average the children in this study established instructional levels about two and one-half grades above their basal grade-levels. This indicates that no child failed to encounter reading difficulties upon his instructional level. It was to be expected, therefore, that at least some slight evidences of tension would appear. The criteria defining the instructional level act, however, as a limiting factor in controlling the incidence of tension behavior at this level. By definition

RESEARCH/TABLE 6
Summary analysis of tension behavior at the probable instructional level

Tension Behavior	PP	P	I	II	III	IV	V	VI	VII	VIII	IX	Number	Percent
Head Movements	1				1	1	1					4	10.0
Body Movements			1				2					3	7.5
Arm Movements							1					1	2.5
Hand Movements													
Picking			1			2	2					5	12.5
Fingering Book									1			1	2.5
Leg Movements						1	1					2	5.0
Foot Movements							1				1		5.0
Facial Movements													
Frowning						3					1	5	12.5
Sucking Finger					1							1	2.5

(p. 169)

of the level, many or severe evidences of insecurity, could not be manifested here.

Research/Table 6 summarizes the findings pertaining to tension behavior at the probable reading level. It reveals that reading performance at this level was accompanied by comparatively few indications of tension. The most characteristic forms in which tension behavior was observed were picking and fingering movements of the hands and frowning. Hand movements were made by 15 percent of the children; 12.5 percent frowned. Just twenty-nine observations were recorded for the entire group (p. 167–168).

Research/Table 7 in which a corresponding analysis is made for the probable reading frustration level gives a different picture. It reveals that frustration is characterized by many and various manifestations of tension. Twenty-seven different items were observed, as compared to ten at the instructional level. Frequency of occurrence ranged from 2.6 percent to 42.1 percent. The extreme types of behavior represented is evidence of the severity of the frustration. Gasping, gritting teeth, biting lips and fingers, and many of the other responses are seldom associated with mild tension (p. 168, 171).

It is apparent that children, confronted with reading difficulties greatly incommensurate with their abilities, tend to make many different inappropriate adjustments. It seems improbable to suppose that situations necessitating these adjustments would in no way affect the mental or physical welfare of the pupils if they were made a part of the daily classroom activities. And the data presented in Chapter IV indicate that this is no uncommon occurrence. According to these data pupils with less than first grade reading ability are being confronted daily by fourth-grade materials. They are required to display their inadequacy before their classmates. They are held responsible for the same standard of achievement. What adjustments they are able to make to such situations are not revealed. The enormity of the adjust-

RESEARCH/TABLE 7
A summary of tension behavior at the probable reading-frustration level

Tension Behavior	IV	V	VI	VII	VIII	IX	Total	Percent
Body Movements	1	6	3	0	3	1	14	36.8
Head Movements	0	1	2				3	7.9
Facial Movements								
Squinting	0	1	2	2	3	1	9	23.7
Sucking in Cheeks	0	0	0	0	1	0	1	2.6
Grimacing	2	0	1	1	0	0	4	10.5
Frowning	1	2	3	3	7	0	16	42.1
Raising Eyebrow	0	0	1	0	1	0	2	5.3
Cheek Twitching	0	0	0	0	1	1	2	5.3
Pursing Lips	0	1	0	0	0	0	1	2.6
Gritting Teeth	0	1	0	0	0	0	1	2.6
Flaring Nostrils	0	0	1	0	0	0	1	2.6
Blinking	0	2	0	1	0	0	3	7.9
Hand Movements								
Pinching	0	1	0	0	0	0	1	2.6
Picking	0	1	0	0	1	1	3	7.9
Fingering Book	0	2	1	0	0	1	4	10.5
Rubbing Chair	0	1	0	0	1	0	2	5.3
Gripping Chair	1	0	0	0	0	0	1	2.6
Scratching	0	0	0	0	0	1	1	2.6
Leg Movements	2	1	0	0	1	0	4	10.5
Foot Movements	0	0	0	0	2	1	3	7.9
Biting								
Lips	0	0	1	0	1	0	2	5.3
Finger	1	1	0	0	0	0	2	5.3
Arm Movement	0	3	0	0	1	1	5	13.2
Blushing	1	3	0	2	0	0	6	15.8
Sighing	1	0	2	1	0	0	4	10.5
Gasping	0	0	0	0	1	0	1	2.6
Voice								
Little Volume	0	1	1	1	0	0	3	7.9
High Pitch	0	0	0	0	1	0	1	2.6

(p. 170)

ment, however, is suggested by the data in Research/Table 7 (p. 171).

CONCLUSIONS

The following results were obtained through the use of the Informal Reading Inventory and depend in some measure upon the subjective judgment of the examiner (p. 171).

1. The average basal reading level of this group of fourth grade children was .86; the range, 0–5.0.

The average probable instructional level was 3.16; the range, 0–9.0. The average probable frustration level was 6.3; the range, 4.0–9.0. The average reading capacity level was 5.10; the range, 3.0–9.0.

2. The Informal Inventory placed the pupils in this group 1.06 grades lower on the average than they were placed by the Gates Reading Survey.
3. The probable instructional level determined for this population was 2.4 grades above the basal level, on the average.
4. The probable frustration level was, on the average, 3.38 grades higher than the instructional level.
5. The reading capacity level was 1.97 grades above the instructional level, on the average.
6. Symptoms of difficulty at the probable instructional level were neither numerous nor severe. The following characteristics are noteworthy:
   a. All but five of the difficulties noted were word-perception errors.
   b. All of the errors at instructional levels above grade five were word-perception errors (p. 172).
   c. Repetitions occurred more frequently than any other error. Eighty percent of the pupils repeated at least one word. Only repetitions and substitutions characterized all grade levels.
7. The probable reading frustration level was characterized by
   a. A greatly increased number of error responses.
   b. A large increase in types of reading difficulties.
   c. A definite increase in the severity of the symptoms of reading difficulty.
   d. A low degree of comprehension.
   e. Much sheer word calling.
   f. Many manifestations of tension behavior of an extreme nature.
8. Comprehension scores on the frustration level ranged from 0 to 13 percent; on the instructional level they ranged from 50 to 95 percent; the means were 11 and 71 percent, respectively.
9. The mean ratio of errors to running words at the probable instructional level was 1:20, or 5 per hundred. The range of error-ratios was 1:100 to 1:16.
10. Ninety-three percent of the pupils in this group were frustrated according to the criteria established for this investigation.
11. Overt tension behavior at the instructional level was not marked. Only 29 occurrences were observed among the entire group. Frowning and picking movements were each observed in 12.5 percent of the cases. Ten types of tension behavior were observed (p. 173).
12. Many, various and pronounced manifestations of tension behavior were observed at the frustration level. Frequency of occurrence ranged from 216 percent to 42.1 percent. Twenty-seven different forms were exhibited. Many of the symptoms of tension were of severe character (p. 174).

REFERENCES

Betts, E. A. Reading problems at the intermediate grade level. *Elementary School Journal, 40,* 1941, 737–746.

Center, S. S. & Persons, G. L. *Reading and thinking.* New York: Macmillan, 1940.

Grady, W. E., Klopper, P. & Gifford, J. C. *Childhood readers.* New York: Charles Scribner's Sons, 1939.

A Critique of P. A. Killgallon's Study: A Study of Relationships Among Certain Pupil Adjustments in Reading Situations

TIMOTHY SHANAHAN

University of Illinois at Chicago

The basic assumption in individualizing reading instruction is that some requisite level of achievement relative to the level of instruction must first be accomplished if instruction or learning are to proceed with maximum success and efficiency. If a student is taught with materials that are either too easy or too difficult relative to ability level, then achievement will not be optimal. If the discrepancy between previous achievement and level of instruction is too great, no learning at all will take place.

The instructional level is often the focus of educational testing or diagnosis. One popular method for establishing the optimal level of instruction is the informal reading inventory. The informal reading inventory consists of a sequential series of reading selections of graded difficulty which students read and answer questions about, and a set of procedures for analyzing the students' reading behavior in an instructional situation. The idea is that an appropriate level of instructional difficulty can be specified on the basis of a quantitative analysis of reading performance. Although many factors (e.g., interests, health, attitudes, social-emotional adjustment, intelligence, etc.) exert influence upon learning, it is assumed that, on the average, instructional placement based on IRI (informal reading inventory) criteria will lead to maximum achievement.

THE SOURCE OF THE CRITERIA

Betts (1946), in his landmark text, described three levels of reading ability that could be measured relative to the difficulty level of the instructional materials used. This description included a specification of what he termed the independent or basal level, instructional level, and frustration level. The instructional level describes the most appropriate level of readability of material to be used for reading instruction. "Maximum development may be expected when the learner is challenged but not frustrated" (p. 449).

The hypothetical construct proposed by Betts was not unique. Wheat (1923), Thorndike (1934), and Durrell (1937) all proposed similar designations of instructional appropriateness. However, Betts did provide a unique, objective set of procedures which a teacher or clinician could use to determine whether materials were appropriate for a given child. These procedures probably led to the widespread adoption of his ideas. Betts's IRI prescribed a rigorous set of procedures with which to observe student reading, and it seemed to provide empirically validated, research-based criteria for the determination of reading levels. Betts suggested that the criteria for the instructional level classification of the IRI had their source in a study conducted by P. A. Killgallon (actually Killgallon's doctoral dissertation under the auspices of Betts). "Among Dr. Killgallon's conclusions, this is pertinent: On average, the ratio of word perception errors to the number of running words at the instructional level is one to twenty" (1946, p. 445). This figure, together with that derived by Thorndike (1934) in his earlier research concerning the independent level, led Betts to propose a 95–98% oral reading accuracy criteria for the instructional level.

Betts's proposal had a widespread impact upon educational practice. Examinations of textbooks designed for reading courses at the graduate and undergraduate levels indicate virtual unanimity in the adoption of Betts's criteria (Powell & Dunkeld, 1971; Pikulski & Shanahan, in press).

The construct validity of a test concerns the meaningfulness of its underlying idea or construct, in this case, the instructional level, and the test's ability to measure this construct. The construct validity question for the IRI asks, "Does providing instruction at the level which can be read with 95–98% accuracy, as measured by the IRI, lead to demonstrably higher levels of achievement than does placement in materials above or below that level?" Killgallon seemed to provide an answer to this question.

THE KILLGALLON STUDY

Killgallon's study leaves the reader who is looking for a validation of the instructional level criteria perplexed. Killgallon claimed the IRI to be "possibly, the best single available index to reading ability at the elementary school level" (p. 101). He also noted the IRI's subjective nature. He suggested that "the extent of this limitation is reduced and the reliability of the instrument is increased in direct proportion to the degree to which results are interpreted according to valid and objective criteria" (p. 102). Although Killgallon clearly understood the limitations of the IRI, his attempts to overcome those differences were insufficient.

First, Killgallon established a set of arbitrary criteria for the derivation of each level.[1] For the "probable instruction level," he suggested a minimal oral reading accuracy of 93.9%, with 50% comprehension minimal. Subjects who exhibited two or more symptoms of difficulty (i.e., vocalization during silent readings, finger pointing, lateral head movement, etc.) had to accomplish a minimum of 75% comprehension to be placed at that level.

[1]The source of these criteria is open to question. Killgallon refers to a "preliminary trial," but reports nothing about it. Betts indicated, in private correspondence (Beldin, 1970), that he assumed Killgallon employed "the criteria we had originally set up" in mimeographed instructional materials at the Reading Clinic of the Pennsylvania State College (now University).

To test the validity of these admittedly arbitrary criteria, Killgallon would have had to divide these students into groups taught above, below, and at the instructional level specified, and then compared their relative progress after instruction. Instead, Killgallon computed the mean percentage of errors exhibited by students whose performances fell in this specified range. In other words, he arbitrarily selected those oral reading performances which he considered, a priori, to be at the instructional level, and then reported the mean number of errors evident in those readings. The average oral reading accuracy for students performing within his arbitrary limits was 95%, or one error per 20 running words. On the basis of this finding, the original minimal oral accuracy for instructional level was changed from 93.9% to 95%. Unfortunately, the mean of an arbitrary set of scores is an arbitrary mean. Therefore, Betts's criteria are likewise arbitrary. Such research does not indicate whether students receiving instruction in materials at this level of difficulty would benefit more than they might from easier or harder materials.

Killgallon also compared the symptoms of tension, types of reading errors, and amount of comprehension at the instructional and frustration levels. Although these comparisons are interesting, they are necessarily circular. Killgallon selected those performances he judged to be at the instructional and frustration levels on the basis of relative numbers of oral reading errors, comprehension accuracy, and tension types. The subsequent comparison of these performances provides no new information. The a priori decision, for example, that less than 20% comprehension is frustration level and more than 50% comprehension is instructional guarantees that instructional level performances will evidence a higher mean level of comprehension.

More important, the comparison of such data could, at best, provide only a very indirect test of the validity of the IRI criteria because the test ignores the basic point of the instructional level designation, which is to indicate level of material difficulty that will lead to maximum learning. In the four decades since Killgallon's original study, several others have attempted to validate the IRI criteria through similar, though less circular tests. Efforts have been made to measure the physiological tension associated with different amounts of difficulty (Ekwall, 1974; Ekwall, Solis, & Solis, 1973), to examine the meaningfulness of miscues at various levels of difficulty (Christensen, 1969; Kibby, 1979; Williamson & Young, 1974), and to indicate the level of accuracy needed to ensure a high degree of comprehension (Powell, 1970). These attempts have sometimes led the investigators to very different conceptions of the instructional level criteria. However, these investigators, too, have failed to provide direct tests of the IRI criteria as a measure of the instructional level construct. They do not indicate whether or not the use of their criteria would lead to optimum achievement.

Beldin (1970), in his otherwise excellent historical review of IRI research, defends the Betts interpretation of the Killgallon data on the grounds that the criteria "have been fairly well validated through use . . . there has been little dissatisfaction or pressure for change based on valid research" (p. 76). However, "validation through use" can be a very misleading approach. It might, for instance, suggest that Killgallon's criteria are not harmful, even that they are usable and that they may enhance achievement. But the instructional level criteria are concerned with optimal match of students to instruction for maximization of achievement. Validation through

critique

use might indicate that a given set of criteria has its benefits, but it does not necessarily provide for an optimal match. Experimental validation of the criteria is the only way to assure the extraction of optimum criteria, and this is precisely what Killgallon failed to provide.

ATTEMPTS TO VALIDATE THE INSTRUCTIONAL LEVEL

Only two attempts to directly validate the instructional level criteria have been reported since Killgallon's dissertation. Cooper (1952) considered arbitrarily established levels of performance. However, he examined the learning as measured by standardized achievement tests for students who were instructed at, above, or below these levels over a six-month period of time. Cooper found that the most appropriate level of difficulty was 98–100%, though achievement gains for students taught at the 94–97% level were not significantly lower. Although Cooper's study reported slightly different results than Killgallon's, it is impossible to say whether or not these criteria are the most appropriate to be specified, because of the arbitrary nature of the range of performance compared (i.e., he found the 98–100% criteria predicted learning better than did a 96–98% accuracy, but slightly different categories might have had very different results).

Dunkeld (1970) also attempted to validate the IRI criteria. He did not establish arbitrary accuracy limits, but instead, examined the scattergrams of the relationship between residual gains in achievement and the appropriateness of the difficulty level of the instructional materials used, as measured by IRI procedures. He then described the instructional level using his subjective analysis of the scattergrams. Dunkeld reported critical differences across levels (second grade: 85.5–95%; third grade: 89–97%; fourth, fifth, and sixth grades: 91.5–96.8%). The mean gain scores of students who performed within these ranges were significantly higher than those of students taught in easier or harder materials.

The Dunkeld study, although it represents the most rigorous effort to validate the instructional level criteria to date, is not without important limitations. For example, Dunkeld was unable to manipulate experimentally instructional placements, and thus high-IQ students were never placed in difficult materials and low-IQ students were never placed in easy materials—a phenomenon that certainly influenced his results. Another, probably more important, weakness, was the lack of a cross-validation sample on which to test the effectiveness criteria. All that we know from this research is that Dunkeld's subjective analysis of the scatter plots was successful in selecting students with maximum achievement. Whether or not the criteria so derived, when applied to a cross-validation sample, would have significantly predicted achievement is undetermined.

Although the Cooper and Dunkeld studies are not without limitations, both represent direct attempts to validate the IRI criteria, something that was not, and could not be done with the Killgallon data. Cooper's criteria appear very similar to those suggested by Killgallon, but Dunkeld's are quite different. So different, in fact,

critique

that if adopted, large numbers of children would be taught at levels different from those generated by Killgallon's method. If the assumption of instructional optimization is correct, then such a gross difference represents a potentially crucial discrepancy. The placement of students at non-optimal levels, which could occur using the popular Killgallon criteria, would lead to less learning than might otherwise be possible.

CONCLUSIONS

Killgallon failed to validate the instructional level criteria. He never claimed to have done so. Despite the circularity of his methods and the indirectness of his research, his study continues to exert a powerful influence upon educational practice. The sheer volume of use of the Killgallon criteria may have created an environment of resistance to the consideration of any experimentally derived alternatives to those criteria. Nevertheless, such experimental studies are needed to ensure that reading instruction will be maximally beneficial to the largest number of children.

With apologies to Voltaire, "If instructional level criteria didn't exist, man would have to invent them." Betts's interpretation of Killgallon's study represents just such an invention. The Cooper and Dunkeld studies suggest that after 40 years, the most optimal instructional criteria have still not been rigorously derived.

FOR FURTHER LEARNING

Those readers who are interested in continuing to explore the topic of informal reading inventories would find the following references helpful:

Allington, R. L. Teacher ability in recording oral reading performance. *Academic Therapy,* 1978, *14,* 187–192.

Bradley, J. M., & Ames, W. S. The influence of intrabook readability variation on oral reading performance. *Journal of Educational Psychology,* 1976, *70,* 101–105.

Bradley, J. M., & Ames, W. S. Readability parameters of basal readers. *Journal of Reading Behavior,* 1977, *9,* 175–183.

Gonzalez, P. C., & Elijah, D. V. Rereading: Effect on error patterns and performance levels on the IRI. *Reading Teacher,* 1975, *28,* 647–652.

Hoffman, J. V. Weighting miscues in informal inventories—a precautionary note. *Reading Horizons,* 1980, *20,* 135–139.

Peterson, J., Greenlaw, M. J., & Tierney, R. J. Assessing instructional placement with the IRI, the effectiveness of comprehension questions. *Journal of Educational Research,* 1978, *71,* 247–250.

Pikulski, J. J. A critical review: Informal reading inventories. *Reading Teacher,* 1974, *28,* 141–151.

---

for further learning

REFERENCES

Beldin, H. O. Informal reading testing: Historical review and review of the research. In W. K. Durr (Ed.), *Reading difficulties: Diagnostic, correction, and remediation.* Newark, Del.: International Reading Association, 1970, 67–84.

Betts, E. A. *Foundations of reading instruction.* New York: American Book Co., 1946.

Christenson, A. Oral reading errors of intermediate grade children at their independent, instructional, and frustration levels. In J. A. Figurel (Ed.), *Reading and realism.* Newark, Del.: International Reading Association, 1969, 674–677.

Cooper, J. L. *The effect of adjustment of basal reading materials on reading achievement.* Unpublished doctoral dissertation, Boston University, 1952.

Dunkeld, C. G. M. *The validity of the informal reading inventory for the designation of instructional reading levels: A study of the relationships between children's gains in reading achievement and the difficulty of instructional materials.* Unpublished doctoral dissertation, University of Illinois, 1970.

Durrell, D. Individual differences and their implications with respect to instruction in reading. *Teaching of reading: A recent report,* The 36th Yearbook of the National Society for the Study of Education, 1937, 325–326.

Ekwall, E. E. Should repetitions be counted as errors? *Reading Teacher,* 1974, *27,* 365–367.

Ekwall, E. E., Solis, J. K., & Solis, E. Investigating informal reading inventory scoring criteria. *Elementary English,* 1973, *50,* 271–274; 323.

Kibby, M. W. Passage readability effect on the oral reading strategies of disabled readers. *Reading Teacher,* 1979, *32,* 390–396.

Killgallon, P. A. *A study of relationshps among certain pupil adjustments in reading situations.* Unpublished doctoral dissertation, Pennsylvania State College (University), 1942.

Pikulski, J. J., & Shanahan, T. Informal reading inventories: A critical analysis. In J. J. Pikulski & T. Shanahan (Eds.), *Informal reading evaluation.* Newark, Del.: International Reading Association, in press.

Powell, W. R. Reappraising the criteria for interpreting informal inventories. In D. DeBoer (Ed.), *Reading diagnosis and evaluation.* Newark, Del.: International Reading Association, 1970, 100–109.

Powell, W. R., & Dunkeld, C. G. Validity of the IRI reading levels. *Elementary English,* 1971, *48,* 637–642.

Thorndike, E. L. Improving the ability to read. *Teachers College Record,* 1934, *36,* pp. 123–144; 229–241.

Wheat, H. G. *The teaching of reading, a textbook of principals and methods.* Boston: Ginn, 1923.

Williamson, L. E., & Young, F. The IRI and RMI diagnostic concepts should be synthesized. *Journal of Reading Behavior,* 1974, *6,* 193–194.

A Commentary on Shanahan's Critique of Killgallon's Study: A Study of the Relationships Among Certain Pupil Adjustments in Reading Situations

KENNETH M. AHRENDT

Oregon State University

Killgallon's unpublished doctoral dissertation states that: "the chief purpose of this investigation is to study individual differences among fourth grade pupils in typical reading situations with respect to reading, spelling, and personality adjustment" (p. 11). This statement assumes that using a standardized test and an informal reading inventory are "typical reading situations" for fourth-grade pupils. Oral and silent reading activities in the intermediate grades have been an established practice in American public schools for many years although most students and adults spend the greatest amount of their time reading silently and in a variety of materials that in no way resemble the basal readers used for reading instruction in the public schools.

Dr. Shanahan believes that to individualize reading instruction, some measure—either formal or informal—must be used to determine an appropriate placement level for instruction. He also suggests that the informal reading inventory has been the most popular method used to determine this placement. Research and usage certainly seem to support this premise.

However, since Betts (1946) described procedures for placement and reading instruction such as the informal reading inventory (IRI) and the Directed Reading Activity (DRA), other methods and means of diagnosis and placement have been developed.

Betts (1946) did state that Killgallon's study was a major source for research conducted concerning the informal reading inventory. Betts used this study to build his criteria for determining the so-called instructional reading level for the IRI. Killgallon's dissertation termed the "probable instructional level" as "(a) a score of fifty percent minimum in comprehension and (b) the maximum ratio of word-perception errors to number of running words . . . one to fourteen" or no more than 7% error in word recognition. If 100% is the absolute score, then 7% is 93% word recognition errors, not 95%. Killgallon did, however, in his suggestion for further research, admit that his percentages were tenuous at best.

Also note that when Killgallon's study was conducted in 1942, no "single series covering the full range of difficulty" was required. An assumption was made that two different series were used, and that the gradation of difficulty was strictly compatible—an assumption that may or may not be entirely valid but which the researcher considered to be a limitation of his study.

Furthermore, Shanahan's critique of this study overlooked one very important statement: "An informal inventory is, however, a useful instrument for diagnosing reading difficulties in highly valid materials, the reading textbooks themselves" (p. 101). In 1942, this statement may have been valid; however, even then, one would hardly agree that these materials had any validity. Furthermore, given these limitations, these factors could question the validity or reliability of not only the instructional level, but also the independent and frustration level.

The purpose of Killgallon's study was not to validate or make reliable the reading levels of the informal inventory, but, "to study individual differences among fourth grade pupils in typical (1942) reading situations with respect to reading, spelling, and personality adjustment" (1942, p. 11). The purpose statement implies that the researcher would investigate various levels of reading achievement as secondary factors. The description of the reading levels for the informal reading inventory described the instrument the researcher used to gather his data, which had been developed and used extensively in Betts's reading clinic.

To argue that Killgallon's dissertation was at fault because Betts used 95–98% oral reading accuracy criteria for the instructional level is a spurious interpretation of Killgallon's data, as he used 93%. Perhaps Betts used Thorndike's (1934) and Killgallon's (1942) criteria to ascertain the 95–98%. However, Table 24 (p. 166) of Killgallon's data does in fact show that the mean fell at 5.00–5.99% errors out of 100. But Killgallon cautions, "It is not suggested that any ratio shall ever dictate the assignment of the instructional level; the mean ratio determined here appears to represent the most suitable one for use as a point of reference or comparison" (p. 167).

Rather than reinvent the wheel, we should attend to the current research concerning oral reading as a diagnostic tool. Oral reading has been used for two purposes: to diagnose a student's ability to use the language and also as a means of oral interpretation of print. However, oral reading does not necessarily reflect the way a person reads silently. Oral reading is only one part of the reading process and usually requires the reader to concentrate on word pronunciation and oral expression in addition to content meaning (Wiesendanger & Birlem, 1981).

Christenson (1969) concluded in a study of oral reading errors of intermediate grade children that undergraduate and graduate reading methods classes should include more training in oral reading as a diagnostic tool. Williamson and Young (1974) concluded that "instructional levels and frustration levels as defined by IRI criteria result in different reading behaviors" (p. 190).

Spache (1981) notes that while a measure of comprehension should be an integral part of an oral reading test to differentiate fluent word-callers from successful readers, many authorities agree that oral reading, unlike silent, is not conducive to comprehension. The reasons seem obvious as the researcher must consider the demands of oral reading in itself, that is, the reader has little or no opportunity to process the data, or to react to the material or ideas presented. The mechanical and vocal demands of oral reading rarely give time for the reader to engage in making judgments or interpretations, and performing other comprehension skills.

There are problems inherent in using an oral reading test, either formal or informal, to evaluate the reading ability level of students when we consider the following factors: (1) many approaches analyzing pupils' oral reading pay little or no attention to the validity of the testing. Selections are combined from various passages of varying readability levels, and many times, from the same series of basal readers. (2) The content of the reading passages varies greatly and may not yield an accurate indication of a child's oral reading ability. If a passage is difficult, according to Kibby (1979), pupils may be misdiagnosed as readers who do not relate meaning to their reading. The content of passages affects oral reading performance, and many times a reader's prior knowledge and experiences, plus his/her ability as an auditory learner, can affect oral reading performance. Killgallon's research alluded to these things but never really treated them in perspective with the results obtained in his study.

(3) The use of short paragraphs in many commercially prepared IRIs raises serious questions about the reliability of oral reading analysis. Spache (1981) states that the nature of a student's errors changes somewhat in selections longer than 250 words from those observed in briefer samples. The Miscue Inventory recognizes this fact and typically uses an entire story for testing.

(4) The examiner's competence is a real problem in testing oral reading. How reliable is the evaluation of a child's oral and silent reading ability when the standards are not understood by trained reading personnel? Furthermore, oral questions asked after oral reading are usually simple recall; no criteria exist for the amount or type of recall that should be expected at various age levels. Therefore, judgment of pupil comprehension tends to be mainly, if not totally, subjective.

In summary, informal reading inventories, including the rigid standards for their construction as outlined by Betts (1946) and Johnson and Kress (1965) and Johnson, and the IRI in Killgallon's study assume that basal readers are graded correctly by the publisher. Bradley (1976) estimated the readability of basal readers using four measures. He found a lack of true scaling within books and between successive books, and little comparability of books of one series with those of another. Unless passages are graded by readability scales such as the Spache for primary materials and the Dale-Chall for upper-grade materials used in constructing an IRI, we accept with faith the readability guide of the publishers. It is impossible to produce a reader in which all content is of stated readability level. Even most of our gifted authors of children's books cannot and do not achieve this noble and unrealistic goal.

IRIs are currently administered to students by reversing the order in the original Killgallon study—oral reading and then silent reading. Killgallon allowed his subjects to read silently first, then orally. Oral reading accuracy changes when a student reads the passage silently and then orally. Children will read better orally after having had the opportunity to read the passage silently first, therefore creating, as in Killgallon's study, artificially high accuracy standards for oral reading.

Independent, Instructional, and Frustrational are terms used in an IRI to indicate reading performances at different oral accuracy levels arbitrarily. These terms have no basis in research, but they are convenient and popular.

Yet teachers and clinicians need some yardstick to place a child in material that will allow a modicum of success. Careful attention to oral reading passages selected from materials used in a classroom—basal readers, science, social studies, health, and other textbooks—can give an accurate measure against the criteria established for oral reading if the reader can relate what was said and what it meant. The criteria consider the student's prior experience and background information.

Killgallon tried to validate and give reliability to arbitrary standards; he failed, and no research has as yet succeeded. To restate a trite phrase—further controlled research is necessary.

REFERENCES

Beldin, H. O. Informal reading testing: Historical review and review of the research. In W. K. Durr (Ed.), *Reading difficulties: Diagnostic, correction, and remediation.* Newark, Del.: International Reading Association, 1970, 67–84.

Betts, E. A. *Foundations of reading instruction.* New York: American Book Co., 1946.

Bradley, J. M. Using readability to improve the content validity of informal placement tests. *Reading Development,* Fall 1976, *13,* 182–191.

Christenson, A. Oral reading errors of intermediate grade children at their independent, instructional, and frustrational levels. In J. A. Figurel (Ed.), *Reading and realism.* Newark, Del.: International Reading Association, 1969, 674–677.

Johnson, M. S., & Kress, R. A. *Informal Reading Inventories.* Newark, Del.: International Reading Association, 1965.

Kibby, M. W. Passage readability affects oral reading strategies of disabled readers. *The Reading Teacher,* Jan. 1979, *32,* 390–396.

Killgallon, P. A. *A study of relationships among certain pupil adjustments in reading situations.* Unpublished doctoral dissertation, Pennsylvania State College, 1942.

Spache, G. *Diagnosing and correcting reading disabilities* (2nd ed.). Boston: Allyn and Bacon, 1981.

Thorndike, E. L. Improving the ability to read. *Teacher's College Record,* 1934, *36.*

Wiesendanger, K., & Birlem, E. Do high school remedial readers comprehend better when reading silently or orally? *Secondary Reading Research Monograph.* Tucson: University of Arizona, 1981, *8.*

Williamson, L. E., & Young, F. The IRI and RMI diagnostic concepts should be synthesized. *Journal of Reading Behavior,* 1974, 6, 193–194.

READABILITY: A NEW APPROACH

JOHN R. BORMUTH

University of California, Los Angeles

One of the great challenges to scientists of this generation is to learn how to predict and control the difficulty of language. It is almost trite to say that further improvement of public and private life depends upon the ability to transmit ever increasing amounts of knowledge to an increasingly large proportion of the population. But, unfortunately, many adults and children fail to understand what they read, not because the concepts are too difficult or because they lack basic reading skills, but simply because of the complexity of the language in which those concepts are presented. The money wasted annually on materials of this sort mounts into millions of dollars. More appalling is the waste in human terms as, for example, when a child fails to learn and drops out of school, when citizens are unable to inform themselves on important matters of government, and when a worker is unemployed because he cannot keep up with advancing technology. But the cost of lives blighted by poverty, ignorance, crime, frustration, and loss of self respect is not easily calculated. Much of this waste must be directly attributed to the present inability to predict and control language difficulty.

The ultimate objective of this and other similar research is to develop accurate formulas for predicting and controlling the readability of language. But before this objective can be attained, certain basic problems must be solved. This study takes up some of these basic problems. The first is to determine whether various features of writing style are linearly related to the comprehension difficulty of language. The second is to find out if the strengths of these relationships change as a function of the reading abilities of subjects. The third is to find out if useful readability prediction can be made on language units as small as a word or an independent clause. The fourth is to gain some idea of how much accuracy can be attained in passage readability formulas when modern testing and linguistic analysis techniques are used to construct these formulas. The fifth is to try out several new types of linguistic variables (measures of features of writing style) to see if they are useful in predicting language difficulty.

From *Reading Research Quarterly,* Vol. 1, No. 3, Spring 1966, pp. 79–132. Reprinted with permission of John R. Bormuth and the International Reading Association.

BACKGROUND

Quality of Present Readability Formulas

It is problematic wherever presently available readability formulas help more than they hinder. Because these formulas are easy and inexpensive to apply, they enjoy widespread use by publishers and educators. Publishers use them for "adjusting" the difficulty of instructional materials, and educators use them to decide if instructional materials are suitable for students of a given level of reading ability. Chall (1958) has made a strong case that the formulas are not sufficiently accurate to warrant either of these uses. Their validity correlations range from .5 to only .7, and experiments have shown that they have little, if any, validity when they are used as style guides for "adjusting" the difficulty of materials. Hence, the publishers' "adjustments" of the materials probably do not have the desired effect on the actual difficulty of the materials. But the practice does mislead educators. Since educators use essentially the same formulas as the publishers, they believe that the materials are suitable for their students when, in fact, they are not.

Advances in Research Techniques

For many years it seemed impossible to improve the formulas because the available research techniques were not equal to the task. In recent years linguists have been making rapid strides in developing objective ways of dealing with language. Also, the cloze test has solved the problem of reliably measuring language difficulty. These new techniques have made it possible to reopen this issue and to deal effectively with many of the basic problems which were beyond the reach of earlier techniques.

The most serious problem encountered in earlier research was the measurement of comprehension difficulty of passages. The best practice available was to give subjects multiple choice tests over the passages. Lorge (1939) criticized this practice because it was uncertain whether the difficulty of the language in the test questions or the difficulty of the language in the passage itself was being measured. The matter was confounded further by the fact that it is notoriously easy to vary the difficulties of these tests simply by changing the alternatives to the question.

The cloze test procedure first conceived by Taylor (1953) was the crucial factor in revitalizing this research. It made possible the accurate measurement of the comprehension difficulty of passages.

A cloze test is made over a passage by replacing every fifth word with an underlined blank of a standard length. Subjects are told to write in the words they think were deleted and responses are scored correct when they exactly match the words deleted. A large amount of research has gone into the development of the cloze procedure. Since Rankin (1965) has written an excellent analysis of this research, only the most relevant studies will be cited. Fletcher (1955) showed that cloze tests are valid measures of comprehension ability. Bormuth (1962) confirmed Fletcher's reports and indicated that cloze tests are valid and highly reliable measures of the comprehension difficulty of passages. MacGinitie (1961) found that cloze items are statistically independent when surrounded by four words of context. Bormuth (1965) found that scoring synonyms correct does not increase the validities of the scores. In every case these results were obtained by administering the cloze tests untimed and without the subjects first reading the passages from which the tests were made.

research

PROBLEMS STUDIED

If the present study has a single central focus, it is to demonstrate that, by marshaling modern techniques of psychological measurement, linguistics, statistics, and automatic data processing, it is once again possible to make large and useful advances in the study of readability. A range of problems whose solutions remained beyond the reach of earlier research methods has been brought under attack in the present study. These problems were selected: first, because they are basic to achieving accurate readability prediction; and, second, because they represent directions in which research must proceed if the applications of readability are to be raised to the status of a science. These problems by no means represent the only directions in which research must proceed. For example, efforts must be made to discover the basic dimensions in which prose style varies. But the effective study of such problems must await the solution of the problems included in the present study.

Linearity of Regressions

Precise readability predictions depend on more than just a knowledge of the sizes of correlations between linguistic variables and comprehension difficulty. Knowledge of whether or not these correlations are linear is required. If they are curvilinear, the shapes of the curves must be determined. Previous investigators have uniformly behaved as if the correlations were linear by using the Pearson product moment correlation model and by using multiple linear regression equations for readability formulas.

While these investigators may have carefully inspected the scatter plots of their correlations for linearity, such an inspection does not necessarily reveal an underlying curvilinearity. These investigators could not measure the difficulties of individual words and clauses. Consequently, they were forced to plot passage difficulty against linguistic variables obtained by averaging values across an entire passage. These averages tend to have distributions that are approximately normal, as can be deduced from the central limits theorem; and two normally distributed variables usually have a linear relationship, if a relationship at all exists between them. While the use of such averages may not violate the correlation models used, it results in the loss of much information that could have been retained by weighting the variable before averaging.

There is evidence that these underlying relationships are not linear. For example, King-Ellison and Jenkins (1954) found a hyperbolic relationship between the Thorndike frequencies of words and the recognition times of subjects. Therefore, there is reason to believe that the precision of readability prediction can be increased by investigating the shapes of these relationships.

Variable Strength as a Function of Reading Ability

One of the most troublesome questions in readability prediction is: Do the linguistic variables that influence difficulty for persons at one level of reading achievement have an equal influence on difficulty for students at other levels of achievement? At least three kinds of speculation are possible on this issue. One theory holds that linguistic variables influence difficulty only for persons who have not yet achieved a high degree of skill in reading. If this were true, readability formulas would be applicable only to persons having low reading achievement. A second theory holds that one set of variables has a strong influence on difficulty for persons at one level of reading ability and other sets for persons at other levels. If this theory is correct, a number of readability formulas must be found and each may be used only for persons within a limited range of reading ability. A third theory states that the linguistic variables influencing difficulty for persons at one level of ability have an equal influence on difficulty for persons at other levels of ability. This theory requires the use of only one formula. Should either of the first two theories be proven correct, the consequences for both psycholinguistic theory and readability prediction would be far reaching.

The literature on readability contains statements to the effect that special readability formulas must be developed for use with subjects at different levels of reading ability (Smith & Dechant, 1961). Chall (1958) cited two types of evidence supporting this notion. First, Chall pointed out that the Lorge formula seemed to be better suited for predicting difficulty for young children than the Dale-Chall formula, while the Dale-Chall formula is superior for older children. Second, Chall pointed out that Gray (1935) observed that the sizes of the correlations between linguistic and difficulty variables differed depending on the reading ability of the groups of subjects used. While these effects could also have been attributed to uncontrolled variables in the studies involved, the evidence was sufficiently strong to warrant further investigation of this question.

Readability of Small Language Units

There is an acute need for readability formulas which measure the readabilities of individual words and sentences. Such formulas can be applied extensively to materials such as tiles, indexes, captions, and test items. They may also be used to locate difficult spots within larger texts. However, most readability formulas have been designed only for measuring the readabilities of passages. The reason is not difficult to find. Until the advent of the cloze test there was no practical way to measure the comprehension difficulties of individual words and sentences. While one formula (Forbes & Cottle, 1953) purportedly measures the readability of test items, the manner in which it was constructed makes its value dubious. In the Forbes and Cottle study several readability formulas were applied to each item in a set of test items and these readabilities were averaged for each of the items. The average was then used as the dependent variable. The question investigated in the present study was whether it is possible to obtain useful readability formulas for these smaller language units.

Validities of Readability Formulas

Probably the most important question raised in the current study is whether it is possible to improve present readability formulas. It is true that formulas currently in use were developed using relatively crude techniques and that they have relatively low validities. At the same time, many of the early investigators made expert use of the techniques available to them. There may be an upper limit on the accuracy with which difficulty can be predicted using just the objectively measurable features of language. If such a limit exists, has it already been reached?

New Linguistic Variables

Without question the most important advances in readability research should result from the development of new linguistic variables. Linguistic scientists have done much in recent years to improve basic understanding of language and to develop objective ways of describing it. Their techniques have been adapted to the study of psycholinguistic problems and to problems of computer translation of language, resulting in the development of several new and potentially useful variables. Several such variables were investigated. The variables included in the present study by no means exhaust the possible variables that could have been included. The ones included were selected because they are representative of types of variables that could be developed further, if the findings suggest the effort would be worthwhile. These variables and their abbreviations are given below. To conserve space, abbreviations are used in all references to the variables in tables.

Word depth (WOR DEP) The method of deriving word depth was developed by Yngve (1960; 1962). It begins with an analysis and diagraming of the syntactic or immediate constituent structure of a sentence. Then a set of counting rules is applied to the diagram of the structure. Because of the complexity of deriving the variable and because Yngve has defined it, only a general description will be offered here.

Research/Figure 1 shows an example of a sentence which has been analyzed to derive the depths of the words in it. The line diagram shows the syntactic relationships among the words and phrases in this sentence. Note that the horizontal lines at the highest level connect the most distantly related elements while the lines at the lower levels connect the more immediately related constituents.

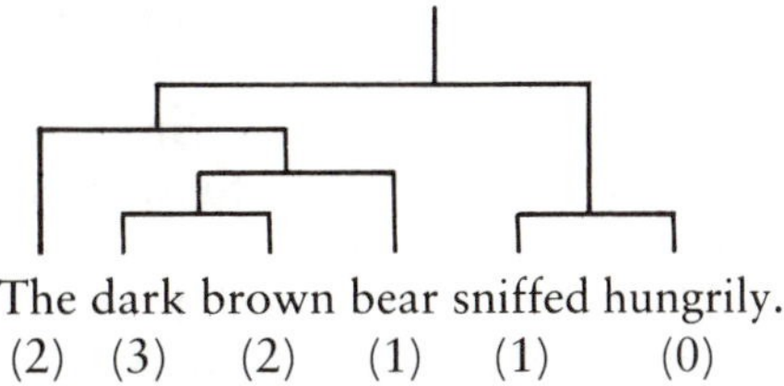
The dark brown bear sniffed hungrily.
(2) (3) (2) (1) (1) (0)

Total depth, 9; net depth, 3; mean depth, 1.5.

RESEARCH/FIGURE 1.
Illustration of the Word Depth Analysis.

The counting rules applied to such diagrams are based on several psychological assumptions about the way in which a sentence is produced. First, it is assumed that a sentence is produced starting at the top of this diagram and working downward through the structure until the first word is produced. The remaining grammatical structures and words are then produced from left to right. At each level in this structure there are two elements that must be produced. For example, at the top level both a subject and a predicate must be produced if the sentence is to be grammatically acceptable. Only one of these structures can be expanded and produced at a time and this must be in a "left to right" order. Consequently, if the sentence is to be completed correctly, the speaker must remember that the production of a predicate must follow the production of the subject. Similarly at each lower level in the structure, he must remember to complete any structure which he has begun. The depth of a given word is found by counting the number of structures a speaker has started but not completed at the time that he is producing that word. For example, in Research/Figure 1 the depth of the word *The* is 2 because he must remember that two structures must follow, a noun and a predicate. But the word *dark* has a depth of three because he must remember to produce an adjective, a noun, and a predicate to complete the sentence correctly. Thus, it is assumed in this model that the difficulty of the structure of a sentence derives from the number of grammatical facts that must be stored in the memory as the sentence is produced or interpreted.

The word depth measure can be used in several ways. The depths of the words can be used individually, or they can be totaled across the sentence. In the latter case, total word depth is necessarily related to measures of sentence length, but the necessity of this relationship can be eliminated by subtracting from total word depth the number of words in the sentence. This variable was labeled net word depth (WOR DEP—WOR). The total can also be divided by the number of words in a sentence or a passage to obtain the mean word depth (WOR DEP/WOR).

The word depth variable has been used in only one other readability study (Bormuth, 1964). A correlation of .78 was found between the mean word depths and the comprehension difficulties of a set of passages. When the vocabulary difficulties and mean sentence lengths of the passages were experimentally held constant, the correlation was .77, indicating that the effect of mean word depth is independent of sentence length.

Letter redundancy (LET RED) Carterette and Jones (1963) described a measure of redundancy of passages and prepared a computer program for performing rather lengthy calculations involved in deriving this measure. Again, because of the complexity of deriving this variable only its general description can be given here. A detailed description of the mathematical procedure is given by Carterette and Jones.

The Letter Redundancy variable is a measure of the sequential dependencies between pairs of letters in the words of a passage. Suppose that the letter *m* occurs a number of times in a passage. The frequencies with which this letter is followed by each of the other letters is tabulated and transformed into probabilities, and these probabilities are then used to calculate the redundancy of the passage using the Shannon-Weiner (Shannon, 1943) function. Such a measure of redundancy was calculated for pairs of letters taken four at a time (LET RED_4) and taken eleven at a time (LET RED_{11}). The purpose in measuring redundancy across these different numbers of letters was to separate the within word redundancy from the between word redundancy. The former was intended as a type of word difficulty measure, while the latter was intended as a type of syntactic redundancy measure.

Carterette and Jones (1963) calculated LET RED_{11} for samples of text drawn from reading textbooks used at the first, second, third, and fifth grade levels. The measured redundancies of the passages correlated perfectly with the grade levels at which the books were used.

Independent clause frequency (IND CLAU FRE) The *IND CLAU FRE* was derived from data gathered by Strickland (1962) who recorded samples of the language of elementary school children enrolled in grades one through six. Strickland analyzed the grammatical pattern of each independent clause, classified it according to its type, and then tabulated the frequency with which each clause pattern occurred.

The independent clauses in the passages used in the present study were classified using Strickland's scheme. Each independent clause was then assigned a number corresponding to the frequency with which that pattern had been observed in Strickland's language sample. The frequencies for the samples of language taken from children enrolled in grades one, three, and six were combined and used to obtain this measure of frequency.

Research/Figure 2 shows an example of a sentence pattern derived by this analysis.

Sentence

We found and caught the brown bear
(1) (2) (4)
when we heard him crashing about
(M_3)
in the underbrush.
(M_3 continued)

The pattern of this sentence is 1, 2, 4, M_3.

RESEARCH/FIGURE 2.
Example of Independent Clause Pattern Analysis.

The major constituents of the sentence were classified and a symbol assigned to each constituent. The pattern of an independent clause is the ordered sequence of symbols associated with it. It should be noted that subordinate clauses and constituents of other major portions of clauses are left unanalyzed. Hence, this analysis accounts for only the gross aspects of the patterns of independent clauses. This variable was derived individually for each independent clause, and a mean was obtained for each passage (IND CLAU FRE/IND CLAU).

Ruddell (1963) wrote three pairs of passages which were carefully matched for Dale-Chall readability, subject matter content, and writing style, but which differed in that one member of each pair was written with high frequency clause patterns and the other with low frequency patterns. The data seemed to show that the passages written in low frequency patterns were more difficult to understand. Unfortunately, there is no way to estimate the confidence that can be placed in this result, since no account was taken of item sample error (Bormuth, 1965) in the analysis.

Letter counts (LET) Flesch (1948) found that a count of the mean number of syllables per word had a correlation of .66 with comprehension difficulty. He theorized that this count measures the "abstractness" of words. A less esoteric theorist might speculate that the length of a word is the factor affecting its difficulty and that counting syllables in words affords a crude measure of this factor. If length is the crucial factor, a more discriminating measure could be obtained by counting the number of letters in words. This variable can be used to measure the lengths of words, independent clauses, or sentences.

Parts of speech Boder (1940) found that authors vary considerably with respect to the ratio of adjectives to verbs used in their writing. Carroll (1960), extending Boder's work, found that authors also vary with respect to the frequency with which they use a number of other parts of speech. He factor analyzed a number of these variables and found that part of speech variables seemed to measure a broad range of characteristics of style. However, no effort seems to have been made to determine whether these variables are in any way related to the comprehension difficulty of language.

There was some problem in deciding what classification scheme should be used to classify words in the present study. First, there was the problem of whether to use the structural or the semantic properties of words for classifying them. Because of their superior objectivity, the structural properties were chosen as the principal attributes used in classifying. Then the question of what categories would be used arose. Almost any part of speech category can be broken down into a number of sub-categories; the total number of possible subcategories is very large. Using a large number of categories results in a more complete understanding of the influence of parts of speech on comprehension, but it also produces categories in which words seldom occur. An attenuation of variance among passages results. Therefore, two different sets of categories were used. One set was similar to the eight categories traditionally used. The other included the four form classes defined by Fries (1952) and a fifth group containing all other structural words. Thus a small number of categories was used in each set and some means of assessing the effects of subclasses was provided. Within each set, the categories were put together in all possible ratios to each other.

Research/Table 1 shows the subcategories used in classifying the words and the major categories into which they were combined.

Variables Previously Studied

Several variables used in a number of earlier studies were included in the present study. Their presence was essential to provide a frame of reference against which to judge the worth of the new variables, and to insure the adequacy of the answers found to the other problems investigated. The abbreviations and descriptions of these variables are given below.

Word frequency index (WOR FRE) The word frequency measure was obtained by assigning an index number ranging from 0 to 52 to each word in each passage used in the study. These index numbers were taken from the combined counts given by Thorndike and Lorge (1944). Zero was assigned to words not observed in the word count studies, and the numbers 51 and 52 were assigned to the two groups of words that occurred most frequently. This variable was used for individual words and also averaged to find the mean frequencies of words in larger language units. Lorge (1948) found a correlation of .51 between difficulties of passages and the mean frequency of the words in the passages.

Syllable counts (SYL) The number of syllables was counted to measure the lengths of words, independent clauses, and sentences. Flesch (1950) found a correlation of .69 between the mean number of syllables per word in passages and the difficulty of the passages. Gray and Leary (1935) found a correlation of .44 between mean sentence length measured in syllables and the comprehension difficulty of passages. A count of the number of syllables in an independent

RESEARCH/TABLE 1
Sub-categories and combined categories of the part of speech analysis

Sub-categories	Traditional parts of speech: Name	Traditional parts of speech: Abbreviation	Form classes
Noun	Noun	n	1
Personal Pronoun	Pronoun	pn	1
Interrogative Pronoun	Pronoun	pn	s
Demonstrative Pronoun	Pronoun	pn	s
Indefinite Pronoun	Pronoun	pn	l
Conjunctive Pronoun	Pronoun	pn	s
Verb	Verb	v	2
Auxiliary Verb	Verb	v	5
"Do" Verb	Verb	v	s
Negative	Adverb	adv	s
Simple Adverb	Adverb	adv	4
Number Adverb	Adverb	adv	s
Degree Adverb	Adverb	adv	s
Introducer (there)	Adverb	adv	s
Preposition	Preposition	prep	s
Conjunction	Conjunction	conj	s
Descriptive Adjective	Adjective	adj	3
Ordinal Adjective	Adjective	adj	4
Cardinal Adjective	Adjective	adj	3
Article and Determiner	Adjective	adj	s
Nominal Adjective	Adjective	adj	3
Possessive Adjective	Adjective	adj	3
Interjection	Interjection	intj	s

clause or sentence is necessarily related to the number of words in that unit. This dependence was eliminated by subtracting the number of words from the number of syllables in the independent clause or sentence to obtain the net syllables (SYL—WOR). Mean number of syllables per sentence was also used as a variable (SYL/WOR).

Count of words (WOR) Sentence lengths have been most commonly measured by counting the number of words in them. The correlation between the mean number of words per sentence and the difficulty of passages was found to be .29 by Dale and Tyler (1934), .40 by Gray and Leary (1935) and .52 by Flesch (1948). This variable has been the best single measure of the grammatical complexity of sentences and is incorporated in nearly all of the widely used formulas.

Words on the Dale List of 769 Words (DL 769) The *Dale List of 769 Words* was compiled by Dale (1931) from those words which were common to both the *International Kindergarten Union List* and to Thorndike's 1,000 most frequently used words. This variable was applied to passages in the present study by determining what proportion of the running words in a passage appeared on Dale's list. The same word could be counted several times if it recurred within a passage. The correlation between the comprehension difficulty of passages and this variable was found to be .35 by Dale and Tyler (1934), .35 by Gray and Leary (1935) and .61 by Lorge (1948).

Words on the Dale List of 3,000 Familiar Words (DL 3000) The words on the Dale list were found (Dale & Chall, 1948) to be known to 80 percent of the children in grade four. The list is used, as is the shorter one, to find the percentage of the words in a passage which appear on the list. Dale and Chall found a correlation of .68 between this variable and the difficulties of passages.

Prepositional phrases (PREP PHR) The PREP PHR variable is usually derived by finding the ratio of prepositions to the total number of words in the passage. The correlation between PREP PHR and comprehension difficulty was found to be .35 by both Dale and Tyler (1934) and Gray and Leary (1935) and .43 by Lorge (1948). It is not entirely clear whether the variable measures sentence length or whether it measures some other attribute of writing style since sentences containing prepositional phrases would seemingly be longer than sentences which do not contain them. In this case, finding the proportions of words appearing in prepositional phrases should result in a higher correlation with difficulty than would the proportion of prepositions. To study the question, the proportion of words in prepositional phrases (WOR PREP PHR) wa also used as a variable.

Independent clause (IND CLAU) The sentence, as defined by an initial capital letter and a final punctuation mark, has been the traditional unit for analyzing the grammatical complexity of syntactic units. Coleman (1962) found some evidence that the independent clause is probably a more valid unit of analysis, since a sentence like *The boy went to the orchard and he picked some apples.* may actually be responded to as if it were two separate syntactic units. The conjunction *and* may serve roughly the same function, psychologically, as a period. If this is true, measures of syntactic complexity based on the independent clause should result in higher correlations than variables based on the sentence as it is traditionally defined. In order to study this problem, measures of syntactic complexity were found for both independent clauses and sentences.

From the foregoing descriptions of the problems investigated, it should be evident that the purpose of the present study was not to develop readability formulas for immediate use. To have done so at this time would have been poor strategy. In research a single new development often opens new areas for progress. But new developments simultaneously present new problems. Readability research has been visited not by just one new development but by three. The cloze test has been responsible for two. It made possible the development of formulas for predicting the readability of units as small as a word and it made possible obtaining information essential to the application of more powerful and sophisticated mathematical models to the treatment of readability data. The growing field of psycholinguistics is rapidly assimilating the *ad hoc* theories of readability into a more integrated body of theory, joining the fields of psychology, linguistics, and literary style, and resulting in new approaches to the measurement of the various attributes of prose style. As expected, these developments have presented new problems for study which must be ordered in priority and studied in a systematic fashion. The author has attempted to begin this task.

PROCEDURE

The data for the present study were obtained by making cloze tests from 20 passages selected to represent a variety of prose styles. This provided data on the difficulties of 5,181 words, 405 independent clauses, and 365 sentences as well as on the 20 passages. The details of how these data were collected are given in the sections that follow.

Materials

Passages Twenty passages of between 275 and 300 words each were selected from materials used for instructional purposes in the areas of literature, history, geography, biology, and physical science. The four passages in each area were selected to provide a roughly even distribution in Dale-Chall readability from about the 4.0 to about the 8.0 grade levels of difficulty. Care was taken to use materials that were not readily available to the subjects, and no two passages were by the same author.

Cloze tests Five cloze test forms were made from each passage with each form made by replacing every fifth word with an underlined blank space 15 spaces in length. No deletions were made from the first and last sentences of each passage. Generally, a word was taken as being defined by the white spaces separating it from other words: *don't, U.S.A., 2,182,* and *re-enter* were deleted as single words. In hyphenated words like *self-made* where both parts were free forms, each part was deleted separately. Commas, apostrophes, and hyphens were deleted along with the rest of the word, except where hyphens separated free forms. The five different test forms, forms A through E, were made by deleting words 1, 6, 11, etc., to make form A, words 2, 7, 12, etc., to make form B, and so on through form E. Every word in a passage, excluding those in the first and last sentences, appeared as a deleted item in exactly one form.

Subjects

The subjects in this study comprised the entire enrollment in grades four through eight of the Wasco Union Elementary School District in Wasco, California. The sample was chosen for its similarity to the general population of school children in the nation with respect to standardized achievement test scores, racial and language backgrounds, and parents' occupational status. The subjects were divided into five form groups, labeled A through E. Their scores on the *California Reading Test* were used to match the means and distributions of reading abilities in the groups. The test had been given by the school personnel several weeks prior to the study. The matching procedure was done a grade level at a time to insure that an approximately equal number of subjects from each grade was in each form group.

Test Administration

The testing extended over a period of eleven school days. On the first day the Standford Achievement Test: Reading,

Form J was administered and the subjects were given a short cloze test to acquaint them with this type of test. For the next ten consecutive school days the subjects then took two cloze tests per day. The test periods were about 50 minutes long and no subject was stopped before he had completed the tests. Each subject took one, and only one, form of the cloze test over each passage and all subjects took a test over each of the twenty passages. A subject was assigned to a form group and all subjects in the same form group took the same cloze test form over each passage. The excellent cooperation of the school authorities and teachers made it possible to administer the tests under almost ideal conditions.

Scoring

Final matching of form groups Subjects who failed to take one or more of the cloze tests were dropped from the study. The form groups were then equated in size by randomly discarding cases from the groups with the larger numbers of subjects. There were 135 subjects in each of the five form groups. The final groups were then checked to see if they were still matched in reading ability. The scores on the Stanford reading test were used as the dependent variable. The F ratio for the between form groups variance shown in Research/Table 2 was not significant. An inspection of the means in the cells also showed that the matching remained extremely close. The over-all mean of the group was 5.5 in grade placement scores, and the range was from about 1.4 to about 12.7 in each form group.

Scoring the cloze tests A subject's response was scored as correct when it exactly matched the word deleted to form the item. Misspellings were scored correct if they were intelligible to the scorer and not ambiguous. A few ambiguities arose in the case of homonyms, each of which could grammatically fit the context of the cloze blank, for example *there* and *their*. The error rate in scoring was held at or below 1 error per 500 items by having a scoring supervisor rescore a 10 percent sample of every group of 100 tests. In point of fact, the error rate seldom reached as high as 1 error per 1,000 items for a scorer. When the errors exceeded the prescribed level, the entire set was rescored. All scorers were trained to read poor handwriting and phonetic spelling.

Dependent Variables

Measures of comprehension difficulty (DIF) The difficulty of each word was found by calculating the proportion of subjects responding correctly when that word appeared as a cloze item. This was

RESEARCH/TABLE 2

Analysis of reading achievement scores by cloze test form groups and levels of reading ability

Source	Degrees of freedom	Mean squares	F ratio
Form Groups	4	12.77	.07
Ability Levels	4	248,223.18	1,320.37
Interaction	16	96.89	.52
Within	650	188.02	

called word difficulty. Independent clause difficulty was determined by taking the mean of the word difficulties in each independent clause. Sentence difficulty and passage difficulty were also found by calculating the mean of the word difficulties within those units.

Difficulties at ability levels One of the major problems studied required that difficulties be calculated separately for subjects at different levels of ability. Thus, the subjects in each form group were ranked by the size of their total scores on the *Stanford* reading test and then divided into quintiles. The mean grade placement scores of these groups were 3.2, 4.2, 5.1, 6.3, and 8.7. The F ratio for the between ability levels in Research/Table 2 shows that this resulted in the formation of strata that differed markedly in reading ability. The very small F ratio for the interaction of form groups and ability levels shows that groups at the same ability level were highly similar regardless of the form group in which they appeared. It also may be taken as evidence that the form groups were well matched in the distribution of reading ability. The measures of word, independent clause, sentence, and passage difficulty were then calculated separately for the groups of subjects at each of these levels of ability.

SUMMARY AND CONCLUSIONS

Improvement in the accuracy of predicting and controlling the readability of printed language is vitally needed. Major research in readability almost ceased after 1948. Dormancy occurred because 1] there were no valid methods for measuring the comprehension difficulty of written language, and 2] there was no organized body of basic research and theory upon which readability research could draw. The development of the cloze test solved the problem of validly measuring difficulty while it simultaneously provided additional power and flexibility in making those measurements. The organization of psycholinguistics as a discipline provided readability research with a body of basic research and theory, and linked readability research more closely to research and theory in psychology, linguistics, and literary style.

While these developments opened vast new areas for advancing knowledge of readability, they also revealed certain basic problems which must be solved before sound readability formulas can be developed. The present study investigated what were considered to be most basic questions. These questions and the related results and conclusions from this investigation are summarized as follows.

Are linguistic variables linearly related to comprehension difficulty? If they are not, non-linear regression techniques must replace the linear equations used in present formulas. An F test of linearity was performed to determine if the regression between each linguistic variable and comprehension difficulty was linear. At the word level of analysis, all regressions departed significantly from linearity where a significant correlation existed to begin with. The shapes of the curves obtained suggested that readability formulas designed to predict difficulties of individual words must utilize quadratic equations.

At the independent clause level of analysis, all but the regression involving words on the Dale List of 3,000 words were linear. However, a note of caution must be injected in interpreting these results. First, several of the F ratios approached a significant level. An inspection of these scatter plots showed that, if curvilinearity existed, its effects were most pronounced at the extreme ends of the distributions. Unfortunately, the F tests of linearity is least powerful in detecting curvilinearity at the extremes because so few cases occur there. Hence the failure to detect curvature may have been due to the limitations of present statistical techniques. Second, several variables were averages of one sort or another. It follows almost automatically from the central limits theorem that averages are normally distributed. Since two normally distributed variables almost invariably exhibit a linear relationship, the results of the F tests were more or less predictable. A good illustration was that syllables per word exhibited a curvilinear relationship at the word level of analysis but a linear relationship at the passage level. Consequently, it must be concluded that this problem must receive further investigation at the independent clause level of analysis to see if curvilinearity actually does exist at the extremes and if transforming the variables before averaging or summing them increases the correlations.

At the passage level of analysis, the results were similar except that no F ratio reached significance at the .05 level. That is, inspections of the scatter plots seemed to reveal a tendency for several of the variables to exhibit curvilinearity at the extremes. This was especially evident in the scatter plots of the Dale List and letter redundancy variables. Since only 20 passages were used, the F test had even less power at this level of analysis. Further investigation of the problem was also needed at the passage level of analysis.

Do linguistic variables more strongly influence difficulty for subjects at one level of reading ability than for subjects at other levels? If they do, different readability formulas must be developed for use with subjects at each level of reading ability. A five by three analysis of variance design was used to determine if linguistic variables influence difficulty more strongly for subjects at one level of reading ability than for subjects at other levels. The subjects were stratified into five levels using their scores on the reading achievement test, and the comprehension difficulty of each word, independent clause, and passage was calculated separately for the subjects at each ability level. The language units were then stratified into three levels using their values on a language variable, and the analysis of variance was calculated. The comprehension difficulties of the language units served as the dependent variable. A significant interaction between linguistic and ability levels in this analysis indicates that a variable is a better predictor of difficulty for subjects at one level of ability than for subjects at other levels.

The results show quite clearly that a linguistic variable can usually be expected to predict difficulty equally well for all subjects regardless of their reading levels. This generalization must, of course, be restricted to subjects whose reading achievement scores fall in the range represented in this study, second through twelfth grade in reading achievement grade placement score terms. But when cell means were plotted, no trend was evident which would suggest that this generalization might not hold equally well for subjects of greater reading ability. Only one exception to this generalization, the independent clause frequency variable, was found. However, this was of little interest because of its low correlation with comprehension difficulty. Because of ceiling effects, this problem could not be studied at the word level of analysis. However, this is not a serious limitation since all the variable occurring at the word level of analysis also occurred at the other levels of analysis where they did receive adequate investigation.

Thus, it was concluded that a single readability formula can be used to predict difficulty for subjects at almost any level of reading ability. This greatly simplified that task of developing readability formulas. Further, it shows that readability analysis should be applied to materials used with students at higher levels of education than has customarily been the case. The amount that even the most able students learn is accurately predictable from the character of the language in their instructional materials.

Can useful readability predictions be made for language units as small as individual words, independent clauses, and sentences? If they can, formulas for making these predictions would be extremely useful for locating difficult parts of texts, and predicting the comprehension difficulties of test items, book indexes, titles, and headings. The objective was to determine if readability formulas designed to predict the difficulties of language units as small as individual words, independent clauses, and sentences have enough validity to warrant their further development. A multiple correlation was found between the linguistic variables and comprehension difficulty at each level of analysis. Had the multiple correlations been low and had the regressions evidenced curvilinearity, non-linear procedures would have been used. The multiple correlation was .51 at the word level of analysis; .67 at the independent clause level; and .68 at the sentence level. While an inspection of the scatter plots showed curvilinearity present, the multiple correlations were high enough to demonstrate the point without further treatment of the data.

Readability formulas found useful in the past had validities ranging from .5 to .7. By these standards, the formulas represented by the regression equations found in the present study must be judged useful. Further, the formulas for predicting the difficulties of small language units can be greatly improved. The most obvious way to improve them is to deal with the problem of curvilinearity. At the word level this will produce a large and easily obtained increase in validity. At the independent clause and sentence levels, correcting for curvilinearity must necessarily be less direct and a large gain in validity is less certain to result. The most important gains in validity will be obtained by developing more valid measures of the attributes of prose style. While this is the most difficult approach, it is the most important, for it will increase our understanding of the psychology of language processes and make important contributions to school curricula in both language composition and comprehension.

Can the validities of readability formulas based entirely upon linguistic variables be improved? If they cannot, research efforts should be diverted to investigate variables which promise to yield gains. Historically, readability prediction formulas utilized only linguistic variables, variables based on objectively measurable features of language, and more or less ignored features that cannot be described objectively. Can the validity of readability formulas based exclusively on linguistic variables be improved beyond the point already reached? The present study with its improved research techniques and large variety of linguistic variables offered an excellent opportunity to study this question. Two multiple regression equations were calculated using the variables at the passage level of analysis. The data were analyzed in two parts because of the large number of variables involved. One multiple correlation was .93; the other, .81. None of the variables used in earlier studies was sufficiently powerful to enter the equations.

It was concluded that much improvement is possible in the validities of readability formulas. The formulas calculated in the present study accounted for 30 to 60 percent more of the comprehension difficulty variance than was possible with earlier formulas. The increase was due almost entirely to the greater validity of the new linguistic variables. Since these new variables only exemplify (and probably do so only crudely) the range of new variables it is possible to develop, it is not unreasonable to expect carefully constructed readability formulas in the future to exhibit validity correlations closely approaching 1.00.

While this conclusion may at first seem too strong, upon further analysis it is quite reasonable. Readability formulas have *prediction* validity only. The variables in them cannot be interpreted as *causing* the difficulty of text material. Difficulty is undoubtedly *caused* by the language itself, but these linguistic features constitute only a part of the causal variables. Semantic, organizational, and content variable undoubtedly constitute other causes of difficulty. However, linguistic variables can index these other types of variables. For example, discussions of highly complex subject matters are usually accompanied by many conjunctions, while discussions of interpersonal trivia are usually accompanied by the use of personal pronouns. Hence, the linguistic variables reflect the content variables in ordinary writing. Consequently, it is not unreasonable to expect readability formulas based exclusively on linguistic variables to *predict* nearly all of the difficulty variance among texts. But it would be most unreasonable to assert that the linguistic variables in those same formulas *caused* nearly all of the difficulty variance. A clever writer could quickly demonstrate that such a statement is nonsense.

Another point that merits discussion deals with the very large correlations which will be routinely observed in modern readability research. Psychologists have become accustomed to rechecking their calculations for errors when they obtain correlations in excess of .8. This is largely because their measurements usually contain a great deal of error. In readability research, error is much smaller. The linguistic variables are based upon exact counts and contain little or no error. Difficulty measurements are based upon test means which involve only the errors of the means which are much smaller, usually, than the errors of individual test scores. Consequently, readability correlations of .98 and .99 are not impossible and will probably be looked upon as commonplace in the future. As long as readability correlations are not interpreted as implying causation, these high correlations need not cause intellectual indigestion for anyone.

Does the use of various new types of linguistic variables improve the accuracy of readability prediction? If the accuracy of prediction is improved, the underlying rationale of new linguistic variables should be fully exploited to explore and refine them. A large number of previously uninvestigated linguistic variables were included in the present study. Some were representative of fundamentally new approaches to the measurement of prose style. Others were simply refinements of well known variables. The purpose was to determine if variables of these types warranted further development. The methods used were appropriate for exploratory purposes only; the value of a variable was judged almost solely by the size of its correlation with comprehension difficulty. When comparisons were made between variables, tests of significance were not attempted because the nature of the data made tests of significance impossible.

Because of the large number of variables involved, only the most important results can be discussed here. Perhaps of greatest immediate importance was the fact that the length and complexity of a sentence can be measured separately; and, though length and complexity are correlated, each has an independent correlation with difficulty. The extent to which their mutual correlation is necessary is an important problem for linguistic research. Another important finding was that the part of speech variables exhibited very high correlations with difficulty. For example, the ratio between the numbers of pronouns and conjunctions in a passage exhibited a correlation of .81 with difficulty. The third major result was that many of the well known variables were markedly improved by making relatively minor refinements in the way they are derived.

If any general conclusion is warranted by the results from this part of the study, it is that the major advances in readability prediction will result from the development of more sophisticated variables with which to measure the attributes of prose style. Whatever the best possible linguistic variables may be, it is certain that only a beginning has been made in their discovery.

IMPLICATIONS

Readability research can again make rapid strides toward the achievement of its two main goals, readability prediction and readability control, and this research must take new directions. Without question the most important advances should come through the development of better linguistic variables developed through the study of psycholinguistics, linguistics, and literary style.

The wholesale introduction of new variables can have only limited value unless some method is used to integrate each new linguistic variable into a general body of readability theory and unless methods are used whereby large numbers of linguistic variables can be simultaneously evaluated. Factor analysis techniques seem to offer an excellent method of solving both problems. Theory in the area of literary style is poorly developed, is stated in vague subjective terms and contains few statements of how the variables of prose style relate either to each other or to responses in a reader. Factor analysis of linguistic variables can reveal the basic dimensions in which prose style varies among authors, thus providing the theoretical framework within which the properties of new linguistic variables can be studied. The factors or dimensions of prose style can themselves be studied to determine how each influences responses in a reader.

This analytic strategy will greatly facilitate experimental readability research. The ultimate goal of readability research is to gain the ability to control the difficulty of language. This can only be achieved through the use of experimental methods which make it possible to determine if a linguistic variable is causally related to difficulty. At present, it is absurd to attempt to apply experimental techniques to the study of readability because of the great number of variables that must be controlled. Over 150 linguistic variables have been shown to correlate with difficulty. If these variables could be held constant, only a few days' work would be required to devise another 150 variables that would also have to be controlled. Fortunately, many of these variables are closely related to each other. Through factor analytic techniques redundancies can be removed and the entire set of variables reduced to a few basic style factors. This small number of factors can then be easily managed in experimental designs.

The introduction of cloze tests into readability research solved the most urgent and important psychological measurement problem in readability. There are still no adequate instruments for measuring the interest and aesthetic responses passages elicit in subjects. As a result these important aspects of readability have not been dealt with by careful researchers. One possibility that should be explored is to determine whether the principles of the semantic differential can be adapted to construct instruments for these purposes.

REFERENCES

Boder, D. The adjective-verb quotient: a contribution to the psychology of language. *Psychological Record,* 1940, *3,* 309–343.

Bormuth, J. R. Cloze tests as a measure of comprehension ability and readability. Unpublished doctoral dissertation, Indiana University, 1962.

Bormuth, J. R. Mean word depth as a predictor of comprehension difficulty. *California Journal of Educational Research,* 1964, *25,* 226–231.

Bormuth, J. R. Comparisons among cloze test scoring methods. In J. A. Figurel (Ed.), *Reading and Inquiry.* Newark, Del.: International Reading Association, 1965.

Carroll, J. B. Vectors of prose style in language. In T. A. Sebeok (Ed.), *Style in language.* Boston: John Wiley and Sons, 1960, pp. 283–292.

Carterette, E. C., & Jones, Margaret H. Redundancy in children's tests. *Science,* 1963, *140,* 1309–1311.

Chall, Jeanne S. Readability: An appraisal of research and application. *Ohio State University Educational Research Monograph,* 1958, No. 34.

Coleman, E. B. Improving comprehensioin by shortening sentences. *Journal of Applied Psychology,* 1962, *46,* 131–134.

Dale, E. A comparison of two word lists. *Educational Records, Bulletin,* 1931, *10,* 484–489.

Dale, E., & Tyler, R. W. A study of factors influencing the difficulty of reading materials for adults of limited reading ability. *Library Quarterly,* 1934, *4,* 384–412.

Dale, E., & Chall, Jeanne S. A formula for predicting readability. *Educational Research Bulletin,* 1948, *27,* 11–20.

Flesch, R. Measuring the level of abstraction. *Journal of Applied Psychology,* 1950, *34,* 384–390.

references

Flesch, R. A new readability yardstick. *Journal of Applied Psychology,* 1948, *32,* 221–233.

Fletcher, J. E. A study of the relationships between ability to use context as an aid in reading and other verbal abilities. Unpublished doctoral dissertation, University of Washington, 1955.

Forbes, F. W., & Cottle, W. C. A new method for determining readability of standardized tests. *Journal of Applied Psychology,* 1953, *37,* 185–190.

Fries, C. C. *The structure of English.* New York: Harcourt Brace, 1952.

Gray, W. S., & Leary, Bernice A. *What makes a book readable,* Chicago: University of Chicago Press, 1935.

Guilford, J. P. *Fundamental statistics in psychology and education.* New York: McGraw-Hill, 1956.

King-Ellison, P., & Jenkins, J. J. The durational threshold of visual recognition as a function of word frequency. *American Journal of Psychology,* 1954, *67,* 700–703.

Lorge, I. Predicting reading difficulty of selections for children. *Elementary English Review,* 1939, *16,* 229–233.

Lorge, I. The Lorge and Flesch readability formulas: a correction. *School & Society,* 1948, *67,* 141–142.

MacGinitie, W. H. Contextual constraint in English prose paragraphs. *Journal of Psychology,* 1961, *51,* 121–130.

Rankin, E. F. The cloze procedure—a survey of research. In L. T. Thurstone (Ed.), *Yearbook, National Reading Conference,* Milwaukee: National Reading Conference, 1965, pp. 50–93.

Ruddell, R. B. An investigation of the effect of the similarity of oral and written patterns of language structure on reading comprehension. Unpublished doctoral dissertation, Indiana University, 1963.

Shannon, C. E. The mathematical theory of communication. *Bell System Technical Journal,* 1948, *27,* 379–423, 623–656.

Smith, H. P., & Dechant, E. V. *Psychology in teaching reading.* Englewood Cliffs, N.J.: Prentice-Hall, 1961.

Strickland, Ruth. The language of elementary school children. *Bulletin of the School of Education.* Indiana University, 1962, *34,* No. 4.

Taylor, W. L. Cloze procedure: a new tool for measuring readability. *Journalism Quarterly,* 1953, *30,* 415–533.

Thorndike, E. I., & Lorge, I. *The teacher's word book of 30,000 words,* New York: Teachers College, Columbia University, 1944.

Yngve, V. H. Computer programs for translation. *Scientific American,* 1962, *206,* 68–76.

Yngve, V. H. A model and hypothesis for language structure. *Proceedings of the American Philosophical Association,* 1960, *404,* 444–466.

A Critique of J. R. Bormuth's Study: Readability: A New Approach

EUGENE A. JONGSMA

Center for Reading Improvement—Dallas, Texas

What makes the Bormuth study a benchmark in reading research? To answer that question, we must first characterize the readability research of the previous 50 years.

Scholars have long been fascinated with documenting those features of a text that make it more or less difficult to read. Klare (1963) wrote an excellent history of readability research in which he summarized the research by eras. Although purposes sometimes changed and methodology was occasionally altered, the basic characteristics of readability research remained the same from 1900 into the 1960s.

CHARACTERISTICS OF EARLY READABILITY RESEARCH

First, early readability research was more subjective than scientific. That is, it was based upon limited theory simply because our knowledge of language was not as advanced as it is today. For example, Gray and Leary (1935) initially sought answers to the question "What makes a book readable?" by obtaining subjective impressions from librarians. Even though their findings have implications for us today, this study exemplifies the rational approach that so characterized readability research.

Second, a primary goal of most researchers was to develop readability formulas. Multiple regression became the predominant statistical means of doing this. Readability formulas, in effect, were regression equations. Selected features of a text (e.g., average sentence length) were correlated with readers' understanding of the same text. The two or three most highly correlated features were weighted and entered into the formulas. These formulas, in turn, described the difficulty of reading material.

The widespread use of regression equations led to a third characteristic of readability research—the assumption of linear relationships. By definition, readability formulas assume that language variables are linearly related to comprehension. That is, as language features such as sentence length or number of syllables increase, so does the difficulty of understanding.

Fourth, the criterion for assessing comprehension was rather limited. Over the years, many researchers came to rely on the McCall-Crabbs *Standard Test Lessons in Reading* (McCall & Crabbs, 1925, 1950, 1961, 1979), a yardstick of graded passages with detailed grade scores. Comprehension was assessed through multiple-choice questions based on the passages. The problem, of course, was that one could never be certain whether poor comprehension was caused by difficulty in understanding the passages or difficulty in understanding the questions. However, alternate types of assessment such as open-ended questions or free recall were not feasible to use with the large number of subjects required in readability research.

A fifth characteristic of early readability research was the focus on longer units of texts. By and large, researchers were interested in the readability of whole passages or books, not smaller units such as phrases, sentences, or paragraphs.

A final characteristic was the assumption that readability formulas applied equally well to readers of all abilities. Sampling procedures usually produced groups of subjects normally distributed in reading ability. But data analysis rarely, if ever, explored whether correlations were consistent across reading ability levels.

DISTINGUISHING FEATURES OF THE BORMUTH STUDY

Given this backdrop of early readability research, we return to our original question. What makes Bormuth's study a benchmark in reading research? Why was it innovative and trend-setting? Four distinguishing characteristics set this study apart from previous readability research.

First, Bormuth approached this study from linguistic theory. Unlike his predecessors, he was more interested in exploring the influence of linguistic variables on comprehension than he was in just developing another readability formula. He saw the ultimate purpose of readability research as not simply to describe but to *control* the difficulty of written language. He believed that, working from a linguistic framework, we could document the effects of linguistic variables and eventually control the comprehensibility of written language systematically. It should be remembered that interest in linguistics grew dramatically in the late 1950s and throughout the 1960s. Chomsky (1957, 1965), for example, had presented an entirely new way of viewing syntax. Katz and Fodor (1963) broadened our concept of semantics. At the time, interest was not only strong in building new linguistic theories but also in applying our new-found knowledge of language to reading. Bormuth, no doubt, was influenced by these developments.

A second distinguishing characteristic was Bormuth's willingness to question assumptions. Specifically, he wondered (1) whether the correlations between linguistic variables and comprehension are in fact linear; and (2) whether linguistic variables influence difficulty equally at all levels of reading ability. So often, in any line of research, certain assumptions are absorbed into the knowledge base and go unexamined. Although not always the most popular stance to take, a re-examination of previously held assumptions often yields new insights and directions for future research.

Third, Bormuth was one of the first investigators to use the cloze procedure as a criterion measure in readability research. Coleman (1965) is credited by Klare (1974–75) as the first to use the cloze procedure in this way. Originally conceived by Taylor (1953), the cloze procedure was widely accepted as a valid and reliable means of measuring reading comprehension by the mid-1960s. Bormuth's (1962) doctoral dissertation a few years earlier supported its usefulness. The cloze procedure offered two important breakthroughs in readability research. It eliminated the problem mentioned earlier regarding multiple-choice questions. It also permitted the assessment of smaller textual units such as sentences, phrases, and individual words. By using an every-fifth deletion pattern and systematically rotating its starting point, Bormuth could obtain difficulty ratings for each individual word in the passages used.

A fourth distinguishing feature, although not unique, was the use of large-scale automatic data processing, which was more commonplace by the mid-1960s. Data processing facilitated the handling of large amounts of data. For example, in Bormuth's follow-up readability study (1969), over two million responses were analyzed.

IMPORTANT FINDINGS OF THE BORMUTH STUDY

What in the Bormuth study broadened our understanding of readability or perhaps influenced the research that was to follow? The sheer volume of the data and the complexity of the analysis make it impossible to discuss all of Bormuth's findings in this critique. Instead, we will focus on four of the most important things we learned from this study.

1. As Bormuth suspected, he found curvilinear relationships between some of the linguistic variables and comprehension. However, the curvilinear relationship appeared at the word level, not the passage level of analysis. The three variables that showed marked curvilinear relationships with word difficulty were (1) number of syllables; (2) number of letters or word length; (3) word frequency.

   What this finding means in a practical sense is this: As was commonly believed, short high-frequency words tend to be of low difficulty. As words increase in length or decrease in frequency, they become more difficult—but only up to a point. Eventually, there is a leveling off, and increases in length or decreases in frequency do not result in corresponding increases in word difficulty.

2. To examine variable strength as a function of reading ability, Bormuth ingeniously stratified subjects, taking each form of the passages into five levels of reading achievement. The linguistic variables, in turn, were stratified into three levels on the basis of difficulty. A series of three by five analyses of variance were then performed to find any significant interactions.

   Results revealed that the correlations between linguistic variables and difficulty remain stable across levels of reading ability. This finding more or less confirmed what had been assumed previously. A single readability formula could be used with the same degree of confidence for low to high readers. Since Bormuth's subjects ranged in reading levels from second through twelfth grade, this finding would appear to be widely generalizable.

3. One of Bormuth's major goals was to determine whether we could accurately predict the difficulty of smaller language units such as individual words, independent clauses, and sentences. As mentioned earlier, previous readability research had focused on whole passages.

   Bormuth found that he could indeed predict the difficulty of smaller language units although perhaps with not as much accuracy as he had hoped. Multiple correlations ranged from .5 to .7, somewhat lower than the validities for passage formulas. The variables accounting for most of the word difficulty were (1) word length; (2) word depth (a measure of the sequential dependencies between pairs of letters in the words of a passage); and (3) word frequency. Independent clause and sentence difficulties were caused by a large number of factors that suggested the complexity of comprehension. In a larger follow-up study, Bormuth (1969) developed 24 readability formulas. Some of these were for sentence-level and word-level analysis (including both words in context as well as words in isolation).

   The cloze procedures also made the analysis of smaller language units possible. Bormuth's study reaffirmed the usefulness of the cloze procedure as a tool for conducting language research.

4. Bormuth discovered that the predictive validity of readability formulas had assumed that sentence length reflected difficulty. Later work by Pearson (1974–75) confirmed this distinction between length and complexity. Pearson found that shorter sentences are not necessarily easier to understand. When shortening sentences, writers often omit words that signal semantic relationships. This places a greater burden on the inferencing ability of readers. This finding questions the simplistic practice of lowering the readability level of material by shortening sentences.

SUMMARY

Bormuth's study was one of the most comprehensive readability studies ever conducted and marked a turning point in readability research. It called into question a number of previously accepted beliefs about readability. Through a combination of linguistic theory and cloze methodology, it provided new ways of examining the complexities of written language.

FOR FURTHER LEARNING

Those readers who are interested in continuing to explore the topic of readability would find the following references helpful:

Carver, R. P. Measuring prose difficulty using the reading scale. *Reading Research Quarterly*, 1975–76, *11*, 660–685. (See also M. Kibby's reaction to Carver's study and Carver's response to Kibby in the same issue.)

for further learning

Halliday, M., & Hasan, R. *Cohesion in English*. London: Longman, 1976.

Harris, A. J., & Jacobson, M.D. A framework for readability research: Moving beyond Herbert Spencer. *Journal of Reading*, 1979, *22*, 390–398.

Hittleman, D. R. Seeking a psycholinguistic definition of readability. *The Reading Teacher*, 1973, *26*, 783–789.

Irwin, J. W., & Davis, C. A. Assessing readability: The checklist approach. *Journal of Reading*, 1980, *24*, 124–130.

Kibby, M. W. Passage readability affects the oral reading strategies of disabled readers. *The Reading Teacher*, 1979, *32*, 390–396.

Marshall, N., & Glock, M. Comprehension of connected discourse: A study into the relationships between the structure of text and information recalled. *Reading Research Quarterly*, 1978–79, *14*, 10–56.

Standal, T. C. Readability formulas: what's out, what's in? *The Reading Teacher*, 1978, *31*, 642–646.

REFERENCES

Bormuth, J. R. *Cloze tests as a measure of comprehension ability and readability*. Unpublished doctoral dissertation, Indiana University, 1962.

Bormuth, J. R. *Development of readability analyses*. Final Report, Project No. 7-0052, Contract No. OEC-3-7-070052-0236. USOE, Bureau of Research, U.S. Department of Health, Education, and Welfare, March, 1969.

Chomsky, N. *Syntactic structures*. The Hague: Mouton, 1957.

Chomsky, M. *Aspects of the theory of syntax*. Cambridge, Mass.: M.I.T. Press, 1965.

Coleman, E. B. *On understanding prose; some determiners of its complexity*. NSF Final Report GB-2604, Washington, D.C.: National Science Foundation, 1965.

Gray, W. S., & Leary, B. A. *What makes a book readable?* Chicago: University of Chicago Press, 1935.

Katz, J. J., & Fodor, J. A. The structure of semantic theory, *Language*, 1963, *39*, 170–210.

Klare, G. R. *The measurement of readability*. Ames, Iowa: Iowa State University, 1963.

Klare, G. R. Assessing readability. *Reading Research Quarterly*, 1974–75, *10*, 62–102.

McCall, W. A., & Crabbs, L. M. *Standard test lessons in reading*. New York: Teachers College, Columbia University, 1925, 1950, 1961, 1979.

Pearson, P. D. The effects of grammatical complexity on children's comprehension, recall, and conception of certain semantic relations. *Reading Research Quarterly*, 1974–75, *10*, 155–192.

Taylor, W. L. Cloze procedure: A new tool for measuring readability. *Journalism Quarterly*, 1953, *30*, 415–533.

A Commentary on Jongsma's Critique of Bormuth's Study: Readability: A New Approach

PRISCILLA A. DRUM

University of California, Santa Barbara

Jongsma's critique aptly describes *Readability: A New Approach* (Bormuth, 1966) as a benchmark in reading research," for the study has served as a major reference point for the extensive use of cloze in both readability and comprehension research in the 1970s. However, cloze is not a panacea; it too has problems as a measure of text difficulty and as an assessment tool for comprehension. We need to examine both its merits and limitations to find out what makes texts difficult and how readers can be helped to more fully understand them.

Dr. Jongsma outlined certain limitations in earlier readability research which Bormuth addressed in his work. The limitations included: (1) the subjective selection of text variables; (2) the use of linear regression analyses to obtain a predictive formula; (3) the selection of multiple-choice tests as the criterion measure; (4) the averaging of responses across subjects representing different reading ability levels; and (5) the focus on longer texts to the exclusion of word, clause, or sentence difficulties. Bormuth's results, described in Jongsma's critique, indicated that the new linguistic variables improved prediction; curvilinear relationships existed between certain predictors and the criterion scores; the correlations between predictors and difficulty scores were stable across reading ability levels; and word, clause, and sentence scores could be predicted, though not as well as passages. The following sections examine these results and the change from multiple-choice answers to cloze insertion scores, for though certain criticisms of readability formulas were resolved by the Bormuth study, others were not. Also, as stated before, cloze presents some new problems in its procedures for either measuring text difficulty or assessing comprehension.

SELECTION OF PREDICTOR VARIABLES

Early researchers asked teachers, librarians, and others what makes a text difficult, and listed the responses so that text selection was based on a perusal of the contents matched with these "difficulty" characteristics. The matching procedures were tedious and limited by the subjective opinion of the analyzer. Later readability researchers, including Bormuth, used countable characteristics of passages: number of words per sentence, number of affixes, number of syllables per word, number of prepositional phrases per 100 words, words on or not on vocabulary lists, etc. (Klare, 1974–75).

Most studies include some measure of vocabulary difficulty since vocabulary level correlates highly with both reading comprehension and intelligence measures. The vocabulary variables are often word-length measures—number of syllables or letters per word—because length and difficulty correlate. The longer the word, the less frequently it occurs. A second common measure of vocabulary difficulty is a word's appearance on some relatively limited vocabulary list, such as the Thorndike-Lorge Count (Thorndike & Lorge, 1944), the Dale List of 769 Words (Dale, 1931), or the Dale List of 3,000 Familiar Words (Dale & Chall, 1948). Bormuth used both types of vocabulary measures. The list approaches are usually scored as *yes* or *no* variables—the word is or is not on the list—rather than scoring the raw-score frequency of the word. Bormuth calculated the percentage of the words on the two Dale lists and applied the scores to his passage analysis. He also indexed the words by the 30,000 Thorndike-Lorge frequency counts on a 0 (not there) to 52 (most frequent) scale for his word analysis.

Bormuth added new variables based on the then-current linguistic theories, such as Yngve's word-depth variable (1960; 1962) from phrase structure analysis, Strickland's independent-clause type frequency (1962), Fries's four form classes (1952), and others. Thus, both readability formulas and cloze procedures are derived from counting certain language characteristics to identify the difficulty of texts for use with a group of readers.

The problem with these "count" approaches is not whether they are theory-driven or not; it is that naturally occurring passages do not vary systematically on the count variables. Passages contain frequent and infrequent words, short and long sentences, common and uncommon clauses. If one tested very long, simple sentences containing all high-frequency words versus very short, simple sentences with similar high-frequency words, one could test the sentence length variable systematically, but passages are not written in this manner. Also, the count variables used do not include semantic or conceptual variables, probably because we cannot easily define them.

Some of the more recent work in comprehension suggests that chronologically ordered fiction that explicitly contains story grammar categories is easier for children to understand than less well-ordered stories (Stein & Glenn, 1979). We need categories for the difficulty of types of genre, quality of writing for each genre, and specific topics. A beginning on the latter requirement is described by Miller and Kintsch (1980). The content of the information should make a greater difference in comprehension than the grammatical representation and the average frequency of the lexicon used.

METHODOLOGY FOR RESEARCH

As noted by Jongsma, most readability researchers' primary goal was to arrive at a summative designation of the difficulty level of a text. Regression procedure is a statistical method for obtaining an index. The following hypothetical example illustrates the procedure. If the fourth-grade sample correctly answers 75% of the items on a passage with a mean syllable length of 1.5 per word and a mean sentence length of 17 words, then the readability level for that passage and other passages with similar syllable and sentence-length characteristics would be designated fourth-grade level passages. The predictive power of the language counts used in readability formulas varies from .5 to .7 (Chall, 1958), which simply means that even for the particular children sampled, the language counts can only explain about half to three-fourths of the variance on the multiple-choice test. The criterion of proportion of correct answers (.50 to .75) required for grade-level designation varies, but the .75 level is often used. Thus, a norming sample's performance on a standardized test provides the basis for readability levels. Bormuth also used regression procedures. His language counts were entered as predictors, but performance on deletions, rather than scores on a multiple-choice test, was the criterion variable.

The multiple-regression procedures used in readability formulas generally have been tested only for linearity and not for quadratic or higher order trends. Bormuth examined his data for departures from linearity, but he did not test such departures for their explanatory power, probably because of the difficulty in defining "the number of distinct values in the (various) independent variable(s)" (Kerlinger & Pedhazur, 1973, p. 209). Instead, he simply noted that a number of variables were curvilinear by dividing them into three categories of Hi, Mid, and Lo, and testing them in univariate tests for each of the five ability groups.

Curvilinear Relationships

The curvilinear relationships found by Bormuth may be telling us more about the limitations on cloze as a measurement procedure than about the relationships of the variables to comprehension.

Bormuth's study (1966) showed curvilinear relationships between all linguistic variables and comprehension at the word level. Words were more difficult in a linear fashion. As the number of letters or syllables per word increased and word frequency decreased, comprehension difficulty also increased until the regression line flattened out, indicating that increases in word difficulty no longer affected the difficulty of inserting the correct word. This effect is comparable to certain athletic events. In pole-vaulting the results are linear up to a certain height; the better the athlete, the more likely he will vault higher levels. At a certain height the difference between good and poor athletic ability is no longer a factor as no one succeeds, and the linear relationship disappears. Many function word deletions and stereotypical phrases, such as "the ______ House, home of the president," are highly predictable; few choices fit this slot. An examination of the following sentence illustrates this point:

> "Education has come into __(1)__ mainstream of our nation's __(2)__, where it is being __(3)__ as a political instrument __(4)__ solve social problems and __(5)__ an economic instrument to __(6)__ industry and government with __(7)__ manpower. (Bormuth, 1970, p. 1)

Deletions (1), (3), (4), and (5) are quite predictable in that only a few words can fit these slots. The words are all highly frequent, short, one-syllable words. But deletion (2) is an attractive nuisance in that many readers would select the word *capitol* because of strong associations with the phrase *our nation's*. There are numerous choices for (6) and (7).

Most readers who have developed some fluency in reading so that they can monitor the sense of the passage could fill in the four predictable words, but to be accurate on the other three requires either luck, not skill, or memory for the particular passage. In a longer sample, there are more clues; the same content words are often repeated. As Finn (1977) noted, each successive repetition of a word in a passage proved easier to guess; the third repetition was easier than the second, and so forth. Passages with few content words repeated many times should prove easier for correct cloze insertion, but this count variable is also amenable to more typical readability approaches.

The curvilinear relationships for first readings of cloze passages are similar to a ceiling effect where the probabilities for exact answers on many of the deletions are so small that no one is likely to guess them. "The difficulty of each word was found by calculating the proportion of subjects responding correctly when that word appeared as a cloze item" (see page 599). The mean proportion correct was 29.66 collapsed across all 5,181 words. It would be useful to examine the proportion correct on specific words with identified characteristics rather than collapsing across words. Until the probabilities can be estimated for each deletion, what is being measured remains moot.

STABILITY OVER READING LEVELS

Reading ability formulas attempt to designate the difficulty levels of text for grade levels with the implicit assumption that reading ability and grade level are in concordance. This assumption may not be accurate. However, not all researchers assume that readability formulas apply equally to all reading ability levels. The literature on readability contains statements to the effect that special readability formulas must be developed for use with subjects at different levels of reading ability (Smith & Dechant, 1961). Chall (1958) cited two types of evidence supporting this notion. First, Chall noted that the Lorge formulas seemed better suited for predicting difficulty for young children than the Dale-Chall formula, while the Dale-Chall formula was superior for older children. Second, Chall pointed out that Gray (1935) observed "the sizes of the correlations between linguistic and difficulty variables differed depending on the reading ability of the groups of subjects used" (see page 590).

Cloze procedures are limited also in determining readers' capacities for understanding texts; these limitations are closely related to the curvilinear relationships noted above. Bormuth states that "the results show quite clearly that a linguistic variable can usually be expected to predict difficulty equally well for all subjects regardless of their reading levels" (see page 600).

To explore ability differences, Bormuth divided the 675 students sampled into five reading ability groups of 135 subjects each. The ability group means from the Stanford reading test were 3.2, 4.2, 5.1, 6.3, and 8.7. Each ability group's cloze scores were tested on each predictor variable. Each predictor had been stratified into three equal groups according to its value. For instance, the syllable variable for the word criterion was divided into a Hi group (the top third of the words with the most syllables per word), a Mid group, and a Lo group. The mean for syllables at the word level of analysis was 1.41 with a standard deviation of .76. Since every word has at least one syllable, this is a positively skewed distribution. Yet the multiple-range tests indicated that for each of the five ability groups tested separately, there was a significant difference at the .05 level (2 and 5,179 df) between Hi versus Mid and Hi versus Lo. The only differences that were not significant were the Mid versus Lo for the top two ability groups. For the more than 650 tests examined for levels of the predictor variables, the differences within ability groups were significant for approximately .64 of the tests.

An examination of Figures 4a to 4e (Bormuth, 1964, p. 63) for the difficulty scores on words by the five ability groups for the three levels (Hi, Mid, and Lo) of the word predictors shows the following patterns. As reading ability increases, there are fewer errors on the Lo and, to some extent, the Mid classifications for all variables except word depth. There are no differences by ability for the Hi classification on any variable or on comprehension difficulty. Only at the easier levels does reading achievement exert a moderately strong influence on number correct. In effect, as words become less predictable because more choices are available for a particular slot, cloze is no longer useful as a measure of reading comprehension, just as a bar at 22 feet does not measure pole-vaulting ability. Able and less able readers alike perform poorly.

In a clinical setting where the reader is tested in a one-on-one situation, cloze insertions could be a useful tool. Questions about why a particular choice was made might be enlightening for diagnosing comprehension difficulties. Even here the *n*th word deletion procedure should probably be modified to specific types of words after the preliminary diagnosis. If a pupil does not note synonym clues, passages with different synonym clues might be prepared so that cloze deletions could be used for instruction geared to a particular problem.

CRITERION MEASURE

Dr. Jongsma notes that "Bormuth was one of the first investigators to use the cloze procedure as a criterion measure in readability research" (see page 608). Most earlier researchers used the language count variables as predictors for the scores on multiple-choice questions. Poor comprehension for the criterion scores was caused by either difficulty in understanding the passages or difficulty in understanding the questions. Any problems in the multiple-choice test used as a criterion for a readability formula lessens the validity of the resulting grade-level designation.

By using the cloze insertion as the dependent measure, the passage versus question confounding can be avoided. The language count variables, similar to those used in readability formulas, are entered as predictors for the cloze results. The materials are easy to prepare; simply select passages, delete every *n*th word, then ask readers or listeners to fill in the blanks. The subjectivity underlying the construction of multiple-choice items, such as which detail to question and which inference to ask, is avoided. The answers cannot be inserted without reading the passage, as many items can be at better-than-chance levels with multiple-choice tests (Tuinman, 1974; Pryczak, 1972). Also, the cloze results correlate highly with the readability designations (Taylor, 1953) and with reading achievement tests (Bormuth, 1969; Taylor, 1957). Each cloze deletion can be scored for various types of linguistic complexity: word characteristics of frequency, number of letters, number of syllables, part of speech, and syntactic context in which the word occurs. The cloze insertion becomes the subject's score, and the characteristics of the original word become the predictor variables.

Using either cloze scores or readability formulas to represent text difficulty indices for future readers is open to the same criticism often cited for multiple-choice tests. The original readers, the norming sample, are not necessarily similar in requisite knowledge to subsequent children who read the text. When cloze scores are based on actual students' performance, the cloze determination of readability is more accurate for those students. However, the easily predicted words are those that are syntactically inappropriate or those that are directly related to a certain topic. The latter group of words depends on one's familiarity with certain reading materials and a background of related experiences. Taylor (1953), at the end of his article on cloze procedure, warns of the dangers of relying on readability results to generalize to specific readers. "It is a little unreasonable that a single readability score for an article on cattle-breeding should apply alike to residents of Texas 'cow country' and metropolitan Brooklyn" (p. 433). Taylor then suggests that cloze be used with the individuals who are to read the material to make sure the readability level is pertinent. The same restrictions apply to generalizing cloze results; readers differ in their reading habits and their background knowledge. The difficulty of the passages as determined by cloze results cannot be generalized to all readers, but only to those who are similar on relevant attributes to those who participated in the original test.

WORD, CLAUSE, AND PASSAGE UNITS

Much print information is given in linguistic units smaller than paragraphs, for example, signs, instructions, questions, etc. Therefore, finding the variables that affect the comprehensibility of smaller discourse units is important. As noted earlier, readability formulas applied to passages account for somewhere between .5 and .7 of the variance in answers to items in multiple-choice tests. With cloze as the criterion measure, language count predictors account for .26 of the variance on 5,181 words, .44 and .46 for the 405 clauses and the 365 sentences respectively, and .87 for the 20 passages. In these predictions, number of letters accounted for .25 of the word difficulty variance, but letters correlated with syllables at .81 and with frequency at −.48. This is an example of multicollinearity, where only one variable predicts; it may be letter length or some complex interaction between syllables, frequency, and length. Without systematic design, including orthogonal predictors, we cannot know. Yet *n*th word random deletions do not lend themselves to systematic design.

For the clause and sentence levels, the best predictors are word length and number of words per unit, two variables quite similar to those used in many readability formulas. The variance accounted for in passages is substantial, an R^2 of .87. Here the mean average for the proportion of subjects selecting the correct words is 29.66 for the 20 passages, but the standard deviation decreases from 21.61 for words to 9.06 for passages. Cloze did provide a stronger relationship between language counts and passage difficulty, but there was less variance to predict.

In conclusion, Bormuth states in his introduction to the 1966 article that "many adults and children fail to understand what they read, not because the concepts are too difficult or because they lack basic reading skills, but simply because of the complexity of the language in which those concepts are presented" (see page 587). Bormuth's studies attempted to isolate the linguistic variables that predict comprehension error. The concomitant assumption was that, once the variables were isolated, textbook authors would simplify their texts so that they would be more easily understood by all readers. Or, as stated by Jongsma, "He (Bormuth) saw the ultimate purpose of readability research as not simply to describe but to *control* the difficulty of written language."

The danger in this assumption is that informative texts might continuously regress into simpler and simpler forms, such as the Newspeak of Orwell's *1984*. Rather than controlling language, the effort of identifying variables of linguistic complexity and their effects on specific aspects of comprehension difficulty should provide direction for teaching comprehension skills with language learning, and not language control, as the ultimate goal.

REFERENCES

Bormuth, J. R. Relationships between selected language variables and comprehension ability and difficulty. *Cooperative Research Project, No. 2082,* Los Angeles, 1964.

Bormuth, J. R. Readability: A new approach. *Reading Research Quarterly,* 1966, *1,* 79–132.

Bormuth, J. R. Factor validity of cloze tests as measures of reading comprehension ability. *Reading Research Quarterly,* 1969, *4,* 358–365.

Bormuth, J. R. *On the theory of achievement test items.* Chicago: University of Chicago Press, 1970.

Chall, J. S. Readability: An appraisal of research and application. *Ohio State University Educational Research Monograph,* 1958, No. 34.

Dale, E. A comparison of two word lists. *Educational Records Bulletin,* 1931, *10,* 484–489.

Dale, E., & Chall, J. S. A formula for predicting readability. *Educational Research Bulletin,* 1948, *27,* 11–20.

Finn, P. J. Word frequency, information theory, and cloze performance: A feature theory of processing in reading. *Reading Research Quarterly,* 1977–78, *13,* 508–537.

Fries, C. C. *The structure of English.* New York: Harcourt Brace, 1952.

Gray, W. S., & Leary, B. A. *What makes a book readable.* Chicago: University of Chicago Press, 1935.

Kerlinger, F. N., & Pedhazur, E. J. *Multiple regression in behavioral research.* New York: Holt, Rinehart, & Winston, Inc., 1973.

Klare, G. R. Assessing readability. *Reading Research Quarterly,* 1974–75, *10,* 62–102.

Miller, J. R., & Kintsch, W. Readability and recall of short prose passages: A theoretical analysis. *Journal of Experimental Psychology: Human Learning and Memory,* 1980, *60,* 335–354.

Pryczak, F. Objective evaluation of the quality of multiple-choice test items designed to measure comprehension of reading passages. *Reading Research Quarterly,* 1972, *8,* 92–111.

Smith, H. P., & Dechant, E. V. *Psychology in teaching reading.* Englewood Cliffs, N.J.: Prentice-Hall, 1961.

Stein, N. S., & Glenn, C. G. An analysis of story comprehension in elementary children. In R. O. Freedle (Ed.), *New directions in discourse processing.* Norwood, N.J.: Ablex, 1979.

Strickland, R. The language of elementary school children. *Bulletin of the School of Education.* Indiana University, 1962, *34*(4).

Taylor, W. L. Cloze procedure: A new tool for measuring readability. *Journalism Quarterly,* 1953, *30,* 415–433.

Taylor, W. L. Cloze readability scores as indices of individual differences in comprehension and aptitude. *Journal of Applied Psychology,* 1957, *41,* 19–26.

Thorndike, E. I., & Lorge, I. *The teacher's word book of 30,000 words.* New York: Teachers College, Columbia University, 1944.

Tuinman, J. J. Determining the passage dependency of comprehension questions in five major tests. *Reading Research Quarterly,* 1973–74, *9,* 206–223.

Yngve, V. H. A model and hypothesis for language structure. *Proceedings of the American Philosophical Association,* 1960, *404,* 444–466.

Yngve, V. H. Computer programs for translation. *Scientific American,* 1962, *206,* 68–76.

section XIII

TECHNOLOGY AND READING

RESEARCH by Roger C. Schank and Charles J. Rieger, *Inference and the Computer Understanding of Natural Language* and Roger C. Schank, *The Structure of Episodes in Memory.*

CRITIQUE by Don H. Nix

FOR FURTHER LEARNING

COMMENTARY by Thomas W. Bean

This section introduces the reader to two studies in the area of computer-technology and reading. Nix critiques both Schank and Rieger's study and the study authored by Schank alone. Nix takes the position that traditional approaches to reading comprehension have tended to mask the complexity involved in comprehending even simple texts. He feels strongly that in order to teach comprehension, a teachably explicit characterization of such complexity is needed. Nix claims that the research by Schank and Rieger and Schank in the field of Artificial Intelligence (A.I.) has considerable potential for developing a specific framework for comprehension instruction. Bean's comments are generally supportive of Nix's critique of these studies. He recognizes that most of our traditional approaches for teaching comprehension stem from pedagogical intuition rather than from empirical research. He questions, however, whether or not an instructional program based on an A.I. model is more promising than our heretofore "armchair" methods and feels that this question cannot or will not be resolved until adequate applied research is conducted.

INFERENCE AND THE COMPUTER UNDERSTANDING OF NATURAL LANGUAGE[1]

ROGER C. SCHANK[2] and CHARLES J. RIEGER III[3]

Computer Science Department, Stanford University, Stanford, Calif. 94305, U.S.A.

Recommended by E. Sandewall

ABSTRACT

The notion of computer understanding of natural language is examined relative to inference mechanisms designed to function in a language-free deep conceptual base (Conceptual Dependency). The conceptual analysis of a natural language sentence into this conceptual base, and the nature of the memory which stores and operates upon these conceptual structures are described from both theoretical and practical standpoints. The various types of inferences which can be made during and after the conceptual analysis of a sentence are defined.

[1]This research was supported by the Advanced Research Projects Agency of the Department of Defense under Contract SD-183.

The views and conclusions contained in this document are those of the authors and should not be interpreted as necessarily representing the official policies, either expressed or implied, of the Advanced Research Projects Agency or the U.S. Government.

[2]Present address: Computer Science Department, Yale University, New Haven, Connecticut 06520, U.S.A.

[3]Present address: Computer Science Department, University of Maryland, College Park, Maryland 20740, U.S.A.

From *Artificial Intelligence* 5(1974), pp. 373–412.

CONTENTS

1. INTRODUCTION

The question of what belongs to the domain of parsing and what is part of the domain of inference inevitably comes up when attempting to put together a system in order to do natural language understanding. This paper is intended to explain the difference within the context of Conceptual Dependency Theory [6, 7, 8], categorize the kinds of inferences that are necessary within such an understanding system, and outline the basic elements and processes that make up the program at Stanford that currently handles these inference tasks.

We shall assume in this paper that it is the desire of those researchers who work on the problems of computational linguistics to have a system that is capable of responding intelligently, on the basis of its own model of the world, in reaction to a given input sentence. Thus, we assume here that a system responds as follows (for example) is both an interesting and useful system if it accomplishes these things:

(1) INPUT: I am going to buy some aspirin for my cold.
OUTPUT: Why don't you try some chicken soup instead?
(2) INPUT: John asked Mary for a book.
OUTPUT: A book about what?
(3) INPUT: Do you want a piece of chocolate?
OUTPUT: No, I don't want to spoil my appetite for dinner.
(4) INPUT: John went to the store.
OUTPUT: What did he want to buy?

Before getting into the descriptions of the various kinds of inferences to which a conceptual memory should be sensitive, the notion of inference and how it differs from logical deductions (for instance in a theorem-prover or question-answerer) should be made clear.

In its broadest sense, we consider an inference to be a new piece of information which is generated from other pieces of information, and which may or may not be true. The intent of inference-making is to "fill out" a situation which is alluded to by an utterance (or story line) in hopes of tying pieces of information together to determine such things as feasibility, causality and intent of the utterance at that point. There are several features of all inferences which should make clear how an inference differs in substance and intent from a formal deduction:

(1) Inference generation is a "reflex response" in a conceptual memory. That is, one of the definitions of "processing conceptual input" is the generation of inferences from it. This means that there is always an implicit motivation to generate new information from old. In a theorem-prover or question-answerer, deductions are performed only upon demand from some external process.

(2) An inference is not necessarily a logically valid deduction. This means that the new information represented by the inference might not bear any formal logical relationship to those pieces of information from which it is generated. A good example of this is called "affirmation of the consequent", a technique fruitfully utilized by Sherlock Holmes, and certainly utilized by people in everyday situations. Briefly, this refers to the "syllogism" $A \supset B$, B; therefore A. In this sense (and there are other examples), conceptual memory is strikingly different from a formal deductive system.

(3) An obvious consequence of (2) is that an inference is not necessarily true. For this reason, it is useful for memory to retain and propagate measures of the degree to which a piece of information is likely to be true. Memory must also be designed with the idea that *no* information is inviolably true, but rather must always be willing and able to respond to contradictions.

(4) The motivations for inference generation and formal deduction are entirely different. Formal deductions are highly directed in the sense that a well-defined goal has been established, and a path from some starting conditions (axioms and theorems) to this goal is desired. Inferences on the other hand are not nearly so directed. Inferences are generally made to "see what they can see". The "goal" of inferencing is rather

amorphous: make an inference, then test to see whether it looks similar to, is identical to, or contradicts some other piece of information in the system. When one of these situations occurs, memory takes special action in the form of discontinuing a line of inferencing, asking a question, revising old information, creating causal relationships or invoking a belief pattern.

(5) A memory which uses the types of inference we will describe needs some means of recourse for altering the credibility of a piece of information when the credibility of some piece of information which was used in its generation changes. In other words, memory needs to remember *why* a piece of information exists. In contrast, a formal deductive system in general doesn't "care" (or need to know) where a fact came from, only that it exists and is true.

Having made these distinctions between conceptual inference and other types of logical deductions, we will describe some distinct types of inference.

2. INFERENCE AND PARSING

We take as one of our operating assumptions, that the desired output for a conceptual analyzer is a meaning representation. Since it is possible to go directly from an input sentence into a meaning representation (see [4, 6, 11] for descriptions of computer programs that do this), we shall disregard any discussion of syntactic parsing output.

What then should be present in a meaning representation? We claim that it is necessary for a meaning representation to contain each and every concept and conceptual relation that is explicitly or implicitly referred to by the sentence being considered.

By explicit reference we mean the concepts that underlie a given word. Thus we have the concept of John for "John" and the concept of a book for "book" in sentence (5):

(5) John bought a book.

However, we claim in addition that an adequate meaning representation must make explicit what is implicit but nonetheless definitely referenced in a given sentence. Thus, in (5) we have the word "bought" which implicitly references two actions of transfer, one whose object is the book and the other whose object is some valuable entity. We assume that hearers of (5), unless specifically told otherwise, will assume that this object is "money".

It is here then that we shall make our first distinction between the province of parsing (or the extraction of explicit and implicit information) and that of inference (the adding-on of probably correct information). The word "buy" has a number of senses in English, but the surrounding information disambiguates "buy" so that in (5) it can only mean that two actions of transfer occurred and that each action caused the other's existence. Furthermore, it is always true what whenever one of these transfer actions is present (hence called ATRANS for abstract transfer) it is also true that an actor did the ATRANSing; there was an object acted upon, and there was a recipient and a donor of this object.

We now state our first inference type which we call LINGUISTIC-INFERENCE:

1. An instance of LINGUISTIC-INFERENCE exists when, in the absence of specific information to the

contrary, a given word or syntactic construction can be taken to mean that a specific but unmentioned object is present in a predicted case for a given ACT with a likelihood of near certainty.

In the above example, the ACT is ATRANS, its predicted cases are OBJECT, RECIPIENT (includes receiver and donor) and INSTRUMENT. The word "buy" by definition refers to the ACT ATRANS and therefore implicitly references its cases. However, in addition "buy" has as a linguistic inference the object "money" as the object of the ATRANS whose actor is the subject of the sentence in which "buy" appears.

We assign to the conceptual analyzer the problem of handling explicit reference, implicit reference, and linguistic inference within a meaning representation because these are consequences of words. Using Conceptual Dependency notation (where ⇔ denotes the relation between actor and action; ←O denotes the relation between action and object; ⇚ denotes causality dependence; and

denotes the relation between action, object, recipient and donor), the conceptual analyzer (described in [4]) outputs the following for (5):

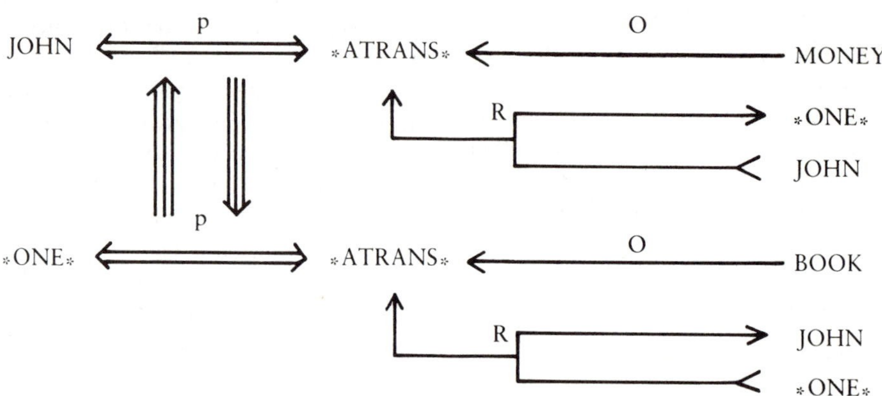

Two more common examples of linguistic inference can be seen with reference to sentences (6) and (7):

(6) Does John drink?
(7) John hit Mary.

In (6), it is reasonable to assume that the referenced object is "alcoholic beverages" although it is unstated. It is a property of the word "drink" that when it appears without a sentential object "alcoholic beverage" is understood. (In fact, this is a property of quite a few languages, but from this it should not be thought that this is a property of the concept underlying "drink". Rather it is an artifact of the languages that most of them share common cultural associations.) Thus, given that this is a linguistic inference, and that our conceptual analyzer is responsible for making linguistic inferences, our analyzer puts out the following conceptual structure for it:

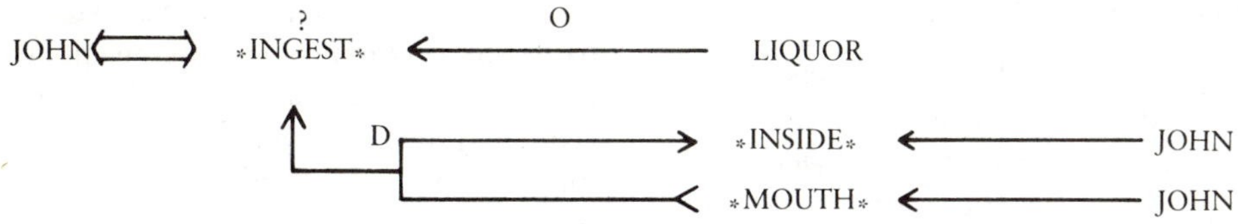

```
                  ?                    O
JOHN <=====> *INGEST* <------------------------- LIQUOR

               ^     D  ----------------> *INSIDE* <------------- JOHN
               |_______|
                       ----------------< *MOUTH* <-------------- JOHN
```

The ACT INGEST is used here. We shall explain the notion of a primitive ACT in the next section.

In (7), we again have the problem that what hearers usually assume to be the meaning of this sentence is in fact quite beyond what the sentence explicitly says. Sentence (7) does not explicitly state what John did. Rather we must call upon some other information to decide if John threw something at Mary or if he swung his hand at her (and whether his hand was holding some object). Notice that the same ambiguity exists if we had sentence (8), but that one meaning is preferred over the other in (9):

(8) John hit Mary with a stick.
(9) John hit Mary with a slingshot.

We shall claim that for (7) when no other information is explicit, the most likely reading is identical with the reading for (10):

(10) John hit Mary with his hand.

Thus, (7) is another example of linguistic inference and it is the responsibility of the conceptual analyzer to assume "hand" as the thing that hit Mary on the basis of having seen "hit" occurring with no syntactic instrument. (Note that syntactic instrument is quite different from the conceptual INSTRUMENTAL case mentioned earlier.) Before we get into inferences that are not linguistic it will be necessary to explain further the elements of the meaning representation that we use as the input to our reference making procedures.

We would like to point out at this point that we assign the problem of extracting conceptual structures and making linguistic references to the domain of the conceptual analyzer. This is because the information that is used for making the decisions involved in those processes is contained in the particular language under analysis. From this point on in this paper we shall be discussing inferences that come from world knowledge rather than from a particular language. It is those interlingual processes that we assign to the domain of a memory and inference program such as we shall describe in Section 6.

3. THE TWELVE PRIMITIVE ACTIONS

Conceptual Dependency theory is intended to be an interlingual meaning representation. Because it is intended to be language free, it is necessary in our representations to break down sentences into the elements that make them up. In order to do this it is necessary to establish a syntax of possible conceptual relationships and a set of conceptual categories that these relate. Furthermore it is necessary that requirements be established for how a given word is mapped into a conceptual construction.

There are six conceptual categories in Conceptual Dependency:

PP	Real world objects,
ACT	Real world actions,
PA	Attributes of objects,
AA	Attributes of actions,
T	Times,
LOC	Locations.

These categories can relate in certain specified ways which are considered to be the syntactic rules of conceptualizations. There are sixteen of these conceptual syntax rules, but we shall list here only the ones that will be used in this paper:

$PP \Leftrightarrow ACT$	indicates that an actor acts.
 $PP \Leftrightarrow PA$	indicates that an object has a certain attribute.
$ACT \xleftarrow{O} PP$	indicates the object of an action.
$ACT \xleftarrow{R} \begin{cases} \rightarrow PP \\ \leftarrow PP \end{cases}$	indicates the recipient and the donor of an object within an action.
$ACT \xleftarrow{D} \begin{cases} \rightarrow PP \\ \leftarrow PP \end{cases}$	indicates the direction of an object within an action.
$ACT \xleftarrow{I} \Updownarrow$	indicates the instrumental conceptualization for an action.
 $X \Uparrow Y$	indicates that conceptualization X caused conceptualization Y. When written with a "c" this form denotes that X COULD cause Y.
$PP \Leftarrow \begin{cases} \rightarrow PA2 \\ \leftarrow PA1 \end{cases}$	indicates a state change of an object.
 $PP1 \leftarrow PP2$	indicates that PP2 is eithr PART OF or the POSSESSOR OF PP1.

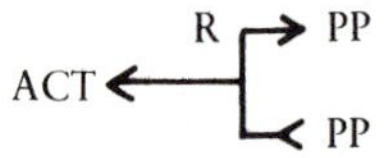

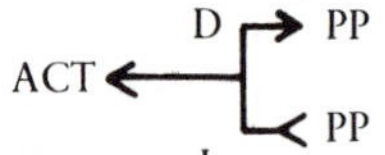

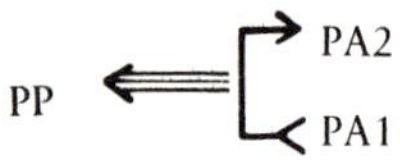

In Conceptual Dependency, tenses are considered to be modifications of the main link between actor and action (⇔), or the link between an object and its state (⟺). The main link modifiers we shall use here are:

p	past,
f	future,
(null)	present,
ts = x	begin a relation at time x,
tf = x	end a relation at time x,
c	conditional,
/	negation,
?	question.

The most important category for our purposes here is the ACT. A word maps into an ACT when it specifically refers to a given possible action in the world. Often verbs only reference unstated actions and make specific reference to states or relationships between these unspecified actions. As an example we have sentence (11):

(11) John hurt Mary.

Here, the real world action that John did is unstated. Only the effect of this action is known: namely that it caused Mary to enter a "hurt" state. Similarly, in (12) the word "prevent" is not a specific real world action but rather refers to the fact that some unstated action caused that some other action (that may or may not be specified later on in the sentence) did not occur.

(12) John prevented Mary from giving a book to Bill.

The analyses of these sentences (11) and (12) are as follows:

JOHN $\overset{p}{\Longleftrightarrow}$ *DO*

MARY $\overset{p}{\Longleftarrow}$ *HEALTH* = (X − 2) / *HEALTH* = (X)

(indicates HEALTH has gone down 2 points on a 10-point scale)

and

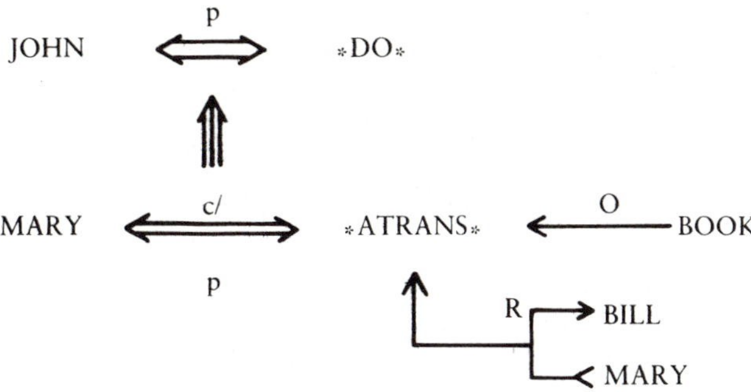

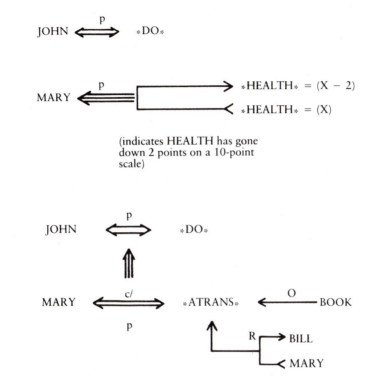

Since many verbs are decomposed into constructions that involve only unstated actions (denoted by DO) and/or attributes of objects (PA's) and since we require that any two sentences that have the same meaning be represented in one and only one way, the set of primitive ACTs that are used is important.

We have found that a set of only twelve primitive actions is necessary to account for the action part of a large class of natural language sentences. This does not mean that these primitives are merely category names for types of actions. Rather, any given verb is mapped into a conceptual construction that may use one or more of the primitive ACTs in certain specified relationships plus other object and state information. That is, it is very important that no information be lost with the use of these primitives. It is the task of the primitives to conjoin similar information so that inference rules need not be written for every individual surface verb, but rather inference rules can be written for the ACTs. This of course turns out to be extremely economical from the point of view of memory functioning.

The twelve ACTs are:

ATRANS	The transfer of an abstract relationship such as possession, ownership, or control.
PTRANS	The transfer of physical location of an object.
PROPEL	The application of a physical force to an object.
MOVE	The movement of a bodypart of an animal.
GRASP	The grasping of an object by an actor.
INGEST	The taking in of an object by an animal.
EXPEL	The expulsion from the body of an animal into the world.
MTRANS	The transfer of mental information between animals or within an animal. We partition memory into CP (conscious processor), LTM (long-term memory), and sense organs. MTRANSing takes place between these mental locations.
CONC	The conceptualizing or thinking about an idea by an animal.
MBUILD	The construction by an animal of new information from old information.
ATTEND	The action of directing a sense organ towards an object.
SPEAK	The action of producing sounds from the mouth.

The following important rules are used within Conceptual Dependency:

(1) There are four conceptual cases: OBJECTIVE, RECIPIENT, DIRECTIVE, INSTRUMENTAL.

(2) Each ACT takes from two to three of these cases obligatorally and none optionally.

(3) INSTRUMENTAL case is itself a complete conceptualization involving an ACT and its cases.

(4) Only animate objects may serve as actors except for PROPEL.

We are now ready to return to the problem of inference.

4. LANGUAGE-FREE INFERENCES

The next class of inference we shall discuss includes those that come from objects and relate to the normal function of those objects. As examples we have sentences (13) and (14):

(13) John told Mary that he wants a book.
(14) John likes chocolate.

These sentences have in common that they refer to an action without specifically stating it. In these examples, this missing act concerns the probable use of some object. In (13) that ACT is probably MTRANS (i.e., people usually want books because they want to MTRANS information from them) and in (14) that ACT is probably INGEST (i.e., people normally "like" chocolate because they like to INGEST it). While it is certainly possible that these were not the intended ACTs (John could like burning books and painting with chocolate) it is highly likely that without contrary information most speakers will assume that those ACTs were referenced. In fact, psychological tests have shown (see [5], [10], for example) that in many cases most hearers will not actually remember whether the ACTs were specifically mentioned or not. Notice in the first example that the missing MTRANS (of information from the book) is an inference which occurs AFTER the meaning representation of the sentence has been established (i.e., this sentence is analyzed as "if someone were to ATRANS a book to me it would cause me pleasure"). On the other hand, the missing INGEST in the second example is inferred during the analysis because the REPRESENTATION itself depends upon the analyzer knowing what it means to "like" a food. Therefore, the determination of an object's probable relation to an actor is never strictly a part of just the analyzer or just the memory, but rather a task of conceptual analysis in general.

It is important to mention that, regardless of the ultimate correctness of the chosen ACT, Conceptual Dependency predicts that an ACT is missing because verbs like "want" and "like" are represented as states. In the parsing of each of these sentences it is found that an actor and an object are present with no ACT to link them. This causes a search to be made for the correct ACT to fill that spot.

We thus have our second and third inference-types:

> 2. An instance of ACT-INFERENCE is present when an actor and an object occur in a conceptualization without an ACT to connect them, and the object in question has a normal function in the world. In this case the normal function is assumed to be the implicitly referenced ACT.

and

> 3. A TRANS-ENABLE-INFERENCE occurs with conceptualizations involving one of the TRANS ACTs. It is inferred that the TRANS conceptualization enables another conceptualization involving the same actor and object to take place. The specific act for this inferred conceptualization then comes about via ACT-INFERENCE. Inferences of this type are frequently useful for inferring the intended use of a physical or mental object.

The finished analyses for (13) and (14) after ACT-INFERENCE and TRANS-ENABLE-INFERENCE take place are then:

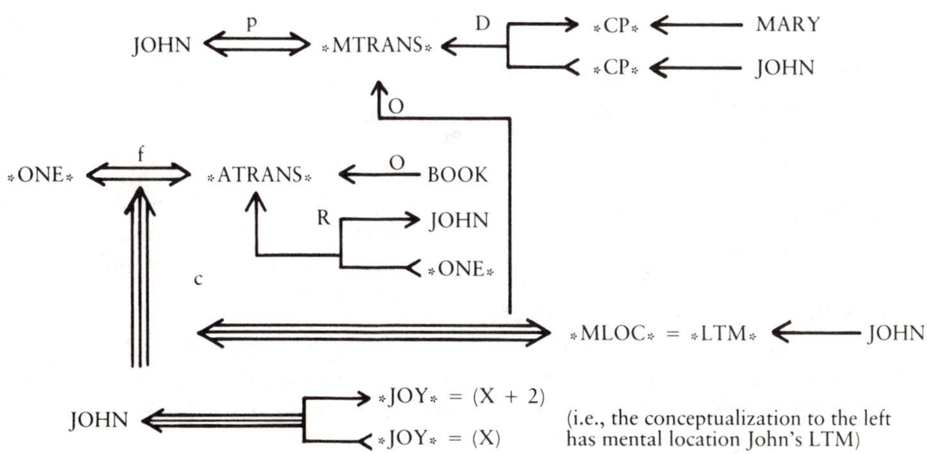

(which eventually leads to:

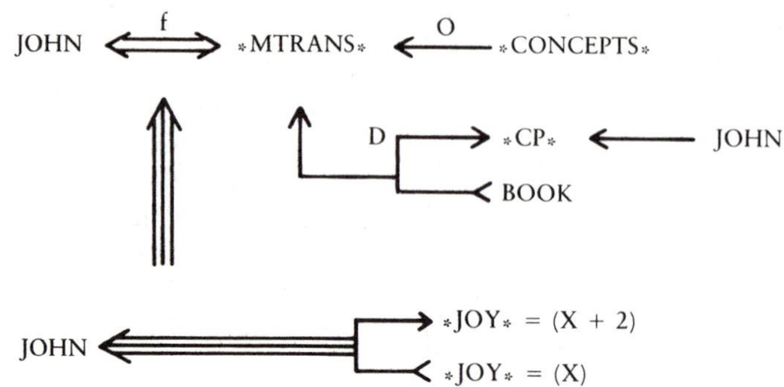

i.e., John wants to read the book), and

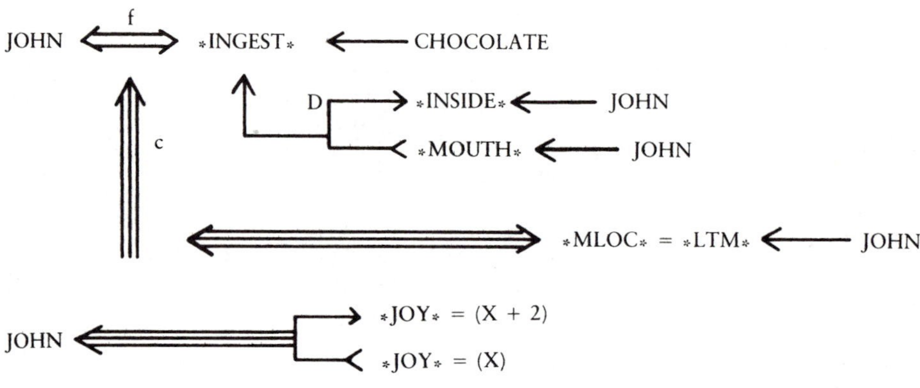

The next kind of inference that we shall discuss has to do with the results of a given ACT. Consider sentences (15), (16) and (17):

(15) John went to South Dakota.
(16) John told Mary that Bill was a doctor.
(17) John gave Mary a book.

Each of these sentences refers to an ACT that has a predictable result. Here again, when no information is given that contradicts this prediction, it is reasonable to assume that the normal result of the action was achieved. (Here, as in most of the examples given in this paper, it is necessary in English to use the conjunction "but" to indicate that the inferred result did not take place. Thus, unless we add "but he didn't get there" to (15), the hearer will assume he did.)

We thus have our fourth example of inference:

4. RESULT-INFERENCE can be made whenever a TRANS ACT is present and no information exists that would contradict the inferred result.

Thus, whenever PTRANS is present, we can infer that the location of the object is now the directive case of

PTRANS. Whenever ATRANS is present we can infer that there is a new possessor of the object, namely the recipient, and lastly, whenever an MTRANS occurs we can assume that the information that was transferred to the conscious processor (CP) of the brain became present there. Thus for (16), Mary can be assumed to "know" the information that was told to her since "know" is represented as "exist in the long term memory (LTM)" and "tell" involves MTRANSing to be the conscious processor which leads to LTM. A program that deals with this problem will be discussed later on in this paper.

The fifth kind of inference that we shall discuss is called OBJECT-AFFECT-INFERENCE. This kind of inference also concerns the result of an ACT but here we mean result to refer to some new physical state of the object involved. Sentences (18) and (19) illustrate this problem:

(18) John hit Mary with a rock.
(19) John ate the egg.

Both (18) and (19) make an implicit statement about a new physical state of the item that is in the objective case. In (18) we can guess that Mary's state of physical health might have been diminished by this ACT (i.e., she was hurt). In (19) we know that the egg, no matter what state it was in before this ACT, is now in a state of not existing at all anymore. Thus we have inference-type 5:

> 5. An instance of OBJECT-AFFECT-INFERENCE may be present with any of the physical ACTs (INGEST, EXPEL, PROPEL, GRASP, MOVE). The certainty of any of these inferences is dependent on the particular ACT, i.e., INGEST almost always affects the object, PROPEL usually does and the effects of the others are less frequent but possible. When OBJECT-AFFECT-INFERENCE is present, a new resultant physical state is understood as having been caused by the given ACT.

The analyses for (18) and (19) are given below. Note that if "rock" is replaced by "feather" in (18) the inference under discussion is invalid. Thus, in order to accomplish this inference correctly on a machine, the specifications for under what conditions it is valid for a given ACT must be given. Obviously these specifications involve mass and acceleration as well as fragility in the case of PROPEL.

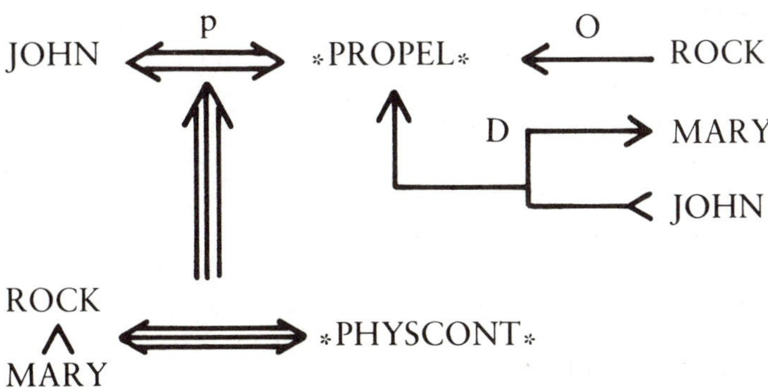

and

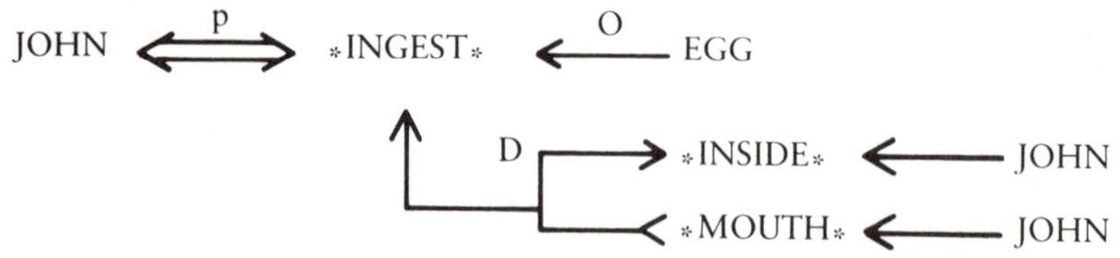

JOHN ⟺(p) *INGEST* ←(O) EGG

D → *INSIDE* ← JOHN
  ← *MOUTH* ← JOHN

The next kind of inference we shall discuss concerns the reasons for a given action. Until now, we have only considered the effects of an action or the unstated pieces of a given conceptualization. However, in order to conduct an intelligent conversation it is often necessary to infer the reason behind a given event. Consider sentences (20), (21) and (22):

(20) John hit Mary.
(21) John took an aspirin.
(22) John flattered Mary.

We would like a computer to have the ability to respond to these sentences as follows:

(20a) What did Mary do to make John angry?
(21a) What was wrong with John?
(22a) What does John want Mary to do for him?

In order to accomplish this, we need to use some of the inference-types discussed above first. Thus, in (20), we must first establish that Mary might be hurt before we can invoke an appropriate belief pattern. By belief pattern we mean a sequence of causally-related ACTs and states that are shared by many speakers within a culture. Such a sequence usually deals with what is appropriate or expected behavior and is often a prescription for action on the part of the hearer.

The belief pattern called by (20) is commonly described as VENGEANCE. It states that people do things to hurt people because they feel that they have been hurt by that person. This belief pattern supplies a reason for the action by the actor. Thus we come to the sixth kind of inference:

> (6) An instance of BELIEF-PATTERN-INFERENCE exists if the given event plus its inferred results fit a belief pattern that has in it the reason for that kind of action under ordinary circumstances.

In example (21) we have an instance of the WANT belief pattern which refers to the fact that people seek to obtain objects for what they can use them for (this is intimately related to inference-type 2 discussed above). Sentence (22) refers to the RECIPROCITY belief pattern (which deals with "good" things (i.e., those that cause positive changes on the JOY scale), VENGEANCE taking care of the "bad" ones). RECIPROCITY comes in two types. The one being used here is anticipatory. That is, the action is being done with the hope that the nice results achieved for one person will encourage that person to do something which will yield nice results for the original actor.

We will further discuss (20) later on in this paper when we outline the procedure by which our computer program produces (20a) in response to it.

The next kind of inference we shall discuss is called INSTRUMENTAL-

INFERENCE. It is the nature of the primitive ACTs discussed earlier that they can take only a small set of ACTs as instrument. Thus, for example, whenever INGEST occurs, PTRANS must be its instrumental ACT because by definition PTRANS is the only possible instrument for INGEST. The reason for this is that in order for someone to eat something it is necessary to move it to him or him to it. Thus, whenever INGEST is present we can make the legitimate inference that the object of INGEST was PTRANSed to the mouth (nose, etc.) of the actor. If this inference is incorrect, it is only because the direction of motion was mouth to object instead. Also, whenever PTRANS appears, the instrument must have been either MOVE or PROPEL. That is, in order to change the location of something it is necessary to move a bodypart or else apply a force to that object (which in turn requires moving a bodypart). Thus we have the seventh inference type:

> 7. INSTRUMENTAL-INFERENCE can always be made, although the degree of accuracy differs depending on the particular ACT. Whenever an ACT has been referenced, its probable instrument can be inferred.

The list of instrumental ACTs for the primitive ACTs follows:

INGEST	instrument is PTRANS.
PROPEL	instrument is MOVE or GRASP (ending) or PROPEL.
PTRANS	instrument is MOVE or PROPEL.
ATRANS	instrument is PTRANS or MTRANS or MOVE.
CONC	instrument is MTRANS.
MTRANS	instrument is MBUILD or SPEAK or ATTEND or MOVE.
MBUILD	instrument is MTRANS.
EXPEL	instrument is MOVE or PROPEL.
GRASP	instrument is MOVE.
SPEAK	instrument is MOVE.
ATTEND	no instrument is needed, although MOVE often applies.

Using this table it is possible, for example, to make the following inferences from these sentences:

(23) John is aware that Fred hit Mary.
(24) John received the ball.

Since (23) refers to CONC and CONC requires MTRANS as instrument, we can infer (from the possible instruments of MTRANS) where John got his information. He could have MBUILDed it (not likely here because Fred hit Mary is an external event); he could have perceived it from his senses by ATTEND eye to it himself; or by ATTEND ear to someone else which MTRANSed it to him. Since (24) refers to PTRANS, we have two possible instruments MOVE or PROPEL. From this we can infer that the ball was handed to him (move someone else's bodypart) or else it was rolled or thrown (or underwent some other manner of applying a force to a ball).

The next type of inference is PROPERTY-INFERENCE:

> 8. Whenever an object is introduced in a sentence, certain subpropositions are being made. The most common instance of this is the predication that the object being

referenced exists. The inference of these subpropositions we call PROPERTY-INFERENCE.

In some instances, PROPERTY-INFERENCE is dependent on other inference types. Thus, in the sentence "John hit Mary", not only is it necessary to make the PROPERTY-INFERENCE that both John and Mary exist, but it is also necessary to realize that John must have arms in order to do this. This inference is thus dependent on the LINGUISTIC-INFERENCE that, unless otherwise specified, "hit" refers to "hands" as the object of the PROPELing.

PROPERTY-INFERENCE is necessary in a computer understanding system in order to enable us to respond either with surprise or a question as to manner if we know that John does not have arms. Furthermore, in answering questions, it often happens that the checking of subpropositions associated with PROPERTY-INFERENCE will allow us to find an answer with less work. Thus for sentence (25):

(25) Did Nixon run for President in 1863?

Two separate subpropositions that can be proved false allow the question to be answered most efficiently. Establishing that "Nixon was alive in 1863" is false or that "there was a presidential election in 1863" is false is probably the best way of answering the question.

We have not discussed to this point the standard notions of logical inference for two reasons: (a) the problems involving logical inference are already fairly well understood, and (b) we do not view logical inference as playing a CENTRAL role in the problem of computer understanding of natural language. However, there exists a related problem that bears discussion.

Consider the problem of two sentences that occur in sequence. Often such sentences have additional inferences together which they would not have separately. For example, consider:

(26a) All redheads are obnoxious.
(26b) Queen Elizabeth I had red hair.
(27a) John wants to join the army.
(27b) John is a pacifist.

In (26), (26b) has its obvious surface meaning, but also can mean either one of two additional things. Either we have the inference that Queen Elizabeth I was obnoxious according to the speaker, or if (26b) were spoken by a different speaker from (26a), there exists the possibility that (26b) is intended as a refutation of (26a).

For (27), a sophisticated language analyzer must discover that (b) is essentially a contradiction of (a) and hence the inference that the speaker of (b) believes that the speaker of (a) is in error is probably correct. We thus introduce inference-type 9:

9. An instance of SEQUENTIAL-INFERENCE is potentially present when one sentence follows another and they share a subject or a proposition. When subpropositions or inferences of subpropositions can be detected as common to both conceptualizations, and satisfy certain set inclusion or contradiction rules, SEQUENTIAL-INFERENCE may apply.

The next kind of inference is quite straightforward:

10. An instance of CAUSALITY-INFERENCE is present if two sentences are connected by an "and" or by their appearing in sequence. Then if one could have caused the other,

it can be inferred that this is what happened.

Consider sentences (28) and (29a) and (29b):

(28) John hit Mary and she died.
(29a) John hit Mary.
(29b) John died.

In these sentences it is usually correct to assume causality. For (28) we infer that the hitting caused Mary's death. For (29) we infer that (a) caused (b). It is our knowledge of the world, however, that would cause us to wonder about the connection in (29) but not in (28). A good program would discover this to be a different kind of causality from the straight result present in (28). Kinds of causality are discussed in [7].

Another important inference type BACKWARD-INFERENCE. This type of inference can be made whenever an action has occurred that required another action to precede. The possible actions that can be inferred for a given ACT as BACKWARD-INFERENCE are often quite similar to those which can be inferred as instruments for a given ACT. We use this kind of inference whenever an object is acted upon. Thus if we have:

(30) John ate a banana.

we can infer that the banana must have been PTRANSed to him at some time. Likewise, whenever a mental item is operated upon its previous MTRANSing can also be inferred. If we have:

(31) John knows where Mary is.

then we can infer that this information must have been MTRANSed to John at some point (either from his eyes or from someone else MTRANSing this information to him). Thus we have reference type 11:

11. All conceptualizations are potentially subject to BACKWARD-INFERENCE. Depending on the nature of the object, one of the TRANS ACTs can be inferred as having enabled the current conceptualization's occurrence.

The last kind of inference we shall discuss concerns the intention of the actor. Consider the following sentences.

(32) John hit Mary.
(33) John told Bill that he wants to go to New York.

We assume that a person does something because he wants to do it and that he wants to do it because of the results that he expects to achieve. Thus a valid inference here is that it is the intention of the actor that the things inferred with OBJECT-AFFECT-INFERENCE or RESULT-INFERENCE will occur, and that these things are desired by the actor.

Thus from (32) using inference-type 6 we get that "Mary is hurt pleases John". From (33), using inference-type 5, we get that "being located in New York will please John" and "Bill knowing this pleases John". Thus we have inference-type 12:

12. INTENTION-INFERENCE is assumed whenever an actor acts unless information to the contrary exists.

5. OBSERVATIONS

Using the inference types discussed above we can see that an effective analysis of a sentence is often quite a bit more than one might superficially imagine. If we start with the sentence "John hit Mary" for example, our conceptual analyzer would perform the following conceptual analysis:

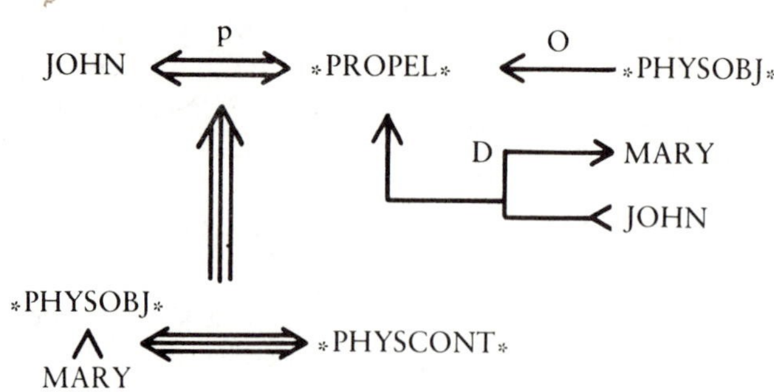

During and after the language analysis the consultation of the above inference processes would yield the following results:

LINGUISTIC	add "hand" as object of PROPEL.
OBJECT AFFECT	add causal "recipient (Mary) be hurt".
BELIEF PATTERN	add potential cause of the entire event as Mary DO cause John be hurt cause John be angry.
INSTRUMENTAL	add instrument of MOVE "hand".
PROPERTY	add prediction that John and Mary exist and that John has hands and that they were in the same place at the same time.
INTENTION	add that John knew that it would cause him pleasure if Mary was hurt and that is why he did it.

The graph after analyzer-initiated inferences have filled out the meaning representation, but before MEMORY gains direct processing control is:

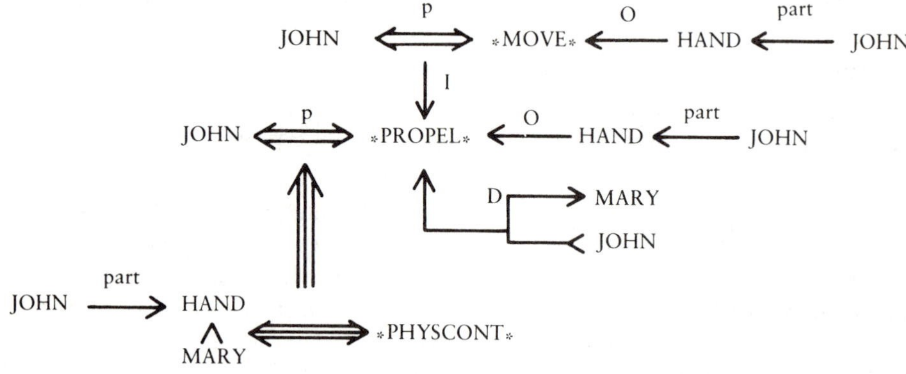

REFERENCES

Fillmore, C. The case for case. *Universals in Linguistic Theory,* E. Bach and R. Harms (eds.), Holt, Rinehart and Winston, New York (1968).

Goldman, N. The generation of English sentences from a deep conceptual base. Ph.D. Thesis, Computer Science Dept., Stanford University, Stanford, Calif. (1974).

Rieger, C. Conceptual memory. Ph.D. Thesis, Computer Science Dept., Stanford University, Stanford, Calif. (1974).

Riesbeck, C. Computer analysis of natural language in context. Ph.D. Thesis, Computer Science Dept., Stanford University, Stanford, Calif. (1974).

Sachs, J. Recognition memory for syntactic and semantic aspects of connected discourse. *Perception and Psychophysics* 2 (1967).

Schank, R. Conceptual dependency: A Theory of natural language understanding. *Cognitive Psychology* 3 (October 1972).

Schank, R. Semantics in conceptual analysis. *Lingua* 30 (1972), 101–140.

Schank, R. The fourteen primitive actions and their inferences. Stanford A.I. Memo 183, Computer Science Dept., Stanford University, Stanford, Calif. (1973).

Simmons, R. and Slocum, J. Generating English discourse from semantic networks. *Commun. ACM* **15** (October 1972).

Wettler, M. Zur Speicherung syntaktischer Merkmale in Langzeitgedächtn *of 28th Congress,* Eckensberger, L. (ed.), DGFP-Hogrefe, Göttingen (in press).

Wilks, Y. An artificial intelligence approach to machine translation. *Computer of Thought and Language,* R. Schank and K. Colby (eds.), Freeman, San Francisco (1973).

Received May 1973; revised September 1973; accepted April 1974

THE STRUCTURE OF EPISODES IN MEMORY

ROGER C. SCHANK

Yale University, New Haven, Connecticut

I. INTRODUCTION

The past few years have significantly altered the direction of research in computer processing of natural language. For nearly the entire history of the field, parsing and generating have been the major preoccupations of researchers. The realization that meaning representation is a crucial issue that cannot be divorced from the above two problems, leads to a concern with the following two questions:

• How much information must be specified, and at what level, in a meaning representation?

• To what extent can problems of inference be simplified or clarified by the choice of meaning representation?

II. CONCEPTUAL DEPENDENCY

These are the principal issues we have been concerned with in our work on conceptual dependency: (1) It is useful to restrict severely the concepts of action such that actions are separated from the states that result from those actions. (2) Missing information can be as useful as given information. It is thus the responsibility of the meaning representation to provide a formalism with requirements on items which must be associated with a concept. If a slot for an item is not filled, requirements for the slot are useful for making predictions about yet to be received information. (3) Depending on the purposes of the understanding processes, inferences must be made that will (a) fill in slots that are left empty after a sentence is completed (b) tie together single actor-action complexes (called "conceptualizations") with other such complexes in order to provide higher-level structures.

Throughout our research it was our goal to solve the paraphrase problem. We wanted our theory to explain how sentences which were constructed differently lexically could be identical in meaning. To do this we used the consequence of (1) and (2) to derive a theory of primitive ACTs. Simply stated, the theory of primitive ACTs states that within a well-defined meaning representation it is possible to use as few as eleven ACTs as building blocks which can combine with a larger number of states to represent the verbs and abstract nouns in a language. For more detail on these acts, the reader is referred to the Appendix and to Schank (1973a) and Schank

From *Representation and Understanding: Studies in Cognitive Science*. New York: Academic Press, 1975. Reprinted by permission of the publisher.

(1975). We claim that no information is lost using these ACTs to represent actions. The advantage of such a system is this:

1. paraphrase relations are made clearer,
2. similarity relations are made clearer,
3. inferences that are true of various classes of verbs can be treated as coming from the individual ACTs. All verbs map into a combination of ACTs and states. The inferences come from the ACTs and states rather than from words.
4. Organization in memory is simplified because much information need not be duplicated. The primitive ACTs provide focal points under which information is organized.

A. Some Caveats about Oversimplification

The simplest view of a system which uses primitive ACTs gives rise to a number of misconceptions. The following caveats, which we subscribe to, must be observed.

(1) There is no right number of ACTs. It would be possible to map all of language into combinations of mental and physical MOVE. This would, however, be extremely cumbersome to deal with in a computer system. A larger set (several hundred) would overlap tremendously causing problems in paraphrase recognition and inference organization. The set we have chosen is small enough not to cause these problems without being too small. Other sets on the same order of magnitude might do just as well.

(2) The primitive ACTs overlap. That is, some ACTs nearly always imply others either as results or as instruments. Our criteria for selecting a given ACT is that it must have inferences which are unique and separate from the set of already existing ACTs.

(3) Information can be organized under each primitive ACT, but it is definitely necessary to organize information around certain standard combinations of these ACTs. Such "super predicates" should be far fewer than those presented by other researchers, but they certainly must exist. Many inferences come from "kiss" for example that are in addition to those for MOVE. Organizing information under superpredicates such as "prevent" is, however, misguided since prevent is no more than the sum of its individual parts.

(4) Information is not lost by the use of primitive ACTs, nor is operating with them cumbersome in a computer program. Goldman (in Schank, 1975) has shown that it is possible to read combinations of ACTs into words very easily. Rieger (1974) has written a program to do inferences based on a memory that uses only those ACTs. Riesbeck (1974) has shown that predictions made from the ACTs can be used as the basis of a parsing program that can bypass syntactic analysis. The MARGIE program (see Schank, Goldman, Rieger, & Riesbeck, 1973) would seem to indicate that objections to ACTs on computational grounds are misguided at the current level of technology.

B. Toward Episode Representation

This chapter outlines our assumptions about how people tie together episodes or stories. We use the notions of conceptual dependency and primitive ACTs to represent and paraphrase entire episodes. We assume that knowing how to build larger structures bears upon the problem of how to use context to direct inferencing, and when to stop making inferences. The program of Goldman and Riebeck (1973) paraphrased sentences semantically but did not go beyond the level of the sentence. The solution that we will present is meant to be a partial solution to the paraphrase problem.

Our goal is to combine input sentences which are part of a paragraph into one or more connected structures which represent the meaning of the paragraph as a whole. While doing this we want to bear in mind the following: (1) A good paraphrase of a paragraph may be longer or shorter (in terms of the number of sentences in it) than the original. (2) Humans have little trouble picking out the main "theme" of the paragraph. (3) Knowing what is nonessential or readily inferable from the sentences of a paragraph is crucial in paraphrasing it as well as parsing it.

We pose the question of exactly how units larger than the sentence are understood. That is, what would the resulting structure in intermediate memory look like after a six-sentence episode or story had been input? Obviously, there must be more stored than just the conceptual dependency representation for each of the six sentences, but we could not store all possible inferences for each of the six sentences. Ideally what we want is to store the six sentences in terms of the conceptualizations that underlie them as an interconnected chain. That is, we shall claim that the amount of inferencing which is useful to represent the meaning of a paragraph of six sentences in length is precisely as much as will allow for the creation of a *causal chain* between the original conceptualizations.

Finally we shall address the question of creating the best model to explain how information is stored in human memory. We do not believe that people remember everything that they hear, but rather that forgetting can be explained partially in terms of what information is crucial to a text as a whole and what information can be easily rediscovered.

C. Causal Links

We shall claim here that the causal chain is the means for connecting the conceptualizations underlying sentences in a text. Conceptual dependency allows for four kinds of causal links. These are:

Result Causation: An action causes a state of change. The potential results for a given action can be enumerated according to the nature of that action. Consider some illustrative examples: *John hurt Mary*—John did something which *resulted in* Mary suffering a negative physical state change. *John chopped the wood*—John propelled something into wood which resulted in the wood being in pieces.

Enable Causation: A state allows for an action to have the potential of taking place. Here too, the states necessary for an action to occur can be enumerated. *John read a book*—John's having access to the book and eyes, etc. *enabled* John to read. *John helped Mary hit Bill*—John did something which *resulted* in a state which enabled Mary to hit Bill. *John prevented Bill from leaving*—John did something which ended the conditions which enabled Bill to go. (This is *unenable* causation.)

Initiation Causation: Any act or state change can cause an individual to think about (MBUILD) that or any other event.

John reminds me of Peter—when I think of John it initiates a thought of Peter. *When John heard the footsteps he got scared*—hearing the footsteps *initiated* a thought about some harm that might befall John.

Reason Causation: An MBUILD of a new thought can usually serve as the reason for an action. Reason causation is the interface between mental decisions and their physical effects. *John hit Mary because he hated her*—John thought about his feelings about Mary which made him decide to hit her which was the *reason* he hit her.

In this chapter causality will be denoted by a line from cause (top) to effect (bottom). A label will indicate which causal it is. Sometimes two or more labels will appear at once, which indicates that all the intermediate conceptualizations exist, but that we simply choose not to write them.

III. UNDERSTANDING PARAGRAPHS

Consider the following three paragraphs constructed from three different introductions (S1, S2 and S3) followed by a paragraph (BP). The base paragraph is:

(BP) John began to mow his lawn. Suddenly his toe started bleeding. He turned off the motor and went inside to get a bandage. When he cleaned off his foot, he discovered that he had stepped in tomato sauce.

(S1) It was a warm June day. (followed by) BP.

(S2) It was a cold December day. (followed by) BP.

(S3) John was eating a pizza outside on his lawn. He noticed the grass was very long so he got out his lawn mower. (followed by) BP.

We will refer to S1 (S2, S3) followed by BP as paragraph I (II, III).

Within the context of a paragraph, a sentence has a dual role. It has the usual role of imparting information or giving a meaning. In addition, it serves to set up the conditions by which sentences that follow it in the paragraph can be coherent. Thus in general, in order for sentence Y to follow sentence X and be understood in a paragraph, the conditions for Y must have been set up. Often these conditions will have been set up by X, but this is by no means necessarily the case. The conditions for Y might be generally understood, that is, part of everyday knowledge, so that they need not be set up at all. If this is not the case then it is irrelevant that X precedes Y.

A. Necessary Conditions

By a *necessary condition,* we mean a state (in conceptual dependency terms) that enables an ACT. Thus one cannot play baseball unless one has access to a ball, a bat, a field to play on, etc. The conditions that are necessary in order to do a given ACT must be present before that ACT can occur.

It is thus necessary, in order to understand that a given ACT has occurred, to satisfy oneself that its necessary conditions have been met. Often this requires finding a causal chain that would lead to that condition being present. That is, if we cannot establish that John has a bat, but we can establish that he had some money and was in a department store, we can infer that he bought one there if we know that he has one now. Obviously there are many possible ways to establish the validity of a necessary condition. Often, it is all right just to assume that it is "normally" the case that this condition holds. Rieger (1974) makes extensive use of this kind of assumption in his inference program. Establishing or proving necessary conditions is an important part of tying diverse sentences together in a story (John wanted to play baseball on Saturday. He went to the department store.). It is also, as we shall see, an important part of knowing when a paragraph does not make sense.

Thus the problem of representing a paragraph conceptually is at least in part the problem of tying together the conditions set up by sentences with the sentences that required those conditions to be set up. In the base paragraph (BP) no conditions have been set up under which tomato sauce could reasonably be considered to be present. Thus BP does not hang together very well as a paragraph. With S3, however, the conditions for tomato sauce being present are set up, the last sentence of BP can be tied to those conditions, and this is an integral paragraph. Note that there is no need to set up "bandage's" existence, since people can normally be assumed to have a bandage in a medicine cabinet in a bathroom in their house. If the third sentence were replaced by: "He took a bandage off of his lawn mower," however, there would be problems.

What we are seeking to explain then is what the entire conceptual representation of a paragraph must be. It can be seen from the above that in our representation of BP, it might well be argued that "bathroom" and "medicine cabinet" are rightfully part of the representation. The representation of a paragraph is a combination of the conceptualizations underlying the individual sentences of the paragraph plus the inferences about the necessary conditions that tie one conceptualization to another or to a given normality condition.

Let us consider the connectivity relationships with S1. We shall do this by looking at the necessary conditions required for each conceptualization and established by that conceptualization for subsequent conceptualizations.

S1, *It was a warm June day,* consists of two details. One is that the time of some unspecified conceptualization was a day in June. The other is that the temperature for that day was warm (or to be more precise greater than the norm for that season). These two states enable all warm weather activities. That is: the *established conditions* invalidate any activities for which contradictory conditions would be necessary.

Consider as an example S1 followed by an S4 such as: S2. John began to build a snowman. The fact that people would find such sequences bothersome, if not absurd, indicates that part of the process of understanding is the tying together of *necessary conditions* and *established conditions.* Necessary conditions are backward looking inferences that must be generated for each input conceptualization. For S4 we would have something like—"check to see if the necessary condition for this action (coldness) has been established. If it has not been, then infer it unless a contradictory condition has been established in which case there is an anomaly."

Established conditions are forward-looking inferences. These are states which are inferable from an input conceptualization. Often established conditions are input directly and need not be inferred at all. Thus S1 provides two established conditions. Neither of these conditions are called into play until a request for their existence is received from a following input conceptualization.

Now the actual S2 in paragraph I is "John began to mow his lawn". S2 requires appropriate necessary conditions to be satisfied. Some of these are: (a) John has a lawn; (b) John has a lawn mower; (c) John's lawn has grown to a length such that it might be moved; (d) It is a pleasant day for being outside. (Obviously, there are an extremely large set of conditions to be satisfied. Part of the problem is knowing how to reduce the search space.)

It can be seen from these four conditions that they are not all equal. That is (a) and (b) are of the class of necessary conditions that we shall call "absolutely necessary conditions" (ANCs). An ANC is a state which must be present in order to enable a given ACT to take place. If an ANC is violated, a sentence sequence is construed to be anomalous. Conditions (c) and (d), however, are the more interesting. They are what we shall call "reasonable necessary conditions" (RNCs). An RNC is a state which is usually a prerequisite for a given ACT. If an RNC is violated, the story sequence is not interrupted. Rather a peculiarity marking is made. These peculiarity markings turn out to be a crucial part of story understanding because they are predictive. That is, the sequence "It was a cold December day. John walked outside in his bathing suit," predicts a to-be-related consequence which is likely the point of the story. What makes this prediction is the peculiarity marking that would be generated from the established violation of the RNC involving warm weather necessary for walking outside scantily clad.

Necessary conditions are thus a subset of the set of possible inferences. They are precisely the set which is commonly used to connect isolated conceptualizations together. Necessary conditions are checked by means of establishing whether there exist records of them in memory. First, there is an attempt to tie them to information already present from previous sentences. This is done by use of the general facts in memory (e.g., about warm weather and lawns) including normality conditions. If such facts are present or can be established, an enable causation link is established between the previously input or inferred state and the new input conceptualization. That is, it is quite usual for people to possess lawns and lawn mowers so the fact that nobody told us this about John is not upsetting. (Of course, if we knew that John lived in an apartment then an ANC would be violated and there would be trouble.) If the connection can be established from normality information, then the new states involving this normality information are inferred as being the case in this particular instance (i.e., John has a lawn is inferred). When none of this can be done, a severe problem in the cohesion of the story (for the listener) exists.

The interesting part of paragraph connectivity comes when we examine the sentence "Suddenly his toe started bleeding." How can we connect this sentence to previous information? In fact humans do it with little trouble. A question is generated, "what can cause bleeding in people?" This question is coupled with an inquiry as to whether the established conditions demandable from any previous information in the text result in "a human bleeding" under the right circumstances. Working in both directions at once, we can establish a chain from "lawn mowing" to "blades turning" to "toe bleeding" if we hypothesize contact between blade and toe. The syntax for causality in this chain follows exactly the same lines as proposed by Schank (1973b). The kind of inference outlined previously has been considered in some detail (including programming some examples on the order of complexity shown here) by Rieger (1974). Let us now consider what the final representation of paragraph I should be.

(In our representation we shall use a simplified conceptual dependency diagram, consisting of a parenthesized expression in the order: (ACTOR ACTION OBJECT X) where X is any other relevant case which we choose to include which we make explicit there. State diagrams are written: (OBJECT NEWSTATE). Necessary conditions are abbreviated as ANCs or RNCs. Ss designate input sentences. INFs designate inferences needed to complete causal chains. The time of an event or state is relative to the others around it with earlier events higher on the page. Story (for the listener) exists. Research/Figure 1 is the final representation of the paragraph except for the following:

(1) Normally the initiation reason causation (from ANC/3) would have to be expanded. In this case there would have to be a belief about what bandages had to do with bleeding body parts. This belief would be part of the MBUILD structure that supplied the reason for going in the house.

(2) All the ANCs would have to be accounted for. This would be done as the paragraph was being processed.

The ANCs for the above paragraph are as follows:

ANC/1, ANC/2, . . . ::	These specify that John has a lawn and a lawn mower and can push it, etc.
ANC/3:	John has a toe and he was not wearing shoes, etc.
ANC/4:	John has a house, it is nearby and he can get in, etc.
ANC/5:	John has a bandage in his house, and he can find and get it.
ANC/6:	This is provided by "John cleaned his toe". Thus the entire structure causally related to ANC/6 established another chain apart from the actual story.
ANC/7:	This is specified by the next part of the last sentence.
ANC/8:	This is the condition that tomato sauce be in a place where John might have stepped in it.

Two important things are illustrated in this diagram of paragraph I: (1) Conceptually, a paragraph is essentially a set of causal chains, some leading to dead ends and at least one carrying on the theme and point of the story. (2) As long as required necessary conditions can be established and inferences necessary to complete causal chains can be resolved, a paragraph is coherent and understandable. When these processes are too difficult or impossible problems result.

In paragraph I, ANCs 1–5 are easily satisfied by everyday normality conditions, but ANCs 6–8 are more of a problem. ANC/6 is provided by the story in C15, but C17 which is initiated by ANC/6 requires John himself to establish (in an MBUILD) ANC/7. In trying to establish ANC/7 John concludes that C19 is true. This leaves the reader with the problem of verifying ANC/8, which is not possible under these conditions.

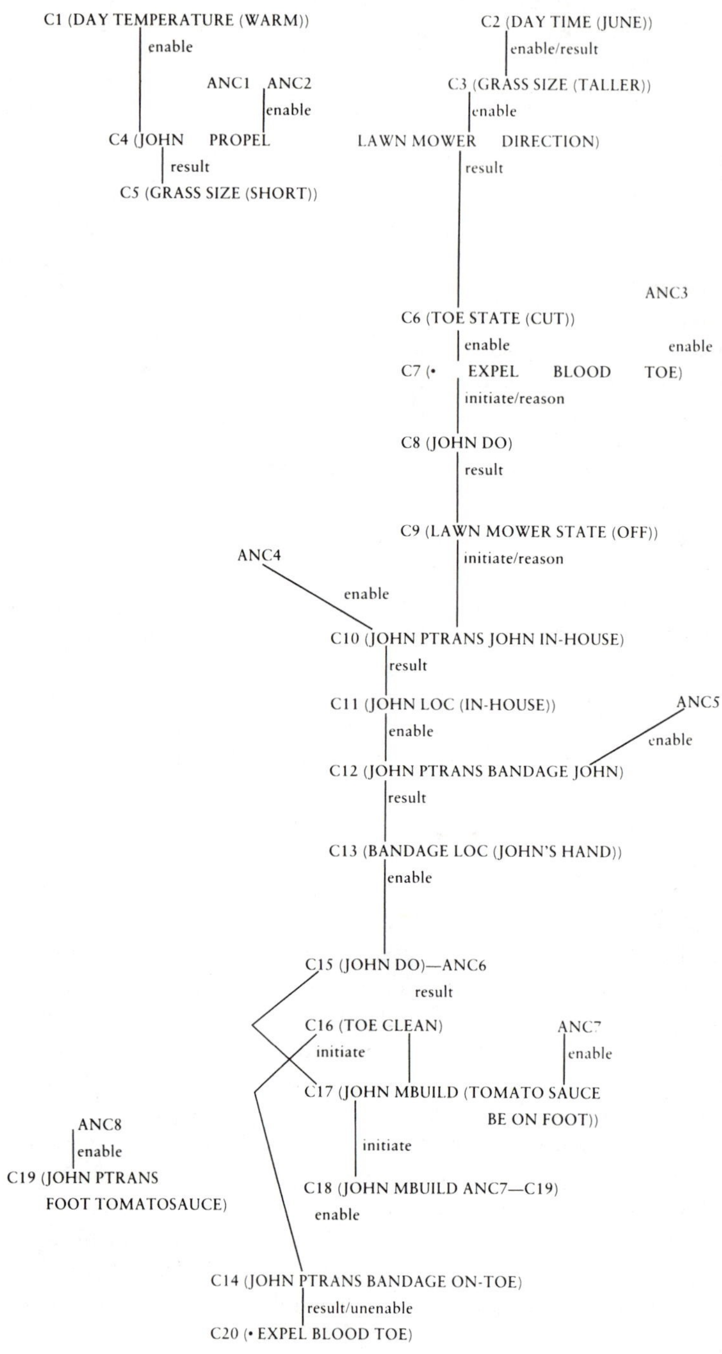

RESEARCH/FIGURE 1.
Conceptual dependency representation of the paragraph.

The rest of the story thus remains incomplete and can never really get to C14 and C20.

Now, in paragraph III on the other hand, ANC/8, when it is discovered, is easily resolvable. (PIZZA LOC (LAWN)) is a possible result of the first sentence (John was eating a pizza outside of his lawn). If the problem of knowing that a pizza contains tomato sauce is resolvable, then so is ANC/8. In that case, an ANC would be resolved from within the given paragraph as was done for ANC/6 and ANC/7 in paragraph I.

Some additional comments that can be made about the representation of paragraph I are:

(1) C5 is a deadend. Short grass may be the condition for something, but this story does not tell us nor make use of it. Deadend paths in a story indicate items of less importance in the story. This information is crucial in the problem of paraphrase of paragraphs since it tells you what you can leave out.

(2) The inference of the result link between C4 and C6 is one of the most important inferences in the story. It serves to tie together two apparently unrelated events into a contiguous whole.

(3) The information about turning the lawn mower off is another deadend. In fact, there was no reason for this information to be in the story at all.

(4) C14 and C20 are crucial to a story that has not been told. What has happened is that the attempted resolution of ANC/6 has interrupted the flow of the story. Inside the resolution of ANC/6 we have had to resolve ANC/8 which causes us to quit.

Diagrammatically we can view the story as in Research/Figure 2 which shows a version of the story structure with only concept labels. From various sources of information we can construct a path that sets up C4. One of the inferences from C4 is fruitful in that it provides a chain to C7. Two paths come from C7, one is fruitful in leading us to C10 (whose conditions can be explained by ANC/4). On our way to C14, we try to establish ANC/6. Doing so leads to a direct path to C18. In order to prove the conditions for C18, however, we need ANC/8 which cannot be determined.

B. Remembering Paragraphs

We have established in the previous section some basic principles regarding what we would expect to be the result in memory after a paragraph has been input. (1) The conceptual dependency representation of each input sentence is included. (2) The conceptualizations that underlie the sentences should connect to each other conceptually. (3) The basic means of connecting the conceptualizations underlying the input sentences to each other is the causal chain. (4) Inferences from the input conceptualizations are part of the representation of the total paragraph if they are used in order to connect input conceptualizations into a causal chain. (5) The necessary conditions must be satisfied for every represented conceptualization. This is done by inferring facts both from inside and outside the paragraph. Inferences made from outside the paragraph proper are still part of the representation of the total paragraph. (6) Stories can be viewed as the joining together of various causal chains that culminate in the "point" of the story. Deadend paths that lead away from the main flow of the story can thus be considered to be of lesser importance.

From the point of view of paraphrasing tasks or the problem of remem-

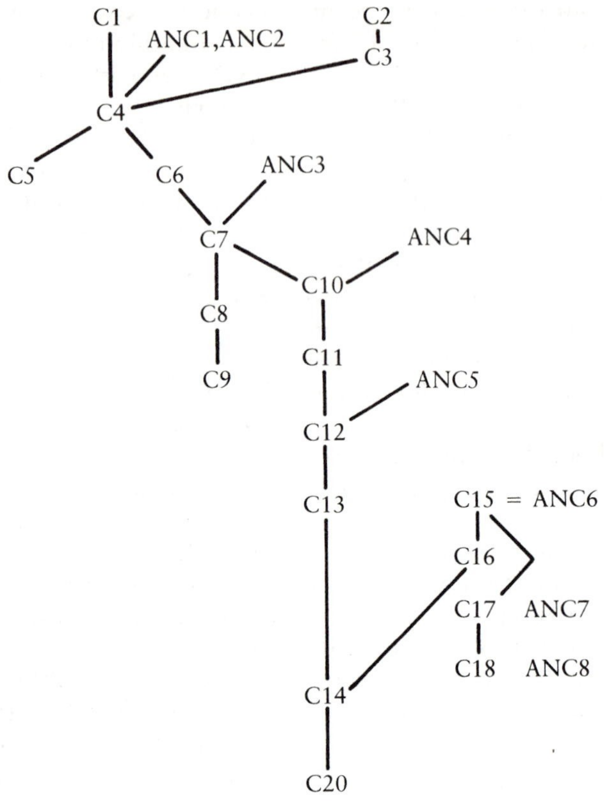

C1 ANC1,ANC2 C2 C3
C4
C5 C6 ANC3
C7 ANC4
C10
C8
C9 C11 ANC5
C12
C13 C15 = ANC6
C16
C17 ANC7
C18 ANC8
C14
C20

RESEARCH/FIGURE 2.
A diagrammatic version of the paragraph.

bering, the things most likely to be left out in a recall task are: the deadend paths; the easily satisfied necessary conditions, whether they were explicit in the original paragraph or not; and the inferences that make up the causal chain that are "obvious" and easy to recover at any time.

In order to better examine the validity of our predictions about memory and the usefulness of our representation for stories, we diagrammed the well known "The War of the Ghosts," a story used by Bartlett (1932) for experiments in memory. We are not interested here in all the facets of memory that Bartlett considered, but some of the problems that he concerned himself with can be handled more easily using our representation. The story is:

One night two young men from Egulac went down to the river to hunt seals, and while they were there it became foggy and calm. Then they heard war-cries, and they thought: "Maybe this is a war-party." They escaped to the shore, and hid behind a log. Now canoes came up, and they heard the noise of paddles, and saw one canoe coming up to them. There were five men in the canoe, and they said:

"What do you think? We wish to take you along. We are going up the river to make war on the people."

One of the young men said: "I have no arrows."

"Arrows are in the canoe," they said.

"I will not go along. I might be killed. My relatives do not know where I have gone. But you," he said, turning to the other, "may go with them."

So one of the young men went, but the other returned home.

And the warriors went on up the river to a town on the other side of Kalama. The people came down to the water, and they began to fight, and many were killed. But presently the young men heard one of the warriors say: "Quick, let us go home: that Indian has been hit." Now he thought: "Oh, they are ghosts." He did not feel sick, but they said he had been shot.

So the canoes went back to Egulac, and the young man went ashore to his house, and made a fire. And he told everybody and said: "Behold I accompanied the ghosts, and we went to fight. Many of our fellows were killed, and many of those who attacked us were killed. They said I was hit, and I did not feel sick."

He told it all, and then he became quiet. When the sun rose he fell down. Something black came out of his mouth. His face became contorted. The people jumped up and cried.

He was dead.

Using a diagram for this story based on causal chains, we followed the rules given below to prune the causal chains to create a summary diagram which would allow a paraphrase to be generated on later remembering. We have not worked out a complete set of rules, but the following give a reasonable first approximation:

1. Deadend chains will be forgotten.
2. Sequential flows (correct chains) may be shortened.
   a. The first link in the chain is most important.
   b. Resolution of questions or problems is too.
3. Disconnected pieces will be either connected correctly or forgotten.
4. Pieces that have many connections are crucial.

Using a diagram with only the causal connections (as shown in Research/Figure 2 for paragraph I) and the above rules, we derived a paraphrase which was:

> *Two men went to the river. While they were there they heard some noises and hid. Some men approached them in canoes. They asked them if they would go on a war party with them. One man went. He got shot. The men took him home. He told the people what happened and then he died.*

The reasonableness of this paraphrase suggests that the above procedural outline for paragraph paraphrase is a good one.

If one compares our paraphrase with the output of Bartlett's subjects, the one striking difference is that the two conceptualizations missing necessary conditions are present in his subjects' output. We hypothesized that peculiarity markings would be generated for violation of necessary conditions. C37 and C52 ("They are ghosts," and "Something black came out of his mouth.") would have generated peculiarity markings. If Bartlett's output is examined, it can be seen that his subjects handled these peculiarity markings in various ways. They were made part of the causal chain in entirely different ways for each speaker and were hardly ever forgotten.

Paraphrases can be generated from meaning representations of text by procedures that read out the conceptualizations which are central to the flow of the diagram. Paraphrases longer than the original text would be generated by realizing all the conceptualizations in the final meaning representation. Paraphrases shorter than the text would be generated by various means. Among these are: (a) leaving out deadend paths, (b) only realizing conceptualizations that have more than two pointers to them in the text, (c) reading out only starting and ending points of the subchains in a text. Summaries would be developed in similar ways.

The main problem in building a computer program to do paraphrases is, at this point, not the generation aspect, but the problem of actually being able to make the crucial inferences that connect texts together. In the base paragraph the inference that the lawn mower may have cut John's toe is difficult to make. In "The War of the Ghosts" the crucial inference that the notion of ghosts somehow resolves the unconnectable causal chain at the end of the story is too difficult for humans to figure out.

E. Scripts

Some of the episodes which occur in memory serve to organize and make sense of new inputs. These episodic sequences we call *scripts*. A script is an elaborate causal chain which provides world knowledge about an often experienced situation. Specifically, scripts are associated as the definitions of certain situational nouns. Words whose definitions are scripts are, for example, restaurant, football game, birthday party, classroom, meeting. Some words that have scriptal definitions have physical senses as well, of course. "Restaurant", for example, has a physical sense which is only partially related to its scriptal sense.

The notion of scripts has been proposed generally and specifically in different forms by Minsky (1975), Abelson (1973), and Charniak (1972). What we call scripts represent only a small subset of the concept as used by others. For our purposes, scripts are predetermined sequences of actions that define a situation. Scripts have entering conditions (how you know you are in one), reasons (why you get into one), and crucial conceptualizations (without which the script would fall apart and no longer be that script). In addition, scripts allow, between each causal pair, the possibility for the lack of realization of that causation and some newly generated behavior to remedy the problem. In general, scripts are nonplanful behavior except when problems occur within a script or when people are planning to get into a script.

Scripts are recognizable partially by the fact that, after they have been entered, objects that are part of the script may be referenced as if they had been mentioned before. For example:

I. John went into a restaurant. When he looked at the menu he complained to the waitress about the lack of choice. Later he told the chef that if he could not make much, at least he could make it right.

II. We saw the Packers-Rams game yesterday. The Packers won on a dive play from the two with three seconds left. Afterwards they gave the game ball to the fullback.

These paragraphs have in common that they set up a script in the first sentence. This script then sets up a set of roles which are implicitly referenced and a set of props which are implicitly referenced. From that point, roles and props can be referenced as if they had already been mentioned. (Actually, we would claim that they *have* been mentioned by the definition of the script word.)

The script also sets up a causal chain with the particulars left blank. The hearer goes through a process of taking new input conceptualizations previously predicted by the script that has been entered. As before, pieces that are not specifically mentioned are inferred. Now, however, we are going further than we went in the first part of this chapter, in saying that the sequences implicitly referenced by the script are inferred and treated as if they were actually input. This is intended to account for problems in memory recognition tasks that occur with paragraphs such as these.

Let us consider the restaurant script in some more detail.

Script: restaurant
Roles: customer, waitress, chef, cashier
Reason: hunger for customer, money for others

Part 1: Entering
*PTRANS (into restaurant)
MBUILD (where is table)
ATTEND (find table)
PTRANS (to table)
MOVE (sit down)

Part 2: Ordering
ATRANS (receive menu)
ATTEND (look at it)
MBUILD (decide)
MTRANS (tell waitress)
MTRANS (waitress tells chef)
DO (chef prepares food)

Part 3: Eating
ATRANS (waitress gets food)
*ATRANS (receive food)
*INGEST (eat food)

Part 4: Leaving
MTRANS (ask for check)
ATRANS (leave tip)
PTRANS (to cashier)
*ATRANS (pay bill)
PTRANS (exit)

In the restaurant script given above, we have oversimplified the issue as well as arbitrarily decided the kind of restaurant we are dealing with. Basically, a restaurant is defined by a script that has only the starred ACTs. Restaurants exist where the maitre d' must be tipped in order to get a table, where you get your own food, and so on. The sequence of ACTs above is meant only to suggest the abstract form of a script. A complete script would have at each juncture a set of "what-ifs" which would serve as options for the customer if some sequence did not work out. In addition, other kinds of restaurants could have been accounted for in one script by having choice points in the script. A still further issue is that this is how the restaurant looks from the customer's point of view. Other things happen in restaurants that have nothing to do with restaurants per se and other participants see them differently.

With all these disclaimers aside, the restaurant script predicts all the conceptualizations whose ACTs are listed above, and in a manner quite similar to the functioning of our language analysis program (Riesbeck, 1974) it is necessary in understanding to go out and look for them.

Stories, fortunately for the hearer, unfortunately for us, usually convey information which is out of the ordinary mundane world. The first paragraph tells that the customer did not like the restaurant. His complaining behavior is part of the "what-if" things which we mentioned earlier. The purpose of the script is to answer questions like "Did he eat?" and "Why did he complain to the chef?" These are trivial questions as long as one understands implicitly the script that is being discussed. Otherwise they are rather difficult.

It is perhaps simplest to point out that the second paragraph is incomprehensible to someone who does not know football yet makes perfect sense to someone who does. In fact, football is never mentioned, yet questions like "What kind of ball was given to the fullback?" and "Why was it given?" are simple enough to answer, as long as the script is available.

V. SUMMARY

We are saying that the process of understanding is, in large part, the assigning of new input conceptualizations to causal sequences and the inference of remembered conceptualizations which will allow for complete causal chains. To a large extent, the particular chains which result are tied up in one's personal experience with the world. Information is organized within episodic sequences and these episodic sequences serve to organize understanding. The simplest kind of episodic sequence is the script that organizes information about everyday causal chains that are part of a shared knowledge of the world.

Human understanding, then, is a process by which new information gets treated in terms of the old information already present in memory. We suspect that mundane observations such as this will serve as the impetus for building programs that understand paragraphs.

ACKNOWLEDGMENTS

The research described here was done partially while the author was at the Institute for Semantic and Cognitive Studies, Castagnola, Switzerland, partially while the author was at Bolt Beranek and Newman, Cambridge, Massachusetts, and partially at Yale University.

REFERENCES

Abelson, R. The Structure of belief systems. In R. Schank & Colby (Eds.), *Computer Models of Thought and Language*. San Francisco: Freeman, 1973.

Anderson, J., & Bower, G. *Human Associative Memory*. Washington, D.C.: Winston-Wiley, 1973.

Bartlett, F. C. *Remembering: a study in experimental and special psychology*. Cambridge: Cambridge University Press, 1932, p. 65.

Charniak, E. He will make you take it back: A study in the pragmatics of language (Technical Report). Castagnola, Switzerland: Instituto per gli studi Semantici e Cognitivi, 1974.

Collins, A. M., & Quillian, M. R. Retrieval time from semantic memory. *Journal of Verbal Learning and Verbal Behavior*, 1969, *8*.

Conrad, C. Cognitive economy in semantic memory. *Journal of Experimental Psychology*, 1972, 92(2).

Goldman, N., & Riesbeck, C. A conceptually based sentence Paraphraser (Stanford AI Memo 196). Stanford, California: Stanford University, 1973.

Minsky, M. A framework for representing knowledge. In P. H. Winston (Ed.), *The psychology of computer vision*, New York: McGraw-Hill, 1975.

Quillian, M. R. Semantic memory. In M. Minsky (Ed.), *Semantic Information Processing*. Cambridge: Massachusetts Institute of Technology Press, 1968.

Rieger, C. Conceptual memory. In R. Schank (Ed.), *Conceptual information processing*. Amsterdam: North-Holland, 1975.

Riesbeck, C. Conceptual analysis. In R. Schank (Ed.), *Conceptual information processing*. Amsterdam: North-Holland, 1975.

Rumelhart, D. E., Lindsay, P. H., & Norman, D. A. A process model for long-term memory. In E. Tulving and W. Donaldson (Eds.), *Organization of memory*. New York: Academic Press, 1972.

Schank R. C. *Conceptual information processing*. Amsterdam: North-Holland, 1975.

A Critique of R. C. Schank and C. J. Rieger's Study: Inference and the Computer Understanding of Natural Language and R. C. Schank's Study: The Structure of Episodes in Memory

DON H. NIX

IBM Thomas Watson Research Center

I. INTRODUCTION

The teaching of inferential reading comprehension is difficult. Part of the reason is that comprehension is complex, and traditional research in models and taxonomies pertaining to reading has not developed a body of knowledge to describe the complexity in an explicit, teachable way. Thus, comprehension is taught without giving the student useful rules. This is analogous to teaching addition, for example, without teaching rules for such processes as borrowing, carrying, and lining up columns.

An orientation characterized by a focus on explicitness in describing complex, inferential connections that must be made to comprehend text has recently arisen from work in the field of Artificial Intelligence. The papers under consideration here were selected because of their importance in introducing this orientation. They will be briefly described, and their potential contributions to a body of knowledge for teaching inferential reading comprehension will be stressed, particularly in terms of their orientation.

The term "teachably explicit" refers to a concept that can be clearly defined in terms of explicit rules for positive and negative examples that highlight the critical attributes of the concept. A teachably explicit concept can be taught in a step-by-step manner in terms of its component parts.

Models and taxonomies from the field of reading comprehension are not teachably explicit. For example, various models (inspired, historically, by Thorndike, 1917; see pages 209–15 of this volume) focus on hypothesis formation during reading, or thinking while reading. Such notions are not explicated so that they can be communicated to a child as a step-by-step program for how to form them. Although the models refer to complex processes, their level of description is itself not detailed in a teachably explicit sense.

stemming from earlier "specific skills" work by Davis (1968). The sentence pair, "Picnic Man was furious. He threw his basket at Snerdpot," can be classified in terms of at least five different specific skills, depending on inexplicit criteria. These skills are: inferred character trait, inferred detail, sequence, outcome, and cause and effect. These skills overlap, and are not explicitly defined. In addition, these and other typical specific skills have not been shown empirically to be distinct, specific skills (Rosenshine, 1980). Thus, these skills are not teachably explicit.

To teach comprehension more effectively, we need, among other requirements, a teachably explicit version of what is to be taught. Of particular interest in the papers selected here is that they provide an orientation for explicitly dealing with the complexities of comprehension. They show a level of complexity and explicitness that a teachably explicit body of knowledge might have. The papers, and the points of view they express, can be an impetus for educational psychologists to begin experimental investigations in developing ways to teach, rather than to "mention" (Durkin, 1978–79; see pages 287–329 of this volume) reading comprehension skills.

II. SCHANK AND RIEGER

The Schank and Rieger paper (1974) stresses the use of "normative inferences" in a computer system programmed to understand natural-language text. Inferences add information to what is already given in the text. Normative inferences are not the same as inferences used in deductive logic; they are based on knowledge of the world rather than knowledge of deduction, and they are contingent rather than provably true. Furthermore, they are reflex responses rather than ancillary options. This notion of inferences as normative, pervasive, action processes is critical to language comprehension.

Twelve types of information-adding inferences are explicated. Each inference is defined by the conditions for applying it, and by the type of information the inference adds. The inferences can be categorized roughly as highlighting various types of world knowledge: functions of objects (inferences #1, #2, #3); results of ACTs (#4, #5); properties of objects (#8); sequences (#9); causes (#7, #10, #11); and mental events (#6, #12).

Inferences add information to the Conceptual Dependency (CD) representation of the meaning of a sentence. The CD system is a set of categories about objects and actions, and a set of relationships for connecting the categories. The CD type of analysis focuses on semantic rather than structural aspects of language. The semantic aspects include commonsense concepts such as moving objects around, thinking, paying attention, and transferring ownership. Thus, making such a set of categories and relationships salient implements a non-linguistic view of language understanding. That is, an individual sentence is not conceptualized in terms of subjects or predicates or direct objects, all of which are relatively non-intuitive, abstract concepts. Instead, the sentence is conceptualized in terms of experiential concepts that generate expectations and associations and explanations.

The process of understanding a sentence in Schank and Rieger's study is as follows: The sentence is parsed into a semantic representation, which explicitly labels the meaning relationships between the various components of the sentence. This parsing is done using a fixed set of conceptual categories (i.e., real-world objects; real-world actions; attributes of objects; attributes of actions, times, and

critique

locations), and using a fixed set of conceptual syntax rules for combining these categories. Next, this meaning representation is expanded with inferential material that is likely true, or possibly true, given the relationship of the components of the sentence to a normative knowledge of the world. The inferential expansions are also done using a fixed set of relationships—the 12 inference types.

As an example of this process, consider the sentence "John hit Mary." The CD analysis for this sentence is shown in (34) in Schank and Rieger. John propelled ("*PROPEL*") some physical object ("*PHYSOBJ*"), in the direction ("D") from John to Mary, and the object came into contact ("*PHYSCONT*") with Mary. The various types of arrows indicate the various relationships between the conceptual categories. For example, the double-lined, double-headed arrow between John and *PROPEL*, where John is a PP (real-world object) and *PROPEL* is an ACT (real-world action), indicates that an actor acts. The three-line, single-headed arrow indicates that what John did causes what happened to Mary.

The simple sentence has been conceptualized in terms of actors, actions, recipients of actions, and causation. This contrasts, as already stated, with conceptualizing the sentence in terms of subject, predicate, and direct object. The CD representation focuses on the experiential aspects, which leads directly into the inferential augmentation.

The 12 inference types add inferential information to the initial CD representation. Elements of the CD representation are inspected to determine which ones are conditions that are part of the criteria for triggering one or more of the inference patterns. Appropriate inferences are then activated to add information. For example, an OBJECT—AFFECT—INFERENCE (inference type #5) may be triggered by one of the physical ACTs (which are INGEST, EXPEL, PROPEL, GRASP, and MOVE). Applying the inference consists of adding the resultant effect the ACT has on the object to the CD. In addition, a new physical state exists. Thus, from (34) it might be inferred that Mary was hurt, since there is a *PROPEL* ACT, and since, according to what we know about the world, hitting can hurt. Another inference of the same type, but leading to a different result, based also on normative information, might be that Mary is mad as an outcome of being hit by John. Another inference is that John probably used his hand (LINGUISTIC INFERENCE), since hitting must be done with some instrument, and in this context a hand is likely. A different LINGUISTIC INFERENCE might be that John used a club. It might be inferred that John might have been angry (BELIEF PATTERN INFERENCE), since that could explain why he would hit Mary. Another explanation can be that he was scared.

Even from such a simple sentence, many other inferences could be made. None of these inferences is necessarily true. Additional context is needed to select which ones apply, and what additional inferences need to be made. These types of inferences are reflexes, rather than optional information. Furthermore, they are based on what is known about the world of experience, rather than based on logical relationships.

critique

The sentences used in the examples in Schank and Rieger are simple in one sense. However, when considering what is necessary to program a computer to understand these sentences, it is clear that they are not simple. Even a sentence like "John hit Mary" requires a reader to organize the meaning using a variety of semantic categories and to inferentially extend the meaning in various directions. The fact that a proficient reader such as a teacher or a researcher who is building a taxonomy or model of reading comprehension can process such a sentence, as well as more complicated text, automatically tends to obscure the complexity of the processing requirements. This may be responsible in part for the lack of teachably explicit conceptualizations of the reading comprehension process.

A significant potential contribution to educational psychology is just this point. Teachers are often unaware of what they are asking children to do when they ask them to comprehend. Such traditional notions of authors' intent, sequence, and so on, mask this. The notions of OBJECT-AFFECT INFERENCE and BELIEF-PATTERN INFERENCE highlight this.

The concept of inference as relevant to reading comprehension did not originate in the field of Artificial Intelligence. The term is regularly used in specific skills and other taxonomies, as well as in descriptions of models of readings. What is new about inferences here is that they are normative and pervasive. Most crucial for a teachably explicit approach to a body of knowledge for teaching reading comprehension, the inferences are specifically delineated and their conditions for application are defined. Although the exact inferences in Schank and Rieger may be difficult to use for actual teaching, partly because their definitions are somewhat unclear and overlapping, the notion of inference they developed has considerable potential.

III. SCHANK

The Schank and Rieger paper focused its analysis on single sentences. The intention was to show how single sentences generate a network of inferential information based on the interaction between the CD representation for the sentence and the way the conceptual content in the sentence related to the world of experience. The Schank paper (1975) extends this analysis to paragraphs using the notion of causal chains and scripts to provide a method for connecting conceptualizations underlying sentences. The causal chains, composed of results, enablements, initiations, and reasons, provide the connections. The causal chains are composed of normative inferential connectives that provide paragraph coherence. They present world knowledge similar to that in Schank and Rieger, but grouped differently. The 12 inferences in Schank and Rieger have been shuffled and streamlined somewhat.

Figure 1 in Schank shows a simplified CD representation for the paragraph about John and the lawn mower. The paragraph, on a surface reading, appears simple. A person is mowing his lawn, notices what he thinks is blood on his toe, goes inside to get a bandage, wipes off his foot to put on the bandage, and realizes, to his surprise, that it is tomato sauce, not blood, on his toe. However, given the task of instructing a computer to understand and paraphrase the passage in terms that would work for other paragraphs as well, the complexity becomes prominent.

Figure 1 depicts this difficulty by showing necessary conditions in causal chains. To comprehend even a simple story, the reader must inferentially link the components together using what he/she knows about the world. A reader must be aware

critique

that certain conditions are absolutely necessary ("ANCs"), for example, it is necessary to have a lawn mower to mow a lawn. Certain other necessary conditions are reasonable necessary conditions ("RNCs"), which are usually required, such as it is usually the case that the lawn has grown high enough to need mowing, if you are going to mow it. In processing a text, a reader can fill in ANCs if they are not overtly stated, and might be cued to look for something unusual when an RNC is contradicted.

The introduction of scripts in Schank (extended in Schank & Abelson, 1977) is a preliminary step to relating elements of a text that do not fit directly into a causal chain. Scripts are packages of inferences that are connected through repeated association in past experiences. Each script has mandatory or optional roles, and various causal chains are invoked. Input text can be fit into a script, and elements missing in the text can be filled by the script that the rest of the text invokes. An internalized script, then, functions to consolidate a reader or listener's comprehension of a text.

In the current context of the Schank notions of causal chains and scripts, the viewpoint that text is a complex entity is important. A reader does not simply understand a text—the reader uses knowledge of various types of expectations based on world knowledge. Furthermore, such expectations need to be explicitly described, along with their rules for interaction.

IV. IMPLICATIONS FOR EDUCATION

Traditionally, the comprehension process has been a mystery. The concepts used to characterize the process and the teaching of the process have systematically masked the underlying complexity. The various skill taxonomies and comprehension models have not been teachably explicit. Teaching materials have not contained sustained teaching, if any teaching at all (Durkin, 1981; see pages 331–53 of this volume), and teacher behavior, in questioning practices or time on task, has not been oriented to teaching inferential aspects of comprehension (Durkin, 1978–79, see pages 263–69 of this volume; Guzak, 1968, see pages 287–329 of this volume, and 1972).

The potential value of the notions discussed in Schank and Rieger (1974) and Schank (1975) is that they are relevant to comprehension (as specific-skill taxonomies and reading-as-thinking models may be), *and* that their complexity is explicitly defined (in contrast to specific-skill taxonomies and reading-as-thinking models). To get from one sentence to the next, the reader must inferentially make connections in terms of what the reader knows about the world, via a fixed set of inferential concepts. Furthermore, empirical studies conducted with children provide supportive evidence for the importance of normative inferences of various types (e.g., Nix, 1978; Omanson, Warren, & Trabasso, 1978; Paris, 1975; Paris & Upton, 1976; Stein & Glenn, 1979; Trabasso & Nicholas, 1980), and for other explicit systems or taxonomies, in terms of children's abilities to comprehend and recall various types of text. What can this do to improve the teaching of reading comprehension?

The specific set of inferences in Schank and Rieger does not constitute the main contribution. Specifically, it is not clear that each inference is well-defined or distinct from each of the others. For example, inferences #4 and #11 both involve the results of TRANS ACTs, and differ only in which sentence is noted first. Inferences

#5 and #10 also seem conceptually the same, and differ only in superficial aspects. An example of an inference not well-defined is the SEQUENTIAL—INFERENCE (#9). This inference covers a wide range of dissimilar situations. Similar problems occur with a set of 14 inferences presented in Rieger (1975), which have much in common with the 12 in Schank and Rieger.

The Artificial Intelligence approach to inferences, instead of being the definition of the specific inferences enumerated, is the notion of a normative, reflexive, pervasive, componentially conceptualized inference itself. Such inferences are used both to extend the meaning of individual conceptualizations and to connect series of conceptualizations in a chain. These inferences comprise a fixed, delineated set. And, they are explicit. This notion of inferences is unique and leads to a teaching plan for demystifying the comprehension process.

The plan is to isolate a fixed set of inferential connectives that are relevant, teachably explicit, and common-sense-oriented; to teach each concept assiduously, stressing supportive positive and negative examples and maintaining a high degree of time on task; and to teach how to apply these concepts to various types of texts. For example, Nix (in press) uses a set of normative inferential connectives developed on the basis of interview sessions with children. One such connective is a "Feeling Reason Link" which, as shown in (*1) below, involves a Feeling World (FW = loves), a Feeler (F = Whole Wheat Dan), a Feeling Reason (FR = F + FW), and what a Feeler Might Do (FMD = call her all the time). A Feeling Reason Link (FRL = FR + FMD) occurs when there is a feeling, and, based on what the reader knows about what happens in the world, there is something that such a feeler might do under those circumstances, if there is no information to the contrary. This type of inference is normative, non-logical, and likely rather than always true.

> (*1)
> Whole Wheat Dan loves Loretta-Too.
> He calls her all the time.
> (FRL = (FR = ((F = Dan) + (FW = (loves)) + FMD = (calls her))

To teach the FRL, the following set of lessons is used: (1) Doing and Finding FWs; (2) Doing and Finding Fs; (3) Doing and Finding FMDs; (4) Using World Knowledge; (5) Doing and Finding FRs; (6) Doing and Finding FRLs; (7) More Doing and Finding FRLs. The point is to teach these in a step-by-step fashion.

Remediation points are integrated, and each point is defined by what has gone before. For example, if children have difficulties with More Doing and Finding FRLs, which uses more complicated paragraphs than Doing and Finding FRLs, these difficulties are not conceptualized simply as not being able to make inferences, or some other inexplicit skill, and then dealt with using another similar question. Instead, there is an interactive, constructive determination of where the problem exists. The problem may be the complexity of the paragraph, for example, as distance between FR and FMD, competing FMDs, direction of the FRL, type of FW. It may be finding FRLs, or FMDs or FRs or Fs or FWs. After this is detected, the teaching goes back up the scale to show how the original FRL question can be answered. Whether the teacher should continue with More Doing and Finding FRLs or should go to the remediation point that has been identified is then determined.

After FRLs have been learned, additional FRL lessons follow to implement various applications. These lessons include: 8 FRLs and Main Ideas; 9 FRLs to Do Pronoun Reference; 10 FRLs and Comprehension Questions; 11 FRLs with Invisible FRs; 12 FRLs and Invisible Main Ideas; and 13 FRL Chains. Lessons 8–10 explain certain tasks that children are routinely required to do, but for which traditionally no explanation is given. Instead of giving unexplained practice items, without follow-up, the approach is to systematically lead up to the concept, for example, of main idea, in terms of FRLs (and other links). Then the concept is defined by how one uses FRLs to identify or produce exemplars of it, and remediation is performed using explicit components of the process. Lessons 11, 12, and 13 deal with additional complexities in text.

Other links are similarly segmented for instructional presentation. In general, the build-up is done carefully, from simple to complex, sensitizing the child to the need to actively use his or her knowledge of the world to tie text together. As a result, children learn two types of skills: (1) how to link (comprehension); and (2) the necessity for linking (meta comprehension).

This type of teaching plan for demystifying the comprehension process requires the central assumptions that comprehension is complex, and that the complexity must be explicitly described. What is important, in this context, about the orientation to explicitness represented by the Schank and Rieger (1974) and Schank (1975) papers selected here, as well as others, is that they made such assumptions salient. They conceptualized comprehension in such a way that may lead to a framework for developing a teachably explicit body of knowledge for teaching reading comprehension. Enough research has been done to delineate various sets of inferential skills, whether packaged in terms of inferences (Nix, in press), causal chains (e.g., Warren, Nicholas, & Trabasso, 1979), scripts (Schank & Abelson, 1977), goals and plans (Black & Bower, 1980), story schema (Johnson & Mandler, 1980), rhetorical predicates (Meyer, 1975), bridges (Clark, 1975), maps (Armbruster & Anderson, 1980), and others (review by Reder, 1980). These can be seriously considered as components of a body of knowledge for experimental efforts to teach inferential reading comprehension. The orientation to explicitness may provide a means for demystification of comprehension, analogous to teaching addition *with* rules, rather than without.

This orientation has not, in general, been concerned with applications to teaching. Thus, an important new set of ideas for education is not being actively explored by educators, and psychologists who are dealing with these ideas are typically, with few exceptions, neglecting educational applications. A central problem now is how to introduce the explicitness point of view into educational research.

FOR FURTHER LEARNING

Those readers who are interested in continuing to explore the topic of technology and reading would find the following references helpful:

Atkinson, R., & Hansen, D. Computer-assisted instruction in initial reading: The Stanford project. *Reading Research Quarterly*, 1966, 2, 5–25.

Cushman, R. The Kurzweil reading machine. *Wilson Library Bulletin,* 1980, *22,* 311–315.

Doerr, C. *Microcomputers and the 3 r's.* Rochelle Park, N.J.: Hayden Book Company, 1979.

Gleason, G. Microcomputers in education: The state of the art. *Educational Technology,* 1981, *21,* 7–18.

Isaacson, D. What's holding back computer use in education? *Classroom Computer News,* 1981, *1,* 1; 28–29.

Just, M., & Carpenter, P. A theory of reading: From eye fixations to comprehension. *Psychological Review,* 1980, *87,* 329–354.

Kintsch, W., & van Dijk, T. Toward a model of text comprehension and production. *Psychological Review,* 1978, *85,* 363–394.

Mason, G. Computerized reading instruction: A review. *Educational Technology,* 1980, *20,* 18–22.

Mason, G., & Blanchard, J. *Computer applications in reading.* Newark, Del.: International Reading Association, 1979.

Mason, G., & Mize, J. Teaching reading with television: A review. *Educational Technology,* 1978, *18,* 5–12.

Rumelhart, D. Toward an interactive model of reading. In S. Dornic (Ed.), *Attention and performance VI.* Hillsdale, N.J.: Laurence Erlbaum Associates, 1977.

Simon, H. Studying human intelligence by creating artificial intelligence. *American Scientist,* 1981, *69,* 300–309.

Vinsonhaler, J., & Bass, R. A summary of ten major studies on CAI drill and practice. *Educational Technology,* 1972, *12,* 29–32.

REFERENCES

Armbruster, B. B., & Anderson, T. H. *The effect of mapping on the free recall of expository text.* (Technical Report No. 160.) Center for the Study of Reading, University of Illinois at Urbana-Champaign, 1980.

Black, J. B., & Bower, G. H. Story understanding as problem solving. *Poetics,* 1980, *8,* 223–250.

Clark, H. H. Bridging. In R. Schank & B. L. Nash-Webber (Eds.), *Theoretical issues in natural language processing.* Arlington, Va.: Center for Applied Linguistics, 1975.

Davis, F. B. Research in reading comprehension. *Reading Research Quarterly,* 1968, *4,* 499–545.

Durkin, D. What classroom observations reveal about reading comprehension instruction. *Reading Research Quarterly,* 1978, *16*(4), 481–533.

Durkin, D. Reading comprehension instruction in five basal series. *Reading Research Quarterly,* 1981, *16*(4), 515–544.

Guzak, F. Teacher questioning and reading. *The Reading Teacher,* 1968, *21,* 227–234.

Guzak, F. *Diagnostic reading instruction in the elementary school.* New York: Harper and Row, 1972.

Johnson, N. S., & Mandler, J. M. A tale of two structures: Underlying and surface forms in stories. *Poetics,* 1980, *9,* 51–86.

Meyer, B. M. F. *The organization of prose and its effect on recall.* Amsterdam: North Holland, 1975.

Nix, D. Linking-mediated syntax in children's sentence comprehension. *Journal of Reading Behavior,* 1978, *10*(1), 79–90.

Nix, D. Links: A teaching approach to developmental progress in children's reading comprehension and meta comprehension. In R. O. Freedle & J. Fine (Eds.), *Developmental studies in discourse (Vol. 4): New directions in discourse processing.* Norwood, N.J.: Ablex, in press.

Omanson, R. C., Warren, W. H., & Trabasso, T. Goals, inferential comprehension, and recall of stories by children. *Discourse Processes,* 1978, *1,* 337–354.

Paris, S. G. Integration and inference in children's comprehension and memory. In F. Restle, R. M. Shiffrin, N. J. Castellan, H. R. Lindman, & D. B. Pisoni (Eds.), *Cognitive Theory* (Vol. 1). Hillsdale, N.J.: Laurence Erlbaum Associates, 1975.

Paris, S. G., & Upton, L. R. Children's memory for inferential relationships in prose. *Child Development,* 1976, *47,* 660–668.

Reder, L. M. The role of elaboration in the comprehension and retention of prose: A critical review. *Review of Educational Research,* 1980, *50*(1), 5–54.

Rieger, C. Conceptual memory. In R. C. Schank (Ed.), *Conceptual information processing.* Amsterdam: North Holland, 1975.

Rosenshine, B. V. Skill hierarchies in reading comprehension. In R. J. Spiro, B. C. Bruce, & W. F. Brewer (Eds.), *Theoretical issues in reading comprehension.* Hillsdale, N.J.: Laurence Erlbaum Associates, 1980.

Schank R. C., & Abelson, R. P. *Scripts, plans, goals, and understanding.* Hillsdale, N.J.: Laurence Erlbaum Associates, 1977.

Stein, N. L., & Glenn, C. G. An analysis of story comprehension in elementary school children. In R. O. Freedle (Ed.), *New directions in discourse processing* (Vol. 2). Norwood, N.J.: Ablex, 1979.

Thorndike, E. Reading as reasoning: A study of mistakes in paragraph reading. *Journal of Educational Psychology,* 1917, *8,* 323–332.

Trabasso, T., & Nicholas, D. W. Memory and inferences in the comprehension of narratives. In F. Wilkening, J. Becker, & T. Trabasso (Eds.), *Information integration in children.* Hillsdale, N.J.: Laurence Erlbaum Associates, 1980.

Warren, W. H., Nicholas, D. W., & Trabasso, T. Event chains and inferences in understanding narratives. In R. O. Freedle (Ed.), *Advances in discourse processes (Vol. 2): New directions in discourse processing.* Norwood, N.J.: Ablex, 1979.

A Commentary on Don H. Nix's Critique of Schank and Rieger's Study: Inference and the Computer Understanding of Natural Language and Schank's Study: The Structure of Episodes in Memory

THOMAS W. BEAN

California State University at Fullerton

Contemporary research in Artificial Intelligence may, as Nix suggests, offer a basis for developing instructional procedures to guide reading comprehension. However, before embracing such a recommendation wholeheartedly, we need to examine two aspects of Nix's proposal: (1) the strengths and limitations of an artificial intelligence (AI) theory of prose comprehension; and (2) a method for evaluating a teaching paradigm based on AI research.

STRENGTHS AND LIMITATIONS OF ARTIFICIAL INTELLIGENCE

Nix finds our traditional reading models and taxonomies to be generally descriptive but lacking in the specificity needed to guide step-by-step instruction in comprehension. Indeed, most of our favored strategies for guiding comprehension such as reciprocal questioning (Manzo, 1968) are based on pedagogical intuition rather than extensive basic research. Whether instructional procedures derived from basic research in AI are more helpful, less helpful, or about as good as our armchair inventions, awaits experimental findings. Nevertheless, Nix finds AI efforts aimed at developing computer programs capable of comprehending sentences (Schank & Rieger, 1974) and paragraphs (Schank, 1975) indicative of the inferential processes underlying human comprehension. What are some of the strengths and limitations of such a view?

In reading any AI description, it is immediately clear that comprehension of the simplest sentence strings is a vastly complex event. Thus, as Nix points out, even the brief sentence "John hit Mary" has the potential for generating upwards of six divergent inferences. The introduction of additional context delimits the number of possible interpretations for a person reading this sentence but undoubtedly complicates the data base needed for a computer to understand it. For example, "John hit Mary because she had a bee on her arm" reduces our confusion about John's possible motives for striking Mary. Yet a program designed to comprehend this new sentence would need to contain a corpus of normative inferences or world knowledge about bees and bee stings. Because an AI conception of comprehension must necessarily restrict the range of possible inferences included in a data base, it can only partially explain or model human comprehension.

An AI model restricts the range of possible inferences for a sentence or paragraph to those that are "normative" or reasonably plausible. Yet many inferences readers make are based on social or cultural experiences that depart from the norm. These idiosyncratic inferences are seemingly limitless, unexpected, and undoubtedly helpful in understanding conceptual miscues that readers often make. Such novel inferences are usually contained in teachers' anecdotes and rarely explained in any systematic fashion (Graesser, 1981).

Taking a real-life example, we can see just how divergent children's inferences can be from a corpus of possible or expected interpretations. Picture a Southeast-Asian child in a first-grade classroom in an urban area of the United States. The child and teacher are gazing at a popular basal reader selection featuring pictures of ducks. The teacher points to a picture with the word "duck" underneath and the child responds "duke." Thinking that "duke" is a dialect pronunciation for "duck," the teacher assumes that this child has the requisite prior knowledge to comprehend this selection. Later, however, she asks the child how he came to know about ducks. He says, "from the Duke boys on television" (i.e., "The Dukes of Hazzard").

The point is, while AI representations of comprehension are impressive in their precise, explicit set of possible inferences, this strength is also their major limitation. Despite its elegance, an AI representation can only attempt to account for the tremendous range of divergent, cross-cultural inferences children actually make. Thus, any teaching plan based on an AI model still will not be fully explicit for some children or it may only be applicable to carefully contrived passages with limited transfer to naturalistic text.

In a unique experimental approach, Nix and Schwarz (1979) demonstrated cross-cultural differences in inferencing by comparing tenth-grade East Harlem children's inferential question-answering processes on Reading for Understanding (SRA, 1963) items with criterion answers. The students completed the items aloud and were then interviewed to determine how they chose particular answers that departed from the expected choice. For example, in the following passage, students' inferential processes departed from what might be expected in a significant, but culturally rational way.

"Summer" Passage

> That summer we bought electric fans, drank gallons of ice water, and spent most of our time by the river, but nothing worked. We simply had to resign ourselves to being:
>
> A. hot B. tired C. poor D. sick (SRA, 1963, p. 186)

For some students, this description implied that these people were "poor" since they did not have an air conditioner or swimming pool. This form of student-centered interview research extends the range of normative inferences that might be derived from an AI perspective. Certainly it holds some promise for examining and improving materials and strategies that purport to teach reading comprehension.

All of this discussion about novel, unexpected inferences should not detract from the possible instructional programs that may arise from a carefully developed theoretical perspective such as that offered by AI. Direct instruction in how to connect text information via normative inferences is a persuasive proposition that needs to be carefully evaluated.

EVALUATING AI-BASED COMPREHENSION INSTRUCTION

A manipulative, direct-teaching approach such as "Links" (Nix, in press), designed to present text in manageable chunks with a step-by-step instructional scheme for fostering and trouble-shooting comprehension, needs to be field-tested in an experimental fashion. One procedure might involve using the same passage of material approached through two different strategies. A condition Y group would go through the material using "Links" and a condition Z group would be guided through the material using a classical, armchair strategy like reciprocal questioning (Manzo, 1968). I suspect that both groups would achieve similar comprehension, in part because the variables of time on task and depth of processing (Bransford, 1979) are positive ingredients of both approaches. Furthermore, Brown (1981) has already demonstrated the facilitative effects of reciprocal questioning with lower-ability students. Yet we still do not have reliable evidence to indicate whether or not students apply inferential strategies on an independent, metacognitive basis. Instituting a transfer task to see if students would spontaneously apply a "Links" or "ReQuest" strategy equally might shed some light on their relative value as systems for guiding comprehension.

In summary, AI research offers a precise, highly specific description of the reading process heretofore lacking in our models and taxonomies. Whether or not an instructional program based on an AI model is more promising than our armchair efforts will remain an enigma until adequate applied research studies are conducted.

REFERENCES

Bransford, J. D. *Human cognition: Learning, understanding, and remembering.* Belmont, Calif.: Wadsworth, 1979.

Brown, A. Metacognition: The development of selective attention strategies for learning from texts. In M. L. Kamil (Ed.), *Directions in reading: Research and instruction.* Thirtieth Yearbook of the National Reading Conference. Washington, D.C.: National Reading Conference, 1981.

Graesser, A. C. *Prose comprehension beyond the word.* New York: Springer-Verlag, 1981.

Manzo, A. V. *Improving reading comprehension through reciprocal questioning.* Unpublished doctoral dissertation, Syracuse University, 1968.

Nix, D. Links: A teaching approach to developmental progress in children's reading comprehension and meta comprehension. In R. O. Freedle & J. Fine (Eds.), *Developmental studies in discourse (Vol. 4): New directions in discourse processing.* Norwood, N.J.: Ablex, in press.

Nix, D., & Schwarz, M. Toward a phenomenology of reading comprehension. In R. O. Freedle (Ed.), *New directions in discourse processing.* Norwood, N.J.: Ablex, 1979.

Science Research Associates. *Reading for understanding.* Chicago: SRA, 1963.